FRIARS' GUIDE
To
NEW ZEALAND
ACCOMMODATION
For The
DISCERNING TRAVELLER
2005

10TH ANNIVERSARY EDITION

DISCLAIMER: The contents of this Guide were believed to be correct at the time of printing.

Prices are subject to change and should be confirmed at time of booking.

All wording in these editorials is based on information provided by the hosts, who approved proofs before publication.

However, the publishers and authors can accept no responsibility for errors, or omissions, or changes to details herein. Nor are they responsible for any guest dissatisfaction with any accommodation included in this Guide.

*We would like to thank our assistants
— Renate Simenauer and Daniel Friar —
for their long hours of work on this tenth edition,
and to all those relatives, friends and hosts who supported us
by kindly offering hospitality on our busy itinerary around New Zealand.*

Front cover: Grasmere Lodge, Cass, Arthur's Pass, South Island *(see page 373)*
Previous page: Cotter House, Remuera, Auckland, North Island *(see page 113)*

ISBN 1-86958-990-4

© 2005 – original text, Jillian Friar, and original photographs, Denis Friar, FRIARS
The moral rights of the authors have been asserted

© Concept – Jillian & Denis Friar and Hodder Moa Beckett Publishers

© 2005 – design and formatting, Hodder Moa Beckett Publishers Limited

Published in 2005 by Hodder Moa Beckett Publishers Limited
[a member of the Hodder Headline Group]
4 Whetu Place, Mairangi Bay, Auckland, New Zealand

Typeset by Jillian & Daniel Friar and Renate Simenauer, FRIARS, Wanganui, New Zealand

Colour separations by Microdot, Auckland, New Zealand
Printed by Everbest Printing Co Ltd, China

All rights reserved. No part of this publication may be reproduced or transmitted in any form or by any means, electronic or mechanical, including photocopying, recording, or any information storage and retrieval system, **without permission in writing from the publisher or authors.**

FRIARS' GUIDE
TO
NEW ZEALAND
ACCOMMODATION
FOR THE
DISCERNING TRAVELLER

◆ LODGES ◆ FARMS ◆ PRIVATE HOMES ◆ BOUTIQUE HOTELS ◆
◆ B&BS ◆ SELF-CONTAINED COTTAGES ◆ APARTMENTS ◆ INNS ◆

2005
10TH ANNIVERSARY EDITION

Text and typesetting by
Jillian Friar

Photography by
Denis Friar

Hodder Moa Beckett

FRIARS' GUIDE TO NEW ZEALAND ACCOMMODATION FOR THE DISCERNING TRAVELLER

PERSONAL INTRODUCTION

WELCOME to our special 10th edition of *Friars' Guide*. These guidebooks differ from all others. How? Each place has been personally selected and recommended by Jillian and Denis Friar, who travel annually throughout the length and breadth of New Zealand inspecting, evaluating and selecting superior and special venues for the book. This year they have again declined a record number of places that are not up to the standard set in the book. A total of over 470 venues have been found that meet the selection criteria and provide accommodation with a level of personal service and quality to put them in a class of their own. Other outstanding features of *Friars' Guide* are its renowned reliability, accuracy, attention to detail and its comprehensiveness.

EVERY PROPERTY offers private facilities for guests. Diverse features make each place unique. Sometimes it is the distinctive architecture, interior design, or quality furnishings, from historical to contemporary, that is special. Fine cuisine may be the outstanding point of difference. Some properties are located in magnificent settings commanding sweeping views over pristine lakes or lush green countryside, to snow-capped mountain ranges beyond. But it is the intangible qualities that make the guest's stay at each place so memorable. It is the personal touches, little surprises and unexpected extras that contribute to the indefinable ambience that sets the places in this directory apart.

THE FRIARS personally endorse the top-class accommodation showcased in this edition. Exterior and interior shots by professional photographer Denis Friar highlight the special features of each establishment. The accompanying editorials are written by Jillian Friar to provide all the information the traveller needs to know. Jillian uses a descriptive, objective and informative style of writing to detail the characteristics of each property clearly, without overstatement, exaggeration, florid prose or mood writing.

THE FRIARS spend most of the spring and summer months travelling throughout New Zealand evaluating, photographing and interviewing for the following edition, which they then take several months to organise and typeset into this top quality product. They run their specialist Friars House and Garden Photo Library in Wanganui, where they live with their son, Daniel, who does the cartography and much of the typesetting, and Jillian's father on the same property. Throughout their itinerary, the Friars meet many guests and overseas visitors, who provide them with valuable insights into the needs of the discerning traveller. Contrary to popular belief, guests tend to prefer a range of different accommodation as offered in this book, some totally private, others providing the opportunity to socialise with their hosts.

Friars' Guide is published annually, to keep the information up-to-date and reliable. Guests who stay at any of the accommodation included in this guide are invited to send feedback to the authors (*see details on page 505*). New hosts who would like to apply to be included in the next edition are also invited to contact the Friars. (As with most accommodation guides, there is a charge for appearing in this full-colour book which assists in offsetting the retail price.) Any property is eligible for inspection and evaluation if it incorporates private bathroom facilities for guests and has special features of sufficient standard to rate it in the class of accommodation included in this book.

A WIDE DIVERSTIY of accommodation is featured in this edition of *Friars' Guide*, as well as two exclusive tours, one by air and the other by motorhome. We are also introducing specialist real estate brokers for buying and selling lodges. Each venue is individual, not conforming to any prescribed pattern. Tariffs range from over $NZ100 to more than $NZ1,000 per couple per night. Guestrooms range from one-bedroom cottages to multi-bedroom boutique hotels. Luxury lodges, bed and breakfast inns, self-contained apartments, homestays, farmstays, resorts, health spas and retreats also feature. Each place specifies whether breakfast, lunch or dinner are offered and if they are included in the tariff or optional. See pages 6 and 7 for a detailed explanation of how to use this Guide.

STRETCHING from the Far North down to Stewart Island, there are over 470 superior accommodation venues featured in this special 10th anniversary 2005 edition to satisfy every discerning traveller's itinerary. Over the past decade *Friars' Guide* has gained a reputation with travel professionals and independent travellers alike of providing access to the best of accommodation in New Zealand. Many loyal users refer to it as their "bible". The current edition upholds this high accolade.

Jillian and Denis Friar

Friars' Guide to New Zealand Accommodation for the Discerning Traveller

Sample Page Key

- host's names, usually also the owners
- accommodation name
- postal address, if different from physical address
- physical/geographical address
- location name indicates local area
- logos indicate smoking restrictions, children accepted, wheelchair access, or chef
- phone, freephone, mobile phone, fax, email and website address
- local map, with accommodation at red dot
- numeral corresponds to numerals on the maps inside the covers of book
- regional map, red dot shows location in either North or South Island
- directions to accommodation
- green tab indicates B&B option is available
- credit cards accepted
- burgundy tab indicates dinner is available
- total number of bedrooms available
- blue tab indicates self-catering is available
- total number of ensuites or private bathrooms available
- powder room available
- logos for virtual tour on web, affiliations, historic places trust category, etc
- tariff in New Zealand dollars includes 12.5% tax
- meals available for extra charge
- meals included in tariff
- description of accommodation
- in-house facilities offered
- activities on site and nearby
- page number
- copyright and Friars' credit

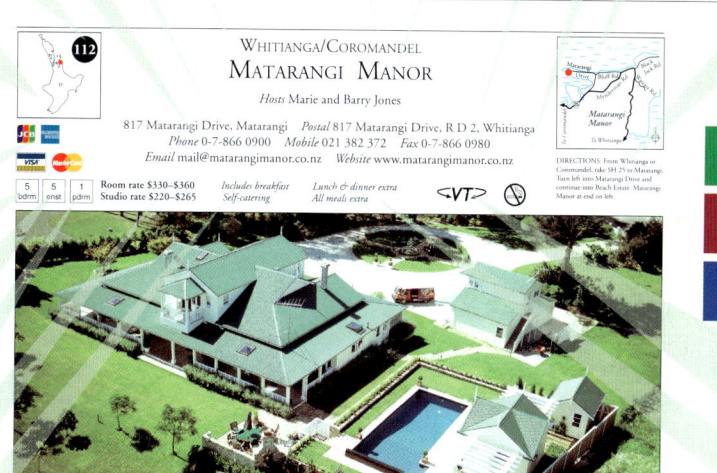

FRIARS' GUIDE TO NEW ZEALAND ACCOMMODATION FOR THE DISCERNING TRAVELLER

How to Use this Guide

The editorials on each page aim to cover all the relevant details the discerning traveller needs to know. Because conventions vary and overseas terminology is not always consistent with that used in New Zealand, we have compiled and updated the following explanations for clarity.

- **Map Numbers**
  These correspond to the numbers on the large North and South Island maps inside the front and back covers of the book, respectively. These maps show the geographical relation of each location, to help travellers plan their itineraries.

- **Phone Numbers**
  The international code for NZ is 64, then drop the 0. Eg 64-9- for Auckland, 64-3- for the South Island. Freephones and freefaxes are for reservations within New Zealand only.

- **Internet**
  Most pages in this book are on the website
  http://friars.co.nz
  Some include Virtual Tours (indicated by our VT symbol). The accommodation properties often have additional websites, usually linked from the Friars' site. Bookings can be made via the Internet booking form to all hosts with email addresses.

- **Tariffs**
  Tariffs are calculated in New Zealand dollars and cents. All tariffs include GST (Goods & Services Tax of 12.5%). Each tariff indicates a nightly rate, unless otherwise stated.
  Double indicates the tariff for two people sharing one double or one twin room.
  Single indicates the tariff for one person occupying a room.
  Room rate indicates the tariff for one room, single or double.
  A **deposit** is often required on booking.
  Cancellation fees usually apply, although these vary.
  All tariffs are subject to change – confirm with your hosts. Tariffs are correct at time of printing in 2003.
  Tariffs include breakfast or provisions unless otherwise stated.
  Sometimes dinner is offered which is either included within the tariff, or is charged for separately as indicated.

- **Booking**
  All accommodation must be booked in advance unless otherwise stated. Cancellation policies usually apply. These vary from place to place, so please check at time of booking. Most hosts take credit cards for deposits, which also vary. These are only refundable if the booking is cancelled within the specified time.
  If hosts also offer lunch or dinner, they usually need prior notice.
  Single, private, exclusive, or one-party bookings mean that only one group of people is booked at a time. If there is a shared bathroom, this means it is shared only within that same party.

- **Bedrooms and Bathrooms**
  The following abbreviations are used:
  bdrm = bedroom
  enst = ensuite bathroom
  prbth = private bathroom
  shbth = guest-share bathroom
  pdrm = powder room (extra guest toilet near the dining room)

  Ensuite: An ensuite means a bathroom directly adjoining a bedroom. An ensuite can include just a shower and toilet, or else it can be a spacious bathroom incorporating a bath or even spa bath. "Ensuite" does not indicate size, only position.

  Private bathroom: A private bathroom, including a shower and toilet and maybe a bath, is separated from the bedroom, perhaps across the hallway, but is dedicated for that bedroom's sole use. If single-party bookings are indicated, then the bathroom is private to that one party. Bathrobes are usually supplied for guests' use.

  Guest-share bathroom: This bathroom is usually shared between two guest bedrooms, occasionally more, within the same party. It is rarely shared with the hosts. If only one bedroom is occupied, it becomes that room's private bathroom. It contains shower, toilet and maybe a bath.

  Powder room: This means an extra separate toilet serving the general living areas, dining room/restaurant or lounge.

  King/twin: This is either a king zipper bed or two singles that can be configured as one king-size or two single beds.

  Super-king: This bed is 15cm longer than king-size.

  Californian-king: This is 15cm wider than super-king.

  Queen: This is 15cm narrower than a king-size bed. A **queen/twin** means either that the bed can be configured as two singles, or that an extra bed is available, as a triple.

  Double: This means one double bed. An additional single bed may be available, sometimes indicated as **double/twin**. This can also be referred to as a triple.

  Twin: This means two separate beds. Often both are single beds, and occasionally one or both twin beds may be double beds. If the twin room can sleep three guests, it is sometimes known as triple.

  King-single: This means a single bed, an extra 15cm long.

  Suite: This means a bedroom and an ensuite bathroom, as well as an additional room, usually a separate lounge that belongs exclusively to that guest's bedroom.

- **Metrics**
  Measurements in this book are calculated in metrics. Eg:
  1 foot = 30cm (centimetres)
  3.28 feet = 1m (metre)
  6 miles = 10km (kilometres)
  5 acres = 2ha (hectares)

Friars' Guide to New Zealand Accommodation for the Discerning Traveller

- MEALS
  Breakfast or a breakfast basket or provisions is included in the tariff unless a separate charge is stated.
  A **continental** breakfast can be buffet style or quite elaborate, but excludes cooked dishes.
  A **cooked** breakfast may also be offered, either included in the tariff or charged in addition to a continental breakfast, as indicated.

  Occasionally tariffs include dinner or **all** meals as stated.

  Sometimes **lunch** is available, by prior request, at an extra charge. This may be either a light luncheon, a full lunch with wine, or picnic hampers may be offered.

  Self-catering means that there is a fully equipped kitchen where guests can make their own meals. If full cooking facilities are not provided, it is referred to as a kitchenette. Tea, coffee and maybe provisions or a pantry are supplied.

  Dinner may be available, usually by prior arrangement. A courtesy car may be provided for nearby restaurants.

  Booking is usually necessary for lunch or dinner, unless included in tariff. Hosts need at least a few hours' notice, unless there is an in-house restaurant. Most hosts cater for **vegetarian** or other dietary requirements if notified in time.

  Lunch and dinner **charges** are per person.

  Drinks are complimentary if indicated, or charged separately.

  À la carte means there is a menu choice.

  Table d'hôte indicates a fixed menu.

  BYO means you can Bring Your Own alcohol.

  Licensed means all the alcohol is sold on the premises. Even without a licence, alcohol or wine with meals can be charged for as long as the number of guests does not exceed 11.

- TOURS
  Exclusive tours can be booked in specific regions or throughout New Zealand. Land or air tours are both available – see pages 11 and 12.

- ROAD TRAVEL
  The directions given beneath each map are intended to guide self-driving guests to their destinations. Vehicles drive on the left-hand side of the roads in New Zealand. Overseas travellers should keep this in mind when starting off after a roadside rest stop, as research has shown that this is the time when many accidents involving tourists happen. The left-hand road rule means that, when turning left, drivers must give way to right-turning traffic. When booking for the winter months, it pays to check road conditions with South Island hosts, in case of icy conditions or snow.
  Off-street or on-site parking is usually indicated, and sometimes garaging is available.

- PETS
  Pets are not welcome, unless specified, by prior arrangement.

- AIR TRAVEL
  A shuttle service delivers passengers to destinations in most major cities. Some hosts operate a courtesy passenger transfer service. Sometimes a helipad is available for helicopters.

- BUSH WALKS
  This activity indicates formed walkways through native forest.

- WEATHER FORECASTS
  Because New Zealand's weather can be unpredictable, it is advisable to listen to a weather forecast before travelling. For the most up-to-date weather information, ring Metphone for the location you will be visiting. There is a charge for these calls:
  0900 99 909 for Northland and Auckland regions
  0900 99 907 for Waikato and Bay of Plenty regions
  0900 99 906 for Gisborne, Hawke's Bay, Taranaki, Wanganui, Manawatu and Wairarapa regions
  0900 99 904 for Kapiti Coast and Wellington region
  0900 99 903 for the South Island

- RADIO FREQUENCIES
  The traveller may wish to tune into the national public non-commercial network. These are the AM National programme (current affairs and light entertainment) and FM concert programme (mainly classical music, with jazz reviews and composer profiles).

- LOCATION GUIDE
  On page 8 is a location guide, showing the traveller the salient features of each region throughout New Zealand. The accommodation properties in each region are indicated by the relevant page numbers.

- EXPLODED PAGE
  On page 5 there is a sample page from this book, with the layout and all the logos, symbols, icons and tabs explained. Each page is designed in a standardised way for ease of reference. The individual logos used are further identified on page 9.

- INDEXES
  At the end of the book, on pages 506–508, is the Accommodation Index. This provides an alphabetical listing of each property featured in this book, including two yachts. Two exclusive tour operators are listed under **Tours**. Then on pages 509–512 is the Hosts Index. This enables the traveller to locate the accommodation by looking up the host's name, again alphabetically listed.

- EVALUATION
  Each place showcased in this book is personally evaluated and recommended by Denis and Jillian Friar who have stayed at most of them. The success of this book depends on its reliability and accuracy. We therefore welcome evaluative comments from guests who stay at the accommodation included in this book. To send your feedback to us, please refer to the address, phone, fax and email details on page 505. We always follow up all feedback, both complimentary and critical, although we are not responsible for any guest dissatisfaction.

FRIARS' GUIDE TO NEW ZEALAND ACCOMMODATION FOR THE DISCERNING TRAVELLER

NEW ZEALAND LOCATION GUIDE

NORTH ISLAND FEATURES

Far North: subtropical beaches, Cape Reinga, Ninety Mile Beach, sparsely populated

Bay of Islands: "winterless north" climate, big-game fishing, watersports, historic sites, Waitangi Treaty House, walking tracks

Northland: warm climate, kauri forests & museums, watersports, northernmost city Whangarei, Poor Knights Islands Marine Reserve, Whangarei Harbour Basin

Auckland: largest city in NZ, "City of Sails", beaches, watersports, Devonport ferry, 48 dormant volcanoes, Kelly Tarlton's Antarctic Encounter & Underwater World, MOTAT Technological Museum, War Memorial Museum, Maritime Museum, zoo, art galleries, parks & reserves, walking tracks, public & private gardens to visit, Muriwai mainland gannet colony, offshore islands

Coromandel: historic gold trails, golden beaches, Hot Water Beach, surfing, fishing, wading and shorebirds, native forest, kauri groves, tramping, crafts, sparsely populated

Bay of Plenty: sunny east coast, orchards, Rotorua with boiling mud pools, geysers & steaming lakes, Maori culture, redwood forest, crafts, surf beaches, big-game fishing, Mayor Island, active White Island volcano

Waikato: longest NZ river, biggest inland city Hamilton, crafts, river sports, mineral pools, rich dairy farmland, horse studs, gardens

King Country: Waitomo Caves, glow-worms, gardens, sheep farming

Central Plateau: Taupo – NZ's biggest lake, trout fishing, watersports, Mt Ruapehu, skiing, Tongariro National Park, walks

Gisborne: sunny, "First City of the Sun", surf beaches, isolated, Lake Waikaremoana, Te Urewera National Park, wineries

Hawke's Bay: sunshine, wineries, Wine Festival (Feb), Blossom Festival (Sept), Art Deco Napier, Cape Kidnappers gannet colony, beaches, fishing, National Aquarium

Taranaki: mountain, skiing, climbing, tramping, gardens, Rhododendron Festival (late Oct), Egmont National Park, New Plymouth city, cheese-making

Rangitikei & Wanganui: river sports, gardens to visit, historic homes, tramping

Manawatu: Palmerston North inland city, farming, agricultural university, wind farms

Wairarapa: wineries, gardens, historic museums, Cape Palliser seal colony, historic Maori sites, farming, wind farms

Kapiti Coast: Kapiti Island wildlife sanctuary, gardens to visit, car museum

CONTENTS

Ninety Mile Beach 14
Ahipara 15, 16
Cable Bay 17
Coopers Beach 18–20
Mangonui 21
Whangaroa 22–24
Cavalli 25–27
Kerikeri 28–35
Paihia 36–41
Opua 42–45, 56
Russell 46–55
Hikurangi 57
Whangarei 58–61
Dargaville 62–64
Lang Cove 65
Mangawhai Heads .. 66–68
Warkworth 69–80
Sandspit 76–78
Puhoi 81
Waiwera 82, 83
Orewa 84
North Shore 92, 93, 105
West Auckland 96, 107
Waiheke Island 95–104
Central Auckland 106–108
Eastern Suburbs .. 109–115
South Auckland .. 116–118
Miranda 119
Coromandel 120–121
Whitianga 122–124
Tairua..................... 125
Whangamata 126–128
Waihi 129
Tauranga 130–138
Mt Maunganui ... 139–140
Whakatane 141
Ngongotaha 142–153
Rotorua 154–161
Te Whaiti 162
Hamilton 163
Matangi 164
Cambridge 165–167
Tirau 168
Otorohanga 169
Te Kuiti 170
Taupo 171–192
Turangi 193–195
Gisborne 196–198
Mahia 199, 200
Napier 201–208
Cape Kidnappers 209
Hastings 219
Havelock North ... 210–218
Waipukurau 220
New Plymouth 221–225
Stratford 226
Raetihi 227
Ohakune 228
Wanganui 229–231
Mangaweka 232
Hunterville 233
Kimbolton 234
Palmerston North...... 235
Woodville 236
Masterton 237–241
Carterton 242, 243
Greytown 244, 245
Martinborough ... 246–249
Palliser Bay 250, 251
Kapiti Coast 252–260

Wellington: capital city, parliament, museum, theatre, arts, political centre, history, Cook Strait ferries, only NZ cable car, Botanic & Native Gardens

SOUTH ISLAND FEATURES

Marlborough: "Gourmet Province", interisland ferries, temperate climate, wineries, Marlborough Sounds, fishing, whale, seal & dolphin watching, boating, tramping, skiing, gardens, history

Nelson: sunny climate, arts & crafts, pottery, limestone caves, river, lakes, golden beaches, city, early colonial buildings, wineries, native forest, walks, deer hunting, watersports, trout/salmon fishing, shellfish, horse trekking, gold trails, gardens, three National Parks, northernmost tip of Island

Westland: gold trails, lakes, trout fishing, rainforest, walks, glaciers, rivers, greenstone, underground coalmine, heron sanctuary

North Canterbury: Southern Alps, glacier lakes, trout fishing, skiing, climbing, hot springs, hunting, river sports, gardens to visit, scenic flights, tramping, plains, farming

Christchurch: largest South Island city, English stone buildings, history, parks & gardens, cycling, arts, River Avon, Antarctic Centre, beaches, Lyttelton Harbour

Banks Peninsula: old French town of Akaroa, bays, seabirds, salmon, shellfish, boating, gardens

Mid & South Canterbury: highest NZ mountain Mt Cook/Aoraki, Southern Alps, glacier lakes, salmon & trout fishing, skiing, climbing, hunting, river sports, gardens to visit, scenic flights, tramping, plains, farming

North Otago: Oamaru historic limestone buildings, quarry, blue penguins, heritage trail

Dunedin: stone buildings, gardens, history, arts, albatross colony, yellow-eyed penguins, Carisbrook sports park

Central Otago: glacial lakes, Clutha River – NZ's largest, gold trails, gold panning, river sports, skiing, climbing, bobsledding, walks, gardens to visit, April Arrowtown Autumn Festival, museums, historic steamer, fishing, golf, bungy jumping, jet boating, stonefruit orchards

Fiordland: glacial lakes, fiords, walking tracks, rainforest, National Park, Doubtful Sounds, Milford Track, fishing, isolation

Southland: trout fishing, hunting, sheep farming, alpine lakes, rainforests, Catlins, southernmost city – Invercargill, gardens

Stewart Island: rainforest, native birds, brown kiwi, penguins, walks, boat charters

Pauatahanui 261, 262
Ohariu Valley 263, 264
The Hutt 265, 267
Lowry Bay 266
Khandallah 268, 269
Wellington 270–277

CONTENTS

The Sounds 279–283
Picton 284–287
Blenheim 288–302
Rai Valley 306
Havelock 303, 305
Nelson 307–324
Port Hills 325–330
Richmond 331–333
Tasman Bay
 ....334, 335, 343–346
Ruby Bay 340–342
Motueka 347, 351, 352
Kaiteriteri 348–350
Golden Bay 353–355
Nelson Lakes 356
Westport 357, 358
Punakaiki 359
Greymouth 360
Kumara 361, 362
Hokitika 363
Awatuna 364
Harihari 350
Franz Josef 367, 368
Fox Glacier 369
Lake Moeraki 370, 371
Arthur's Pass ...371–373
Kaikoura 374–379
Hanmer Springs ..380–383
Amberley 384, 385
Rangiora 386, 388
Oxford 387
Christchurch 389–404
West Melton 405
Lincoln 406
Tai Tapu 407–409
Lyttelton 410
Banks Peninsula ..411–418
Darfield 419
Methven 420
Ashburton 421
Geraldine 422, 423
Winchester 424
Timaru 425
Lake Tekapo 427–429
Twizel 430, 431
Tokarahi 432
Palmerston 433
Dunedin..........434–440
Mosgiel 441
Alexandra 442
Dublin Bay 445, 446
Wanaka 443–462
Cardrona 463
Arrowtown 464–467
Lake Hayes 468, 469
Queenstown 477–490
Te Anau 491–494
Gore 495, 496
Winton 497, 498
Invercargill 499
Riverton 500
Catlins 501
Stewart Island 502–504

Friars' Guide to New Zealand Accommodation for the Discerning Traveller

Key to Logos, Symbols and Tabs

- **Affiliation Logos**
Accommodation establishments are members of the following affiliations wherever the relevant logos are displayed:

 Heritage & Character Inns of New Zealand

 @ Home

 Small Luxury Hotels of the World

 New Zealand Lodge Association

 Superior Inns of New Zealand

 Select Hotels & Resorts International

 NZ Federation of Bed & Breakfast Hotels

 Boutique Hotels of New Zealand

 New Zealand Historic Places Trust (category 1 or 2)

 NZ Beef & Lamb Hallmark of Excellence

 New Zealand Tourism Awards winner/finalist (only awards from 2002 onwards displayed)

 Qualmark 5-star – defined by Qualmark as "Exceptional. Among the best available in New Zealand"

 Qualmark 4-star plus and Qualmark 4-star – defined by Qualmark as "Excellent. Consistently achieves high quality levels with a wide range of facilities and services"

 Qualmark 3-star plus – defined by Qualmark as "Very good. Provides a range of facilities and services and achieves good to very good quality standards"

 Qualmark without any stars indicates that the establishment has applied for Qualmark rating and is awaiting grading

Qualmark category "guest & hosted" corresponds to the *Friars' Guide* green or burgundy tabs

Qualmark category "self-contained & serviced" corresponds to the *Friars' Guide* blue tab

NOTE: All Qualmark gradings are assessed and rated by Qualmark, **not** Friars

- **Coloured Tabs**
The coloured tabs at the side of each page indicate categories of accommodation.
Green means that a full bed and breakfast option is offered – continental and/or cooked breakfast is served; if breakfast provisions are supplied for self-catering a green tab is **not** used.
Burgundy means dinner is offered – either within the tariff, or at an extra charge.
Blue means that a full kitchen is provided for self-catering. A kitchenette does **not** qualify for a blue tab. Provisions are supplied if indicated.

> Green tab – indicates B&B option available
>
> Burgundy tab – indicates dinner available
>
> Blue tab – indicates self-catering available

- **Symbols**
The following apply wherever the symbol is used:

 this means that smoking restrictions are to be observed – these vary, but often limit smoking to outdoors. Some establishments do not permit smoking at all. Please enquire. If there is no smoking restriction symbol, then smoking is permitted.

 this means there is wheelchair access to at least one bedroom, and there are wheelchair facilities available in at least one ensuite or private bathroom.

 this indicates child-friendly accommodation and it means children are accepted by arrangement. Children are the responsibility of their parents or guardians unless otherwise arranged with the hosts. Reduced tariffs may apply. Age restrictions often apply. Some places are unsuitable for children and for pets.

 this means that there is a professionally qualified chef. Dinner may be offered, ranging from home cooking to gourmet cuisine, and vegetarians may be catered for. Meals are usually available only by prior arrangement.

 this means there is a Virtual Tour available on the host's website, usually on http://friars.co.nz

- **Credit Cards**
The following are accepted wherever displayed:

 Visa

 Mastercard

 Amex (American Express)

 JCB (Japanese)

 Diners

 Eftpos

- **Friars' Plaque**
The solid cast bronze plaque depicted on page 505 graces many of the establishments in this book. It reassures guests that the accommodation has been recommended by Friars, and is relinquished if hosts are no longer in the *Friars' Guide*.

 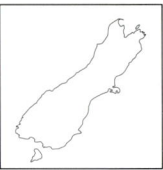

Christopher Brown & Associates Ltd, MREINZ
Lodges – Hotels – Business Brokers

Brokers Alison Marks, AREINZ and Olaf Eady, AREINZ, ACA

Level 9, 17 Albert Street, Auckland Central, Auckland
Postal P O Box 106 019, Downtown, Auckland
Phone 0-9-377 7741   *Mobile* 021 974 203   *Fax* 0-9-377 7742
Email alison@businessbrokers.co.nz   *Website* www.businessbrokers.co.nz

Alison and Olaf specialise in the buying and selling of lodges and hotels. Their emphasis is on providing a high level of professionalism and confidentiality focused on fulfilling their clients' needs. As brokers they are practised at concluding transactions outside the public gaze. They are part of a team of highly experienced and well supported brokers, each in a specialist field. They are members of Christopher Brown and Associates Ltd, a specialist company in the field of business mergers, acquisitions and sales. The company operates an extensive database system tailored to each individual broker's needs. Specified in the company mission statement is the mandate to be the "quiet achievers". Alison and Olaf value the relationships they build with both the vendors and purchasers. By specialising in selling lodges and hotels they are familiar with the particular features pertaining to that part of the market. The majority of their sales and transactions are effected by knowing their industries and identifying their buyers. Alison and Olaf are pleased to provide their services to both members and readers of *Friars' Guide*. They can offer advice on either purchasing or selling lodges. They travel extensively throughout New Zealand whenever possible, and are only a phone call away.

Features

Alison & Olaf:

- have 25 years' experience in the selling of commercial investments in NZ
- are skilled negotiators
- a high level of industry knowledge & strong industry networking skills
- travel throughout NZ
- understand the needs of vendors & puchasers
- have access to the company's large database of purchasers
- undertake to maintain confidentiality
- are only a phone call away

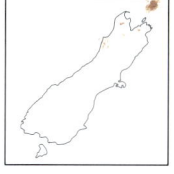

NEW ZEALAND FLIGHT SAFARIS

Operator Dolphin Travel

P O Box 15 358, Tauranga 3001
Phone 0-7-578 8950   *Email* enjoy@flightsafaris.com
Fax 0-7-578 3299   *Website* www.flightsafaris.com

DIRECTIONS: Guests are met at Auckland Airport & taken to airline's passenger lounge before departure, or to selected accommodation, depending on personal itinerary.

2–9 passengers per plane

Day tour rate $1,250–$1,350 per person
Multiple-day tour rate $2,075–$23,800 pp for 2–14 days
Valid for 4-person group   *Includes flightseeing, transport, selected meals & other arrangements*

New Zealand Flight Safaris are designed for couples and small groups for touring the length and breadth of New Zealand. Tailor-made flightseeing itineraries from two days to six weeks are created by Dolphin Travel to care for guests' every need. Launched in 1997, this inbound tour operator was established to provide individual personalised service. Christian Aviation, which runs the three well-maintained twin-engined aircraft, has an accident-free record. Their four pilots have lengthy flying experience. The pilot is also the in-flight tour guide, or a qualified local tour guide can accompany passengers. The passengers' favourite beverages and snacks are available on board, and lunch options include alfresco luncheons, silver-service picnics and local restaurants. A range of vehicles are available for sightseeing tours and transport to the selected accommodation.

Facilities
- 3 twin-engine charter aircraft:
  – 4-seater *Piper Seneca,*
  – 7-seater *Piper Navajo,*
  – 9-seater *Piper Chieftain*
- 4 experienced pilots
- passengers' favourite snacks & beverages on board
- lunch options from light on-board snacks to silver-service picnics, or local restaurants
- personalised itinerary
- travel wallet comprising: itinerary, region & activity information, tour-service vouchers, NZ travel guidebook, NZFS' 24-hr multi-lingual emergency number, brochures, maps
- accommodation included, with range of vehicles for passenger transfer

Activities available
- variety of tour options such as:
  – nature tours
  – golfing
  – fishing
  – hunting
  – arts & crafts tours
  – bird-watching
  – diving
  – Maori culture
  – food & wine gourmet tours
  – vintage cars or aeroplanes
- flightseeing & sightseeing
- viewing New Zealand's landscape
- information provided by pilot and driver/guides
- if requested, pilot will land wherever safe & legal, including comfort stops
- boutique accommodation or luxury lodges included

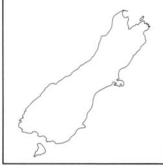

Dream Places

Host Tony Lilleby

P O Box 1504, Nelson

Phone 0-3-548 1081 *Email* enquiries@dreamplacesnewzealand.com
Fax 0-3-548 1691 *Website* www.dreamplacesnewzealand.com

DIRECTIONS: Guests are collected & dropped off at selected airports & towns by arrangement. Driver is Nelson-based & charges will reflect distances incurred.

4 passengers maximum

Motorhome rate $415–$655 for 2 persons Extra persons, $125 each *Includes all meals*
Motorhome rate $370–$550 for 2 persons Extra persons, $75 each *Self-catering*

Dream Places features flexible guided travel in a motorhome that provides customised touring for guests according to their interests. The 10.5-metre motorhome is fully self-contained, with spacious interiors for comfortable accommodation in back country locations. Guests can either cater for themselves, or have all meals provided. Menus are arranged with guests prior to travel. Dream Places offers a range of tours, personalised to suit individual interests, or guests may choose to travel with no pre-arranged or set timetable at all. Tony, your host, driver and guide, has a background of working in New Zealand's National Parks and back country, and uses a network of special and secluded places for overnight stops.

Facilities

- single-party bookings only in 10.5m motorhome
- 1 king bedroom & vanity
- lounge/dining area with extra fold-down king/twin bed
- driver sleeps in cab or tent
- large, high-pressure hot shower
- separate full-size flush toilet
- quality linen & towels
- air-conditioning & heating
- meals catered, optional; local food & menus arranged with guests
- full kitchen with fridge/freezer & gas cooker
- BBQ & outdoor furniture
- sound system
- phone, computer & email
- collection & drop-off at selected airports & cities of guests' choice, extra

Activities available

Guided or individual:

- 3 quality serviced road & mountain bikes, extra
- kayaks, paddles & life jackets, extra
- personalised itineraries
- walking; hiking
- road cycling; mountain biking
- sea & lake kayaking
- photography & film making
- *The Lord of the Rings* tours
- fly fishing
- watersports
- rural golf
- national parks
- back country travel
- garden tours
- horse trekking
- customised sightseeing & tours throughout NZ

FRIARS' GUIDE TO NEW ZEALAND ACCOMMODATION FOR THE DISCERNING TRAVELLER

NORTH ISLAND

Hokianga Harbour, on the west coast of Northland, see pages 14–16, and page 62.

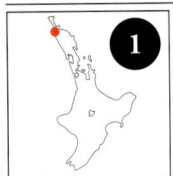

Ninety Mile Beach
Taharangi Marie Lodge

Hosts Ron Adams and Connie Simon

700 Sandhills Road, Ninety Mile Beach, Far North   *Postal* P O Box 59, Kaitaia
Phone 0-9-406 7462   *Mobile* 027 492 6949   *Fax* 0-9-408 3085
Email taharangi@xtra.co.nz   *Website* friars.co.nz/hosts/taharangi.html

2 bdrm   2 enst   Room rate $300   Winter rates available   Includes continental breakfast   Dinner extra

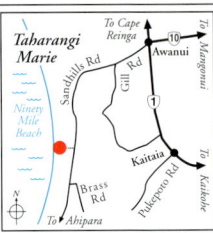

DIRECTIONS: From Awanui, take Gill Rd west. Turn right before end of tarseal into Sandhills Rd. Travel 7km to gate on right. Take driveway approx. 0.75km to Taharangi Marie. From Ahipara, take Sandhills Rd for 8.8km.

Built among the sand-dunes bordering Ninety Mile Beach, Taharangi Marie is aptly named "peaceful horizon". The relative isolation of the accommodation, with the ocean only 50 metres away, makes it a tranquil get-away for relaxation and rejuvenation. Guests find the constant sound of the waves soothing, complemented by activities for the energetic. Opened in 1998, the house features stone pillars, timber ceilings, a mezzanine floor separating the two ensuite guestrooms, extensive decking and uninterrupted sea views. Guests enjoy breakfast indoors, or alfresco, and in season, freshly gathered seafood is a highlight of the dinner menu. The hosts are willing to share knowledge and experience of their Maori culture and tradition.

Facilities

- 1 king & 1 queen ensuite bedrooms upstairs
- 2 ensuite bathrooms with toiletries & hair dryers
- cotton bed linen
- tea/coffee facilities in both bedrooms
- lounge with open fire
- Sky TV & video in lounge
- panoramic ocean views
- continental breakfast
- dinner with wine, by prior arrangement, with fresh local seafood gathered from adjacent beach
- extensive decking
- laundry available
- courtesy passenger transfer
- garaging for guests
- beach access

Activities available

- hiking over sand-dunes
- beach, 50-metre walk
- swimming; surfing
- tuatua shellfish gathering
- beach walks
- historic kauri log site
- fishing; diving
- sand-dune adventures
- Ninety Mile Beach drive
- quad bike hire
- personalised tours in Far North
- restaurants, 15-min drive
- horse treks
- gum fields; glow-worms
- golf
- Ancient Kauri Kingdom
- Maori arts & crafts
- Cape Reinga, 1-hour drive

Ninety Mile Beach
Siesta Guest Lodge & Villa Apartment

Hosts Carole and Alan Harding

Tasman Heights Road, Ahipara   *Postal* P O Box 30, Ahipara, Northland
Phone 0-9-409 2011   *Mobile* 021 965 085   *Fax* 0-9-409 2011
Email ninetymile@xtra.co.nz   *Website* www.ahipara.co.nz/siesta

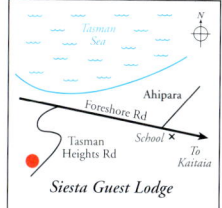

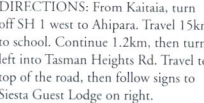

DIRECTIONS: From Kaitaia, turn off SH 1 west to Ahipara. Travel 15km to school. Continue 1.2km, then turn left into Tasman Heights Rd. Travel to top of the road, then follow signs to Siesta Guest Lodge on right.

5 bdrm	3 enst	1 prbth	1 pdrm

Room rate $150–$195
Apartment rate $150–$250

Includes breakfast, or extra in apartment
Long-stay rates available   *Self-catering*

Alan and Carole's Mediterranean-style house overlooks Ninety Mile Beach. Facing north, the upstairs guest wing is warmed by all-day sun, the guest balconies overlook the secluded subtropical gardens and sheltered bay below. The guest dining and lounge areas are quiet and spacious, with native rimu wood panelling and terracotta tiles. Guests enjoy sleeping to the sound of the sea, and relaxing in the privacy and tranquillity. Carole and Alan have lived locally since 1974 and know all the sunny local white-sand beaches and hidden treasures. Long-stay guests have the option of adjacent Siesta Villas with two self-contained apartments, where guests can self-cater and stay in spacious comfort with panoramic ocean views, even from their bed.

Facilities

Main house:
- 2 ensuite queen bedrooms with tea/coffee & ocean views
- continental breakfast, or cooked on request
- private guest balconies
- guest lounge & reading room
- courtesy transfer from Kaitaia airport or bus depot

2 Villa apartments:
- 1 upstairs apartment with king bedroom & ensuite
- 1 studio downstairs with 1 queen & 1 twin bedroom, 1 bathroom
- Sky TV, video & stereo with CDs
- full kitchen with dishwasher
- breakfast available, extra
- indoor/outdoor living & BBQ
- panoramic seaviews, east & west

Activities available

- licensed restaurant 400m away
- beach, 5-min walk
- safe swimming; surfing; diving
- fishing, on or off-shore
- sand-dune wilderness, close by
- guided hikes
- personalised luxury 4WD tours
- bush, coastal & wilderness walks
- horse riding on beaches & sandhills
- local award-winning winery
- Cape coach tours
- Ninety Mile Beach
- links golf course, 5 mins
- Glow-worm Grotto & Kiwi House, 30 mins
- quad bike hire
- local kauri forests, 1 hour
- Bay of Islands, 1¼-hr drive
- Kauri Coast, 2-hour drive

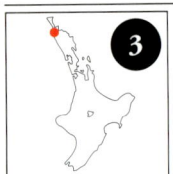

Ninety Mile Beach
Shipwreck Lodge

Hosts Laura and Roger Raduenz

70 Foreshore Road, Ahipara   *Postal* 70 Foreshore Road, R D 1 Kaitaia
Phone 0-9-409 4929   *Mobile* 021 126 7294   *Fax* 0-9-409 4928
Email shipwrecklodge@xtra.co.nz   *Website* www.shipwrecklodge.co.nz

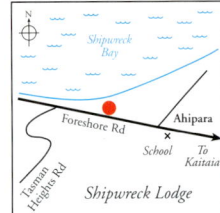

DIRECTIONS: From Kaitaia, turn off SH 1 at clock tower, west to Ahipara. Travel 15km to school. Continue for 1km on Foreshore Rd to 90 Mile Beach House on right.

3 bdrm   3 enst   1 pdrm   Room rate $165–$295   Includes breakfast   Wine extra

Located on the beachfront at Shipwreck Bay, this lodge was purpose-built in 2000 at the southern end of Ninety Mile Beach. Guests at Shipwreck Lodge enjoy the special features which include direct beach access, unlimited views of the bay and reef, and the sunsets. This Tuscan-style villa was designed for easy living, with large airy rooms, high studs and fold-out doors. The spacious king and queen ensuite bedrooms upstairs overlook the beach, each with a private balcony for uninterrupted vistas. Breakfast is served in the dining area downstairs which opens directly towards the beach. Wine is also available in-house. Fishing, golf, surfing and four-wheel-drive trips over the nearby sandhills are popular activities with guests. Restaurants are nearby.

Facilities

- 1 queen & 2 king spacious ensuite bedrooms upstairs
- demist mirrors & toiletries in all 3 bathrooms
- cotton bed linen
- writing desk & phone jacks in each bedroom
- tea/coffee on bedroom landing
- TV available
- phone, fax & email available
- full breakfast served in dining area
- extensive wine list, extra
- powder room downstairs
- laundry available
- wide sea views
- private guest balconies from all 3 bedrooms
- "winterless north" climate
- on-site parking

Activities available

- direct beach access & views to Shipwreck Bay from site
- barbecue on site
- Ahipara village nearby
- safe swimming
- 4WD bike tours
- 90 Mile Links Golf Course & Carrington Club nearby
- Ninety Mile Beach for walking, driving, swimming, 4WD tours
- restaurants nearby
- award-winning winery
- fishing
- boating
- surfing
- walks
- horse riding
- Kaitaia township, 15km
- Cape Reinga, 1½-hr drive
- Auckland City, 4½-hr drive

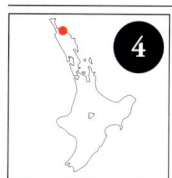

Cable Bay
Carneval Ocean View

Hosts Martha and Roly Fasnacht

360 State Highway 10, Cable Bay, Mangonui
Phone 0-9-406 1012   *Mobile* 021 214 6524   *Fax* 0-9-406 1012
Email holiday@carneval.co.nz   *Website* friars.co.nz/hosts/carneval.html

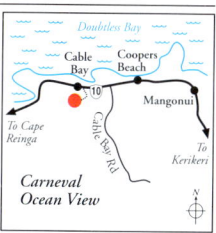

DIRECTIONS: From the turn-off to Mangonui, follow SH 10 to Coopers Beach. Continue to Cable Bay. Cross bridge & opposite rest area turn left up driveway 500m to top of hill, to Carneval Ocean View at end.

| 2 bdrm | 2 enst |

Room rate $140–$170

Includes breakfast
Picnic baskets & dinner extra

Located 80 metres above sea level, Carneval Ocean View provides panoramic vistas of Doubtless Bay. Carneval is Swiss for the hosts' surname. Martha and Roly speak Swiss-German and French, and Roly is a qualified chef. Swiss-style cooked breakfast is served in the dining room or alfresco on the terrace. Swiss-French style or Kiwi cuisine is also available for dinner using fresh local fish and produce. Built in Mediterrean style, Carneval overlooks the pink sand beach at Cable Bay where guests enjoy swimming and diving or fishing trips can be arranged. European-style accommodation comprises two king-size ensuite bedrooms with Finnish Tulikivi wall heating and a Tulikivi fire warms the lounge in winter.

Facilities

- one-party booking; sea views
- 2 ensuite king bedrooms
- dressing room, TV, tea/coffee, soda water, mini-fridge & Finnish Tulikivi wall heater in bedrooms
- hair dryers, toiletries, bathrobes, heated towel rails in ensuites
- guest lounge with Tulikivi fire, tea/coffee, cable TV, video, books, CD-player & writing desk
- email, fax & phone available
- Swiss-style cooked breakfast
- 3–5-course Swiss/French-style dinner, $35–$55 pp
- Swiss-German & French spoken by hosts
- beach towels supplied
- laundry, $5
- wheelchair access
- on-site parking
- courtesy passenger transfer

Activities available

- sauna room on site
- dartboard & darts available
- windsurfer & snorkelling gear
- large landscaped gardens on site
- kayak available
- pink-sand beach, 3–5-min walk
- Coopers Beach village, 3 mins
- Mangonui township, 8 mins
- diving & fishing trips arranged
- restaurants & cafés, Coopers Beach & Mangonui
- safe swimming
- golf, 15-min drive
- gardens & potteries to visit
- Butler Point historic visit
- Glow-worm Grotto & Kiwi House, 45-min drive away
- day trips & tours arranged
- www.carneval.co.nz

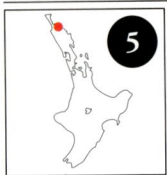

Coopers Beach
COOPERS BEACHFRONT SUITES

Hosts George Van Valkenburg and Janet Brennan

18 Bayside Drive, Coopers Beach   *Postal* P O Box 385, Mangonui
Phone 0-9-406 1018   *Freephone* 0800 169 020   *Fax* 0-9-406 1018
Email stay@coopersbeach.net   *Website* www.coopersbeach.net

DIRECTIONS: From the turn-off to Mangonui, follow SH 10 to Coopers Beach. Past the shopping centre, turn right into Bayside Drive to Coopers Beachfront Estate. Bear left to Coopers Beachfront Suites at end of private road.

Suite rate $175–$290
Weekly rates available

Includes continental breakfast provisions for 1st morning
Winter rates available   Self-catering

Coopers Beachfront Suites were purpose-built in 1997 beside the ocean, with only native pohutukawa trees separating them from the seashore. Adjacent is George and Janet's home, ensuring total guest privacy, yet accessibility if desired. Guests have exclusive use of either the upstairs suite with balcony overlooking the beach, or the similar downstairs suite with larger verandah providing direct access to the beach. Each totally smoke-free suite comprises a queen-size bedroom with ensuite bathroom, kitchenette, lounge and dining area, all facing the ocean. The peace and quietness of the setting is broken only by the soothing sound of the waves breaking on the shore. There is no traffic noise, yet the shops are only two minutes' walk away.

Facilities

- 1 upstairs & 1 downstairs suite
- 1 queen bedroom per suite
- sea views from both beds
- quality bed linen, bathrobes, reclining chair & insect screens
- hair dryer, heated towel rails & toiletries in both ensuites
- ceiling fan, TV, music in suites
- teas & plunger coffee in suites
- global cable television

- unsuitable for pets or children
- fridge/freezer, microwave, water filter & frypan in kitchenettes
- guest phone in both lounges
- laptop computer with free internet access available
- email, fax & laundry available
- gas barbecue available
- private guest entrances to suites
- off-street parking

Activities available

- direct access to beach
- sea kayaks for hire
- walking; swimming
- scuba diving; jogging
- deep-sea fishing
- historic sites; hiking
- Whaling Museum
- cinema with latest releases, 15-min drive
- ATM; Medical Centre

- restaurants & cafés, 5-min drive
- historic Mangonui, 2.5 km away
- 3 golf courses, range of difficulty
- arts & crafts; gardens to visit
- day trips to Cape Reinga
- Ninety Mile Beach, sand-dune buggies
- Ancient Kauri Kingdom, 20-min drive
- Matai Bay, 30-min drive, for picnics, swimming, snorkelling
- northernmost award-winning winery

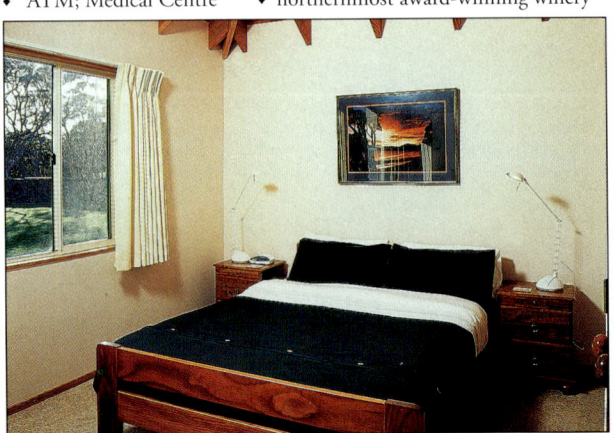

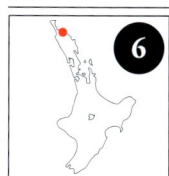

COOPERS BEACH
35 BAYSIDE

Hosts Jenny and John Baird

35 Bayside Drive, Coopers Beach   *Phone* 0-3-332 5996
Postal P O Box 28–118, Beckenham, Christchurch   *Fax* 0-3-332 8947
Email jenny@35bayside.co.nz   *Website* www.35bayside.co.nz

| 4 bdrm | 1 enst | 1 shbth |

House rate $250–$380
Minimum 4-night stay

Self-catering, no meals available
Long-term rates available

DIRECTIONS: From the turn-off to Mangonui, follow SH 10 to Coopers Beach. Travel past shops, then turn right into Bayside Drive, to Coopers Beachfront Estate. Continue to 35 Bayside on right at end.

Located on the Coopers Beachfront Estate is 35 Bayside, a self-contained holiday home built in 2001 to sleep 10 persons, including children. Set in fully landscaped gardens, with tropical plantings, this contemporary house provides extensive views of the pohutukawa-lined beach and Doubtless Bay. Four bedrooms are provided on two levels, with the full kitchen and two bathrooms by a multi-award-winning kitchen designer. Quality fittings and furnishings feature throughout and there are ceiling fans to enhance comfort. Guests can relax to the sound of the waves from the beach only 30 metres away via a private accessway, and the large paved patio area with gas barbecue is well sited for alfresco dining in the "winterless north" climate.

Facilities

- private-party bookings only
- self-contained house for 10
- 1 queen ensuite bedroom downstairs with bath
- 1 queen bedroom & 2 rooms with 1 bunk & 1 single upstairs share 1 bathroom
- cotton bed linen
- heated towel rails
- extra toilet; outdoor shower
- full kitchen for self-catering
- lounge with TV, video, CD-player, games & books
- children's TV area upstairs
- 2 phones; ceiling fans
- fully equipped laundry
- stair-guards, highchair & cot
- children welcome; no pets
- double garage
- on-site parking for boats

Activities available

- paved gas BBQ area on site
- 30m private accessway to Coopers Beach
- safe swimming
- shops & restaurant, 100m walk away
- historic Mangonui, 2km
- scuba diving
- deep-sea fishing
- 3 wineries within 45 mins
- restaurants & cafés, 5 mins
- boat launching ramps, 5 mins
- golf courses – Carrington Estate 15 mins, Kauri Cliffs 30 mins
- kauri forest, 30 mins
- Kauri Kingdom, 30 mins
- historic Bay of Islands, 45-min drive south
- Ninety Mile Beach, 35 mins
- day trips to Cape Reinga

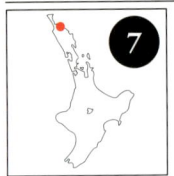

Coopers Beach
BEACH LODGE

Host Margaret Morrison

121 State Highway 10, Coopers Beach *Postal* P O Box 190, Mangonui
Phone 0-9-406 0068   *Email* margaret@beachlodge.co.nz
Fax 0-9-406 0068   *Website* www.beachlodge.co.nz

DIRECTIONS: From the turn-off to Mangonui Village, follow SH 10 for 2km. Beach Lodge is the last dwelling on the beach side of the road (45 minutes north of Kerikeri, or 25 minutes east of Kaitaia).

10 bdrm   5 prbth   Chalet rate $250–$380   *Self-catering, no meals available*

Overlooking the Pacific Ocean, Beach Lodge comprises a series of separate self-contained chalets sited directly above Coopers Beach. The waves breaking on the shore create a constant soothing sound and beachcombing is a relaxing pursuit. Native pohutukawa trees edge the beach, their red blossoms in December giving them the name "New Zealand Christmas Trees". The two-storey chalets are architecturally designed using native timbers, with each kitchen and bathroom built in solid rimu. Double-doored showers are a feature of the bathrooms. Total privacy is ensured with double French doors opening on to private decking surrounded by an attractive garden. Guests are welcomed with fresh flowers and confectionery.

Facilities
- 5 self-contained chalets
- single-party booking per chalet
- 1 queen downstairs & 1 twin upstairs bedroom per chalet
- 1 bathroom per chalet
- 50-channel cable TV in each chalet's lounge
- direct-dial phone per chalet
- ocean views from every room
- children over 8 years welcome
- 1 fully equipped kitchen for self-catering per chalet
- fax, email & BBQ available
- sundecks overlooking ocean
- Margaret speaks German
- gym facilities on site
- self-serve guest laundry
- "winterless" North climate
- off-street parking
- courtesy passenger transfer

Activities available
- private access to beach
- boogie boards & kayaks
- safe swimming
- shellfish gathering
- restaurants & cafés nearby
- shops easy walk; golf courses
- historic Mangonui, 2km away
- fishing trips; dolphin swims
- Glow-worm Grotto & Kiwi House, 24km away
- sailing trips to Cavalli Islands
- Maori pa sites, Butler Point
- Karikari Peninsula beaches, golf course & restaurant
- door-to-door tour service to: Cape Reinga, gum fields, kauri forests, Ninety Mile Beach, sand-hills with Paradise Connections
- arts & crafts – paintings, Maori weaving, fabric design, carving, pottery & swamp kauri turning

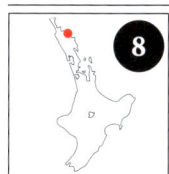

Mangonui
MILL BAY HAVEN

Hosts Anette and Anthony Norman

19 Silver Egg Drive, Mangonui   *Postal* P O Box 295, Mangonui
Phone 0-9-406 1113   *Mobile* 021 346 118   *Fax* 0-9-406 1130
Email anthonynorman@xtra.co.nz   *Website* www.millbayhaven.co.nz

5 bdrm   5 enst

Double $200–$400
Single $90–$140

Self-catering
No meals available

DIRECTIONS: Take SH 10 north & turn right to Mangonui. Travel thru village, turn right into Mabel Thorburn Dr & continue into Mill Bay Rd. Turn right into Silver Egg Dr & travel thru boat ramp area to end.

Mill Bay Haven is sited on the waterfront of Mangonui Harbour and backs onto a nature reserve. This historic kauri mill site now offers three self-contained options. Mill Lodge (*behind trees to left above*) still retains original rimu and kauri panelling, and provides three ensuite guestrooms, all with harbour views through mature pohutukawa trees at the lawn edge on the sea wall, from where guests can fish. A spa pool is located on a large deck backed by subtropical gardens. Rose Cottage (*also behind trees*) is set in a private garden and Seaview Studio (*to right of hosts' house above*) looks onto Mill Bay Haven's private beach. Moored in front of Mill Lodge are boats available for fishing or sailing charters. Anthony enjoys hosting guests on his yacht *Hinemoana*.

Facilities

- Mill Lodge: 1 twin & 2 queen ensuite bedrooms with bathrobes; 1 double basin, powder room, mezzanine & self-serve laundry
- Rose Cottage: 1 queen bedroom, ensuite & living room
- Seaview Studio: 1 queen ensuite bedroom with harbour views
- heated towel rails, hair dryers & toiletries in all 5 ensuites
- cotton bed linen; fresh flowers
- 3 kitchens for self-catering, or caterer by arrangement
- fruit baskets on arrival
- Sky TV in all 3 venues
- lounge in Lodge with open fire, phone, video & CDs
- children welcome
- spaniel dog & cat on site
- French & Swedish spoken
- parking; courtesy transfer

Activities available

- spa pool on Lodge deck
- BBQ on site
- fishing from front lawn or jetty
- private beach access
- safe swimming nearby
- 13.5m (44 ft) yacht *Hinemoana* on site, for hosted sailing charters with Anthony to Cavalli Islands, Karikari Peninsula, or Whangaroa
- golf courses
- Maori pa site & walks in nature reserve adjacent
- cafés & restaurants within walking distance
- Mangonui township 1km
- Coopers Beach, 2km
- Cable Bay pink sand, 5 mins
- door to door Cape Reinga day trips via 90 Mile Beach & sandhill tobogganing

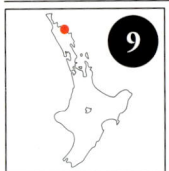

WHANGAROA
KINGFISH LODGE

Hosts Bernice and Roger Cairns

Kingfish Cove, Whangaroa Harbour, R D 1, Kaeo, Northland
Freephone 0800 100 546   Phone 0-9-405 0164   Fax 0-9-405 0163
Email fish@kingfishlodge.co.nz   *Website* www.kingfishlodge.co.nz

DIRECTIONS: Take SH 1 north from Whangarei, through Kawakawa, to Pakaraka. Turn right into SH 10. Travel to Kaeo then turn right & continue 10 mins to Whangaroa. Boat for Kingfish Lodge leaves from wharf.

12 bdrm | 12 enst

Double $375   Single $300
All meals extra
Inclusive packages available

Built in 1947, Kingfish Lodge is the oldest coastal fishing lodge in New Zealand. It now provides 12 waterside guest bedrooms, including two family suites. Guests need no fishing experience, as total tuition is provided. Under new management, this family-owned historic lodge is set in Kingfish Cove at the headland of Whangaroa Harbour. Surrounded by water and native bush, it provides tranquil isolation, accessible by helicopter or by boat from Whangaroa Wharf. After the courtesy 10-minute scenic cruise, guests land at the jetty adjacent to the lodge set in a subtropical garden. All dietary needs are catered for, including Japanese cuisine. Meals are served in the dining room or alfresco with harbour views.

Facilities

- 10 guest bedrooms with ensuite bathrooms
- 2 family suites each including 1 double/twin bedroom & 1 ensuite bathroom
- hair dryers, toiletries & heated towel rails in each ensuite
- TV, tea/coffee, iron & board, & phone in each bedroom
- weddings, functions, business groups, conferences catered for

- English breakfast, extra
- picnic or lunch, extra
- 4-course fine dining, extra
- fully licensed
- private guest entrances
- laundry available
- courtesy boat transfer
- 2 helipads
- full business facilities

Activities available

- full sauna & gym on site
- conferences catered
- complimentary fishing tuition
- kayaking
- clay-bird shooting
- lawn games eg croquet, volley ball, beach pétanque
- board games
- yachting
- hiking in 220ha native bush

- swimming & snorkelling
- salt fly-fishing & all light tackle fishing options
- big-game fishing – marlin, tuna & shark
- scuba diving by arrangement
- small power fishing boats, extra charge
- off-site: golfing; horse trekking; & sea kayaking

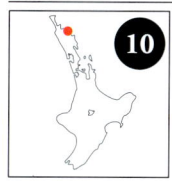

Whangaroa
Butterfly Bay

Host Amanda Kennedy

Butterfly Bay, Whangaroa   *Postal* P O Box 78, Kaeo
Phone 0-9-407 5957   *Email* butterflybay@actrix.co.nz
Fax 0-9-407 5977   *Website* friars.co.nz/hosts/butterflybay.html

House rate $565
Multiple-night & low-season rates available

Self-catering
No meals available

DIRECTIONS: Take SH 10 north to Kaeo. Continue 4km on Whangaroa Rd. Turn right into Wainui Rd. Travel 8km, then turn left into Tauranga Bay Rd. Travel 3km then turn left. Turn left again, then take right fork in drive.

3 bdrm | 3 enst

Butterfly Bay is a natural butterfly-breeding sanctuary, being a sunny secluded spot, sheltered from the wind. Riparian rights provide access to a private beach below the multi-level contemporary house, which is built into a rock-face, the hills creating an amphitheatre bordered by the sweeping beach of finely ground coloured shell. This self-contained house includes a fully equipped kitchen for self-catering. There is one king and one queen-size bedroom with ensuite bathrooms, and a mezzanine floor with two single beds and ensuite bathroom. All rooms face the ocean and doors open to a spacious deck where meals can be enjoyed alfresco. The peacefulness of the location is enhanced by the constant rhythm of the waves on the shore.

Facilities

- single-party bookings
- 1 king & 1 queen bedroom
- 1 mezzanine twin bedroom
- 3 ensuites with bathrobes
- extra outdoor shower
- sundeck overlooking ocean
- library
- guest phone
- fax available

- fully equipped kitchen for self-catering
- self-catering provisions
- spacious lounge with videos, CD-player & CDs
- self-serve laundry
- children & pets welcome
- off-street parking; helipad
- courtesy passenger transfer to/from Kerikeri Airport

Activities available

- swimming/surf beach with riparian rights
- gas BBQ on sundeck
- spa pool set in private grotto
- surf shack on beach with fishing tackle, pétanque, croquet, kites, volleyball, cricket, boogie boards, snorkels, masks, flippers, frisbees
- surf-casting, fishing from beach
- 5 18-hole golf courses nearby

- restaurants nearby
- guided scuba diving arranged
- coastal kayaking; horse treks
- big-game fishing; local fishing from boat
- guided salt-water fly fishing
- DOC walking tracks; sailing
- day trips to Cape Reinga, Puketi Kauri Forest, Ninety Mile Beach, sand-dunes

23   © Friars' Guide to New Zealand Accommodation for the Discerning Traveller

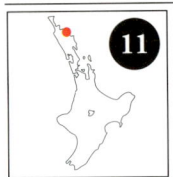

Tauranga Bay
Shearwater

Hosts Helen and Graham Ashman

Tauranga Bay, Northland *Postal* P O Box 192, Kaeo
Phone 0-9-405 0089 *Email* enquiries@shearwaternz.com
Fax 0-9-405 1233 *Website* www.shearwaternz.com

DIRECTIONS: Take SH 10 north to Kaeo. Continue 4km on Whangaroa Rd. Turn right into Wainui Rd. Travel 8km & turn left into Tauranga Bay Rd. Turn left at phone kiosk & travel 600m up to Pukemarama gates. 300m to Shearwater.

4 bdrm	4 enst	Villa rate $575 for 4 persons	*Includes continental breakfast*
		Apartment rate $275–$375	*Lunch & dinner extra Self-catering*

Located on the cliff edge overlooking Tauranga Bay (*see below right, centre*), Shearwater offers two self-contained accommodation options. Security gates open to a 300-metre driveway leading to Shearwater Retreat. The Villa is totally separate, featuring two ensuite bedrooms with spacious decks that lead to a spa pool and private six-metre swimming pool overlooking the ocean. The Apartment is a private wing of Helen and Graham's house, also offering two ensuite bedrooms and a large deck with spa pool and barbecue. Both venues include a fully equipped kitchen with breadmaker, and there is a dishwasher in the Villa. Guests can self-cater for lunch and dinner or a chef can be arranged to cater for them. A continental breakfast is provided.

Facilities

- Villa: 1 super-king/twin & 1 king bedroom, each with ensuite & bathrobes
- Apartment: 2 king ensuite bedrooms with wheelchair access
- cotton bed linen in both
- heated towel rails & toiletries in all 4 ensuite bathrooms
- lounge with tea/coffee, TV, CD-player, books & phone in both
- complimentary laundry
- continental breakfast
- lunch & dinner, by prior arrangement only, extra
- full kitchen for self-catering in both
- open fire in Villa
- email & fax available
- children by arrangement
- on-site parking
- courtesy passenger transfer

Activities available

- Apartment: large private deck with spa pool & BBQ
- Villa: private deck with spa pool, BBQ & 6m plunge pool
- kayaks & boogie boards available for guest use
- complimentary use of 4WD to beach
- day trips arranged
- 'winterless north' activities
- swimming beaches
- surf-casting; diving
- golf including Kauri Cliffs
- rock & big-game fishing
- 4WD tours arranged
- bush & beach walks
- vineyards
- scenic boat trips
- day trips to Cape Reinga & Ninety Mile Beach

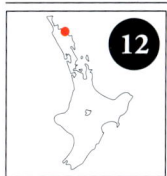

Mahinepua/Cavalli
Waiwurrie

Hosts Vickie and Rodger Corbin

Mahinepua Road, R D 1, Kaeo, Whangaroa, Northland
Phone 0-9-405 0840   *Email* wai.wurrie@xtra.co.nz
Fax 0-9-405 0854   *Website* www.coastalfarm-lodge.co.nz

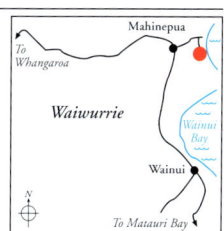

DIRECTIONS: Take SH 10 north & turn right into Matauri Bay Rd for 15 km. Turn left into Wainui Rd for 10km & right into Mahinepua Rd. Turn right thru gates to Ronaki, then 2nd drive right uphill to Waiwurrie.

 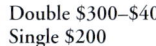

Double $300–$400
Single $200

Includes breakfast & dinner
Lunch extra

The new Kauri Cliffs golf course is less than 15 minutes' drive away from Waiwurrie. Located on the sunny east coast, surrounded by private farmland and forestry, Waiwurrie provides two large bedrooms and bathrooms, and a guest balcony featuring panoramic sea views. Situated near the Cavalli Islands, Whangaroa, Waiwurrie offers game fishing in the deep-sea fishing ground which is renowned marlin territory. Alternatively, guests may enjoy the Bay of Islands, sightseeing to Cape Reinga, diving to see the *Rainbow Warrior*, fishing, swimming, or just relaxing on the beach. Dinner is New Zealand cuisine and included in the tariff. It is served with a complimentary bottle of wine, overlooking Mahinepua Bay to Cavalli Islands.

Facilities

- 1 king ensuite bedroom upstairs
- 1 queen bedroom with bathroom & bathrobes downstairs
- heated towel rails & toiletries
- private guest balcony opens from upstairs bedroom with sea views
- fresh flowers in bedrooms
- guest lounge with open fire, tea/coffee, TV, video & music
- phone, fax & email available
- home-made bread & cooked breakfast available
- lunch by arrangement, extra
- dinner served with bottle of complimentary wine
- complimentary laundry
- black labrador & cat on site
- garaging available
- on-site parking
- boating access

Activities available

- walks on site
- swimming & fishing from site
- golf at Kauri Cliffs, Kerikeri, Whangaroa & Waitangi
- fishing for marlin at Cavalli Islands, Whangaroa
- sightseeing; watersports
- Cavalli Islands trips
- Bay of Islands boat trips
- friars.co.nz/hosts/waiwurrie.html
- restaurants, 10km
- deep-sea fishing at Whangaroa, 20-min drive
- diving to *Rainbow Warrior* & Cavalli Islands
- Kerikeri township, 45km
- Paihia township, 60km
- ferry trip to Russell from Paihia or Opua, 1 hr drive
- Cape Reinga day trips

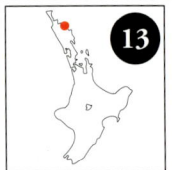

Mahinepua/Cavalli
Cavalli Beach House Retreat

Hosts Carrie and Richard Barron

Mahinepua Road, Whangaroa   *Postal* P O Box 690, Kerikeri
Phone 0-9-405 1049   *Email* info@cavallibeachhouse.com
Fax 0-9-405 1043   *Website* www.cavallibeachhouse.com

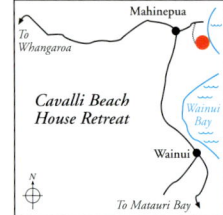

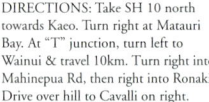

DIRECTIONS: Take SH 10 north towards Kaeo. Turn right at Matauri Bay. At "T" junction, turn left to Wainui & travel 10km. Turn right into Mahinepua Rd, then right into Ronaki. Drive over hill to Cavalli on right.

3 bdrm   3 enst   Room rate $525–$625   *Includes breakfast*
House rate available   *Lunch & dinner extra*

Cavalli Beach House is an exclusive private beachfront retreat, only 20 metres from a private secluded bay. Featuring wide, unimpeded ocean views from all rooms to the Cavalli Islands, this sail house concept was architecturally designed by Martyn Evans and Chris Howe, and purpose-built in 1999 to cater for six guests. The three king-size guestrooms all include generous ensuites and the entire house is also available for private-party bookings. The interior design reflects the tones of the sand and the atmosphere of the Pacific enhanced by Island tapa cloth. Meals are served in the dining room or alfresco on the balcony in summer. The cuisine emphasises ocean fresh and Pacific tastes, accompanied by home-grown organic produce.

Facilities
- 1 super-king/twin & 2 king bedrooms with balcony decks
- 3 large ensuites with double basins, hair dryers, bathrobes, heated towel rails & toiletries
- cotton bed linen
- guest lounge with open fire, tea/coffee, TV & video
- private guest entrance
- email facilities available
- breakfast with local fruits, Greek yoghurt & full cooked options, served in dining room or alfresco
- 2-course lunch, $30 pp
- 3-course table d'hôte dinner, with NZ wine list, $90 pp
- dietary requirements catered
- laundry, by arrangement
- on-site parking
- airport transfers arranged

Activities available
- hillside spa pool on site
- kayaks available
- swimming in private bay
- snorkelling gear available
- dinghy available
- fishing gear available
- star gazing, star charts available
- picnicking, baskets on request
- sketching easel & pastels available for guest use
- Kauri Cliffs Golf Course, 10-min drive away
- Wildlife Reserve coastal walks
- Cavalli Islands
- deep-sea diving
- big-game fishing
- wine & cheese tasting tours
- art & design stores tour
- historical day trips

Te Ngaere Bay
Huntaway Lodge Northland

Hosts Mary and Greg Hunt

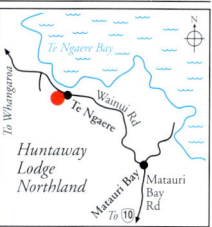

Wainui Road, Te Ngaere Bay   *Postal* Te Ngaere Bay, R D 1, Kaeo
Phone 0-9-405 1611   *Mobile* 021 405 161   *Fax* 0-9-405 1612
Email greg@huntawaylodge.com   *Website* www.huntawaylodge.com

3 bdrm   3 enst   Room rate $365–$420   Includes breakfast
House rates available   Lunch & dinner extra

DIRECTIONS: Take SH 10 north towards Kaeo. Turn right into Matauri Bay Rd for 15km. Turn left into Wainui Rd for 5km. Continue past Te Ngaere Bay to black gates on left. Take private road & turn right at top to Huntaway.

At Huntaway Lodge Northland, Greg and Mary specialise in personalised accommodation. Their contemporary cedar beach house, built in 2000 overlooking Te Ngaere Bay, is just 10 minutes from the Kauri Cliffs Golf Course. Huntaway's logo is inspired by the labradors, Barley and Chester, who with the outside cat, Thompson, complete the family. Guests are offered three queen ensuite bedrooms, all opening to the expansive deck with 180-degree ocean views. Each bedroom includes a ceiling fan and a kit of beach towels for guest use. Full home-baked breakfasts are served on the solid kauri dining table or alfresco on the deck. Greg and Mary enjoy providing personal service and offer lunch and dinner according to guests' wishes.

Facilities

- 3 queen ensuite bedrooms opening to deck, each with fan, TV, CD-player, CDs & tea/coffee
- cotton bed linen; beach towels
- hair dryer, toiletries, heated floor, heated towel rails & bathrobes
- guest lounge with teas/coffee, nibbles, bar, Sky TV, CD-player, games, books & magazines
- children welcome in private parties only; honeymoons catered for
- breakfast served in dining room or alfresco on balcony
- lunch, $30 pp
- 3-course table d'hôte dinner with wine list, $75 pp
- vegetarians catered for
- phone jack in lounge
- fax & email in office
- 2 labradors & 1 cat on site
- on-site parking; helipad

Activities available

- therapeutic massage
- pétanque court on site
- kayaks, snorkelling gear & surf-casting fishing gear available
- swimming at white sand beaches
- coastal walkways; native bush
- big-game fishing; sailing
- deep-sea diving, *Rainbow Warrior*
- private gardens to visit
- restaurants, 30-min drive
- wineries; arts & crafts trail
- golf courses, Kauri Cliffs
- Cavalli Islands
- Far North day tours
- Kerikeri, 30-min drive
- Paihia, 45-min drive
- Waitangi, 45-min drive
- Auckland, 3.5 hours south

Takou Bay, Kerikeri
Magic Cottage

Hosts Ian and Anna Sizer   *Mobile* 021 457 633

Takou Bay Road, Takou Bay   *Phone* 0-9-407 8065   *Fax* 0-9-407 8403
Postal P O Box 55, Waipapa, State Highway 10, Kerikeri
Email takouriver@xtra.co.nz   *Website* www.takouriver.com

DIRECTIONS: From Kerikeri turn-off, take SH 10 north for 14km. Turn right into Takou Bay Rd. Travel 7km, veering left at fork, & continue to very end of unsealed road. Magic Cottage is at the end.

1 bdrm	1 enst

Cottage rate $150
2-night minimum stay

Self-catering
Includes breakfast basket

Magic Cottage has been designed as a private retreat. Situated on the riverside with extensive estuarine river views, on the edge of the two-hectare private subtropical Magic Garden, this rustic cottage provides total privacy. The temperate climate is suitable for the indoor/outdoor living facilities of this cosy timber-lined cottage. Magic Cottage is self-contained, comprising a king-size bedroom, ensuite, seating area and fully equipped kitchen for self-catering. The cottage is powered by gas, not electricity. Built in 1995 on a pioneer farm site with historic sea access, Magic Cottage offers a floating jetty, canoe and row boat for exploring the estuary and Takou River with its birdlife. The five-bedroom Lodge is also available for family bookings.

Facilities

- 1 self-contained cottage
- single-party bookings
- 1 king ensuite bedroom
- all gas heating & lighting, no electricity available
- guest laundry
- private sundeck over river
- estuarine river views
- email & fax access available in main house
- complimentary gourmet organic breakfast basket
- fully equipped kitchen for self-catering
- private barbecue
- total seclusion & privacy
- 2ha private mature subtropical garden
- Lodge for family bookings
- on-site parking

Activities available

- private jetty & boat ramp
- private access to river for boating, swimming & fishing
- kayak, canoe & row boat available for guest use
- mountain bikes available
- 60ha (150-acre) organic farm, native bush, waterfall & stream
- Maori historic sites, scenic riverside, garden, farm & beach walks on site
- restaurants, 15–20 mins
- wineries; arts & crafts
- private gardens to visit
- horse riding; scenic flights
- golf, eg: at Kauri Cliffs
- kauri forest, 30-min drive
- Cape Reinga day trips
- historic Kerikeri, 14km
- Bay of Islands maritime attractions, 40-min drive

© Friars' Guide to New Zealand Accommodation for the Discerning Traveller

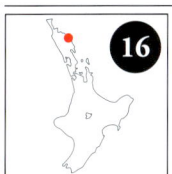

Kerikeri
The Summer House

Hosts Christine and Rod Brown

424 Kerikeri Road, Kerikeri, Bay of Islands   *Mobile* 025 409 288
Phone 0-9-407 4294   *Email* summerhouse@xtra.co.nz
Fax 0-9-407 4297   *Website* www.thesummerhouse.co.nz

| 3 bdrm | 2 enst | 1 prbth | 1 pdrm | Double $195–$245 Single $175 | Includes breakfast |

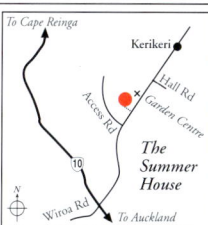

DIRECTIONS: From Whangarei, take SH 1 north to Pakaraka. Turn right into SH 10 & travel 18km. Then turn right into Kerikeri Rd & travel 1.7km to The Summer House on left, 1.5km from Kerikeri village.

The Summer House is an architecturally designed French Provincial-style home, built in 1999 using energy conservation principles. Set in a hectare of citrus orchard with a subtropical garden and pond, The Summer House offers a peaceful retreat close to Kerikeri village. Upstairs are two ensuite guest bedrooms, one with a queen-size Victorian brass bed and the other a queen antique French bed. A comfortable guest lounge provides tea and coffee-making facilities. Downstairs is the self-contained Pacific Pavilion with super-king/twin bed, dressing room, private bathroom, kitchenette for self-catering, and a private guest entrance and deck. Christine serves gourmet breakfasts in the dining room or patio overlooking the water feature.

Facilities

- 1 super-king/twin suite with kitchenette & decking
- 2 queen bedrooms upstairs, both with ensuite bathrooms
- hair dryer, toiletries & heated towel rails in all bathrooms
- cotton bed linen
- guest lounge with tea/coffee-making facilities
- TV, phone, fax, email available
- gourmet breakfast served in dining room, or alfresco on patio with garden view
- environmentally approved by Green Globe 21
- fresh flowers
- bar facilities
- German & French spoken
- off-street parking
- courtesy passenger transfer

Activities available

- picking citrus fruit in orchard
- subtropical garden & pond
- cafés/restaurants/shops, 1.5km
- diving, fishing, sailing, kayaking
- Kerikeri Golf Course, nearby
- Waitangi Golf Course & Treaty House, 20-min drive
- Kauri Cliffs Golf Course, 25 mins
- pre-European Maori fishing village
- kiwi viewing by night, in season
- vineyards & wineries
- craft shops & galleries trail
- boat charters arranged
- historic buildings & sites
- guided eco forest walks
- beaches, swimming
- gardens open to visit
- dolphin watching, 20 mins
- day trips to Cape Reinga, Doubtless Bay, etc

Kerikeri
Villa-Maria Petit Boutique Hotel

Hosts Mieke and Catharina Van Dyck

306 Kerikeri Inlet Road, Kerikeri, Bay of Islands
Postal P O Box 230, Kerikeri   *Phone* 0-9-407 9311   *Fax* 0-9-407 9311
Email villa-maria@xtra.co.nz   *Website* www.villa-maria.co.nz

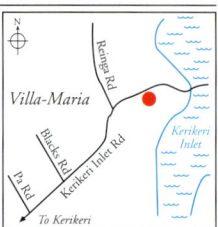

DIRECTIONS: From SH 10 turn east to Kerikeri. At roundabout turn right into Hobson Ave, then right again into Cobham Rd. Turn left into Kerikeri Inlet Rd. Travel 3.5km to Villa-Maria on right.

| 7 bdrm | 4 prbth | Double $200–$400
Single $135–$200 | Extra persons $75 each
2-night minimum stay | *Includes breakfast*
Single-night surcharge $50 |

With views over the Kerikeri Inlet to the ocean beyond, Villa-Maria Petit Boutique Hotel is set in a subtropical park. The Spanish-style landscaping features a salt-water swimming pool, with the 2,800-hectare Waitangi forest for a backdrop. Three separate villas in Mediterranean style are individually designed and named after the artists Salvador Dali, Toulouse-Lautrec and Paul Gauguin. Each villa includes a queen and a twin bedroom with private bathroom, lounge, full kitchen, undercover parking and tiled courtyard terrace. There is also the Hippocampus suite, with four-poster bed, and views overlooking the Waitangi forest. An eco Belgian-Pacific breakfast, mostly organic, is served alfresco on the house terrace or in the breakfast room.

Facilities

- private-party booking per villa
- 3 villas with sea views, each with 1 queen & 1 twin bedroom, bathroom, kitchen, lounge, terrace & garage
- 1 queen suite with 4-poster, ensuite, tea/coffee, rural view
- toiletries, hair dryers, heated towel rails, bathrobes, TV & ironing per villa & suite
- fine Belgian bed linen/towels
- eco Belgian-Pacific breakfast
- complimentary arrival drink
- NZ organic wines, extra
- guest privacy & quietness
- French, German, Flemish, Italian & English spoken
- children over 8 yrs welcome
- villas/suite serviced daily
- entrance gate with security feature

Activities available

- salt-water swimming pool on site
- boutique health shop on site
- orange trees for picking & pedigree pet goats on site
- Kerikeri airport, 8km by courtesy car
- bookings for massage, aromatherapy, facials, manicures, pedicures, skin packs, homeopathic consultations
- private sailing, flying, diving
- day trips to Cape Reinga & bays
- heritage NZ buildings to visit in local area
- Kerikeri township, 4 mins
- 6 golf courses in area
- tennis complex, 5km
- horse treks; kayaking
- walks eg to Kerikeri Falls
- arts & crafts trail
- Rewa's Village & historic Maori pa site

Above: Breakfast is offered alfresco on the terrace overlooking the salt-water swimming pool, or in the breakfast room.
Below left: The bedroom of the Salvador Dali villa, featuring a rimu ceiling and New Zealand sheep skins on the tiled floor.
Below right: The large Italian marble bathroom in the Salvador Dali villa, similar to the bathroom in the Paul Gauguin villa.
Opposite top: Private entrance, with security features, to Villa-Maria Petit Boutique Hotel, looking towards the three villas.
Opposite bottom left: The lounge in the Salvador Dali villa opens to outside terraces overlooking the park and ocean.
Opposite bottom right: Three Mediterranean-style villas and suite are set in a subtropical park on a hill overlooking the inlet.

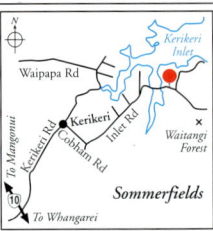

KERIKERI
SOMMERFIELDS LODGE

Hosts Sandra and Bob Murphy

405A Inlet Road, Kerikeri   *Postal* P O Box 726, Kerikeri
Phone 0-9-407 9889   *Mobile* 027 441 1689   *Fax* 0-9-407 1648
Email hosts@sommerfields.co.nz   *Website* www.sommerfields.co.nz

3 bdrm   3 enst   Room rate $335–$435   *Includes breakfast*   *Dinner extra*

DIRECTIONS: From SH 10 turn east to Kerikeri. At roundabout turn right into Hobson Ave, then right again into Cobham Rd. Turn left into Inlet Rd. Travel 4km & cross one-way bridge to Sommerfields on left.

Sommerfields provides uninterrupted views from every room over pastureland to the historic Kerikeri Inlet waterway. Architecturally designed to capture the all-day sun, Sommerfields offers three super-king or twin guestrooms, each with an ensuite bathroom and private deck. An exclusive-use guest entrance and guest lounge ensure privacy and comfort. Personalised service in a relaxing environment is enhanced by the tranquil surroundings. Evening dining is by prior arrangement and features the freshest of local produce. Sommerfields is only minutes from Kerikeri's cafés, restaurants, shops and historic buildings. Guests enjoy the Kauri Cliffs Golf Course, award-winning wineries, watersports and other Bay of Islands attractions.

Facilities

- 3 super-king/twin bedrooms
- 3 ensuites with hair dryers, heated floors, heated towel rails, bathrobes & toiletries
- spa bath, dual basins & double shower in Premium ensuite
- cotton bed linen, writing desk, internet jack, TV, coffee/tea, ceiling fan, fridge, iron & board in all 3 bedrooms
- phone, fax, email, photocopying
- full cooked breakfast
- 3-course dinner, $60 pp, wine list available
- laundry by arrangement
- private guest lounge with open fire
- private decks from bedrooms
- Japanese spoken
- courtesy B of I airport transfer; on-site parking

Activities available

- 18-hole golf courses inluding Kauri Cliffs
- award-winning wineries, 5 mins
- Historic Stone Store
- Kemp Mission House
- historic Treaty House at Waitangi, 20-min drive
- walk into Waitangi Forest
- steam sawmill, 5-min drive
- Kerikeri centre, 5.1km
- restaurants, 7-min drive
- arts & crafts trails
- private boat charters
- Rainbow Falls; Rewa's Village
- Kerikeri Inlet steamboat rides
- all-weather tennis club
- numerous beach excursions
- deep-sea fishing
- Cape Reinga trips & Bay of Islands boat tours

© Friars' Guide to New Zealand Accommodation for the Discerning Traveller

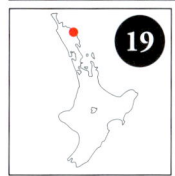

Kerikeri
Kerikeri Village Inn

Hosts Sandrine and Peter Vansevenant

165 Kerikeri Road, Kerikeri, Bay of Islands
Phone 0-9-407 4666   *Email* kerikeri.village.inn@xtra.co.nz
Fax 0-9-407 4408   *Website* www.kerikerivillageinn.co.nz

3 bdrm 3 enst   Room rate $145–$235   *Includes breakfast*

DIRECTIONS: From Whangarei, take SH 1 north to Pakaraka. Turn right into SH 10 & travel 18km. Then turn right into Kerikeri Rd & travel 5km. Kerikeri Village Inn is on the right, past the village centre.

This adobe-style masonry villa was inspired by Frank Lloyd Wright's work. Situated on the Stone Store Hill at Kerikeri, it is located a short walk from the village centre in one direction and the Stone Store Basin in the other. Facing north, the Kerikeri Village Inn is warmed by all-day sun and cooled by the prevailing breezes. Panoramic rural views can be enjoyed during the gourmet breakfast served either inside or alfresco on the verandah. Freshly squeezed orange juice and fresh fruit salad, home-made muesli and muffins are accompanied by Eggs Benedict, salmon'n'eggs, omelettes, pancakes with bacon and pure maple syrup or traditional bacon'n'eggs. Sandrine and Peter are happy to recommend and make dinner reservations at local cafés and restaurants.

Facilities

- 3 queen ensuite bedrooms
- toiletries, hair dryer & heated towel rails in all bathrooms
- fine bed linen & electric blankets in bedrooms
- complimentary tea/coffee, port, home-made cookies & evening chocolates
- guest lounge with open fire, TV, VCR, CDs, phone & fax
- bookings for tours & cruises
- gourmet breakfast menu
- picnic lunch by request
- laundry by arrangement
- guest iron & board available
- beach towels supplied
- party games available
- children welcome; cot available
- off-street parking
- courtesy passenger transfer

Activities available

- pétanque/boules on site
- cafés & restaurants, short walk
- craft shops & galleries trail
- 3 championship golf courses
- fishing; diving; kayaking; sailing
- NZ's oldest Stone Store & Kemp House/Kerikeri Mission Station
- Aroha Island ecological centre
- award-winning tours & cruises; Cape Reinga day trip
- tennis court & swimming pool nearby
- scenic flights
- 4WD tours; horse treks
- scenic walks & beaches
- Maori fishing village
- local wineries & distillery
- Puketi Kauri Forest
- Kerikeri gardens, avocado, citrus & macadamia orchards

Kerikeri
Ora Ora Resort

Hosts Inge Bremer and Rolf Mueller-Glodde

28 Landing Road, Kerikeri, Bay of Islands
Phone 0-9-407 3598 *Email* inge@oraoraresort.co.nz
Fax 0-9-407 8712 *Website* www.oraoraresort.co.nz

DIRECTIONS: From Auckland, take SH 1 north to Pakaraka. Turn right into SH 10. Then turn right to Kerikeri. Continue on Landing Rd past the Stone Store & cross bridge. Ora Ora Resort is 200m on left.

| 7 bdrm | 5 enst | 1 prbth | 1 pdrm | Villa rate $150–$450 |

Includes breakfast
Lunch & dinner extra

Ora Ora Resort is set in a subtropical garden above historic Kerikeri with heritage buildings on the river inlet, backed by park reserves. The six separate villas have been refurbished and feature East Asian art and Chinese silk or Turkish wool rugs. Two include kitchenettes and all have decks with garden views. The in-house licensed Makai Restaurant provides seven tables looking out to the illuminated water garden. The new hosts, Inge and Rolf, who have lived in the Far East since 1980, serve organic food, juices and wines and have planted a kitchen garden and orchard. They now offer spa treatments, including reflexology, massage, Kneipp hydrotherapy, sauna and plunge pool at Ora Ora, which is Maori for zest, health and contentment.

Facilities

- 6 villas: 2 king, 1 super-king/ twin, 1 queen/twin, 1 single & 1 with king/twin & queen bedrooms; 2 with kitchenettes
- all villas include ensuite, lounge area, private deck, mineral water, tea/coffee, cookies, fruit basket, TV, radio, & direct-dial phone
- hair dryers, toiletries, bathrobes, slippers & 1 double spa bath
- guest laundry on site
- à la carte organic breakfast
- individual dining & wining in licensed, fully organic Makai Restaurant, $35–$70
- Makai music event, monthly
- German, Spanish & French spoken
- family reunions, caucus meetings & yoga seminars
- 12 parking spaces on-site; courtesy passenger transfer

Activities available

- massage & hydrotherapy rooms
- sauna & plunge pool on site
- meditation pond; open gardens
- star gazing from pond deck
- historic Stone Store & Kemp House, Rewa's Maori Village
- Ngawha Springs, 30-min tour
- Matauri Beach, 30-min tour
- Kerikeri township, 3-min drive
- walking to Rainbow Falls
- native kiwi watching, 12km
- sailing on 17m (51-ft) yacht
- cruises in Doves Bay, 13km
- 4 golf courses; horse riding
- Inlet trip on steamboat
- steam sawmill
- art galleries & shops
- fishing; swimming with dolphins; scuba diving
- air trips to Cape Reinga

© Friars' Guide to New Zealand Accommodation for the Discerning Traveller

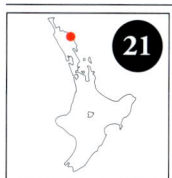

Rangitane, Kerikeri
Fernbrook

Hosts Margaret and Robert Cooper

Kurapari Road, Rangitane, R D 1, Kerikeri
Phone 0-9-407 8570 *Email* tfc@igrin.co.nz
Fax 0-9-407 8572 *Website* friars.co.nz/hosts/fernbrook.html

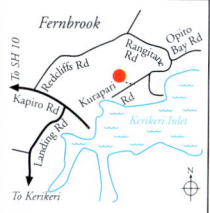

5 bdrm	5 enst

Room rate in house $200 Includes breakfast Dinner extra
Apartment rate $220 Cottage rate $250–$400 Self-catering Breakfast extra

DIRECTIONS: Take SH 10 north & bypass Kerikeri turn-off. Turn right into Kapiro Rd & travel 4km. Turn left into Redcliffs Rd. Continue to T junction, turn right & travel 1km. Take Kurapari Rd to Fernbrook. 2nd drive on right

Fernbrook covers 27 hectares (65 acres) that reach from the Kerikeri Inlet uphill to the homestead, through native bush with tree ferns, a stream and waterfall. Set in an extensive garden including olive, macadamia nut and citrus trees, the large cedar homestead offers two ensuite guestrooms. The library and sitting room are furnished with antiques, oriental rugs and original artworks. Self-catering accommodation is also provided in a semi-detached one-bedroom apartment, and a restored two-bedroom waterfront cottage (*see below, left*) originally built in 1917. Meals are served in the homestead dining room or on the terrace overlooking the bay, and guests can listen to the evening call of the kiwi, and walk through the bush to the secluded beach.

Facilities

- homestead:
  2 queen ensuite bedrooms
- self-contained apartment:
  1 queen ensuite bedroom upstairs
- self-contained cottage:
  2 queen ensuite bedrooms
- hair dryers, toiletries, double basins & heated towel rails in bathrooms
- cotton bed linen, fresh flowers, TV
- open fire, Sky TV, video, CD-player, & piano in sitting room in house
- gourmet breakfast served in house or alfresco on terrace; $15 pp for cottage/apartment guests
- picnic lunch on request
- 3-course dinner in house with wine, $55 pp
- 2 self-catering kitchens
- French spoken; laundry available
- on-site parking

Activities available

- BBQ on site
- pétanque & croquet on site
- brown kiwi sanctuary on site
- private beach & bush walks
- swimming; scuba diving
- charter sailing by arrangement
- fishing; watersports
- boat tours in bay
- horse riding; hiking
- Kerikeri restaurants, 12km
- Kerikeri gardens & orchards open to visit
- Kerikeri Stone Store & Kemp House, 12-min drive
- historic sites; kauri forest
- scenic flights; paragliding
- golf course
- arts & crafts trail
- day trips to Cape Reinga

Paihia/Kerikeri, Bay of Islands
Appledore Lodge

Hosts Janet and Jim Pugh

624 Puketona Road, Paihia/Kerikeri *Phone* 0-9-402 8007
Mobile 021-179 5839 *Email* appledorelodge@xtra.co.nz
Fax 0-9-402 8007 *Website* www.appledorelodge.co.nz

4 bdrm	4 enst	Apartment rate $160–$225	Includes breakfast basket	Self-catering
		Room rate $140–$150	Includes breakfast	

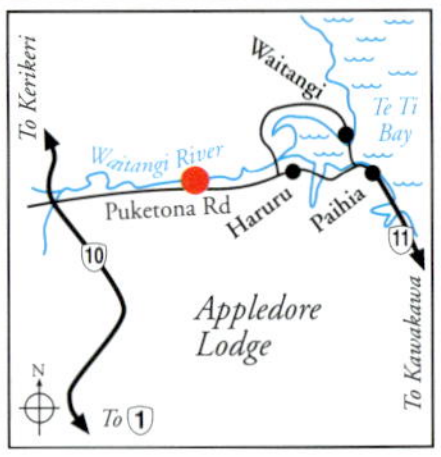

DIRECTIONS: From Paihia travel towards Waitangi & turn left into Puketona Rd. Travel 6km to Appledore on right. From Kawakawa take SH 10 north to Puketona Junction, turn right & travel 6km.

Set in a large garden on Waitangi River, Appledore Lodge features private river frontage with uninterrupted rural views over farmland to the forest beyond. The main house offers the Riverside Suite furnished in native rimu, and the Victoria Room with Queen Anne-style furniture including the draped four-poster double bed. An adjacent cottage purpose built in 2002 accommodates four guests and has a spacious lounge with river views. Adjoining is a self-contained studio with wheelchair access. A full English breakfast is available for main house guests on the ancient kauri table in the dining room or alfresco on the grand deck overlooking the river. A continental breakfast basket is supplied to the cottage and the studio.

Facilities

- main house: Riverside Suite with 1 super-king/twin ensuite bedroom, dressing room & TV; Victoria Room with 1 double ensuite & bath
- cottage: 1 super-king/twin ensuite bedroom, 1 double sofa bed, writing desk & TV in lounge, kitchen & laundry
- studio: 1 queen ensuite bedroom with wheelchair access & kitchen
- full breakfast for house guests; continental breakfast basket for cottage & studio guests
- hair dryer, toiletries & heated towel rails in all 4 ensuites
- email, fax & phone available
- children over 12 years
- in-house laundry service, $10
- courtesy passenger transfer
- on-site parking; helipad

Activities available

- golden retriever, Misty, on site
- outdoor spa pool on site
- 2 mountain bikes for guest use
- reserve walk on site
- jet ski hire; kayaks, parasailing
- sailing/motorised yacht trips
- deep-sea fishing for marlin
- scenic flights; microlite flying
- watersports; sky-diving; zorb ride
- restaurants in Paihia, 6km
- horse or quad bike treks
- Waitangi Treaty House & Golf Course, 6 mins
- Paihia beach, 6km
- Kerikeri, 15-min drive
- gardens open to visit
- swimming with dolphins
- day trips to Cape Reinga
- Auckland, 3½ hours south

© Friars' Guide to New Zealand Accommodation for the Discerning Traveller

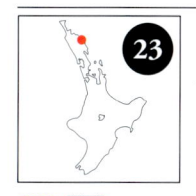

Paihia, Bay of Islands
Abri Apartments

Hosts Terrie and Bill Wood

10/12 Bayview Road, Paihia, Bay of Islands   *Postal* P O Box 509, Paihia
Phone 0-9-402 8003   *Email* abriaccom@xtra.co.nz
Fax 0-9-402 8035   *Website* www.abri-accom.co.nz

Apartment/suite rate $130–$250   *Includes breakfast basket for 1st morning*
Self-catering in apartments

3 bdrm | 3 prbth

DIRECTIONS: From Kawakawa, travel for about 20 mins towards Paihia. Continue down Seaview Rd. into Marsden Rd. Turn left into Bayview Rd. Abri Apartments on left.

Located in the heart of the Bay of Islands, in the small coastal town of Paihia, Abri Apartments comprise two studios and one suite, all in contemporary design and with sea views. With single-party bookings per studio and suite, each is spacious and individually styled, incorporating native timbers. Abri Apartments are nestled in native bush, north facing to benefit from all-day sun, with private decks providing panoramic views of the Bay of Islands to Russell and beyond. Guests enjoy the short stroll to the beach and to Paihia's shops, cafés and restaurants, or they can self-cater in the full kitchens of Abri's two self-contained apartments if preferred. A breakfast basket is supplied for the first morning and a barbecue is available on request.

Facilities
- 2 self-contained studios each with 1 queen bedroom & 1 private bathroom with double spa bath in each
- 1 suite with queen bedroom & private bathroom
- hair dryer, heated towel rails, demist mirror, bathrobes & toiletries in all 3 bathrooms
- 3 lounges with tea/coffee, TV, video & music
- complimentary breakfast basket on 1st morning
- full cooking facilities for self-catering & filtered water in 2 studio apartments
- fresh flowers in rooms
- air-conditioning
- private decks with BBQ
- private guest entrances
- off-street parking

Activities available
- boat & bird-watching on site
- beach, 2-min walk
- restaurants in walking distance
- marlin & line fishing
- watersports; scuba diving
- Cape Reinga bus tour
- vehicular & passenger ferries
- Hole-in-the-Rock cruise
- historic Waitangi
- golf course; tennis courts
- sailing & parasailing
- swimming with dolphins
- bush walking
- horse riding
- sea kayaking & canoeing
- kauri forest, 1-hour drive
- Russell, by ferry or car
- Kerikeri, 20-min drive

PAIHIA, BAY OF ISLANDS
PAIHIA BEACH RESORT AND SPA

Hosts Helen and Ray Arnesen

116 Marsden Road, Paihia *Postal* P O Box 180, Paihia
Freephone 0800 870 111 *Phone* 0-9-402 6140 *Fax* 0-9-402 6026
Email pbr@xtra.co.nz *Website* www.paihiabeach.co.nz

Room rate $400–$670   Includes breakfast   Self-catering
Lunch & dinner extra

23 bdrm   23 enst

DIRECTIONS: From Auckland, take SH 1 to Kawakawa turn-off. Continue straight ahead for 17km to Paihia. Travel on Marsden Rd along waterfront to Paihia Beach Resort on the left.

Paihia Beach Resort and Spa is part of La Spa Naturale Day Spa (*see opposite page 39*). Offering an international spa experience, this five-star waterfront property features unobstructed sea views from every studio and suite, and is located on Ti Bay – one of the premier beaches in Paihia. All apartments are spaciously furnished, with air-conditioning, DVD-players and hi-fi systems. Each ensuite includes a spa bath with candles and bath gel, bathrobes, slippers and chocolates. Guests enjoy the resort facilities such as the 20-metre salt-water heated swimming pool and large jacuzzi, licensed poolside restaurant, and the new Day Spa, offering a full range of body and water treatments and Corporate Wellness programmes, from 30 minutes to five-day packages.

Facilities
- 2 family 2-bedroom suites, each with 2 ensuites & 2 baths
- 10 king suites each with ensuite & full kitchen
- 9 queen/twin studios, each with ensuite & kitchenette
- bathrobes, hair dryers & toiletries in all bathrooms, 18 with whirlpool spa baths
- direct-dial phone per bedroom
- 1 wheelchair access bathroom
- full à la carte gourmet breakfast
- The Black Rocks in-house poolside restaurant open for breakfast, Spa lunch, cocktail hour & dinner, extra
- La Spa Naturale Day Spa, extra
- mini-bar; email & fax service; guest laundry
- air-conditioning, TV, DVD & hi-fi equipment in rooms
- under-cover parking

Activities available
- in-house conferences & Corporate Spa Wellness programmes
- panoramic heated 20m swimming pool & jacuzzi
- private sauna & steam-rooms
- massages, facials, body treatments, manicures, pedicures by qualified therapists, extra
- Day Spa packages for couples
- sailing, fishing & dolphin watching trips
- Paihia shops & wharf, easy walk away
- Waitangi & Kauri Cliffs golf courses
- Waitangi Treaty House
- bush & coastal walks
- boutique vineyard nearby
- Bay of Islands cruises
- day trips to Cape Reinga
- Auckland, 3-hr drive south

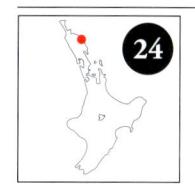

Paihia, Bay of Islands
La Spa Naturale Day Spa

Hosts Helen and Ray Arnesen

116 Marsden Road, Paihia   *Postal* P O Box 180, Paihia
Freephone 0800 870 111   *Phone* 0-9-402 6140   *Fax* 0-9-402 6026
Email pbr@xtra.co.nz   *Website* www.paihiabeach.co.nz

Treatment rate $25–$415   Day packages include Spa lunch

21 trtmnt rm   6 day-spa rm

DIRECTIONS: From Auckland, take SH 1 to Kawakawa turn-off. Continue for 17km to Paihia. Travel on Marsden Rd along waterfront to Paihia Beach Resort. Turn left into Davis Cres. La Spa Naturale immediately on left.

La Spa Naturale is the Day Spa located at Paihia Beach Resort (*see opposite page 38*) on the waterfront at Paihia. Opened in 2003, this five-star facility offers an international health spa experience. Located in a private garden setting, La Spa Naturale features cascading waterfalls and candlelit treatment rooms with tranquil music throughout. Fully qualified beauty and massage therapists offer a range of day treatments from half an hour to five-day packages. La Spa Naturale provides relaxing, nourishing and revitalising treatments for in-house guests, day visitors and also Corporate Spa Wellness programmes.

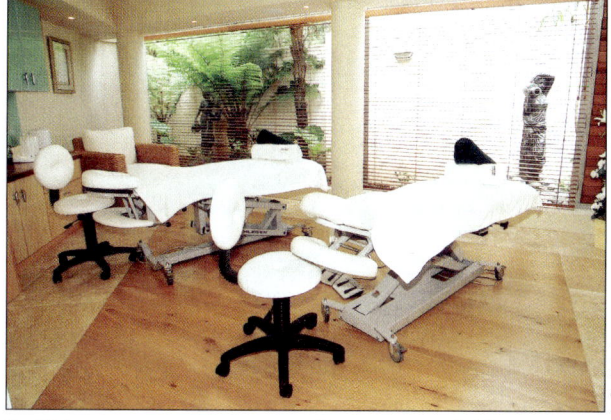

Facilities
- 21 in-house treatment rooms
- 6 day-spa treatment areas
- selection of herbal teas
- quality spa products for sale
- pedicure chair with heat & massage controls & foot spa
- manicure & make-up areas
- double massage room
- Vichy shower room with 8-head shower roses
- fusion shower room for wet treatments & mud wraps
- changing room with private lockers & toilet facilities
- private sauna with double shower & changing area
- private steam-room with shower & changing area
- 20m saltwater heated pool & jacuzzi spa pool
- licensed poolside restaurant with panoramic sea views

Treatments available
- Corporate Wellness Programme: for health & well-being
- packages for her: "Girls Day In", "Bride-to-be-Day", "Aromarine Bliss", "Delightful Indulgence"
- packages for him: "Relaxation Day for Men", "Executive Break", "Groom's Day"
- facial treatments for him & her: deep cleansing & Darphin signature treatments
- massage: Swedish, deep tissue, aromatherapy, reflexology, shiatsu, Indian head massage
- body treatments: "Darphin Signature", "Absolute Heaven", "Marine Magic", "Vichy Shower", "Jet Lag Solution"
- manicure & pedicure
- waxing for him & her
- Darphin make-up: weddings & bridal parties, special occasions
- gift vouchers for Mother's Day, Valentine's Day, special occasions

Paihia, Bay of Islands
Sanctuary Palms

Hosts Rob and Raewyn Wilson

31 Bayview Road, Paihia, Bay of Islands
Phone 0-9-402 5428 *Mobile* 021 166 0707 *Fax* 0-9-402 5427
Email info@sanctuarypalms.co.nz *Website* www.sanctuarypalms.co.nz

3 bdrm | 1 enst | 2 prbth Suite rate $300 *Includes breakfast basket for 1st morning* *Self-catering*

DIRECTIONS: From Auckland, take SH 1 to Kawakawa turn-off. Continue straight ahead for 17km to Paihia. Continue on Marsden Rd along waterfront & turn left into Bayview Rd. Sanctuary Palms on right.

Located on a hillside overlooking Paihia and the Bay of Islands, Sanctuary Palms offers three self-contained guest apartments. Individually themed with artwork from various New Zealand artists, each apartment features quality fittings and furnishings. The design is contemporary, with the original building totally renovated and extended to provide the three self-catering apartments. Each has one king-size bedroom, bathroom including a double spa bath, and separate lounge. The Pacifika and Moulin Rouge Suites both have a fully equiped kitchen while the Waterfall Suite has a kitchenette. A range of restaurants is within walking distance, down the hill from Sanctuary Palms, and watersports and fishing are popular with the guests.

Facilities
- Moulin Rouge & Pacifika Suites: each with 1 king bedroom, bathroom, spacious lounge with stereo & kitchen & private bathroom
- Waterfall Suite: 1 king ensuite bedroom, lounge, dining area & kitchenette
- double spa bath, candles, hair dryers, heated towel rails & toiletries in all bathrooms
- breakfast basket provided for 1st morning
- TV, cotton bed linen & bathrobes in bedrooms
- each lounge with Sky TV, video, CD-player, phone, electric fire, artwork, books & opens to balcony
- self-service laundry in suites
- courtesy passenger transfer
- off-street parking

Activities available
- Paihia wharf & beach, 5-min walk
- Paihia shops & restaurants, easy walk away
- golf courses
- historic Waitangi Treaty House
- bush & coastal walks
- boutique vineyards nearby
- marlin & line fishing; guided fishing trips
- swimming with dolphins
- sailing, sea kayaking, canoeing & watersports
- Bay of Islands cruises
- kauri forest, 1-hour drive
- Cape Reinga bus tours
- Kerikeri, 20-min drive
- Russell, by ferry or car
- Auckland, 3-hour drive south

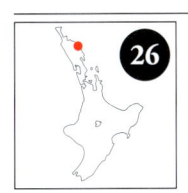

PAIHIA, BAY OF ISLANDS
CHALET ROMANTICA

Hosts Inge and Ed Amsler

6 Bedggood Close, Paihia, Bay of Islands   *Phone* 0-9-402 8270
Freephone 0800 124 253   *Email* chalet-romantica@xtra.co.nz
Fax 0-9-402 8278   *Website* chaletromantica.homestead.com/accom1.html

| 3 bdrm | 2 enst | 1 prbth |

Room/suite rate $115–$225
Off-season rates available

Breakfast extra
Self-catering in suites

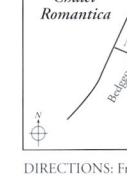

DIRECTIONS: From Auckland, take SH 1 to Kawakawa turn-off. Continue straight ahead for 17km to Paihia. Turn left into MacMurray Rd, then left again up Bedggood Close. Chalet Romantica at top of road.

Swiss owners, Inge and Edi, designed and built Chalet Romantica in 1994 as a large family home with three private guest suites featuring balconies overlooking the bay. Two of the suites are king size with ensuites and kitchen facilities for self-catering. The third is queen size with a separate private bathroom, tea and coffee facilities and fridge. Breakfasts are optional, Inge serving Swiss-style breakfasts of fresh fruits, breads, cheeses, yoghurt and muesli in the suites or in the conservatory by request. Edi skippers day and overnight charters on his Catalina 14-metre yacht. The Chalet is set on almost a hectare (two acres) with secure parking for guests' cars and boats. Indoor activities include the exerjet swimming pool, spa pool and gym.

Facilities

- 2 super-king/twin suites with ensuite bathrooms, kitchen facilities & private lounges
- 1 queen bedroom with private bathroom & bathrobes, tea/coffee facilities & fridge
- hair dryers, heated towel rails
- full-length mirror, sewing kit & fresh flowers in each guestroom
- phone, TV, video & CD-player in each guestroom
- Swiss-style breakfast served in guestrooms, $15
- hosts' Swiss Café & Grill for meals in Paihia, 5-min walk
- fax & email available
- private balconies with sea views
- German & French spoken
- self-service laundry, $3
- courtesy passenger transfer
- ample secure parking

Activities available

- in-house gym equipment
- indoor spa pool & heated swimming pool with exerjets
- skippered private yacht charter, www.yachtcharter.homestead.com/nz1.html
- safe, sandy swimming beaches
- Waitangi Treaty House, 2 mins
- historic Russell, 15-min car ferry
- marlin & light tackle fishing
- restaurants & Paihia township, 5-min walk
- tennis court, short walk
- sailing; kayaking
- dolphin/whale watching
- Bay of Islands cruises
- golfing, 2-min drive
- gardens to visit; hiking
- day trips to Cape Reinga & Ninety Mile Beach

41

© Friars' Guide to New Zealand Accommodation for the Discerning Traveller

OPUA, BAY OF ISLANDS
CROWS NEST HOLIDAY HOMES

Manager Marj Browning

20 Sir George Back Street, Opua, Bay of Islands Postal P O Box 176, Paihia
Phone 0-9-402 7783 Mobile 027 210 5242 Fax 0-9-402 7783
Email info@propertymatters.co.nz Website friars.co.nz/hosts/crowsnest.html

4 bdrm | 4 enst

Room rate $280–$550
Low-season rates available

Includes continental breakfast for 1st morning
Self-catering

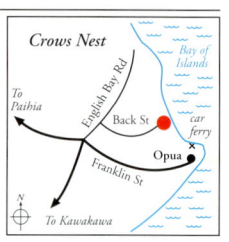

DIRECTIONS: 3-hour drive from Auckland. From Kawakawa, turn right & travel towards Opua. At intersection, continue into English Bay Rd. Turn 1st right into Back St. Crows Nest at end of cul-de-sac. Yacht moorings.

Crows Nest Holiday Homes are perched on a cliff above the sea at Opua, where the port activities and yacht haven provide endless interest below. Two individually designed and crafted villas offer exclusive accommodation for up to four guests each. A nautical theme unifying the villas includes porthole windows. The "Bridge Deck", built in 1995, offers two queen ensuite bedrooms, separated by the living area featuring swing couches, kwila flooring and canopied deck beyond overlooking Opua Bay. "Sails" was built in 1994, with queen and twin ensuite bedrooms, featuring a waterfall plunge pool at the private entrance. The queen bedroom opens to a private sundeck for relaxing above the bay. Guests need to phone, in order to be met on arrival.

Facilities
- single-party bookings
- 2 separate self-contained villas
- Bridge Deck: 2 queen bedrooms with ensuite bathrooms
- Sails: 1 queen & 1 twin ensuite bedroom & waterfall plunge pool
- host off-site ensuring guest privacy
- servicing by arrangement
- cotton bed linen
- hair dryers, heated towel rails
- continental breakfast supplied for 1st morning
- 2 fully equipped kitchens for self-catering
- 1 lounge with TV & music per villa
- laundry in each villa
- 1 villa with sundeck
- children & pets welcome
- secure off-street parking

Activities available
- yacht moorings adjacent
- yacht charter from Opua Wharf
- restaurant at Opua Wharf
- historic Waitangi Treaty House
- boat tours around the bay
- golf at Waitangi, 10-min drive
- car ferry to Russell from Opua
- dolphin watching from Paihia
- historic Kerikeri, 30-min drive
- cafés & restaurants at Paihia & Russell
- watersports
- swimming & diving
- Hole-in-the-Rock cruise
- Fullers cruises
- deep-sea fishing charters
- private gardens to visit
- Ninety Mile Beach
- Cape Reinga day tour

© Friars' Guide to New Zealand Accommodation for the Discerning Traveller

OPUA, BAY OF ISLANDS
CLIFF EDGE BY THE SEA

Hosts Peter and Glennis Meier

Richardson Street West, P O Box 8, Opua, Bay of Islands
Phone 0-9-402 6074 *Email* stay@cliffedge.co.nz
Fax 0-9-402 6074 *Website* www.cliffedge.co.nz

| 4 bdrm | 4 enst | 1 pdrm |

Room rate $380–$450

Includes breakfast & bar
Dinner extra

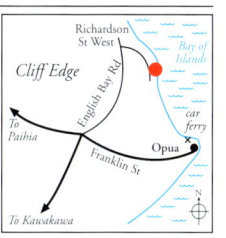

DIRECTIONS: 3-hour drive from Auckland. From Kawakawa, turn right & travel towards Opua. At intersection, continue into English Bay Rd. Turn right into Richardson St West. Cliff Edge near end of cul-de-sac on left.

With panoramic water views over Opua Harbour, Cliff Edge was purpose-built into the cliff-face on five levels to provide four ensuite guestrooms. Each bedroom opens to a private balcony, and the king-size room includes a spa bath. Guest also enjoy the outdoor spa pool sheltered below on the sundeck. The design of this cedar-clad guest lodge is contemporary, with the extensive use of native timbers complemented by antiques, and Persian rugs adding a warm ambience. From breakfast to gourmet dinner options, Peter offers innovative Mediterranean and Asian-inspired cuisine, with emphasis on seasonal and local produce. As chef, Peter draws from his long experience owning award-winning Casuarina Resort in Australia's Hunter Valley wine region.

Facilities

- 1 queen & 3 king ensuite bedrooms, each with private balcony
- spa bath in 1 king
- underfloor bathroom heating, hair dryers & quality toiletries
- cotton bed linen & bathrobes
- TV, video, CDs, safes, direct-dial phone in each bedroom
- laundry facilities available laundry service, extra
- full cooked breakfast
- gourmet dinner, extra
- spacious lounge with sea views, open fire, TV, video, DVD, CDs, piano, games & library
- complimentary open bar
- fax, email, internet access & small conference equipment
- courtesy transfer to Paihia
- on-site parking

Activities available

- outdoor spa pool & sauna
- excursion bookings arranged
- fishing – recreational, big-game & from rocks or wharf
- golf at Waitangi nearby, Kerikeri, or Kauri Cliffs
- ferries to Russell, 5-min drive
- arts & crafts in Kerikeri
- scenic walking tracks
- tall ship sailing
- dolphin & whale watching
- watersports – scuba diving, parasailing, sailing, snorkelling, kayaking, jet skiing, windsurfing
- Island cruises eg Hole-in-the-Rock & Cream Trip
- Mahoe cheese factory; wineries
- glow-worm caves; gardens to visit
- historic visits to Waitangi Treaty House, Pompallier, Kemp House, Stone Store, kauri forest, etc

43

© Friars' Guide to New Zealand Accommodation for the Discerning Traveller

OPUA, BAY OF ISLANDS
HARBOUR HOUSE VILLA

Hosts Robert and Masae Serge

7 English Bay Road, Opua, Bay of Islands
Phone 0-9-402 8087   *Email* stay@harbourhousevilla.com
Fax 0-9-402 8688   *Website* www.harbourhousevilla.com

3 bdrm / 3 enst / 2 pdrm

Room rate $200–$295
Apartment rate $260–$590

Includes breakfast   Lunch & dinner extra
Includes breakfast provisions   Self-catering

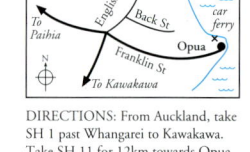

DIRECTIONS: From Auckland, take SH 1 past Whangarei to Kawakawa. Take SH 11 for 12km towards Opua. At intersection, cross into English Bay Rd. Travel 500m to Harbour House Villa on right.

Featuring panoramic sea views of the Bay of Islands, Harbour House Villa is located on a promontory overlooking the scenic Opua recreational harbour. All guestrooms have water views. The Villa has been refurbished to include aspects of Masae's Japanese culture. The upstairs living room opens to a large viewing deck where guests can watch sailing races, boating activities and some of the 500 yachts from around the world that enter the harbour each summer to escape the northern winter. If notified the night before, Masae serves Japanese breakfast, in the dining room or alfresco on the deck. Bob prepares the western cuisine. Lunch and dinner are available by arrangement, or guests can use the barbecue and self-cater if preferred.

Facilities
- 1 king & 1 queen/twin ensuite bedroom, can be 2-bedroom apartment with lounge, TV & kitchen
- 1 super-king/twin bedroom apartment with ensuite, lounge, TV & kitchen
- hair dryers, toiletries, heated towel rails, demist mirrors & bath or spa bath in ensuites
- 2 powder rooms; laundry; children welcome
- full breakfast or supplies
- lunch & à la carte dinner by request; complimentary wine
- 2 full self-catering kitchens
- upstairs lounge with Sky & World TV, DVD, CDs, books, grand piano, artwork, desk, phone, fax & computer station
- Japanese spoken
- on-site parking; courtesy passenger transfer

Activities available
- tours & itinerary assistance
- playing & listening to acoustic/digital grand piano
- small spa pool
- access via on-site garden & bush to coastal walking path & beach for swimming, fishing or shellfish collecting
- Opua wharf, boat charters & sea fishing, 15-min walk
- rainforest, 20-min walk
- Paihia restaurants, 3-hour scenic walk or 7-min drive
- sea kayaking, scuba diving, scenic flights, golf & horse riding at Paihia
- swimming with dolphins
- historic Russell by Opua ferry
- Waitangi Treaty grounds, Maori culture, golf course
- Cape Reinga day trips
- Auckland, 3½ hours south

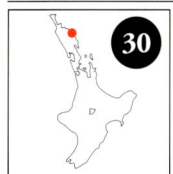

OPUA, BAY OF ISLANDS
THE BOATHOUSE OPUA

Manager Wendy Younger

Beechy Street, Opua   *Postal* c/- 5 Richardson Street, Opua
Freephone 0800 683 722   *Email* info@theboathouseopua.com
Phone 0-9-402 6800   *Website* www.theboathouseopua.com

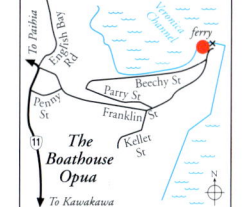

3 bdrm | 1 enst | 1 prbth   Apartment rate $500   Winter & weekly rates available   *Self-catering*   *No meals available*

DIRECTIONS: 3-hour drive from Auckland. From Kawakawa, turn right into SH 11 & travel towards Paihia. At intersection turn right into Franklin St & travel to ferry ramp. Turn left into Beechy St to The Boathouse on right.

The Boathouse provides over-water accommodation in two contemporary self-contained apartments, designed with a nautical theme. Upstairs is The Bridge apartment and downstairs is The Landing, both with spacious decks over the water, reminiscent of the prow of a boat. Opened in 2002, both apartments feature a large, fully equipped kitchen, each including dishwasher drawer, fridge/freezer with ice-maker, full oven, coffee machine and floating floor. The Bridge offers a king-size bedroom with dressing room and office, and The Landing has two bedrooms. Located adjacent to the Opua car ferry, the Boathouse offers endless 270-degree views of boating activities from the deck, where guests can also enjoy fishing and barbecues.

Facilities
- The Bridge upstairs apartment: 1 king ensuite bedroom with dressing room, 1 queen sofa-bed in office, dining/lounge & writing desk
- The Landing downstairs apartment: 1 king/twin & 1 twin bedroom, 1 bathroom & dining/lounge
- central heating
- hair dryer, toiletries, heated towel rails, heated floor, bidet in bathrooms
- Sky TV, video, DVD, music & CDs
- full kitchen for self-catering in each apartment
- phone, fax & jacks
- guest laundry
- children welcome
- spacious decking
- monitored security system
- 270° sea views
- off-street parking

Activities available
- gas BBQ on decks on site
- on-site fishing from lower deck
- Opua marina; beach; diving
- sailing charters; kayaks
- coastal walkway; golf courses
- swimming with dolphins
- bus tours; boat tours
- vineyards & wine trails
- car rental; scenic flights
- restaurants in Paihia, 10 mins
- superette & bakery adjacent
- car ferry, 4-min crossing every 20 mins, 5-min drive to Russell
- arts & crafts in Kerikeri, ½ hour
- Hole-in-Rock trips
- gardens open to visit in Kerikeri
- Waitangi Treaty House; Kemp House; Stone Store; Pompallier
- Auckland City, 3½ hours south

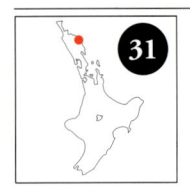

ORONGO BAY, RUSSELL
ORONGO BAY HOMESTEAD

Hosts Michael Hooper and Chris Wharehinga Swannell

Aucks Road, R D 1, Russell, Bay of Islands
Freephone 0800 242 627   *Phone* 0-9-403 7527   *Fax* 0-9-403 7675
Email bookings@thehomestead.co.nz   *Website* www.thehomestead.co.nz

| 4 bdrm | 4 enst | Double $650 Single $400 | Includes breakfast Weekend & off-season rates available | Dinner extra |

DIRECTIONS: Take Twin Coast Discovery Route 1 hour north of Whangarei. Travel via Kawakawa to Opua. Take car ferry to Russell. Travel 2 mins towards Russell township. At Orongo Bay, Homestead is on right.

This fully restored historic homestead was built in the 1860s for the first Amercian Consular Agent in New Zealand. Now set in organic gardens with sweeping views of Orongo Bay, this country home features original native timbers including the kauri ceilings, large open fire and 1000-bottle underground wine cellar. Peacefully sited on seven spring-fed hectares (17 acres), the two-bedroom homestead is complemented by the separate garden Retreat, with the new Pacific Suite upstairs overlooking the duck pond. There are sea, bush or meadow views from each bedroom. The resident hosts serve gourmet dinners by prior arrangement, matching each course with wine from the cellar. Healthy organic luxury food is the keynote at Orongo Bay Homestead.

Facilities
- 4 super-king/twin bedrooms
- 4 ensuites; 1 with spa bath & 1 with double basin
- hair dryers, heated towel rails, bathrobes & toiletries
- wheelchair access to The Retreat only
- home theatre in 2 bedrooms
- fine art collection
- laundry available, $30
- "Bubbly Bakehouse Breakfast" with à la carte options, served until midday in dining room
- 4-course gourmet table d'hôte dinner, served in dining room, fireside, or on verandah, $120 pp
- complimentary coffee, teas & cookies available
- turn-down service
- open fire & grand piano in lounge
- helicopter landing area

Activities available
- dry Finnish lakeside sauna
- massage by appointment
- native bush walk on 7ha (17 acres) of private coastal land, including wildlife pond on site
- swimming at nearby beaches
- boating
- kayaking
- organic culinary garden tours
- aquatic activities
- several golf courses nearby, including Kauri Cliffs
- Russell township, 5-min drive
- world record big-game fishing
- restaurants nearby
- vineyard visits & tastings
- swimming with dolphins
- Bay of Islands sightseeing
- flightseeing, including fly/ 4WD to tip of North Island

© Friars' Guide to New Zealand Accommodation for the Discerning Traveller

ORONGO BAY, RUSSELL
HARDINGS' – AOTEAROA LODGE

Hosts Barbara and Trevor Harding

Orongo Bay Farm, Aucks Road, R D 1, Russell, Bay of Islands
Phone 0-9-403 7277 *Mobile* 021 184 2023 *Fax* 0-9-403 7277
Email info@the-lodge.co.nz *Website* www.the-lodge.co.nz

Double $200–$285   Single $185–$250   *Includes breakfast*

DIRECTIONS: From Auckland take SH 1 north to Kawakawa. Turn right to SH 10 & travel to Opua. Take car ferry for Russell. Drive 2 mins towards Russell township. At Orongo Bay, Hardings' – Aotearoa is on right.

Overlooking Orongo Bay and a scenic reserve, midway between the car ferry and Russell, is Hardings' – Aotearoa Lodge. Set in two and a half hectares (seven acres) of rolling countryside, the Lodge provides two ensuite guestrooms upstairs, with adjoining lounge and balcony, and two further ensuite super-king rooms in Brook Barn down the driveway. Originally built in the late 1970s, the Lodge was refurbished in 2002 to provide quality accommodation. A full breakfast of fresh fruit and home-made muesli, as well as a special cooked dish daily using free-range eggs from the property, is served in the breakfast room or alfresco on the deck. The sauna and spa pool are popular on the separate secluded deck, and guests enjoy dining at historic Russell nearby.

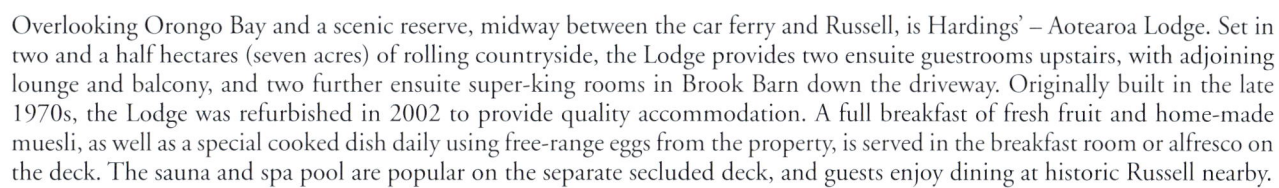

Facilities

- 2 super-king/twin ensuite bedrooms in Brook Barn, each with lounge & deck
- 2 queen ensuite bedrooms upstairs in house
- cotton bed linen
- hair dryers, heated towel rails, bathrobes & toiletries
- fans, tea/coffee & mineral water in bedrooms
- laundry available, $15
- breakfast served in breakfast room or alfresco on deck
- lounge downstairs with open fire, Sky TV, CD-player & games
- guest lounge upstairs with phone jack & balcony; phone available
- decks & patios from lounges & barn; large spa pool decking
- on-site parking
- outdoor pets on site

Activities available

- sauna & spa pool on site
- bicycles for guest use
- snorkelling; scuba diving
- fishing; swimming; sailing
- swimming with dolphins
- canoes & kayaks for hire
- Waitangi Treaty House
- historic buildings & locations
- Russell township, 5-min drive
- restaurants, 5-min drive
- scenic flights & cruises
- vineyards & wine tasting
- golf courses; gardens to visit
- 4WD day trips to Cape Reinga & 90 Mile Beach
- car ferry, 3-min drive
- Kerikeri, 25-min drive
- Auckland 3½ hours south

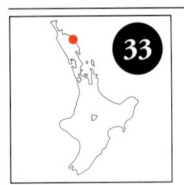

MATAUWHI BAY, RUSSELL
OUNUWHAO – HARDING HOUSE B & B

Hosts Allan and Marilyn Nicklin

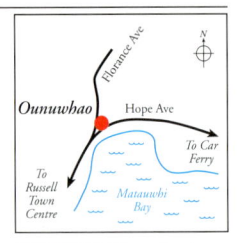

16 Hope Avenue, Matauwhi Bay, Russell
Phone 0-9-403 7310   *Email* thenicklins@xtra.co.nz
Fax 0-9-403 8310   *Website* friars.co.nz/hosts/ounuwhao.html

VISA MasterCard

| 6 bdrm | 4 enst | 2 prbth |

Double $185–$250
Single $135–$170

Cottage rate $200–$290 for 2–4 persons
Includes breakfast, or extra for cottage guests

Self-catering

DIRECTIONS: Take car ferry from Opua. Travel 10 mins from car ferry towards Russell. Continue on Hope Ave to 50km sign. Travel another 100 metres. Ounuwhao on right.

This heart kauri Edwardian villa, originally the farmhouse of Edward and Emily Harding, was built in 1893. The Nicklins, fourth-generation New Zealanders, moved it from Dargaville in 1991 and faithfully restored it, furnishing it in period style with colonial furniture and patch-work quilts. Their adjacent garden suite is similarly furnished, and also the garden cottage, where guests can self-cater in the fully equipped kitchen, or join the house guests for breakfast in the dining room or alfresco on the wrap-around verandah of the guesthouse. Breakfast begins with squeezed orange juice, home-made yoghurt and fresh fruit salad, followed by a special cooked option which changes daily. Ounuwhao features views of Matauwhi Bay.

Facilities
- 4 queen bedrooms in house with 3 ensuites & 1 private bathroom
- antique wash-stands & hand-made quilts in bedrooms
- guest lounge with open fire
- self-serve tea/coffee facilities
- sunny verandahs & conservatory
- laundry available, $10
- cottage garden with brick & shell pathways
- 2 double bedrooms in fully self-contained cottage
- breakfast in cottage optional extra, $15 pp
- kitchen & laundry in cottage
- detached garden suite with 1 king/twin bed, dressing room, spa bath in ensuite & private verandah overlooking garden
- closed June & July

Activities available
- pétanque/boules on site
- cafés & licensed restaurants
- historic Russell village, 1km
- Russell Museum, 1km
- historic Pompallier, 1km
- safe swimming beaches
- art & craft shops, 1km
- sailing charters; sea & island excursions
- coastal, bush & kauri walks
- Cape Reinga day trip
- Hole-in-the-Rock & Cream trips
- kayaking; cycling; golf
- flagstaff walk & heritage trails
- Christ Church – oldest in NZ
- sport & big-game fishing
- swimming with dolphins
- Waitangi Treaty House & garden
- Kerikeri craft & wine trails

© Friars' Guide to New Zealand Accommodation for the Discerning Traveller

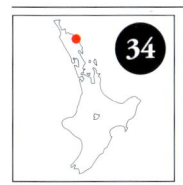

Russell
Aomotu Lodge

Hosts Geraldine and Roy Franklin, and Jacqui and Clinton Bradley

6 Ashby Street, Russell, Bay of Islands
Phone 0-9-403 7693   Email info@aomotulodge.com
Fax 0-9-403 7683   Website www.aomotulodge.com

4 bdrm   4 enst   Room rate $300–$400   *Includes breakfast*

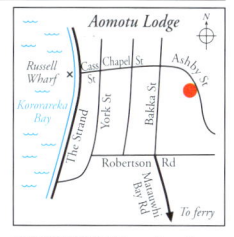

DIRECTIONS: Take car ferry from Opua. Drive to Russell. Turn left into Robertson Rd, then right into York St. Turn right into Chapel St, continuing through intersection into Ashby St. Drive up hill to Aomotu on right.

Aomotu Lodge (pronounced "our-more-too") means "World Island" and is nestled in an elevated and central position overlooking the bay and village of Russell. The Lodge is an architecturally unique home, built with an emphasis on native timber and stained-glass windows which create a warm and welcoming environment. All guestrooms are newly renovated and feature spacious ensuites and sea views. The front balcony, with its vistas over the sea, is popular for alfresco breakfast, or just relaxing and watching the sunset at the end of the day. Local restaurants in Russell village are only a short stroll down the hill. The new owners/hosts at Aomotu Lodge welcome weddings and provide consultations by arrangement.

Facilities

- 1 super-king/twin ensuite bedroom
- 3 queen ensuite bedrooms, 1 with private spa pool room
- organic toiletries, hair dryers & heated towel rails in ensuites
- cotton bed linen & bathrobes
- TV, fridge, tea/coffee, herbal teas, fresh fruit, chocolates & treats in all bedrooms
- native timber; cathedral ceilings
- continental or cooked breakfast served in bedrooms, dining room, or on balcony
- fresh flowers; sea views
- air-conditioning & heating
- phone, fax, 24-hr internet & laptop computers available
- wedding arrangements & consultations, extra
- courtesy airport transfers; off-street parking

Activities available

- detailed itineraries arranged
- mountain bikes, beach chairs & towels available
- beaches in walking distance
- local restaurants, short stroll
- historic sites in Russell, Waitangi & surrounding areas
- wine, heritage, art & craft trails
- guided island tours, including dolphin & whale encounters
- swimming; diving; kayaking
- parasailing; jet-skiing; caves
- golf; tennis; horse riding
- scenic coastal & bush walks
- gardens open to visit
- boat charters for fishing & sailing round 144 islands
- ferry to Opua, 8km
- bus & air tours to Cape Reinga & other day trips

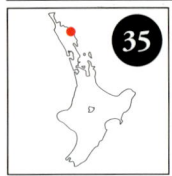

Russell
Pukematu Lodge

Hosts Kay and Colwyn Shortland *Mobile* 025 245 7640

Top Flagstaff Hill, Russell *Postal* P O Box 145, Russell
Phone 0-9-403 8500 *Email* pukematu.lodge@clear.net.nz
Fax 0-9-403 8501 *Website* www.pukematulodge.co.nz

2 bdrm 2 enst
Double $295
Single $250
Includes breakfast Picnic hampers extra

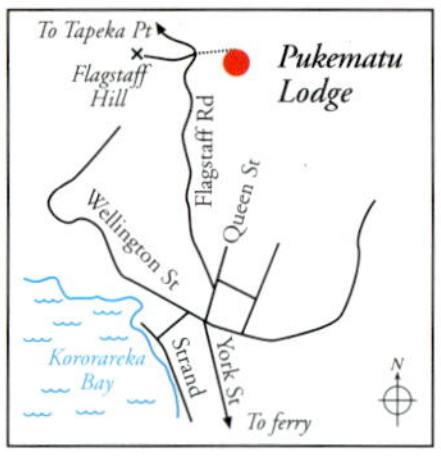

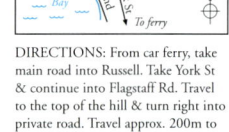

DIRECTIONS: From car ferry, take main road into Russell. Take York St & continue into Flagstaff Rd. Travel to the top of the hill & turn right into private road. Travel approx. 200m to Pukematu Lodge on right.

Pukematu, the name of the hill on which the Lodge is sited, means "hill of hospitality", echoed by their byword: "Haere mai ki to tatou kainga i roto i nga kapua" meaning "Welcome to your home within the clouds". Overlooking almost five hectares (12 acres) of native bush with panoramic views of the Bay of Islands and Russell, Pukematu was built in 1992, and offers two guestrooms with private entrances. Breakfast is often served alfresco on the spacious decking where small weddings are held. Colwyn is a marriage celebrant and fluent Maori speaker, and Kay's floral expertise enhances such occasions. Pukematu is a specialist location for both weddings and honeymoons. Home baking is provided and organic produce is used in season.

Facilities
- 2 ensuite queen bedrooms
- seating area, TV, fridge & coffee/tea in both guestrooms
- hair dryers & toiletries
- cotton bed linen & bathrobes
- both bedrooms open to balcony
- chocolates & fresh flowers
- phone & fax available
- complimentary laundry
- continental and full cooked breakfast, alfresco or indoors
- picnic hampers by request
- large deck overlooks bay
- Colwyn, marriage celebrant, speaks fluent Maori
- wedding consultant, Kay
- private guest entrance
- small functions venue
- on-site parking

Activities available
- ceremonies, celebrations, small conferences, small weddings & honeymoons catered
- outdoor spa pool on site
- almost 5ha (12 acres) native bush on site with pheasants, quails, tui, kingfishers, kiwi & morepork at night
- Flagstaff Hill walk to Hone Heke's flagpole
- picnicking on islands
- 8 restaurants & shopping in Russell township, 3-min drive
- boat trips & fishing arranged
- swimming with dolphins
- historic buildings – hotel, police station & church
- kiwi eco tours; oyster farm visits
- Waitangi Treaty House & golf
- Ninety Mile Beach tours
- day trips to Cape Reinga

© Friars' Guide to New Zealand Accommodation for the Discerning Traveller

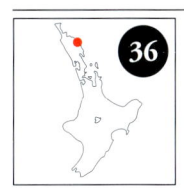

Russell
Titore Lodge

Host Carolyn Mills

32 Titore Way, Russell, Bay of Islands
Phone 0-9-403 7335   *Mobile* 021 138 8337   *Fax* 0-9-403 7335
Email cmillswriter1@aol.com   *Website* attitorelodge.com

3 bdrm | 3 enst | Suite rate $200–$450   Includes breakfast   Dinner extra   **2-night minimum stay**
Lodge rate $4,500–$10,000 per week   Low-season rates available

DIRECTIONS: From car ferry, take Matauwhi Rd into Russell. Turn west into York St & continue into Flagstaff Rd. Continue around top of hill. Turn left into Titore Way. Travel to end to Titore Lodge on left.

Perched on a hill surrounded by native forested reserve land, Titore Lodge overlooks the historic harbour of the oldest whaling village in New Zealand. Pathways take guests down to the village of Russell with its range of fine dining restaurants, cafés, shops and museums. A private sandy beach cove is also a short walk away. Titore Lodge offers three quiet suites, each opening on to a private patio where continental breakfast can be served. Alternatively guests are welcome to join other guests for a full breakfast in the dining room, and evening dining can be arranged. Guests can enjoy books from the library, relax in the hammock and watch the abundant birdlife. Titore is an eco-friendly Lodge, environmentally sensitive and minimises the use of chemicals.

Facilities

- 1 super-king/twin & 2 queen suites each with ensuite, living room & water views
- hair dryer, toiletries, heated towel rails & bathrobes
- fine bed linen; beach towels; fresh flowers & fruit
- heated floors in suites; both open to private patios
- extensive library; TV, phone, fax & email available
- full breakfast in dining room, continental on patio, or in suite
- dinner arranged with chef
- complimentary apéritifs & hors d'oeuvres
- kitchenette in each suite
- original artwork throughout
- private guest entrances
- courtesy transfer from wharf
- off-street parking

Activities available

- walk to private sandy beach cove
- watersports – scuba diving, sailing, sea kayaking, deep sea fishing, parasailing, snorkelling, swimming & fishing
- bird-watching from site
- Flagstaff Hill, coastal, mangrove & forest walks
- wine tasting at vineyards
- restaurants, cafés, museums & shops in Russell village, short walk
- Hole-in-the-Rock trip to watch dolphins & whales
- golf; tennis; lawn bowling; croquet
- Paihia township, ferry trip
- horse riding; mountain biking
- historic church & Pompallier
- day trips to Ninety Mile Beach & Cape Reinga

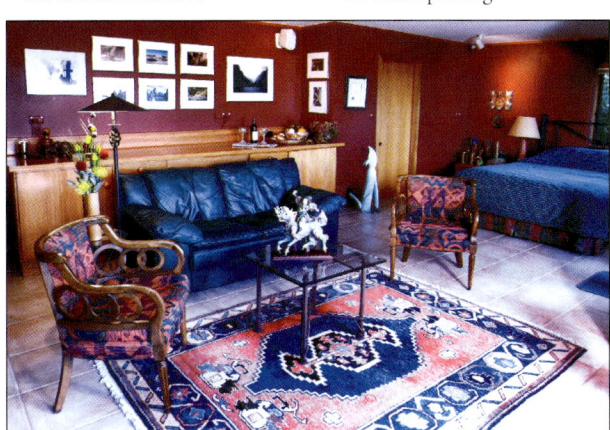

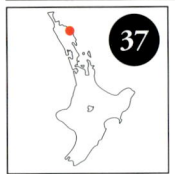

TAPEKA POINT, RUSSELL
EAGLES NEST VILLA RETREAT

Manager Lorraine Fowell

60 Tapeka Road, Russell, Bay of Islands   *Phone* 0-9-403 8333
Postal P O Box 60, Russell, Bay of Islands   *Fax* 0-9-403 8880
Email manager@eaglesnest.co.nz   *Website* www.eaglesnest.co.nz

| 11 bdrm | 10 enst | 2 prbth | 2 pdrm |

Villa rate $1,700–$3,940

*Includes breakfast provisions
Chef extra, or self-catering*

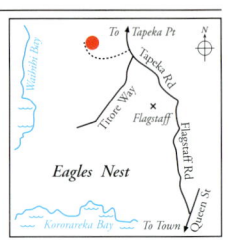

DIRECTIONS: Take car ferry from Opua to Russell. Travel thru Russell & up Flagstaff Hill. Continue on Tapeka Rd, past Titore Way & take 1st driveway left. Follow stone wall & take 4th drive on right to Eagles Nest.

Eagles Nest is a secluded retreat with panoramic views overlooking the Bay of Islands. Located on a 30-hectare (74-acre) estate, Eagles Nest comprises four separate self-contained villas, just two minutes' drive from the old seaport village of Russell. The elegant but simple interiors of each villa are complemented by the expansive ocean views and sunsets. Sacred Space is the largest villa and is set in private subtropical gardens. Accommodating eight guests, it has its own 25-metre lap pool, spa pool and sauna. First Light Temple is Eagles Nest's honeymoon retreat, with a mezzanine suite. Eyrie includes a gourmet chef's kitchen, private lap pool and jaccuzi. Eagle Spirit is set on the cliff edge and has its own private lap pool and jaccuzi.

Facilities
- Sacred Space: 1 king & 3 queen bedrooms, each with ensuite or private bathroom
- First Light Temple: 1 king bedroom with ensuite
- Eyrie & Eagle Spirit: 3 ensuite bedrooms in both villas
- Egyptian cotton bed linen, hair dryers, toiletries & bathrobes
- air conditioning & central heating in all 4 villas
- each villa includes lounge, gourmet kitchen, laundry, sunset decks & ocean views
- breakfast provisions supplied
- on-site catering by request
- extensive wine cellar
- tour desk; business centre
- private lap pool & spa pool/jacuzzi for 3 villas; 1 sauna
- on-site parking; helipad

Activities available
- native fauna track to private sandy beaches
- extensive subtropical & native bush gardens
- deep-sea fishing; boat tours
- resident fishing guide available
- yachting, cruising & sailing
- water-skiing
- sea kayaking
- resident gourmet chefs available
- restaurants & shops, 4 mins
- dinner cruises
- eco tours
- dolphin & whale watching
- golf at Kauri Cliffs, Kerikeri or Waitangi
- diving & snorkelling
- helicopter, heritage & wine tours

© Friars' Guide to New Zealand Accommodation for the Discerning Traveller

Above: The spacious Kingfisher Suite, located in the Sacred Space villa, with panoramic ocean views and ensuite bathroom.
Below: Set in subtropical gardens, the architecturally designed First Light Temple is a honeymoon retreat with wide ocean views.
Opposite top: Guests enjoy the heated horizon-edge infinity lap pools, with uninterrupted views over the Pacific Ocean.
Opposite bottom left: Eagle Spirit accommodates six guests and features sea views, a private lap pool and jacuzzi.
Opposite bottom right: The open-plan living area in the Eyrie Villa which includes an open fire, dining table and full kitchen.

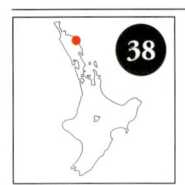

Tapeka Point, Russell
Anchorage of Russell

Hosts Anna and John Boulter

43 Tapeka Road, Russell *Postal* P O Box 170, Russell, Bay of Islands
Phone 0-9-403 8410   *Mobile* 021 293 0360   *Email* anchorage.boi@xtra.co.nz
Fax 0-9-403 8410   *Website* www.bay-of-islands.co.nz/accomm/anchorage.html

3 bdrm 3 enst   Double $150–$195   Single $120–$150   *Includes breakfast*

DIRECTIONS: Take car ferry from Opua to Okiato. Drive to Russell. Continue on Tapeka Rd, over Flagstaff Hill towards Tapeka Point. Turn left into continuation of Tapeka Rd. Anchorage of Russell on left.

Built opposite Tapeka Beach, which is framed by two historic Norfolk Island pines, The Anchorage offers three guestrooms on the ground level, each opening towards the beach. The Endeavour Suite is named after Captain Cook's ship that landed in 1769 at the Bay of Islands, the Hazard Suite after the ship which was involved in the "sacking" of Russell by local Maori in 1845, and the Charlotte Jane, a migrant ship from England. The beachside guestrooms are contemporary and tiled, with private guest entrances. Breakfast can be served in the suites or the upstairs dining room if preferred. Guests are welcome to use the barbecue and the mountain bikes, dinghy and kayaks. Swimming, fishing and other watersports are popular activities around Tapeka Point.

Facilities

- 3 queen ensuite bedrooms
- hair dryers & toiletries
- all 3 guestrooms open to private verandah
- fresh flowers
- seating area with tea/coffee, herbal teas, nibbles, mineral water, Sky TV, CD-player & writing desk in all 3 guestrooms
- 3 private guest entrances
- gourmet continental breakfast; cooked on request
- cordless phone, fax & email available on request
- sea views from all rooms
- children by arrangement
- courtesy passenger transfer
- off-street parking
- mooring available
- closed June to August

Activities available

- 2 mountain bikes, 2 kayaks & dinghy for guest use
- BBQ on site
- safe swimming – towels & beachchairs supplied
- snorkelling, diving, fishing & rock pools across road
- boating; kayaking; sailing
- boat tours & Cape Reinga tours
- Waitangi Treaty House & golf
- 6 restaurants nearby
- paragliding; heritage trail
- sport & big-game fishing
- dolphin watching
- historic Russell buildings
- gardens to visit; tramping
- Christ Church in township
- historic Pompallier & garden
- Kerikeri crafts; wine tours
- scenic coastal & bush walks

© Friars' Guide to New Zealand Accommodation for the Discerning Traveller

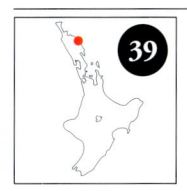

Tapeka Point, Russell
Villa du Fresne

Hosts Maureen and Ron Redwood

23 Du Fresne Place, Tapeka Point, Russell   *Phone* 0-9-403 7651
Postal P O Box 208, Russell   *Mobile* 021 636 121   *Fax* 0-9-403 7651
Email m.redwood@xtra.co.nz   *Website* friars.co.nz/hosts/dufresne.html

2 bdrm	2 enst	Villa suite rate $230–$295	Minimum 2-night stay	Includes breakfast provisions	Self-catering
		Roberton Room rate $150–$180	Low-season rates available	Includes continental breakfast	

DIRECTIONS: Take car ferry from Opua to Okiato. Travel through Russell. Continue over Flagstaff Hill into Tapeka Rd. Turn right into Du Fresne Place & continue to Villa du Fresne (pronounced "Frane") on right.

Located on Tapeka Point, just two kilometres from Russell, is Villa du Fresne. This Mediterranean-style villa offers a spacious self-contained guest suite with one or two ensuite bedrooms. A full kitchen, with stocked pantry, fridge and breakfast supplies for self-catering, is complemented by a vege garden and grapevine in season. The Roberton Room, king/twin with ensuite, is available for the bed and continental breakfast option. The bedrooms and lounge lead into a conservatory opening to the lawn overlooking the beach. The uninterrupted sea views and sound of waves provide a relaxing atmosphere where guests can escape from day-to-day stress beside the ocean. The hosts live in a separate wing of the villa, which assures guest privacy.

Facilities

- 1 super-king/twin ensuite & 1 queen ensuite bedroom
- hair dryers, toiletries, bathrobes & beach towels
- fresh fruit, flowers, TV, video, CD-player, fridge & tea/coffee facilities in all bedrooms
- laundry available
- private guest lounge with log fire, TV & piano in villa suite
- guest conservatory
- continental or self-serve breakfast in conservatory; or self-catering breakfast provisions for suite
- full kitchen with provisions for self-contained option
- phone & fax available
- honeymooners welcome
- private guest entrance; off-street parking
- courtesy passenger transfer

Activities available

- unimpeded sea views from site
- direct access to 2 beaches
- gas barbecue on site
- swimming; snorkelling
- fishing off rocks
- walk up hill to Tapeka Reserve
- boat trips
- swimming with dolphins
- chartered sailing
- deep-sea fishing
- "Hole in the Rock" trips
- high-speed scenic boat
- restaurants, 2km away
- historic buildings & gardens
- forest walks
- historic Pompallier, 2km
- Cape Reinga Day Trip
- heritage trails
- Waitangi Treaty House
- ferry services

© Friars' Guide to New Zealand Accommodation for the Discerning Traveller

Opua, Bay of Islands
Tio Bay Lodge

Hosts Dawn and Richard Wall

Waikino Road, Opua   *Postal* P O Box 19, Opua Post Office, Bay of Islands
Phone 0-9-403 7963   *Mobile* 027 496 2885   *Fax* 0-9-403 7963
Email stay@tiobay.com   *Website* www.tiobay.com

3 bdrm | 3 enst | Double $550 | Single $275 | Includes breakfast & dinner | Lunch extra

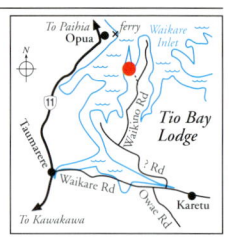

DIRECTIONS: Take SH 1 north to Kawakawa. Turn right & travel towards Opua for 3km. Turn right into Waikare Rd. Travel 5km & turn left into Waikino Rd. Travel 8km on gravel to end. Take left gate & follow drive down to Lodge.

Set on the water's edge in over eight hectares (20 acres) of private land, Tio Bay Lodge offers privacy and tranquillity. Separate from the main house, each of the three ensuite guestrooms is individually styled with wide sea views and sunny decks. Extra touches include the fresh fruit, freshly roasted home-grown macadamia nuts and the bottle of wine in the bedrooms. Tio Bay Lodge operates its own 10-metre high-speed launch and qualified skipper, available for sightseeing and fishing, by arrangement. Trips to the Hole-in-the-Rock are always popular. Included in the tariff is a three-course dinner with wine, featuring innovative dishes using fresh local produce and seafood. Richard is happy to cook guests' own catches of fish.

Facilities
- 3 queen ensuite bedrooms with private decks & sea views
- hair dryers, toiletries & bathrobes
- CD-player, fridge, bottle of wine, macadamia nuts, fresh fruit, tea/coffee & mineral water in all 3 bedrooms
- cotton bed linen; fresh flowers
- private guest entrance
- lounge with open fire, Sky TV, video, CDs, bar & tea/coffee
- breakfast served in dining room or alfresco on deck
- lunch, $25 pp
- 3-course dinner with wine
- powder room
- phone, fax & internet access
- complimentary laundry
- transfer by boat from Opua
- on-site parking; helipad
- closed June, July, August

Activities available
- BBQ & spa pool on site
- Tio Bay's 10m (30-ft) launch with skipper for sightseeing & fishing trips, extra charge
- walking on 8ha (20-acre) site
- hobi-cat sailing from site
- oyster collecting at Tio Bay
- Hole-in-the-Rock boat trips
- sailing; boating
- sea kayaking
- diving; snorkelling
- dolphin watching
- fishing; swimming
- golf; walks
- saltwater fly fishing
- kauri forest
- Ninety Mile Beach tours
- Waitangi Treaty House
- ferries from Paihia to historic Russell

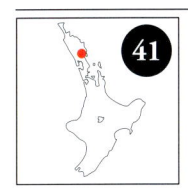

Bland Bay, Whangaruru Harbour
Pawhaoa Bay Lodge

Hosts Bill and Claire Hurst   *Fax* 0-9-433 6563

Whangaruru North Road, Bland Bay, R D 4, Hikurangi, Northland
Phone 0-9-433 6566   *Mobiles* 025 399 440 or 021 714 243
Email cbhurst@ihug.co.nz   *Website* www.pawhaoabaylodge.co.nz

4 bdrm	4 enst	1 pdrm	**Room rate** $240–$260 *Includes breakfast*	$400–$440 *Includes breakfast & dinner*
			Villa rate $220 **Extra persons** $30 each	*Self-catering*

DIRECTIONS: From Whangarei take SH 1 north for 20km. Turn right into Old Russell Rd. Travel 40km & turn right at Bland Bay sign into Whangaruru Nth Rd. Travel 1km past Bland Bay camping ground to Pawhaoa on right.

Pawhaoa Bay Lodge is located on the water's edge and consists of the main house/Lodge and two separate self-contained villas. The house, opened in 2003, offers two spacious ensuite bedrooms, a large open-plan lounge, dining and outside living area. The Villas, completed in 2001, each comprise a super-king/twin ensuite bedroom, guest lounge and fully equipped kitchen for self-catering. French doors from the house and villas open onto decks, lawn and beach. Set in established subtropical landscaped gardens, the Lodge provides panoramic views over the harbour to the bush-clad hills beyond. Pawhaoa is surrounded by conservation land, and provides access to scenic walking tracks, safe swimming and boating and fishing charters.

Facilities

- 2 Villas, each with 1 super-king/twin bedroom, with ensuite & extra rollaway bed
- 2 super-king ensuite bedrooms in Lodge
- cotton bed linen
- bath, hair dryer, toiletries, heated towel rails, heater & bathrobes per ensuite
- lounge area with tea/coffee, herbal teas, DVDs & CDs
- full kitchen for self-catering in each villa with provisions
- dinner by request, $60 pp
- powder room
- laundry facilities in Villas & Lodge
- balcony overlooking harbour & garden from bedroom & living room per villa
- on-site parking

Activities available

- BBQ & pétanque on site
- large subtropical garden on site for relaxing
- small boat mooring available on request
- direct beach access from villas
- kayaks available to guests
- holistic health massage available by appointment
- bush & beach walks; fishing
- swimming & snorkelling
- Bland Bay shop, 5-min away
- charter fishing from local company available
- bird-watching
- beaches, wide selection
- surfing & diving
- Whangarei, 1 hr south
- Paihia or Russell, both 40-min drive away

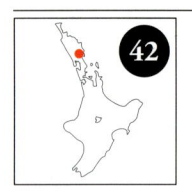

Tutukaka, Whangarei
Poor Knights Lodge

Hosts Yvonne Clark and Jim Mason

Tutukaka Block Road, Tutukaka *Postal* P O Box 1526, Tutukaka, Whangarei
Phone 0-9-434 4405 *Email* jamesandyvonne@poorknightslodge.co.nz
Fax 0-9-434 4401 *Website* www.poorknightslodge.co.nz

2 bdrm 2 enst Room rate $240 Includes breakfast Picnic lunch & wine extra

DIRECTIONS: From Whangarei bypass, turn right before Advocat Stadium & left at 2nd lights into Mill Rd. Travel 24km to Ngunguru, then 2km & turn right into Tutukaka Block Rd. Lodge is 0.5km on left.

Named after the Poor Knights Islands, 20 kilometres off-shore, Poor Knights Lodge offers an exclusive guest floor downstairs. Two separate super-king-size ensuite bedrooms open to a spacious guest deck for relaxing and appreciating the views over the Marina and Oturu Bay. Privacy is ensured and a full breakfast is served in the guestrooms or alfresco on the guests' decking in the warm Northland weather. Picnic lunches and wine are available, there is a barbecue for guest use and restaurants are a short drive away at Tutukaka Marina. The secluded setting is landscaped with native plants and overlooks the harbour out to the ocean. Nearby activities are popular with guests, including swimming, diving, fishing, the surf beaches and coastal walks.

Facilities

- 2 super-king/twin ensuite bedrooms downstairs
- hair dryers, bathrobes, heated towel rails & toiletries
- cotton bed linen, writing desk, phone jack, fruit, tea/coffee & fridge in bedrooms
- TV & stereo in bedrooms
- fresh flowers
- phone, fax & email available
- continental or cooked breakfast served in guestrooms or alfresco on guests' decking
- picnic lunch, $25 pp
- large, sunny guest deck with views over Oturu Bay & Marina
- private guest entrance for each bedroom downstairs
- off-street parking

Activities available

- BBQ available; wine extra
- honeymoons catered for
- diving around Poor Knights, shipwrecks, *Tui* & *Waikato*
- game & line fishing
- snorkelling
- swimming at local beaches
- surfing
- beach & coastal walks
- restaurants at Tutukaka Marina, 5-min drive away
- horse trekking
- gardens open to visit
- bush walks
- golf, 5-min drive, or 20-min drive for Whangarei golf
- Whangarei City, 20-min drive
- Bay of Islands, 1 hour north
- Auckland City, 2⅓ hours south

KAMO, WHANGAREI
MULRYANS COUNTRY ACCOMMODATION

Hosts Val and Kevin Ryan

Crane Road, Kauri, R D 1, Kamo, Whangarei
Phone 0-9-435 0945 *Email* info@mulryans.co.nz
Fax 0-9-435 5146 *Website* www.mulryans.co.nz

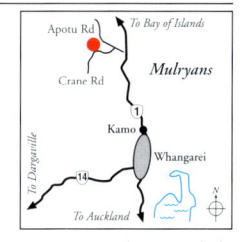

| 2 bdrm | 1 enst | 1 prbth | Room rate $165–$245 | *Includes breakfast*
Platters, BBQ & dinner extra |

DIRECTIONS: Take SH 1 north of Whangarei & bypass Kamo. Travel 5.6km & turn left into Apotu Rd, then left again into Crane Rd. Travel 0.5km to Mulryans on right. (Approx. 14 minutes north of Whangarei.)

Set in large gardens with established trees in a rural spot just off the motorway north of Whangarei, this kauri villa has been restored to provide a quiet retreat for guests. The upper floor comprises two queen-size bedrooms with bathrooms and tranquil views over the established gardens and surrounding countryside. Val serves gourmet breakfast downstairs in the country kitchen, dining room, or alfresco on the verandah overlooking the pond. In summer, food platters or a barbecue can be served alfresco by the swimming pool, and in winter, a three-course dinner is offered indoors. Mulryans still features the original homestead's kauri floors and mantelpieces and is a member of the Heritage and Character Inns of New Zealand.

Facilities

- Rose Room: queen bed, private bathroom & balcony
- Magnolia Room: queen bed, ensuite, stained glass feature window & balcony
- bathrobes, hair dryers, heated towel rails & toiletries
- cotton bed linen, feather pillows & feather duvets
- phone, fax & email available
- turn-down service
- hearty farmhouse breakfast, with cooked options
- food platters or BBQ by pool in summer; 3-course dinner offered in winter only, extra
- happy hour drinks
- fresh flowers, tea/coffee, herbal teas, home-made biscuits, hot chocolate with marshmallows & chocolates in each bedroom
- undercover on-site parking

Activities available

- swimming & spa pools on site
- pétanque; grass tennis courts
- Manx cat, dogs, donkeys, goat, chickens, coloured sheep on site
- Poor Knights Island Marine Reserve for diving, courtesy transport available
- big-game fishing charters & other aquatic activities
- 3 golf courses within 10-min drive
- award-winning restaurants, 8 mins; vineyard visits/tastings, local boutique brewery
- Tutukaka coast, 20-min drive
- Bay of Islands, 40-min drive
- beaches, wide selection
- private gardens open to visit
- antique & collectible shops
- Whangarei town & Basin, 12-min drive south

ONERAHI, WHANGAREI

SAIL INN

Host Jan Malcolm   *Mobile* 021 136 5702

148 Beach Road, Onerahi, Whangarei   *Phone* 0-9-436 2356
Postal 7/8 Madeira Lane, Grafton, Auckland   *Fax* 0-9-436 2356
Email sailinn@xtra.co.nz   *Website* friars.co.nz/hosts/sailinn.html

1 bdrm   1 enst   Room rate $195   Includes breakfast   Lunch & dinner extra

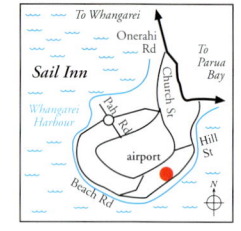

DIRECTIONS: From Auckland, take SH 1 to Whangarei. From Whangarei township, travel through Onerahi towards Whangarei Heads. Turn right into Beach Rd. Continue about 1km to Sail Inn on right.

Jan designed Sail Inn in 1990 to be spacious and airy with expansive harbour views. Sited directly across the road from the harbour inlet, Sail Inn is strategically positioned for viewing craft of all shapes and sizes, for swimming, fishing and boating. This peaceful retreat offers an ensuite bedroom with private decks, walk-in dressing room and sunken sitting room. Tea, coffee and fresh baking are provided for guests on arrival and flexi-time breakfast is served alfresco on the deck or indoors overlooking the harbour. Picnic hampers can be arranged for hosted day trips to the Bay of Islands. A barbecue or dinner can also be provided, with apéritifs, wine and port, and guest are welcome to cook in collaboration with Jan who operates on relaxed "island time".

Facilities

- 1 queen ensuite bedroom with walk-in dressing room, fridge, & sitting room
- sitting room with tea/coffee, TV, extensive CD collection & decks
- toiletries, hair dryers, heated towel rail in ensuite
- phone & fax available
- French & Japanese spoken
- complimentary laundry
- fresh flowers
- full breakfast served alfresco on deck or at dining table
- 3-course dinner or BBQ, with wine, $50 pp
- picnic hampers on request
- on-site parking
- courtesy airport transfer
- Scottish terrier, Mac, in residence
- massage & facials on request

Activities available

- pétanque court, spa pool & BBQ area
- feeding doves on site
- restaurant, 5-min walk
- swimming beach across road
- viewing yachts to tankers passing by window up harbour
- spearing flounder across road
- fishing for snapper & tarakihi
- tennis court, 2-min walk
- hosted day trips within Bay of Islands
- Town Basin for shopping & restaurants, 10-min drive
- golf course, 10-min drive
- gardens open to visit
- deep-sea game fishing
- chartered scenic flights
- airport, 5-min drive
- Auckland City, 2 hours south

© Friars' Guide to New Zealand Accommodation for the Discerning Traveller

Parua Bay, Whangarei Heads
Parua Bay Cottage

Hosts Marian and Greg Innes   *Phone* 0-9-436 5626

Parua Bay Cemetery Road, Parua Bay, Whangarei Heads
Postal P O Box 1370, Whangarei   *Website* friars.co.nz/hosts/parua.html
Freephone 0800 116 626   *Email* paruabaycottage@innes-strategy.com

2 bdrm | 1 prbth

Cottage rate $150 for 2 persons
Extra persons $30 each

Self-catering, no meals available
5-day minimum stay in peak season

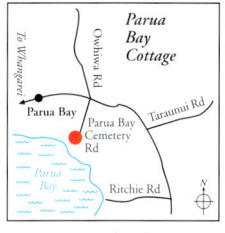

DIRECTIONS: Take Whangarei Heads Rd to Onerahi. Fork left & travel 10 mins to Parua Bay. Continue past tavern, then turn right into Parua Bay Cemetery Rd. Travel 1km to end of road to Parua Bay Cottage.

Set beside a secluded private beach, on eight hectares of bush including ecologically significant kauri forest, this historic cottage is fully self-contained for one-party bookings. Originally built with three rooms circa 1860, Parua Bay Cottage was carefully restored in 1995 to sleep seven, and kitchen, bathroom and laundry were added. The kitchen is fully equipped for self-catering and the verandahs are popular for alfresco dining. Fishing, diving and sightseeing trips can be arranged and mooring is available for large yachts and other boats. There is direct access from the cottage to Parua Bay with its safe swimming and an extra shower on the beach. Children are welcome to view the farm animals on site and the mature kauri forest attracts native songbirds.

Facilities

- one-party bookings only
- 1 twin & 1 double bedroom with private bathroom
- cotton bed linen
- hair dyer, toiletries & heated towel rail in bathroom
- extra double fold-out beds in lounge and in dining area
- lounge with open fire, TV, music, CD-player, games, magazines & writing desk
- full kitchen for self-catering
- self-serve laundry
- children welcome
- phone jack for email
- fax available
- fresh flowers
- Marian speaks basic German
- pets welcome if supervised
- on-site parking; helipad

Activities available

- private beach from site
- sheep, ducks & hens on site
- safe swimming beach from site
- mature kauri forest on 8-ha (20-acre) property
- bush & beach walks on site
- native bird-watching on site
- kayaking; boating
- mooring available in bay, extra
- fishing in bay
- restaurants, 2km drive
- golf, 3km drive
- surf beaches, 15-min drive
- diving trips
- boat charters for fishing, diving & sightseeing
- walkways at Bream Head reserve, 15-min drive
- tramping, 15-min drive
- Whangarei Basin, 20 mins

WAIPOUA FOREST, KAURI COAST
WAIPOUA LODGE

Hosts Nicole and Chris Donahoe

State Highway 12, Katui, Waipoua Forest *Phone* 0-9-439 0422
Postal Waipoua Lodge, R D 6, Dargaville *Fax* 0-9-439 0422
Email nicole@waipoualodge.co.nz *Website* www.waipoualodge.co.nz

| 5 bdrm | 3 enst | 1 prbth | 1 pdrm |

Apartment rate $310–$340 for 2 persons
Extra persons $30 each
Includes breakfast
Self-catering
Lunch & dinner extra

DIRECTIONS: Take SH 12 north to Dargaville. Turn left through township & continue on SH 12 for 48km. Waipoua Lodge on right of highway, 2km before forest.

Located on the southern boundary of the Waipoua Forest, Waipoua Lodge was built over a century ago as a private residence, and has housed guests to the forest over these years. Restored in 2003, the Lodge features native kauri timber construction and rimu ceilings in the dining room, bar and guest lounge. Guests can enjoy notable New Zealand wines while relaxing on the leather couches in front of the original fireplace. Historical antique farm and kauri milling implements hang in the lounge, and the sunroom/library overlooks the gardens and forest beyond. Adjacent to the lodge, the original working sheds have been transformed into four pupose-built apartments, each opening to private balconies with views to the forest beyond.

Facilities
- Stables: 1 king bedroom, ensuite with bath, lounge, kitchenette, balcony
- Calf Pen: 1 king bedroom, ensuite, lounge, kitchenette & balcony
- Woolshed: 1 king bedroom, ensuite with bath, kitchen, lounge, twin mezzanine over lounge (suitable for children), wrap-around balcony
- Tack Rooms: 1 super-king & 1 king bedroom opening to balcony, 1 bathroom, lounge, kitchenette

- full breakfast
- picnics/lunch, extra
- organic local produce; guests' trout prepared
- licensed restaurant & bar
- quality linen, hair dryer, toiletries, bathrobes, TV, stereo/CDs per apartment
- laundry, extra
- on-site parking; helipad

Activities available
- bush walk on site – native birds
- guided night walk in kauri park to view NZ's rare & endangered kiwi
- forest headquarters adjacent
- Kai Iwi Lakes for swimming, water skiing, kayaking & fishing, 20 mins
- guided trout fishing from boat
- longest beach in NZ, golden sand, unpopulated, beach fishing, 15km
- biggest kauri tree in NZ, 16km

- waterfall, 15-min drive
- Waipoua Forest walks
- swimming in river waterhole
- horse trekking
- 4WD beach tours
- gardens to visit
- Hokianga Harbour views, 30-min drive
- Matakohe Museum, 1 hour
- Dargaville, 30-min drive

© Friars' Guide to New Zealand Accommodation for the Discerning Traveller

Dargaville
Kauri House Lodge

Host Doug Blaxall   *Mobile* 025 547 769

Bowen Street, Dargaville   *Postal* P O Box 382, Dargaville
Phone 0-9-439 8082   *Email* kaurihouse@xtra.co.nz
Fax 0-9-439 8082   *Website* friars.co.nz/hosts/kaurihouse.html

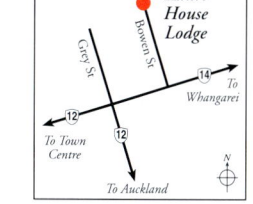

3 bdrm | 3 enst
Double $200–$275
Single $200
Includes breakfast
Weekend & off-season rates available

DIRECTIONS: Take SH 12 north to Dargaville. At cross-road junction, turn right into SH 14. Turn first left into Bowen St. Continue to end of road, to driveway entrance to Kauri House Lodge.

Kauri House Lodge is set among mature trees, three kilometres from the township of Dargaville. The historic style and ambience of this 1880s villa has been retained, with the original kauri panelling and period antiques in all rooms. Surrounded by extensive landscaped grounds, the quiet at Kauri House Lodge is broken only by native birds. In summer guests enjoy the large swimming pool. In winter, the billiards room is popular with its log fire and library for relaxing in the evening. The hosts also invite guests to explore the mature native bush on their nearby farm overlooking the Wairoa River and Kaipara Harbour. Some of the activities available in the area include the deserted beaches, lakes, river tours, horse treks, walks and restaurants.

Facilities
- 1 super-king, 1 king & 1 twin bedroom, each with ensuite
- hair dryers & toiletries
- wheelchair access to 1 bedroom
- children over 9 years welcome
- piano & open fire in billiards room
- verandah overlooks 3ha garden
- TV lounge & library
- satellite Sky TV & VCR
- fresh flowers
- continental or cooked breakfast, served in dining room
- teas & coffee available
- night-store heating
- self-serve laundry
- Spud, the dog, & Spook, the black cat, in residence
- courtesy passenger transfer
- on-site parking

Activities available
- in-house billiards & piano
- cattle farm tour on site
- large swimming pool on site, available in summer season only
- surfing, swimming & cliff views from 100km beach, 10km away
- 16ha (40 acres) native bush, steers & donkeys, 5km away
- horse rides/treks on beach
- walking tracks; garden visits
- licensed restaurants, 3km
- trout fishing in Kai Iwi lakes, guides available
- river cruises & boat trips
- Waipoua kauri forest treks
- Matakohe Kauri Museum
- wood turning & crafts
- Dargaville shops, 3km
- Whangarei, 40-min drive
- Auckland, 2½ hrs south

POUTO POINT, DARGAVILLE
LIGHTHOUSE LODGE

Hosts Christine Findley and Bob Benseman

6577 Pouto Road, Pouto Point, Dargaville *Phone* 0-9-439 5150
Postal 6577 Pouto Road, R D 1, Te Kopuru *Fax* 0-9-439 5150
Email email@lighthouse-lodge.co.nz *Website* www.lighthouse-lodge.co.nz

| 6 bdrm | 3 enst | 1 prbth | 1 pdrm |

Room rate $210–$420

Includes breakfast
Lunch & dinner extra

DIRECTIONS: Take SH 12 north to Dargaville. Turn left into Pouto Rd & travel south for 1 hr to Lighthouse Lodge. Alternatively 4WD along Ripiro Beach at low tide, or access Lodge via boat, or helicopter.

With uninterrupted ocean vistas, Lighthouse Lodge is sited at the tip of Pouto Point, on the secluded headland of Kaipara Harbour, one hour south of Dargaville. Set in a subtropical garden, this contemporary cedar-clad Lodge has been designed on a nautical theme incorporating local historical artefacts. The spacious interiors open to the balcony, with sea views from every room. Accommodation comprises three guest suites, which can be configured as six bedrooms. Full breakfast is served in the dining room, or alfresco on the deck, with special diets catered and seafood a speciality. A three-course table d' hôte dinner is also offered. Lighthouse Lodge has direct access to the longest drivable beach in New Zealand, 101 kilometres in length.

Facilities
- 1 king/twin suite with private access
- 2 queen suites open to balcony & patio
- TV, writing desk, fridge & tea/coffee in suites
- hair dyers, toiletries, heated towel rails & bathrobes
- wood burner, bar, Sky TV & books in lounge
- cotton bed linen
- continental & cooked breakfast
- lunch & picnic baskets, extra
- dinner, $40–$60 pp; seafood speciality; special diets catered
- email, fax & phone available
- fresh flowers
- laundry available
- conferences & weddings
- on-site parking
- helipad

Activities available
- private jacuzzi under stars
- bird-watching on site
- picnicking on beach
- golf, 45-min drive via beach
- wilderness coastal walks
- 1884 wooden lighthouse, 7km
- 4WD truck tours
- Pouto sand dune tours; quad bike safaris
- gannets & seals
- restaurants, 1 hour north
- beach & boat fishing; fishing gear & charters
- swimming & surfing
- pétanque & clay bird shooting
- scenic Kaipara boat cruises
- Dargaville, 1 hour north
- Auckland, 3-hour drive or 20-min heliflight

© Friars' Guide to New Zealand Accommodation for the Discerning Traveller

LANG COVE, WAIPU
ROYAL PALM LODGE

Hosts Jan and John Allen   *Mobile* 025 948 863

19 Highland Lass Place, Lang Cove, Northland   *Phone* 0-9-432 0120
Postal P O Box 88, Thistle Post Office, Waipu, Northland   *Fax* 0-9-432 0368
Email hosts@royalpalmlodge.co.nz   *Website* www.royalpalmlodge.co.nz

7 bdrm   3 enst   2 prbth   1 shbth

Room rate $250–$400
Off-season rates available

Includes breakfast   *Lunch & dinner extra*
Self-catering available downstairs

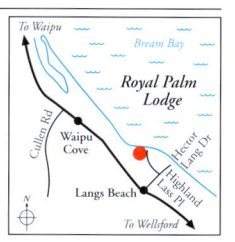

DIRECTIONS: From SH 1, turn right at Wellsford into coastal road & travel towards Mangawhai. Continue towards Waipu. At Langs Beach turn right into Hector Lang Drive & left into Highland Lass Pl. Royal Palm Lodge on left.

Royal Palm Lodge is set right on the beachfront at Lang Cove. Constructed in 1997, in a classical style with spacious covered balconies overlooking the sea, the Lodge provides a variety of accommodation options. An exclusive guest floor is situated at beach level, which offers self-catering with a full kitchen. On the main level of the Lodge are another three bedrooms and the dining facilities. Meals are served upstairs in the spacious dining room with ocean views, or alfresco on the extensive sundeck. Restaurants are ten minutes' drive. There is a relaxed beach-house ambience at Royal Palm Lodge. Popular on-site activities include an exercise gym, spa pool, billiards table, pétanque, swimming, walking, jet skiing and kayaking at the beach.

Facilities

- Royal Palm & King Palm Rooms: king/twin bed in each & ensuite
- Queen Palm Room: queen/twin bed with private bathroom
- Phoenix Palm Room: super-king/twin with private bathroom & bath
- Music Room: king bed & ensuite
- Arabian Room: queen bed & Tulip Room: queen/twin bed share 1 bathroom
- hair dryers, toiletries & bathrobes
- continental or cooked breakfast served upstairs or alfresco on sundeck
- light lunch by request, extra
- 3-course dinner by arrangement, extra
- full kitchen & lounge downstairs with Sky digital TV, stereo & tea/coffee
- guest laundry, email, fax & phone facilities

Activities available

- direct access to safe swimming beach from site
- ocean kayaks, wave ski & jet ski, all available on site
- spa pool & BBQ on site
- pool table; pétanque on site
- massage & facials by arrangement
- honeymoons/conferences catered
- 2 golf courses; tennis courts
- fishing charters; coastal walks
- Mangawhai & Waipu restaurants, 10-min drive
- horse riding; fishing
- glow-worm caves
- gardens open to visit
- Scottish Heritage Museum
- Mangawhai & Waipu, 10-min drive
- Whangarei City, 30 mins
- Auckland City, 1½ hours

65

© Friars' Guide to New Zealand Accommodation for the Discerning Traveller

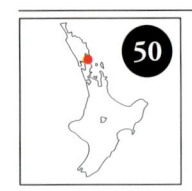

Mangawhai Heads
Milestone Cottages

Host Gael McConachy

27 Moir Point Road, Mangawhai Heads
Phone 0-9-431 4018   *Email* gael@milestonecottages.co.nz
Fax 0-9-431 4018   *Website* www.milestonecottages.co.nz

5 bdrm | 5 prbth | Cottage rate $140–$250
Extra persons $35 each
Self-catering, no meals available
2-night minimum on weekends

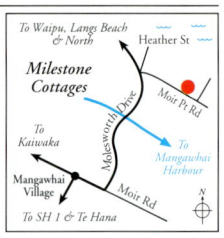

DIRECTIONS: From Te Hana, turn right on to coastal road & travel to Mangawhai. Turn right into Moir Rd, then left into Molesworth Drive. Cross causeway & turn right into Moir Point Rd. Travel 200m to Cottages on left.

Milestone Cottages are individually designed by Gael's architect sister, Philippa Johnson, to complement the natural setting of the private estuary with sandy beach and coastal bush at Mangawhai Heads. Gael's husband, Ian, built and hand-crafted the cottages in an environmentally sensitive way. The Schooner and Gumdiggers Cottages overlook the estuary, while the Puka (with sea views) and Palm Cottages are nestled in the hectare of subtropical gardens around the swimming pool. A second earth-brick cottage, The Gardners Cottage, is adjacent to the thatched adobe and manuka wharekai where guests enjoy barbecues. Palm trees fringe the croquet lawn and steps lead from a tree-framed viewing platform down to the private beach below.

Facilities
- private-party bookings per cottage
- 5 fully equipped self-contained cottages – individually named
- 1 queen or twin bedroom & bathroom in each cottage
- lounge area with TV & fully equipped kitchen in each cottage
- private decking overlooking garden
- barbecue/wharekai area available
- conference facilities
- self-catering for all meals
- videos in all cottages
- wheelchair access to Palm Cottage
- extensive subtropical garden with fish pond
- BBQ per cottage
- total privacy
- ocean views
- native bush setting

Activities available

On site:
- swimming pool
- croquet lawn
- pétanque court
- gazebo in garden
- kayaks available
- safe sandy swimming beach
- sheltered estuary & sand-dunes
- horse rides

Off site:
- coastal walkways
- café serving breakfast, restaurant & hot bread shop, 150m walk
- white sandy surf beaches
- bird sanctuary; gardens to visit
- 18-hole golf links nearby
- tennis courts; bowls
- Matakohe Museum
- Goat Island Marine Park

Mangawhai Heads
Mangawhai Lodge

Host Jeannette Forde

4 Heather Street, Mangawhai Heads
Phone 0-9-431 5311   *Email* mlodge@xtra.co.nz
Fax 0-9-431 5312   *Website* www.seaviewlodge.co.nz

| 5 bdrm | 3 enst | 2 prbth | 1 pdrm |

Double $150–$165   *Includes breakfast*
Single $120–$140   **House rate & seasonal rates available**

DIRECTIONS: From Te Hana, turn right into Twin Coast Discovery Route to Mangawhai. Turn right into Moir Rd, then left into Molesworth Drive. Cross causeway & turn right into Heather St. Lodge on right corner.

This two-storey colonial-inspired house features wrap-around verandahs which provide panoramic ocean views. Vistas extend to the sheltered harbour and sand-dunes, upper reaches of the Hauraki Gulf, and the Hen and Chickens Islands. Mangawhai Lodge is sited adjacent to an 18-hole championship all-weather golf course and a licensed café. The Lodge caters for couples, small conferences, and social and golfing groups of up to 10 guests. The five guestrooms open to verandahs with tables and chairs. Continental or cooked breakfast is served upstairs or alfresco on the adjacent verandah. The guest kitchenette downstairs provides tea and coffee facilities and the upstairs reading lounge includes a television. A barbecue is also available.

Facilities

- 2 queen ensuite bedrooms
- 1 super-king/twin ensuite bedroom & 2 super-king/twin bedrooms with private bathrooms
- hair dryers & toiletries
- high quality bed linen
- verandahs opening from all bedrooms, with table & chairs
- TV in all 5 guestrooms
- groups catered for
- full breakfast served in upstairs dining room, or alfresco on verandah
- tea/coffee facilities in guest kitchenette
- guest lounge with TV, video, CDs & books
- sea views
- email, fax & phone & barbecue available
- on-site parking

Activities available

- beach, 2-min walk away
- licensed café opposite
- 18-hole golf course adjacent
- safe swimming beach, 300m
- kayaking; boogie boarding
- bird sanctuary
- coastal walkway; gardens to visit
- sand-dunes; surfing; watersports
- mountain bike tracks, 10 mins
- 5 restaurants nearby
- white sandy surf beaches
- tennis; bowls; horse riding
- quality crafts
- Matakohe Kauri Museum
- boat charters – fishing/diving
- Goat Island reserve, 35 mins
- midway between Auckland Airport & Bay of Islands, 2 hours drive north or south

Te Arai Point, Mangawhai
Lake View Chalets

Hosts Gabi and Sven Oltersdorf

662 Ocean View Road, R D 5, Wellsford   *Postal* P O Box 243, Wellsford
Freephone 0800 LAKEVIEW   Phone 0-9-431 4086   Fax 0-9-431 4886
Email info@chalets.co.nz   *Website* www.chalets.co.nz

12 bdrm | 6 prbth

Chalet rate $130–$170 for 2 persons
Extra adults $35 each   Extra children $20 each

Self-catering
Breakfast extra

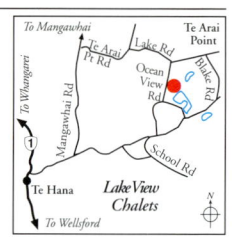

DIRECTIONS: From Auckland take SH 1 north to Te Hana. Travel 13km & turn right into Mangawhai Rd. Turn right into Te Arai Pt Rd. Take Lake Rd to right, & turn right into Ocean View Rd. Chalets on left.

Lake View Chalets were built by the Pierau family in 1996, on their 80 hectares (200 acres) of farmland, with access to the Slipper and Spectacle Lakes. All six Chalets are positioned for lake views and privacy, and set in planted gardens. Each Chalet is self-contained for self-catering, with a full kitchen, although breakfast is available on request. And guests are welcome to pick citrus from the on-site orchard in season. There are two bedrooms per Chalet – super-king/twin and twin – one bathroom and a private sundeck with outdoor furniture and barbecue. Kayaks are available for guest use on the two adjacent lakes, and mountain bikes can take guests through the adjacent Mangawhai pine forest to 14 kilometres of unspoiled white-sand beaches.

Facilities

- 6 Chalets, each with private-party bookings only
- each Chalet includes 1 twin & 1 super-king/twin bedroom with 1 private bathroom
- cotton bed linen
- hair dryer & toiletries
- dining lounge in each Chalet, with Sky TV & phone jack
- video, games, books available
- breakfast available, $20 pp
- full kitchen for self-catering in each Chalet
- guest deck from each Chalet
- lake views from all Chalets
- phone & email available
- complimentary laundry
- German spoken
- on-site parking
- children welcome

Activities available

On site complimentary:
- access to Slipper, Spectacle & Tomarata Lakes
- spa pool on site
- row-boat & kayaks available
- walks around lakes
- citrus for guests to pick
- mountain bikes available
- pétanque/boules
- swimming in lakes

Off site:
- restaurants, 15-min drive
- golfing; walking; horse riding
- gardens open to visit
- boat charters
- big-game fishing
- Wellsford shops, 20km south
- Whangarei, 30km north
- Warkworth village, 50km south
- Auckland City, 1 hour south

Leigh, Warkworth
Tera del Mar Country B & B

Hosts Teresa Gibson and Marshall Lefferts

140 Rodney Road, Leigh, R D 5, Warkworth
Phone 0-9-422 6090 *Mobile* 027 478 8202 *Fax* 0-9-422 6090
Email be@teradelmar.co.nz *Website* www.teradelmar.co.nz

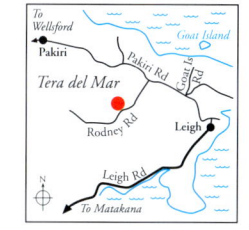

| 4 bdrm | 3 enst | 1 prbth | Double $220–$320 Single $180–$280 | *Includes breakfast* |

DIRECTIONS: From Auckland take SH 1 north to Warkworth. At 2nd lights turn right & veer left to Matakana & Leigh. Continue on Pakiri Rd past Goat Island. Turn left into Rodney Rd. Travel 1.4km to Tera del Mar on right.

Designed in Victorian style, Tera del Mar was opened in 2003 on Teresa and Marshall's 40-hectare (100-acre) property, just over an hour north of Auckland. Four open fireplaces feature in the upstairs guestrooms, and all bedrooms open to the extensive wrap-around verandahs overlooking the landscaped garden, with expansive ocean and rural views to Pakiri Beach and beyond. The two-course gourmet breakfast or brunch is served downstairs in the lounge or library, alfresco on the verandah, or room service is available. Surround sound entertainment is enjoyed in the guest lounge. Teresa and Marshall's two young sons and Misty, their friendly Samoyed dog, complete the family. Cafés and restaurants are nearby in Leigh and Matakana.

Facilities
- 3 queen bedrooms with ensuites
- 1 super-king/twin or 1 queen bedroom with 1 private bathroom & double spa bath
- hair dryer, toiletries & bathrobes
- phone jacks, tables & 4 open fireplaces in bedrooms
- guest lounge with open fire, tea/coffee, herbal tea, filtered rainwater, glass of wine, surround-sound, DVDs & CD-player
- 2-course gourmet breakfast
- library with open fire, games, magazines & writing desk; fax & email in office
- children by arrangement
- private guest entrance
- weddings, anniversaries, honeymoons & group bookings welcome
- ample on-site parking; helipad

Activities available
- outdoor spa pool/jacuzzi, sauna & changing room
- lawn pétanque & croquet
- gazebo, landscaped gardens & scenic ridge walk on site
- children's sandpit, tree house & trampoline on site
- Goat Island Marine Reserve & glass-bottom boat, 5 mins
- safe swimming beach & playground, 7-min drive
- restaurants & cafés, 5–25 mins
- scenic & fishing charter tours
- coastal & bush walks, 5–8 mins
- diving; snorkelling; kayaking
- Pakiri Beach surfing & horse riding
- art & craft galleries, 5–30 mins
- Matakana wine trails, 20 mins
- pottery & café, 20-min drive
- Tawharanui Regional Park, 40 mins
- Auckland airport, 2 hours south

MATAKANA, WARKWORTH
SANDPIPER LODGE

Hosts Robin and Louise Fischer

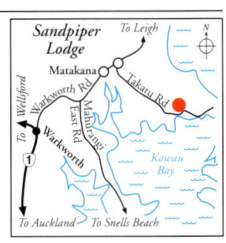

Takatu Road, R D 6, Warkworth
Phone 0-9-422 7256   *Mobile* 025 283 6853   *Fax* 0-9-422 7816
Email sandpiper.lodge@xtra.co.nz   *Website* www.sandpiperlodge.co.nz

Room rate $250–$450   Includes breakfast
Lunch & dinner, extra

| 9 bdrm | 9 enst | 1 prbth |

DIRECTIONS: From Auckland, take SH 1 north to Warkworth. At lights turn right & veer left to Matakana. Continue through Matakana & take 2nd right into Takatu Rd. Travel 10km & turn right 150m to Sandpiper Lodge.

Overlooking a tidal estuary with views to Kawau Island, Sandpiper Lodge is located in over two hectares (6.5 acres) of sub-tropical and native gardens at Christian Bay on the Takatu Peninsula. This boutique hotel includes an à la carte restaurant and is also suitable for hosting conferences. Accommodation comprises nine ensuite super-king/twin bedooms each with direct dial phone, television and tea/coffee facilities. Meals prepared by an award-winning chef are offered alfresco on the pool deck, or in the fully licensed restaurant, featuring wine from local vineyards. Picnics are available for trips to Tawharanui Regional Park and the beach. Sandpiper Lodge is a tranquil country hotel, 15 minutes from the colonial township of Warkworth.

Facilities

- 9 super-king/twin ensuite bedrooms with dressing rooms
- cotton bed linen, writing desk, phone, tea/coffee, mineral water & TV in all 9 bedrooms
- bathrobes, hair dryers, toiletries, demist mirrors, heated towel rails
- guest lounge with open fire, tea/coffee, mineral water, bar, TV, CD-player & games
- fax & email available

- à la carte breakfast
- à la carte lunch, $40 pp
- à la carte dinner with wine at licensed restaurant, $60 pp
- picnics on request, $25 pp
- laundry services, $10
- German & French spoken
- guest entrances & balconies
- courtesy passenger transfer
- on-site parking; helipad

Activities available

- croquet & pétanque on site
- 2ha landscaped gardens on site
- swimming pool on site
- rowboat on estuary
- kayaking, diving, fishing & sailing access from site
- 2 golf courses; quad bikes
- clay pigeon shooting
- walks; horse riding
- tennis court

- vineyards; wine tours
- antiques shops at Warkworth
- Matakohe Kauri Museum
- marine farm; surf beaches
- local crafts, artwork & pottery
- historic Mansion House on Kawau Island
- Tawharanui Regional Park
- helicopter sightseeing
- Goat Island; nature trails

© Friars' Guide to New Zealand Accommodation for the Discerning Traveller

MATAKANA, WARKWORTH
CASA D'ORO

Hosts Noreen and Norm Harvey

4/449 Whitmore Road, Matakana *Mobile* 021 971 562
Postal 4/449 Whitmore Road, R D 6, Warkworth *Phone* 0-9-422 7903
Email harville@clear.net.nz *Website* www.casadoro.co.nz *Fax* 0-9-422 7904

Double $190–$215 *Includes breakfast & apéritifs*
Single $170 Multiple-night rate available

1 bdrm 1 enst

DIRECTIONS: At Warkworth turn right into Matakana/Leigh Rd. Travel 1km past Matakana & turn right at Omaha sign. Turn right into Takatu Rd, travel 2km, right into Whitmore Rd & travel 2km to Casa d'Oro on right.

Architecturally designed in 2002 in Italianate style, Casa d'Oro is a single-level home, providing one queen-size guestroom with ensuite bathroom. Guests can park at their own entrance, and have television and tea and coffee-making facilities in their room. The bedroom opens to a private guest terrace with table and chairs overlooking the Matakana River estuary, where a full breakfast can be served alfresco. Apéritifs are offered before dinner and restaurants are only five or 10 minutes drive away in the village of Matakana or the township of Warkworth. Guests enjoy the art and craft at Warkworth and the local wine trail. Ferry trips to Kawau Island and glass-bottom boat trips to the Goat Island Marine Reserve are also popular.

Facilities

- 1 queen ensuite bedroom
- guest terrace opens from bedroom with view over estuary
- cotton bed linen
- hair dryer, toiletries & heated towel rails in bathroom
- bathrobes
- TV in bedroom
- tea/coffee facilities in bedroom
- fresh flowers
- continental or full breakfast served in dining room, alfresco in courtyard, or on guest terrace
- lounge with TV, CD-player & magazines
- complimentary apéritifs
- private guest entrance
- phone, fax & email available
- on-site parking

Activities available

- Matakana coast wine trail
- golf courses
- Tawharanui Regional Park, beaches & walks
- art & craft markets & galleries
- Warkworth Museum
- Omaha & Pakiri beaches
- fishing trips & charters
- swimming; snorkelling
- restaurants & cafés 5–10 mins
- pottery & café, 10-min drive
- Cape Rodney lookout
- Goat Island marine reserve
- glass-bottom boat trips
- ferry trips to Kawau Island & historic Mansion House
- Matakana village, 5-min drive
- Warkworth township, 10 mins
- Auckland, 1¼-hr drive south

MATAKANA, WARKWORTH
THE CASTLE MATAKANA

Hosts Val and Ross Sutherland

378 Whitmore Road, Matakana, R D 6, Warkworth
Phone 0-9-422 9288   *Fax* 0-9-422 9289
Email mail@the-castle.co.nz   *Website* www.the-castle.co.nz

Room rate $270–$342

Includes breakfast & apéritifs
Lunch, dinner & liquor extra

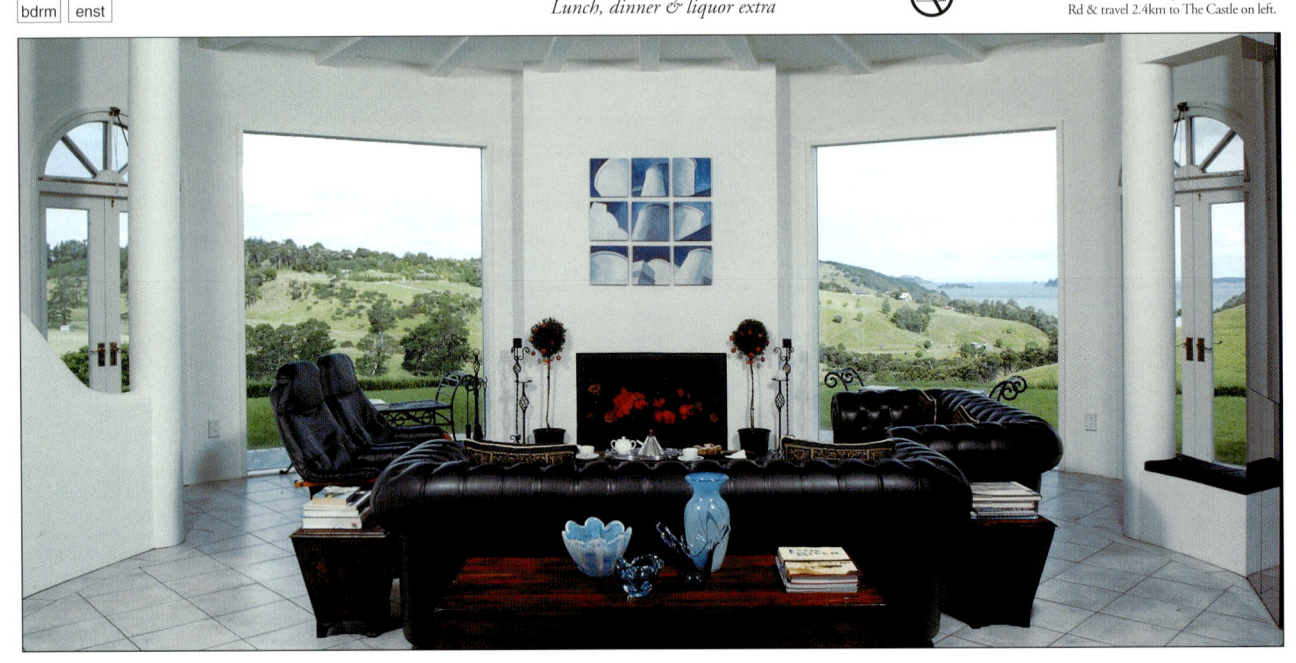

3 bdrm   3 enst

DIRECTIONS: At Warkworth, turn right into Matakana/Leigh Rd. Travel 1km past Matakana & turn right at Omaha sign. Turn right into Takatu Rd, travel 2km, turn right into Whitmore Rd & travel 2.4km to The Castle on left.

The Castle Matakana is a boutique lodge with vineyard in the Matakana Coast Wine Country near Warkworth. It is an easy hour north of Auckland and en route to the Bay of Islands. The contemporary architecture is designed to capture the rural and sea views over historic Kawau Bay, from every room. Upstairs is a spacious guest suite opening to a private balcony, with two further bedrooms in the guest wing on the ground floor, adjacent to the circular entrance lounge with log fire. Val's cuisine is a speciality at The Castle, featuring local produce and catering for individual requirements. Ross offers his own wines from his wine cellar, along with fine wines from Matakana's vineyards. Special occasions can be catered by arrangement.

Facilities

- 3 super-king/twin ensuite bedrooms, 1 with dual basins, bidet, dressing room, balcony
- cotton bed linen; iron & board
- hair dryers, heated floors, heated towel rails, toiletries & bathrobes
- fresh flowers, fruit, chocolates
- all rooms open to deck; views
- guest lounge with open fire, tea/coffee, music & artwork
- continental & cooked breakfasts served in dining room, or alfresco
- lunch/picnic on request, extra
- dinner, by prior arrangement, $75 pp, wine extra
- welcome tea/coffee on arrival
- laundry; central heating
- phone, fax & email access
- on-site parking

Activities available

- giant chess board on balcony
- barbecue; pétanque/boules
- vineyard on site
- wine trail
- golfing
- art & craft galleries
- swimming; diving; sailing
- glass bottom boat trips
- ferry to Kawau Island
- local vineyard restaurant
- horse riding
- snorkelling
- Goat Island marine reserve
- white sand beaches
- surfing; wind surfing
- walking & tramping tracks
- Warkworth restaurants & township, 15-min drive
- Auckland, 1 hour south

MATAKANA, WARKWORTH
HURSTMERE HOUSE

Hosts Anne and Bob Moir

186 Tongue Farm Road, Matakana   *Phone* 0-9-422 9220
Postal P O Box 37, Matakana, Warkworth   *Fax* 0-9-422 9220
Email hurstmere@ihug.co.nz   *Website* www.hurstmerehouse.co.nz

4 bdrm   4 enst   Room rate $230–$250   Self-contained suite rate $250   *Includes breakfast*   *Self-catering in suite*

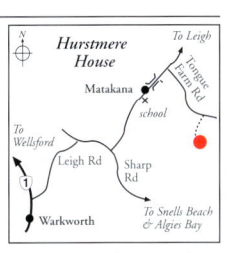

DIRECTIONS: Take SH 1 north to Warkworth. Turn right at traffic lights towards Leigh. Travel 10 mins to Matakana, cross bridge & turn right into Tongue Farm Rd. Hurstmere at end on right. White entrance to drive.

Originally built in 1930 on Hurstmere Road in Takapuna, Auckland, Hurstmere House was moved to its present rural site in 1995, then extended to provide four guest ensuite bedrooms, including one suite which is self-contained. The two-storey home features original native timber panelling and is furnished with antiques and rimu furniture. The No Exit road ensures peaceful surroundings, although Warkworth town and beaches are only a few minutes' drive away. Guests can enjoy viewing the sheep and cattle, as well as the sunsets, from the wrap-around verandahs which face due west. Anne and Bob serve continental and cooked breakfasts in the dining room, alfresco on the verandah, or in the self-contained suite if required.

Facilities

- 2 queen suites, 1 self-contained queen suite & 1 king/twin bedroom
- 4 ensuites with heated towel rails
- hair dryer & iron in bedrooms
- electric blankets, cotton linen
- TV, fridge & tea/coffee in 3 suites
- fresh flowers in all rooms
- phone, fax & email available
- laundry, $10 per load
- wrap-around verandah
- continental/cooked breakfast served in dining room or alfresco on verandah; self-contained suite on request
- kitchen for self-catering in self-contained suite
- summer house in garden
- sheep & cattle on site
- on-site parking
- www.heritageinns.co.nz

Activities available

- Matakana Coast Wine Trail
- restaurants & cafés, 3-min drive
- Pottery & Café, 2-min drive
- 2 golf courses, 8–10-min drive
- horse trekking
- snorkelling at Goat Island, a national maritime reserve
- Tawharanui Regional Park with beaches & walks
- wine tasting at vineyards nearby
- licensed fishing launch trips
- picnicking at beaches
- tramping; walking
- museum at Warkworth
- Sheep World; tennis courts
- boating; fishing
- shopping in Warkworth
- Antiques & Craft Market
- Kawau Island trips to Mansion House

73

© Friars' Guide to New Zealand Accommodation for the Discerning Traveller

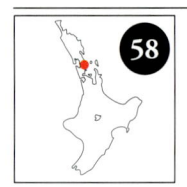

MATAKANA, WARKWORTH
ROSEMOUNT HOMESTEAD

Host Libby Dykes

25 Rosemount Road, Matakana, Warkworth
Phone 0-9-422 2580   *Mobile* 027 496 6654   *Fax* 0-9-422 2583
Email enquiries@rosemount.co.nz   *Website* www.rosemount.co.nz

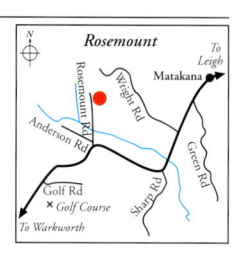

3 bdrm   3 enst   Room rate $195–$225   *Includes breakfast*

DIRECTIONS: Take SH 1 north to Warkworth. Turn right at traffic lights towards Matakana & Leigh. Pass Warkworth Golf Course on right, then turn left into Rosemount Rd. Travel up hill to Rosemount on right.

Originally built in 1900, Rosemount Homestead was constructed from a twin-trunk native kauri, felled by an early settler in the Matakana valley and sawn on the property. Libby and her late husband, Charlie, restored this two-storey villa with care and attention to detail to provide three ensuite guestrooms, each opening to a balcony. Set in a landscaped garden on six hectares of grazing land, Rosemount provides extensive rural views of rolling hillsides from its elevated site. Just one hour north of Auckland, in the heart of the Matakana wine region, Rosemount is close to vineyards and Warkworth restaurants. A full breakfast is served in the dining room or alfresco by the swimming pool. Toto, the miniature schnauzer, is a friendly family member.

Facilities
- 2 queen ensuite bedrooms
- 1 twin ensuite bedroom
- cotton bed linen, writing desk, TV & tea/coffee in bedrooms
- heated towel rails & hair dryers in all 3 ensuites
- balcony opening from each bedroom with rural views
- fresh flowers
- unsuitable for children
- full country cooked breakfast
- email, fax & phone available
- lounge with open fire, Sky TV, CD-player & writing desk
- full wedding & honeymoon facilities available
- swimming pool & spa pool
- courtesy passenger transfer by arrangement
- on-site parking

Activities available
- Matakana wine trail
- vineyards
- Ascension Vineyard music events & shows, 1km away
- many craft shops
- local produce stalls in surrounding area
- Sheep World
- Leigh fishing village
- Warkworth, 4km away
- several restaurants nearby, closest 5-min walk away
- Morris & James pottery
- Goat Island marine reserve with glass bottom boat trips
- walks & beaches on Tawharanui Peninsula
- Warkworth Golf Club & course, 3-min drive away
- Warkworth historical museum; kauri forest

© Friars' Guide to New Zealand Accommodation for the Discerning Traveller

WARKWORTH
STARGATE LODGE

Hosts Tracie Lee and Kevin Martin

139 Clayden Road, Warkworth   *Postal* P O Box 275, Warkworth
Phone 0-9-425 9995   *Mobile* 021 665 401   *Fax* 0-9-425 0102
Email info@stargate-lodge.co.nz   *Website* www.stargate-lodge.co.nz

| 3 bdrm | 2 enst | 1 prbth | 1 pdrm |

Room rate $260–$285

Includes breakfast
Lunch & dinner extra

DIRECTIONS: From Auckland, take SH 1 north to Warkworth. Turn right at 2nd traffic lights & take left fork into Matakana Rd. Travel about 1km & turn left into Clayden Rd. Travel 1.4km, veering left to Stargate Lodge.

Featuring 360-degree rural vistas, Stargate Lodge is surrounded by a hectare of pastureland and three hectares of native bush, with walks throughout. Purpose-built in 2002 to provide contemporary accommodation, Stargate offers guests a choice of a king-size suite or two spacious super-king-size ensuite bedrooms, each opening to a private balcony. There is a spa bath in one of the bathrooms. Kevin, the in-house award-winning pastry chef, prepares gourmet food to suit guests' requirements.

A breakfast menu is chosen the evening before and served in the formal dining room, the breakfast nook, or in the guestrooms. Lunch and three-course dinner are also available at Stargate Lodge, and there is a bar beside the open fire in the guest lounge.

Facilities
- 1 king suite & bathroom, with queen sofa-bed in private lounge
- 2 super-king ensuite bedrooms
- hair dryers, toiletries & heated towel rails in all bathrooms; spa bath in 1 ensuite
- TV, tea/coffee, fridge & private balcony for each guestroom
- phone, fax & email available
- fresh flowers; laundry available
- cotton bed linen
- choice from full gourmet breakfast menu
- lunch by arrangement
- 3-course à la carte dinner, $50–$75 pp; wine extra
- guest lounge with open fire, bar, Sky TV, video, DVD & CD-player
- 2 cats, 4 guinea pigs & 9 sheep on site
- on-site parking

Activities available
- walks in 4-ha of native bush & pasture on site
- BBQ area on site; star gazing
- wineries; golf courses
- swimming beaches
- snorkelling at Goat Island, a national maritime reserve
- boating, fishing & diving
- gardens open to visit
- Tawharanui Regional Park
- restaurants, cafés & shopping at Warkworth, 10-min drive
- art galleries & antique shops
- Morris & James pottery
- museum at Warkworth
- Sheep World
- Honey Centre
- Ascension music events
- Waiwera hot pools, 25 mins
- Auckland, 1 hour south

SANDSPIT, WARKWORTH
The Saltings

Hosts Maureen and Terry Baines

1210 Sandspit Road, Sandspit   *Phone* 0-9-425 9670
Postal 1210 Sandspit Road, R D 2, Warkworth   *Mobile* 021 625 948
Fax 0-9-425 9674   *Email* relax@saltings.co.nz   *Website* www.saltings.co.nz

3 bdrm   3 enst   Room rate $165–$225   *Includes breakfast*

DIRECTIONS: From Auckland, take SH 1 north to Warkworth. At 2nd lights turn right towards Sandspit/Snells Beach. Travel 5 mins then turn left into Sandspit Rd. Continue 2km to The Saltings driveway on right.

Located at Sandspit, overlooking the estuary, The Saltings was built in 1970 and converted to accommodation in 1996. The Mediterranean atmosphere is enhanced by the small vineyard, olive grove and lavender paths, complemented by the rustic interiors featuring oiled timber and plaster walls. French doors open from each of the three guestrooms to private patios, and the ensuites include tiled mosaics. Downstairs are the Tuscany Suite with its own lounge, the Palm Room, Lavender Room, and the guest coffee lounge. A full gourmet breakfast is served upstairs with sea views. Set in three hectares of landscaped gardens, The Saltings also offers self-contained accommodation at the Vintner's Haven (*see page 77 opposite*).

Facilities

- Tuscany Suite: 1 super-king ensuite bedroom with lounge, French doors to patio, writing desk, phone jack & tea/coffee
- Palm Room: 1 super-king ensuite bedroom opens to patio
- Lavender Room: 1 king ensuite bedroom opens to patio
- cotton bed linen; fresh flowers
- hair dryer, toiletries, bathrobes & heated towel rails
- full breakfast served upstairs in dining room with sea views
- private guest coffee lounge downstairs with TV
- email, fax & phone available
- German spoken
- golden retriever, Samantha
- private guest entrance
- on-site parking
- closed 24 Dec. – 2 January

Activities available

- pétanque/boules on site
- 3ha (8 acres) landscaped grounds
- Matakana wine trail
- safe swimming at local beaches
- snorkelling at Goat Island Marine Reserve
- sea kayaking
- hiking in regional parks
- pottery & cafés
- mailboat cruise
- restaurants & cafés, 5 mins
- local artists
- antique shops
- Warkworth township, 10 mins
- 3 golf courses
- Kawau Island & historic Mansion House, by ferry
- gardens open to visit
- Waiwera hot pools, 25 mins
- Auckland, 1 hour south

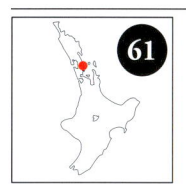

Sandspit, Warkworth
The Vintner's Haven

Hosts Maureen and Terry Baines

1210 Sandspit Road, Sandspit, R D 2, Warkworth
Phone 0-9-425 9670   *Mobile* 021 625 948   *Fax* 0-9-425 9674
Email relax@saltings.co.nz   *Website* www.saltings.co.nz

3 bdrm   3 enst

Room/suite rate $150–$215   *Self-catering*   *Breakfast basket, extra*
House rate $490–$545

DIRECTIONS: From Auckland, take SH 1 north to Warkworth. At 2nd lights turn right towards Sandspit/Snells Beach. Travel 5 mins then turn left into Sandspit Rd. Continue 2km to The Saltings driveway on right.

The Vintner's Haven is a three-bedroom home built in 1980 and converted in 2003 to provide self-catering accommodation. Secluded and overlooking the small vineyard and estuary, this self-contained house extends the accommodation available next-door at The Saltings (*see opposite page 76*). The Bordeaux Suite includes a full kitchen, large decks for alfresco dining in summer, a log fire in the lounge for winter evenings, and a claw-foot bath. The Merlot Suite downstairs has a kitchenette, lounge and deck, and the Olive Room upstairs has a fridge and dining area. All three ensuites feature timber ceilings and local Morris and James tiles. Located in the heart of Matakana wine country The Vintner's Haven is close to restaurants and beaches.

Facilities
- Bordeaux Suite: 1 super-king bedroom upstairs, with claw-foot bath in ensuite, spacious kitchen, lounge, log fire, phone & balcony
- Merlot Suite: 1 queen bedroom downstairs, with ensuite, lounge, kitchenette & deck
- Olive Room: 1 super-king ensuite bedroom upstairs with fridge, tea/coffee, dining area & balcony
- hair dryers, heated towel rails & toiletries
- breakfast basket by prior arrangement, $15 pp
- self-catering in both suites
- fresh flowers, bathrobes, cotton bed linen & phone jacks in all guestrooms
- TV, CD-player & books in both lounges
- self-service laundry
- on-site parking

Activities available
- golden retriever, Samantha, on site
- 3ha (8 acres) of vines, olives & landscaped gardens
- Matakana wine trail
- safe swimming at local beaches
- snorkelling at Goat Island Marine Reserve; sea kayaking
- hiking in regional parks
- local pottery
- restaurants & cafés, 5 mins
- mailboat cruise
- local artists; antique shops
- Warkworth township, 10 mins
- 3 golf courses
- Kawau Island & historic Mansion House, by ferry
- gardens open to visit
- Waiwera hot pools, 25 mins
- Auckland, 1 hour south

© Friars' Guide to New Zealand Accommodation for the Discerning Traveller

Sandspit, Warkworth
Sandspit Retreat

Hosts Sue and Dennis Anderson

18 Beach Street, R D 2, Sandspit, Warkworth
Phone 0-9-425 7128   *Mobile* 021 782 979   *Fax* 0-9-425 7128
Email sandspitretreat@value.net.nz   *Website* www.sandspitretreat.co.nz

Apartment rate $300 for 2 persons
Extra persons $50 each

Self-catering
Includes breakfast provisions for 1st morning

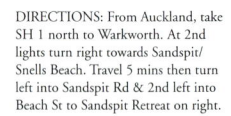

DIRECTIONS: From Auckland, take SH 1 north to Warkworth. At 2nd lights turn right towards Sandspit/Snells Beach. Travel 5 mins then turn left into Sandspit Rd & 2nd left into Beach St to Sandspit Retreat on right.

Set in a large subtropical garden, on the water's edge, Sandspit Retreat is a contemporary self-contained guesthouse. Designed with good utilisation of space, the retreat comprises a super-king/twin-size bedroom, private bathroom with garden view and open-plan lounge, dining and kitchen area. The bedroom opens onto a balcony where there is a spa pool with sea vistas. The spacious lounge is heated with a solid-fuel wood burner in winter, and the doors open to the decking with sea views for dining alfresco in the summer. Guests can self-cater and the gardens provide privacy from the hosts' residence. Guests have access to a gamesroom and indoor rock-climbing wall, and by arrangement the gymnasium and home theatre in the main house.

Facilities
- 1 private guesthouse with single-party bookings only
- 1 super-king/twin bedroom with Sky digital TV, phone & bathroom
- cotton bed linen; fresh flowers
- hair dryer, heated towel rails & toiletries in bathroom with 1-way glass garden view
- double sofa-bed in lounge
- home theatre by arrangement
- breakfast provisions
- full self-catering kitchen
- wood burner in lounge
- phone & email available
- self-serve laundry
- children by arrangement
- spacious deck from lounge/bedroom to spa pool
- passenger transfer
- on-site parking

Activities available
- gamesroom with table tennis & pool table; indoor rock climbing wall; gym by request
- archery, sailing & kayaking from site
- beaches, fishing & wharf, within 2-min drive
- customised tours by hosts
- 3 golf courses; fishing trips
- Waiwera thermal pools, 15 mins
- Matakana wine trail
- restaurants, galleries, shops in Warkworth, 5-min drive
- Kauri Park; Sheep World
- horse riding; bush & beach walks; heritage trails
- Goat Island Marine Reserve snorkelling & boat trips
- white sand dune beaches
- cruises to Kawau Island
- Auckland, 45 mins south

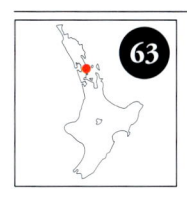

Cowan Bay, Warkworth
The Shanty

Hosts Megan Brice and Peter Sullivan

592 Cowan Bay Road, Pohuehue, Warkworth   *Postal* P O Box 387, Warkworth
Phone 0-9-425 0133   *Mobile* 021 806 060   *Fax* 0-9-425 0134
Email info.shanty@xtra.co.nz   *Website* www.cowanbayfarm.com

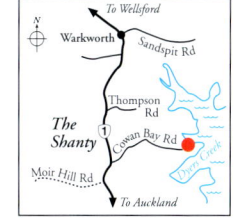

3 bdrm | 1 prbth

Cottage rate $295 for 2 persons
2-night minimum stay on weekends

Extra persons $50 each
Self-catering

DIRECTIONS: From Orewa take SH 1 north for 10 mins & turn right into Cowan Bay Rd. Travel 6km unsealed to Cowan Bay Farm at end. Veer left down to The Shanty. From Warkworth take SH 1 south for 5 mins & turn left.

The Shanty, as the hosts affectionately call their restored beachfront cottage, is set in a secluded private bay on Mahurangi Harbour. High tide comes up to the sundeck, from where guests can watch fish jumping by day and the moonlight shining a path on the water at night. The sandy tidal beach is private for guest use only, offering safe swimming, fishing, kayaking and boating, with all equipment provided. The Shanty is suitable for families, where parents can relax on the deck and watch their children playing safely on the beach. Birdlife can be seen in the native bush on the 160-hectare farm, with bush walks in the adjacent reserve. The cottage is fully self-catering, with Warkworth township just 15 minutes' drive away.

Facilities
- 1 self-contained cottage
- single-party bookings only
- 1 king & 2 queen bedrooms
- 1 spacious bathroom with separate toilet
- hair dryer, toiletries & heated towel rails
- writing desk in 1 queen bedroom
- all bedrooms open to sundecks
- private beachfront location
- children welcome
- children's toys supplied
- full kitchen for self-catering
- basic supplies in pantry
- lounge with video, CDs, board games & books
- large sundeck opens from lounge & dining area
- pets welcome
- on-site parking

Activities available
- 2 kayaks & 2 boogie-boards available for guest use
- aluminium dinghy with motor, oars & life-jackets for guest use
- swimming & fishing from sandy beach on site; fishing net
- 160ha (400-acre) farm with rare cattle, sheep, 2 horses & 3 dogs
- bush walks & bird-watching, adjacent 160ha reserve
- gardens open to visit
- restaurants, cafés & shops in Warkworth, 15 mins north, or Orewa, 20-min drive south
- Matakana wine trail & Horse Museum
- Waiwera hot pools, cheese factory, Honey Centre, & Sheepworld
- Morris & James Pottery
- snorkelling at Goat Island
- Auckland City, 50 mins south

© Friars' Guide to New Zealand Accommodation for the Discerning Traveller

MAHURANGI WEST
UHURU

Hosts Sue and Bob Stevenson

390 Pukapuka Road, R D 3, Warkworth
Phone 0-9-422 0585   *Mobile* 021 739 294   *Fax* 0-9-422 0545
Email suestevenson@xtra.co.nz   *Website* friars.co.nz/hosts/uhuru.html

| 3 bdrm | 1 enst | 1 prbth | Apartment rates $225–$425 $50 surcharge for 1-night stay | Includes breakfast provisions Long-stay rates available | Self-catering Dinner extra |

DIRECTIONS: From Auckland, travel north to Orewa. Continue 14.4km to Mahurangi Regional Park sign. Turn right & travel 0.8km. Turn left into Pukapuka Rd & travel 3.9km, taking left fork, then right to Uhuru at end.

Uhuru, meaning "Freedom" in Swahili, was purpose-built in March 2000, on a private peninsula, just 40 minutes north of the Auckland Harbour Bridge. Designed by architect Greg Turner, this contemporary home was built partly from schist with two separate self-contained apartments adjoining the main house. The library and games room opens to the heated swimming pool and spa pool with a ha-ha view overlooking the native bush and private bays of Mahurangi Harbour below. Uhuru is set on 160 hectares (400 acres) of farmland, including 40 hectares (100 acres) of mature native kauri trees and over eight kilometres of varied coastline. Guest privacy is ensured, with a popular activity being the many walks on the farm, all with ocean views.

Facilities

- private-party bookings per apartment
- upstairs apartment with 1 king bedroom & ensuite bathroom
- downstairs apartment with 1 king & 1 queen/twin bedroom, & private bathroom with bath
- heated towel rails, heated floors & wheelchair access
- laundry available
- email, fax & phone available
- kitchenette in each apartment for self-catering; BBQ on deck
- breakfast supplies included for 1st 2 mornings only
- casual dinner with hosts by request, $40 pp with wine
- both apartments include TV, with Sky & videos available
- games room/library
- on-site parking; helipad

Activities available

On site complimentary:

- heated swimming pool & spa
- floodlit astroturf tennis court
- sea swimming in private bay
- 160ha (400 acres) farm with native bush & coastline walks
- farm tours; birdwatching
- canoes & dinghy available
- shooting; fishing
- horses for experienced riders

Off site:

- restaurants & cafés, 20-min drive
- wine trails
- sculpture park & local artists
- Puhoi pub, honey centre & cheese factory, 15-min drive
- Waiwera hot pools, 15 mins
- Regional Parks
- river & harbour boating trips

© Friars' Guide to New Zealand Accommodation for the Discerning Traveller

Puhoi
The Ridge Contemporary Country Lodge

Hosts Maralyn and Ian Bateman

147 Greenhollows Road, Puhoi *Postal* P O Box 182, Puhoi, North Auckland
Freephone 0508 THE RIDGE *Phone* 0-9-426 3699 *Fax* 0-9-426 3695
Email relax@theridge.co.nz *Website* www.theridge.co.nz

3 bdrm | 3 enst | 1 pdrm
Double $250
Single $175

Includes breakfast
Lunch & dinner extra

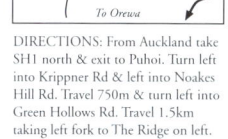

DIRECTIONS: From Auckland take SH1 north & exit to Puhoi. Turn left into Krippner Rd & left into Noakes Hill Rd. Travel 750m & turn left into Green Hollows Rd. Travel 1.5km taking left fork to The Ridge on left.

Located in the hills in a peaceful native bush setting, about 45 minutes north of Auckland, The Ridge Contemporary Country Lodge was purpose built in 2001 to offer accommodation for six guests in three spacious ensuite guestrooms. Designed in contemporary style, fitting into the environment, the Lodge is north-facing, capturing all-day sun, with extensive decking from all rooms providing 180-degree views over the landscaped native garden, pastureland and bush to the sea beyond. A special cooked breakfast is served in the guest dining room or alfresco on the deck, and dinner with wine is available by arrangement. Guests enjoy visiting the historic village of Puhoi, only four kilometres away, and there are three regional parks nearby.

Facilities
- 3 super-king/twin ensuite bedrooms open to balcony
- hair dryer, toiletries & heated towel rails in all 3 ensuites
- bathrobes; cotton bed linen
- wheelchair access
- open fire, tea/coffee, nibbles, books, Sky TV, video, DVD & CD-player in lounge, opening to deck
- 1 powder room
- special cooked breakfast served in guest dining room
- lunch available, extra
- 3-course dinner with wine served in dining room, $60 pp
- fresh flowers
- email & fax available
- private guest entrance
- pets on site
- on-site parking

Activities available
- pétanque/boules on site
- on-site walks in native bush & landscaped native garden
- historic village of Puhoi:
  – Bohemian Museum
  – Puhoi Pub
  – cheese factory
  – Art of Cheese Café
  – Puhoi Cottage Tea Rooms
- kayak & canoe hire
- horse riding
- restaurants, 20-min drive
- Matakana vineyards
- native bird sanctuary at Tiritiri Matangi Island
- 3 regional parks, all with beach & bush walks
- surfing at Orewa/Tawharanui
- Waiwera hot pools
- gardens open to visit
- Auckland City, 45 mins south

Waiwera
Island View Lodge

Hosts Melanie and John Schischka

122 State Highway One, Waiwera *Postal* P O Box 113, Waiwera, Auckland
Phone 0-9-426 7839 *Mobile* 021 268 8272 *Fax* 0-9-426 7839
Email guest@islandviewlodge.co.nz *Website* www.islandviewlodge.co.nz

| 2 bdrm | 1 enst | 1 prbth | Double $145–$195 Single $110–$170 Winter rates available | *Includes breakfast* *Lunch & dinner extra* |

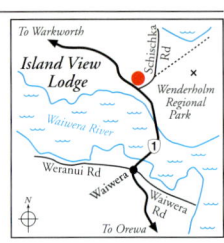

DIRECTIONS: From Auckland, take SH 1 north to Orewa. Continue approx. 8 mins to Waiwera, then travel 1.5km over bridge & uphill past Wenderholm Regional Park on right, to Island View Lodge on right.

Located adjacent to Wenderholm Regional Park, Island View Lodge overlooks Puhoi River to Motuora Island and the Hauraki Gulf beyond. Set on six and a half hectares (17 acres), the Lodge offers rural tranquillity, yet proximity to beaches and Auckland City. Guests enjoy the native pigeons, tui and other birdlife abounding in the bush on site. Converted to accommodation in 2002, Island View Lodge provides two guestrooms with bathrooms, opening to a large deck, and a private lounge with wood burner and a picture window. A full breakfast is served on the dining table or alfresco on the deck, and room service is available. Dinner is also offered according to guests' tastes, and restaurants are a short drive south in Orewa.

Facilities
- 1 king bedroom, dressing room & ensuite including bath
- 1 queen bedroom with bathroom
- hair dryers, toiletries, heated towel rails, heated floors & bathrobes
- cotton bed linen, phone jack, TV, fridge, tea/coffee, fruit, home-made biscuits & table in both bedrooms opening to deck
- guest lounge with wood burner, CD-player & telescope
- breakfast served in dining room, alfresco, or room service
- lunch by arrangement
- 2–3-course dinner, $35–$45 pp, wine extra
- email, phone & fax in office
- self-serve laundry; fresh flowers
- children over 13 yrs welcome
- friendly German shepherd, Kiri
- sea views; on-site parking

Activities available
- BBQ, pétanque, spa pool on site
- 2 double kayaks for guest use
- bird-watching & bush walking on site & park; tours arranged
- Wenderholm Park adjacent
- Waiwera thermal pools, 2 mins
- safe swimming beaches
- artists, pottery & wineries
- 2 golf courses, 15 mins
- Kawau Island trips
- restaurants in Orewa, 7 mins
- marina, 30-min drive
- historic Puhoi & cheese factory
- Kauri Park & Museum in Warkworth
- Goat Island marine reserve & glass-bottom boat, 30 mins
- Tiritiri bird sanctuary on island
- Auckland City, 35 mins
- airport, 1-hour drive

© Friars' Guide to New Zealand Accommodation for the Discerning Traveller

WAIWERA
GREENHILLS VILLA

Host Lisa Shrimpton   *Mobile* 021 623 083

982 Hibiscus Coast Highway, Waiwera   *Phone* 0-9-426 5737
Postal P O Box 6661, Wellesley Street, Auckland   *Email* greenhills@xtra.co.nz
Website www.warkworth-information.co.nz/greenhills   *Fax* 0-9-426 5737

DIRECTIONS: From Auckland, take SH 1 north for 30 mins to Orewa. Pass lights at West Hoe Rd & continue 4.2km to Greenhills on right. Turn right into private road & travel to Villa, 1st house on right.

2 bdrm   2 enst

Villa rate $335   Includes breakfast provisions   *Self-catering*

Greenhills Villa is completely private accommodation on over seven hectares (18 acres) overlooking the secluded beach, with panoramic northern views of the Hauraki Gulf. Purpose-built in 1999, Greenhills is a fully self-contained villa for single-party bookings, comprising two ensuite bedrooms, lounge, laundry and fully equipped kitchen for self-catering. Breakfast provisions are supplied. Both bedrooms and the guest lounge feature French doors opening to private sunny decks. Guests enjoy swimming at the private beach, in the swimming pool adjacent to the main house, or in the Waiwera thermal pools just five minutes' drive away. Although Greenhills offers total seclusion, it is only half an hour's drive north of Auckland City.

Facilities

- private-party bookings only
- self-contained villa
- 1 super-king/twin & 1 king bedroom, both with ensuites
- claw-foot bath, hair dryer, toiletries, heated towel rails & bathrobes in both ensuites
- percale cotton bed linen, TV, & lounge area in both bedrooms
- both bedrooms open to decking
- breakfast provisions
- fully equipped kitchen for self-catering
- guest lounge with log burner, phone, Sky TV & books, opens to verandah
- children over 3 yrs welcome
- self-serve guest laundry
- outdoor spa pool
- on-site parking

Activities available

- activities on 60ha (150-acre) working farm on site
- swimming pool on site
- tennis court on site
- private beach via golf cart
- native bush walks on farm
- Waiwera thermal pools nearby
- Wenderholm Regional Park
- 2 golf courses
- public beaches
- restaurants in Orewa, Gulf Harbour & Whangaparaoa
- Puhoi historic village
- gardens open to visit
- horse trekking
- walking tracks
- Gulf Harbour Village & marina
- ferry to bird sanctuary on Tiritiri Matangi Island
- Auckland, 30-min drive south

HATFIELDS BEACH, OREWA
MOONTIDE LODGE

Hosts Ronnie and Andy Lee

19 Ocean View Road, Hatfields Beach, Orewa
Phone 0-9-426 2374   *Mobile* 025 263 0102   *Fax* 0-9-426 2398
Email moontde@nznet.gen.nz   *Website* friars.co.nz/hosts/moontide.html

| 4 bdrm | 3 enst | 1 prbth | 1 pdrm |

Room rate $150–$200   Includes breakfast   Lunch extra

DIRECTIONS: From Auckland, take SH 1 north to Orewa. Continue north towards Hatfields Beach for 3km. Turn right into Ocean View Rd. Moontide Lodge on left, at end of driveway.

Moontide Lodge is perched on a clifftop overlooking Hatfields Beach and the ocean beyond. Only five minutes north of Orewa and south of the popular Waiwera hot pools, Moontide enjoys private access to the beach below. Renovated in 1998 to maximise the view, Moontide offers four guestrooms, each individually styled with ensuite or private bathroom. The Whangaparaoa Suite includes a private conservatory and deck, Hatfields Beach Room overlooks the beach below, Coromandel Room provides an ocean vista towards Coromandel, and Kauri View Room looks out on native bush and the beach. A full breakfast is served in the dining room or alfresco, lunch is also available, and there are small conference facilities at Moontide.

Facilities
- 4 queen bedrooms, 2 balconies
- 3 spacious ensuites & 1 private bathroom with robes & slippers
- phone, TV, desk, hair dryer & tea/coffee in each bedroom
- video & fax available
- guest lounge
- beach & ocean views
- children over 12 yrs welcome
- guest laundry, $10 per load
- continental or cooked breakfast served in dining room, or alfresco on deck
- lunch by arrangement, in garden, on decking, or picnic, extra
- complimentary drinks
- small conferences catered
- on-site parking
- passenger transfer arranged

Activities available
- private access to beach
- boat ramp
- safe swimming from site, at Hatfields Beach
- horse trekking
- Waiwera hot pools, 5-min drive north
- Wenderholm Regional Park
- Puhoi historic village
- gardens open to visit
- choice of recommended restaurants nearby
- Orewa shops, 5 mins
- tennis
- golf courses & golf equipment available
- kayak tours
- Auckland City, 30 mins
- Auckland airport, 45-min drive south

© Friars' Guide to New Zealand Accommodation for the Discerning Traveller

MILFORD, AUCKLAND
THE MILFORD LODGE

Hosts Viv and Brian Gilfoyle

104 Kitchener Road, Milford, North Shore, Auckland
Phone 0-9-486 3838 *Email* viv.brian@xtra.co.nz
Fax 0-9-486 4636 *Website* www.themilfordlodge.co.nz

4 bdrm	4 enst	Room rate $230–$240	*Includes breakfast or provisions*	*Self-catering in apartment*
		Apartment rate $270	Multiple-night & low-season rates available	

DIRECTIONS: From Auckland City, take SH 1 north over Harbour Bridge. Take Barry's Pt exit & turn right into Anzac St. Turn left into Hurstmere Rd, then veer left into Kitchener Rd. The Milford Lodge on left.

Purpose-built in 2003, in the heart of Milford, with views of the Hauraki Gulf, The Milford Lodge provides quality accommodation. There is a spacious king-size ensuite bedroom at the front of the house, and two queen-size ensuite bedrooms opening to a private back courtyard. Between the guestrooms is a private lounge with guest facilities. Viv serves a full English breakfast upstairs in the breakfast room, or alfresco on the covered balcony with sea views. Alternatively guests are welcome to breakfast in the formal dining room, where wine is also available. There is a separate entrance to a self-contained one-bedroom apartment upstairs which has a full kitchen for self-catering. Children are accepted by arrangement only.

Facilities

- 1 king bedroom; 2 queen bedrooms open to courtyard
- self-contained apartment, with 1 double bedroom & laundry
- hair dryers, toiletries & heated towel rails in all ensuites; heated floor in king ensuite
- cotton bed linen
- dressing rooms
- guest lounge with TV, phone, fridge, tea/coffee, home baking
- family lounge upstairs with TV & open fire
- porta-cot & highchair
- full English breakfast; provisions for apartment
- morning newspaper
- wine available
- laundry facilities
- internet facilities
- secure off-street parking

Activities available

- Milford Beach, 3-min walk
- public transport from site
- coastal & bush walks
- tennis; cycling
- horse trekking
- sea kayaking; canoeing
- jet-skiing; surfing
- fishing; parapenting
- harbour cruises & boat trips to Rangitoto Island
- over 20 restaurants within walking distance
- Pupuke & Takapuna golf clubs nearby
- art & craft galleries
- gardens open to visit
- Milford shopping mall, 3-min walk
- downtown Auckland, 10-min drive, or 15 mins by ferry

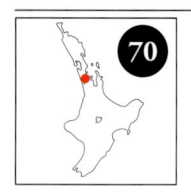

Takapuna, Auckland
Emerald Cottage

Manager Janice Heffernan

5 Alison Avenue, Takapuna   Phone 0-9-488 3500
Postal P O Box 33 303, Takapuna, Auckland   Fax 0-9-488 3555
Email info@emerald-inn.co.nz   Website www.emeraldcottage.co.nz

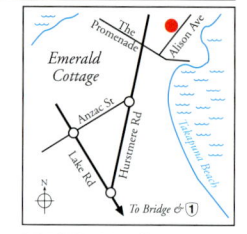

| 3 bdrm | 1 enst | 1 prbth |

House rate $675
Extra persons $50 each

Self-catering
Long-term rates available

Breakfast extra

DIRECTIONS: Travelling north, cross Harbour Bridge. Take Takapuna exit. At 3rd set lights, turn left into Lake Rd. Next lights veer right into Hurstmere Rd. Turn right into The Promenade, then left into Alison Ave. Cottage on left.

The exclusive use of Emerald Cottage provides guests with privacy and seclusion overlooking Takapuna Beach with views to Rangitoto Island. This Cape Cod style house was totally renovated in 1998, retaining the seaside cottage ambience, but incorporating high quality fittings, furnishings and New Zealand artwork to provide a luxurious yet casual feel. Emerald Cottage is fully self-contained for self-catering or a chef can be arranged. Breakfast is available at Emerald Inn adjacent. Next door, Emerald Villas are also available for accommodation (*see page 87 opposite*). An indoor spa pool is set in the conservatory looking out to the private landscaped garden. The downstairs lounge and upstairs honeymoon suite overlook the bay.

Facilities

- 1 king & 1 twin bedroom downstairs with bathroom including bath
- 1 super-king bedroom with double bath & double basin in ensuite, dressing room, fridge, tea/coffee, lounge & balcony
- heated towel rails, hair dryers & toiletries in all bathrooms
- TV & video in all bedrooms
- fresh flowers & original NZ art
- full kitchen for self-catering or chef by arrangement
- breakfast at Inn, $10–$15
- complimentary teas, coffee, fruit juice & cookies
- guest phone & fax
- individual climate control
- guest laundry
- off-street parking
- passenger transfer arranged

Activities available

- beach across road
- indoor spa pool
- 19.4m (65 ft) yacht extra, skipper available
- swimming pool adjacent
- 32 restaurants in walking distance
- downtown Auckland, 10-min drive, or 15 mins by ferry
- 6 golf courses; tennis; surfing
- cycling; horse trekking; canoeing
- Lake Pupuke nearby
- harbour cruises & boat trips to Rangitoto Island
- sea kayaking; jet-skiing
- fishing; parapenting
- 2 boating marinas
- coastal & bush walks
- gardens to visit
- art & craft galleries
- boutique shopping

© Friars' Guide to New Zealand Accommodation for the Discerning Traveller

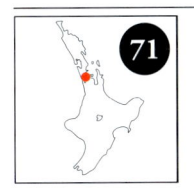

TAKAPUNA, AUCKLAND
EMERALD VILLAS

Manager Janice Heffernan

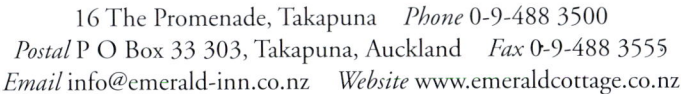

16 The Promenade, Takapuna   *Phone* 0-9-488 3500
Postal P O Box 33 303, Takapuna, Auckland   *Fax* 0-9-488 3555
Email info@emerald-inn.co.nz   *Website* www.emeraldcottage.co.nz

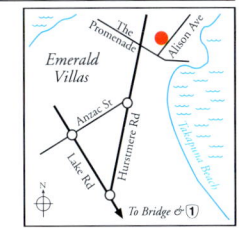

4 bdrm   2 prbth   Villa rate $450
Long-term rates available   *Self-catering*   *Breakfast extra*

DIRECTIONS: Travelling north, cross Harbour Bridge. Take Takapuna exit. At 3rd set lights, turn left into Lake Rd. Next lights veer right into Hurstmere Rd. Turn right into The Promenade, then left into Alison Ave. Cottage on left.

Next door to Emerald Cottage (*see page 86 opposite*) are the Emerald Villas. These two villas offer spacious, fully self-contained accommodation, especially designed for families on transfer or holiday. Adjacent to Takapuna Beach, each holiday home is able to accommodate four people. Both family villas have a lounge, full kitchen for self-catering, bathroom including bath, guest laundry and two king-size bedrooms. Emerald Villas have private grounds with barbecue facilities, and are connected to the Emerald Inn complex for use of the heated swimming pool, spa pool and breakfast room. The Takapuna business area, shops, cafés and restaurants are within walking distance of Emerald Villas.

Facilities

- single-party bookings
- 2 self-contained villas
- 2 king bedrooms in each villa
- 1 bathroom, including bath, in each villa
- heated towel rails, hair dryers & toiletries in both bathrooms
- lounge with phone, Sky TV, video & CD-player in villas
- fresh flowers & original NZ art
- full kitchen for self-catering
- breakfast at Inn, $20 pp
- complimentary teas & coffee
- BBQ on site
- children welcome
- full laundry facilities
- off-street parking
- passenger transfer arranged

Activities available

- beach across road
- swimming pool adjacent
- 32 restaurants in walking distance
- downtown Auckland, 10-min drive, or 15 mins by ferry
- 6 golf courses
- cycling; horse trekking
- Lake Pupuke nearby
- sea kayaking; jet-skiing
- fishing
- 2 boating marinas
- harbour cruises & boat trips to Rangitoto Island
- coastal & bush walk
- tennis; surfing
- canoeing
- parapenting
- gardens to visit
- art & craft galleries
- boutique shopping

© Friars' Guide to New Zealand Accommodation for the Discerning Traveller

DEVONPORT, AUCKLAND
EARNSCLIFF

Hosts Jenny and Graeme Dickey

44 Williamson Avenue, Devonport, Auckland
Phone 0-9-445 7557   Mobile 021 444 392   Fax 0-9-445 7602
Email earnscliff@xtra.co.nz   Website www.earnscliff.co.nz

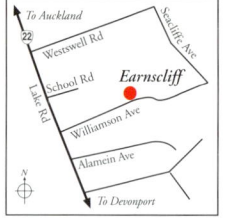

2 bdrm   2 prbth   Room rate $245–$285   *Includes breakfast*

DIRECTIONS: Travelling north, cross Auckland Harbour Bridge. Travel 1.5km & take Esmonde Road exit. Follow Lake Rd towards Devonport. At Belmont, turn left into Williamson Ave. Earnscliff on left at end of driveway.

This historic home, originally built for Englishman Charles Williamson in 1882, has been restored and refurbished to provide two ensuite guestrooms upstairs and the living rooms downstairs. The entrance portico, supported by Greek-style columns, leads into the English Gothic-style house, set in park-like grounds now featuring a disciplined blue, cream and lemon-toned garden. Breakfast is served in the country kitchen, dining room, conservatory looking into the garden, or alfresco in the summer house weather permitting, framed by the historic trees. Jenny's breakfast menu offers everything from Eggs Benedict to French toast, with seasonal fruits and home-made muesli. Transport is available to and from Devonport village and ferry.

Facilities
- 2 queen ensuite bedrooms
- hair dryer, demist mirror, toiletries & heated towel rails in each ensuite
- bath in Louisa Hampton Suite
- cotton bed linen
- TV & tea/coffee in bedrooms
- wheelchair access
- guest study with writing desk, phone, books & magazines
- full breakfast menu
- weddings & honeymoons catered for
- guest verandah, opening from guest study
- fresh flowers
- email & fax available
- pets on site
- transfer from ferry available
- off-street parking

Activities available
- park-like grounds on site, including woodland planting, summer house & pergola
- 2 bicycles on site for guest use
- sailing
- fishing
- beaches nearby
- swimming
- Devonport heritage walk; golf
- ferry, 5-min drive
- restaurants & cafés nearby
- old world shopping
- Devonport village, 1km
- art galleries; library
- day trips
- gardens open to visit
- Auckland airport, 40-min drive
- Auckland City, 15-min drive or 10 mins by ferry

© Friars' Guide to New Zealand Accommodation for the Discerning Traveller

Devonport, Auckland
Duder Homestead

Hosts Helen and Kerry McNae

11 Church Street, Devonport, Auckland   *Mobile* 021 125 5643
Phone 0-9-445 8310   *Email* enquiries@duder-homestead.co.nz
Fax 0-9-445 8311   *Website* www.duder-homestead.co.nz

| 2 bdrm | 1 prbth | 1 pdrm | Double $275–$375
Single $250–$375 | Extra persons $50 each
Minimum 2-night stay | *Self-catering*
Continental breakfast tray extra |

DIRECTIONS: Travel north across harbour bridge. Take Esmonde Rd exit. At "T" turn right into Lake Rd for 5km. At "T" turn left into Albert St & right into Vauxhall Rd. Continue into Church St to Duder Homestead on right.

Originally built in the 1860s and occupied for 90 years by the Duder family, this is one of Devonport's earliest homes, now with a category A listing. The hosts live in Duder Homestead, with the re-fitted self-contained apartment in a separate wing. Two bedrooms are available upstairs overlooking the garden, and the living areas downstairs include a guest office, opening from the spacious lounge and dining room. Guest can self-cater in the fully equipped kitchen with native rimu benchtop and quality contemporary fittings. An organic fruit bowl, chocolates, sherry and port are provided and, by arrangement, a continental breakfast tray with organic produce. There is a barbecue in the courtyard and many restaurants are within walking distance.

Facilities
- private-party bookings only
- 1 self-contained apartment
- 1 super-king/twin & 1 queen bedroom upstairs, with extra toilet adjacent
- 1 private bathroom downstairs, including double basin, double bath & double shower
- hair dryer, toiletries, bathrobes, demist mirrors, heated floor & heated towel rails
- breakfast tray by arrangement
- full kitchen for self-catering
- fruit bowl, chocolates, sherry
- cotton bed linen; fresh flowers
- lounge/dining area with open fire, Sky TV, DVD, CD-player, phone & artwork
- guest office with phone jack
- children over 12 welcome
- monitored security system

Activities available
- BBQ, patio & garden on site
- Duder Beach in walking distance
- fishing; boating; sea kayaking
- mountain bikes; yacht club
- 2 dormant volcanoes
- Mt Victoria & North Head lookouts nearby
- historic fort & walks
- Devonport & naval museums
- 2 wedding venues, 5-min walk
- 20+ restaurants & cafés, 10-min walk away
- historic Devonport village & shops, 3-min drive
- golf; squash; tennis
- art galleries
- gardens open to visit
- Auckland CBD, 12-min ferry or 15-min drive
- airport, 40-min drive

© Friars' Guide to New Zealand Accommodation for the Discerning Traveller

BIRKENHEAD POINT, AUCKLAND
LITTLE SHOAL BAY

Hosts Suzanne and William Hindmarsh

14 Peregrine Place, Birkenhead Point, Auckland
Phone 0-9-480 8500   *Mobile* 021 531 253   *Fax* 0-9-480 8501
Email littleshoalbay@xtra.co.nz   *Website* www.littleshoalbay.co.nz

2 bdrm   2 enst   Suite rate $450   *Includes breakfast*

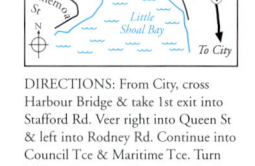

DIRECTIONS: From City, cross Harbour Bridge & take 1st exit into Stafford Rd. Veer right into Queen St & left into Rodney Rd. Continue into Council Tce & Maritime Tce. Turn left into Peregrine Pl to Little Shoal.

Little Shoal Bay provides accommodation just four kilometres from Auckland City Centre, yet in a quiet private location with panoramic bay views framed by dense native bush which attracts native birdlife. A guest suite occupies the ground floor of the four-storey architecturally designed house, 75 metres from the bay. One-party or family bookings ensure privacy, with the main bedroom large enough to be the sitting room as well, featuring Persian rugs and windows opening to the adjacent bush. Extensive decking wraps around the guestrooms and provides opportunities for bird-watching and private sunbathing. The hosts, Willy and Suzanne, who are fourth generation New Zealanders, serve breakfast and apéritifs on the floor above.

Facilities

- one-party bookings only
- 1 king bedroom with spa bath in ensuite, living area, gas fire, tea/coffee, Sky TV, video, CD-player, games, books, writing desk & baby grand piano upstairs
- 1 twin ensuite bedroom
- hair dryer, heated towel rails, toiletries & bathrobes
- guestrooms open to balcony
- complimentary wine & hors d'oeuvres before dinner
- full breakfast served with hosts in 2nd floor breakfast room; organic food where possible
- children welcome
- fresh flowers; central heating
- laundry available
- email, fax & phone available
- off-street parking

Activities available

- BBQ & spa pool on site
- native bird-watching
- black labrador, Bart, on site
- bush walks from site to bay & beach walks at low tide
- riparian rights & views to Little Shoal Bay; Little Shoal Bay reserve, 1km
- ferry from Birkenhead to Auckland, 1km away
- 5 restaurants, 2 bars & shopping centre within 2km
- Bridgeway Cinema art films, 2km
- Auckland CBD & arts centre, Takapuna or Ponsonby, all 10-min drive away
- gardens open to visit
- Viaduct Basin & Hauraki Gulf ferry terminal, 10-min drive or 15 mins by ferry
- Takapuna beach, 10 mins

© Friars' Guide to New Zealand Accommodation for the Discerning Traveller

BIRKENHEAD POINT, AUCKLAND
STAFFORD VILLA

Hosts Chris and Mark Windram

2 Awanui Street, Birkenhead Point, Auckland
Phone 0-9-418 3022   *Email* rest@staffordvilla.co.nz
Fax 0-9-419 8197   *Website* www.staffordvilla.co.nz

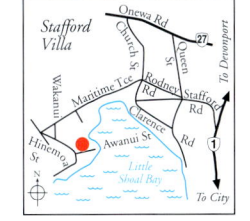

Room rate $300–$335   *Includes breakfast*
Multiple-night rates available

DIRECTIONS: From Harbour Bridge, take Stafford Rd exit & veer right into Queen St. Turn left into Rodney Rd & continue into Maritime Tce. At top, turn left into Hinemoa St. Take 2nd left into Awanui St. Villa on left.

Set in a quiet street near the Waitemata Harbour, Stafford Villa was built in 1903 in Victorian style. Thoughtfully restored and elegantly furnished, this two-storey twin-bay villa provides two spacious ensuite guestrooms overlooking the large established garden with bush views. The China Blue Room features an antique four-poster bed, dressing room and spa bath in the ensuite. The Tuscany Summer Room overlooks the original Victorian orchard. Both guestrooms are designed to provide privacy. Gourmet breakfast is served in the dining room downstairs, in the conservatory or alfresco in the garden where native birds abound. The ferry to the city is within walking distance and there are restaurants of many nationalities nearby.

Facilities
- China Blue Room: 4-poster king bed, ensuite, spa bath, dressing room & private balcony
- Tuscany Summer Room: king/twin bed, ensuite; orchard views
- heated towel rails, hair dryers & toiletries in both ensuites
- bathrobes in winter & silk kimonos in summer
- damask linen, feather pillows & quilts on all beds
- full breakfast menu
- antiques, TV, video & central heating in all rooms
- fruit, sherry, port, chocolates, tea/coffee, cookies, filtered water & fresh flowers
- library & business facilities
- laundry available
- off-street parking
- bridal package available

Activities available
- Central Auckland, 10 mins by ferry or car
- Viaduct Basin
- Maritime Museum
- historic maritime suburb
- park & harbour
- SH 1 motorway, 5 mins
- sailing
- antique & boutique shopping
- gardens open to visit
- wide range of restaurants
- 3 private beaches, nearby
- art gallery trail
- bush walks
- golf course nearby
- tennis courts
- public library, 5-min walk
- private gym, 5-min walk
- personalised tours
- cinemas

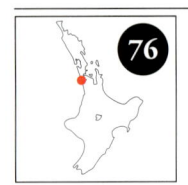

ORATIA, AUCKLAND
THE SHAW

Host Eva Knausenberger

72 Shaw Road, Oratia, Auckland
Phone 0-9-813 6662 or 0-9-813 6652 *Fax* 0-9-813 6664
Email eva2@ware.co.nz *Website* friars.co.nz/hosts/theshaw.html

1 bdrm 1 enst Suite rate $250 *Includes continental breakfast*

DIRECTIONS: From Auckland, take SH 16 to Great Nth Rd exit. At Kelston turn left into West Coast Rd & continue through Glen Eden. At roundabout turn left & travel 400m to Shaw Rd on left. The Shaw on left.

With panoramic views to the surrounding native bush, The Shaw is located adjacent to the Waitakere forest ranges on the outskirts of West Auckland. The guest suite includes a queen-size bedroom, spacious ensuite bathroom with spa bath, and dressing room. Privacy, peace and quiet are ensured, with the single-party guest suite opening to a private terrace overlooking the bush setting. The host, Eva, lives in the adjoining house, and speaks both German and French as well as English. She serves a continental breakfast in the guest suite and there is a barbecue available. Three restaurants are nearby. The Shaw was architecturally designed and built from stone circa 1995, including a pool house for the spa pool which guests enjoy.

Facilities

- single-party bookings only
- 1 queen/twin bedroom with dressing room & writing desk
- spa bath, double basin, hair dryer, toiletries, bidet & heated towel rails in ensuite
- bathrobes & cotton bed linen
- wheelchair access
- private guest entrance
- fresh flowers; central heating
- continental breakfast including nuts, home-made muesli & bread served in guestroom
- tea/coffee, nibbles, CD-player, music, games, artwork, books & writing desk in TV lounge
- children & pets welcome
- email & fax available
- French & German spoken
- 2 terraces; garaging

Activities available

On site:
- swimming pool & spa pool
- BBQ for guest use
- pétanque/boules
- extensive gardens with walks among flowers & fruit trees

Off-site:
- vineyards
- golf courses

- restaurants nearby
- bushwalks & hiking in Waitakere forest ranges
- Piha & Laingholm beaches
- sailing & harbour cruises
- arts & crafts
- Titirangi village
- gardens open to visit
- Sky Tower & casino
- Auckland City, 25 mins away

© Friars' Guide to New Zealand Accommodation for the Discerning Traveller

Above: The private guest suite at The Shaw opens to the guest terrace with views of the garden and native bush beyond.
Below: The tiled ensuite bathroom in the guest suite includes spa bath, bidet, double basin and shutters revealing garden views.
Opposite top: Set in gardens, surrounded by native bush, The Shaw was architecturally designed and built from stone circa 1995.
Opposite bottom left: The driveway to The Shaw sweeps through the extensive gardens with mature exotic and native trees.
Opposite bottom right: The guest suite includes a queen-size bed, desk, dressing room, ensuite, and tea/coffee facilities.

Taupaki, West Auckland
Ashbourne Lodge

Hosts David and Veronica York

214 Hunters Road, Taupaki, Auckland
Phone 0-9-810 9352   *Fax* 0-9-810 9852   *Email* yorkey@xtra.co.nz
Mobile 021 938 202   *Website* friars.co.nz/hosts/ashbourne.html

Double $245
Single $225

Includes breakfast
Lunch & dinner extra

DIRECTIONS: From Auckland, take Nth-Wst Motorway to end. Turn left & continue on SH 16. Turn left into Taupaki Rd. Travel 5km & turn left into Waitakere Rd. Travel 1.5km & turn right into Hunters Rd. Travel 2km to end.

Ashbourne Lodge was originally built in 1895 as a farmhouse for millers of kauri trees in the area. Set in the foothills of the Waitakere Ranges, Ashbourne Lodge offers the peace and quiet of the countryside yet Auckland City is only 30 minutes away. There have been many additions to the homestead over the years, the most recent being the adjacent separate purpose-built accommodation with a spacious suite above the guest lounge/gamesroom. A further guestroom is provided in the house. Guests have full use of the park-like setting and on-site activities. Continental or cooked breakfast is served either in the suite, in the dining room of the main house, or alfresco. Three-course dinner with local wine is also available in the house by arrangement.

Facilities
- 1 super-king/twin upstairs bedroom, with marble ensuite, in separate guesthouse adjacent
- 1 twin bedroom in house, with private bathroom
- cotton bed linen, phone, writing desk, TV & seating in bedroom
- separate guest lounge/gamesroom with tea/coffee, Sky TV, video, CD-player, piano & billiards table
- fresh flowers; laundry available
- full breakfast served
- lunch extra, by request
- 3-course dinner with complimentary local wine, in house, $65pp
- hair dryer, heated towel rails, toiletries & bathrobes in both bathrooms
- email & fax available
- on-site parking; helipad

Activities available
- guest gamesroom
- fitness equipment
- swimming pool
- tennis court
- pétanque on site
- equestrian facilities
- 0.8ha (2-acre) garden & 12ha (30-acre) farm with macadamia nut orchard
- vineyards
- restaurants nearby
- golf
- beaches
- arts & crafts
- trap shooting
- bush walks, hiking & tramping in Waitakere Ranges
- gardens open to visit
- Waitakere Ranges Visitor Centre
- Auckland City, 30km away

© Friars' Guide to New Zealand Accommodation for the Discerning Traveller

Matiatia Bay, Waiheke Island
The Moorings

Hosts Lyn and Warren Lincoln   *Phone* 0-9-372 8283

9 Ocean View Road, Matiatia Bay, Waiheke Island
Postal P O Box 377, Oneroa, Waiheke Island   *Fax* 0-9-372 8283
Email wlincoln@xtra.co.nz   *Website* www.themoorings.gen.nz

2 bdrm   2 prbth   Studio rate $215–$280   *Includes breakfast provisions*
Self-catering

DIRECTIONS: From Auckland City in Quay St, take ferry to Waiheke Island. Take taxi or rental car up Ocean View Rd. Turn left into 1st driveway. Continue 100m to The Moorings at top. Well sign-posted.

Overlooking Matiatia Bay's moorings and the ferry wharf is The Moorings, purpose-built, self-contained accommodation. With uninterrupted views out to Rangitoto Island and the Hauraki Gulf to Auckland City beyond, The Moorings is popular for rest and recreation with constant boat activity to watch. Honeymooners find it a romantic retreat, yet still close to the amenities at Oneroa. The Moorings comprises two semi-detatched studio apartments, each open-plan with one king bed and a kitchette for self-catering. Continental breakfast provisions are supplied and the hosts live in the adjacent house. The entrance is through a private courtyard featuring lavenders, lemons and olives, and the studios open to private decks above the bay.

Facilities
- 2 studio apartments; one-party booking per studio
- each studio with 1 king bed & 1 private bathroom
- hair dryers, heated towel rails & toiletries in bathrooms
- spacious & sunny deck opening from each studio with seating, BBQ & panoramic sea views
- fresh flowers & magazines
- fax & email available
- self-contained kitchenette in each studio for self-catering
- continental breakfast provisions
- lounge area in each studio with Sky TV, stereo, CD-player, phone jacks & books
- laundry facilities available
- on-site parking; courtesy passenger transfer
- studio serviced on request, extra fee

Activities available
- pétanque court on site
- bay access via private track
- honeymoons catered for
- guest barbecues on decks
- coastal walks; snorkelling
- rental cars, bikes & kayaks for hire at bottom of driveway
- fishing charters; fishing off rocks
- day trips around Waiheke
- gardens open to visit
- restaurant, 2-min walk away
- Oneroa beach, 10-min walk
- arts & crafts; olive groves
- wine tours & art tours
- restaurants, cafés, vineyards & shopping, 2-min drive
- Rangitoto Island, 20-min ferry
- Devonport, 30 mins by ferry
- Auckland City, 35 mins by ferry from Matiatia

© Friars' Guide to New Zealand Accommodation for the Discerning Traveller

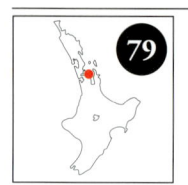

OWHANAKE BAY, WAIHEKE ISLAND
DELAMORE LODGE

Host Roselyn Barnett-Storey   *Mobile* 021 471 344

83 Delamore Drive, Owhanake Bay, Waiheke Island   *Phone* 0-9-372 7372
Postal P O Box 572, Oneroa, Waihkeke Island   *Fax* 0-9-372 7382
Email reservations@delamorelodge.com   *Website* www.delamorelodge.com

4 bdrm   4 enst   Suite rate $894   *Includes breakfast, hors d' oeuvres & apéritifs*
Dinner extra

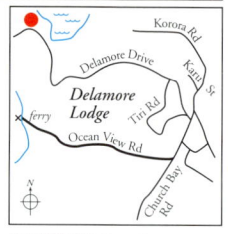

DIRECTIONS: From City, 35 mins by ferry to Waiheke Island. Take taxi or rental car along Ocean View Rd. Turn left into Korora Rd & left again into Delamore Dr. Delamore Lodge on right. 12 mins by helicopter.

Overlooking Owhanake Bay on Waiheke Island, Delamore Lodge was completed in 2003 without a straight wall in the entire complex. Built into the side of a rolling hill, leading directly to the beach, the curves and soft edges were designed to blend in with the sky, sea and earth. The interior walls and ceiling were all carefully hand-plastered and the result is an ambience that complements the sea vistas. Eight guests can be accommodated in the private suites, and special features include the starlit grotto, deep cave jacuzzi, sauna cove with all-over body shower, and the spa treaments available. Gourmet dining is enjoyed alfresco by the Mediterranean-style log fireplace, or indoors at individual dining tables or the shared table.

Facilities
- 4 super-king/twin suites with private courtyard gardens
- baths, double basins, heated towel rails, demist mirrors, hair dryers, toiletries, slippers & bathrobes
- phone, Sky TV, DVD, CDs, full mini-bar, teas/coffee, writing desk & artwork in suites
- wheelchair access; powder rooms
- open lounge with fire & sea vistas; Mediterranean outdoor log fire
- gourmet breakfast indoors, alfresco, or room service
- 4-course table d'hôte dinner with wine, extra
- fax & email available
- wedding ceremonies, honeymoons & functions catered
- 2 spa treatment rooms
- private guest entrances; on-site parking; helipad

Activities available
- alfresco dining beside outdoor log fire
- grotto, jacuzzi, sauna, beauty & spa treatments on site
- lithos massage on site
- library & board games
- golf; beaches
- arts & crafts
- vineyard tours
- gardens; walks
- olive-grove cafés
- restaurants, 2-min drive
- music festivals
- kayaking; sailing; fishing
- wine festivals
- scenic flights
- scuba diving; paragliding
- tramping; horse riding
- Auckland City, 35 mins by ferry
- air services from Auckland

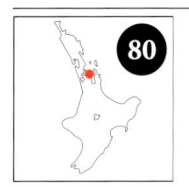

LITTLE ONEROA BAY, WAIHEKE ISLAND
THE BOATSHED

Host Jonathan Scott   *Phone* 0-9-372 3242

Corner of Tawa and Huia Streets, Waiheke Island   *Fax* 0-9-372 3262
Postal P O Box 91-742, Auckland Mail Centre   *Mobile* 021 512 127
Email enquiries@boatshed.co.nz   *Website* www.boatshed.co.nz

| 5 bdrm | 5 enst | 1 prbth | Room rate $600–$760 | *Includes breakfast* Lunch & dinner extra |

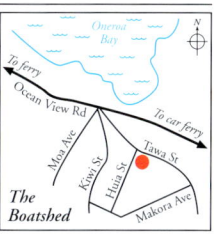

DIRECTIONS: From Auckland City, take ferry to Waiheke Island. Take taxi or rental car along Ocean View Rd through Oneroa to Little Oneroa. Turn right into Tawa St. The Boatshed on right, on corner of Huia St.

The Boatshed, boutique seaside accommodation, is located on Waiheke Island's northern sun-drenched shores, set above the clear waters and white sandy swimming beaches of Oneroa. The contemporary architecture is designed to capture the feeling of Waiheke's historical boatsheds of the early 1900s. The five Boatshed guestrooms offer panoramic sea views, each with private balcony, open fire and ensuite bathroom. Fine dining is available with traditional and Pacific Rim cuisine matched to an extensive New Zealand wine list. A short walk takes guests to Oneroa village, with access to extensive coastal walks. Exclusive use of the Boatshed is available for family gatherings, small weddings, and management retreats.

Facilities

- 4 super-king/twin bedrooms, each with ensuite bathroom
- 3-storey Lighthouse, queen bed, ensuite & separate lounge suite
- cotton bed linen, writing desk, TV, CD, DVD, mini bar, open fire, IDD phone & wireless Internet in all 5 guestrooms
- hair dryer, bathrobes, scuffs, heated floors, toiletries & beach bag of amenities
- full continental & cooked breakfast; lunch $25–$35 pp
- 4-course dinner, $85 pp
- guest lounge with open fire, tea/coffee, nibbles, bar, Sky TV, video & writing desk
- children by arrangement
- laundry available; wheelchair access
- courtesy passenger transfer on-site parking

Activities available

- pétanque/boules on site
- masseuse available on site by prior arrangement
- conferences, weddings, honeymoons catered for
- Little Oneroa Beach, 3-min walk; swimming
- coastal walks
- fishing & kayaking
- bicycle hire
- village, 8-min walk
- vineyard lunches & tours
- beaches & watersports
- art galleries & tours
- golf courses
- beauty therapy
- horse riding
- hiking
- passenger ferry wharf, 5-min drive
- Auckland City, 35 mins by ferry

ONEROA BAY, WAIHEKE ISLAND
GIVERNY INN

Hosts Gabrielle and Bruce McLelland

44 Queens Drive, Oneroa, Waiheke Island
Phone 0-9-372 2200   *Email* relax@giverny.co.nz
Fax 0-9-372 2204   *Website* www.giverny.co.nz

| 2 bdrm | 1 enst | 1 prbth | Room rate $290–$380 | *Includes breakfast* *Self-catering in cottage* |

DIRECTIONS: From ferry hosts will arrange transfer, or take rental car & travel along Ocean View Rd, through Oneroa village, to Little Oneroa. Turn left into Goodwin Ave. Turn left again into Queens Dr. Giverny on left.

Sited on the brow of a hill with views to the Hauraki Gulf and its islands, Giverny comprises a home built in the 1990s, adjacent to a colonial-style cottage built circa 1939. Sundecks from both buildings open to the Mediterranean-style gardens which complement the Tuscan style of the main house. The upstairs Venus Suite in the house has a private balcony overlooking the garden to the ocean beyond, and is shaded by a flame tree. Bacchus Cottage is fully self-contained with polished floors, country furnishings and a kitchen for self-catering. Gabrielle and Bruce serve a gourmet breakfast in the house dining room each morning, and are happy to provide recommendations on the best way to spend time on Waiheke Island.

Facilities
- Venus Suite: queen bedroom, day room with single bed, ensuite & balcony upstairs in house
- Bacchus Cottage: queen bedroom with bathroom, extra couch-bed in sitting room, kitchen & decking
- hair dryer, toiletries & heated towel rails in both bathrooms
- cotton bed linen; fresh flowers
- TV, video, stereo & chocolates
- children welcome
- continental & full American-style breakfasts
- wine & liquor available for guests
- tea/coffee; fresh fruit
- spa pool & decks with sea views
- safe available
- laundry facilities
- email available

Activities available
- Tuscan picnic, extra
- garden ramble on site
- walking tracks
- swimming
- golf course
- horse riding
- fishing from rocks
- watersports
- vineyard visits
- artists & potters
- restaurants & cafés, in walking distance, or transport available
- island tours
- Oneroa village shops
- coastal walks
- beaches
- viewing Gulf & harbour
- bicycles for hire, rental cars
- kayaking
- Auckland City, 35-min ferry trip

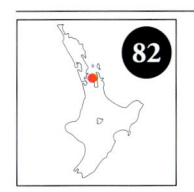

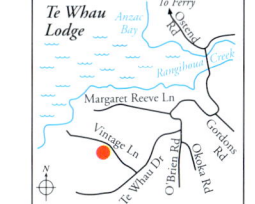

Te Whau Point, Waiheke Island
Te Whau Lodge

Hosts Liz Eglinton and Gene O'Neill

36 Vintage Lane, R D 1, Te Whau Point, Waiheke Island
Phone 0-9-372 2288 *Mobile* 027 430 8222 *Fax* 0-9-372 2218
Email lizandgene@tewhaulodge.co.nz *Website* www.tewhaulodge.co.nz

| 4 bdrm | 4 enst | 2 pdrm | Double $360 / Double $560 | Single $300 / Single $440 | Includes breakfast / Includes breakfast, apéritifs & dinner |

DIRECTIONS: Take ferry to Waiheke Island. From Matiatia or Kennedy Pt, follow signs towards Rocky Bay. From O'Brien Rd, turn right into Te Whau Drive. Turn right again into Vintage Lane. Te Whau Lodge on left.

Surrounded by native planting and regenerating bush on Te Whau Peninsula, the Lodge features an outdoor spa pool and extensive decks, with outdoor seating overlooking Putiki Bay and the Waitemata Harbour. Panoramic views across the sea to Rangitoto Island and Auckland City beyond are complemented by the evening sunsets. Set in a rural location with vineyards and olive groves close by, Te Whau Lodge is a tranquil retreat, architecturally designed and purpose built in a contemporary New Zealand style. Te Whau accommodates up to eight guests in four ensuite bedrooms and offers fine food and wine. Dining is a key feature at Te Whau, with local produce used wherever possible, and Waiheke wines included on the wine list.

Facilities

- 4 super-king ensuite bedrooms
- hair dryers, toiletries, heated towel rails & wheelchair access
- cotton bed linen
- CD-player in each guestroom
- TV in rooms on request
- guest lounge with open fire, TV, video & CD-player
- full breakfast served in dining room or alfresco on spacious sundecks
- 4-course dinner & apéritifs available - menu changes daily
- fully licensed
- phone, fax & email available
- complimentary laundry
- courtesy passenger transfer to & from ferry or local airfield

Activities available

- outdoor spa pool with sea views
- in-house massage by arrangement
- pétanque/boules on site
- spacious decks for dining, relaxing & reading
- extensive library & CD collection
- conference facilities
- beaches; watersports
- many local walking trails
- art galleries & artist studios
- cafés for lunch nearby
- vineyards
- golf
- boating; fishing
- horse riding
- shopping, 10-min drive
- Auckland City, 35 mins by passenger or car ferry
- Auckland International Airport, 12-min flight

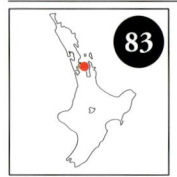

ROCKY BAY, WAIHEKE ISLAND
THE GLASS HOUSE

Host David Eyre

33 Okoka Road, Rocky Bay, Waiheke Island
Phone 0-9-372 3173   *Mobile* 021-234 3455   *Fax* 0-9-372 4145
Email info@theglasshouse.co.nz   *Website* www.theglasshouse.co.nz

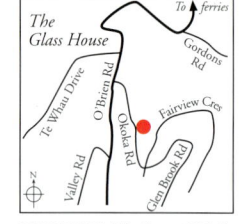

Room rate $520–$580   Includes breakfast
Lunch & dinner extra

3 bdrm   3 enst

DIRECTIONS: Take ferry to Waiheke Island. Take taxi or rental car on Ocean View Rd. Continue into Ostend Rd. Turn right into O'Brien Rd, then left into Okoka Rd. Travel to The Glass House on left.

Purpose built in 2003, this state-of-the-art minimalist glass structure is set in native bush on the highest point of Waiheke Island, with 320-degree views from the cliff edge of Rocky Bay. Surrounded by a nature reserve, The Glass House provides views to Rangitoto Island, Auckland City and Coromandel Peninsula. Three super-king-size guestrooms, with spacious ensuites, open to private balconies overlooking the ocean. A range of organic breakfast and dinner options is served in the dining room or alfresco on the deck, and room service is available. Picnic hampers with wine can be arranged and a four-course dinner is also offered. Guests enjoy the on-site swimming and spa pools, with massage and yoga available.

Facilities

- 3 super-king bedrooms, each with large deck, phone, Sky TV, DVD, CD-player, mini-bar & home-made snacks
- 3 ensuite bathrooms, each with dual bath & double basin
- hair dryers, toiletries, demist mirrors & bathrobes
- cotton bed linen; fresh flowers
- children by arrangement
- fax & email available

- breakfast in dining room, alfresco, or room service
- picnic hampers including wine, $50 pp
- 4-course dinner, $95 pp
- 2 kitchenettes for self-catering
- guest lounge with open fire
- 1 powder room
- private guest entrance
- parking; courtesy transfer

Activities available

- cedar hot tub & cliff-hugging infinity-edge swimming pool on site
- in-room massages, beauty treaments & yoga
- bush walking trail from site into nature reserve
- beaches; swimming
- wineries & tastings
- olive oil tasting
- Waiheke Island tours

- restaurants, 2-min drive
- snapper fishing; sea kayaking
- boating; water skiing
- local art studios & art for sale
- village shopping
- car rental; bicycle hire
- golf courses; horse trekking
- native bird-watching
- Auckland airport, 12-min flight
- Auckland City, 35-min ferry

© Friars' Guide to New Zealand Accommodation for the Discerning Traveller

ONETANGI, WAIHEKE ISLAND
WAIHEKE SANDS APARTMENT

Managers Tony and Raewyn Lancaster   *Phone* 0-9-372 4484

Apartment 16, 141–145 The Strand, Onetangi Beach, Waiheke Island
Postal P O Box 188, Oneroa, Waiheke Island   *Mobile* 027 448 5741
Email lansands@pl.net   *Website* www.waihekeluxury.com   *Fax* 0-9-372 4558

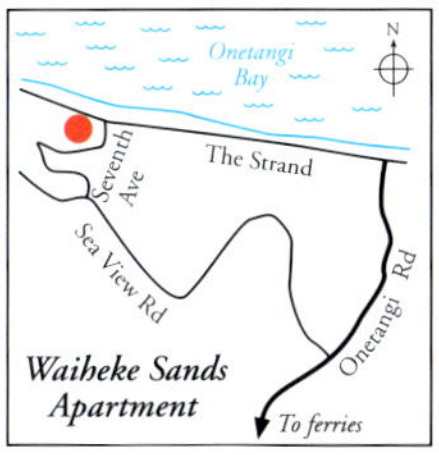

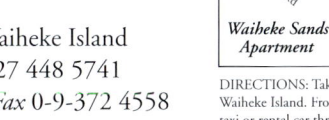

3 bdrm | 1 enst | 1 prbth   Apartment rate $350–$450   *Self-catering*   *Platters extra*

DIRECTIONS: Take ferry to Waiheke Island. From Matiatia take taxi or rental car through Oneroa, past Ostend into Onetangi Rd. Turn left into The Strand & travel to The Sands on Onetangi on left, to apartment 16.

Opened in 2003, Waiheke Sands Apartment is part of The Sands on Onetangi complex located on the sheltered quiet western end of the north-facing beach. The apartment commands panoramic views over Onetangi Beach from the lounge, dining room, two bedrooms and the deck. Designed in a contemporary style, the self-contained apartment provides quality fittings and furnishings including leather sofas and granite benches, and original New Zealand artwork is featured. Guests can self-cater in the fully equipped kitchen and alfresco dining can be enjoyed on the spacious terrace where there is a gas barbecue and outdoor furniture. There are many restaurants and wineries from five to 15 minutes away, and Auckland City is 35 minutes by ferry.

Facilities
- single-party bookings only
- 1 king ensuite bedroom
- 1 king & 1 twin bedroom share 1 bathroom
- king bedrooms open to deck
- hair dryer, toiletries & heated towel rails in both bathrooms
- lounge with tea/coffee, Sky TV, DVD, CD-player, artwork & magazines
- quality fittings
- self-service laundry
- platter meals by arrangement, extra
- full kitchen for self-catering
- large terrace with gas BBQ & outdoor furniture
- lift access
- wheelchair access
- sea views
- on-site parking

Activities available
- direct beach access from apartment
- variety of restaurants, cafés & village shops, 5–15-min drive
- bush walks
- native bird-watching
- scenic drives
- wineries & tastings
- snapper fishing
- sea kayaking
- boating
- water skiing
- local art studios & art for sale
- bicycle hire
- golf course, 5-min drive
- horse trekking
- Waiheke Island tours
- Auckland City, 35 mins by passenger or car ferry
- Auckland International Airport, 12-min flight

… 85

CONNELLS BAY, WAIHEKE ISLAND
CONNELLS BAY

Hosts Jo and John Gow

Connells Bay, Cowes Bay Road, R D 1, Waiheke Island
Phone 0-9-372 8957   *Mobile* 021-363 613   *Fax* 0-9-377 4877
Email info@connellsbay.co.nz   *Website* www.connellsbay.co.nz

| 2 bdrm | 1 enst | 1 prbth |

Cottage rate $350
Minimum 2-night stay

Includes breakfast provisions
Self-catering

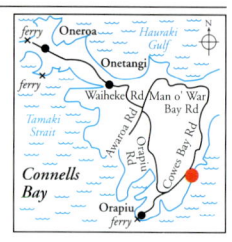

DIRECTIONS: Take ferry to Waiheke Island. Take hire vehicle on Waiheke Rd. Continue into Orapiu Rd. At "T" junction turn left into Cowes Bay Rd. Travel just over 1km to Connells Bay to yellow letterbox on left.

Sited at the historic trading depot in Connells Bay since circa 1890, the colonial guest cottage is one of three on 24 hectares (60 acres) at the privately owned bay on the eastern side of Waiheke Island. The century-old cottage has recently been restored and refurbished to provide self-contained accommodation just 10 metres from the beach, backed by native trees and rolling farmland. The guest cottage is set in a fenced garden, beyond which is a unique sculpture park comprising commissioned and purchased contemporary works by some of New Zealand's most renowned sculptors. Walking tracks are cut through the park and surrounding bush, which includes an ancient stand of kauri trees. Guests also enjoy kayaking to nearby islands.

Facilities

- one-party bookings only
- 2 double bedrooms, with ensuite or private bathroom, opening to deck
- hair dryer & quality toiletries in both bathrooms
- lounge with open fire, artwork, tea/coffee facilities, CDs, phone, books & magazines
- sunrise over sea from bedrooms & lounge
- full self-catering kitchen
- breakfast provisions
- outdoor BBQ area
- cotton bed linen
- fresh flowers
- self-serve laundry facilities
- on site-parking
- vehicle for hire, extra
- helipad; boat mooring

Activities available

On site:
- pétanque or boules
- contemporary sculpture park
- walks in 24ha (60 acres) of bush & rolling farmland
- fishing boat with motor & gear; wharf
- 3 kayaks for guest use
- snapper fishing in bay
- safe swimming in bay

Off site:
- kayaking to nearby islands
- Stoney Batter historic site, 10-min drive
- vineyards; art galleries
- golf course, 20-min drive
- Waiheke Island tours
- Auckland airport, 12-min flight
- Auckland City, 35-min ferry

Above left: The contemporary sculpture park at Connells Bay features large works such as the bronze feather by Paul Dibble.
Above right: "Oi Oi Bridge" at Connells Bay is a seven-metre aluminium bridge sculpted by Virginia King.
Below: Large sculptures feature in the park, such as "Other Peoples' Houses", an eight-metre tower by sculptor Neil Dawson.
Opposite top: The historic guest cottage is just 10 metres from the beach and backed by native trees & rolling farmland.
Opposite bottom left: The cottage offers two bedrooms, each with its own bathroom and views of the sunrise over the beach.
Opposite bottom right: The guest living room in the cottage opens to the verandah and the beach at Connells Bay beyond.

PATIO BAY, WAIHEKE ISLAND
PATIO BAY

Hosts Ian and Frances McIndoe

Patio Bay, Waiheke Island *Postal* 115 Victoria Avenue, Remuera, Auckland
Phone 0-9-524 7565 *Mobile* 021 728 829 *Fax* 0-9-520 5864
Email fox-home@xtra.co.nz *Website* friars.co.nz/hosts/patiobay.html

| 5 bdrm | 2 enst | 1 shbth | House rate $1,200 up to 6 adults
Minimum 2-night stay | *Self-catering, or qualified chef available* |

DIRECTIONS: From Quay St in City, take ferry to Waiheke Island. Take rental car on Waiheke Rd, into Orapiu Rd. At "T", turn left into Cowes Bay Rd. Take 5th drive on right at white cow letterbox to end of steep driveway.

Patio Bay is a private home available for up to six adults for a minimum two-night stay. Situated on the eastern coast of Waiheke Island, Patio Bay is accessible by rental car or private transfer from the ferry terminal. The private beach with safe anchorage offers secluded tranquillity enhanced by pohutukawa trees, terraced garden, floodlit all-weather tennis court, golf chipping green and six hectares of land. The two-storey home was custom-built in pine in 1989 and provides five bedrooms and three bathrooms. The king-size bedroom features a raised central spa bath, dual shower and private viewing balcony. All meals can be self-catered, although a professional chef is available if preferred.

Facilities
- private-group bookings
- 1 king ensuite bedroom, with double basins, dual shower, spa bath & balcony
- 1 queen ensuite bedroom
- 1 double & 1 twin bedroom & 1 bunkroom share 1 bathroom with bath & additional 2 toilets
- 2 hair dryers, 3 heated towel rails
- lounge with open fire, large screen Sky TV, VCR, & hi-fi
- fully equipped state-of-the-art kitchen, with ice-maker, for self-catering & entertaining
- chef by arrangement
- walk-in coolroom
- self-service laundry
- guest phone & fax
- unsuitable for children
- passenger transfer, extra

Activities available
- boat mooring
- indoor & outdoor BBQs
- spa pool & swimming pool
- floodlit all-weather tennis court on site
- golf chipping green
- billiards, snooker, pool
- terraced garden
- row boat available
- swimming in bay
- fishing from bay
- Waiheke Channel
- Pakatoa Island, 2km by sea
- Ponui Island, 1km by sea
- 9-hole golf course, 20 mins
- Waiheke Island Walkways
- restaurants & cafés, 20km
- ferry from Orapiu Wharf, 2km
- ferries from Matiatia Wharf, 24km
- Auckland, 35-min ferry trip

© Friars' Guide to New Zealand Accommodation for the Discerning Traveller

Western Springs, Auckland
Hastings Hall

Host Malcolm Martel

99 Western Springs Road, Western Springs, Auckland
Phone 0-9-845 8550   *Mobile* 021 300 006   *Fax* 0-9-845 8554
Email unique@hastingshall.co.nz   *Website* www.hastingshall.co.nz

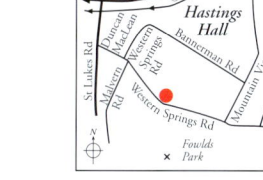

10 bdrm	6 enst	2 prbth	1 pdrm	Double $165–$375	Includes breakfast	Lunch extra
				Single $145–$325	Breakfast for invited friends of guests, extra	

DIRECTIONS: From city, take NW Motorway (SH 16). Take St Lukes exit & turn left into St Lukes Rd. Turn 1st left into Duncan McLean Link & veer right into Western Springs Rd. Hastings Hall on left.

Hastings Hall is a heritage home, originally built in 1876, refurbished and now providing accommodation for 20 guests. The main house offers three bedrooms upstairs and two downstairs, with a further five guestrooms in the adjacent Stables. The colonial interiors are furnished with antiques, and each bedroom includes tea and coffee-making facilities, television and phone. The breakfast menu changes daily with a full range of dishes served in the dining room or spacious indoor/outdoor conservatory. Room service is offered, and lunch is available by request. A small conference or seminar room for staff-training sessions is available, and swimming and spa pools. Children are welcome, and there is a golden retriever, Barney, on site.

Facilities
- House: 1 king, 1 queen & 1 double ensuite bedroom upstairs; 1 king/twin & 1 queen bedroom with 1 private bathroom & wheelchair access downstairs
- Stables: 5 queen bedrooms, 3 with ensuites & 2 share 1 private bathroom
- cotton bed linen, phone, TV, tea/coffee, writing desk & fresh flowers in all bedrooms
- full breakfast menu
- lunch by arrangement
- private guest lounge with open fire, Sky TV, video, CD-player, grand piano, library & bar
- hair dryers, toiletries, heated towel rails, heaters & bathrobes
- powder room
- laundry, $5; fax & email
- off-street parking

Activities available
- BBQ on site
- swimming & spa pools on site
- conference/seminar room on site
- in-house music lounge & library
- Auckland Zoological Gardens
- feeding ducks at Western Springs & chickens at Cornwall Park
- parks, reserves & private gardens
- museum & Auckland Domain
- art & craft galleries
- wide selection of cafés, restaurants & bars
- sightseeing & harbour tours
- Auckland City Centre & Viaduct Basin, 5–10 mins
- Sky Tower & casino
- Tahuna Torea Bird Sanctuary
- wine & antique shop trails
- Waitakere ranges, 30 mins
- airport, 30–45 mins

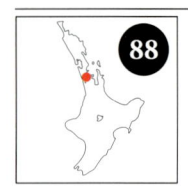

Herne Bay, Auckland
Moana Vista

Hosts Tim Kennedy and Matthew Moran

60 Hamilton Road, Herne Bay, Auckland   *Phone* 0-9-376 5028
Freephone 0800 213 761   *Mobile* 021 376 150   *Fax* 0-9-376 5025
Email info@moanavista.co.nz   *Website* friars.co.nz/hosts/moanavista.html

3 bdrm | 2 enst | 1 prbth

Double $120–$220
Single $90–$140

Includes breakfast

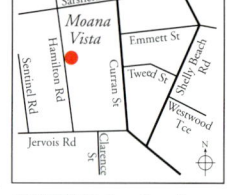

DIRECTIONS: From Ponsonby, take Jervois Rd & turn right into Hamilton Rd. Moana Vista on right. From Harbour Bridge, take 1st exit into Shelley Beach Rd. Turn right into Sarsfield St & left into Hamilton Rd.

Moana Vista is located close to the Waitemata Harbour, in the prestigious suburb of Herne Bay. Originally built as a private residence in the 1890s, this two-storey villa has been renovated to offer accommodation. There are three guestrooms each with a bathroom, as well as an extra family bedroom, as Moana Vista is a child friendly establishment. Two of the upstairs bedrooms provide harbour views, which give Moana Vista its name. Guests can relax in two living areas, one with a grand piano, and the outside decking and subtropical sunken garden area are also popular. Breakfast includes fresh seasonal fruits, yoghurts and a bakery selection. A short evening stroll takes guests to a range of local award-winning restaurants in Ponsonby.

Facilities

- 2 queen ensuite bedrooms
- 1 queen bedroom with 1 private bathroom including bath
- extra family bedroom
- hair dryers, toiletries & heated towel rails
- cotton bed linen
- bathrobes
- children welcome
- continental breakfast served in dining room downstairs
- complimentary glass of wine
- TV, tea/coffee & mineral water available
- lounge with open fire, Sky TV, video, DVD, CD-player, grand piano & artwork
- high-speed internet access
- city location

Activities available

- restaurants & cafés on Jervois & Ponsonby roads
- kayak available for guest use
- swimming & kayaking
- Waitemata Harbour & beach
- walk to city via waterfront, under harbour bridge, 20 mins
- boating/sailing
- private gardens open to visit
- Cornwall Park & One Tree Hill
- Sky tower restaurant & casino
- Auckland CBD, 20-min walk
- boutique shopping
- Britomart rail centre
- museum & art gallery
- The Domain
- antiques shops
- Viaduct Basin & America's Cup Village
- Auckland airport, 30 mins

© Friars' Guide to New Zealand Accommodation for the Discerning Traveller

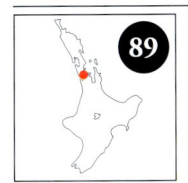

Ponsonby, Auckland
The Great Ponsonby B & B

Hosts Sally James and Gerard Hill

30 Ponsonby Terrace, Ponsonby, Auckland
Freephone 0800 766 792   *Phone* 0-9-376 5989   *Fax* 0-9-376 5527
Email info@greatpons.co.nz   *Website* www.greatpons.co.nz

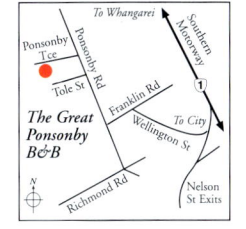

| 11 bdrm | 11 enst |

Suite rate $215–$330
Room rate $180–$210

Includes breakfast

DIRECTIONS: Travelling north take Nelson St exit from Motorway. Turn into Wellington St, then left into Franklin Rd. Turn right into Ponsonby Rd, then left into Ponsonby Tce. Great Ponsonby on left, at bottom of road.

This 1898 Victorian villa has been carefully restored to reflect the city's Pacific heritage, with bold use of colour and New Zealand artwork. Features include Pacific masks, tapa cloth, work by local ceramic artists, John Papas and Jeannie van der Putten tiles, sand-blasted windows by Kara Dodson, and floor rugs from Baluchistan. Soft leather couches create a comfortable lounge, and breakfast in the adjoining dining room ranges from self-serve continental to the Shearer's Special. Alternatively guests can enjoy their breakfast alfresco on the verandah overlooking the courtyard in the quiet cul-de-sac setting. The Great Ponsonby is within walking distance of many restaurants, cafés, shops, and city attractions, and not far from the beaches.

Facilities

- 1 large suite with balcony
- 5 super-king/twin suites, with ensuites & kitchenettes, 3 with baths
- 5 queen/twin ensuite bedrooms, with tea/coffee
- hair dryers, heated towel rails, demist mirrors & bathrobes
- cotton bed linen
- guest lounge with tea/coffee, music, artwork
- full breakfast cooked to order, from extensive menu
- morning paper
- direct dial phone in bedrooms
- fax, email & laundry available
- central heating
- children/dog by arrangement
- high-speed internet access
- quiet peaceful location
- off-street parking

Activities available

- 2 bicycles available
- relaxing in sunny garden & courtyard on site
- beach towels available
- cat & dog on site
- pétanque in adjoining park
- bus passes every 10 mins
- Ponsonby historic walk
- Auckland CBD, 5-min drive
- motorway nearby
- large range of Ponsonby restaurants, outdoor cafés & bars in walking distance
- gym & swimming pool, 18-min walk
- art galleries nearby
- cinemas & museum nearby
- Herne Bay beaches nearby
- gardens open to visit
- airport, 30-min drive

… PARNELL, AUCKLAND
ST GEORGES BAY LODGE

Hosts Carol and Steven Quilliam   *Mobile* 021 214 1473

43 St Georges Bay Road, Parnell, Auckland   *Phone* 0-9-303 1050
Postal P O Box 42 036, Orakei, Auckland   *Fax* 0-9-360 7392
Email carol@stgeorge.co.nz   *Website* friars.co.nz/hosts/stgeorge.html

Double $215–$255
Single $195–$215   *Includes breakfast*

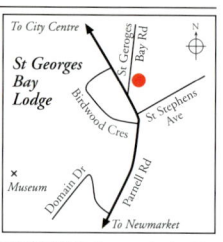

4 bdrm / 4 enst

DIRECTIONS: From south take SH 1 Motorway to Khyber Pass exit. Turn right to Newmarket & then left into Parnell Rd. Turn right into St Georges Bay Rd. Lodge on right. From North, take Fanshawe St exit to Customs St.

One of the four original villas built in St Georges Bay Road in the 1890s, this Lodge has been totally renovated with tasteful modern amenities. Set in Parnell, a prestigious inner city location, this Victorian-style weatherboard villa, typical of the late 19th century, still includes original sash windows, turned verandah posts, fretwork detailing, bay windows and high ceilings. St Georges Bay Lodge now features native timber furniture and a new conservatory with arched windows, flowing on to a balcony overlooking a city park, with views of the central city, across the harbour to Rangitoto Island. A healthy breakfast is served alfresco on the balcony on sunny mornings, which is also a popular spot for night-time viewing of the harbour.

Facilities

- Gold Room: super-king/twin ensuite bedroom
- Blue Room & Cream Room: 2 king/twin ensuite bedrooms
- Lavender Room: double ensuite bedroom
- marble/tiled ensuites with toiletries & heated towel rails
- NZ woollen underlays
- library & private guest lounge
- full healthy continental & English-style cooked breakfast
- complimentary NZ port
- office facilities & PC with internet access
- central heating
- children by arrangement
- city & harbour views
- verandahs open to small private landscaped garden

Activities available

- Parnell Village, 2-min walk
- Parnell cafés, restaurants, nightclubs, designer boutiques & speciality shops in Village
- Holy Trinity Cathedral, nearby
- Auckland City CBD, 1.5km
- world class yacht & tennis clubs, nearby
- health centres; gymnasiums
- swimming pools
- Parnell Rose Gardens, easy walk
- Auckland Museum, Domain & Winter Garden
- public & private gardens; parks & reserves
- sandy beaches; watersports
- art galleries; casino
- University of Auckland
- Waitemata Harbour
- airport, 30-min drive

© Friars' Guide to New Zealand Accommodation for the Discerning Traveller

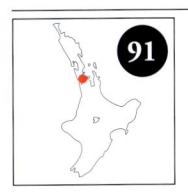

REMUERA, AUCKLAND
AACHEN HOUSE BOUTIQUE HOTEL

Hosts Joan and Greg McKirdy

39 Market Road, Remuera, Auckland
Freephone 0800 AACHEN *Phone* 0-9-520 2329 *Fax* 0-9-524 2898
Email info@aachenhouse.co.nz *Website* www.aachenhouse.co.nz

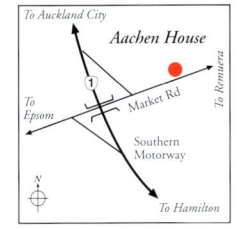

9 bdrm | 9 enst | 1 pdrm

Room rate $275–$475   Includes breakfast & apéritifs
Dinner extra

DIRECTIONS: Travelling either north or south on Southern Motorway, take Market Rd exits. Travel east towards Remuera for 100m. Aachen House Boutique Hotel on the left.

Aachen House, a restored Edwardian gentleman's residence, is nestled at the foot of the Mount Hobson reserve in the affluent suburb of Remuera. Sympathetically renovated to provide modern facilities, yet retaining the elegance of the Edwardian era with antique fittings and period pieces, Aachen House features many original details including ornate plaster ceilings, hand-carved fireplace mantels, timber wall-panels and the hand-crafted staircase. All nine bedrooms have large ensuite bathrooms, and five have direct access to private balconies and the garden. A gourmet breakfast selection is served in the spacious conservatory with its marble floor and antique furnishings, and an outlook over the private garden featuring an Edwardian-style pavilion.

Facilities
- 3 Californian-king, 2 super-king, & 2 king ensuite bedrooms
- 2 king single ensuite bedrooms, 1 with wheelchair access
- Egyptian cotton bed linen
- hair dryer, toiletries, bathrobes
- direct-dial phones, fax, modem
- 5 private balconies/verandahs
- powder room serves guest lounge
- children over 16 yrs welcome

- full gourmet breakfast
- dinner by request, extra
- complimentary tea/coffee & pre-dinner drinks
- satellite TV, classic films
- central heating
- laundry service; ironing
- conference facilities
- fire safety system
- ample on-site parking

Activities available
- sheltered sunny garden, with Edwardian-style pavilion
- Mt Hobson park adjacent, with daffodils in springtime
- Mt St John walks & city views, easy 500m walk
- horse racing & trots, 5-min drive
- golf driving range & golf courses
- tennis & squash courts
- quality shopping, 10-min walk

- restaurants, 5–10-min walk
- antique shops, 300m walk
- City Centre, 10-min drive
- beaches, harbour, 10 mins
- museum & art galleries, 10-min drive away
- private gardens to visit
- bus transport, 300m away
- railway station, 300m away
- airport, 20-min drive

REMUERA, AUCKLAND
AMERISSIT

Host Barbara McKain

20 Buttle Street, Remuera, Auckland
Phone 0-9-522 9297   *Mobile* 027 284 4883   *Fax* 0-9-522 9298
Email barbara@amerissit.co.nz   *Website* www.amerissit.co.nz

3 bdrm	3 enst	1 pdrm	Room rate $185–$325	Includes breakfast
			House rate $600	Self-catering available

DIRECTIONS: Take SH 1 Motorway to Market Rd exit. Travel east towards Remuera. Turn left into Remuera Rd, right into Bassett Rd & 1st right into Arney Rd. Take 1st right into Buttle St to Amerissit at end.

Amerissit is architecturally designed and located in a quiet cul-de-sac near Newmarket. Although the emphasis is on privacy and tranquillity, Amerissit is only a few minutes' drive to restaurants, cafés, shopping, art galleries and museums. The motorways and beaches are also within easy access. The three mimimalist-style guestrooms at Amerissit include slim-line televisions with Sky, DVD-players, in-wall or ceiling speakers, direct dial phone and high-speed internet access. Each room opens to a balcony or patio, offering total privacy with views over the peaceful garden surrounded by mature trees to Remuera and Mt Hobson beyond. A choice of continental or gourmet breakfasts are served in the guestrooms, dining room, or alfresco on the balcony.

Facilities
- 1 queen & 2 king ensuite bedrooms, 1 with dressing room & spa bath
- TV, phone, tea/coffee, fridge & balcony for all 3 bedrooms
- hair dryer, toiletries & heated towel rails in all 3 ensuites
- fresh flowers
- fax & email available
- self-serve laundry, $3 per load
- gourmet breakfast menu with a selection of cooked dishes
- full kitchen available
- private guest lounge with open fire, tea/coffee, nibbles, bar, Sky TV, DVD, CD-player, piano, games, artwork & magazines
- children by arrangement
- small conferences & weddings
- off-street parking

Activities available
- walks on Mt Hobson, through daffodils in early spring
- One Tree Hill & Mt St John walks nearby
- golf courses
- horse racing
- Viaduct Harbour, 10-min drive
- art galleries & museums
- Parnell Rose Gardens
- local bush & beach walks
- restaurants, cafés & shopping at Newmarket, Parnell & Remuera, less than 5-min drive
- public & private gardens
- Hauraki Gulf cruises
- watersports
- Underwater World, 10 mins
- Sky Tower
- Auckland City CBD, 1.5km
- airport, 20-min drive

© Friars' Guide to New Zealand Accommodation for the Discerning Traveller

Above: The guest living areas include open fireplace, piano, TV, tea/coffee facilities, nibbles and a bar opening to a patio area.
Below: One of the three guest bedrooms with LCD TV, Arne Jacobson swan chairs, and view to the balcony and garden beyond.
Opposite top: Amerissit is located at the end of a quiet cul-de-sac in Remuera and is set in a garden surrounded by mature trees.
Opposite bottom left: A spa bath is included in one of the three spacious ensuite bathrooms, with view overlooking Mt Hobson.
Opposite bottom right: Gourmet breakfast can be served in the dining room, or alfresco on the balcony overlooking the garden.

REMUERA, AUCKLAND
THE DEVEREUX BOUTIQUE HOTEL

Hosts Shannon McAuley and Mark Bishop

267 Remuera Road, Remuera, Auckland
Phone 0-9-524 5044 *Email* bookings@devereux.co.nz
Fax 0-9-524 5080 *Website* www.devereux.co.nz

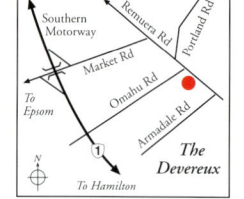

12 bdrm / 10 enst

Room rate $190–$290

Includes breakfast
Lunch & dinner extra

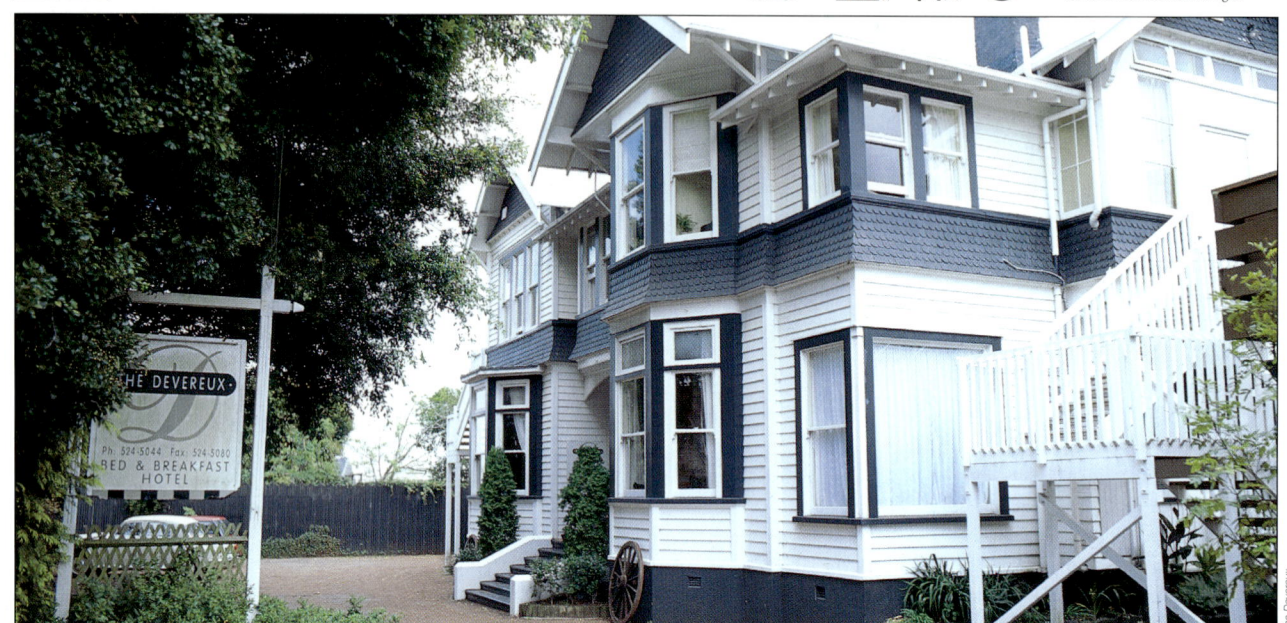

DIRECTIONS: From Motorway, take Market Rd exit. Travel east along Market Rd & turn right into Remuera Rd. The Devereux on right. From Newmarket, take Remuera Rd south for 2km. The Devereux on right.

The Devereux Boutique Hotel offers 12 bedrooms, each individually decorated in a different global theme. Guests can choose from themes as diverse as Provence, Antigua, Cairo, Taj, Zambezi, Tuscany, Bodrum, South Pacific, and the Orient. Originally built in the 1890s, this historic villa features spacious living areas, including a private reading room, sunny conservatory and a small seminar room. Breakfast, such as scrambled eggs with smoked salmon, or blueberry pancakes with warm maple syrup and crème fraîche, is served in the conservatory or alfresco by the fountain. Set in a large garden, The Devereux is located in the prestigious suburb of Remuera, making inner Auckland activities and the waterfront readily accessible.

Facilities

- 2 Master king/twin rooms; 1 family suite for 3–5 people
- 3 Executive king/twin ensuite rooms; 4 queen or double suites
- 2 single or double bedrooms; 1 self-contained 2-bedroom cottage
- cotton bed linen, Sky TV, modem, direct dial phone, hair dryers & toiletries in all rooms
- private garden & courtyard
- complimentary internet/computer
- open fire, lounge, board room, conservatory & library
- early check-in service
- lunch, dinner & special diets catered for, by arrangement
- intimate private functions & business conferences
- laundry & dry cleaning
- children by arrangement
- off-street parking

Activities available

- tours organised: caving, wine, farms, nature trails & sailing
- gardens & parks to visit
- bus & trains, few mins
- Sky Tower, 10-min drive
- downtown Auckland, 10 mins
- Viaduct Harbour, 10 mins
- Underwater World, 10 mins
- Mission Bay, 10-min drive
- tennis & squash courts nearby
- restaurants/cafés, 5-min walk
- speciality shops, 5-min walk
- swimming; gym; golf nearby
- walks up One Tree Hill & Mt Hobson nearby
- harbour & beaches, 10 mins
- island & ferry trips
- cultural displays, galleries & museum
- theatres & cinemas

© Friars' Guide to New Zealand Accommodation for the Discerning Traveller

REMUERA, AUCKLAND
COTTER HOUSE

Host Gloria Poupard-Walbridge

4 Saint Vincent Avenue, Remuera, Auckland   *Postal* P O Box 28 528, Auckland
Phone 0-9-529 5156   *Mobile* 021 672 989   *Fax* 0-9-529 5186
Email info@cotterhouse.com   *Website* www.cotterhouse.com

Room rate $385–$565   *Includes breakfast/brunch*
Double $665–$1,015   Single $330–$510   *Includes all meals*

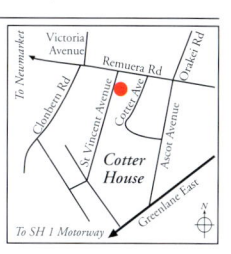

DIRECTIONS: From SH 1 Motorway, take Greenlane exit. Travel east on Greenlane East towards Remuera. Take 2nd left into St Vincent Ave. Cotter House on right.

Cotter House has re-positioned itself as an inner city luxury retreat for pampered holidays, offering a secluded setting for weddings, honeymoons, business conferences and entertaining. Built in 1847 and carefully restored, preserving the original regency architecture, Cotter House features an 1892 ballroom, and is furnished with antiques complemented by Gloria's contemporary art collection. Guests are served four-course breakfasts or brunches, and enjoy access to the heated swimming pool, exercise pavilion and yoga classes. Either the bed and breakfast or all-meal option is available, the latter including gourmet dining accompanied by the extensive wine list from the house bar. In-room health spa treatments are available.

Facilities

- Suite: Bronze Room with queen bed & Empire Room with single bed; & 1 ensuite with bath
- Oriental Room: 1 double bedroom with ensuite
- Blue Provencal Room: 1 king/twin bedroom with private bathroom
- desks, Sky TVs, tea/coffee, DDI phones, CDs, DVDs, safes & irons
- hair dryers, toiletries, robes, slippers & turbans, heated floor/towel rails
- gourmet breakfast/brunch
- 4-course dinner, hors d'oeuvres with apéritifs; wine extra
- 2 guest lounges with open fires, Sky digital TV, CDs, DVDs & guest mini-fridges
- fluent French & Spanish, some Italian & Portuguese
- fully equipped guest office; laundry, dry cleaning available
- central heating; 7 carparks

Activities available

- private bricked courtyard, heated swimming pool & BBQ area on site
- summer conferences, corporate seminars, banquets, weddings, receptions & other functions catered for guests only
- spa pool, massages, exercise pavilion & complimentary yoga classes available to guests
- Hauraki Gulf cruises
- wide selection of restaurants, bars & cafés, walking distance
- antique shops & cinemas
- Newmarket & Parnell shopping area, 5-min drive
- wine trail & harbour tours
- Auckland sightseeing tours
- CBD shopping, 10-min drive
- city museums & art galleries
- airport, 20-min drive

© Friars' Guide to New Zealand Accommodation for the Discerning Traveller

St Heliers Bay, Auckland
Seaview Heights

Hosts Anthea and John Delugar

23A Glover Road, St Heliers, Auckland
Phone 0-9-575 8159   *Mobile* 027 485 4659   *Fax* 0-9-575 8155
Email seaview@seaview.co.nz   *Website* www.seaview.co.nz

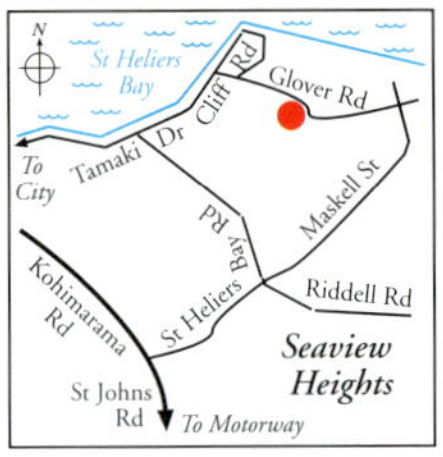

3 bdrm | 2 enst | 1 prbth   Room rate $180–$260   Long-stay & off-season rates available
Minimum 2-night stay in summer   *Includes breakfast*

DIRECTIONS: From City, take Tamaki Dr into Cliff Rd. Turn right into Glover Rd. Seaview Heights on right, up driveway. Or from St Johns Rd, travel down Kohimarama Rd. Turn right into Tamaki Dr, then as above.

Seaview Heights is set high on a hill 250 metres from the cliffs of St Heliers Bay. This 1960s large family home, an Auckland Tourism Award finalist, comprises three levels, with a circular staircase leading to the spacious guestrooms on the top floor. The king Bay View Suite features a double Roman spa bath and a private balcony provides views over the bay. The queen Park View Suite also has a private balcony with sea views, and overlooks Glover Park, with its tree-lined scenic walking track. Furnished with native kauri and mahogany antiques, the soft colourings create a restful yet stylish Mediterranean ambience. Breakfast – of hot muffins, fresh fruit platter, croissants, muesli, eggs Benedict, salmon and avocado – is served in the dining room.

Facilities

- 1 king/twin, 1 king & 1 queen bedroom, all with seaviews, TV, private balconies & bathrooms
- hair dryers, toiletries & bathrobes
- double spa bath in 1 king ensuite
- flowers, chocolates, teas, coffee, biscotti & wine in bedrooms
- children welcome, by request
- honeymoon hideaway
- laundry & iron available

- gourmet breakfast served in middle-floor dining room, with sea view & balcony
- fluent German, French, Spanish & Italian spoken
- guest lounge with seaviews
- phone/fax, email available
- courtesy car to restaurants
- Jasmine, the cat, & Fergus, the border collie, on site

Activities available

- private lessons in English, German, French, Spanish, or Italian, with Anthea
- garden & swimming pool
- restaurants & bistros, wide selection, 10-min walk
- St Heliers Bay, 5-min walk
- aquatics centre, close by
- Tahuna Torea Bird Sanctuary
- scenic beach & cliff walks

- Auckland City, 15-min drive
- Gulf cruises; kayaking; sailing
- swimming; boutique shopping
- Kelly Tarlton's Antarctic Encounter & Underwater World
- private gardens to visit
- Auckland highlights tours
- aromatherapy by arrangement
- art galleries & museums
- theatres, concerts, cinemas

ST HELIERS BAY, AUCKLAND
CLIFF VIEW

Hosts Jill Mathew and Geoff Annesley-Smith   *Mobile* 025 769 405

51 Cliff Road, St Heliers, Auckland   *Phone* 0-9-575 4052
Postal P O Box 25 233, St Heliers, Auckland   *Fax* 0-9-575 4051
Email cliffview@xtra.co.nz   *Website* friars.co.nz/hosts/cliffview.html

| 1 bdrm | 1 enst | Room rate $250
Long-stay & off-season rates available | Includes breakfast supplies
Self-catering |

DIRECTIONS: From the City, take Tamaki Drive & travel around the waterfront for 8km. Continue past St Heliers Bay & into Cliff Rd. Cliff View on right at Ladies Bay.

With 180-degree uninterrupted harbour panorama, Cliff View offers a private king-size guest suite upstairs, with three balconies all providing different aspects of the view. Native pohutukawa trees on the cliff edge frame the vista and the spacious lounge invites relaxation and contemplation of the boating activities below. A secluded beach, Ladies Bay, is only a minute's walk down the hillside. A fully self-contained kitchen including breakfast supplies and dishwasher opens on to a sundeck for alfresco dining. The king-size bedroom has a private sundeck and ensuite bathroom, and a study provides a separate spot for letter writing, peace and quiet. Cliff View is only 11 kilometres from the City Centre, via a picturesque waterfront drive.

Facilities
- 1 self-contained private guest suite upstairs, with 1 king ensuite bedroom opening to sundeck
- heated towel rails, hair dryer & toiletries in ensuite bathroom
- TV, video & radio in lounge
- guest phones in bedroom & study
- complimentary guest laundry
- breakfast supplies include fresh fruit, orange juice, cereals, breads, yoghurt, cheeses, eggs, bacon
- fully equipped kitchen
- tea/coffee selection
- fresh flowers
- private guest lounge
- separate guest study
- 180° views over harbour
- 3 private sundecks
- non-smoking
- off-street parking

Activities available
- swimming beach, 1-min walk
- St Heliers shops, 5-min walk
- restaurants & cafés, 5-min walk
- Kelly Tarlton's Underwater World, 4km away
- cliff edge walks adjacent
- Churchill & Glover Parks
- kayak & motor launch hire
- cycles & roller blades for hire on waterfront
- City & Sky Tower, 8km
- harbour cruises
- Tahuna Torea Bird Sanctuary
- fishing & sailing
- Auckland Museum
- gardens to visit
- golf courses
- Rangitoto & Waiheke Islands
- Tiritiri Matangi Island bird sanctuary

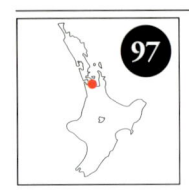

CLEVEDON, SOUTH AUCKLAND
PURIRI HILLS

Hosts Judy and Paul Fowler

398 North Road, Clevedon, R D 2, Papakura
Phone 0-9-292 9264   *Email* judy.fowler@puririhills.co.nz
Fax 0-9-292 9265   *Website* www.puririhills.co.nz

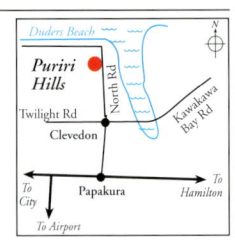

| 2 bdrm | 1 prbth |

Suite rate $500 for 1 or 2 persons
1 or 2 extra persons $100 each

Includes breakfast   *Dinner extra*

DIRECTIONS: Take Papakura exit from Southern Motorway (SH 1). Turn right into Beach Rd & follow signs for 13.3km to Clevedon village. Continue on North Rd another 3.98km to Puriri Hills on left.

The luxury guest suite at Puriri Hills provides exclusive access to a 37-hectare (93-acre) wine-growing estate. Planted in 1997, this boutique vineyard features merlot, cabernet franc and malbec grapes from which Bordeaux-style red wine is made on site. The surrounding hills are home to native puriri trees, which live to a great age, developing massive trunks. Panoramic rural views extend to the Hunua Range and over the Hauraki Gulf to the Coromandel Peninsula beyond. The spacious guest suite has quality furnishings and fittings including the spa bath which looks into a private fernery. Breakfast is provided in the suite and dinner is also offered in the suite, conservatory, or alfresco overlooking the vineyard. A comprehensive wine list is available.

Facilities
- private-party bookings only
- 1 guest suite with 2 super-king/twin bedrooms, 2 dressing rooms, bathroom, lounge & kitchenette
- spa bath, double basin, hair dryer, toiletries, heated floor & heated towel rails in bathroom
- fresh flowers; cotton bed linen
- fridge & tea/coffee in kitchenette
- phone, Sky TV, video, library & writing desk in guest lounge
- hearty country or continental breakfast served in suite
- 3-course dinner served in suite, conservatory, or alfresco, $75 pp, wine extra
- Puriri Hills wine list
- email & fax available
- children over 11 yrs welcome
- private guest entrance
- on-site parking

Activities available
- extensive walking trails on 37-ha (93-acre) property on site
- pets on site
- observing vineyard & winery activities on site
- polo in season
- tours & wine tasting at Puriri Hills & other local vineyards
- sightseeing in vintage aircraft
- botanic gardens
- restaurants, 4km away in Clevedon village
- beaches; boating
- tramping
- horse riding
- private gardens to visit
- scenic coastal drive
- tours of Auckland
- airport, 30-min drive
- Auckland City, 35 mins

© Friars' Guide to New Zealand Accommodation for the Discerning Traveller

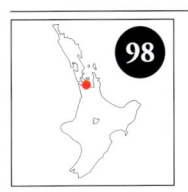

Papakura
Hunua Gorge Country House

Hosts Ben, Amy and Joy Calway

482 Hunua Road, Papakura   *Postal* P O Box 27, Papakura
Phone 0-9-299 7926   *Mobile* 021 669 922   *Fax* 0-9-299 7926
Email hunuagorge@xtra.co.nz   *Website* friars.co.nz/hosts/hunua.html

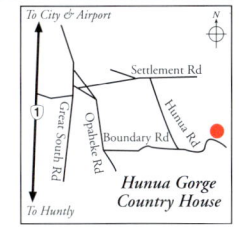

| 5 bdrm | 1 enst | 1 prbth | 1 shbth |

Room rate $110–$150

*Includes breakfast
Lunch & dinner extra*

DIRECTIONS: From Auckland, take SH 1 south to Papakura exit. Turn left into Beach Rd. At lights continue ahead into Settlement Rd. Turn right into Hunua Rd. Travel across bridge & up gravel drive to house at top left.

After crossing the gorge, guests reach this large country house set in 20 hectares (50 acres) with expansive rural views. Built in 1980, the architecture is simple country style in harmony with the rural location of Hunua Gorge, adjacent to the Hunua Ranges, popular for hiking and tramping, yet just 25 minutes from the airport. Night views are special with sunsets followed by the city lights and Manukau Harbour under the starry skies. Innovative meals include breakfast in bed if desired, or brunch, alfresco dining and picnics in the fresh country air. The best of seasonal produce is accessible daily, with regional wines and particular dietary needs Joy's speciality. Guests have the choice of four bedrooms, plus a bunkroom for children.

Facilities
- 1 king suite with ensuite
- 1 queen bedroom with private bathroom & bath
- 1 double & 1 twin bedroom & 1 bunk room with 1 bathroom
- cotton bed linen; fresh flowers
- hair dryers, toiletries & heated towel rails
- private guest lounge with open fire, tea/coffee, TV & video
- breakfast or brunch served
- lunch, $20 pp
- 3-course à la carte dinner, $35 pp
- wheelchair access
- email facilities
- complimentary laundry
- children & pets welcome
- verandah overlooking garden
- on-site parking

Activities available
- pétanque/boules on site
- ponds, streams, bush & trees on site for walks
- slug-shot shooting
- pony rides
- picnicking spots
- golf courses
- fishing
- bush walking & hiking
- tramping in Hunua Ranges
- variety of restaurants, nearby
- shopping & cinemas, 10 mins
- scenic flights
- beaches for swimming, surfing & relaxing
- yachting
- gardens open to visit
- motorway (SH 1), 5-min drive
- airport, 25-min drive
- Auckland City, 30-min drive

117

© Friars' Guide to New Zealand Accommodation for the Discerning Traveller

DRURY, SOUTH AUCKLAND
THE DRURY HOMESTEAD

Hosts Carolyn and Ron Booker

349 Drury Hills Road, R D 1, Drury, Auckland South
Phone 0-9-294 9030   *Email* druryhome@paradise.net.nz
Fax 0-9-294 9035   *Website* friars.co.nz/hosts/drury.html

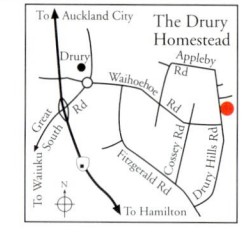

| 4 bdrm | 3 enst | 1 prbth | Double $100–$130 Single $70 | Includes breakfast or provisions in studio Dinner extra   Self-catering in studio |

DIRECTIONS: Take SH 1 Southern Motorway to Drury exit. Turn nor'east & travel 800m to roundabout. Take Waihoehoe Rd east to "T" junction. Turn left into Drury Hills Rd. Drury Homestead 2nd driveway on right.

This early colonial home, circa 1879, was built as the original homestead in the Drury area. It has been fully restored and refurbished to provide quality accommodation. The three upstairs bedrooms provide rural views, and downstairs there is a self-contained studio. A full cooked breakfast is served in the dining room and family dinner is also available. Studio guests can self-cater in their fully equipped kitchen if preferred, and restaurants are nearby. Guests enjoy relaxing on the deep verandahs, and for the more active, bush walks or jogging on the forested property. The Waihoehoe Stream in the garden features large rocks and the native bush attracts birdlife. Two dogs, a Jack Russell and a giant schnauzer, live on site.

Facilities
- 2 queen ensuite bedrooms upstairs
- 1 twin bedroom with private bathroom upstairs
- 1 self-contained queen studio
- hair dryers, heated towel rails & toiletries in all 4 bathrooms
- cotton bed linen; fresh flowers
- 2 lounges with tea/coffee, nibbles, TV & books
- children welcome
- full cooked or continental breakfast in dining room
- 3-course family dinner, $30–$40 pp; BYO
- breakfast provisions in full studio kitchen for self-catering
- fax, phone & email available
- self-serve laundry
- extensive verandahs with rural outlook; on-site parking

Activities available
- garden & bushwalks on site
- farm animals, pasture, native bush & stream on site
- gliding club nearby
- Pukekohe township & motor racing, 15-min drive
- Auckland harbours & beaches for swimming & surfing
- gardens open to visit
- Manurewa Botanic Gardens, 15-min drive
- 3 restaurants within 2km
- variety of restaurants in Pukekohe & Bombay
- tramping in Hunua Ranges
- scenic flights
- yachting; fishing
- golf courses
- Auckland CBD, 35-min drive on southern motorway
- airport, 20-min drive

© Friars' Guide to New Zealand Accommodation for the Discerning Traveller

MIRANDA
UMOYA LODGE

Host Johann van den Berg

30 Rataroa Road, R D 3, Pokeno   *Mobile* 021 655 599
Phone 0-9-232 7636   *Email* relax@umoyalodge.co.nz
Fax 0-9-232 7636   *Website* www.umoyalodge.co.nz

2 bdrm | 2 enst | 1 pdrm

Double $360
Single $260

*Includes breakfast
Lunch & dinner extra*

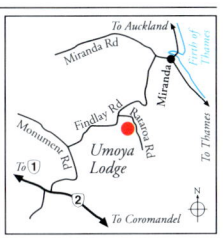

DIRECTIONS: From SH 1 turn off to SH 2 & travel east. Turn left into Monument Rd & travel 4km. Turn right into Findlay Rd & travel 4km. Turn right into Rataroa Rd & travel to Umoya Lodge on right.

Umoya is Zulu for soul, spirit and breath, alluding to the tranquillity and sea views from the secluded setting atop Mount Rataroa. Surrounded by 14 hectares (35 acres) of native bush, with rural vistas across farmland to mountains, Umoya Lodge was custom designed and purpose built to provide the Umoya Luxury Suite and the new Hilltop Studio, adjacent to the main lodge. A full breakfast is served in the guestrooms and three-course lunch and fine dining in the evening are also available by arrangement. The contemporary suite and studio feature antiques, oriental rugs and international artwork and open to private gardens. Guests can enjoy the extensive bush walks on site that abound with wood pigeons and other native birds.

Facilities

- 1 suite with 1 king bedroom, spa bath in ensuite; TV, writing desk, tea/coffee, bar & art in lounge; opens to private deck & enclosed watergarden
- 1 studio with king/twin ensuite bedroom, 2 private decks & cast iron bath in tropical garden with bush & mountain views
- hair dryers, toiletries, heated towel rails, heated floor, bidets, demist mirrors & bathrobes
- full breakfast in guest suites
- 3-course lunch, $40 pp
- 4-course dinner, $90 pp; licensed
- lounge with open fire in lodge
- phone, fax & internet in lodge
- cotton bed linen; fresh flowers
- separate guest entrance
- parking & garaging
- helipad

Activities available

- BBQ on site
- in-house massage
- fine dining on site
- pétanque on site
- extensive bush walks on site
- hot pools
- bird sanctuary
- beach walks
- fishing
- Hunua National Park
- restaurants
- wine & cheese tasting
- golf; squash
- sky diving
- antique stores
- gardens open to visit
- Sky Tower, Viaduct Basin
- Auckland City, 55-min drive
- airport, 40-min drive or 10 mins by helicopter

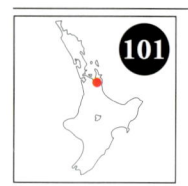

Te Puru, Thames
Te Puru Coast View Lodge

Host Pam Kopecky

468 Thames Coast Road, Te Puru *Postal* P O Box 241, Thames
Phone 0-7-868 2326 *Email* tepuru-lodge@xtra.co.nz
Fax 0-7-868 2376 *Website* friars.co.nz/hosts/tepuru.html

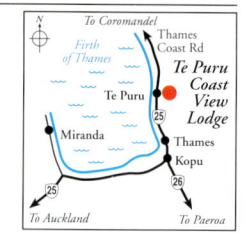

| 4 bdrm | 3 enst | 2 prbth | 1 pdrm |

Room rate $120–$165   *All meals extra*

DIRECTIONS: From Thames, take SH 25 north for 11km, to Te Puru. Te Puru Coast View Lodge on right up driveway.

Built on a historic Maori pa site, Te Puru Coast View Lodge commands spectacular views of the Coromandel coastline, as the name suggests. This Mediterranean-style lodge was refurbished with hand-crafted native rimu and kauri furniture, before opening in 1989. Te Puru's award-winning licensed restaurant features premium New Zealand meats, Coromandel seafoods, and fine wines. After viewing panoramic sunsets, guests can enjoy intimate candlelit dining while the lights come on in the township below. Surrounded by native bush rich in history, the lodge is ideally sited for exploring the peninsula. The developing native heritage garden attracts varied birdlife, including the native kiwi, which can often be heard calling at night.

Facilities
- 4 ground-level bedrooms with views, TV, tea/coffee facilities, ceiling fans, electric blankets, & winter heating
- 1 ensuite king bedroom with sitting area & patio
- 1 ensuite queen bedroom
- 1 ensuite double bedroom
- 1 twin bedroom, with 2 double beds & 2 private bathrooms
- à la carte breakfast, served in dining room with coast view, or alfresco on sunny patio
- lunch by arrangement
- award-winning à la carte licensed restaurant with coast views, & log fire in winter
- spacious lounge with TV, VCR, stereo, library, open fireplace, & bar service
- on-site parking

Activities available
- western gateway to scenic & historic Coromandel Peninsula
- full range shopping & services, in Thames, 10-min drive south
- Maori cultural heritage trail & site interpretation
- Thames Heritage Museum
- vineyard trail
- private gardens to visit
- beach & river swimming
- wide range of bush & beach walks close by
- historic walkways & sites
- arts & crafts trails
- rock prospecting
- bird-watching
- Coromandel forest park
- wading birds at Miranda
- special requests & activities organised

© Friars' Guide to New Zealand Accommodation for the Discerning Traveller

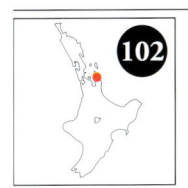

COROMANDEL
BUFFALO LODGE

Host Evelyne Siegrist

Buffalo Road, Coromandel   *Postal* P O Box 11, Coromandel
Phone 0-7-866 8960   *Email* buffalo@wave.co.nz
Fax 0-7-866 8960   *Website* www.buffalolodge.co.nz

3 bdrm | 3 enst | 2 pdrm

Room rate $220–$265   *Includes breakfast*   *Dinner extra*

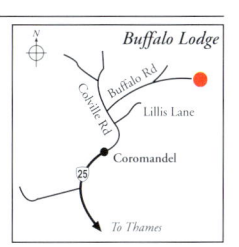

DIRECTIONS: From Coromandel, take Colville Rd north for 2km. Turn right into Buffalo Rd, continue past the Gold Stamper Battery & drive slowly on narrow road, following signs to Buffalo Lodge.

Perched on a hillside with sweeping views over the Coromandel hills, Hauraki Gulf and as far as Waiheke Island, Buffalo Lodge is a contemporary country retreat, tucked away in four hectares (10 acres) of native bush. From here guests can explore the peninsula, and sample the superb sunsets, tranquil sounds of nature and native birdlife. The accent is on culture, with a contemporary art gallery displaying Evelyne and her late husband Raouf's paintings and sculptural work. Slippers are provided for guests to wear on the native miro floors. Buffalo Lodge is unsuitable for children and is open from October to the end of April. Evelyne recommends bookings of at least two days, to take in the scenic attractions of Coromandel and the surrounding area.

Facilities
- honeymoon queen suite, with panoramic view from bath
- 2 queen ensuite bedrooms
- heated towel rails, designer bathrobes & hair dryers
- private sundecks from bedrooms
- Swiss-quality bedding
- slippers provided
- 2 powder rooms
- contemporary art gallery
- Swiss-style breakfast
- cooked breakfast on request
- dinner by request, $85 pp
- BYO licence; no TV
- meals served in dining room with bush & ocean views
- extensive sundeck overlooking Hauraki Gulf
- German, French & Mandarin spoken

Activities available
- Evelyne & Raouf's paintings for sale from on-site art gallery
- massage by arrangement
- bird-watching
- bush walking & climbing
- historic goldmine exploring
- gold stamper battery
- mining museum
- botanic & private gardens
- exploring Coromandel Peninsula
- restaurants, 5-min drive
- narrow-gauge railway
- swimming beaches
- golf course nearby
- fishing & diving
- native kauri tree grove
- pottery & craft trails
- horse riding
- historic township of Coromandel

© Friars' Guide to New Zealand Accommodation for the Discerning Traveller

WHITIANGA/COROMANDEL
MATARANGI MANOR

Hosts Marie and Barry Jones

817 Matarangi Drive, Matarangi   *Postal* 817 Matarangi Drive, R D 2, Whitianga
Phone 0-7-866 0900   *Mobile* 021 382 372   *Fax* 0-7-866 0980
Email mail@matarangimanor.co.nz   *Website* www.matarangimanor.co.nz

| 5 bdrm | 5 enst | 1 pdrm |

Room rate $405–$430
Studio rate $270–$310

Includes breakfast
Self-catering

Lunch & dinner extra
All meals extra

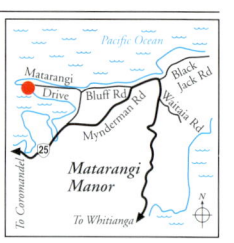

DIRECTIONS: From Whitianga or Coromandel, take SH 25 to Matarangi. Turn left into Matarangi Drive and continue into Beach Estate. Matarangi Manor at end on left.

Opening on to Matarangi Golf Links, with the Pacific Ocean beyond, Matarangi Manor was built in 2000 in authentic Carolina style. Located on Matarangi Beach, on the north-east of the Coromandel Peninsula, the Manor provides peace and quiet on almost half a hectare of landscaped gardens, yet just a 20-minute scenic drive from either Whitianga ot Coromandel townships. The homestead provides four ensuite bedrooms all opening to the covered verandah, where breakfast is often served alfresco overlooking the golf course. A self-contained studio is also available for guests who wish to self-cater. Gourmet dinner is offered with fish, venison, steak or vegetarian set menus and wine. A golf package is also available.

Facilities

- 4 super-king/twin ensuite bedrooms with verandah access
- 1 self-contained studio with 1 queen ensuite bedroom
- cotton bed linen; fresh flowers
- hair dryers, toiletries, heated floors, bathrobes in all bathrooms, 1 with bath & heated towel rails
- internet access, TV, writing desk & tea/coffee in bedrooms
- 1 powder room; laundry available

- Manor: full breakfast served in dining room or alfresco; Studio: breakfast provisions
- lunch/picnic hamper, $20 pp
- 4-course dinner, $65–$100 pp; wine extra
- 2 lounges, open fires, Sky TV, video, DVD, CDs, piano, artwork, library & games
- courtesy passenger transfer
- on-site parking; heli access

Activities available

- outdoor fireplace, BBQ area; swimming & spa pools on site
- putting green, pétanque on site
- cat, Lucy, on site
- Matarangi Golf Links adjacent, golf clubs & golf carts for hire
- Matarangi Beach adjacent; 2 Blokarts/beach yachts provided
- kayaks for hire; tennis nearby
- Matarangi Airfield, 2-min drive

- café, 3-min drive
- restaurants at Matarangi & Whitianga, 5–20 mins
- Matarangi Golf Club 5-min walk
- beach fishing, charters arranged
- walking or trekking in Coromandel Ranges
- Mercury Bay, Cathedral Cove & Whitianga, each 20-min drive
- Coromandel township, 20 mins

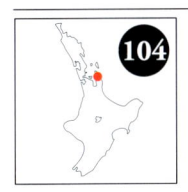

WHITIANGA
SILENCIO LODGE

Hosts Jane and Martin Jackson

251 Old Coach Road, R D 1, Whitianga   *Postal* P O Box 186, Whitianga
Phone 0-7-866 0304   *Mobile* 025 792 980   *Fax* 0-7-866 0275
Email silenciolodge@silenciolodge.co.nz   *Website* www.silenciolodge.co.nz

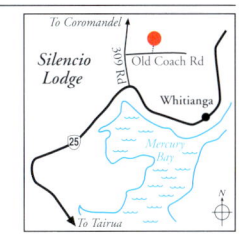

| 4 bdrm | 4 enst | 1 pdrm | Double $280 | Single $250 | Includes breakfast |

DIRECTIONS: From Tairua, take SH 25 north for 35km. Turn left into 309 Rd. Travel 4km to 2nd bridge & turn right into Old Coach Rd. Travel 1.5km to Lodge on left. Take driveway 200m, cross ford & travel to Silencio.

Silencio Lodge features the sounds of silence – from over four hectares (12 acres) of surrounding native bush, home to many birds including the elusive native kiwi. Meandering through the grounds is a pristine stream providing two private swimming spots for guests, as well as sheltered picnicking areas. A double spa bath is also privately sited in the bush. The four ensuite bedrooms are separated from the Lodge to ensure privacy for the guests. The Lodge itself feaures timber interiors and includes spacious decks for relaxing in the summer and a log fire in the lounge for conviviality in the winter. Home-made bread and muffins or croissants and a cooked option are served for breakfast in the Lodge dining room or alfresco on the sundeck.

Facilities
- 1 king/twin & 3 queen bedrooms, all with ensuite bathrooms
- quality bed linen
- heated towel rails, hair dryers & toiletries in all 4 bathrooms
- bathrobes
- wheelchair access
- lounge with log fire, tea/coffee, Sky TV, video & music
- library
- home-baked breakfast & cooked option served in Lodge or alfresco on deck
- powder room
- fax & email facilities
- complimentary laundry
- views of native bush
- private guest entrance
- on-site parking
- courtesy passenger transfer

Activities available
- native bush walks on site
- swimming in stream on site
- pétanque court on site
- double spa bath in bush on site
- massaging & beauty therapy arranged
- beaches – watersports
- 18-hole golf course
- horse riding
- gardens open to visit
- restaurants/cafés nearby
- chartered fishing arranged
- diving; boating
- sailing arranged
- kayaking; windsurfing
- arts & crafts trails
- Hot Water Beach
- local craft shops
- Whitianga township, 10-min drive

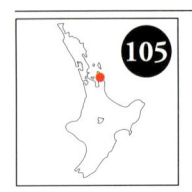

WHITIANGA
VILLA TOSCANA

Hosts Giorgio and Margherita Allemano

Ohuka Park, Whitianga *Postal* P O Box 43, Whitianga
Phone 0-7-866 2293 *Fax* 0-7-866 2269 *Mobile* 025 871 833
Email giorgio@villatoscana.co.nz *Website* www.villatoscana.co.nz

| 2 bdrm | 1 prbth | 1 pdrm | Suite rate $440–$640 for 2 persons
Extra persons $70 each | *Includes breakfast*
Dinner extra | *Self-catering* |

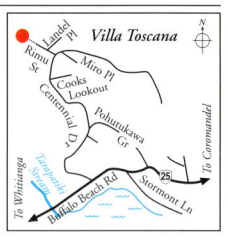

DIRECTIONS: From Whitianga, take Buffalo Beach Rd (SH 25) north for 2km. Turn left into Centennial Dr. At top of hill, turn left into Rimu St. At Ohuka Park continue 1km, sign up private concrete drive to Villa Toscana.

Villa Toscana is a veritable piece of Tuscany – with everything imported from Italy, including 13 tonnes of terracotta tiles, over 12 square metres of granite and marble slabs, Italian antique furniture and paintings, even a genuine terracotta pizza oven! Opened in 1998, this true Tuscan villa is set in two hectares of native bush with panoramic views over Whitianga and Mercury Bay to the islands beyond. Genuine Italian hosts, Giorgio and Margherita, with their young family, dog and cat, enjoy sharing their dream with guests. A fully self-contained suite provides guests with total privacy, although they are welcome to partake of the Italian gourmet cuisine, with wine from the cellar. Giorgio, who loves the sea life, is also happy to take guests game fishing.

Facilities
- single-party bookings only
- 1 king/twin & 1 king bedroom
- 1 bathroom including bidet, hair dryer, heated towel rails, toiletries, bathrobes & slippers
- antique bed linen, fresh flowers, fruit, chocolates & champagne
- fully self-contained guest kitchen
- self-serve guest laundry
- children welcome
- Italian continental breakfast, in suite, alfresco on terrace, or upstairs dining room
- 5-course dinner, $95 pp; wine from cellar, extra
- TV, VCR & CD-player in private guest lounge
- under-tile heating throughout
- Italian & French spoken
- airport courtesy transfer; security gates; helipad

Activities available
- private outdoor spa pool with views; gym adjacent to suite
- Italian billiards table
- in-house art gallery
- guest BBQ; archery on site
- mountain bikes available
- bush walks on site & peninsula
- duplicate bridge arranged
- horse riding on beach, 4-min drive away
- *Mamma Mia!* – 32ft Bertram launch, available for skippered game fishing
- massage & beauty therapists
- swimming & watersports
- kayaking; windsurfing
- scenic flights
- Whitianga, 8-min drive
- 18-hole golf course, 12 mins
- Hot Water Beach, 30 mins

Tairua, Coromandel Peninsula
Colleith Lodge

Hosts Maureen and Colin Gilroy

8 Rewa Rewa Valley, Tairua   *Postal* P O Box 25, Tairua
Phone 0-7-864 7970   Mobile 025 721 423   Fax 0-7-864 7972
Email info@colleithlodge.co.nz   *Website* www.colleithlodge.co.nz

3 bdrm | 3 enst | 1 pdrm

Room rate $220–$295

*Includes breakfast & apéritifs
Dinner extra*

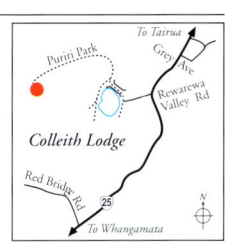

DIRECTIONS: From Whangamata, take SH 25 north towards Tairua. Just after 50km sign, turn left into Rewarewa Valley Rd. Turn right over causeway & right into Puriri Park. Travel up hill to Colleith Lodge at top on left.

Set in native bush full of birdlife, with views over the harbour and ocean to Slipper Island, Colleith Lodge was purpose built in 2002 from kiln-fired Hinuera stone. Three ensuite queen-size bedrooms are available for guests, each opening to a private patio on the terrace overlooking the estuary. A full breakfast is served indoors or alfresco on the terrace, and a barbecue or full dinner is available by arrangement. A small wine cellar stocks a selection of New Zealand wines, and complimentary pre-dinner drinks and nibbles are offered to the guests each evening. Colin or Maureen will drive guests to the local restaurants at Tairua, or a ferry will provide transport to Paku. An outdoor fox terrier, Sam, and border collie, Jip, complete the family.

Facilities

- 3 queen ensuite bedrooms open to private patios with sea views
- 1 ensuite with spa bath; 2 ensuites with wheelchair access
- bathrobes, toiletries, heated floors & heated towel rails
- phone jacks in bedrooms
- 1 guest lounge with open fire, books, desk, phone & bar, extra
- television lounge with Sky TV, video, DVD & CD-player
- breakfast indoors or alfresco
- complimentary apéritifs
- 3-course dinner, $50 pp, by arrangement
- wine from cellar, extra
- BBQ; tea/coffee available
- self-serve laundry
- email, phone & fax available
- passenger transfer, extra
- fresh flowers; on-site parking

Activities available

- easy bush walk on site
- 2 kayaks for guest use
- swimming & spa pools on site
- 2 outdoor dogs, Sam & Jip
- bird-watching; fishing
- tramping, hiking & walking
- sightseeing; bush scenery
- golf; boating; goldmines
- Coromandel day tour, guided by hosts, extra
- restaurants at Paku via ferry 2km drive
- restaurants in Tairua, 1km
- cafés, crafts & galleries
- Hot Water Beach, 20 mins
- Cathedral Cove
- gardens to visit
- Whangamata town, 26km
- Auckland airport private transfer, extra

125

© Friars' Guide to New Zealand Accommodation for the Discerning Traveller

WHANGAMATA
Bushland Park Lodge

Hosts Reinhard and Petra Nickel

Wentworth Valley Road, Whangamata *Postal* P O Box 190, Whangamata
Phone 0-7-865 7468 *Email* bushparklodge@xtra.co.nz
Fax 0-7-865 7486 *Website* www.bushlandparklodge.co.nz

4 bdrm | 4 enst | 1 pdrm Room rate $200–$350 *Includes breakfast* *Dinner, sauna, spa & treatments extra*

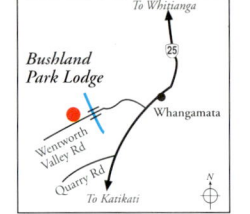

DIRECTIONS: From Thames, take SH 25A south to SH 25. Turn right to Whangamata. Then turn right into Wentworth Valley Rd. Travel 5km & cross ford. Bushland Park on right. Or from Waihi take SH 25 north.

Bushland Park Lodge and Nickel Strausse was a finalist in the 1998, 1999 and 2000 New Zealand Tourism Awards. The recently extended Lodge is set in two hectares (five acres) of native rainforest, close to Wentworth Falls, south of Whangamata. The Nickels have incorporated their German Black Forest Strausse as a winery style gourmet dining room suitable for special occasions. The ambience of the boutique five-table dining room, as well as the newly built lounge with open fireplace, is popular with guests celebrating anniversaries and birthdays. On request, the Nickels will send their complimentary eight-minute video clip on CD-ROM for special occasion planners. Pamper and special occasion packages are available.

Facilities
- 2 queen ensuite bedrooms with sunny balcony
- 2 super-king twin honeymoon suites with verandah
- hair dryers, heated towel rails, toiletries & bathrobes
- TV & video in suites
- phone, fax & email available
- tea/coffee facilities for rooms
- German & French spoken
- fully licensed Black Forest-style gourmet dining
- 3-course candlelit dinner, $75 pp
- special dietary needs catered, by prior arrangement only
- alfresco dining, open fireplaces
- Scandinavian sauna, $15 pp
- hydrotherapeutic spa pool, $10
- massage & beauty treatments

Activities available
- in-house gourmet dining
- various games on site
- glow-worm grotto in 2ha park
- rainforest on site & walk to waterfall nearby
- safe beach & township at Whangamata, 10-min drive
- all outdoor & watersport activities arranged
- bush walks & beach walks for all fitness levels
- 18-hole golf course, 5km away
- Health Spa Treatments: yoga, massage, sauna, spa pool, beauty treatments & relaxation treatments, extra
- off-season package: 4-day Coromandel trip with "Culture & Cuisine" theme see www.touchofeurope.co.nz
- hosted bush tour – see www.bushlandparklodge.co.nz

© Friars' Guide to New Zealand Accommodation for the Discerning Traveller

Above: The entrance to Bushland Park Lodge and Nickel Strausse with the accommodation facilities in the background.
Below: Two hectares (five acres) of native bushland feature a water-lily pond, glow-worm grotto and outdoor sauna and spa pool.
Opposite top: The Nickel Strausse is the boutique five-table gourmet dining room at Bushland Park Lodge.
Opposite bottom left: Bushland Park Lodge caters for all special celebrations, such as honeymoons, anniversaries and birthdays.
Opposite bottom right: The Presidential Suite, with an open fireplace, is popular for special occasions at Bushland Park Lodge.

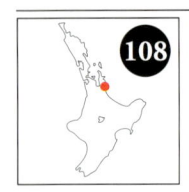

WHANGAMATA
BRENTON LODGE

Hosts Rosa and John Ashton

1 Brenton Place, Whangamata   *Postal* P O Box 216, Whangamata
Phone 0-7-865 8400   Mobile 021 120 0574   Fax 0-7-865 8400
Email brentonlodge@xtra.co.nz   *Website* www.brentonlodge.co.nz

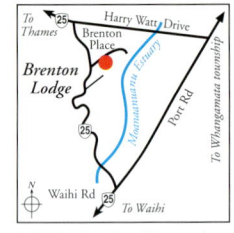

| 3 bdrm | 3 enst | Double $295 | Single $275 | Includes breakfast |

DIRECTIONS: From Thames take SH 25A south to SH 25. Turn right to Whangamata. Or from Waihi take SH 25 north to Whangamata. Turn east into Brenton Place. On the corner is Brenton Lodge on right.

Brenton Lodge features two contemporary guest chalets, Rose and Lavender Cottages, and also The Garden Room, which is adjacent to the house with its own private entrance. All are designed in keeping with the 1984 house. The chalets are built and decorated in country style with weathered timber, leadlight windows and pleated calico curtains. Set in a garden featuring mature native and English trees, the chalets are sited upstairs with sea views to Mayor Island. A gourmet breakfast is served in the privacy of guest chalets or alfresco on the balcony, the menu including crêpes, croissants and various egg dishes. A popular summer attraction for guests is the in-ground swimming pool and the spa pool house, set in the landscaped garden.

Facilities
- 3 separate upstairs guestrooms, with private balconies
- each room includes open-plan queen bedroom/lounge & ensuite
- tea/coffee-making facilities, microwave, fridge & TV
- crisp white cotton bed linen
- each suite includes bathrobes, toiletries, hair dryer
- sea views to Mayor Island from all rooms
- gourmet breakfast menu
- breakfast served in suite or alfresco on guest balcony
- fresh flowers
- separate guest laundry
- large garden with mature trees & pergola
- swimming pool
- aviary with doves
- off-street parking

Activities available
- fishing & diving trips arranged locally
- in-ground swimming pool
- surf beach, 1.5km away
- bush walks
- 2 golf courses, 9-hole & 18-hole – golf clubs available
- craft trail
- garden visits
- bird sanctuary
- restaurants nearby
- gateway to the Coromandel – beaches, native bush, regenerating kauri forests, historic gold trails, & glow-worms
- Hot Water Beach, 45-min drive away
- Hahei marine reserve, 45-min drive away
- Whangamata town 1.5km

WAIHI
WOODLAND PARK LODGE

Hosts Barbara and Ken Hogg

418B Woodland Road, R D 2, Waihi
Phone 0-7-863 8168 *Email* barbara@woodlandpark.co.nz
Fax 0-7-863 8596 *Website* www.woodlandpark.co.nz

4 bdrm	2 enst	2 prbth	Room rate $425	*Includes breakfast or provisions*	*Lunch & dinner extra*	*Self-catering*
			House rate $375–$475	Extra persons, $150 each		Minimum 2-night stay in house

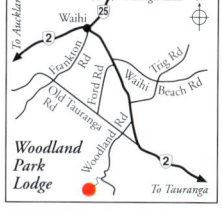

DIRECTIONS: From Waihi or Tauranga, take SH 2 & turn south into Woodland Rd. Travel 4km & turn right into 418B driveway. Travel 1km & take left-hand fork. Travel uphill & take middle fork to Lodge.

The philosophy of Woodland Park Lodge is to provide for guests' every need, from fine cuisine to health and beauty treatments in a relaxing environment. Set in a restful rural location, with views down the valley to the ocean beyond, Woodland Park is a 112-hectare farm with extensive native bush walks designed for rejuvenation. Guest are offered hosted accommodation in the lodge, or self-contained privacy in the separate Punga House, both with quality furnishings and attention to detail. Breakfast provisions are supplied in the Punga House, or breakfast is served in the dining room upstairs in the Lodge, with guests' choice from a comprehensive breakfast menu the evening before. Lunch, gourmet picnic hampers and dinner can also be requested.

Facilities

- Lodge: 2 super-king bedrooms, 1 with ensuite & spa bath, 1 with private bathroom
- Punga House: 1 super-king bedroom with double bath & double shower in ensuite; & 1 queen bedroom with bathroom
- hair dryer, bathrobes, toiletries, demist mirror & heated towel rails & floors in all 4 bathrooms
- 1-party bookings in Punga House
- full breakfast or provisions
- lunch, $20–$40 pp; dinner, $80–$95 pp; wine extra
- complimentary apéritifs; special diets catered for
- Lodge guest lounge opens to courtyard; Punga lounge to decking; both with Sky TV, music, games, books, artwork, bar & nibbles
- 2 full kitchens; phone jacks

Activities available

- in-house beauty & body therapy, extra
- large private classic car collection on site & tours
- gourmet picnicking; birdlife
- garden & bush walks on site
- seasonal farm activities on site
- beaches; watersports, 15 mins
- golf course adjacent
- guided forest treks
- Coromandel Peninsula tours
- heritage sites
- gardens open to visit
- steam train to Karangahake Gorge walkway
- open-cast working goldmine; historic Waihi, 10 min drive
- wine tours, collectables, antiques, art & craft trails
- murals at Katikati, 25 mins

KATIKATI, TAURANGA
FANTAIL LODGE AND GARDEN VILLAS

Hosts Harrie and Barbara Geraerts

117 Rea Road, R D 2, Katikati   *Postal* P O Box 1174, Tauranga
Phone 0-7-549 1581   *Email* info@fantaillodge.co.nz
Fax 0-7-549 1417   *Website* www.fantaillodge.co.nz

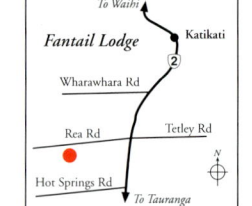

| 12 bdrm | 12 enst | 12 villas | Room rate $405 Villa rate: Double $790 | Includes breakfast Single $395 | Dinner extra Includes all meals |

DIRECTIONS: From Tauranga, take SH 2 towards Katikati. Turn left into Rea Rd. Travel 1.17km to Fantail Lodge on left. From Waihi, take SH 2 to Katikati. Continue 3km on SH 2, then turn right into Rea Rd to Lodge.

Fantail Lodge is located in the tranquillity of the countryside 10 minutes north of the City of Tauranga. The rural ambience is enhanced by the rich natural timbers used. The park-like setting inludes 16 hectares (40 acres) of gardens, rocky creeks and subtropical plantations, all with the dramatic backdrop of the Kaimai Forest Park. Many activities are available on site including the new spa facilities that are open daily. Fantail Lodge has an international reputation for its cuisine, which is recognised by membership in the prestigious French organisation Chaine des Rotisseurs. The Lodge's main building has 12 spacious suites overlooking the extensive gardens, while the 12 secluded garden villas emphasise privacy and comfort.

Facilities
- 12 queen ensuite bedrooms
- honeymoon suite includes spa bath & garden views
- 12 themed garden villas, each with either 1 or 2 ensuite bedrooms, kitchenette, phone, gas fire, heated floors, covered sundeck & covered parking
- phone in each bedroom
- hair dryers, toiletries & heated towel rails
- sunny breakfast room in Lodge
- lunch by arrangement
- licensed in-house restaurant
- laundry, $15 per load
- internet/laptop plugins
- full conference facilities
- French, German, Dutch spoken
- seasonal rates available
- on-site parking; helipad

Activities available
- wedding packages
- tennis court & pétanque
- in-ground swimming pool
- 7-day in-house spa facilities
- Katikati mural tours
- private gardens to visit
- arts & crafts trails
- Oddysey's nature walks
- subtropical orchards
- beaches – Waihi & Mt Maunganui
- trout & deep-sea fishing
- bush walks in Kaimai Range
- 3 golf courses, 2–20km away
- Katikati Bird Gardens
- native bird photography
- diving, canoeing, hunting
- full-day guided tours, $300 pp
- www.dreamers.co.nz

© Friars' Guide to New Zealand Accommodation for the Discerning Traveller

KATIKATI
MATAHUI LODGE

Hosts Kay and Trevor Mitchell

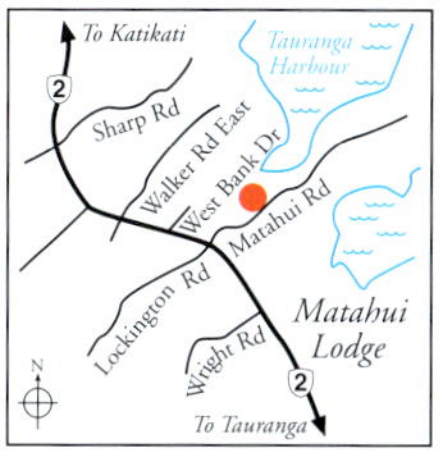

187 Matahui Road, R D 2, Katikati, Bay of Plenty
Phone 0-7-571 8121 *Mobile* 021 416 632 *Fax* 0-7-571 8121
Email info@matahui-lodge.co.nz *Website* www.matahui-lodge.co.nz

Room rate $325–$425

Includes breakfast
Lunch & dinner extra

DIRECTIONS: From Katikati take SH 2 south for 7.7km. Turn left into Matahui Rd. Travel 1.87km to Matahui Lodge on left. From Tauranga take SH 2 north, 500m past Morton Estate Vineyard. Turn right to Lodge.

North-facing with extensive rural views to Tauranga Harbour, Matahui Lodge is set in over two hectares (six acres) including a golf-driving range. Purpose built in 2001, the Lodge is designed for indoor/outdoor living, with a blend of contemporary and period furnishings and original New Zealand artwork. The two guest bedrooms include mini-bars with complimentary juice, wine and beer. A chauffeur's room is also available. Guests enjoy the in-house library and gymnasium, and private golf lessons with Trevor are popular. Membership privileges are offered at the local championship golf course. Matahui is fully licensed and complimentary pre-dinner drinks can be followed by indoor or alfresco dining. There is light plane or helicopter access.

Facilities

- 2 super-king/twin bedrooms, each with ensuite, tea/coffee, fridge with courtesy drinks, iron, phone jack & views
- wheelchair access to 1 bedroom
- 1 chauffeur's queen ensuite bedroom upstairs
- cotton bed linen; fresh flowers
- hair dryers, toiletries, heated towel rails & bathrobes
- laundry available
- breakfast served in dining room, alfresco or room service
- lunch indoors or alfresco, $20 pp
- 3–4 course dinner, $55 pp; licensed; complimentary apéritifs
- lounge with open fire, Sky TV, video, DVD & CD-player
- library upstairs; original NZ art
- email, phone & fax available
- on-site parking; helipad

Activities available

- in-house gym & massage
- outdoor fireplace & BBQ
- spa pool on site
- golf-driving range on site
- golf lessons from Trevor
- clay target shooting on site
- picnicking; scenic flights
- sea & freshwater fly fishing
- hot air ballooning
- restaurants, 3–20 mins
- Katikati murals, 4 mins north
- horse riding; surfing beaches
- bush walking; gardens to visit
- vineyard tours & wine tasting
- kiwifruit & avocado orchards
- hot mineral pools, 16 mins south
- Mt Maunganui, 30 mins south
- Tauranga airport, 30 mins south

131

© Friars' Guide to New Zealand Accommodation for the Discerning Traveller

WHAKAMARAMA, TAURANGA
LA HACIENDA

Hosts Julie and Terry Smith

26 Plummers Point Road, R D 2, Tauranga
Phone 0-7-548 1949 *Mobile* 027 280 1076 *Fax* 0-7-548 1939
Email albacora@clear.net.nz *Website* friars.co.nz/hosts/hacienda.html

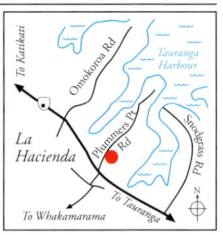

DIRECTIONS: From Tauranga, take SH 2 north through Bethlehem & Te Puna. At Whakamarama turn-off, turn right into Plummers Point Rd. Travel about 50m & take 1st drive on right to La Hacienda at end.

1 bdrm 1 prbth Room rate $250 Includes breakfast Lunch & dinner, extra

Guests have the exclusive use of the upstairs floor at La Hacienda. This suite comprises a queen-size bedroom, bathroom, and a spacious lounge, with views to Mt Maunganui, Tauranga Harbour and Mayor Island. Just a 15-minute drive from Tauranga City, La Hacienda is set in a mature garden surrounded by an avocado orchard, in a rural location. The guest lounge includes a bar and dining area overlooking the garden to the sea beyond. Guests are served a full breakfast upstairs, and offered à la carte dinner either downstairs with the hosts, or upstairs in the suite. Alternatively, there are restaurants at Bethlehem, just 10 minutes south. The hosts, Julie and Terry, speak Spanish and there is a South American influence at La Hacienda.

Facilities
- 1 queen bedroom upstairs with private bathroom, TV, writing desk & phone
- hair dryer & toiletries
- tea/coffee, nibbles, bar, Sky TV, video, CDs, books & desk in private guest lounge
- kitchenette, dining area & balcony from guest lounge
- children & pets welcome
- cotton bed linen
- full breakfast served in suite or with family downstairs
- lunch in suite, on patio, or downstairs with hosts, or picnics available, extra
- à la carte dinner, $45 pp; wine extra, fully licensed
- laundry, fax & email available
- Spanish spoken; guest parking
- courtesy passenger transfer

Activities available
- BBQ on site
- garden & orchard walks on site
- horse riding
- Tauranga Harbour; surf beaches
- avocado & kiwifruit orchards
- 18-hole golf courses
- native bush walks
- white water rafting; sailing
- deep-sea fishing & diving
- shops, bars, restaurants & cafés, 10-min drive south
- wine tours
- gardens open to visit
- swimming with dolphins
- White Island
- Tauranga City, 10-min drive
- Mt Maunganui & hot salt water pools, 20-min drive
- Rotorua City, 45-min drive

© Friars' Guide to New Zealand Accommodation for the Discerning Traveller

BETHLEHEM, TAURANGA
HOLLIES

Hosts Shirley and Michael Creak

Westridge Drive, Bethlehem, Tauranga
Phone 0-7-577 9678   *Email* stay@hollies.co.nz
Fax 0-7-579 1678   *Website* www.hollies.co.nz

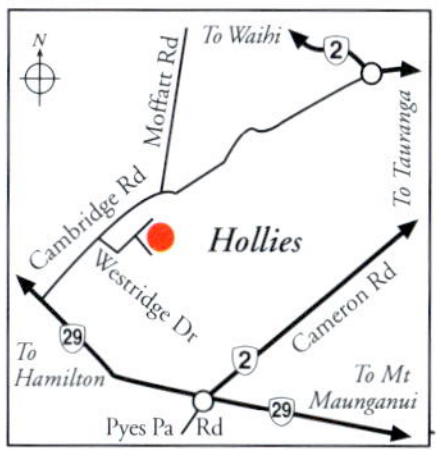

| 3 bdrm | 1 enst | 2 prbth | Double $120–$250 Single $95–$165 | *Includes breakfast Dinner extra* |

DIRECTIONS: From SH 2, turn into Cambridge Rd. Travel 4km, then turn left into Westridge Drive. Hollies on right. Or from SH 29, turn right into Cambridge Rd. Travel 2km, then turn right into Westridge Drive to Hollies.

Named after a family home in England, Hollies is set in almost half a hectare of landscaped gardens featuring roses, camellias, holly hedge, swimming pool with rock waterfall, gazebo and citrus trees. Hollies is a semi-rural contemporary home furnished in Mediterranean colours complementing tiled floors. The staircase sweeps up to the guest wing which comprises a spacious suite and two bedrooms overlooking the gardens. The suite includes kitchenette, bedroom, ensuite, lounge, balcony and guest entrance providing privacy suitable for honeymooners. Breakfast consists of a fresh fruit platter, home-made fare including muffins, bread and muesli, and a cooked option, and Shirley also offers dinner with New Zealand wine by arrangement.

Facilities

- 1 king/twin suite (honeymoon) with lounge, TV, kitchenette, private balcony, & entrance
- 1 queen & 1 king/twin bedroom, each with private bathroom
- toiletries, hair dryers, robes
- crisp bed linen
- luggage racks; garden views
- TV, wood burner in family room
- guest lounge with TV
- breakfast served alfresco in garden, family room, or suite
- dinner by arrangement, $40 pp
- teas/coffee, laundry, phone, fax, email facilities available
- fresh flowers
- children by arrangement
- Muffy, the white tabby cat
- courtesy passenger transfer
- secure off-street parking

Activities available

- pétanque/boules on site
- in-ground swimming pool
- croquet on site
- viewing Michael's Jaguar cars
- hot mineral pools, 2-min drive
- canoeing & kayaking, 5 mins
- wineries nearby
- climbing Mt Maunganui, 15-min drive away
- safe beaches
- licensed award-winning restaurants, 3–6-min drive
- deep-sea fishing
- jet boating; horse racing
- private gardens to visit
- potteries; walks
- swimming with dolphins
- 5 18-hole golf courses
- kiwifruit & avocado orchards
- shopping in Tauranga, 7 mins

BOSCABEL, TAURANGA
VAUCLUSE

Hosts Jan and Paul Campbell

11c Zapote Place, Boscabel   *Postal* P O Box 7033, Maungatapu, Tauranga
Phone 0-7-544 1279   *Mobile* 021 780 134   *Fax* 0-7-544 1279
Email vauclusetga@xtra.co.nz   *Website* friars.co.nz/hosts/vaucluse.html

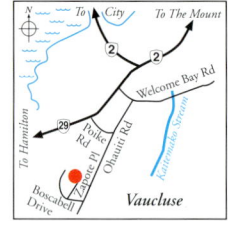

2 bdrm   2 enst   1 pdrm   **Room rate** $395   *Includes breakfast*

DIRECTIONS: From SH 29 or SH 2 turn east into Welcome Bay Rd. Take 1st right into Ohauiti Rd & travel 3km. Turn right into Boscabel Drive & right into Zapote Pl. At end, take right-of-way. Vaucluse at end on right.

Built in 1998 in Tuscan style, Vaucluse provides spacious accommodation in a quiet cul-de-sac. The tranquil garden setting provides views over a natural spring-fed pond surrounded by lush plantings and mature trees. Guests enjoy watching the native birds and wild ducks in their natural habitat at the large pond. A separate guest wing comprises two queen-size bedrooms with ensuite bathrooms and quality furnishings. Special breakfasts are served at the dining table or alfresco on the terrace along the front of the house overlooking the pond. On-site activities include swimming in the pool, pétanque and relaxing around the outdoor fireplace. Guests can also arrange fishing trips with the hosts, Jan and Paul, on their boat.

Facilities

- 2 queen ensuite bedrooms
- cotton bed linen
- hair dryers, toiletries & heated towel rails
- bathrobes
- fresh flowers
- tea/coffee & phone jacks in both bedrooms
- guest lounge with open fire, Sky TV & CD-player
- full breakfast indoors or alfresco on terrace
- 1 powder room
- library with writing desk; phone, fax & email available in library
- self-serve laundry
- guest terrace
- honeymoons & special occasions catered for
- off-street parking

Activities available

- swimming pool on site
- outdoor fireplace on site
- pétanque court on site
- ½ or full-day hosted boat trips
- surf beaches; golf
- swimming with dolphins
- white water rafting; sailing
- native bush walks
- deep sea fishing & diving
- bars, restaurants, cafés, 10 mins
- wineries & wine tours
- avocado & kiwifruit orchards
- gardens open to visit
- White Island
- Tauranga City, 10-min drive
- Mt Maunganui & hot salt water pools, 20-min drive
- Rotorua City, 45-min drive

Tauranga
Boscabel Lodge

Hosts Rosemary and Peter Luxton

98D Boscabel Drive, R D 3, Tauranga, Bay of Plenty
Phone 0-7-544 6647   *Mobile* 021 744 441   *Fax* 0-7-544 6647
Email boscabellodge@yahoo.com   *Website* friars.co.nz/hosts/boscabel.html

5 bdrm | 1 enst | 2 prbth | 1 pdrm

Apartment rate $150–$200
Suite rate $150–$160

Self-catering
Includes breakfast

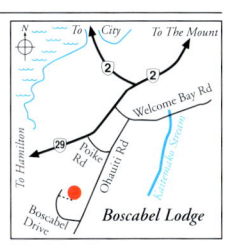

DIRECTIONS: From SH 29 or SH 2 travel towards Welcome Bay. Turn east into Welcome Bay Rd. Take 1st right into Ohauiti Rd. Travel 3km & turn right into Boscabel Dr. Towards end, turn right up a narrow right of way.

Boscabel Lodge, meaning "beautiful wooded area" in Spanish, is set beside a native bush walk and surrounded with avocado trees from the orchard that originally occupied the site. Guests are offered the choice of a spacious suite in the house downstairs, or two fully self-contained two-bedroom apartments with rural and sea views. The 12-metre solar-heated swimming pool and spa pool are popular on-site activities with vistas across the fields to Mt Maunganui which is visible in the distance. Continental breakfast is served in the conservatory, or in the apartments if preferred. Both apartments include a fully equipped kitchen for self-catering and there are many restaurants 15 minutes' drive away in the township of Tauranga.

Facilities
- 1 queen bedroom with ensuite, dressing room & 4-poster bed
- 2 apartments each with 1 king or queen & 1 twin bedroom, private bathroom, lounge, & full kitchen with dishwasher, fridge & microwave
- hair dryers, heated towel rails, toiletries & cotton bed linen
- children welcome
- complimentary laundry
- continental breakfast for all guests; served in conservatory or apartment
- phone, fax & email available
- German, Dutch/Flemish & French spoken by hosts
- separate guest entrances & terraces
- babysitting by arrangement
- off-street parking; garaging

Activities available
- 12-m solar-heated swimming pool on site
- in-ground pétanque court
- heated spa pool; table tennis
- avocado orchard on site
- native bush walk & stream, 2-min walk away
- private gardens to visit
- fishing & big-game charters
- surf beaches, 15-min drive
- restaurants, cafés & bars, 15-min drive
- diving & hunting trips
- choice of golf courses
- scenic flights arranged
- swimming with dolphins
- shopping in downtown Tauranga or Mt Maunganui, 10–15-min drive
- Rotorua City, 45-min drive

WELCOME BAY, TAURANGA
VILLA COLLINI

Hosts Margrit Collini and Andy Wurm

36 Kaiate Falls Road, R D 5, Welcome Bay, Tauranga
Phone 0-7-544 8322   *Mobile* 021 047 8394   *Fax* 0-7-544 8322
Email villacollini@pl.net   *Website* www.naturetours-nz.com

Double $110–$150
Single $80–$110

*Includes breakfast
Dinner extra*

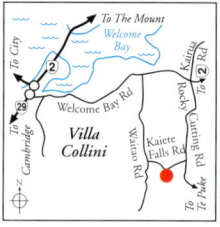

DIRECTIONS: From SH 29 or SH 2 turn east into Welcome Bay Rd. Travel 6.5km & turn right into Waitao Rd. Travel 5km then turn left into Kaiate Falls Rd. Travel 400m to Villa Collini on right.

With panoramic views from the open-plan lounge over the surrounding valleys to the ocean and Mt Maunganui beyond, Villa Collini was architecturally designed in contemporary style in 1996. Accommodation is provided for single-party bookings only in two spacious bedrooms, sharing a private ensuite. A special continental breakfast, including home-made breads, fresh fruit and Italian coffee, is served alfresco on the terrace or indoors, where guests can enjoy the sea vistas. Dinner with wine is also available by arrangement, specialising in Mediterranean and international cuisine. Guests can relax in the spa pool and sauna on site, or take a bush walk to the Kaiate waterfalls close by. Andy and Margrit also operate guided nature tours.

Facilities

- one-party bookings only
- 1 super-king & 1 queen bedroom share ensuite with bath
- toiletries & heated towel rails in ensuite
- tea/coffee, TV, CD-player, music, books, magazines & writing desk in lounge
- 1 powder room
- German spoken by hosts
- continental breakfast with home-made breads
- dinner with wine, $40 pp
- self-serve laundry, $5
- email, fax & phone available
- children welcome
- set on hilltop with extensive lawns & garden on 1.5ha (4 acres) grounds
- on-site parking

Activities available

- BBQ, spa pool & sauna on site
- boules/petanque & basketball courts on site
- hosted nature tours
- bush walk to Kaiate waterfalls close by
- hot mineral pools, 5-min drive
- golf courses, 10–15-min drive
- Mt Maunganui & Papamoa
- sandy east coast surf beaches
- restaurants & shops, 15 mins
- dolphin watching
- gardens open to visit
- White Island by helicopter or boat
- Tauranga airport, 15 mins
- kiwifruit orchards & adventure park, at Te Puke, 20 mins
- Rotorua City, 50-min drive

WELCOME BAY, TAURANGA
RIDGE COUNTRY RETREAT

Hosts Joanne O'Keeffe and Penny Oxnam

300 Rocky Cutting Road, Welcome Bay, Tauranga
Phone 0-7-542 1301 Email relax@rcr.co.nz
Fax 0-7-542 2116 Website www.rcr.co.nz

Includes breakfast & dinner Lunch extra
Off-season rates available

Double $950
Single $565

5 bdrm | 5 enst | 1 pdrm

DIRECTIONS: From south take SH 2 thru Te Puke & travel 10km. Turn left into Welcome Bay Rd. Take 2nd turn on left into Rocky Cutting Rd for 3km to Retreat. From north turn right at roundabout, then left at 2nd roundabout.

Ridge Country Retreat is set in native bush on 14 hectares (35 acres) of rural hills with panoramic views of Tauranga's coastline and farmland. Purpose built and opened in 2003, the Retreat offers five ensuite guestrooms, small conference facilities and a range of recreational opportunities including in-house beauty and body therapies. Ridge Country Retreat has been designed for guests with the motto in mind: "relax, reflect, replenish, recharge and revitalise". A full cooked breakfast is served in the dining room, then in the evening complimentary pre-dinner drinks and nibbles are followed by a five-course dinner served in the formal lounge, or alfresco on the private balcony. The Retreat is fully licensed and lunch is also available.

Facilities
- 5 super-king/twin bedrooms each with private bathroom & balcony
- cotton bed linen; powder room
- writing desk, TV, teas, ground coffee, mini-bar, phone, fax, email, iron & board in bedrooms
- bathrobes, hair dryers, toiletries, heated floors, heated towel rails, demist mirrors, double basins, spa baths with views in all ensuites
- laundry, $5; wheelchair access
- full gourmet breakfast menu
- 2-course lunch menu, $35 pp
- apéritifs & 5-course dinner
- guest lounge with open fire, Sky TV, DVD, CD-player, artwork, tea/coffee & fully licensed bar; library
- 2 Colourpoint Persian cats
- on-site parking; helipad
- local courtesy transfer

Activities available
- corporate functions catered
- outside open stone fireplace with BBQ on site
- 15m heated lap & spa pools
- in-house gym & massage room
- strolls along native bush walks
- sandy east coast beaches
- Bayfair shopping centre
- kiwifruit orchards
- golf club with rural views, 3km
- cafés/restaurants with Japanese, Thai, Turkish, Chinese, Italian, Mediterranean & NZ cuisine
- deep-sea fishing; harbour cruises
- dolphin watching
- jet boating
- Tauranga City, 15-min drive
- Mt Maunganui, 10-min drive
- Rotorua thermal villages & trout fishing, 40 mins south

Pyes Pa, Tauranga
Cassimir Lodge

Host Reg Turner

20 Williams Road South, Pyes Pa, R D 3 Tauranga
Postal R D 3, Tauranga   *Phone* 0-7-543 2000   *Fax* 0-7-543 1999
Email cassimir@xtra.co.nz   *Website* www.cassimir.com

Room rate $680–$1,000
Includes all meals & cocktail hour

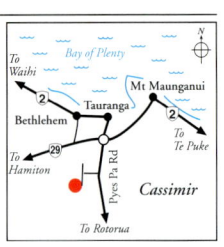

6 bdrm | 4 enst | 2 prbth | 2 pdrm

DIRECTIONS: From Auckland, take SH 2 to Bethlehem. Turn right into Moffat Rd, then left into SH 29. Turn right at roundabout into Pyes Pa Rd. Travel 12km & turn right into Williams Rd, then left to Lodge.

Originally built in 1890, Cassimir was totally redesigned in 1993, by the architect John Little of Ambientie, to feature early 19th-century colonial-style architecture, with Queen Anne-style turrets and dormer windows. Contemporary furnishings complement the native timber flooring, doors and furniture. Set in a private estate of 20 hectares with deer, sheep, cattle and horses, Cassimir offers a peaceful rural retreat. All meals are prepared by the host or chef. Five-course candlelit dinners specialise in fresh New Zealand seafood, lamb, venison and local wines. The East Wing comprises four suites and belvedere with expansive views to the Pacific Ocean, while the West Wing comprises two further suites, with similar attention to detail.

Facilities
- 6 king/twin bedrooms, 4 ensuites & 2 private bathrooms in 2 guest wings
- bath in 1 marble bathroom
- spa bath in bathhouse
- solarium conservatory
- spacious bar lounge with grand piano & feature fireplace
- children with nannies welcome
- sea views from viewing belvedere
- full country breakfast, with any cooked preference
- light lunches, picnic hampers
- 5-course candlelit dinner, with local wines extra
- liquor licence
- library with fireplace
- phone, fax & email available
- laundry available
- on-site parking; helipad

Activities available
- in-house board games
- lawn games – tennis, croquet, pétanque/boules
- telescope for star gazing
- native bird photography
- horse riding
- 9-hole pitch'n'putt
- trout fishing in estate stream
- bush walks
- wine trails
- mountain hiking
- deep-sea fishing
- white water rafting
- 2 golf courses
- shopping in Tauranga, 15km
- Mt Maunganui, 20 mins
- Rotorua lakes, 30-min drive
- Maori history at Rotorua

© Friars' Guide to New Zealand Accommodation for the Discerning Traveller

Mount Maunganui
Thornton Lodge

Hosts Judy and Bob Thorne

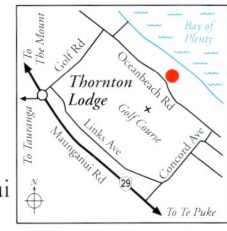

171 Oceanbeach Road, Mount Maunganui   *Postal* P O Box 4352, Mount Maunganui
Phone 0-7-575 5555   *Mobile* 027 273 0021   *Email* thorntonhouse@clear.net.nz
Fax 0-7-575 5554   *Freephone* 0508 846 763   *Website* www.thorntonlodge.co.nz

| 7 bdrm | 6 enst | 1 prbth | 1 pdrm | Room rate $450–$650 | Includes breakfast | Self-catering in apartment |

DIRECTIONS: From Tauranga, cross harbour bridge into Hewletts Rd. Take Golf Rd & turn right into Oceanbeach Rd. Thornton Lodge on left. From Te Puke, turn right into Girven Rd. Then left into Oceanbeach.

Located on the beachfront, Thornton Lodge offers guests a choice of four ensuite bedrooms, and a one or two-bedroom apartment. All the guestrooms overlook the ocean or adjacent top links golf course. Private access to Omanu Beach enables guests to relax and enjoy the watersports at leisure from the comfort of Thornton Lodge. Purpose-built in 1999 in Mediterranean style, the Lodge features classic Italian interior design with guestrooms both upstairs and down. A guest kitchen allows guests to be independent. The fully equipped self-contained apartments enable guests to self-cater. A full English breakfast is served in the dining room for the other guests, and restaurants are close by, within walking distance.

Facilities
- 4 super-king/twin & 3 queen bedrooms, all with bathrooms
- hair dryers & toiletries in all bathrooms
- beachfront self-contained apartment with private lounge & full kitchen
- Sky TV, phone, fax & modem in all bedrooms
- secretarial services
- conference facilities
- full English breakfast
- minibar, fridge & tea/coffee facilities in all suites
- tea/coffee in guest kitchen
- grand piano in lounge
- library
- spa pool for guest use
- courtesy passenger transfer
- off-street parking
- ocean views

Activities available
- outdoor spa pool on site
- surfing & boogie boards
- shellfish gathering
- fishing from beach & diving
- 7 golf courses
- kiwifruit country; farm parks
- game & deep-sea fishing
- hot mineral & salt-water pools
- dolphin swimming; safaris
- restaurants & shopping, 2-min drive
- cruises & sightseeing tours
- jet ski & boat hire
- bush & mountain walks
- scenic flights
- wineries; arts & crafts
- horse trekking; tennis
- white water rafting
- Rotorua, 40-min drive

Mount Maunganui
Augusta Lodge

Hosts Karen Gravatt and Keith Smith

198 Oceanbeach Road, Mount Maunganui
Phone 0-7-575 9677   *Mobile* 0274 822 177   *Fax* 0-7-575 3632
Email enquiry@augustalodge.co.nz   *Website* www.augustalodge.co.nz

| 6 bdrm | 5 enst | 1 pdrm |

Suite rate $340–$400
Apartment $220–$270

Includes continental breakfast
Self-catering

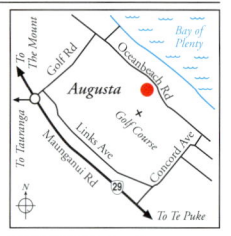

DIRECTIONS: From Tauranga, cross harbour bridge into Hewletts Rd. Take Golf Rd & turn right into Oceanbeach Rd. Augusta Lodge on right. From Te Puke, turn right into Girven Rd. Then left into Oceanbeach.

Augusta Lodge overlooks the prestigious Mount Golf Course with its eighth green and fairway only 20 metres away, popular with golf enthusiasts. Guests enjoy swimming at the white sandy beach of the Pacific Ocean directly across the road, or in the in-ground 10-metre swimming and spa pool complex. Built in 2000, in neo-American colonial style, the Lodge is set in a landscaped garden of palms, herbs and flowers, complemented by cobblestones and a natural rainbow sandstone pool surround. The guest lounge opens to the verandah with expansive views over the adjacent golf course. Accommodation comprises four spacious ensuite bedrooms, each with private balcony or verandah, and a separate two-bedroom self-contained apartment.

Facilities
- 1 queen & 3 super-king/twin ensuite bedrooms, each with balcony/verandah
- cotton bed linen, writing desk, phone, Sky TV, tea/coffee, fridge & air conditioning in bedrooms
- hair dryers, toiletries, heated towel rails, bathrobes, phones; corner baths in 3 ensuites
- children welcome
- laundry available
- continental breakfast in Lodge for suite guests
- 2-bedroom apartment with bathroom & tub, full kitchen for self-catering
- guest lounge with open fireplace & library
- private guest entrance
- secure off-street parking
- courtesy passenger transfer

Activities available
- in-ground 10m swimming pool
- spa pool & sauna
- exercise treadmill
- golf cart available; golfing access from site
- 6 golf courses in area
- white sand beach across road
- climbing the Mount
- game & fly fishing
- clay bird shooting
- award-winning restaurants, cafés & shops 5-min drive
- swimming with dolphins
- wine tour; scenic flights
- Kiwifruit Country
- animal farms
- Longridge Park; jet boating
- Vintage Auto Barn
- airport, 5-min drive
- Tauranga, 10-min drive

© Friars' Guide to New Zealand Accommodation for the Discerning Traveller

WHAKATANE
Motuhora Rise B & B

Hosts Toni and Jeff Spellmeyer

2 Motuhora Rise, Whakatane   *Postal* P O Box 553, Whakatane
Phone 0-7-307 0224   *Email* jtspell@xtra.co.nz
Fax 0-7-307 0541   *Website* friars.co.nz/hosts/motuhora.html

2 bdrm | 2 enst

Double $205
Single $190

Includes continental breakfast
Dinner extra

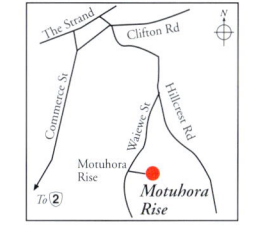

DIRECTIONS: From The Strand, turn right at roundabout into George St. Veer right into Hillcrest Rd, then turn right again into Waiewe St. Take 1st left into Motuhora Rise. 1st house on right at top of drive.

Nestled into the hilltops of Whakatane, Motuhora Rise overlooks the Rangitaiki Plains and Whale Island with the active volcanic White Island beyond. This purpose-built Bed and Breakfast offers an entire guest floor for peace and quiet, with only two guest bedrooms, an entertainment centre, and refreshment area. Guest privacy is ensured, with hosts Toni and Jeff living upstairs, accessible by intercom. Accommodation comprises two spacious bedrooms, each with ensuite bathroom featuring dual-headed showers. A hot tub/spa pool can be enjoyed on the guest decking under the stars. Toni serves guests fresh fruit with yoghurt, croissants or home-made muffins in the parlour, or alfresco. Dinner is offered, by request, and diets catered for.

Facilities
- 1 super-king/twin bedroom with wheelchair access, & 1 queen bedroom
- 2 ensuite bathrooms with double-headed showers
- hair dryers, toiletries, bathrobes & heated towel rails
- ceiling fans, chocolates & fresh flowers in bedrooms
- laundry available, $5
- fax & email available, extra
- continental breakfast served in parlour, or alfresco on guest patio
- 3-course dinner with lamb or venison & NZ wine, $45 pp
- cheeseboard on arrival
- refreshment centre with coffee, teas, fridge & microwave
- home theatre, VCR, DVD, satellite TV, CD, stereo
- off-street parking

Activities available
- outdoor cat, Tigger, on site
- outdoor hot tub/spa pool on decking
- fishing rods & golf clubs available
- half-day walking tours
- 4 local golf courses
- White Island volcanic tour
- surf beaches; scuba diving
- swimming with dolphins
- restaurants & shops, 10-min walk
- beach walks; bush safaris
- museums; gardens open to visit
- trout & deep-sea fishing
- charter boats & cruises
- Tarawera Falls
- 4WD adventures; hunting
- gateway to East Cape
- Rotorua & Tauranga, each 1 hr

Lake Rotoiti, Rotorua
Lakestay Rotoiti

Hosts Raewyn and Graeme Natusch

173 Tumoana Road, Lake Rotoiti, R D 4, Rotorua
Phone 0-7-345 4089 *Mobile* 0274 188 404 *Fax* 0-7-345 4089
Email lakestayrotoiti@xtra.co.nz *Website* friars.co.nz/hosts/rotoiti.html

3 bdrm | 3 enst | Room/Studio rate $150 Off-season rates available | *Includes breakfast* *Self-catering in studio* | *Dinner extra*

DIRECTIONS: North of airport turn east into SH 30. Travel 5.35km & turn left into pumice rd. Travel 100m, turn left into Main Race Rd, travel 1km & fork right into Tumoana Rd. Travel 1.73km to Lakestay Rotoiti on left.

One of just three lakefront sites on a secluded sandy beach bay, Lakestay Rotoiti offers two ensuite guestrooms as well as a fully self-contained studio only 26 metres from the lake edge. Built in 2004 to maximise lake views, Lakestay Rotoiti offers a peaceful quiet retreat, with both hosted and self-catering options available. The two guestrooms are upstairs in the main house, with elevated lake vistas, even from one of the ensuites, while the studio opens to a level grass lawn stretching to the lake shore. Guests have the use of kayaks, windsurfer and dinghy for exploring Lake Rotoiti, and bicycles are available for the bike tracks and forest walks. A full breakfast is served in the dining room or sunroom, and speciality vegetarian dinners are popular.

Facilities
- 2 queen ensuite bedrooms upstairs in house, with lake views
- 1 self-contained studio with queen bed, ensuite, writing desk, phone & kitchen, opens to garden & lake
- toiletries & heated towel rails in all 3 ensuites
- cotton bed linen, phone, TV & DVD in all 3 bedrooms
- TV, DVD, piano & wood burner in lounge in house
- continental & cooked breakfast for house guests, includes home-baked muesli, breads & muffins
- dinner by arrangement, extra – vegetarian speciality
- underfloor heating
- email, fax & phones
- on-site parking
- courtesy airport transfer

Activities available
- dinghy, windsurfer, kayaks & bicycles for guest use
- private beach access from site
- bush & forest walks from site
- many cycling tracks
- trout fishing
- hot mineral pools, short boat trip away
- glow-worm caves by night
- Redwood Grove, 10-min drive
- restaurants & cafés, 15 mins
- safe swimming, windsurfing, sailing & water skiing on lake
- Maori cultural activities
- gondola rides
- geothermal areas – mud pools & geysers
- gardens open to visit
- airport, 8km
- Rotorua CBD, 20-min drive

Hamurana, Rotorua
Panorama Country Homestay

Hosts Christine King and Dave Perry

144 Fryer Road, Hamurana   *Postal* 144 Fryer Road, R D 2, Rotorua
Phone 0-7-332 2618   *Mobile* 021 610 949   *Fax* 0-7-332 2618
Email panorama@wave.co.nz   *Website* friars.co.nz/hosts/panorama.html

3 bdrm | 2 enst | 1 prbth
Double $145–$185   Extra person $50   *Includes continental breakfast*
Single $110   Multiple-night rates available   *Dinner extra*

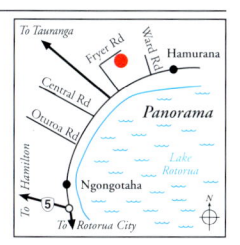

DIRECTIONS: Take SH 5 to roundabout. Travel north round lake through Ngongotaha, towards Hamurana. Turn left into Fryer Rd & travel 1.5km, turning right at end of bitumen. Take 2nd driveway on right to Panorama.

Panorama is named for its panoramic views over Lake Rotorua and the surrounding countryside. Sited on over a hectare of farmland, this architecturally designed cedar and brick home is set in landscaped gardens with private areas for guests to relax. Panorama features a private guest entrance and spacious rooms with native timber cathedral ceilings in the living areas. Panorama specialises in country hospitality offering dinner, with the emphasis on home-grown, home-made and local produce. Three-course dinners are served on the native rimu table in the formal dining room. Outdoor pursuits at Panorama include petting and feeding the sheep and working dog, playing a game of tennis, or relaxing in the therapeutic spa.

Facilities
- 1 super-king ensuite bedroom
- 1 super-king/twin bedroom with wheelchair access ensuite
- 1 queen bedroom with private bathroom & bath
- hair dryers, toiletries, heated towel rails & heaters
- cotton bed linen; fresh flowers
- children over 12 years welcome
- phone, fax & email available
- cooked breakfast, $15 pp
- 3-course dinner, $45 pp, with wine extra
- open fire in guest lounge
- Sky TV & wood fire in casual lounge
- laundry available
- courtesy passenger transfer
- on-site parking
- lake views

Activities available
- tennis court on site
- outdoor massage spa pool
- farm activities on site
- feeding pet sheep & dog
- fishing, boating on lake
- 3 golf courses, within 15 mins
- Maori culture, hangi, & concert
- geothermal attractions
- Hamurana & Rainbow Springs
- City restaurants, 15 mins
- Polynesian Spa
- private gardens to visit
- Skyline Gondola rides
- Agrodome
- Buried Village
- Redwood Grove walks
- Mt Tarawera
- Blue & Green Lakes

NGONGOTAHA, ROTORUA
HAMURANA COUNTRY ESTATE

Hosts Kim and Andrew Martin

415 Hamurana Road, Ngongotaha   *Phone* 0-7-332 2222
Postal 415 Hamurana Road, R D 2, Rotorua   *Fax* 0-7-332 2284
Email stay@hcestate.co.nz   *Website* www.hcestate.co.nz

12 bdrm | 12 enst | Room rate $295–$550 | Includes breakfast | Dinner extra

DIRECTIONS: From Rotorua take SH 5 north to Ngongotaha turn-off. Travel through Ngongotaha village & continue 5km around lake to Hamurana Country Estate on left.

With rural and lake views, this secluded country lodge is located just 15 minutes north of Rotorua City. The Tudor-style manor is set in six hectares (15 acres) of farmland and gardens and offers 12 ensuite bedrooms, each individually furnished. Kim and Andrew, the Kiwi hosts, enjoy escorting guests on strolls around the estate where horses, donkeys, sheep and pet pigs graze. The boutique restaurant serves fresh country cuisine prepared by the in-house chef, complemented by a select range of New Zealand wines. The large balcony features in the summer months for alfresco dining. Hamurana Country Estate is popular with independent travellers and small groups, or as an exclusive venue for conferences and weddings.

Facilities
- 1 super-king suite with private lounge & spa bath in ensuite
- 6 superior king/twin bedrooms, 4 with spa bath in ensuite
- 5 standard king or queen bedrooms, each with ensuite
- toiletries, hair dryers, bathrobes
- phone, TV, tea/coffee in rooms
- laundry available
- guest lounge with open fire
- chef's à la carte breakfast
- à la carte restaurant, extra
- lunch by arrangement, extra
- rimu bar & billiards room
- balcony for alfresco dining
- guest & luggage lift; covered portico
- conference room for 20
- courtesy passenger transfer
- on-site parking; helipad

Activities available
- BBQ areas on site
- heated swimming pool
- in-ground tennis court
- farm walks on site
- pétanque terrain on site
- in-house billiards table
- native bird-watching
- local trout guide
- relaxing in gardens on site
- golf putting green
- 6 golf courses, 3–15-min drive
- horse riding, 5-min drive away
- Hamurana springs & gardens
- Maori arts & crafts
- luge & gondola, 10-min drive
- Polynesian Spa, 15-min drive
- Hell's Gate thermal area, 20 mins
- redwood forest walks at springs
- Rotorua City & shops, 15 mins
- airport, 20-min drive

© Friars' Guide to New Zealand Accommodation for the Discerning Traveller   144

NGONGOTAHA, ROTORUA
Clover Downs Estate

Hosts Lyn and Lloyd Ferris

175 Jackson Road, Ngongotaha, R D 2, Rotorua   *Phone* 0-7-332 2366
Freephone 0800 3687 5323   *Mobile* 021 712 866   *Fax* 0-7-332 2367
Email reservations@cloverdowns.co.nz   *Website* www.cloverdowns.co.nz

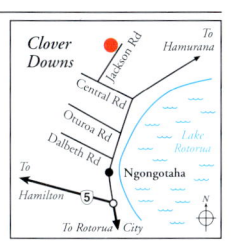

| 4 bdrm | 4 enst | 1 pdrm |

Double $195–$275
Single $180–$260

Includes breakfast

DIRECTIONS: Take SH 5 to roundabout. Travel north round lake, through Ngongotaha, on Hamurana Rd. Take 3rd left into Central Rd, then turn right into Jackson Rd. Travel 1.75km to Clover Downs on left.

Sited on a 14-hectare deer and ostrich farm, Clover Downs is a brick ranch-style home built in 1987 with views to Lake Rotorua. The guest wing comprises the super-king/twin Governor's Suite, super-king/twin Gone Fishing Room, super-king/twin Rose Room and king-size Going Flying Room. All four bedrooms have ensuite bathrooms, and open to outdoor decks with lake or farm views. Rural vistas to the lake can also be enjoyed from the private guest lounge. A brick courtyard extends to a viewing deck overlooking the garden and farm. Lyn serves flexi-time full breakfasts with her home-made preserves and a variety of breads, croissants and muffins, and a cooked selection, either in the family room or alfresco overlooking the farm in summer.

Facilities
- 1 king & 3 super-king/twin ensuite bedrooms with decks
- bathrobes, hair dryers, toiletries, & heated towel rails in ensuites
- 1 bath & dual basins in suite
- cotton bed linen
- TV, video, ceiling fan, iron & ironing board in all 4 bedrooms
- fridge, tea/coffee, bottled mineral water, cookies, fruit & fresh flowers in each bedroom
- full continental breakfast, or cooked selection, extra
- private guest lounge with open fireplace
- decking for alfresco dining
- phone, fax, email available
- children welcome
- laundry available
- small conference facilities
- on-site parking

Activities available
- pétanque/boules court
- deer & ostrich farm tour
- barbecue on site
- helicopter tours from site
- farm & forest horse riding
- 4 golf courses, 5–20-min drive
- clay-bird shooting
- guided fishing trips arranged
- traditional Maori hangi & Maori concerts
- city restaurants, 15-min drive
- watersports in lake
- 4WD tours & motorbikes – off-road, farm, bush or Mt Tarawera, 5–40 mins away
- gondola & luge
- private gardens to visit
- Orchid Garden & water organ
- thermal attractions
- Rotorua City shops, 15km

Ngongotaha, Rotorua
COUNTRY VILLA

Hosts Anneke and John van der Maat

351 Dalbeth Road, R D 2 Ngongotaha, Rotorua   *Fax* 0-7-357 5843
Phone 0-7-357 5893   *Local UK call phone* 0871 474 1573
Email countryvilla@xtra.co.nz   *Website* www.countryvilla.biz

| 5 bdrm | 3 enst | 1 prbth | Double $215–$235 Single $195–$215 | *Includes breakfast* Extra persons $85 each |

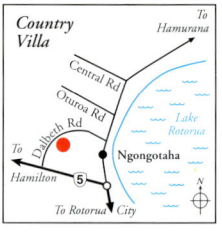

DIRECTIONS: From City, travel through Ngongotaha & over railway. Turn left into Dalbeth Rd & travel 3.5km to Villa on left. Or from SH 5, turn left after golf course into Dalbeth Rd. Travel 2.5km to Villa on right.

This large Victorian-style villa was originally built in Auckland in 1906, and transported in 1996 to its present site in Ngongotaha, Rotorua. Totally renovated and refurbished, Country Villa offers three ensuite guestrooms downstairs, as well as an upstairs guest suite for single-party bookings. The turret provides rural views from the upstairs guest lounge, and there is another guest lounge downstairs with garden and lake views. Anneke serves breakfast in the conservatory with croissants or muffins, pancakes and fresh home-made bread and yoghurt, fresh fruit salad, and omelettes, or ham, cheese and tomatoes if preferred. Recommended restaurants are only a 10-minute drive away, and Ngongotaha village is just five minutes.

Facilities

- 3 queen bedrooms downstairs with ensuites, 2 with baths
- 1 suite upstairs with 1 queen/twin & 1 twin bedroom, 1 private bathroom & bath
- hair dryers, robes & toiletries
- wheelchair access to 1 ensuite
- private-party bookings upstairs; children welcome upstairs
- fluent Dutch & basic German spoken by hosts
- full breakfast, served downstairs in conservatory
- BBQ available for guest use
- turret lounge upstairs with tea/coffee, TV & writing desk
- guest lounge downstairs with piano, log fire & tea/coffee
- complimentary laundry
- phone, fax & email in office
- on-site parking

Activities available

- native bird-watching in large gardens
- feeding lambs in season; farm & garden walks on site
- trout fishing, 3-min drive
- golf, 3-min drive
- jetboats at Agrodome, 5 mins
- Maori cultural activities
- bungy jumping & Zorb
- 4WD at Mount Tarawera
- restaurants, 10-min drive
- Ngongotaha village, 5-min drive
- Rainbow & Fairy Springs, 7 mins
- Gondola, glass-blowing 7 mins
- Hamurana Springs, 8-min drive
- Redwood Grove, 15-min drive
- white water rafting & glow-worms at Okere Falls, 15 mins
- Rotorua City, 12-min drive
- airport, 20-min drive

NGONGOTAHA, ROTORUA
NICARA LAKESIDE LODGE

Hosts Heather and Mike Johnson

30–32 Ranginui Street, Ngongotaha   *Postal* P O Box 327, Ngongotaha
Phone 0-7-357 2105   *Mobile* 021 838 412   *Fax* 0-7-357 5385
Email info@nicaralodge.co.nz   *Website* www.nicaralodge.co.nz

| 4 bdrm | 4 enst | 1 pdrm | Double $350 Single $300 | *Includes breakfast* 2-night minimum stay |

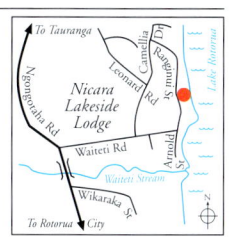

DIRECTIONS: From north, take SH 5 to roundabout. Travel north round lake, through Ngongotaha village. Turn right into Waiteti Rd. At "T" junction turn left into Ranginui St to Nicara Lakeside Lodge on right.

Nicara Lakeside Lodge, opened in 2004, is sited on the edge of Lake Rotorua, close to the Waiteti trout stream. Nicara is constructed from cedar, plaster and schist, and all four guestrooms overlook the lake. Local trout can be prepared for breakfast, served in the dining room downstairs, or alfresco on the patio opening to the extensive grounds and private beach on the lake shore. Guests have the use of kayaks and bicycles, and a private jetty allows access for fishing and floatplane flightseeing excursions. Nicara includes a fully equipped 25-seat conference room. Heather and Mike are happy to assist with local information on sightseeing, restaurants and conference needs. Rotorua City, with its many attractions, is a 12-minute drive away.

Facilities
- 4 king/twin ensuite bedrooms with panoramic lake views
- hair dryer, toiletries, heated floor & heated towel rails
- cotton bed linen, TV, phone, fridge & tea/coffee in all 4 bedrooms
- open fire, TV, video, DVD, CD-player, home theatre, piano, keyboard, games, artwork & books
- full breakfast menu can include local trout caught by guests
- patio for alfresco dining
- underfloor heating
- conference room available
- phone, fax & email available
- children over 12 yrs welcome
- laundry available, $10
- pets on site
- on-site parking

Activities available
- kayaks & bikes for guest use
- private beach & jetty
- assistance with activities/bookings
- Waiteti trout stream for fly fishing, 500m away
- fly-casting lessons arranged
- Agrodome, zorb & gondolas, 5-min drive
- several golf courses nearby
- watersports on lake
- restaurants, 5–10km
- traditional Maori hangi & Maori concerts
- geothermal attractions
- horse riding
- walkways & hikes
- private gardens & farms to visit
- scenic flights; hot pools
- Rotorua City, 10km

NGONGOTAHA, ROTORUA
WAITETI LAKESIDE LODGE

Hosts Brian and Val Blewett

2 Arnold Street, Ngongotaha *Fax* 0-7-357 2311
Phone 0-7-357 2311 *Local UK call phone* 0871 474 1575
Email waitetilodge@xtra.co.nz *Website* www.waitetilodge.co.nz

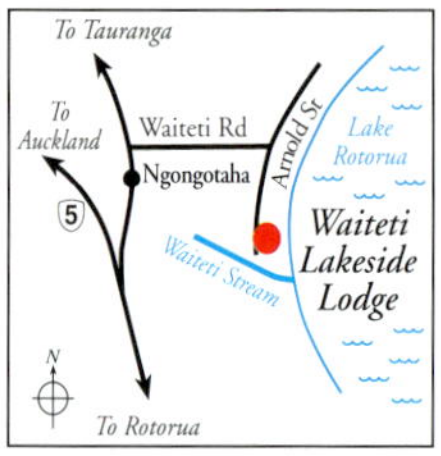

| 5 bdrm | 3 enst | 1 shbth | Double $150–$250 Single $140–$240 | *Includes breakfast* Multiple-night rates available |

DIRECTIONS: From Rotorua City, take SH 5 to Ngongotaha. Continue to Waiteti Rd on right. Travel along Waiteti Rd to "T" intersection. Turn right into Arnold St. Waiteti Lakeside Lodge on the left.

Right on the lake edge, at the mouth of the Waiteti Stream, Waiteti Lakeside Lodge has private access for trout fishing, with its own jetty. Brian and Val built their home from cedar timber and Hinuera stone, with pine wood panelling inside and native rimu stairs leading to the private guest floor. Neither traffic noise nor the characteristic Rotorua sulphur fumes intrude on the peaceful setting, with panoramic bedroom and balcony views over the lake to the city, forest and surrounding countryside. Rainbow and brown trout can be caught beneath the bedroom windows! Brian and his professional guides offer fly and boat fishing, and he enjoys taking guests on a scenic cruise to the Mokoia Island wildlife sanctuary with its endangered native birds.

Facilities
- 4 queen & 1 king/twin bedroom with heating, electric blankets & flyscreens
- 3 bedrooms with ensuites & TV
- 4 bathrooms with hair dryers & heated towel rails
- children over 10 yrs welcome
- spacious guest lounge overlooking lake, with Sky TV, video, pool table, library, fridge & tea/coffee facilities
- separate conservatory/breakfast room with log fire
- continental or cooked breakfast selection
- phone & fax available
- laundry available
- wide, sunny verandahs
- stream & lake views
- gardens featuring natives, rhododendrons & azaleas

Activities available
- guided boat trips to bird sanctuary
- year-round fishing on lake & in Waiteti Stream adjacent
- Canadian canoeing in stream & lake
- dinghy & outboard motor for hire
- guided fly fishing & charter boat with RPTFGA professional guides, equipment & licences provided
- restaurants & shopping, 5–10km
- Maori hangi & concert
- 5 golf courses nearby, golf clubs available
- 4WD fly fishing trips to remote streams
- hunting
- horse riding
- white water rafting
- helicopter tours
- gardens open to visit
- Rotorua City, 10km

NGONGOTAHA, ROTORUA
NGONGOTAHA LAKESIDE LODGE

Hosts Lyndsay and Graham Butcher

41 Operiana Street, Ngongotaha   *Phone* 0-7-357 4020
Freephone 0800 144 020   *Email* lake.edge@xtra.co.nz
Fax 0-7-357 4020   *Website* friars.co.nz/hosts/ngongotaha.html

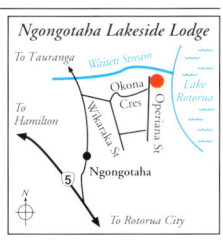

3 bdrm | 3 enst

Double $130–$190
Single $110–$170

Includes breakfast
Dinner extra

DIRECTIONS: From Rotorua, take SH 5 to Ngongotaha turn-off. Turn right & continue round lake. After railway crossing, turn right into Wikaraka St, left into Okona Cres & left into Operiana St. Lodge on right.

With lawn stretching to the lake edge, this contemporary home offers trout fishing in Lake Rotorua all year round. The quiet garden setting, free of sulphur fumes, is broken by the sounds of birds which frequent the sandspit. The upper floor of this two-storey home is designed for guests, including three ensuite bedrooms, dining room, large lounge and conservatory with panoramic views over the lake. Graham is willing to share his knowledge of fishing in the lake and at the mouth of the Waiteti Stream, only metres away, and enjoys cooking guests' catches. Fishing rods and canoe are available. Lyndsay serves a continental and cooked breakfast and is happy to provide an evening meal, by prior request. Activities can be arranged.

Facilities

- 1 super-king/twin, 1 king & 1 twin ensuite bedroom
- toiletries, hair dryers & heated towel rails in all 3 ensuites; 1 demist mirror & heated floor
- tea/coffee, electric blanket, TV & flyscreens in all 3 bedrooms
- guest floor with lounge, TV, video, CDs, library & fridge
- conservatory overlooking lake
- children over 12 years welcome

- continental & cooked breakfast in dining room
- dinner by arrangement, $45 pp
- guests' catches cooked
- central heating
- phone & fax available
- laundry service available, extra
- lake edge site & lake views
- BBQ on site
- off-street parking

Activities available

- fishing rods & canoe provided
- direct lake access from site
- trout fishing in lake & stream adjacent, all year round
- bird-watching
- guided fishing trips
- Ngongotaha village, 10-min walk
- agricultural Agrodome
- boiling mud pools & geysers
- thermal & volcanic areas

- Rotorua City, 10-min drive
- hot pools
- Maori hangi & concert
- gondola & luge
- white water rafting
- Redwood Memorial Grove in Whakarewarewa Forest
- walkways & tramping
- heli or float plane scenic flights

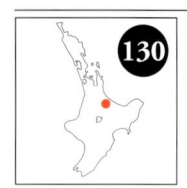

NGONGOTAHA, ROTORUA
THE HOME OF HARDY

Hosts Brent and Shirley Hardy

104 Parawai Road, Ngongotaha, Rotorua
Phone 0-7-357 4753   *Mobile* 021 959 192   *Fax* 0-7-357 4758
Email base@hardy.co.nz   *Website* www.hardy.co.nz

10 bdrm | 5 enst | 3 prbth
Double $195–$225
Single $175–$200
Includes continental breakfast
Cottage rate $210–$265
Lunch & dinner extra
Self-catering in cottages

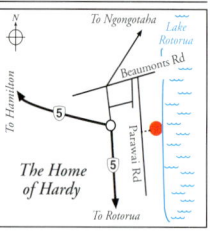

DIRECTIONS: From north, take SH 5 to roundabout. Turn left, then 2nd right into Beaumonts Rd. Turn right again into Parawai Rd. Home of Hardy on left. From Rotorua, take SH 5 to roundabout to Ngongotaha.

The Home of Hardy comprises a lakefront lodge and two self-contained cottages, built in 1995 from brick. Native rimu is used extensively on the interiors which creates a warm ambience. The hunting-fishing lodge theme throughout extends to the private jetty which provides lakeside moorings. Six guest bedrooms are offered within the lodge, with two further bedrooms in each cottage. Continental breakfast is served either in the main dining room, or alfresco on the deck beside the lake, or room service is available. Lunch or picnic hampers and dinner can also be provided by prior arrangement. The Home of Hardy offers a relaxing retreat on the shores of Lake Rotorua, both cottages and lodge set in quiet gardens with mature trees.

Facilities
- dinner by request, $60 pp, BYO
- lunch/picnic hamper, $15–$25 pp
- lodge: 1 twin & 3 queen ensuite bedrooms, 1 ensuite bunkroom with extra single bed, 1 single rm shares powder room/bathroom
- 2 cottages: each with 1 queen & 1 twin bedroom & 1 bathroom
- toiletries, hair dryers & heated towel rails in all 8 bathrooms
- TV in every bedroom
- single-party bookings in cottages include children
- complimentary morning & afternoon tea/coffee
- Sky TV, phone, fax, email
- 1 kitchen & 1 laundry in both cottages
- decking overlooking lake
- courtesy transfer
- off-street parking

Activities available
- spa pool on site
- in-house billiards table
- croquet on site
- boules/pétanque
- boat jetty & moorings on site
- private access to lake
- fly, boat & helicopter fishing year-round in lake, professional guide available
- Indian-style canoe available
- trout stream nearby
- golf matches arranged
- rabbit shooting by arrangement
- Ngongotaha shops, 5-min drive
- restaurants, 15-min drive away
- agricultural Agrodome
- public & private gardens to visit
- Rotorua City, 15-min drive
- airport, 30-min drive away

© Friars' Guide to New Zealand Accommodation for the Discerning Traveller   150

Above: Lakeside lodge showing main lounge and dining room, looking through folding doors across decking to Lake Rotorua.
Below: One of the two cottages, showing open-plan lounge, dining area and kitchen with doors opening into private garden.
Opposite top: The lodge exterior, looking across the lawn from the lake to the main lounge, showing the garden and gazebo.
Opposite bottom left: Interior of one of the two cottages, showing a queen-size bedroom with its warm native rimu ceiling.
Opposite bottom right: The private driveway leads past the two brick cottages, set in private gardens, to the lakefront lodge.

NGONGOTAHA, ROTORUA
ARIKI LODGE

Hosts Wendy and Robert Forgie

2 Manuariki Avenue, Ngongotaha   *Postal* P O Box 578, Rotorua
Phone 0-7-357 5532   *Mobile* 025 288 6642   *Fax* 0-7-357 5562
Email rgforgie@xtra.co.nz   *Website* www.arikilodge.co.nz

| 3 bdrm | 3 enst | Double $130–$195 | Single $110–$175 | Includes breakfast |

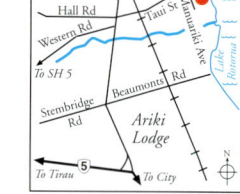

DIRECTIONS: From Hamilton, take SH 5 towards Rotorua. Just before Agrodome turn left into Western Rd. At "T" junction turn left, then 1st right into Taui St. Turn right again into Manuariki Ave. Ariki Lodge on left.

Set on the lake edge at Ngongotaha, with views across to Mokoia Island, Ariki Lodge offers accommodation for individuals or small groups. This single-storey home was built in the 1940s, but has been totally renovated to provide one suite with spacious ensuite, conservatory and private lounge, and two other guestrooms with two tiled ensuites in Italian marble and access to a spacious guest lounge. Breakfast is served in the dining room, or alfresco overlooking the lake. This lakeside accommodation is well suited for fishing from the Ngongotaha trout stream, just a few metres away, and the Waiteti trout stream, a short stroll along the beach. And yet the Lodge is sited only eight kilometres from Rotorua City Centre.

Facilities
- 1 suite with queen/twin bedroom, ensuite, spa bath, bidet, private sitting room, fridge, conservatory
- 1 super-king/twin & 1 queen bedroom, both with ensuites
- cotton bed linen
- electric blankets
- TV & video in both lounges
- tea/coffee facilities in each room
- breakfast served in dining room
- central heating
- hair dryer & toiletries in all 3 bathrooms
- fresh flowers
- phone, fax & email
- laundry available
- children welcome
- courtesy passenger transfer
- barbecue available on site
- off-street parking

Activities available
- pétanque/boules on site
- trout fly fishing adjacent
- Agrodome
- Maori cultural performances; Maori arts & crafts
- Rainbow Springs
- geothermal attractions
- lake cruises
- scenic flights
- Polynesian Spa
- restaurants nearby
- 7 golf courses
- white water rafting
- tandem skydiving
- gondola & luge
- gardens open to visit
- 4WD tours; horse trekking
- Ngongotaha village, 5-min walk
- Ngongotaha trout hatchery
- Rotorua City, 8km away

Mamaku, Rotorua
Rotorua Country Lodge

Hosts Sharon and Zak Love

691 Dansey Road, R D 2, Rotorua   *Postal* PO Box 129, Ngongotaha
Phone 0-7-332 5892   *Mobile* 027 486 4341   *Fax* 0-7-332 5891
Email sharon@reddeer.co.nz   *Website* friars.co.nz/hosts/rotoruacountry.html

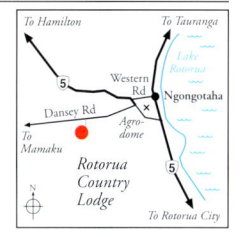

| 4 bdrm | 1 enst | 1 prbth | 1 pdrm |

Double $180–$234
Single $140–$168

Includes breakfast
Lunch & dinner extra

DIRECTIONS: From Hamilton, take SH 5 towards Rotorua. Turn right into Dansey Rd, travel 6.91km towards Mamaku. Turn left to Rotorua Country Lodge through gully for 1km. From Rotorua, take SH 5 for 8km.

A kilometre's drive via a dramatic gully of natural rock formations leads through the woodland garden to Rotorua Country Lodge. The homestead overlooks the extensive gardens, featuring rhododendrons in springtime, to the native bush and 100-hectare red deer and sheep farm beyond. Built in 1977, Rotorua Country Lodge provides a Deluxe Suite and Family Suite upstairs. The Lodge offers private dining downstairs in the conservatory or in the formal dining room, both with garden views. As a qualified chef, Sharon serves a menu of cooked dishes to complement the buffet breakfast, and lunch is available, using seasonal produce. Dinner can be arranged either as a family meal, or silver service, and special requirements and functions can be catered.

Facilities

- 1 Deluxe Suite with 1 queen/twin bedroom & ensuite
- 1 Family Suite with 1 king/twin, 1 queen, 1 single bedroom, & 1 private bathroom including bath
- cotton bed linen, writing desk, TV & tea/coffee in bedrooms
- demist mirror, bathrobes, toiletries & hair dryer in both bathrooms
- laundry available
- full breakfast in conservatory
- light lunch, $20 pp
- 2–4 course dinner, family or silver service, $45–$75 pp
- guest lounge with drinks, nibbles, TV, video & music
- central heating; fresh flowers
- phone available
- email & fax services
- on-site parking

Activities available

- garden & native bush walks
- pet red deer, Emma
- free 4-wheel drive tour to view deer, sheep & farm activities; wild game spotting & photography
- geothermal activity; Maori culture
- agricultural shows
- scenic flights; horse riding
- museums; maze
- variety of cafés & restaurants
- lake cruises; trout fishing; guided hunting; shooting range & clay birds
- bush hiking; hot pools
- bike riding; 4WD safaris
- 6 golf courses; gondola
- white water rafting
- jet boating; sky diving; zorbing
- Central Rotorua, 15km south

153

© Friars' Guide to New Zealand Accommodation for the Discerning Traveller

… 134

KAWAHA POINT, ROTORUA
KAWAHA POINT LODGE

Hosts Margaret and Tony Seavill

171 Kawaha Point Road, Kawhaha Point, Rotorua
Phone 0-7-346 3602 *Email* kawaha.lodge.rotorua@xtra.co.nz
Fax 0-7-346 3671 *Website* www.kawahalodge.co.nz

| 8 bdrm | 8 enst | 1 pdrm | Double $832–$1,040 Single $561–$702 | *Includes breakfast & dinner Lunch extra* | Double $640–$800 Single $435–$544 | *Includes breakfast Lunch extra* |

DIRECTIONS: From north, take SH 5 towards Rotorua City. Turn left into Kawaha Pt Rd, left into Koutu & right again. Travel to Lodge on right. From City, take SH 5 north. Turn right into Kawaha Pt Rd. Then as above.

Set on the shores of Lake Rotorua, Kawaha Point Lodge provides panoramic views across the lake to Mt Tarawera. A private jetty enables professional fishing guides to collect guests interested in fishing for rainbow and brown trout. Alternatively guests can enjoy relaxing in the half-hectare (one-acre) mature gardens which feature statues, terracing, a gazebo and 1930s stone grotto. Additional on-site pursuits include swimming in the pool and unwinding in the sauna. The Lodge is licensed and five-course silver service dinner can be covered in the tariff and served in either the formal dining room, the more intimate library, the garden room, or alfresco on the wide verandah. Each of the eight ensuite guestrooms also has garden or lake views.

Facilities

- 8 king bedrooms, each with ensuite bathroom
- 2 spa baths, 5 baths, toiletries, hair dryers, heated towel rails
- 1 wheelchair access bathroom
- cotton bed linen, fresh flowers
- air-conditioning; lake views
- TV, music, library, garden room
- laundry available, extra
- chauffeur/guide accommodation

- full breakfast
- picnic baskets & buffet lunch available, $25–$35 pp
- 5-course dinner; fully licensed
- vegetarian alternatives
- fridge, tea/coffee, home-made biscuits in each room
- phone, fax & email
- off-street parking
- private jetty; helipad nearby

Activities available

- lakeside setting & activities
- swimming pool & sauna on site
- mature garden, stone grotto on site
- pétanque & croquet on site
- private access to lake; lake cruises
- fishing guides & seaplane rides from private jetty on site
- trout fishing in lakes & rivers
- Rainbow Springs, Agrodome
- traditional Maori hangi & concert

- 3 professional golf courses
- Maori culture, arts & crafts
- helicopter & 4WD tours
- Polynesian Spa
- geothermal areas
- bush walks; horse riding; mountain biking
- gardens open to visit
- Rotorua City, 5-min drive
- airport, 15-min drive

© Friars' Guide to New Zealand Accommodation for the Discerning Traveller

Rotorua City
Regal Palms

Hosts Alison and Graeme Pike

350 Fenton Street, Rotorua City *Freephone* 0800 743 000
Phone 0-7-350 3232   *Email* experience@regalpalmsml.co.nz
Fax 0-7-350 3233   *Website* www.regalpalmsml.co.nz

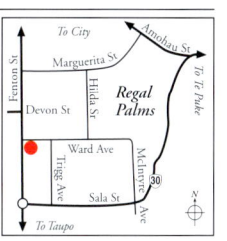

52 bdrm | 24 enst | 23 prbth | 1 pdrm

Suite rate $150–$260
Apartment rate $285–$320

Self-catering
Breakfast extra

DIRECTIONS: From north take SH 5 to Rotorua. Turn left into Devon St. Turn right into Fenton St to Regal Palms on left. From south, take SH 5 & veer right into Hemo Rd. Continue into Fenton St to Regal Palms on right.

Regal Palms is a city resort, centrally located within walking distance of cafés, restaurants and shops, and with many on-site activities for all age groups. The first 26 suites were opened in 2001, then the south wing added in 2003 comprising 15 more suites and three two-bedroom apartments. All suites and apartments include indoor spa pools and full kitchens for self-catering, although meals are available with local restaurants offering a charge-back and delivery service. In-house facilities include the Phoenix Lounge with open fire, bar and internet café, which is used as a break-out room for boutique conferences in the Kentia Room above. Guests enjoy alfresco dining, the heated swimming pool, sauna, gym and playing mini-golf or tennis.

Facilities

- 3 apartments each including 2 king bedrooms, 2 bathrooms, laundry & original artwork
- 17 suites, 5 with 2 bedrooms & 12 with 1 bedroom, all with 1 bathroom & extra sofa-bed/s
- 24 studio-suites, 18 king & 6 queen/twin beds with ensuites
- spa pool, hair dryer, toiletries, heated towel rails & demist mirror in each suite/apartment
- room service meals available; breakfast, $11–$21.50 pp
- 44 full kitchens for self-catering, 11 with dishwasher drawers
- 44 lounges each with phone, mini-bar, digital Sky TV, video, CD-player & writing desk
- 18 DVDs/stereos; 18 bathrobes
- air-conditioners; double glazing
- guest laundry, extra; children welcome; parking on site

Activities available

- 2 BBQ & outdoor dining areas
- heated swimming pool, sauna & gymnasium on site
- Phoenix Lounge, internet café & house bar opens to garden patio
- Kentia Room for boutique in-house conferences
- tennis court & mini-golf on site
- children's playground on site
- horse trekking; mountain biking
- restaurants & cafés, nearby
- Rotorua City, 2-min drive
- watersports at lake, 5 mins
- geothermal sights & pools
- Maori culture & hangi
- golf; gardens to visit
- gondola & luge; springs
- farm shows; trout fishing
- airport, 15-min drive
- Redwood Grove walks

HOROHORO, ROTORUA
TREETOPS LODGE

Hosts The Sax Family

351 Kearoa Road, Horohoro, R D 1, Rotorua
Phone 0-7-333 2066   Fax 0-7-333 2065
Email info@treetops.co.nz   Website www.treetops.co.nz

| 12 bdrm | 12 enst | 1 pdrm | Double $1,103–$2,171 Single $821–$1,890 | Includes breakfast & dinner Extra persons in villa $400–$450 each | Lunch extra |

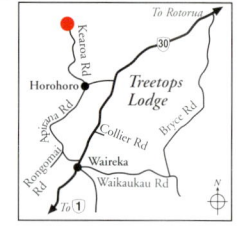

DIRECTIONS: From Rotorua take SH 5 & turn right into SH 30. Travel 10km & turn right into Apirana Rd. Travel 1km to fork & into Kearoa Rd. Travel 3.3km up unsealed road to intercom at 2nd gates to Treetops.

Located high in native bush on a 1,000-hectare (2,500-acre) eco and wilderness park, Treetops Lodge provides peace and quiet only half an hour from Rotorua City. Guest privacy is ensured with the siting of eight separate Villas, and a further four ensuite bedrooms in the Lodge. The chef provides a four-course menu for evening dining in the licensed dining room, and breakfast is served in the sunny conservatory or alfresco in the courtyard. Lunch is also available by arrangement. Small conferences, and weddings or other functions, can be catered for, either private, exclusive or formal as required. The many on-site activities include guided fly fishing, bird-watching, horse riding, abseiling and four-wheel drive experiences.

Facilities
- 8 Villas each with 1 super-king bedroom, ensuite, mini-bar, phone & lounge
- 4 super-king ensuite bedrooms in Lodge, each with phone
- cotton bed linen
- spa bath, double basin, hair dryer, toiletries, bidet, heated floors, heated towel rails & demist mirror in all ensuites
- children welcome
- full breakfast, indoors or alfresco
- lunch, $50 pp
- 4-course table d'hôte dinner, wine extra
- open fire, Sky TV, video, CD-player in all Villas & Lodge
- fax & email available at Lodge
- laundry facilities
- on-site parking
- helipad

Activities available
- hiking on site
- in-house massage
- fly fishing & tutorial, on site
- kayaking, archery & clay target shooting, on site
- horse riding; mountain bike riding, on site
- bird-watching & native animal spotting, on site
- eco tours, on site
- photographic safari, on site
- heli packages; cruises; golf
- sightseeing; cultural tours
- sailing & fishing in lake
- hot air ballooning
- tandem skydiving
- wilderness heli fishing
- big-game fishing; jet fishing
- water & snow skiing

© Friars' Guide to New Zealand Accommodation for the Discerning Traveller

LAKE TARAWERA, ROTORUA
PUKEKO LANDING

Manager Jennifer McBrearty

6 Ronald Road, Lake Tarawera, Rotorua *Freephone* 0800 ESSENCE
Postal P O Box 5231, Mount Maunganui *Mobile* 027 542 4202
Fax 0-7-574 8096 *Email* stay@essencenz.com *Website* www.essencenz.com

3 bdrm | 1 enst | 1 prbth

House rate $900–$1,200 for up to 4 persons *Self-catering*
Extra persons $100 each *Provisions & all meals extra*

DIRECTIONS: From Rotorua take Te Ngae Rd & turn right at the 1st roundabout into Tarawera Rd. Travel 13km then continue into Spencer Rd. Travel 7km & turn right into Ronald Rd. Travel 300m to Pukeko Landing on left.

Pukeko Landing is a self-contained cottage overlooking Lake Tarawera. North-facing, the accommodation enjoys all-day sun with a garden walk through native bush and exotic plantings to the private jetty. Here guests can leave on chartered excursions, moor their boat, swim and fish. Bird-watching is a popular activity in this secluded location, the frequent visits of the native pukeko bird to the lawn that stretches to the edge of the lake inspiring the name of the cottage. A fully equipped kitchen allows for self-catering, with provisions and a qualified chef available by arrangement. Lodge-style dining is available within easy walking distance, while the shops, restaurants and thermal pools of Rotorua City are only 20 kilometres away.

Facilities

- self-contained cottage
- single-party bookings
- 1 super-king/twin bedroom with spa bath, double basin & demist mirror in ensuite
- 1 super-king/twin & 1 twin bedroom share 1 bathroom
- hair dryer, toiletries, heated towel rails, heated floor & bathrobes in each bathroom
- cotton bed linen; fresh flowers
- full kitchen for self-catering
- basic or full provisions supplied
- qualified chef available
- all meals by arrangement, extra
- open fire in lounge; tea/coffee, Sky TV, video DVD, CD-player
- computer, printer, phone & fax
- self-serve laundry on site
- on-site parking; security gates
- helipad by arrangment

Activities available

- garden/bush walk & seating; bird-watching on site
- private jetty for swimming, fishing & boat mooring; row boat for guest use
- lawn area adjacent to lake edge
- petanqué on site
- massage by arrangement
- charter boat tours, pick-up from private jetty on site
- self-drive or skippered pontoons
- guided trout fishing in river, stream & lake
- scenic/fishing helitours
- scenic float plane tours
- art gallery & handcraft centre
- jet-skiing; cultural experiences
- natural hot pools; buried village
- guided tours of Tarawera volcano
- Rotorua City shops, 20 mins
- 'Hobbiton', 1-hr 20-min drive

159

© Friars' Guide to New Zealand Accommodation for the Discerning Traveller

138

LAKE OKAREKA, ROTORUA
OKAREKA LAKE HOUSE

Host Barbara Cook

Acacia Road, Lake Okareka *Postal* P O Box 10 044, Rotorua
Phone 0-7-349 8123 *Mobile* 021 797 049 *Fax* 0-7-3498 4990
Email enquiries@okareka.co.nz *Website* www.okareka.co.nz

| 5 bdrm | 5 enst | 1 pdrm | House rate $1,250–$6,500 | *Includes breakfast & dinner* *Self-catering available* | Lunch extra |

DIRECTIONS: From Airport, take SH 30 towards Rotorua. Turn left into Tarawera Rd. Travel to Holiday Park. Turn left into Okareka Loop Rd. Take 2nd on right into Acacia Rd. Travel to Okareka Lake House at end.

Set in secluded surroundings on the lake edge, Okareka Lake House was opened in 2003 to provide accommodation for guests in a peaceful retreat. Purpose built from timber and schist, with quality furnishings and fittings, the Lake House offers a super-king-size and four king-size ensuite bedrooms all opening to balconies overlooking the lake. Guests enjoy watersports on the lake, with a jet ski, kayaks and fishing gear available for their use. Float planes have acccess to the private jetty and there are many scenic bush walks in the area. The breakfast room seats 10 guests and dinner is served in the wine cellar or formal dining room, with a chef on call specialising in Thai cuisine. Guests can choose to self-cater if they prefer.

Facilities

- 1 super-king/twin suite with lounge area, office & ensuite with private spa pool, bidet, double basins & heated floor
- 4 king ensuite bedrooms
- bathrobes, double shower, hair dryer, toiletries & heated towel rails in all 5 ensuites
- 2 guest lounges, with open fire, tea/coffee, Sky TV, video, DVD, CD-player, games, artwork, books & desk
- flexible breakfast & dinner menus; licensed; wine cellar
- lunch by arrangement, extra
- full kitchen for self-catering
- 5 phones; fax, computers, printers & broadband internet
- complimentary laundry
- garaging; helipad; secure gate; courtesy passenger transfer
- central heating; balconies; cotton bed linen; flowers

Activities available

- hot tub, BBQ, outdoor furniture & water feature in landscaped park-like gardens
- in-house theatre with large screen projection
- outdoor illumination & audio systems
- fly fishing from lake edge; private jetty
- boat trolling
- kayaks & jet ski for guest use
- private safe swimming beach
- glow-worm caves
- windsurfing; water skiing
- sailing
- Okareka Walkway over wetland & farmland, 5.5km return
- Rotorua City, 15-min drive
- Maori cultural activities
- geothermal attractions – geysers, mud pools & hot springs

© Friars' Guide to New Zealand Accommodation for the Discerning Traveller

Above: The main super-king/twin bedroom includes an office and lounge area that opens to a balcony overlooking the lake.
Below: Okareka Lake House is located on the lake edge with views across the lake to Mt Tarawera and the surrounding hills.
Opposite top: Watersports are popular on the lake at Okareka Lake House, with a jet ski and kayaks available for guest use.
Opposite bottom left: The main super-king/twin bedroom has a spacious ensuite including a spa bath, double basin and bidet.
Opposite bottom right: The dinner menu is planned to suit guests' wishes, and a chef specialising in Thai cuisine is on call.

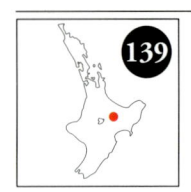

Te Whaiti, via Rotorua
Hukitawa Country Retreat

Host Lesley Handcock

279 Minginui Road, Te Whaiti   *Phone* 0-7-366 3952
Postal Private Bag 3054, Te Whaiti, via Rotorua   *Fax* 0-7-366 3950
Email lesley@hukitawa.co.nz   *Website* www.hukitawa.co.nz

3 bdrm | 3 enst | 1 pdrm   Double $390–$410   Single $280   *Includes all meals*

DIRECTIONS: From Rotorua, take SH 5 south to SH 38. Turn left & travel 60km to Te Whaiti. Turn right into Minginui Rd. Travel 2.79km to Hukitawa, on left. Travel 2.4km up drive.

Nestled in the Whirinaki Valley, Hukitawa is a rural retreat in a New Zealand home set on 80 hectares (200 acres) of farmland featuring deer, sheep and cattle. Nearby is the well-known Whirinaki podocarp forest where guests enjoy exploring the native bush, streams and waterfalls. Hukitawa is elevated above the surrounding farmland with views across the duck pond to the bush-clad Ikawhenua Ranges. Accommodation comprises three ensuite guestrooms, and an extra room for guides, pilots or children. From the privacy of the indoor spa pool, guests can enjoy panoramic views or star-gaze through the clear glass roof in the evening. All meals are included in the tariff, featuring New Zealand home-made cuisine and fresh produce served indoors or alfresco.

Facilities

- 1 super-king/twin, 1 king/twin & 1 double bedroom; 3 ensuites
- 1 extra king/twin bedroom & 1 shared bathroom for guides, pilots, or children
- hair dryers, heated towel rails, bathrobes & toiletries in ensuites
- open fire in lounge; tea/coffee, Sky TV, video & NZ art
- laundry, phone, fax & email available for guests
- full cooked breakfast served in dining room or patio
- light lunch or picnic wherever guests choose
- à la carte dinner, NZ style including roast meats, home-grown veges & BBQ
- cotton bed linen; flowers
- garaging; helicopter access on site; airstrip 7km
- courtesy passenger transfer

Activities available

- indoor spa pool on site
- clay-target shooting on site
- garden & farm walks on site
- bird-watching on site – native birds, pond with ducks, stilts, herons & shags
- observing farming activities on neighbouring farmland
- painting & photography sites
- trout fishing, guide available
- guided horse riding
- 4WD tours, professional guide
- bush walking in Whirinaki podocarp forest 10km away, guided or independent, overnight trips available by prior arrangement
- Maori culture
- river rafting & kayaking, 25km
- Rotorua, 70 mins north; Lake Taupo, 80 mins south

© Friars' Guide to New Zealand Accommodation for the Discerning Traveller

Hamilton
Anlaby Manor

Hosts Halina and Pryme Footner

91 Newell Road, R D 3, Hamilton
Phone 0-7-856 7264 *Email* anlaby.manor@xtra.co.nz
Fax 0-7-856 5323 *Website* www.anlabymanor.co.nz

Room rate $180–$200
Cottage rate $220

Includes breakfast
Dinner extra

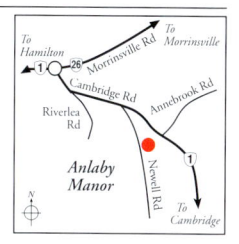

DIRECTIONS: From Hamilton, take SH 1 towards Cambridge. Turn right into Newell Rd. From Cambridge, take SH 1 towards Hamilton. Travel 12km, then turn left into Newell Rd. Continue 1km to Anlaby on left.

Built in 1971 as a replica Yorkshire stately home after a Sir Edwin Lutyens design, Anlaby Manor features a large central staircase replicated from that in *Gone With the Wind*. A formal English garden is planted round a century-old pin oak, with neo-Roman statuary, fountains, wishing well, box hedging, old roses and cottage plants. Leadlight windows are complemented by antique furniture, heirloom china and silver and English-style oil paintings. Families or honeymooners are catered for in a self-contained secluded cottage, which is timber-lined and furnished in blue and white. A full cooked breakfast is served at times to suit the guests, and gourmet dinners are by arrangement. Guests enjoy the billiards room with its full-size table.

Facilities

- 2 queen ensuite bedrooms & 2 double bedrooms with 1 share bathroom in Manor
- self-contained cottage with 1 queen & 2 single beds & ensuite bathroom
- children welcome in cottage; cot supplied
- bathrobes, hair dryers & extra towels supplied
- wheelchair access to 1 ensuite
- full cooked breakfast
- complimentary apéritifs, hors d'oeuvres & afternoon tea
- 4-course dinner, $60 pp
- formal dining room seats 38
- video, fax & email available
- small conference & corporate meeting facilities
- full-size billiards table
- 1ha formal English garden

Activities available

- in-ground swimming pool, sauna
- tennis court, croquet lawn on site
- riverboat cruises, 5-min drive
- 2 golf courses, 5-min drive
- river, lake & rose garden walks, 5-min drive away
- Hamilton Gardens, 5-min drive
- private garden visits; farm tours
- Hamilton City, 10-min drive
- restaurants, 5- & 10-min drive
- antiques & craft shops in English-style Cambridge township, 12 mins south
- horse studs at Cambridge
- Mystery Creek Field-days in June, 5-min drive
- Waikato University, 5 mins
- Hamilton Airport, 5 mins
- Waitomo Caves, Rotorua City, Auckland City, each 1½-hour drive away

163

© Friars' Guide to New Zealand Accommodation for the Discerning Traveller

MATANGI, HAMILTON
MATANGI OAKS

Hosts Gloria and Clyde Morriss

634 Marychurch Road, R D 4, Hamilton
Phone 0-7-829 5765   *Mobile* 025 242 7429   *Fax* 0-7-829 5765
Email matangi.oaks@xtra.co.nz   *Website* www.matangioaks.co.nz

3 bdrm | 1 enst | 1 prbth

Double $130–$145
Single $100

Includes breakfast
Dinner extra

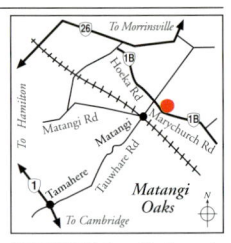

DIRECTIONS: From Hamilton, take SH 1 south towards Cambridge. At Tamahere cross-roads, turn left into Tauwhare Rd. Cross railway line at Matangi & turn right into Marychurch Rd. Matangi Oaks on left.

Matangi Oaks is set in spacious gardens on 15 hectares with rural views, midway between Hamilton and Cambridge. Built in 1997, this two-storey home offers two upstairs bedrooms with one private bathroom, as well as a queen ensuite bedroom downstairs with underfloor heating. Gloria enjoys cooking, using fresh locally grown produce complemented by fine New Zealand wines. Matangi Oaks is surrounded by thoroughbred breeding stud farms, enabling guests to visit some of the country's famous horse studs. Mystery Creek is also nearby, where the annual agricultural field-days are held each June, with major indoor sports other times. Other local features include a well-known sporting memories collection and a military museum.

Facilities
- 1 queen bedroom with ensuite
- 1 super-king/twin bedroom (with 1 extra single bed available) & 1 double bedroom share 1 bathroom in single party, with bathrobes
- hair dryers, heated floor, heated towel rails & toiletries
- complimentary laundry
- fresh flowers in bedrooms
- complimentary tea & coffee
- TV in bedrooms & lounge
- full breakfast served in dining room or alfresco on patio
- dinner with wine, $45 pp
- central heating
- powder room
- private guest lounge
- email, fax & phone available
- unsuitable for pets
- children over 11 yrs welcome
- on-site parking

Activities available
- historic military museum
- sports memorabilia
- horse stud visits
- Hot Air Balloon Festival each April
- gardens open to visit
- Waikato University, 10 mins
- Mystery Creek, 10-min drive
- airport, 10-min drive
- Hamilton City, 10-min drive
- restaurants, 10-min drive
- 9 golf courses nearby
- Cambridge antique shops & activities, 10-min drive
- Waitomo Caves, 1-hr drive
- Raglan Beach for surfing & swimming, 1-hour drive
- Mount Maunganui, 1 hour
- Tauranga, 1-hour drive
- Rotorua, 1-hour drive

© Friars' Guide to New Zealand Accommodation for the Discerning Traveller

CAMBRIDGE
THORNTON HOUSE

Hosts Christine Manson and David Cowley

2 Thornton Road, Cambridge — *Phone* 0-7-827 7567
Postal P O Box 1037, Cambridge — *Fax* 0-7-827 7568
Email b&b@thorntonhouse.co.nz — *Website* www.thorntonhouse.co.nz

2 bdrm / 2 enst

Double $170–$210
Single $150–$175

Includes breakfast
Lunch & dinner extra

DIRECTIONS: Take SH 1 to Cambridge. On Victoria St, opposite St Andrews Church, turn right into Thornton Rd. Thornton House is 1st property on the left corner.

Originally built in 1902, this Queen Anne-style villa features a Marseilles tiled roof and was named "Orongo" by its first owners. Renamed, restored and renovated, Thornton House provides two ensuite guestrooms, the larger Garden Room opening to a private verandah. Set in landscaped gardens with mature trees and an abundance of roses, it is a peaceful location just minutes from the centre of Cambridge where guests can enjoy the antiques, craft shops and restaurants. A full breakfast menu is offered with breakfast served either in the guestrooms or alfresco on the sunporch, verandah or in the garden. Lunches and dinners are also available by prior arrangement. An old moggie and two Burmese cats complete the family.

Facilities

- 2 queen ensuite bedrooms
- hair dryer, toiletries, heated towel rails & bathrobes
- 1 bath in Garden Room ensuite
- cotton bed linen
- tea/coffee, home-baked biscuits, TV & radio/CD/cassette-player in bedrooms
- lounge with open fire, Sky TV, video, CD-player, music, books, magazines & verandah
- full gourmet breakfast
- lunch or dinner by prior arrangement, extra
- picnic baskets available
- central heating
- fresh flowers
- phone, fax & email
- wine list available
- off-street parking
- courtesy passenger transfer

Activities available

- Burmese cats on site
- pétanque/boules on site
- wine cellar
- small weddings & honeymoons hosted
- therapeutic massage by arrangement
- relaxing in garden on site
- antiques & craft shops
- Lake Te Koutu opposite
- farm & horse stud tours
- greyhound & harness racing
- restaurants nearby
- rowing & canoeing on Lake Karapiro
- garden tours
- golfing
- Mystery Creek Field-days
- Hamilton City, 20-min drive
- airport, 15-min drive

165

© Friars' Guide to New Zealand Accommodation for the Discerning Traveller

Cambridge
Huntington Stables Retreat

Hosts Carol and Colin Townshend

106 Maungakawa Road, Cambridge *Postal* P O Box 177, Cambridge
Phone 0-7-823 4120 *Mobile* 027 441 1425 *Fax* 0-7-823 4126
Email hunt.stables@xtra.co.nz *Website* www.huntington.co.nz

2 bdrm 2 prbth

Double $390
Single $350

Includes breakfast provisions
Self-catering

DIRECTIONS: Take SH 1 south from Hamilton. At Cambridge, cross Victoria Rd into Thornton Rd. Travel to Robinson Rd. Continue right on Thornton Rd 2km. Turn left into Maungakawa Rd. Stables on right.

Huntington Stables Retreat accommodation is located adjacent to the Maungakawa Scenic Reserve, just five minutes from Cambridge village. The stables-style accommodation complex comprises two spacious self-contained studios. These open onto decks with rural vistas overlooking the pétanque court and horse paddocks beyond where Carol's Arab horse Springbok grazes. The South Stable is designed with romantic Caribbean-style bed linen in the king-size bedroom and the North Stable has a super-king/twin bedroom with paisley bed linen. A claw-foot bath is included in each studio's bathroom and both kitchens are fully equipped for self-catering and feature local pottery. Honeymooners enjoy a complimentary bottle of champagne.

Facilities
- 2 spacious self-contained studios
- South Stable: 1 king bedroom & Caribbean-style bed linen
- North Stable: 1 super-king/twin bedroom & paisley bed linen
- private bathroom in each studio with claw-foot bath, hair dryers, toiletries, robes & heated floors
- lounge in each studio with tea/coffee, nibbles, bar, Sky TV, video, CD-player, NZ artwork & books
- fully self-catering kitchen & dining area in each studio, with lavish provisions, utensils & local pottery; or breakfast by request
- wine cellar on site with wine for sale & BYO accepted
- central heating
- complimentary laundry
- 2 private guest entrances
- courtesy passenger transfer

Activities available
- swimming & spa pools
- sauna & wine cellar on site
- barbecue & pétanque
- horses in adjacent paddock
- Maungakawa Scenic Reserve
- golf courses within 5km
- Cambridge village, 5 mins
- bush walk tracks
- Lake Karapiro for fishing, waterskiing & kayaking
- restaurants, 5-min drive
- jet boat & horse stud tours
- antique stores
- tennis & squash courts nearby
- harness racing
- Hamilton City, 20-min drive
- Airport, 15-min drive away
- *Waipa Delta* river boat tours
- Waitomo Glow-worm Caves, 30-min drive away

© Friars' Guide to New Zealand Accommodation for the Discerning Traveller

LAKE KARAPIRO
MAUNGATAUTARI LODGE

Hosts Christine and Peter Scoular

844 Maungatautari Road, Lake Karapiro   *Postal* P O Box 1060, Cambridge
Phone 0-7-827 2220   *Mobile* 021 866 873   *Fax* 0-7-827 2221
Email reservations@malodge.com   *Website* www.malodge.com

| 7 bdrm | 7 enst | 1 pdrm | Double $450–$900 Single $350–$570 | Includes breakfast & dinner Packages available   Lunch extra |

DIRECTIONS: From Cambridge, take SH 1 south for 6km towards Karapiro Village. Turn right across dam, then left into Maungatautari Rd. Travel 3km to Maungatautari Lodge on right.

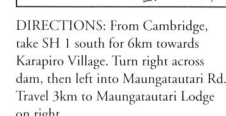

Set in two and a half hectares (six acres) of park-like gardens on a fertile 16-hectare farm, Maungatautari Lodge was purpose-built in 2002. On-site guest activities include a swimming pool, pétanque court, and a chip and putt golf area, with views of Lake Karapiro beyond. Upstairs in the Lodge are four guest suites with private balconies, and in the garden are three guest villas. All are individually styled with a super-king/twin bedroom, ensuite bathroom with double spa bath, walk-in dressing room and guest-controlled heating and air-conditioning. A fully equipped conference room can cater for 20 people. Apéritifs are served in the lounge, followed by table d'hôte fine dining prepared by the chef. A hearty breakfast is served in the conservatory.

Facilities
- 4 super-king/twin suites
- 3 super-king/twin villas
- cotton bed linen, dressing room, writing desk, phone, TV, fridge, minibar & tea/coffee in all suites
- spa baths, hair dryers, bathrobes, heated towel rails & toiletries
- wheelchair access to all villas
- guest lounge with open fire, Sky TV, music, writing desk & books
- email & fax available; fresh flowers
- full cooked & continental breakfast in conservatory
- lunch by request, extra
- 4-course dinner with home-grown veges, NZ organic beef, lamb, fish or game
- central heating throughout
- French spoken by hosts
- courtesy passenger transfer
- on-site parking

Activities available
- in-ground swimming pool
- pétanque/boules on site
- chip & putt mini-golf
- croquet lawn on site
- 2.5ha (6-acre) park-like garden on 16ha farm
- massage, hair dressers & facials by arrangement
- Lake Karapiro adjacent
- stud tours; team building
- 6 golf courses within 30 mins
- fishing trips; canoeing
- gardens open to visit
- Maungatautari Mountain Reserve
- Cambridge, 5-min drive
- Karapiro Dam, 2-min drive
- Rotorua & Tauranga, 1 hour
- Waitomo Caves, 1-hr drive
- Lake Taupo, 1½-hour drive

Tirau, Waikato
Oraka Deer Park

Hosts Linda and Ian Scott

71 Bayly Road, R D 1, Tirau *Phone* 0-7-883 1382
Freephone 0800 835 838 *Mobile* 027 473 2657 *Fax* 0-7 883 1384
Email oraka@xtra.co.nz *Website* www.oraka-deer.co.nz

2 bdrm | 1 prbth

Cottage rate $180 for 2 persons
Extra persons $15 each

Self-catering
All meals extra

DIRECTIONS: From Hamilton take SH 1 or from Rotorua take SH 5 to Tirau. Take SH 27 north for 3km. Turn right into Langlands Rd. Travel 2km & turn left into Bayly Rd. Travel 710m to Oraka Deer Park on left.

The cottage on Oraka Park Deer Farm is fully self-contained with a well equipped kitchen for self-catering. Farm vistas from every window ensure a tranquil stay on this 56-hectare farm. The 48 hectares of wapiti deer provide year-round interest for guests, from the growth of deer velvet in spring to the birth of fawns in summer and bottle feeding pet fawns, then the noisy mating roar of the stags in autumn. In addition there are walks in the large established garden, through the eight-hectare pine forest and beside Oraka Stream that borders the farm. The country cottage comprises two bedrooms, bathroom, fully appointed kitchen, lounge area and laundry. It is suitable for honeymooners or families, and meals can be catered by prior arrangement.

Facilities

- private-party bookings only
- 1 self-contained cottage
- 1 super-king & 1 double/twin bedroom in cottage
- 1 private bathroom with hair dryer & heated towel rails
- cotton bed linen
- lounge with TV & video
- full kitchen for self-catering
- guest phone & laundry
- breakfast, $15 pp
- lunch & dinner by arrangement, extra
- children's books, toys & playground available
- fresh flowers
- wheelchair access
- children welcome
- on-site parking; helipad
- swimming & spa pools

Activities available

- walks in over 1ha (3 acres) garden, with 70-yr-old trees & roses
- tour of Deer Park; feeding deer
- 48ha deer farm & 8ha pine forest & stream on site
- deer roaring in autumn
- deer fawns born from mid-Nov.
- tennis court & croquet on site
- pétanque/boules on site
- shop & restaurant on site
- other restaurants nearby
- hot springs, 15km
- gliding
- 2 golf courses nearby
- antiques & collectables, 6km
- Tirau village, 6km
- Matamata township, 15km
- Rotorua, 50 mins south
- day trips to Tauranga beach, Hamilton, Waitomo caves

© Friars' Guide to New Zealand Accommodation for the Discerning Traveller

Rewarewa, Otorohanga
Kamahi Cottage

Hosts Evan and Elisabeth Cowan

229 Barber Road, Rewarewa, R D 5, Otorohanga
Phone 0-7-873 0849   *Mobile* 025 643 6172   *Fax* 0-7-873 0849
Email enquiries@kamahi.co.nz   *Website* www.kamahi.co.nz

1 bdrm 1 prbth

Cottage rate $225 for 2 persons
Extra persons $55 each
Includes breakfast
Lunch & dinner extra   Self-catering

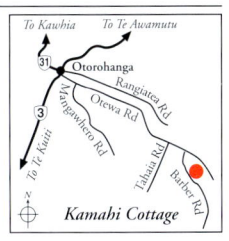

DIRECTIONS: Take SH 3 to Otorohanga. At south end of town, turn east into Otewa Rd, under railway bridge. Travel 12 km & turn right into Barber Rd. Travel 2.29km to Kamahi Cottage & homestead on left.

Set in over a hectare of landscaped garden, Kamahi Cottage was purpose built to blend into the surrounding countryside. This self-contained cottage opens to a verandah with hammock chairs. Uninterrupted panoramic views extend over rolling pastureland to Mount Pirongia and Kakapuka beyond. The hand-crafted cottage has been designed to be light and airy with wooden beams and staircase, concealed kitchen and mezzanine bedroom. A full breakfast is served in the homestead, or cottage if preferred, and lunch or picnic basket is available by prior arangement. Elisabeth enjoys serving two or three-course dinner with changing menus by prior request. Quality New Zealand wines are available for purchase.

Facilities

- private-party bookings only
- 1 queen bedroom with cotton bed linen; sofa bed in lounge
- private bathroom with hair dryer, heated towel rails, bathrobes & toiletries
- guest lounge with tea/coffee, home-made baking, sound system, CDs & writing desk
- Swiss-German spoken by hosts
- laundry available, $10
- full continental or cooked breakfast in homestead or in cottage if preferred
- picnic basket or lunch, $25 pp
- 3-course dinner with home-grown produce, $40 pp, BYO
- kitchenette for self-catering
- email, fax & phone available in homestead
- on-site parking

Activities available

- 1.25ha (3-acre) landscaped garden, native & exotic trees
- 2 elderly cats in homestead
- farm tours & walks on site
- deck area with hammock chairs
- honeymoons catered for
- professionally guided trout fishing tours, by arrangement
- black water rafting
- Waitomo Caves, 30-min drive
- Otorohanga township & shops, 15-min drive
- Woodlyn Park Waitomo Farmshow
- Otorohanga kiwi house
- gardens open to visit
- Waitomo golf course
- Kawhia harbour & west coast beaches, 1 hr away
- Hamilton, 1-hour drive

Waitomo
Tapanui Country Home

Hosts Sue and Mark Perry

Tapanui, 1714 Oparure Road, R D 5, Te Kuiti
Phone 0-7-877 8549   Mobile 025 949 873   Fax 0-7-877 8541
Email info@tapanui.co.nz   Website www.tapanui.co.nz

| 3 bdrm | 1 enst | 1 prbth |

Double $165–$180
Single $155–$170

*Includes breakfast
Lunch & dinner extra*

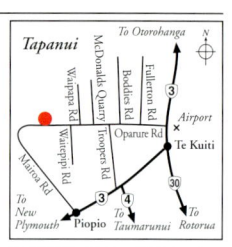

DIRECTIONS: From Te Kuiti, take SH 3 north for 3km. Turn left into Oparure Rd and continue for 17km. Tapanui Country Home is on the right, through limestone entrance.

After a dramatic entrance through the limestone outcrop, peace and quiet abound at Tapanui Country Home. Sue's extensive garden including rhododendrons and camellias bounded by a ha-ha provides uninterrupted views of the countryside. Designed to the Perrys' concept by Darryl Bell in 1981, the purpose-built homestead offers three spacious guestrooms, two in the main house sharing a private bathroom, and one with ensuite in the guest wing. Tapanui features exposed rimu ceilings, quiet-toned furnishings, Warner printed fabrics, original New Zealand art and handknotted oriental carpets. Guests enjoy meeting the family hand-reared sheep, kune pig and donkey on the 770-hectare (1900-acre) sheep and beef farm.

Facilities

- 3 super-king/twin bedrooms, with quality beds, feather or angora/wool mix duvets
- bathrobes for private bathroom
- 1 ensuite in guest wing
- toiletries, hair dryers, heaters & heated towel rails
- central heating
- phone, fax & email available
- laundry available, extra
- continental/cooked breakfast
- lunch by arrangement
- dinner with NZ wine, $50 pp, by prior arrangement
- formal lounge
- casual lounge with TV & leather couches
- separate dining room & patio
- outdoor furniture
- rural & mountain views

Activities available

- piano in sitting room
- garden & farm walks
- farm pets/activities when available, eg bottle-feeding lambs
- Waitomo Caves & glow-worms, 25-min drive
- BBQ luncheons at Roselands
- Waitomo Golf Course & horse trekking
- Natural Bridge walks, 4–25km from Waitomo Caves
- restaurants at Te Kuiti, 20km
- Kiwi House & native birds
- Marokopa Falls; Lost World
- Waitomo Museum of Caves
- private garden visits
- angora rabbit shearing
- black water rafting
- Altura gardens & wildlife park
- kiwi culture show at Woodlyn Park Waitomo

© Friars' Guide to New Zealand Accommodation for the Discerning Traveller

TAUPO
HUKA LODGE

General Manager Co Engels

Huka Falls Road, Taupo   *Postal* P O Box 95, Taupo
Phone 0-7-378 5791   *Email* reservations@hukalodge.co.nz
Fax 0-7-378 0427   *Website* friars.co.nz/hosts/huka.html

20 bdrm | 20 enst | 1 pdrm

Double $1,462–$2,419
Single $1,098–$1,817

Includes breakfast & dinner
Lunch extra

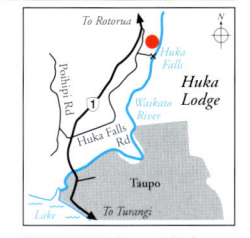

DIRECTIONS: From north take SH 1 towards Taupo. Turn left into Huka Falls Rd. Travel to Huka Falls & continue 300m to Huka Lodge on left. From Taupo Centre, take SH 1 north. Turn right into Huka Falls Rd.

Award-winning Huka Lodge is set in seven tranquil hectares on the banks of the Waikato River. "Huka" meaning "white foaming water" refers to the Huka Falls, only 300 metres downstream. The 20 guestrooms are nestled amongst native bush along the river's edge, each comprising a spacious king-size bedroom, dressing room and ensuite bathroom. Four can be configured into large suites with a separate sitting room. A hearty country breakfast and five-course table d'hôte dinner are included in the tariff and prepared by the executive chef. Meals are served in the Lodge dining room, or any of the private dining options such as the Trophy Room, Wine Cellar, Gazebo, or beside an outside fireplace. Special winter event programmes are also organised.

Facilities

- 20 king ensuite bedrooms, including 4 suites; 1 self-contained cottage
- dual basins, demist mirrors, hair dryer, toiletries, heated towel rails, heated floor, & bathrobes in all ensuite bathrooms
- dressing room & verandah with each bedroom
- cotton bed linen, fresh fruit, tea, coffee & refrigerator in bedrooms
- 5-course dinner & complimentary cocktail hour, 7–8 pm, included
- à la carte lunch, extra
- TV, phone, fax & email
- children & pets welcome
- Dutch, German & French spoken
- laundry available; helipad
- Taupo airport transfers

Activities available

- all-weather tennis court
- heated pool; 2 jacuzzi spa pools
- pétanque/boules
- croquet court on site
- fly fishing from site
- riverside & bush walks
- Huka Falls, 300m downstream
- Taupo township, 7km south
- 5 golf courses within 30 mins
- rainbow trout fishing
- Lake Taupo, 7km
- white & black water rafting
- horse riding; pony trekking
- jet boating; sailing
- guided deer hunting
- skydiving; bungy jumping
- geothermal sights
- snow skiing, 100km away

LAKE TAUPO
AWAHURI GARDEN LODGE

Hosts William and Suzanne Hindmarsh

70 Hindmarsh Drive, Rangatira Park, Taupo
Freephone 0800 426 538   *Phone* 0-7-378 9847   *Fax* 0-7-378 5799
Email hindmarsh@awahuri-lodge.co.nz   *Website* www.awahuri-lodge.co.nz

3 bdrm | 2 enst

Double $300–$400
Single $300

Includes breakfast
Dinner & wine extra

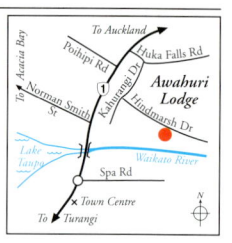

DIRECTIONS: Turn east from SH 1 into Huka Falls Rd, north of Taupo. Opposite radio mast turn into Kahurangi Drive, Rangatira Park, then left into Hindmarsh Drive. Awahuri Lodge on right, on lower terrace.

Awahuri Garden Lodge is set in over one hectare of colourful water gardens bordering the Waikato River, two kilometres north of Taupo. The garden, which features mature trees, rhododendrons, camellias, perennials and roses, is enhanced by the seclusion, views and rural tranquillity. The separate Garden Suite has a spacious super-king bedroom and single room, with a sunny private aspect. Its furnishings include Persian rugs and original oil paintings. The Heron Suite inside the Lodge is configured as a double or twin. Guests enjoy Suzanne's candlelit dinners, complemented by William's wine selection. As the hosts are fourth generation New Zealanders and have lived at Awahuri since 1963, they are well qualified to advise guests about local restaurants and attractions.

Facilities

- Garden Suite: 1 ensuite super-king/twin & 1 single bedroom, separate from Lodge
- Heron Suite: 1 double/twin ensuite bedroom in Lodge
- quality bed linen; fresh flowers
- hair dryer, toiletries & heated towel rails in both bathrooms
- tea/coffee, TV in Garden Suite
- complimentary laundry
- children welcome

- continental/cooked breakfast at times to suit, in dining room
- candlelit dinner, $65 pp, by arrangement
- vegetarians catered
- Suzanne can cook guests' trout catch, or William can smoke, vacuum pack & post to guests
- international wine selection, extra
- phone, fax & email available

Activities available

- walks in over 1ha (3 acres) garden, with lawn, trees, 3 ponds & waterfall
- grass tennis court on site
- fishing & swimming in Waikato River on boundary
- river walks; hot thermal pools
- Huka Falls & Aratiatia rapids
- fly fishing & charter launches on Lake Taupo, 3-min drive

- recommended restaurants, 1km
- 3 golf courses, 3km, including Wairakei International
- guided deer hunting
- Classic Jaguar car tours & scenic river tours available
- hot-air ballooning
- mountain tramping & snow-skiing, 100km away
- warm clothing/gear available

© Friars' Guide to New Zealand Accommodation for the Discerning Traveller   172

ACACIA BAY, TAUPO
TE MOENGA

Hosts Jay (Jennefer) and Bruce McLeod

Reeves Road, Acacia Bay, Taupo   *Phone* 0-7-378 7901
Freephone 0800 663 642   *Mobile* 025 457 729   *Fax* 0-7-378 7909
Email temoenga@reap.org.nz   *Website* www.temoenga.co.nz

6 bdrm | 6 enst

Double $150–$295
Single $110–$220

Includes breakfast
Dinner extra

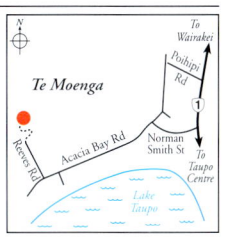

DIRECTIONS: North of Taupo, turn west to Acacia Bay, following signs. Travel another 2km, then take 1st right into Reeves Rd. Travel to end, then follow private road to Te Moenga at top of hill.

Te Moenga, designed by Jack Cantlon in 1982, is set on a working deer, sheep and cattle farm of 24 hectares, overlooking Lake Taupo, the largest lake in New Zealand. Four separate cottages and two guest suites, upstairs and down, are well-appointed with private lounge facilities and lake views. This prairie-style spacious farmstay features native New Zealand timber-panelling in kauri and rimu. Bruce provides guests with the opportunity to tour the farm and learn about the different breeds of farm animals and associated farm activities, including sheep dog demonstrations. Jay and Bruce have a detailed knowledge of Lake Taupo and enjoy assisting guests to arrange trout fishing, golf, tramping and visits to the many scenic attractions.

Facilities
- 2 king/twin suites
- 4 cottages with king beds, spa baths & private decks
- private lounge, TV, fridge, tea/coffee, radio/clock, iron & board per suite/cottage
- children welcome
- laundry service, $15 per load
- lake views from guest lounges in all cottages & suites
- continental or cooked breakfast served in dining room or suite
- 3-course dinner with apéritifs & wine, $60 pp; BBQ $55 pp
- 3ha-garden with roses, proteas, camellias, rhododendrons, azaleas, fuchsias & native ferns
- farm setting; on-site parking
- pétanque; farm walks on site
- tours of deer, cattle, sheep farm

Activities available
- sheepdog demonstrations
- outdoor badminton
- 3 golf courses within 5-min drive
- restaurants/cafés/shopping, 5 mins
- tennis & swimming at Acacia Bay, 2-min drive away
- thermal pools, 5-min drive
- pleasure & fishing boats
- trout fishing in lake & streams
- Huka Falls, 5-min drive
- scenic bush walks
- skiing – water, jet, snow
- tandem skydiving
- helicopter & fixed-wing flights
- gardens open to visit
- Taupo airport, 15-min drive
- Wairakei geothermal area
- Tongariro National Park, 1 hr
- Bay of Plenty beaches, 1½ hrs

LAKE TAUPO
SCENIC HEIGHTS LODGE

Hosts Maureen and Gavin McDonald

24 Scenic Heights, Acacia Bay, Taupo *Postal* P O Box 183, Taupo
Phone 0-7-376 5866   *Mobile* 021 515 803   *Fax* 0-7-376 5867
Email info@scenicheightslodge.com   *Website* www.scenicheightslodge.com

| 5 bdrm | 5 enst | 1 pdrm | Double $440–$890 Single $290–$580 | Includes breakfast & airport transfers Dinner extra   Self-catering in apartment |

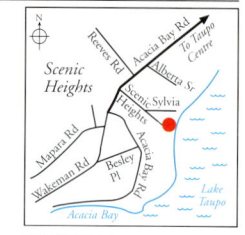

DIRECTIONS: From SH 1 just north of Taupo, turn west into Norman Smith St. Turn left into Acacia Bay Rd & pass Acacia Bay shops. Take 1st left into Scenic Heights & travel to Lodge at end. (5 mins from town.)

Overlooking Lake Taupo in a peaceful, private and secure location, five minutes' drive from Taupo, Scenic Heights Lodge was architecturally designed and purpose built in 2003. Upstairs is a studio apartment and a suite, both with balconies and lake vistas. Downstairs are two further ensuite guestrooms opening to terraces, one with garden views and the other overlooking the heated swimming pool to the lake beyond. A full English or continental breakfast is served in the breakfast room or alfresco on the terrace, and room service is available. A four-course dinner is also offered featuring seasonal contemporary New Zealand and Pacific cuisine. Courtesy transport is provided to the restaurants in Taupo township, five minutes away.

Facilities

- 1 queen bedroom in self-contained studio apartment upstairs
- 1 super-king/twin suite upstairs
- 2 super-king bedrooms downstairs in Lodge
- hair dryer, toiletries & heated towel rails in all 5 ensuites
- terrace/balcony, fridge, drinks, central heating, phone, cotton linen & bathrobes in all rooms
- full breakfast served
- 4-course à la carte dinner, $90 pp
- open fire, nibbles, bar, Sky TV (50"plasma screen), DVD, CDs, games, artwork, books & desk
- computer, fax, copying & email
- elevator; wheelchair access
- fresh flowers; laundry available
- garaging; security gates
- courtesy passenger transfer

Activities available

- home theatre, BBQ & heated pool with swim jets on site
- 2 tennis courts within 500m
- Lake Taupo, 10-min walk
- lake & river trout fishing
- lake cruises; sailing
- Huka Falls, 6-min drive
- jet boating; white water rafting
- international golf courses
- Maori cultural activities
- fine restaurants, 5-min drive
- flight-seeing; tandem sky diving
- bungy jumping
- wilderness walks & treks
- Wairakei geothermal area; hot mineral pools
- horse riding
- public & private open gardens
- Tongariro National Park, 1 hr
- Taupo centre, 5-min drive

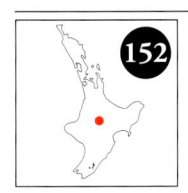

ACACIA BAY, TAUPO
THE LOFT

Hosts Grace Andrews and Peter Rosieur

3 Wakeman Road, Acacia Bay, Taupo
Phone 0-7-377 1040   *Mobile* 0274 851 347   *Fax* 0-7-377 1049
Email book@theloftnz.com   *Website* www.theloftnz.com

Room rate $125–$175

Includes breakfast
Lunch & dinner extra

3 bdrm   3 enst

DIRECTIONS: From SH 1, just north of Taupo, turn west into Norman Smith St. Turn left into Acacia Bay Rd & continue into Wakeman Rd. The Loft is immediately on left.

Set in a small cottage garden, adjacent to a native bush reserve, The Loft was purpose built in 1999 to provide accommodation for up to six guests. The guest floor is upstairs, comprising three ensuite bedrooms, with the living rooms downstairs. Breakfast is a highlight, with fresh fruit, baking, and the guests' choice of a cooked option, served in the dining room or alfresco in the courtyard. Peter and Grace also enjoy providing home-cooked dinners and summer barbecues. They are happy to arrange guides and activities for their guests. Sweetie, the cat, and Turtle, the red-eared turtle, complete the family. Lake Taupo, which is popular for its watersports, fishing and cruises, is only a few minutes' walk away and the township is just five minutes' drive.

Facilities
- upstairs guest floor
- 3 queen ensuite bedrooms with cotton bed linen, robes & TV
- 1 single bed available
- hair dryer, heated towel rails & toiletries in all 3 ensuites
- tea/coffee, mini-fridge & bookshelf on landing
- full laundry service, extra
- children over 12 yrs welcome
- full continental & choice of cooked breakfasts
- home-cooked dinner, or summer BBQ, $30–$45 pp
- BYO or wine available for sale
- lounge with open fire, Sky TV, video & CD-player
- email, fax & phone available
- courtesy passenger transfer
- on-site parking

Activities available
- small cottage garden on site, with courtyard for relaxing
- native bush reserve adjacent for bird-watching
- honeymoons catered for
- fly fishing, guides arranged
- Wairakei International Golf Course, 5 mins
- tramping & walking
- lake & river cruise
- restaurant, 200m away
- Taupo town centre, 5 mins
- kayaking; boating; rafting
- watersports; jet boating
- thermal activities
- gardens open to visit
- hunting tours
- horse riding, 5-min drive
- Lake Taupo, 7-min walk

175

© Friars' Guide to New Zealand Accommodation for the Discerning Traveller

ACACIA BAY, TAUPO
TAUHARA SUNRISE

Hosts Becky and Rob McEwen

38 Mapara Road, Acacia Bay, Taupo
Phone 0-7-376 8555   *Mobile* 021 177 3961   *Fax* 0-7-376 8557
Email rob@tauharasunrise.com   *Website* www.tauharasunrise.com

3 bdrm   3 enst

Room rate $250–$425   Includes breakfast & apéritifs
Room rate $410–$585   Includes breakfast, apéritifs, dinner & wine

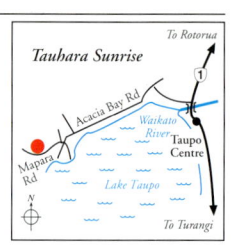

DIRECTIONS: From SH 1, cross bridge & turn left into Norman Smith St. Follow Acacia Bay signs & travel 5km to shops. Continue into Wakeman Rd & turn right into Mapara Rd. Tahaura Sunrise 200m on right.

The panoramic sunrises across Lake Taupo, viewed from all rooms in the lodge, give Tauhara Sunrise its name. The city lights of Taupo also reflect in the lake by night. Purpose built from stone and plaster in 2001, in contemporary style with original artwork, Tauhara Sunrise offers three ensuite guestrooms. The spacious upstairs room includes a double spa bath, and there is a guest kitchenette with fully stocked refrigerator between the two downstairs rooms. A full breakfast menu is provided and dinner is available after the happy hour. A state-of-the-art entertainment system, with plasma television, features in the media room, with open fire in the lounge/reading room. Becky offers therapeutic massage, and Pillpot, the cat, is also in residence.

Facilities
- 1 super-king ensuite bedroom, double basin & spa bath, upstairs
- 1 super-king/twin ensuite bedroom with wheelchair access, downstairs
- 1 queen ensuite bedroom downstairs
- hair dryers, toiletries, heated towel rails & demist mirrors
- cotton bed linen; robes & slippers; bedrooms open to patios
- entertainment room with CD-player, plasma Sky TV, video, DVD
- full breakfast menu
- complimentary apéritifs
- dinner with wine, extra
- guest kitchenette
- lounge with open fire
- high-speed internet, email, fax & phone available
- complimentary laundry
- courtesy passenger transfer
- off-street parking

Activities available
- complimentary bar opening to spacious balcony & 6-person hot tub overlooking landscaped garden & lake
- in-house massage therapist
- weddings, honeymoons & conferences catered for
- tennis across road
- kayaking; rafting; lake cruises
- boutique shops; thermal resort
- sidewalk cafés & restaurants
- golf courses; hunting
- boat hire; fishing; sailing
- gliding; flight-seeing
- mountain biking & boarding
- gardens open to visit
- eco-tours; bush walking
- bungy jumping; skydiving
- skiing in winter, 1½ hours

© Friars' Guide to New Zealand Accommodation for the Discerning Traveller

Acacia Bay, Taupo
West Wellow Lodge

Hosts Ian and Mary Smith

39 Mapara Road, Acacia Bay, R D 1, Taupo
Phone 0-7-378 0435 *Mobile* 021 455 975 *Fax* 0-7-378 0635
Email mary@westwellow.co.nz *Website* www.westwellow.co.nz

5 bdrm | 4 enst | 1 prbth
Double $375–$495
Single $165–$335
Includes breakfast
House rate available
Dinner extra

DIRECTIONS: From Taupo Centre, take SH 1 north. Cross bridge & turn left into Norman Smith St. Following Acacia Bay signs, travel 5km to Acacia Bay shops. Take 2nd right into Mapara Rd. West Wellow is 150m on left.

Set in a landscaped garden overlooking Lake Taupo, West Wellow is a tranquil venue for guests, just minutes' walk from Acacia Bay. Designed in historic style, West Wellow offers one ensuite guestroom downstairs and another three upstairs, each with access to the guest balcony with views across the lake to the township of Taupo and Mt Tauhara beyond. Guests enjoy the lights of Taupo by night. The close proximity to the lake enables guests easy access to the outdoor and watersports. Breakfast is usually served in the conservatory downstairs or alfresco, and dinner is available by prior arrangement. Tea and coffee facilities are provided on the landing, and a guest study includes a writing desk and television. Children are welcome in single-party bookings.

Facilities
- 1 super-king/twin bedroom including ensuite, bath & bidet
- 1 king & 2 queen bedrooms both with ensuites
- 1 chauffeur or guide's single bedroom with private bathroom
- cotton bed linen; fresh flowers
- hair dryers, toiletries, heated towel rails & bathrobes
- guest balconies overlooking Lake Taupo from bedrooms
- complimentary wine bottle, cheese & fruit in bedrooms
- open fire, tea/coffee, Sky TV, video & writing desk
- phone, fax & email in study
- self-service laundry
- children by arrangement
- wheelchair access
- courtesy passenger transfer
- off-street parking

Activities available
- BBQ for guest use, on site
- gourmet dinner by professional chef, by arrangement next-door, $135 pp, wine extra
- tennis court, 2-min walk
- hot mineral pools, 5km
- mini golf, 5km away
- Lake Taupo, 2-min walk
- Taupo shopping, 5-min drive
- scenic bush walks
- restaurants & bars, 1–5km
- trout fishing; lake & rivers
- golf courses, 5km away
- rafting; jet boats
- geothermal activity
- boating hire, 5-min walk
- Rotorua, 45-min drive
- ski-fields & mountain walks
- tandem skydiving

ACACIA BAY, TAUPO
LAKE TAUPO LODGE

Hosts Gary and Shirley Akers

41 Mapara Road, Acacia Bay, Taupo *Postal* P O Box 83, Taupo
Phone 0-7-378 7386 *Mobile* 027 453 3454 *Fax* 0-7-377 3226
Email lodge@reap.org.nz *Website* friars.co.nz/hosts/laketaupo.html

Double $1,110–$1,330
Single $645–$745

Includes breakfast & dinner
Lunch extra

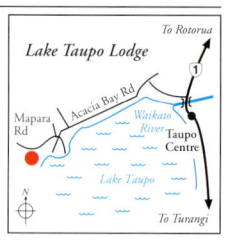

7 bdrm / 7 enst

DIRECTIONS: From Taupo Centre, take SH 1 north. Cross bridge, then turn left into Norman Smith St. Following Acacia Bay signs, travel 5km to Acacia Bay shops. Take 2nd right into Mapara Rd. Lodge is 200m on left.

Sited above Acacia Bay on the north-western shores of Lake Taupo, the Lodge commands panoramic views over the water to the mountains beyond. Guests can relax in the quiet surroundings of the Lodge, yet it is only five minutes' drive from the centre of Taupo township. Built in 1984 in stone and mahogany timber, the Lodge was inspired by Frank Lloyd Wright architecture. The Art Nouveau interiors incorporate spacious living areas and seven guest suites. After dining on the chef's special cuisine, guests can enjoy themselves in the billiards room, music area, reading gallery, or in front of a log fire in winter. A stroll on the pathways through the park-like gardens is popular, with its ponds and mature trees attracting bellbirds and tui.

Facilities
- 7 super-king suites
- 7 ensuites, 5 include spa bath
- cotton bed linen
- private guest lounge, with log fire in winter
- laundry available
- music area includes grand piano
- reading gallery
- lake & garden views
- continental, or cooked breakfast prepared by chef
- lunch by arrangement, extra
- 4-course dinner included in tariff, wine extra, fully licensed
- vegetarian alternative available
- courtesy Taupo Airport transfer
- children 12 yrs & over welcome
- off-street carpark
- helipad

Activities available
- in-house billiards room with full-size table
- boules/pétanque on site
- park-like gardens with birdlife
- tennis court on site
- 3 golf courses nearby, including the Wairakei International Golf Course
- rainbow trout fishing in lake, rivers & streams
- Lake Taupo township, 5 mins
- watersports in Lake Taupo
- trekking
- bush walking
- boating
- Wairakei geothermal fields
- snow skiing at Mt Ruapehu, in winter, 60 mins away
- Taupo airport, 15-min drive

Acacia Bay, Taupo
Acacia Point Lodge Taupo

Host Maureen West

11-13 Sylvia Place, Acacia Bay, Taupo
Phone 0-7-378 9089   *Email* info@acaciapointlodgetaupo.co.nz
Fax 0-7-377 1936   *Website* www.acaciapointlodgetaupo.co.nz

4 bdrm | 4 enst
Double $1,220–$1,990
Single $799–$1,440
Includes breakfast, apéritifs & dinner
Lodge rate available   *Lunch extra*

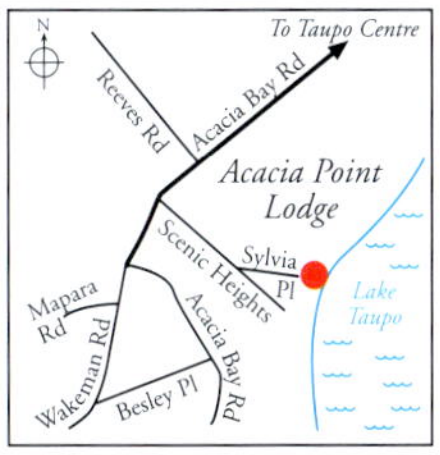

DIRECTIONS: From Taupo Centre, take SH 1 north across bridge. Turn left into Norman Smith St. Turn left into Acacia Bay Rd. Travel 3km, turn left into Scenic Heights & turn left into Sylvia Pl. Lodge at end.

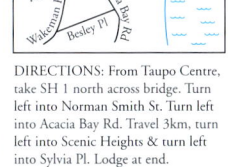

Set on a clifftop, on the edge of Lake Taupo, Acacia Point Lodge is surrounded by a hectare of landscaped park-like gardens which include a nine-hole putting green, floodlit tennis court and heated swimming pool. Designed by renowned American architect, Charles Sutton, in 1992, the residence was converted into an exclusive Lodge in 2002 to provide four large ensuite guestrooms. The Master Room includes a spacious dressing room and ensuite with spa bath. Cuisine is a speciality with breakfast and dinner served in the licensed dining room or alfresco with panoramic views over the lake, to the mountains beyond. Golf parties, small conferences, and honeymoons can be catered for, with trout fishing and golfing popular guest pursuits.

Facilities

- Master Room: 1 super-king bed, dual ensuite with spa bath & large dressing room
- 3 super-king/twin ensuite bedrooms with baths
- Egyptian cotton bed linen, writing desk, phone, TV, fresh fruit & flowers in rooms
- hair dryer, bathrobes, toiletries, heated towel rails & floor
- email, fax & laundry available
- tariff includes full buffet & à la carte breakfast, apéritifs & dinner, with wine extra
- lunch by arrangement, extra
- additional lounge with open fire, tea/coffee, bar, Sky TV, video, DVD, music & library
- children by arrangement
- central heating; courtesy airport transfer; garaging
- wheelchair access to 1 bedroom

Activities available

- swimming pool, spa pool, tennis court, sauna & gym on site
- barbecue available
- home theatre, billiards table, library & games on site
- 9-hole putting green on site
- 1ha of landscaped lakeside gardens with walk on site
- brown & rainbow trout fishing
- Taupo Centre, 5-min drive
- 3 golf courses, including Wairakei, within 10 mins
- shopping, 5 mins
- treks & scenic bush walks
- watersports – boating, jet skiing & rafting
- hot mineral pools, 5 mins
- 3 thermal & volcanic wonderlands within 30 mins
- winter sports within 1 hour

179   © Friars' Guide to New Zealand Accommodation for the Discerning Traveller

ACACIA BAY, TAUPO
THE TOP HOUSE

Hosts Jack and Margy Gower

42 The Point, Taupo   *Postal* P O Box 104, Taupo
Phone 0-7-377 0169   *Email* bookings@pointhouse.co.nz
Fax 0-7-377 3134   *Website* www.pointhouse.co.nz

4 bdrm | 1 enst | 2 prbth | 1 pdrm

House rate $600–$1500   *Self-catering*

DIRECTIONS: From Taupo, take SH 1 north. Turn left into Norman Smith St. Follow Acacia Bay Rd to end to The Point. At security gates punch in code & continue uphill to end of last drive on right to The Top House.

With extensive views over Lake Taupo and the mountains beyond, The Top House is set in private gardens with native planting in The Point enclave at Acacia Bay. Designed by Fraser Cameron in 2002, The Top House is constructed from timber and stone to create a New Zealand feel and ambience. With plenty of living areas, this self-contained house is suitable for small groups and families of up to 12 guests. It provides four bedrooms, three bathrooms and two sitting rooms, one of which can be used as a fifth bedroom. A full kitchen with a double oven enables guest to self-cater, and barbecue facilities are popular for alfresco dining. Catering can be arranged and restaurants are a short drive away. A golf buggy takes guests to the on-site tennis courts.

Facilities
- private-party bookings
- 4 super-king/twin bedrooms
- 1 ensuite with bath & 2 private bathrooms
- cotton bed linen
- hair dryers, toiletries, demist mirror, heated towel rails & double basin in all bathrooms
- children welcome
- self-service laundry
- full self-contained kitchen for self-catering
- catering can be arranged
- guest lounge with open fire, Sky TV, CD-player & NZ art
- billiards table in games room & living room downstairs
- basic French & Italian spoken
- security gates
- on-site parking; helipad

Activities available
- gas barbecue facilities
- in-house games room
- fly fishing, guided by Jack, within 5-min walk away
- golf buggy available to go to tennis courts & fly fishing
- 2 boat ramps available
- beach access & summer swimming in sheltered harbour
- fishing from rocks; watersports
- restaurants, 5–10km
- bush walks nearby
- 4 golf courses, 3 international standard, 15–20 mins
- boutique shopping, 10 mins
- thermal pools, 10-min drive
- horse riding
- rope & rock climbing
- geothermal activities
- ski-field, 1 hour 20-min drive

Acacia Bay, Taupo
The Point Villas

Manager Kerry Lynch

24 The Point, Acacia Bay Road, Taupo
Phone 0-7-376 5131 *Email* kerrysmile@hotmail.com
Mobile 027 490 6717 *Website* www.thepointvillas.co.nz

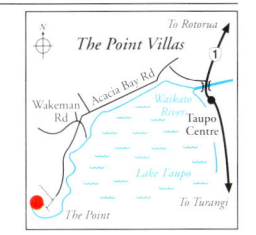

4 bdrm 4 enst Villa rate $600–$1,125 *Self-catering* *Catering extra*

DIRECTIONS: From Taupo, take SH 1 north. Turn left into Norman Smith St. Follow Acacia Bay Rd to end to The Point. At security gates punch in code & continue to "T" & turn right to The Villas, 100m on left.

Set among the native trees surrounding the lake edge to provide privacy, The Point Villas capture the panoramic views over Mine Bay. Designed by award-winning architect, David Page, the two large bedrooms in each villa open into Italian Travatine stone and double-glazed glass bathrooms overlooking the secluded native bush. Guests can relax in the spacious interiors, designed to blend with the natural surroundings to give a feeling of space and privacy. The Villas are furnished with antique oak furniture and seagrass and leather lounge suites. Full kitchens enable guests to self-cater, or an on-site chef can provide full catering. The Point Villas were named in *Condé Nast Traveller 2003* as one of the 80 best new resorts in the world.

Facilities
- single-party bookings
- 2 self-contained villas each with 2 super-king/twin ensuite bedrooms including dressing rooms & double baths
- cotton bed linen
- hair dryers, heated towel rails & toiletries in both bathrooms
- underfloor heating
- living rooms with log fire, TV, VCR, DVD, CDs & stereo
- breakfast provisions supplied
- fully equipped kitchen in both villas for self-catering
- full catering by on-site chef by request, extra
- phone & fax in living rooms
- self-serve laundry in each villa
- daily servicing on request
- security gates; on-site parking
- helipad

Activities available
- gas barbecues on decking
- private decks with sun loungers
- tennis raquets available
- 2 all-weather floodlit tennis courts on site
- swimming pool on site
- sheltered harbour & beaches for swimming
- 2 boat ramps
- rocks for fly fishing
- restaurants, 5–10km
- Taupo township, 10 mins
- thermal pools, 10-min drive
- Maori rock carvings
- bush walks & birdlife
- gardens open to visit
- 4 golf courses, 3 courses international standard, 15–20 mins
- ski-field, 1 hr 20-min drive

BONSHAW PARK, TAUPO
THE PILLARS

Hosts Ruth and John Boddy

7 Deborah Rise, Bonshaw Park, R D 3, Taupo
Freephone 0800 200 983   Phone 0-7-378 1512   Fax 0-7-378 1511
Email enquiries@pillarshomestay.co.nz   *Website* www.pillarshomestay.co.nz

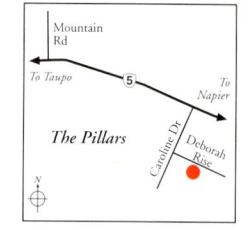

4 bdrm	4 enst	1 pdrm	Room rate $275–$475	Includes breakfast	Lunch & dinner extra
			House rate $1,100	Winter rates available	

DIRECTIONS: Take SH 1 to Taupo. From Lake Tce, south of town, turn east into SH 5. Travel 5.7km towards Napier, then turn right into Caroline Drive. Take 1st turn on left into Deborah Rise. The Pillars on right.

Overlooking Lake Taupo with views to Mount Ruapehu beyond, The Pillars was built in Mediterranean style. The landscaped gardens featuring a pond, gazebo and in-ground swimming pool enhance the tranquillity. Upstairs are the four ensuite guest bedrooms, three with private balconies, and one including a bath. A chauffeur's or guide's room is available downstairs. Breakfast and dinner on request are served in the dining room, conservatory or alfresco in the courtyard. But it is the extra little touches such as the complimentary writing paper and pens, chocolates, and wine that help make The Pillars special. Guests enjoy all-day sun and sunsets over the lake. The Pillars is an exclusive wedding venue and popular with honeymooners.

Facilities
- 1 super-king/twin, 1 king/twin & 2 Californian king/twin ensuite bedrooms; heated floors
- TV, radio-clock, tea/coffee, & fresh flowers in each guestroom
- fridge, fruit, wine, bottled water, & home-made biscuits in all bedrooms
- bathrobes, hair dryers, toiletries
- guide/chauffeur room available
- children over 13 years welcome
- 3-course dinner, with apéritifs, nibbles & nightcaps, $65 pp
- lunch & BBQ by request
- NZ continental breakfast alfresco on courtyard, or in dining room or conservatory
- phone, fax & email available
- complimentary laundry
- off-street parking
- courtesy passenger transfer

Activities available
- swimming pool; pétanque
- all-weather tennis court, raquets & balls provided
- alpaca adjacent
- hot mineral pools, 5km
- Lake Taupo, 6km away
- Taupo shopping, 7km
- trout fishing in lake/rivers
- rafting; jet boats
- golf courses, 6km
- restaurants & bars 5–7km, transport provided
- bungy jumping; paragliding
- tandem skydiving
- horse trekking; mountain biking
- scenic bush walks; Mt Tauhara
- geothermal activity; hunting
- ski-fields, 1-hour drive away
- Rotorua, 45-min drive on SH 5
- Auckland, 3-hour drive on SH 1

© Friars' Guide to New Zealand Accommodation for the Discerning Traveller

LAKE TAUPO
KARAKA COTTAGE

Host Delia Barnes

42 Gillies Avenue, Taupo   *Postal* P O Box 1622, Taupo
Phone 0-7-378 4560   *Mobile* 027 496 9432   *Fax* 0-7-378 3145
Email rugs@reap.org.nz   *Website* www.rugsoriental.co.nz

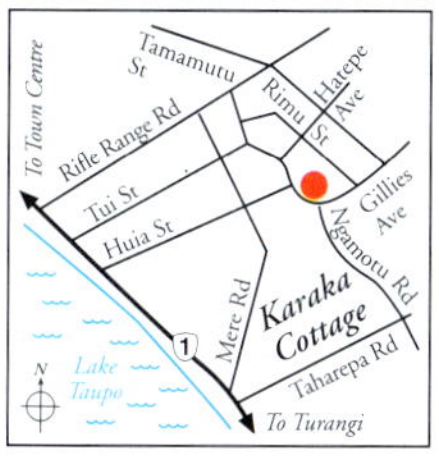

2 bdrm | 2 enst

Double $250–$280
Single $200–$220

Includes breakfast
Winter rates available

Dinner extra
Self-catering in cottage

DIRECTIONS: From north on SH 1, turn left into Tamamutu St. Travel to "T" junction & turn right into Gillies Ave. Cottage 200m on right. From south, on SH 1, turn right into Rifle Range Rd, then right into Gillies Ave.

Set in a quiet garden with mature trees overhead, Karaka Cottage has been purpose-built to provide total guest privacy, adjacent to the main house. The deck from the cottage opens directly to the swimming pool, creating a relaxed atmosphere. Single parties can be accommodated in the super-king/twin bedroom of the self-contained cottage with its fully equipped kitchen for self-catering. Breakfast provisions are supplied for the cottage, or served in the dining room of the house or alfresco in the landscaped garden. One queen bedroom with ensuite bathroom is also available for guests in the house. Oriental rugs are a feature of both cottage and house. Dinner can also be provided – either in the dining room or in the cottage by arrangement.

Facilities

- private-party booking for cottage
- 1 super-king/twin ensuite bedroom in cottage
- 1 queen ensuite bedroom in house
- hair dryers, toiletries, heated towel rails, bathrobes & fresh flowers
- private lounge in cottage with TV
- open fire in lounge in house
- tea/coffee & TV available in house
- self-catering kitchen in cottage

- breakfast served in house or alfresco, or provisions in cottage if preferred
- 3-course dinner with pre-dinner drinks, $60 pp
- guest deck opens from cottage to swimming pool
- phone, fax, email & laundry available
- basic French spoken
- off-street parking

Activities available

- swimming pool on site
- barbecue available
- restaurants, 1–2km away
- golf matches arranged – member Wairakei International Golf Course
- guided fishing
- boating trips arranged
- tourist shopping, 2km away
- sailing; paragliding

- Delia's *Rugs Oriental*, 2km
- thermal pools, 2km away
- Lake Taupo, 5-min walk
- lake activities – watersports
- jet skiing; water skiing
- gardens open to visit; horse riding & trekking
- Wairakei Park – jet boating
- Huka Falls – Aratiatia Rapids
- skiing in winter, 1-hour drive

© Friars' Guide to New Zealand Accommodation for the Discerning Traveller

LAKE TAUPO
AMAKAYA

Hosts Liz and Tony Giesen

2/70 Harvey Street, Taupo   *Postal* P O Box 804, Taupo
Phone 0-7-378 0747   *Email* amakaya@xtra.co.nz
Fax 0-7-378 6892   *Website* www.amakaya.co.nz

| 3 bdrm | 1 enst | 1 prbth |

Room rate $250–$350   Includes breakfast   Lunch & dinner extra

DIRECTIONS: Take SH 1 to Taupo. From Lake Tce, south of township, turn east into SH 5 towards Napier. Take 1st turn right into Harvey St. Turn right up small lane to Amakaya.

Located close to Lake Taupo, Amakaya is set in spacious grounds with hideaway native and water gardens. Built in 1993 with a Mediterranean influence, it affords panoramic views over the lake to the mountains beyond. Amakaya's three spacious guest bedrooms open to the downstairs terrace, garden and solar-heated swimming pool. Breakfast is served in the family room and lunch or dinner are offered by prior arrangement. Two guest lounges, one with a log fire, provide relaxation after dinner in the formal dining room, and the expansive tiled balcony provides an alfresco setting for lunches in summer. For the more active, rounds of golf with Liz and Tony can be arranged. Ollie, the Cavalier King Charles spaniel, is an extra family member.

Facilities
- 1 king bedroom with ensuite
- 1 queen/twin & 1 twin share 1 private bathroom with bathrobes, in single-party booking
- hair dryers, toiletries, heated towel rails in both bathrooms
- TV in king & queen bedrooms
- double-glazed windows
- tea/coffee & fresh flowers
- children welcome
- 3-course dinner with wine, in formal dining room, $65 pp
- lunch by arrangement, $25 pp
- guest kitchenette with fridge
- central heating
- phone & fax available
- laundry, $10 per load
- off-street parking
- courtesy passenger transfer

Activities available
- solar-heated swimming pool
- pétanque/boules on site
- BBQ in large garden area
- Taupo Hot Springs nearby
- botanical gardens nearby
- Lake Taupo, 0.4km away
- Taupo shops & cafés, 5 mins
- trout fishing
- tennis; bush walks
- 3 golf courses, hosts members of Wairakei International
- restaurants in walking distance
- guided lake & river fly fishing
- watersports
- bungy jumping
- tandem skydiving
- horse riding nearby
- Huka jet boats
- winter snow skiing, 1-hr drive

© Friars' Guide to New Zealand Accommodation for the Discerning Traveller

Two Mile Bay, Taupo
Te Kowhai Landing

Manager Jennifer McBrearty

325 Lace Terrace, Two Mile Bay, Taupo *Freephone* 0800 ESSENCE
Postal P O Box 5231, Mount Maunganui *Mobile* 027 542 4202
Fax 0-7-574 8096 *Email* stay@essencenz.com *Website* www.essencenz.com

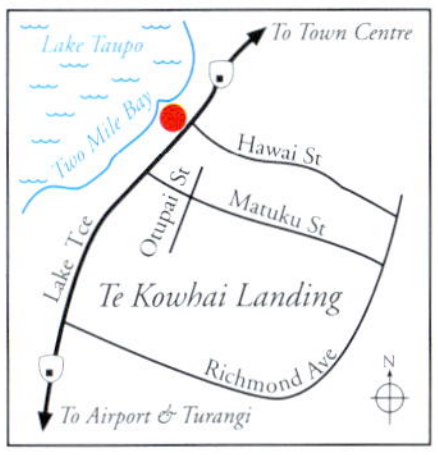

2 bdrm	2 enst	1 prbth	House rate $1,500–$1,800 for up to 4 persons	Self-catering
			Extra persons $100 each	Chef service for any meal, extra

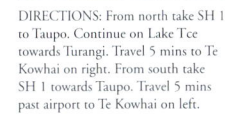

DIRECTIONS: From north take SH 1 to Taupo. Continue on Lake Tce towards Turangi. Travel 5 mins to Te Kowhai on right. From south take SH 1 towards Taupo. Travel 5 mins past airport to Te Kowhai on left.

Located on the shores of Lake Taupo, Te Kowhai Landing was purpose built in 2003 to provide state-of-the-art self-contained accommodation. Architectually designed to resemble a traditional New Zealand-style twin boatshed, this accommodation is "Smart Wired" to provide automated electronic fittings. With interiors designed by Sally Motion, Te Kowhai Landing features quality furnishings to complement the lake views from every room. There are two suites upstairs, with a balcony overlooking the lake, and below are the living and dining areas. The chef-designed kitchen enables guests to self-cater, or their dining needs can be catered for by a chef. The lounge opens towards the beach and a row boat is available for guest use.

Facilities
- single-party bookings only
- 2 super-king bedrooms upstairs, each with ensuite, dressing room, cotton bed linen, tea/coffee, fridge
- hair dryers, toiletries, heated floor, heated towel rails, demist mirrors & bathrobes; 1 double bath
- 2 lounges with wine, Sky TV, DVD, music, CD-player, games, artwork, books & writing desk
- central heating; log fire
- full kitchen for self-catering
- catered meals by arrangement
- computer, printer, email, fax & phones for guest use
- children welcome; twin beds in downstairs lounge
- conferences, weddings, cooking schools, product launches & art displays
- off-street parking; security gates

Activities available
- spa pool; petanque on site
- lake swimming & trout fishing direct access from site
- row boat for guest use
- customised scenic tours; wine tasting excursions
- guided trout fishing & hunting
- bush, mountain, lake-edge walks
- mineral pools, 3-min drive
- Huka Falls; aerial adventures
- Taupo shops, cafés & restaurants, 5-min drive
- golf courses; water pursuits
- mountain biking
- horse-riding; farm visits
- private gardens to visit
- wilderness & volcanic trips
- winter snow skiing, 1 hour
- "Middle-earth", 1½ hours
- airport, 5-min drive

187

© Friars' Guide to New Zealand Accommodation for the Discerning Traveller

LAKE TAUPO
ALBION LODGE

Hosts David and Susie Pierce

358 Lake Terrace, Two Mile Bay, Taupo   *Postal* P O Box 1810, Taupo
Phone 0-7-378 7788   *Mobile* 021 116 8496   *Fax* 0-7-378 2966
Email friars@albionlodge.co.nz   *Website* www.albionlodge.co.nz

3 bdrm   3 enst

Double $240–$330
Single $175–$255

Includes breakfast
Lunch & dinner extra

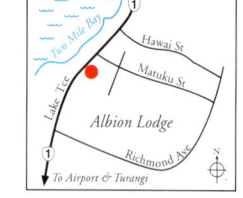

DIRECTIONS: From north take SH 1 to Taupo. Continue past SH 5 turn-off for 1.5km towards airport. Albion Lodge on left beside Anchorage. From south, take SH 1 to airport. Continue 2km to Albion Lodge on right

Albion Lodge is set in a native plant garden with views over Lake Taupo. Each of the three spacious guestrooms offer a super-king size bed and an ensuite including spa bath. Mealtimes are flexible and ingredients are fresh, and wherever possible, organic. A full cooked breakfast is served in the dining room, and a four-course table d'hôte dinner is offered. There is a 70-item wine list featuring all the major varieties of New Zealand wines. An extensive collection of information on all the activities and attractions in Taupo is available. The lake is within walking distance from Albion Lodge. Hosts Susie and David are happy to advise on itineraries and arrange bookings for the guests during their stay in Taupo. Fishing guides can be arranged.

Facilities

- 3 super-king/twin bedrooms, all with ensuites & spa baths
- cotton bed linen; central heating
- hair dryer, toiletries, bathrobes, heated floor & towel rails
- lounge with gas fire, tea/coffee, nibbles, bar, CD-player, games, books & writing desk
- wheelchair access
- fresh flowers

- full cooked breakfast
- lunch hampers available
- 4-course table d'hôte dinner, $75 pp
- phone, fax, internet & email
- laundry available
- drying & ski storage room
- off-street parking
- courtesy passenger transfer

Activities available

- guided lake & fly fishing for rainbow & brown trout
- beach; watersports
- boat trips
- boat fishing
- rafting & kayaking
- parasailing; gliding
- sky diving
- floatplane, fixed wing & helicopter flights

- many restaurants, 10 mins
- shopping, 5-min drive
- bush walking
- bungy jumping
- horse riding
- 4 golf courses within 15 mins
- arts & crafts; volcanic centre
- 3 thermal parks within 30 mins
- Taupo town centre, 7-min drive

© Friars' Guide to New Zealand Accommodation for the Discerning Traveller

Rainbow Point, Lake Taupo
Tuscany on Taupo

Hosts Beryl and Richard Newman

28B Oregon Drive, Taupo   *Mobile* 025 241 4426
Phone 0-4-499 9309   *Email* c.newman@xtra.co.nz
Fax 0-4-384 8675   *Website* friars.co.nz/hosts/tuscany.html

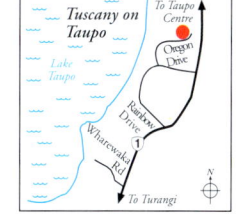

3 bdrm   1 enst   1 prbth   House rate $400   *Self-catering*

DIRECTIONS: From north take SH 1 through Taupo township towards airport. Turn right into Rainbow Dr. Turn 2nd right into Oregon Dr. Tuscany on Taupo on left. From south turn left off SH 1 into Rainbow Drive.

Set in a secluded garden, Tuscany on Taupo offers self-contained accommodation for up to six guests in a contemporary Mediterranean-style home. This four-level house provides three bedrooms, two bathrooms, and a full kitchen for self-catering. Basic provisions are supplied including the first morning breakfast. The dining room opens to a sheltered patio for alfresco dining and barbecues on the ground floor. There is a another barbecue on the first floor deck opening from the second lounge with adjacent kitchenette. The large bedroom on the top floor features a deck with a gimpse of the lake, the other floors looking onto the garden which shelters Tuscany on Taupo and provides lake access. Restaurants and shops are a few minutes away.

Facilities
- Top floor: 1 super-king/twin bedroom with ensuite, double basin, dressing room & patio
- First floor: 1 twin/king bedroom, lounge, kitchenette, computer with internet, patio
- Ground floor: 1 bathroom with spa bath & double basin, lounge with open log fire, TV, DVD & air-conditioning, full kitchen & dining area opening to patio
- Downstairs: 1 queen bedroom & full laundry
- phone on top & ground floors
- fax & email available
- hair dryers, toiletries, heated towel rails & demist mirrors
- cotton bed linen
- pets & children welcome
- single-party bookings only
- off-street parking; garaging

Activities available
- 2 BBQs on patio/decks
- golf clubs for guest use
- fishing equipment & waders
- river or lake fishing
- Lions Lake Taupo walk
- watersports
- walks
- botanic gardens
- 4 golf courses within 10-min drive
- private gardens to visit
- restaurants, 2-min walk
- shopping, 5-min drive
- mineral pools, 3-min drive
- Taupo town centre, 5 mins
- prawn farm
- jet boating
- Huka Falls
- air sports
- winter skiing, 1-hour drive

… 167

LAKE TAUPO
BESIDE LAKE TAUPO

Hosts Irene and Roger Foote

8 Chad Street, Taupo
Phone 0-7-378 5847   *Mobile* 025 804 683   *Fax* 0-7-378 5847
Email besidelaketaupo@xtra.co.nz   *Website* besidelaketaupo.co.nz

3 bdrm | 1 enst | 1 prbth | 2 pdrm   Room rate $220–$250   *Includes breakfast*

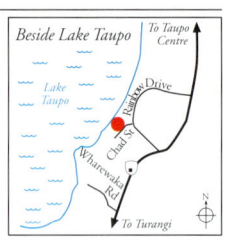

DIRECTIONS: From north, take SH 1 through Taupo township towards airport. Turn right into Rainbow Drive at 1st entrance. Turn right into Chad St. Homestead on right. From south, turn left off SH 1 into Rainbow Drive.

Beside Lake Taupo is in fact located right on Lake Taupo. This two-storey home was architecturally designed for its lakeside setting and built in 1999. With lake views from all rooms, the accommodation comprises one queen and two super-king/twin bedrooms, each with its own bathroom and balcony or terrace. Another terrace opens from the dining room, also overlooking the lake, where guests can breakfast alfresco and enjoy the view. Beside Lake Taupo is adjacent to a tranquil lakeside reserve and yet only 10 minutes' drive from the Taupo township to the north, and the airport to the south. The house is double-glazed and air-conditioned for guest comfort, and an elevator takes guests and their luggage to the upstairs bedrooms.

Facilities

- 1 super-king/twin bedroom with ensuite & terrace
- 1 super-king/twin & 1 queen bedroom with share bathroom & powder room for single-party
- TV & tea/coffee in bedrooms
- hair dryers, heated towel rails & toiletries in both bathrooms
- phone, fax & email available
- central heating; double glazing
- breakfast served in dining room or alfresco on terrace
- central lounge with sound system, Sky TV, video, CD-player & books
- air-conditioning
- laundry available
- internal elevator
- garage with direct internal access to house

Activities available

- lake swimming from site
- fishing from site
- lakeside walks from site
- boating from site
- bush walks; tramping
- lake excursions; river cruises
- canoeing; kayaking
- trout fishing in lake & rivers
- horse trekking
- bike riding
- restaurants & shops nearby
- golf; bridge
- river rafting; rock climbing
- bungy jumping; sky-diving
- rain forests; hunting
- Tongariro National Park
- volcanic terrain, hot springs & pools
- airport, 10-min drive
- winter skiing

Four Mile Bay, Lake Taupo
Wharewaka Lodge

Hosts Susan and Tony Dalby

87 Wharewaka Road, Four Mile Bay, Taupo *Mobile* 021 164 1308
Phone 0-7-378 8169 *Email* wharewakalodgetaupo@xtra.co.nz
Fax 0-7-376 9145 *Website* friars.co.nz/hosts/wharewaka.html

Double $250–$280 Includes breakfast Lunch & dinner extra
Single $200–$220 Off-season rates available

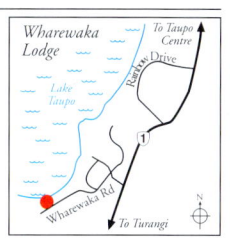

DIRECTIONS: From north take SH 1 through Taupo township towards airport. Turn right into Wharewaka & left into Wharewaka Rd to Lodge on right. From south, turn left off SH 1 into Wharewaka, then as above.

Located on the lake edge with direct access to a safe swimming beach, Wharewaka Lodge is a contemporary home built in 2003 to provide accommodation for six guests in three ensuite guestrooms. A courtyard and small private garden are popular with guests and trout may be caught from the bottom of the landscaped garden. Each bedroom includes a seating area, fridge, tea/coffee facilities, home-made biscuits, juice, mineral water and fruit, and opens to a private balcony with lake views. Breakfast is served either indoors or alfresco on the terrace looking out to Lake Taupo. Lunch or picnic baskets and dinner are also available by arrangement. Guests enjoy kayaking on the lake in front of the Lodge in the two kayaks provided.

Facilities
- 1 super-king, 1 super-king/twin & 1 queen bedroom, all with TV, fridge, tea/coffee, private balcony & lake views
- 3 tiled ensuites, each with bath, hair dryer, toiletries, heated floor & heated towel rails
- cotton bed linen; bathrobes
- guest elevator to 1 queen bedroom
- central heating; double glazing
- fresh flowers
- breakfast indoors or alfresco
- lunch or picnic basket & dinner, by arrangement, extra
- lounge with open fireplace & Sky TV
- laundry facilities
- fax & internet available
- courtesy passenger transfer
- off-street parking

Activities available
- beach & lake access from site
- 2 kayaks available
- swimming, kayaking, cycling, walking & fly fishing from site
- small business retreats catered
- boat tours on Lake Taupo
- 3 golf courses, 1 international
- hot mineral pools, 10 mins
- bush walks; horse trekking
- restaurants & shops, 7km
- watersports; trout fishing
- bungy jumping; parasailing
- sky-diving; airport, 5 mins
- jet boating to Huka Falls
- thermal areas, 15-min drive
- winter snow skiing, 1 hour
- Rotorua, 1¼ hours
- Hawke's Bay vineyard & gannet tours, 1½ hours
- Waitomo Caves, 1¾ hours

LAKE TAUPO
LAKE EDGE LODGE

Host Jean Hughes

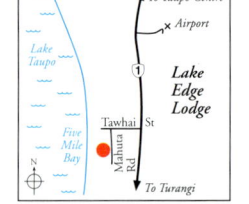

60 Mahuta Road, Five Mile Bay, R D 2, Taupo
Phone 0-7-378 0563   *Mobile* 021 112 2822   *Fax* 0-7-378 0563
Email jean@lakeedgelodge.co.nz   *Website* www.lakeedgelodge.co.nz

| 4 bdrm | 2 enst | 1 prbth | Room rate $180–$300
Seasonal or long-stay rates available | Breakfast or continental hamper extra
Self-catering |

DIRECTIONS: From Taupo township take SH 1 south for 8km to Five Mile Bay. Turn right into Tawhai St & left into Mahuta St. Lake Edge Lodge halfway along on right. From Turangi, take SH 1 north towards airport.

Located right on the water's edge at Five Mile Bay on Lake Taupo, Lake Edge Lodge has been renovated and refurbished to provide three self-catering options. The Boat Shed is a totally self-contained apartment comprising two bedrooms, a bathroom and a full kitchen, and opens to a garden setting. The Kowhai and Tui Rooms have an ensuite bathroom and kitchenette each, and open directly to the lake, with views of Mt Ruapehu across the water. A full breakfast is offered in the upstairs dining room, or a continental breakfast hamper can be provided. Restaurants and cafés are 10 minutes north at Taupo town centre. A sailing dinghy and canoe are available for guest use, and the beach is popular for swimming and watersports.

Facilities

- Boatshed apartment: 1 queen & 1 twin bedroom share 1 bathroom & double spa bath
- Kowhai: 1 king/twin ensuite bedroom with double spa bath
- Tui: 1 queen ensuite bedroom
- hair dryers, toiletries, heated towel rails & bathrobes
- fresh flowers
- central heating
- breakfast, $12.50 pp, or continental hamper, extra
- kitchen or kitchenette
- open fireplace, nibbles, TV, video, CDs, games, artwork, books & desk in lounge
- email, fax & phone available
- laundry available, $5
- secure car & boat parking
- courtesy passenger transfer

Activities available

- outdoor cocker spaniel on site
- sailing dinghy & canoe for guest use
- walks, swimming beach, watersports & fly fishing at lake edge from site
- white water rafting, transport available from door
- fishing pools at Waitahanui Stream, 2-min drive
- parasailing; bungy jumping
- bush walks; horse trekking
- Taupo restaurants & cafés, 10-min drive north
- hot mineral pools
- scenic flights
- jet boating
- trout fishing at Tongariro River, 30 mins south
- Tongariro National Park & skiing at Whakapapa, 1-hour drive

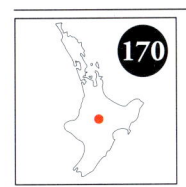

TURANGI
IKA LODGE

Hosts Suzanne and Kerry Simpson

155 Taupahi Road, Turangi *Postal* P O Box 259, Turangi
Phone 0-7-386 5538 *Fax* 0-7-386 5538
Email ikalodge@xtra.co.nz *Website* www.ika.co.nz

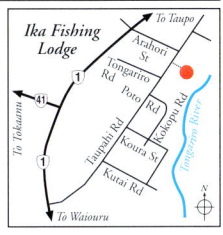

Double $140–$180
Single $120–$140
Apartment rate $160–$260

Includes breakfast

Lunch & dinner extra
Self-catering in apartment

4 bdrm | 2 enst | 1 prbth

DIRECTIONS: From Taupo take SH 1 to Turangi. Turn left into Arahori St. At "T" junction turn right into Taupahi Rd. Take 1st driveway on left to Ika Fishing Lodge. From south take SH 1 to Turangi. Turn right into Taupahi Rd.

Originally designed as a fishing lodge in 1955, Ika was renovated and extended under the guidance of architect John Wilcox in 1998 to offer two guestrooms and two-bedroom self-contained apartment. The highlight for guests is fly fishing for trout with the resident guide Kerry, who is a member of the New Zealand Professional Fishing Guide Association. The Lodge has direct access to the Tongariro River, a haven for brown and rainbow trout, as well as being close to Lake Taupo. Guided river excursions are available for anglers of all levels of experience, or the Lodge's own six-metre boat can be used on the lake. Heli-fishing can also be arranged. Kerry's fishing is complemented by Suzanne's cuisine – as resident chef she offers all meals to suit guests' requirements.

Facilities

- 1 queen ensuite bedroom downstairs
- 1 queen/twin ensuite bedroom upstairs
- 1 self-contained apartment with 1 queen/twin & 1 king/twin bedroom
- hair dryers, toiletries & heated towel rails in all 3 bathrooms
- cotton bed linen, flowers, Sky TV & tea/coffee in all 4 bedrooms
- phone, fax & email in office
- open fire in guest lounge
- resident chef
- 3-course dinner, $50 pp, BYO
- lunch by request, $25 pp in guests' dining room
- full kitchen in apartment for self-catering
- powder room
- off-street parking
- courtesy passenger transfer

Activities available

- garden seating on site
- direct river access from site
- fly fishing for trout in lake & rivers, resident guide
- raft & heli-fishing arranged
- golf course, 1km away
- white water rafting
- walking & hiking
- Turangi shopping centre & township, 5-min drive
- restaurants, walking distance
- Lake Taupo, 10-min drive
- thermal pools, 1km drive
- eco river raft tours
- Tongariro National Park, world heritage area
- horse trekking
- skiing, 30-min drive, July–October
- Taupo airport, 40-min drive

Turangi
Rainbow Trout Lodge

Hosts Jenny Shieff and Heather Macdonald

213 Taupahi Road, Turangi
Phone 0-7-386 6501   *Mobile* 021 729 081   *Fax* 0-7-386 6502
Email jenny@turangi-nz.co.nz   *Website* www.turangi-nz.co.nz

| 3 bdrm | 1 enst | 1 prbth |

Double $185–$270
Single $125–$210

Includes breakfast
Lunch & dinner extra

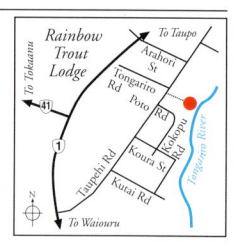

DIRECTIONS: From Taupo take SH 1 to Turangi. Turn left into Arahori St. At T junction turn right into Taupahi Rd. Travel 500 m to Rainbow Trout Lodge on left. From south, turn right into Taupahi Rd, at "Welcome" sign.

Opening directly onto the Tongariro River, Rainbow Trout Lodge is the closest accommodation (*see centre of photograph above*) to the renowned Major Jones Pool, just opposite the back gate. Named after the rainbow trout that are frequently caught at this spot, the Lodge provides three guestrooms and everything the beginner or expert needs for fishing, including a resident professional fishing guide and adviser, Heather. Guiding for anglers and hunters is available on request. Jenny complements the fishing or other activities with her cuisine – there is a full breakfast, followed by lunch and dinner by arrangement. Dinner menus reflect guests' tastes, use the best of local produce and are inspired by the cooking of New Orleans and the Pacific Rim.

Facilities
- 1 king bedroom with double shower in ensuite & TV
- 1 super-king/twin & 1 queen bedroom share 1 bathroom
- cotton bed linen; fresh flowers
- hair dryers, bathrobes, toiletries, & towel rails in both bathrooms
- lounge with open fire, nibbles, tea/coffee, Sky TV, DVD, video, CDs, desk & original artwork
- through gate to river walks
- breakfast indoors or alfresco
- lunch, $12–$15 pp
- 3-course table d'hôte dinner, $65 pp
- phone, fax & email
- library & music
- complimentary laundry
- fish-cleaning table outside
- passenger transfer; on-site parking

Activities available
- 3 decks for dining, relaxing or reading
- fishing tuition & guided fly fishing by Heather, NZPFGA
- fishing equipment available
- fishing catch cooked or smoked
- pétanque/boules on site
- spaniel, Lottie, & 2 cats on site
- hot mineral pools, 7-min drive
- golf course, 3-min drive
- bistro in walking distance
- boating on lake
- lake & river fishing
- river rafting
- bicycles & kayaks for hire
- tramping; hiking
- Taupo township, 35 mins
- Tongariro Crossing
- Tongariro National Park & winter ski-fields, 35 mins

Pukawa Bay, Lake Taupo
Paratiho-by-the-Lake Cottage

Hosts John and Valda Milner

10 Kowhai Drive, Upper Pukawa Bay, R D 1, Turangi
Phone 0-7-386 6318 *Email* milners@paratihonz.co.nz
Fax 0-7-386 6418 *Website* www.paratihonz.co.nz

Cottage rate $160 for 2 persons
Extra persons $50 each

Self-catering
No meals available

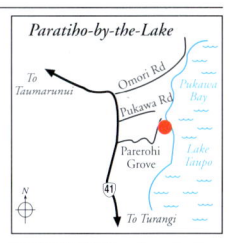

2 bdrm | 1 prbth

DIRECTIONS: From Turangi, take SH 41 north for 14km. Turn right into Parerohi Grove. After 300m, turn left into Kowhai Drive. Continue 100m to drive on left, to Paratiho-by-the-Lake. Cottage on right.

Meaning "Paradise", Paratiho-by-the-Lake is located overlooking the western shores of Lake Taupo with views to Taupo township with relected lights at night in the distance. Purpose-built in 1996, this self-contained cottage is 100 metres from the main homestead, which ensures guest privacy for single-party bookings. A full kitchen enables guests to self-cater. French doors open to a large sundeck with a gas barbecue and outdoor furniture for alfresco dining. Paratiho is set in 2.6 hectares (6.5 acres) of developing gardens including 7,000 trees, a small vineyard, olive grove and pond, with native trees attracting birdlife. John is a retired fishing guide, and enjoys assisting fishing enthusiasts. Turangi township is just 14 kilometres' drive south.

Facilities
- private party bookings only
- 1 self-contained cottage with 2 super-king/twin bedrooms & 1 private bathroom
- hair dryers, toiletries, heated towel rails, bath & bathrobes
- panoramic lake views
- self-serve laundry facilities
- phone, fax, email available
- children & pets welcome
- full kitchen for self-catering
- breakfast basket, $15 pp
- home-made biscuits
- lounge with log fire & TV
- gas BBQ & loungers on patio
- garaging; boat parking
- friendly labrador retriever dog, Travis, on site
- courtesy guest transfer to & from Taupo Airport

Activities available
- 2.6ha developing gardens with small vineyard & olive grove
- fly fishing for trout in Tongariro River & streams, resident guide
- guided trout fishing by boat on Lakes Taupo or Otamangakau
- watersports – white water rafting, kayaking, canoeing, yachting, waterskiing & swimming
- eco tours on *Tongariro Delta*
- private gardens open to visit
- restaurants, Tokaanu 8km & Turangi 14km
- choice of local bush/lake & Tongariro National Park walks
- thermal pools, 8km; horse trekking; scenic flights
- 18-hole golf course
- Tongariro National Trout Centre complex, 15 mins
- snow skiing, July–Sept

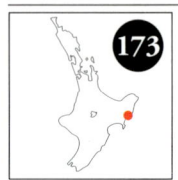

GISBORNE
CEDAR HOUSE

Hosts Derek and Carole Green

4 Clifford Street, Gisborne
Phone 0-6-868 1902   *Email* stay@cedarhouse.co.nz
Fax 0-6-867 1932   *Website* www.cedarhouse.co.nz

| 4 bdrm | 3 enst | 1 prbth | 2 pdrm | Room rate $190–$265 | *Includes breakfast* |

DIRECTIONS: From Gladstone Rd (SH 35), turn north-east at Peel St lights. Continue straight ahead through roundabout into Fitzherbert St. At end, turn left into Clifford St. Cedar House 1st on left.

Originally built in 1909, Cedar House has a colourful history including a period as a girls' school. With substantial renovations 90 years later, it now provides quality accommodation, while retaining original features include timber panelling, over three-metre high ceilings, and leadlight windows. The original cedar tree, after which the house was named, is now being used for cedar fences and landscaping timber. This Edwardian home offers four spacious guestrooms and bathrooms, a guest lounge and a 24-hour accessible refreshment area. Guests meet for hosted pre-dinner drinks and hors d'oeuvres prior to dining out at a choice of restaurants within walking distance. Special breakfast diets, including gluten-free ones, are catered for.

Facilities
- 4 super-king/twin bedrooms
- 3 ensuites & 1 private bathroom
- 2 double spa baths
- heated towel rails & mirrors, hair dryers, robes, slippers
- Sky TV in each room
- internet access available
- magazines & newspapers
- basic French & German spoken
- cooked breakfast menu
- complimentary apéritifs
- 24-hr tea/coffee & minibar
- artwork & fresh flowers
- balcony/deck for smoking
- children over 10 yrs welcome
- courtesy passenger transfer
- special weekends; small seminars & conferences catered
- off-street parking

Activities available
- beaches nearby for swimming, surfing, walking & relaxing
- Maori meeting houses/marae
- trout fishing, guide available
- wineries, cidery & brewery visits
- Wine & Food Festival, in Oct.
- 15 restaurants within walking distance
- sea & freshwater fishing
- City Centre, 7-min walk
- historical sites, eg Captain Cook's landing place
- Morere Hot Springs
- Eastwoodhill Arboretum
- 4WD coast & farm tours
- river kayaking; horse treks
- gardens to visit
- craft trail
- museums & galleries
- East Cape tours

WAINUI BEACH, GISBORNE
BIG TREE HIDEAWAY

Hosts Kim Holland and Glen Mills

9 Cleary Road, Wainui Beach, Gisborne
Phone 0-6-868 5867   *Fax* 0-6-868 5857   *Mobile* 027 439 9012
Email stay@bigtree.co.nz   *Website* friars.co.nz/hosts/bigtree.html

3 bdrm | 2 enst | 1 prbth

Double $220–$250
Single $180

Includes breakfast
Self-catering in 1 cottage only

DIRECTIONS: 5 mins' drive from Gisborne. Take SH 35 from Gisborne City to Wainui. Turn right into Oneroa Rd, then right again into Murphy Rd. Take 1st right into Cleary Rd. Big Tree Hideaway at end.

Set in a native garden, within walking distance of Wainui Beach, is Big Tree Hideaway, with a big macrocarpa tree sheltering the spa pool. Two turn-of-the-century shearers' cottages have been salvaged and meticulously restored. Original features include the corrugated iron exteriors, native timber walls, hand-forged fittings, crafted wooden bed-ends, and polished wooden floors. The "Shearer-tin" cottage provides two spacious sunny ensuite guestrooms, while "The Hideaway" is a self-contained queen-size cottage offering self-catering for longer stays. Breakfast is served in the cottages, in the garden, or in the hosts' home. Big Tree Hideaway is located close to the ocean, yet only five minutes' drive from Gisborne City, the first in the world to greet each day.

Facilities
- 1 cottage with 1 super-king/twin & 1 queen ensuite bedroom
- 1 self-contained cottage with 1 queen ensuite bedroom & kitchen for self-catering
- cotton bed linen
- fresh fruit, flowers & chocolates
- teas/coffee & home-made biscuits
- fridge & minibar; CD-player
- TV, email, fax & phone
- breakfast in guests' room, with hosts, or on guest verandah
- Shearers' Special breakfast of fresh orange juice, home-made muesli, bread/muffins & special cooked options
- hair dryers, bathrobes, heated towel rails & toiletries
- laundry facilities, extra charge
- not suitable for children or pets
- courtesy passenger transfer

Activities available
- spa pool under big tree
- swimming, surfing & sea fishing in walking distance
- beach walks
- golf courses
- vineyards, wineries & cidery
- Wainui Beach close by
- trout fishing
- Botanic Gardens, 7-min drive away
- restaurants, café/bar nearby
- horse trekking
- set of *Whale Rider*, 20-min drive away
- viewing lit bridges in evening
- museum & art gallery
- private gardens open to visit
- local working artists & craftspeople
- Gisborne City, 5-min drive

Manutuke, Gisborne
Opou – A Country House

Hosts Robyn Bickford and Manav Garewal

95 Whakato Road, Manutuke   *Postal* P O Box 139, Manutuke, via Gisborne
Phone 0-6-862 8732   *Mobile* 025 209 6431   *Fax* 0-6-862 8042
Email stay@opoucountryhouse.co.nz   *Website* www.opoucountryhouse.co.nz

| 4 bdrm | 2 enst | 2 prbth | 2 pdrm | Double $420–$675 Single $420–$506 | Includes breakfast Lunch & dinner extra House rate $1,690 up to 8 persons |

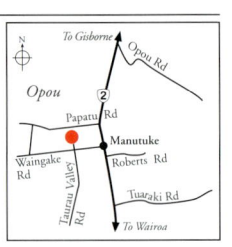

DIRECTIONS: From Gisborne take SH 2 south for 13.5km to turnoff for Manutuke. Turn right past church into Manutuke. Turn right into Whakato Rd & cross 2 cattle stops to Opou – A Country House.

Opou was built in the 1880s by Captain Read, a well known trader in Gisborne. From 1910 it has been owned by the Clarks, a pioneering landowning family of the Gisborne area. Opou is set in almost two hectares of garden surrounded by a further 12 hectares (30 acres) of farmland. This large house is suitable for family groups, small conferences and retreats, as well as individual travellers. The four bedrooms are upstairs, spacious and furnished with an eclectic mix of furniture. A full Western or Asian breakfast is served downstairs or alfresco, and lunch or picnics are available by arrangement. Opou is licensed, and complimentary pre-dinner drinks can be folllowed by dinner, or a driver can take guests into the restaurants 15 minutes away.

Facilities
- 2 super-king/twin ensuite bedrooms
- 2 super-king/twin bedrooms with private bathrooms
- bathrobes, demist mirrors, hair dryers, double basins & toiletries
- cotton bed linen, fresh flowers, chocolates, tea/coffee in rooms
- Sky TV, video, DVD, CDs, library, nibbles, licensed bar
- 4 open fireplaces

- Western or Asian breakfast
- picnic/lunch menu $55 pp
- 3–4-course dinner, $80 pp
- courtyard with open fire for alfresco dining
- phone, fax & email available
- children welcome
- laundry available, extra charge
- Hindi, Urdu & Malay spoken
- on-site parking; helipad

Activities available
- swimming pool on site
- garden tours, pheasant, quail, 2 dogs & 1 cat on site
- croquet & pétanque on site
- in-house beauty treatments, massage & cooking classes
- Gisborne Wine & Food Festival in October
- vineyards; farm activities
- sea & river fishing; boat tours

- restaurants, Gisborne, 15-min drive, driver available
- shopping; arts & crafts; golf
- safe beaches; horse trekking
- Maori culture & arts; picnics
- Eastwood Hill Arboretum
- back country 4WD adventures
- helicopter tours; charter flights
- airport, 12-min drive
- Gisborne City, 13.5 km north

OPOUTAMA, MAHIA
TUNANUI STATION COTTAGES

Hosts Leslie and Ray Thompson

1001 Tunanui Road, R D 3, Opoutama, Mahia, Northern Hawke's Bay
Phone 0-6-837 5790 *Mobile* 027 240 2421 *Fax* 0-6-837 5797
Email tunanui@xtra.co.nz *Website* www.tunanui.co.nz

4 bdrm	2 prbth	3 bdrm	1 prbth	Cottage rate for 2 persons $195 Low-season weekly rates *Self-catering*
				Extra adults $50 each, children $30 *Breakfast provisions & dinner extra*

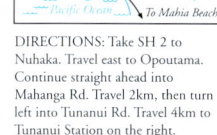

DIRECTIONS: Take SH 2 to Nuhaka. Travel east to Opoutama. Continue straight ahead into Mahanga Rd. Travel 2km, then turn left into Tunanui Rd. Travel 4km to Tunanui Station on the right.

Tunanui Station is a 2,000-hectare sheep and cattle farm in the hills overlooking Mahia Peninsula, in Northern Hawke's Bay. Owned and hosted by a third-generation farming family, Tunanui offers two separate fully self-contained cottages providing guests with privacy and seclusion. The Cottage (*above*) is nestled among trees, backed by five hectares of native bush. Built in 1898, The Cottage still features the Edwardian layout of the rooms, with original kauri doors, rimu flooring and open fireplace in the lounge. A few hundred metres down the road, set in its private garden, is The Farmhouse (*below*) with panoramic views of farmland, the peninsula and the ocean beyond. The Farmhouse, built in 1975, is larger and more spacious than The Cottage. Both are well-appointed and furnished in a comfortable country style with some antique furniture. They are suitable for longer stays to provide time for unwinding in the seclusion of Tunanui Station and for exploring the farm and surrounding region.

Facilities
- 2 self-contained cottages
- single-party bookings
- 3 bedrooms & 1 bathroom with dual-shower in The Cottage
- 4 bedrooms & 2 bathrooms with bath in The Farmhouse
- cotton bed linen, hair dryers, feather & wool bedding
- fresh flowers & fresh herbs
- lounges with open fire, TV, video, CD & NZ books
- children welcome
- phone card guest phones
- fax available
- guest laundries with irons
- 2 full kitchens for self-catering
- breakfast provisions, by arrangement, extra
- dinner/BBQ with hosts, by arrangement, extra
- verandahs with BBQs
- underfloor heating, separate dining room & dishwasher in The Farmhouse only
- secure parking
- 2 car garaging with The Farmhouse
- helipad
- farm airstrip
- low-season May-September weekly rates available

Activities available
On site:
- 2,000-ha (5,100-acre) farm
- seasonal farm activities with sheep, cattle, working dogs & horse-riding for advanced riders arranged, extra
- farm roads for scenic walks & mountain biking
- secluded river valley
- private river swimming
- picnics; trout fishing
- historic concrete viaduct
- indigenous forest & birds
- guests' horses welcome
- grass tennis court

Off site:
- Mahia Beach; fishing charters
- hot mineral pools at Morere
- private gardens to visit
- guided caving trips
- 9-hole golf course, clubs hire
- guided tours to carved Maori meeting house on marae
- marae community dinners
- wineries, 60-min drive north
- 2 arboretums, 90-min drive
- Lake Waikaremoana, 90 mins
- bar at Bistro at Mahia Beach
- Gisborne City, 60 mins north
- Wairoa town, 40 mins south

MAHIA, GISBORNE
THE QUARTERS

Hosts Malcolm and June Rough

867 Mahanga Road, Mahia Postal R D 8, Nuhaka
Phone 0-6-837 5751   Email m.rough@xtra.co.nz
Fax 0-6-837 5721   Website www.quarters.co.nz

2 bdrm | 1 prbth | Double $165–$185
Extra persons $25–$30 each

Self-catering
Breakfast provisions & dinner extra

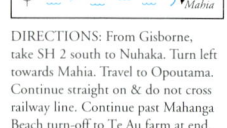

DIRECTIONS: From Gisborne, take SH 2 south to Nuhaka. Turn left towards Mahia. Travel to Opoutama. Continue straight on & do not cross railway line. Continue past Mahanga Beach turn-off to Te Au farm at end.

With unimpeded ocean views, the site on Te Au Farm was carefully chosen for The Quarters. The fully renovated shearers' quarters were relocated to this coastal farm to provide total privacy and comfort for those wanting to get away from it all. Single-party bookings of eight people can be accommodated. The queen-size bedroom, designer bunkroom and living room all open to the large deck for dining and taking in the truly panoramic sea vistas. A fully equipped kitchen makes self-catering easy, with fresh crayfish when available. Home-cooked meals can also be provided. Guests can join in activities on the sheep and beef farm. Fishing from the rock is popular and there are extensive marked walks with coastal, farm and bush views.

Facilities

- self contained accommodation
- single-party bookings only
- 1 queen bedroom
- 1 twin room with 2 sets of designer bunks
- 1 private bathroom
- toiletries & heated towel rails
- self-serve laundry
- panoramic views over ocean
- children welcome
- fresh bread & crayfish (when available) on arrival
- fully equipped kitchen for self-catering
- breakfast provisions by arrangement, extra
- dinner by arrangement: frozen home-made meals or BBQ with hosts, extra
- large glass doors opening to peaceful deck

Activities available

- BBQ with hosts, by request
- walks on 711ha sheep & beef farm & Bush Reserve
- viewing sunrise over ocean
- mountain bikes for hire
- limestone tennis court
- farm activities on site
- hunting – pig & goat
- crayfish & paua collecting
- marae visits; golf courses
- trout fishing & river swimming
- Mahanga Beach, nearby, 2-min drive to 6km sandy shoreline for swimming, surfing, boogie boarding & walking
- social excursions around Mahia Peninsula
- 2 restaurants & cafés, 15 mins
- wineries; Morere Hot Pools
- Gisborne City, 1-hour drive

Ahuriri, Napier
Hardinge Cottage

Host Gilda Swayn   *Mobile* 027 249 3613

51 Hardinge Road, Ahuriri   *Postal* 20 Havelock Road, Napier
Phone 0-6-835 0584   *Email* gilda@hardingecottage.co.nz
Fax 0-6-835 5114   *Website* www.hardingecottage.co.nz

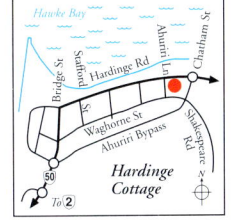

2 bdrm   1 prbth

Cottage rate $450   *Includes breakfast provisions*   *Self-catering*

DIRECTIONS: From north, take SH 2 past airport & turn left into West Quay St. Turn left into Bridge St & right into Hardinge Rd. Cottage on right. From south, take Marine Pde past port into Hardinge Rd.

Located across the road from the ocean, Hardinge is a single-storey cottage that survived the 1931 Napier earthquake. Originally a fisherman's bach built in the 1920s, Hardinge was restored and refurbished in 2000 to offer quality self-contained accommodation. The two bedrooms open into the elegant lounge with expansive harbour views. A small fully equipped kitchen provides for self-catering and alfresco dining is popular in the secluded sunny courtyard. Shopping, cafés, restaurants and art gallery are just 10 minutes' walk away in the historic precinct at the marina, and a sandy beach is five minutes' walk along the harbour. The Art Deco City of Napier offers guided tours and there are activities to suit all interests.

Facilities
- single-party bookings
- self-contained cottage
- 1 queen & 1 double bedroom
- 1 private bathroom
- hair dryer, toiletries, heated towel rails & bathrobes
- cotton bed linen; fresh flowers
- lounge with electric fire, TV, VCR, CD-player, stereo, desk, books, games & phone
- breakfast provisions supplied
- kitchen for self-catering
- fruit, nibbles, confectionery
- children by arrangement
- beach towels & picnic basket
- large self-serve laundry
- Arabic & basic French & German spoken by host
- 2 verandahs & rear courtyard
- off-street parking; transfer

Activities available
- BBQ in courtyard on site
- sandy beach, 5-min walk
- fishing & sailing nearby
- art galleries, 10-min walk
- beautician, 10-min walk
- guided Art Deco tours
- local wineries; wine tours
- saltwater swimming pool
- museum; gardens to visit
- Ahuriri shops, restaurants & cafés, 10-min walk away
- marina & historic precinct
- golfing; hiking; heritage walks
- Hastings & Havelock North village, 20-min drive
- gannet colony at Cape Kidnappers, 30-min drive
- scenic flights arranged
- airport, 15-min drive

BLUFF HILL, NAPIER
COBDEN VILLA

Hosts Amy and Cornel Walewski

11 Cobden Road, Napier *Mobile* 021 121 6666
Phone 0-6-835 9065 *Email* stay@cobdenvilla.com
Fax 0-6-833 6979 *Website* www.cobdenvilla.com

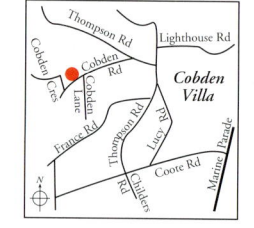

DIRECTIONS: From Marine Pde, travel towards Port, then turn left into Coote Rd. Turn right into Thompson Rd & keep left. Then turn left again into Cobden Rd. Cobden Villa on right.

| 4 bdrm | 3 enst | 1 prbth | Room rate $225–$395 | Includes breakfast |

Set in a garden on Bluff Hill is Cobden Villa, built in 1870 as a residence for Nathaniel Kettle, one of the first homes in the area. Recently restored and refurbished in Art Deco-style, each of the four guest bedrooms is furnished in individual design and colours. The Chiparus honeymoon suite includes an ensuite with double jet spa bath and separated double steamroom shower, opening onto a balcony overlooking the garden with ocean views. Guests enjoy watching the sunset over the harbour from the verandah and can see the ocean sunrise from the conservatory where gourmet cooked breakfast is served, with fresh baking and homemade jams. Amy and Cornel live in a separate wing, their love of Art Deco bringing them from America in 2001.

Facilities

- Chiparus Room: king ensuite & spa bath & double shower steam-room
- Érte Room: queen ensuite
- Cassandre Room: queen ensuite
- Vargas Room: twin bedroom with private bathroom
- cotton bed linen, robes, hair dryers, heated towel rails & toiletries
- lounge with open fire, tea/coffee, nibbles, piano, artwork & books
- gourmet cooked or continental breakfast
- picnic basket, $25–$75
- conservatory with Sky TV, video, books & magazines
- verandahs or balcony opening from all bedrooms
- email, fax & phone
- private guest entrance
- off-street parking

Activities available

- large garden & grounds on site with over 100 roses
- marineland
- Earthquake Museum
- Napier Beach
- gannet colony
- wineries
- Art Deco tours
- gardens open to visit
- water sports & activities
- restaurants & shopping within walking distance
- golf courses
- aquarium
- fishing
- hiking & walks
- art galleries
- Hastings, 20-min drive
- Taupo, 1½-hr drive
- Gisborne, 3½-hr drive

© Friars' Guide to New Zealand Accommodation for the Discerning Traveller

BLUFF HILL, NAPIER
MORNINGTON LODGE

Host Diana Swayn

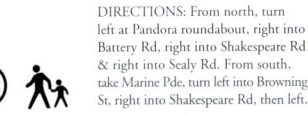

20A Sealy Road, Napier
Phone 0-6-835 4450   *Mobile* 025 538 820   *Fax* 0-6-835 4452
Email stay@mornington.co.nz   *Website* www.mornington.co.nz

Double $250
Single $220

Includes breakfast   *Dinner extra*
Family $370 for up to 4 persons

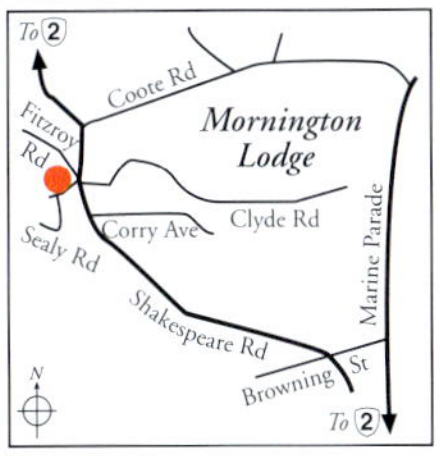

2 bdrm / 1 prbth

DIRECTIONS: From north, turn left at Pandora roundabout, right into Battery Rd, right into Shakespeare Rd & right into Sealy Rd. From south, take Marine Pde, turn left into Browning St, right into Shakespeare Rd, then left.

Renowned Napier architect Louis Hay designed Mornington in 1921 on Napier Hill. Named after the home of the original owners in Dunedin, Mornington overlooks the city with views to the Pacific Ocean and Cape Kidnappers. The bungalow-style house is complemented by the Arts and Crafts interiors with period furniture and William Morris fabrics and wallpapers and attention to detail. Accommodation comprises the red queen room, green twin room, each with fine linen, fresh flowers & quality confectionery. Both rooms open to a sunny east-facing verandah providing panoramic sunrises. Single-party bookings ensure privacy with the spacious bathroom including clawfoot bath and the lounge is available for entertaining friends.

Facilities
- private-party bookings only
- 1 queen & 1 twin bedroom
- 1 private bathroom with clawfoot bath, hair dryer, bathrobes & toiletries
- cotton bed linen
- both bedrooms open onto verandah with sea views
- lounge with open fire, tea/coffee, nibbles, Sky TV, video, stereo & books
- continental or cooked breakfast in dining room
- dinner by arrangement, extra
- email, fax & phone available
- laundry facilities available
- fresh flowers
- children welcome, unsuitable for toddlers
- garaging for 1 car
- courtesy passenger transfer

Activities available
- barbecue available
- 2 friendly cats on site
- beauty therapy & massage available by arrangement
- Art Deco walks
- wineries
- golf; fishing
- country tours
- Maori culture
- cafés, restaurants, bars & shopping, walking distance
- gardens to visit
- gannet safaris
- marineland
- chauffeured deco tours
- earthquake exhibition
- Hastings, 20 mins
- Taupo, 1½-hour drive
- Gisborne, 2½-hour drive

BLUFF HILL, NAPIER
FREEMANS ON CLYDE

Hosts Anthony and Sue Freeman

17 Clyde Road, Bluff Hill, Napier   *Mobile* 021 171 0209
Phone 0-6-835 9124   *Email* freemo@iprohome.co.nz
Fax 0-6-835 9129   *Website* hawkesbaynz.com/pages/freemansonclyde

3 bdrm   3 enst   Room rate $180   Winter rates available   *Includes breakfast*

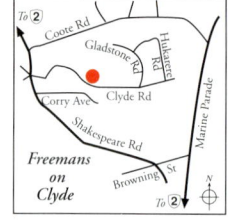

DIRECTIONS: From north take SH 2 to Hyderabad roundabout. Turn left into SH 50. Turn right into Coote Rd, left into Shakespeare Rd & left into Clyde Rd. From south, take Marine Pde & turn left into Coote Rd as above.

Originally built in 1854, Freemans on Clyde is one of Napier's earliest farmhouses that has survived the devastating 1931 earthquake. Located on Napier Hill, this colonial farmhouse features Cape Cod-style settler architecture and now offers three ensuite guestrooms. Guests enjoy relaxing on the large verandah and patio in the summer and beside the open fire in the guest lounge in winter. An extensive cottage garden includes an orchard of citrus trees, plums, olives and avocados. For breakfast guests wander five minutes down the hill to the city to Sue and Anthony's *Caffe Aroma*. Here they can choose from the full café menu included in the room rate. Waffles, bagels, a full English breakfast, Eggs Benedict or other cooked options are available.

Facilities
- 2 queen ensuite bedrooms
- 1 double ensuite bedroom with deck
- cotton bed linen
- heated towel rails
- phone in family room
- private guest lounge with open fire, tea/coffee, herbal teas, TV, CD-player, library, artwork, games & magazines
- breakfast in *Caffe Aroma*, hosts' café downtown, with full cooked & continental breakfast menu
- email available
- fresh flowers
- private guest entrance
- off-street parking
- Molly the fox terrier in residence

Activities available
- half acre cottage garden on site with orchard, citrus trees, olives, avocados & plums
- downtown Napier shops, 5-min walk away
- bush walks
- Art Deco walks
- gardens to visit
- golf courses
- vineyard tours
- many restaurants, bars & cafés within walking distance
- gannet colony
- national aquarium of NZ
- marineland
- public gardens
- earthquake exhibition
- Hastings, 20 mins
- Taupo, 1½-hour drive
- Gisborne, 2½-hour drive

Napier
Gladstone Villa

Hosts Raewyn and Peter Dailey

21 Gladstone Road, Napier   *Phone* 0-6-835 6413
Email gladstonevilla@xtra.co.nz   *Mobile* 021 366 613
Fax 0-6-835 9865   *Website* friars.co.nz/hosts/gladstonevilla.html

2 bdrm   1 prbth

Villa rate $155 for 2 persons
$25 pp for 3 extra persons

Includes continental breakfast provisions
Self-catering

DIRECTIONS: Take SH 2 to Napier. From Marine Pde turn left into Coote Rd, left into Shakespeare Rd & left into Clyde Rd. Turn left again into Gladstone Rd to Gladstone Villa on right towards end.

Gladstone Villa is the lower self-contained floor of the home designed in 1889 by renowned heritage architect, Tilleard Natusch. The hosts live upstairs and the newly renovated Villa below now provides accommodation for up to five guests. Set in a garden on a private hill location, Gladstone Villa is on a quiet sunny north-facing site, just minutes from the Art Deco township of Napier via pedestrian steps and walkways. Local shops, restaurants and cafés abound, and a kitchenette enables guests to self-cater. Fresh fruit and continental breakfast provisions are supplied each day and guests can dine indoors or alfresco. Two bedrooms, the lounge including a sofa-bed, spacious tiled bathroom and separate laundry complete the Villa.

Facilities
- single-party bookings
- 1 self-contained villa
- 1 queen & 1 single bedroom
- 1 private tiled bathroom
- cotton bed linen
- hair dryer, toiletries & heated towel rails
- lounge with Sky TV, phone, magazines & double sofa-bed
- children welcome
- continental breakfast provisions supplied daily
- large kitchenette for self-catering
- dining area
- full self-serve laundry
- iron & ironing board
- private sunny guest terrace
- hosts in separate home above
- off-street parking
- outdoor cat, Tiger, on site

Activities available
- outdoor seating area
- Centennial Gardens, 3-min walk
- Ocean Spa pool complex, 5 min walk
- Art Deco tours, 5-min drive
- national aquarium of NZ
- wineries; walks
- gardens open to visit
- cinemas
- gannets at Cape Kidnappers
- cafés & restaurants, 5-min drive or 10-min walk
- swimming beaches
- heritage trails
- art gallery
- golf courses
- Napier shops, 5-min drive
- Hastings, 20-min drive
- Havelock North, 25 mins
- Napier airport, 15 mins

© Friars' Guide to New Zealand Accommodation for the Discerning Traveller

NAPIER
THE MASTER'S LODGE

Hosts Joan and Larry Blume

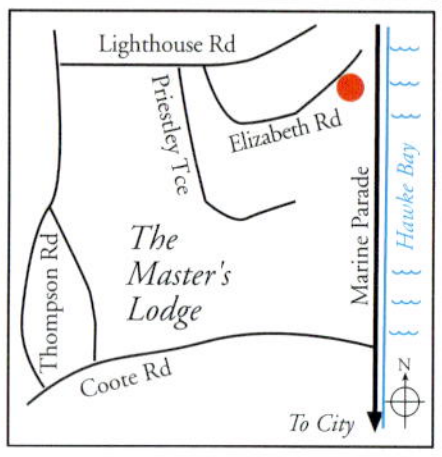

10 Elizabeth Road, Napier *Postal* P O Box 104, Napier
Phone 0-6-834 1946 *Email* unwind@masterslodge.co.nz
Fax 0-6-834 1947 *Website* www.masterslodge.co.nz

2 bdrm	2 enst	Room rate $740	Includes breakfast	Dinner extra
		Lodge rate $980	Includes breakfast & dinner	**Honeymoon specials available**

DIRECTIONS: From the City Centre, follow signs towards Bluff Hill Lookout. Travel 200m on Lighthouse Rd & take 2nd right into Elizabeth Rd. The Master's Lodge on right. Or follow map above.

High above the Art Deco City of Napier, overlooking the Pacific Ocean, The Master's Lodge offers tranquillity and privacy with exclusive accommodation and dining for four guests. Set in mature landscaped gardens, this historic 1900s home has been painstakingly restored to recapture the ambience of the times of the original master, pioneer Gerhard Husheer. Enlarged by famous architect Louis Hay in 1931, the Lodge features Art Deco/Nouveau detailing, leadlights and filigree woodwork which led to its 1997 Art Deco Merit Award. Guests are offered the Kidnappers Suite with panoramic views over Hawke Bay, or the Deco Suite with sea views from its private blacony and elevated bathtub. The Lodge's chef enjoys providing gourmet dinner on request.

Facilities
- 1 super-king/twin & 1 queen ensuite bedroom
- damask & pure cotton bed linen
- both ensuites include bath, hair dryer, toiletries & bathrobes
- direct-dial phone, modem, stereo system, writing desk in bedrooms
- dining room, guest lounge, drawing room, solarium & museum
- Sky TV & video available
- à la carte breakfast
- gourmet dining, extra
- extensive wine cellar
- Deco & antique furnishing
- historic architecture & Mediterranean landscaped gardens
- unsuitable for children/pets
- off-street parking & lock-up garaging

Activities available
- massage therapy available
- exclusive day/evening tours
- dinner with local winemaker
- Art Deco architecture
- earthquake museum
- shopping & galleries
- award-winning wineries
- 4 championship golf courses
- heritage trails
- restaurants, cafés & bars at City Centre, 10-min walk
- 1 of only 3 mainland gannet colonies in world
- horse riding
- gardens & parks to visit
- guided fly & deep-sea fishing
- flight-seeing; hot air ballooning
- gliding & paragliding
- start of Pacific Coast Highway

NAPIER
THE COUNTY HOTEL

Hosts Christopher and Angela Barons

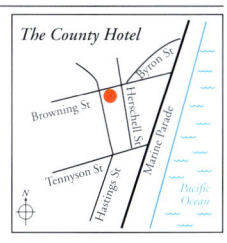

12 Browning Street, Napier   *Postal* P O Box 345, Napier
Phone 0-6-835 7800   *Freephone* 0800 THE HOTEL   *Fax* 0-6-835 7797
Email countyhotel@xtra.co.nz   *Website* www.countyhotel.co.nz

18 bdrm   18 enst   1 pdrm   Room rate $150–$550   *All meals extra*
Seasonal and B&B rates available

DIRECTIONS: In the CBD of Napier. Follow "Port" signs to Marine Pde. Turn west into Browning St. The County Hotel & Anatole's Café are on the left.

Originally built in 1909, The County Hotel is the only example of the Victorian-Edwardian classical revival style that survived the devastating 1931 Napier earthquake. Redevelopment since 1993 has transformed the former County Council building into a boutique hotel and popular restaurant. Original Edwardian Gothic features with Art Deco influences have been preserved, including the high ceilings and wood panelling. Each of the 18 queen bedrooms has been named after a different New Zealand native bird and includes writing bureau, dedicated modem line and Sky television. The library on the first level houses more than 1,000 books and has complimentary port for guests. Children can be accommodated on portable beds.

Facilities

- 2 twin & 16 queen bedrooms, each with ensuite bathroom
- 1 Regal Suite with 2 queen bedrooms, lounge, balcony & 2 bathrooms
- each ensuite bedroom includes writing bureau, Sky TV, phone, fax & electric blanket
- 2 wheelchair-access rooms
- central heating
- children welcome
- Chambers Restaurant on site, all meals extra
- Churchill's Champagne & Snug Bar
- complimentary newspaper
- guest library
- function rooms
- business centre
- foreign currency exchange
- 15 carparks

Activities available

- Chambers Fine Dining Restaurant on site
- Napier city shopping precinct
- museums
- art gallery
- theatres
- Marineland
- fountains
- aquarium
- Kiwi House
- Art Deco walk
- restaurants & cafés
- private gardens to visit
- public parks & seaside gardens
- beach
- fishing
- vineyards & orchards
- heritage trails
- 1 of only 3 mainland gannet colonies in NZ & the world

Puketapu, Napier
Silverford

Hosts Chris and William Orme-Wright

358 Dartmoor Road, Puketapu, Napier
Phone 0-6-844 5600   *Email* homestay@paradise.net.nz
Fax 0-6-844 4423   *Website* www.silverford.co.nz

3 bdrm | 1 enst | 1 prbth   Double $145–$165   Single $115   *Includes breakfast*

DIRECTIONS: From Napier, travel west to Puketapu. Turn left into Dartmoor Rd. Travel 3.5km to Silverford on right, & up oak driveway. From Hastings, cross bridge into Swamp Rd, turn right, then left twice.

Built from native kauri in 1906, with Tudor-style architecture, Silverford is a paradigm country residence designed by Tilleard Natusch to suit New Zealand timbers and conditions. The original rimu interiors with panelling and fireplaces remain intact, as does the inner courtyard garden. The deep verandahs provide shade from Hawke's Bay sunshine and open to the extensive garden. Guests are served breakfast in the country kitchen or alfresco on the verandah. Sited at the end of a half-kilometre oak-lined driveway, Silverford is set in seven hectares (17 acres) where guests enjoy the spacious lawns, established trees, ponds and orchards, in the quiet of the countryside, yet within easy access of the nearby cities. Dinner is available at The Mission Winery nearby.

Facilities
- 1 queen ensuite bedroom
- 1 king & 1 double bedroom share 1 guest bathroom
- 1 bath available
- heated towel rails & hair dryers
- electric blankets
- central heating
- use of family lounge with Sky TV
- guest lounge
- fresh flowers
- breakfast served in kitchen, or alfresco on verandah
- tea & coffee available
- phone, fax, email available
- laundry available
- historic architecture
- garden setting with ponds
- rural views
- on-site parking
- helipad

Activities available
- swimming pool on site
- friendly farm animals
- pétanque/boules on site
- à la carte dinner at The Mission Winery, 8km
- horse trekking
- golf courses
- gardens open to visit
- hot air ballooning; paragliding
- bush walks; beaches
- Taradale restaurants, 10-min drive
- restaurants at Napier & Hastings, 20-min drive
- wine tasting & vineyard lunches
- trout fishing
- croquet; aquarium
- gannet colony
- Napier airport, 25 mins

208

© Friars' Guide to New Zealand Accommodation for the Discerning Traveller

MANGATAHI, HASTINGS
MERRIWEE COUNTRY HOME

Host Jeanne Richards

29 Gordon Road, Te Awanga, Hawke's Bay
Phone 0-6-875 0111   *Mobile* 021 214 5023   *Fax* 0-6-875 0111
Email merriwee@xtra.co.nz   *Website* www.merriwee.co.nz

4 bdrm | 2 enst | 1 prbth

Room rate $110–$220
House rate $900

Includes breakfast
Self-catering in suite

Dinner extra

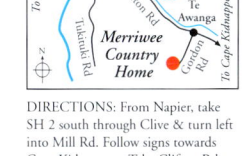

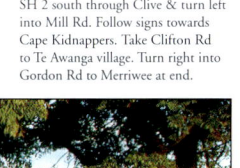

DIRECTIONS: From Napier, take SH 2 south through Clive & turn left into Mill Rd. Follow signs towards Cape Kidnappers. Take Clifton Rd to Te Awanga village. Turn right into Gordon Rd to Merriwee at end.

Set in a rural garden surrounded by two hectares of apricot orchards, Merriwee Country Home is an original villa built in 1908 on an elevated site overlooking the ocean. Te Awanga beach is just a stroll away and the mainland gannet colony at Cape Kidnappers is nearby. Merriwee offer guests four spacious bedrooms, including a self-contained suite, with French doors opening to large verandahs and a courtyard. A full breakfast with crêpes and other cooked options is served in the large country kitchen, and dinner is available by arrangement. Three wineries are within walking distance and restaurants at Napier, Hastings and Havelock North are all 15 minutes' drive away. Guests enjoy relaxing in the swimming pool area on site.

Facilities

- 1 self-contained suite with queen bedroom, ensuite, sitting room, kitchenette & private entrance
- 1 queen ensuite bedroom
- 1 king & 1 queen bedroom share 1 bathroom, with bath & bathrobes
- hair dryer, toiletries & heated towel rails in all 3 bathrooms; 1 with wheelchair access
- cotton bed linen; fresh flowers
- children welcome; cat & dog on site
- full breakfast served
- 3-course dinner & glass of wine, $45 pp; BYO
- tea/coffee, fruit, nibbles & home baking
- 3 living rooms with open fireplaces, TV, CDs, piano, games, artwork, books & writing desk
- email, fax & phones
- off-street parking

Activities available

- salt-water swimming pool, pétanque, cricket & soccer on site
- walks in 2ha grounds with gardens, lawns & apricot orchard on site
- wineries & vineyards, within walking distance
- Cape Kidnappers gannet colony & golf course, short drive away
- beach walks & ocean swimming
- hotwater pools; theatre & galleries
- restaurants & cafés, 15 mins
- guided walking, wine & art trails; horse riding
- gardens open to visit
- hot air balloons
- fishing – river & beach
- art deco Napier, 15 mins
- National Aquarium of NZ
- Marineland & model railway town, Lilliput

209   © Friars' Guide to New Zealand Accommodation for the Discerning Traveller

HAVELOCK NORTH
WELDON BOUTIQUE BED & BREAKFAST

Host Pracilla Hay

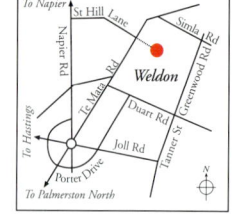

98 Te Mata Road, Havelock North *Postal* P O Box 8170, Havelock North
Freephone 0800 206 499 *Phone* 0-6-877 7551 *Fax* 0-6-877 7051
Email pracilla@weldon.co.nz *Website* www.weldon.co.nz

| 5 bdrm | 2 prbth | 1 shbth |

Double $130–$150
Single $90–$110

Includes breakfast
Dinner extra

DIRECTIONS: Take SH 2 to Havelock North. From roundabout in centre of village, take Te Mata Rd north for 0.9km. Opposite St Hill Lane, turn right into driveway to Weldon Boutique B&B.

Located at the end of a lavender-edged driveway at Weldon is the restored 90-year-old two-storey residence, with French Provençal style ambience. Accommodation is offered in spacious bedrooms elegantly furnished with period and antique furniture. Weldon is located away from the road in a quiet and peaceful setting, complementing the historic architecture, yet within easy walking distance of the cafés, restaurants and Irish pub in the village of Havelock North. Breakfast of fresh local fruits and gourmet cooked options is served alfresco in the garden among the roses in the spring and summer, or in the dining room during winter. Alternatively, continental breakfast can be served in the guests' bedrooms. Dinner is also available.

Facilities
- 1 single & 2 double bedrooms with bathroom upstairs, heated towel rails & toiletries
- 1 queen & 1 twin bedroom with 1 private bathroom & clawfoot bath downstairs
- cotton bed linen & bathrobes
- hair dryer, fresh flowers, TV, tea/coffee, biscuits, water & port in each bedroom
- laundry available

- full breakfast with fresh local fruits & cooked option
- 2-course dinner with wine, $45 pp, by arrangement; light snack, $10 pp
- guest lounge with tea/coffee, TV, video, library & piano
- phone, fax & email available
- courtyard to relax in
- private guest entrance; off-street parking

Activities available
- 2 toy poodle dogs, James & Thomas, on site
- wineries tours
- arts & crafts trails
- garden visits
- beaches
- walking
- golf courses
- Havelock North, 10-min walk away

- village cafés, restaurants & shops within walking distance
- bush walks
- Te Mata peak
- golden beaches, 20 mins away
- horse riding
- paragliding
- gannet safari tours
- Hastings, 10-min drive
- Art Deco Napier, 20 mins

© Friars' Guide to New Zealand Accommodation for the Discerning Traveller

HAVELOCK NORTH
The Villa

Host Sally Thompson

80 Napier Road, Havelock North   *Postal* P O Box 8867, Havelock North
Phone 0-6-877 8608   *Mobile* 021 896 710   *Fax* 0-6-877 4478
Email thevilla_hb@xtra.co.nz   *Website* the-villa.co.nz

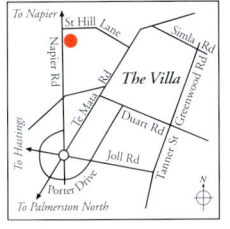

Villa rate $195 for 2 persons
Extra adults $40 each, children $20 each

Breakfast provisions extra
Self-catering

3 bdrm | 1 prbth

DIRECTIONS: From Napier, travel south towards Havelock North on SH 2. Take Havelock North turn-off & continue on Napier Rd just past St Hills Lane to The Villa on left. Or from village take Napier Rd north.

One of the original homes of Havelock North, The Villa was built in 1906 and now offers self-contained accommodation, just a short walk from the village. This colonial villa comprises three bedrooms, one bathroom including a bath, a lounge with wood burner, laundry, and full kitchen for self-catering. Plunger coffee, milk and a fruit bowl are supplied, with further breakfast provisions available on request. Shops, cafés and restaurants are within walking distance and Hawke's Bay wineries are popular with guests. Set in a cottage garden, The Villa also features a barbecue area for alfresco dining and swimming pool which is used by guests all summer. Children are welcome and The Villa sleeps up to six members of single party bookings.

Facilities
- single-party bookings
- 1 self-contained villa
- 1 queen, 1 double & 1 twin bedroom
- 1 private bathroom with bath
- hair dryer, toiletries & heated towel rails
- cotton bed linen; fresh flowers
- lounge with wood burner, Sky TV, video, CDs & piano
- breakfast provisions by arrangement, extra
- full kitchen for self-catering
- complimentary wine
- phone in dining area
- children welcome
- extra outdoor toilet
- self serve laundry
- off-street parking

Activities available
- BBQ on site
- pétanque/boules on site
- swimming pool on site
- parks & gardens to visit
- wineries & vineyards
- golf courses; bush walks
- swimming; jet boating
- scenic flights; hot air ballooning
- sea or river fishing
- restaurants & cafés nearby
- shopping, walking distance
- Havelock North village, within walking distance
- Art Deco tours in Napier
- Cape Kidnappers gannet tours, 20-min drive
- Hastings, 10-min drive
- Napier, 20-min drive
- airport, 30-min drive

HAVELOCK NORTH
THE GREENHOUSE

Hosts Bridget and Chris Jarvis

288 Te Mata Road, Havelock North   *Postal* R D 12, Havelock North
Phone 0-6-877 4904   *Mobile* 021 773 779   *Fax* 0-6-877 2097
Email the.greenhouse@xtra.co.nz   *Website* www.thegreenhouse.co.nz

| 3 bdrm | 1 prbth |

House rate $195 for 2 persons
Extra adults $50 each
Children $20 each

All meals extra
Self-catering

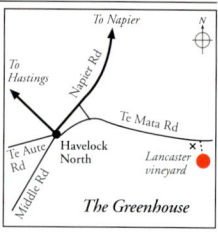

DIRECTIONS: From Napier, travel south towards Havelock North. Turn left into St Hill Lane. At "T" turn left again into Te Mata Rd. Continue to Lancaster vineyard on right. The Greenhouse is next door.

The Greenhouse is nestled in a corner of the Lancaster vineyard, overlooking chardonnay and merlot grapes. The ambience of the cottage is reminiscent of French farmhouses, with terracotta pots in wrought-iron window boxes and cedar shutters on the French doors and windows. Furnishings in natural tones complement the Italian dinnerware, seagrass matting and Country Road linen. Guest privacy is ensured through single-party bookings, with family groups and children welcome. The Greenhouse is totally self-contained with a fully equipped kitchen for self-catering if desired, or all meals can be provided by prior arrangement. Set in the heart of the Hawke's Bay wine trail, the cottage is within strolling distance of winery restaurants.

Facilities
- single-party bookings
- 2 queen & 1 single bedroom
- roll-away bed, cot, high-chair
- Country Rd bed linen, towels, bathrobes, & table napkins
- 1 private bathroom, hair dryer, toiletries & heated towel rail
- complimentary Te Mata Estate wine, fruitbowl & chocolates
- fresh flowers
- lunch at Black Barn Bistro, 7 days a week
- lunch Tues.–Sun., & dinner Fri.–Sat., from Bradshaw Estate Winery & Restaurant
- full kitchen for self-catering
- TV, phone, music, library, & log fire in sitting room
- fully equipped laundry
- off-street parking

Activities available
- gas BBQ, alfresco dining
- croquet & boules on site
- wine tours & tastings
- Tukituki River, end Te Mata Rd – scenic picnic spots, safe swimming holes, rafting
- 3 golf courses nearby
- 2 beaches – swimming, diving, surfing & deep-sea fishing
- guided fly fishing trips
- 3 winery restaurants & 5 wineries, strolling distance
- shopping nearby
- gannet safaris
- horse riding
- helicopter flights
- paragliding; jet boating
- hot air ballooning
- garden visits
- Art Deco tours

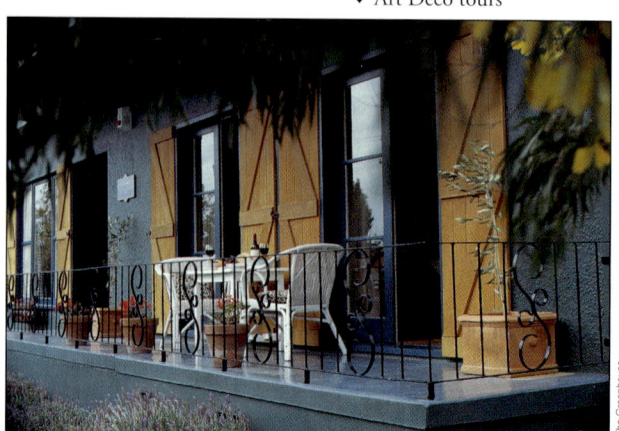

HAVELOCK NORTH
TELEGRAPH HILL VILLA

Hosts Rose and Jeremy Gresson

334 Te Mata Road, R D 12, Havelock North   Mobile 025 243 0508
Freephone 0800 672 681   Phone 0-6-877 5140   Email gresson@xtra.co.nz
Fax 0-6-877 5508   Website friars.co.nz/hosts/telegraph.html

Villa rate $195 for 2 persons   Includes breakfast provisions
Extra persons $30 each   Self-catering, or dinner extra

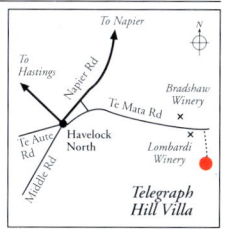

DIRECTIONS: From Napier, travel south towards Havelock North. Turn left into St Hill Lane. At "T" turn left again into Te Mata Rd. Continue to Bradshaw Estate Winery on left. Turn right up 0.8km drive to Telegraph Hill.

Set in the heart of Hawke's Bay's renowned wine country, on an olive grove, Telegraph Hill Villa offers a peaceful hilltop retreat with panoramic views over the plains to the mountains and ocean beyond. This self-contained 1996 Villa provides total privacy, separated from the hosts' house by an olive grove of 100 trees. The two bedrooms each have an adjoining dressing room and direct access to the ensuite bathroom. One bedroom is queen-size, the other offers twin king-size singles. A fully equipped kitchen allows for self-catering, with breakfast provisions supplied. The barbecue is popular for alfresco dining and the north-facing verandah catches all-day sun. The adjacent floodlit tennis court and the hosts' swimming pool provide exercise for the more active.

Facilities
- single-party bookings
- 1 queen & 1 twin bedroom
- dressing room with each bedroom
- cotton bed linen
- 1 ensuite bathroom, directly accessible from both bedrooms
- hair dryer, toiletries, heated towel rail & heated mirror
- Sky TV, phone, & ironing facilities
- laundry available in house
- breakfast provisions
- dinner by arrangement, extra
- fully equipped kitchen for self-catering
- fresh flowers; stereo
- guest barbecue
- fax & email available
- children welcome
- off-street parking

Activities available
- BBQ on Villa site
- pétanque/boules on site
- floodlit tennis court
- swimming pool on site
- walks among 2,000 olive trees on 7ha olive estate on site – olive products for sale
- wine trails
- fishing
- scenic flights
- restaurants & shopping
- golf
- gardens to visit
- rivers, beaches & mountain walks close by
- gannets at Cape Kidnappers
- Splash Planet
- Napier, 28km
- Hastings, 10km
- Havelock North, 4km

HAVELOCK NORTH
PROVIDENCIA COUNTRY HOUSE

Hosts Fiona and Neville Baker

225 Middle Road, Havelock North   *Postal* 225 Middle Road, R D 2, Hastings
Phone 0-6-877 2300   *Mobile* 021 253 4792   *Fax* 0-6-877 3250
Email nfdr.baker@xtra.co.nz   *Website* www.providencia.co.nz

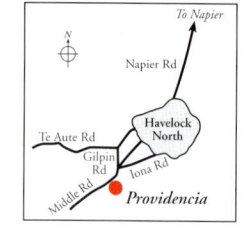

2 bdrm | 1 enst | 1 prbth
Double $210–$240
Single $185
Includes breakfast

DIRECTIONS: From Havelock North, take Middle Rd south for 2km. Cross intersection with Gilpin & Iona Rds. Take 3rd driveway on left to Providencia Country House.

In 1994, Providencia was moved to this peaceful rural location, set in two hectares of grounds, with white fantail pigeons and a backdrop of Te Mata Peak. Built in 1903 with extensive native wood panelling and Queen Anne-style turret, Providencia is Spanish for "Providence". Featuring the original kauri and rimu panelling, leadlight windows and deep verandahs, Providencia was refurbished with high-quality period detailing, including the gold-leafed hexagonal turret dome, floodlit at night. The breakfast menu is arranged the previous evening, Fiona uses fresh regional produce, served in the guest lounge, bedrooms or alfresco. The family lives in a separate wing with Suzy, the friendly dog. A two-bedroom self-contained cottage is also available on site.

Facilities
- 1 king suite includes private bathroom
- 1 ensuite queen/twin bedroom
- lavender toiletries, hair dryers & bathrobes
- mineral water, port decanter, fresh fruit & chocolates in bedrooms
- quality beds with cotton bed linen
- children over 8 years welcome
- pets catered for outside
- breakfast menu
- wine list
- guest fridge with complimentary drinks
- guest sitting room with teas/coffee & biscuits
- turret reading room
- email & fax available
- 2-bedroom cottage, extra
- on-site parking

Activities available
- pétanque pit
- wine trails
- beaches
- antiques
- golf courses
- horse riding
- paragliding
- bush walking
- parachuting
- mainland gannet colony
- trout fly fishing, guide available
- guided Maori culture tours
- country garden & house trails
- parks & public gardens
- private gardens open to visit
- Havelock North town, 2km
- Hastings, 10-min drive
- Art Deco Napier, 25-min drive

HAVELOCK NORTH
FALKIRK COTTAGE

Host Neil Macdonald   *Phone* 0-6-877 8089

236 Middle Road, Havelock North   *Postal* 236 Middle Road, R D 2, Hastings
Freephone 0800 21 495 011   *Mobile* 021 495 011   *Fax* 0-6-877 8089
Email falkirk@clear.net.nz   *Website* www.falkirk.co.nz

2 bdrm   2 enst

Cottage rate $200 for 1 bedroom
2nd bedroom $100

Includes breakfast provisions for 1st morning
Self-catering   *Dinner by chef, extra*

DIRECTIONS: From Havelock North villge, take Middle Rd south for 2km. Cross intersection with Gilpin & Iona Rds. Travel 0.36km to Falkirk Cottage on right.

Set on a farm just two kilometres from Havelock North village, Falkirk Cottage was built in 2002 in a 1920's style, with a rough-cast plaster finish and a clay-tiled roof. Recycled native timber is used throughout this self-contained farm cottage. Guests are welcome to view the Clydesdale horses, Highland cattle and abundant birdlife on the 10-hectare (25-acre) farm. Set in a semi-rural location, Falkirk Farm is within easy driving distance of the ocean, the gannets at Cape Kidnappers, and Hawke's Bay vineyards and wineries. A full kitchen is provided for guests to self-cater, or chef and waiting staff are available by arrangement. Suitable for small business meetings, the living area includes a century-old 10-seater dining table and log fire.

Facilities
- single-party bookings only
- 1 self-contained cottage
- 2 super-king ensuite bedrooms opening to balconies
- cotton bed linen; fresh flowers
- hair dryer, toiletries, claw-foot bath
- lounge with log fire, tea/coffee, TV, video, CDs, piano, books, artwork
- children over 11 years welcome
- powder room; air-conditioning
- full kitchen for self-catering
- breakfast provisions for 1st morning
- chef & waiting staff by arrangement
- self-serve laundry
- phone in kitchen
- private guest entrance
- on-site parking; helipad

Activities available
- small business meetings
- Clydesdale horses & Highland cattle on site
- bird-watching on site
- Havelock North village, 2km
- country walks
- Hawke's Bay vineyards
- winery trail
- golf courses
- Waimarama beach
- restaurants & cafés, 2km
- guided fly fishing
- parks & public gardens
- private gardens open to visit
- paragliding
- hot air ballooning
- Hastings, 10-min drive
- Art Deco Napier, 20 mins
- Cape Kidnappers gannet colony, 30-min drive

215
© Friars' Guide to New Zealand Accommodation for the Discerning Traveller

HAVELOCK NORTH
ENDSLEIGH COTTAGES

Hosts Margie and Denis Hardy

22 Endsleigh Road, Havelock North   *Postal* P O Box 8218, Havelock North
Phone 0-6-877 7588   *Mobile* 027 444 3800   *Fax* 0-6-876 0275
Email endsleigh.cottages@xtra.co.nz   *Website* www.endsleighcottages.co.nz

| 4 bdrm | 2 enst | 2 prbth |

Cottage rate $100–$200
Extra persons $50 each

Includes breakfast
Self-catering in 2 larger cottages

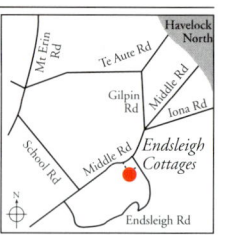

DIRECTIONS: From Havelock North, take Middle Rd south for 3km. Cross intersection with Gilpin & Iona Rds, then turn left into Endsleigh Rd. Endsleigh Cottages are on the right.

The three Endsleigh Cottages are located adjacent to the 1914 homestead set in an established garden among rural hills. The smallest cottage (*see above and below left*) dates from the early 1900s, while the middle cottage (*above right*) is a classic 1920s Arts and Crafts-style construction. The largest cottage (*below right*) has been constructed more recently with recycled components. Guests enjoy the mature garden that Margie and Denis have created since 1967. The two larger cottages are self-contained, each with a fully equipped kitchen for self-catering. All three cottages feature verandahs with garden views to the valley and mountains beyond. The smallest cottage is popular with honeymooners and the two larger cottages are suitable for entertaining.

Facilities

- smallest cottage: 1 king ensuite bedroom
- middle cottage: 1 king bedroom, 1 bathroom, 2 extra beds in sitting room
- largest cottage: 1 ensuite king, 1 queen bedroom with bathroom, 1 extra bed
- 8-seat dining table & piano in largest cottage
- phone in each cottage
- dinner by arrangement, $50 pp
- breakfast provisions supplied
- fully equipped kitchen & guest laundry in 2 larger cottages
- fresh flowers, cotton bed linen, claw-foot baths, toiletries, pedestal basins & hair dryers
- open fires, Sky TV, videos, VCR, CDs, cassettes, books & magazines in 2 larger cottages
- single-party bookings per cottage

Activities available

- entertaining in 2 larger cottages
- gas BBQs & outdoor furniture
- 1ha garden on site with mature trees, lawns, borders, ponds, shrubberies & large aviary
- pétanque/boules, croquet & grass tennis court on site
- 6 mountain bikes available
- 2 golf courses, short drive
- friars.co.nz/hosts/endsleigh.html
- restaurants, cafés & shopping in Havelock North
- best trout fishing river in region close by, guide available
- country walks; garden visits
- vineyard trails & restaurants
- watersports; beaches
- Art Deco Napier, 20 mins
- gannet colony & reserve at Cape Kidnappers, 30 mins

HAVELOCK NORTH
MURITAI

Hosts Margie and Denis Hardy   *Mobile* 027 444 3800

68 Duart Road, Havelock North   *Phone* 0-6-877 7588
Postal P O Box 8218, Havelock North   *Fax* 0-6-876 0275
Email endsleigh.cottages@xtra.co.nz   *Website* www.muritai.co.nz

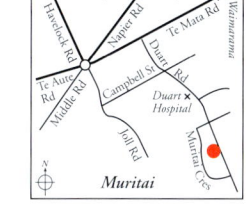

| 6 bdrm | 4 enst | 1 prbth | 1 pdrm | **House rate $700 per night**
Multiple-night rates available | *Includes breakfast provisions*
Self-catering |

DIRECTIONS: From Havelock North village roundabout, take Te Mata Rd north-east. Turn right into Duart Rd. Muritai on right.

Muritai is one of several major houses established in Hawke's Bay in the 1890s. It now offers self-contained accommodation for up to 10 guests in four king-size and two single bedrooms with four bathrooms. There are quality furnishings including many antiques and notable contemporary paintings. Muritai is suitable for entertaining indoors in the spacious living rooms or outdoors where there is a large barbecue facility. Verandahs on all sides open to the established gardens surrounding the house, with views over Havelock North village and out to the coast. Generous breakfast provisions are supplied, with a full kitchen for self-catering, or catering services are available. Restaurants in Havelock North village are within walking distance.

Facilities

- single-party bookings only
- 4 king ensuite bedrooms
- 2 single bedrooms & 1 private bathroom
- cotton bed linen
- hair dryers & toiletries in all 5 bathrooms
- sitting room with open fire, Sky TV & music system to all main rooms
- fully equipped kitchen for self-catering
- breakfast provisions supplied
- catering services available by arrangement, extra
- full laundry facilities
- guest phone; fresh flowers
- children welcome
- central heating
- on-site parking & garaging

Activities available

- barbecue area with outdoor furniture
- croquet on site
- pétanque/boules on site
- extensive garden on site
- 2 golf courses, short drive
- garden visits
- friars.co.nz/hosts/muritai-endsleigh.html
- restaurants in Havelock North, in walking distance
- best trout fishing river in region close by, guide available
- watersports; beaches
- country walks
- vineyard trails & restaurants
- Art Deco Napier, 20 mins
- gannet colony & reserve at Cape Kidnappers, 30 mins

Tukituki Valley, Hawke's Bay
Tom's Cottages

Hosts Linda and Van Howard

116 Matangi Road, Tukituki Valley, Havelock North　*Phone* 0-6-874 7900
Postal P O Box 8642, Havelock North, Hawke's Bay　*Mobile* 027 431 9086
Email vanh@clear.net.nz　*Website* www.tomscottages.co.nz　*Fax* 0-6-874 7909

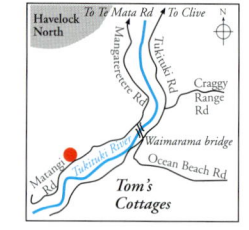

3 bdrm　3 enst　Cottage rate $180–$300　*Includes breakfast provisions*　*Self-catering*

DIRECTIONS: From Havelock North take Te Mata Rd for 3km. Turn right into Mangateretere Rd. Travel 4km towards Waimarama bridge & turn right into Matangi Rd. Travel 1km to Tom's Cottages on right.

With rural views over the Tukituki River valley to Te Mata peak, Tom's Cottages are tucked away in a secluded spot just eight kilometres from Havelock North. The two cottages, built in 1920 and 1940, are fully restored and self-contained, offering total privacy by being set 500 metres apart from each other. The larger of the two, Big Tom's Cottage, provides two ensuite bedrooms, a bath, laundry, kitchen and living room including television and DVD-player. The smaller, Tom's Cottage, has one ensuite bedroom, kitchen and separate living room with television. Both cottages feature an additional open air bathtub, for wood-fired alfresco bathing, overlooking the river below. Farm fresh breakfast provisions are supplied daily.

Facilities

Big Tom's Cottage:
- 1 king & 1 queen bedroom & 2 ensuites, 1 with bath
- open-plan kitchen & living room with open fire, TV & DVD; self-service laundry
- phone jack

Tom's Cottage:
- 1 queen ensuite bedroom
- self-catering kitchen
- living room with TV

Both cottages:
- breakfast provisions daily
- hair dryer, toiletries & bathrobes in ensuites
- cotton bed linen; fresh flowers
- CD-player, books & magazines
- children & pets welcome
- cot or crib available
- 2 secluded outdoor baths
- on-site parking

Activities available

- alfresco dining on decks
- BBQ on site
- local rivers & beaches
- farm, bush & mountain walks
- trout fishing
- wineries & wine trails
- private gardens to visit
- golf courses
- Splash Planet
- scenic flights
- restaurants & cafés nearby
- orchard & olive grove tours
- Havelock North village, 8km
- historic homes to visit
- Cape Kidnappers gannet colony
- Hastings, 20-min drive
- Art Deco Napier, National Aquarium of NZ & Marineland, 30-min drive
- Wellington, 3 hours south

© Friars' Guide to New Zealand Accommodation for the Discerning Traveller

MANGATAHI, HASTINGS
NETHERBY COTTAGE

Hosts Deborah and Graham de Gruchy

195 Mangatahi Road, Hastings, Hawke's Bay   *Postal* R D 1, Hastings, Hawke's Bay
Phone 0-6-874 9807   *Mobile* 021 240 5346   *Fax* 0-6-874 9638
Email netherby@xtra.co.nz   *Website* friars.co.nz/hosts/netherby.html

3 bdrm | 1 prbth | Double $175 | *Self-catering*
Single $150 | Extra persons $50 each

DIRECTIONS: From Napier take SH 50 south, or from Hastings, travel west for 20km to Maraekakaho. Veer right over bridge into Kereru Rd & travel 5km to cross-roads. Continue into Mangatahi Rd for 2km to Cottage.

The rural location of Netherby Cottage ensures its peace and tranquillity where guests wake to the sound of birdsong. Just 20 minutes west of Hastings, in the Mangatahi district, Netherby Cottage is surrounded by wineries and restaurants for the connoisseur. Directly across the road from Netherby are fields of lavender at the lavender farm which guests also enjoy. Close by are two top golf courses and the Ngaruroro River for fishing and jet boating. The self-contained cottage sleeps up to six guests in single parties, in three bedrooms on hand-crafted slat beds by Kevin Osmond. The kitchen and laundry are well appointed with AEG appliances for self-catering, and a barbecue area features outdoor furniture for alfresco dining with rural views.

Facilities
- single-party bookings only
- self-contained cottage
- 1 super-king & 1 king bedroom, each with hand-crafted slat beds
- 1 twin bedroom with designer bunks
- 1 bathroom with bath, hair dryer, heated towel rails & toiletries
- 100% cotton bed linen
- open fire, TV & CDs in lounge
- full kitchen with AEG appliances
- all meals self-catering
- 3 guest phones
- fax & email available
- fresh flowers
- children by arrangement
- outdoor furniture & guest BBQ
- garaging
- helipad

Activities available
- bird-watching on site
- cycling – bicycles available
- lavender farm opposite, lavender products for sale
- gourmet store, restaurant, café & cooking school nearby
- wineries nearby
- Ngaruroro River nearby
- fishing in river
- swimming in river
- jet boating on river
- 2 golf courses, 15 mins
- gardens open to visit
- walks
- Hastings, 20-min drive east
- Napier, 35-min drive north
- Havelock North village, 25-min drive
- Wellington, 3½ hours south
- Auckland, 5½ hours north

WAIPUKURAU
Mynthurst Farmstay

Hosts Annabelle and David Hamilton

912 Lindsay Road, Waipukurau, R D 3, Hawke's Bay
Phone 0-6-857 8093   Mobile 027 2322458   Fax 0-6-857 8093
Email mynthurst@xtra.co.nz   *Website* friars.co.nz/hosts/mynthurst.html

| 3 bdrm | 1 enst | 1 prbth | 1 pdrm |

Double $150
Single $85

Includes breakfast
Lunch & dinner extra

DIRECTIONS: From north, turn right into Onagonga Rd. Travel 6km & turn left into Lindsay Rd. Travel 3km to Mynthurst on left. Or from south, turn left into Lindsay Rd. Travel 9km to Mynthurst on right.

Mynthurst Farmstay is a family homestead on a working 560-hectare sheep and beef farm. Three guestrooms with two bathrooms are available for accommodation in this farmstay. Guests are welcome to observe farm activities, participate in farm tours, walk on the farm, or relax on the extensive terrace overlooking the garden with views to the Ruahine Range.
A separate sitting room is also available for relaxation. Annabelle serves a continental breakfast of seasonal fruits, cereals, scones or muffins alfresco on the terrace in summer, with eggs or other cooked dishes on request. Three-course dinner featuring local produce and wine is also available, by prior arrangement. Alternatively there are restaurants 10 minutes away in Waipukurau.

Facilities
- 1 super-king/twin, 1 double & 1 single bedroom
- 2 bathrooms, each with hair dryer, heated towel rails, bathrobes & toiletries
- cotton bed linen; fresh flowers
- children welcome, cot available
- central heating
- open fire, tea/coffee, TV, & artwork in sitting room
- powder room
- continental breakfast served in dining room or alfresco on terrace, cooked on request
- lunch by arrangement, extra
- 3-course dinner with wine, by arrangement, $35 pp
- complimentary laundry
- email facilities available
- courtesy passenger transfer
- on-site parking

Activities available
- farm walks & tours
- observing 560-ha sheep, bull & beef farm activities
- trout fishing, guide available
- tennis court on site
- trampoline on site
- private gardens to visit
- bush walks
- 3 golf courses, within 10km
- local beaches, 30km drive
- restaurants, 9km
- wineries & wine trails
- orchard tours
- hot air ballooning
- helicopter sightseeing arranged
- Waipukurau & Waipawa, 9km
- gannet colony at Cape Kidnappers, 60km drive
- Art Deco Napier, 55km drive
- Wellington, 3 hours south

OKATO, TARANAKI
PATUHA FARM LODGE

Owners Peter and Susan Henderson   *Managers* Dawn and George Walker

575 Upper Pitone Road, Okato   *Postal* R D 4, New Plymouth
Phone 0-6-752 4469   *Email* patuha.farm.lodge@clear.net.nz
Fax 0-6-752 4470   *Website* www.patuhafarmlodge.co.nz

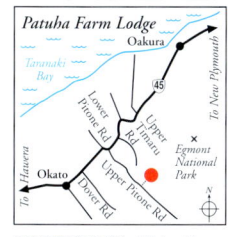

| 10 bdrm | 10 enst | 1 pdrm |

Double $180
Single $100

Includes breakfast & dinner
Lunch extra

DIRECTIONS: Take SH 3 to New Plymouth. Travel south-west on SH 45 for 15km to Oakura. Travel another 10km & turn left into Upper Pitone Rd. Travel 5.75km & turn into Lodge driveway on left. Travel 2km to Lodge.

Patuha is a third generation family farm, taking its name from the highest peak of the nearby Kaitake Range. The 160-hectare (400-acre) sheep and beef farm provides a peaceful site for guests and seasonal farming activities. Twenty hectares of native rainforest surround the lodge which borders Egmont National Park, with a 20-minute bush walk leading guests to the renowned Pukeiti Rhododendron Gardens. Built in the 1980s, Patuha Farm Lodge *(see centre of photo above)* is being progressively updated and caters for small conferences, with 10 ensuite bedrooms comprising four queen and six twin, three with double and single beds. Meals feature traditional farm cuisine which is served in the dining room, adjacent to the licensed bar.

Facilities

- 4 queen & 6 twin bedrooms, including electric blankets
- 10 ensuite bathrooms
- 1 separate spa bathroom
- TV & phone in each bedroom
- central heating
- seasonal flowers
- children welcome
- conference room & facilities
- fax & email available
- continental & cooked breakfast
- 3-course dinner included
- traditional farm cuisine
- lunch or picnics available by request, extra
- wood burner in lounge & dining area; licensed bar
- tea/coffee & cookies area
- courtesy passenger transfer
- on-site parking

Activities available

- games room in-house
- farm walks on site
- seasonal farm activities eg shearing, docking, haymaking, stock work
- native bush walks on site
- bird-watching on site
- Pukeiti Rhododendron Gardens adjacent
- snow skiing at Mt Egmont
- surf-casting from beach, 10km
- trout fishing at Stoney River
- golf course, 12km away
- Egmont National Park
- private gardens open to visit
- Rhododendron Week, Oct./Nov.
- short local walks & day tramps
- New Plymouth, 30-min drive
- ski-field in winter, 1-hour drive

NEW PLYMOUTH
THE WATERFRONT HOTEL

Host David Walter

1 Egmont Street, New Plymouth
Freephone 0508 843 928   *Phone* 0-6-769 5301   *Fax* 0-6-769 5302
Email stay@waterfront.co.nz   *Website* www.waterfront.co.nz

Room rate $130–$165
Suite rate $250–$400

All meals extra

42 bdrm   42 enst

DIRECTIONS: From north take SH 45 (Vivian St). Turn right to Brougham St & left into Devon St. Turn right into Egmont St to The Waterfront on corner Molesworth St. From south take SH 45 (Powderham St) & turn left.

The Waterfront is New Plymouth's newest hotel, located on the shores of the Tasman Sea. Accommodation comprises 39 rooms and three suites all with spacious ensuite bedrooms and sea views. The in-house Salt restaurant is open for breakfast, lunch and dinner, or simply for coffee, a light meal or leisurely drink, and features ocean views from all tables and the balcony. The Pepper room offers a meeting or reception venue for up to 50 guests. The Waterfront is located adjacent to Puke Ariki, the new museum and library complex. The *Wind Wand* landmark by artist Len Lye is directly across the road, where guests enjoy the scenic seven-kilometre seaside boardwalk. The central business and shopping district is but a stroll away.

Facilities

- 3 suites, each with separate bedroom, living area & kitchen
- 33 super-king bedrooms & 6 queen/twin bedrooms
- 42 ensuites, each with hair dryer, toiletries & demist mirror
- cotton bed linen; bathrobes
- Sky TV, phone, ISDN access, desk, tea/coffee & mini-bar in bedrooms
- sea view from all bedrooms, most with balcony
- Salt restaurant open from 7am daily
- room service available
- full kitchen in suites for self-catering
- non-smoking rooms
- laundry service
- wheelchair access to 3 rooms
- children welcome
- covered off-street parking

Activities available

- Pepper room for meetings, weddings & functions
- *Wind Wand* opposite
- 7-km seaside boardwalk
- Festival of Lights, Dec.–Jan.
- Pukekura Park
- Rhododendron Festival, early November
- Pukeiti & gardens to visit
- golf
- New Plymouth CBD & shops, easy stroll away
- Puke Ariki museum
- surfing; wind-surfing; surf fishing
- heritage trails
- Mt Egmont walking/trekking trails
- winter skiing Mount Egmont
- airport, 10-min drive
- Tawhiti Museum, 1 hour south
- Dairyland, 1-hour drive south

© Friars' Guide to New Zealand Accommodation for the Discerning Traveller

New Plymouth
Issey Manor

Hosts Carol Thompson and Lewis Roach

32 Carrington Street, New Plymouth
Phone 0-6-758 2375 *Mobile* 027 248 6686 *Fax* 0-6-758 2375
Email issey.manor@actrix.co.nz *Website* www.isseymanor.co.nz

4 bdrm | 4 enst | Room Rate $160 Multiple-night rates available | Includes breakfast Picnic hampers extra | Self-catering

DIRECTIONS: From Wanganui take SH3 to New Plymouth. Turn left into Pendarves St & left into Carrington St. Issey Manor on right. From City, turn left at Liardet St lights & right into Pendarves St. Then as above.

Drawing inspiration from the clean lines used by the Japanese designer Issey Miyake, Issey Manor has been refurbished in a contemporary style, with a distinctive coloured exterior. Originally built as a two-storey coach house in 1860, and extended into a 1910 villa, Issey Manor now provides four ensuite guestrooms upstairs, five minutes' walk from the city. A self-catering guest kitchen adjoins the guest lounge, featuring original contemporary New Zealand artwork and library. Eclectic furnishings include antique, Asian and retro pieces. Café-style breakfast, continental or cooked, is served downstairs in the dining room and a delivery service for dinner is available. The summer Festival of Lights, at Pukekura Park, is a short walk away.

Facilities

- 1 super-king & 3 queen ensuite bedrooms
- double shower, hair dryer, toiletries, heated towel rails in 4 ensuites; 2 spa baths
- TV, desk, phone, tea/coffee, fridge, bathrobes & cotton bed linen in bedrooms
- Sky TV, video, DVD, CDs, NZ artwork, library & writing desk in guest lounge
- continental or cooked breakfast
- picnic hampers available, extra
- full self-catering kitchen
- email & fax available
- fresh flowers
- pets welcome; dog on site
- laundry available, $10
- courtesy passenger transfer
- off-street parking

Activities available

- BBQ on large guest deck
- Pukekura Park; Festival of Lights (Dec. – Feb.)
- Brooklands Bowl for outdoor concerts
- TSB Stadium & Showplace
- Govett Brewster Art Gallery & other galleries
- Pukekura Raceway
- seaside promenade
- restaurants & shops, 5-min walk
- Pukeariki Museum
- private gardens open to visit
- Rhododendron festival, October
- historic St Mary's Church
- Marsland Hill Observatory
- heritage trails
- Top Town cinema
- Mt Egmont for snow skiing, walking, hiking & climbing

New Plymouth
Henwood House

Hosts Lynne and Graeme Axten

314 Henwood Road, R D 2, New Plymouth
Phone 0-6-755 1212   *Mobile* 027 248 4051
Fax 0-6-755 1212   *Email* henwood.house@xtra.co.nz

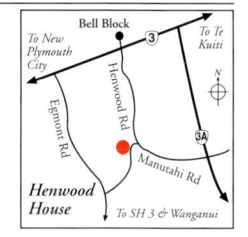

| 5 bdrm | 3 enst | 1 shbth | Double $120–$150
Single $100 | Includes breakfast
Dinner extra |

DIRECTIONS: From north, take SH 3 to Bell Block. Turn left into Henwood Rd. Travel 3.14km to House on right. From south, take SH 3 to Egmont Rd on right. Turn left again into Henwood Rd. House on left.

Henwood House is set in a peaceful rural one-hectare garden, with ponds and mature specimen trees including century-old *Magnolia grandiflora*, chestnuts, rimu and puriri trees. Built as a country residence in 1890, this colonial homestead has been fully renovated, but retains the original heart rimu panelling, kauri trims and matai flooring. Privacy and independence is provided for guests upstairs in five bedrooms and four bathrooms. Breakfast is served either downstairs in the country-style kitchen, alfresco on the verandah, or in the honeymoon suite upstairs, with its own private balcony overlooking the garden. Dinner is also available in the honeymoon suite, the downstairs dining room or in front of the open fire in the guest lounge.

Facilities
- 3 queen ensuite bedrooms
- 2 twin bedrooms share bathroom
- cotton bed linen & fresh flowers
- phone, fax & email facilities
- guest fridge & tea/coffee
- open fire, TV, video, music, tea/coffee & artwork in guest lounge
- private guest entrance
- laundry available
- children welcome
- full cooked breakfast, such as special omelettes, pancake dishes, fresh fruit & home-made bread
- 3-course dinner, $40 pp served in dining room, verandah, garden or honeymoon suite
- diet preferences catered
- powder room downstairs
- on-site parking

Activities available
- 1ha (2½ acres) garden on site for walking
- pétanque court; BBQ
- private gardens to visit
- lavender farm
- wineries
- beaches; fishing
- 5 golf courses; driving range
- Pukeiti Gardens, 30 mins
- Rhododendron Festival, early Nov.
- restaurants, 10-min drive
- Pukekura Park
- Festival of Lights, January
- art galleries; Tawhiti Museum
- Mount Taranaki/Egmont
- Methanex Visitors Centre
- New Plymouth, 10-min drive
- airport, 5–10-min drive

© Friars' Guide to New Zealand Accommodation for the Discerning Traveller

NEW PLYMOUTH
OAK VALLEY MANOR

Hosts Paul and Pat Ekdahl

248 Junction Road, R D 1, New Plymouth
Phone 0-6-758 1501   *Mobile* 027 442 0325   *Fax* 0-6-758 1052
Email kauri.holdings@xtra.co.nz   *Website* www.oakvalley.co.nz

2 bdrm   2 enst   1 prbth
Double $125
Single $65–$85

Includes breakfast
Multiple-night rates available

DIRECTIONS: Take SH 3 towards New Plymouth. From south, travel to Junction Rd. Oak Valley Manor is on left. From north, turn left into Mangorei Rd. Turn right into Junction Rd. Oak Valley Manor is 50m on left.

Oak Valley Manor was purpose-built in 1995 to provide a private wing for guests. Comprising two bedrooms with ensuite bathrooms, and a private lounge, the wing offers views of Mt Egmont/Taranaki on one side, and opens to a private courtyard on the other. Guests can choose their own privacy or are welcome to socialise with Pat and Paul in the shared lounge. The breakfast menu is provided the night before and is served in the dining room. Animals on this two-hectare rural property include donkeys, fallow deer, pigs, peacocks, hens, ostriches and Yale the dog. Ducks and geese enjoy the lake which is surrounded by a developing oak grove and landscaped garden. Tours through the family owned and operated organic brewery are available.

Facilities
- 1 twin & 1 queen bedroom
- cotton bed linen
- 2 ensuite bathrooms, 1 including bath
- private lounge in guest wing with TV, tea/coffee, phone
- 1 shared lounge with hosts
- library
- children & pets welcome
- laundry available
- continental or cooked breakfast served in dining room; menu chosen night before
- fax available
- private guest entrance
- guest courtyard
- landscaped garden
- courtesy passenger transfer
- animals on site
- on-site parking

Activities available
- organic brewery tours
- winery, 1.5km away
- renowned surf beaches
- surfing & windsurfing
- 2 golf courses, 4km
- Tupare Gardens, 1km
- Pukekura Park
- Brooklands Bowl for outdoor summer concerts
- restaurants/shopping, 5-min drive
- private gardens to visit
- New Plymouth, 5-min drive
- walking & hiking at Mt Egmont
- Pukeiti Rhododendron Gardens & Restaurant, 30-min drive away
- Rhododendron Week, Oct./Nov.
- Festival of Lights, 24 Dec.–Feb.
- snow skiing at Mt Egmont, learning & advanced ski tows

EGMONT NATIONAL PARK
MOUNTAIN HOUSE MOTOR LODGE AND ANDERSONS' ALPINE LODGE

Host Berta Anderson

Pembroke Road, Stratford *Postal* P O Box 303, Stratford *Mobile* 025 412 372
Mountain House Phone and Fax 0-6-765 6100 *or Andersons'* Phone 0-6-765 6620
Freephone 0800 MOUNTAIN *Email* mountainhouse@xtra.co.nz
Website friars.co.nz/hosts/mountainhouse.html

13 bdrm 13 enst Room rate $155–$195 *All meals extra*

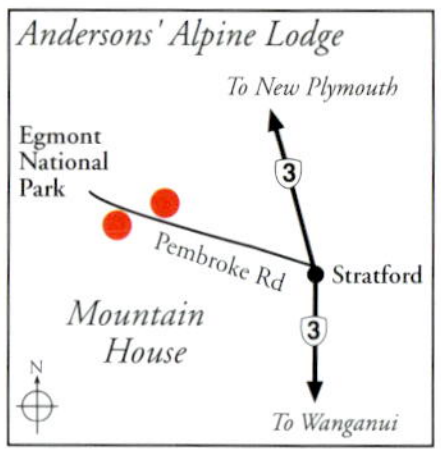

DIRECTIONS: From New Plymouth or Wanganui, take SH 3 to Stratford. Turn west into Pembroke Rd. Travel 9km to Andersons' Alpine Lodge on right, or another 5km to Mountain House Motor Lodge on the left.

Set five kilometres apart on the edge of the Egmont National Park, at the foot of Mt Taranaki, are Andersons' Alpine Lodge and the Mountain House Motor Lodge. Offering diverse accommodation, these venues provide spectacular views of the mountain, sunsets and native bush. Andersons' is a three-storey, Swiss-style chalet featuring oil paintings by the late Keith H. Anderson. The Mountain House comprises a 10-bedroom lodge, family chalet and à la carte licensed restaurant, winner of many awards, with an extensive game menu. Restaurant meals are available at the Summit and Egmont Rooms with adjoining lounge bar. Sited on the eastern flank of Mt Egmont/Taranaki, this is an ideal base for mountain walks from 15 minutes' to five days' duration.

Facilities

- Mountain House restaurant with full à la carte menu for all meals, licensed lounge bar & open fire
- continental breakfast at Andersons'
- 1 king & 2 twin ensuite bedrooms at Andersons', king with spa bath
- 10 king, queen, double & twin bedrooms at Mountain House
- art by the late Keith H. Anderson
- sauna & spa complex at Mountain House
- children welcome at Mountain House
- pets welcome at Andersons'
- laundry available
- farm pets at Andersons'
- mountain views
- German spoken
- courtesy passenger transfer
- helipad
- on-site parking

Activities available

- east Egmont bush walks
- family tramping
- guided summit climbs
- trout stream, opposite
- 3–5-day round mountain trek
- rainforest walking tracks
- walks from Plateau
- Heritage Trails
- Taranaki Rhododendron Week, October/November annually
- scenic helicopter flights
- Manganui Ski-field, 3km
- golf courses
- museums
- Stratford, 5–10-min drive
- Taranaki Pioneer Village, 15km north
- Hollard Gardens, 20km
- Dawson Falls, 20km away
- beach, 40km away

Mt Ruapehu, Central Plateau
Lahar Farm and Lodge

Hosts Brent and Noeline Bishop

Matapuna Road, Horopito   *Postal* R D 6, Raetihi
Phone 0-6-385 4136   *Mobile* 025 223 4292   *Fax* 0-6-385 4136
Email lahar@xtra.co.nz   *Website* www.laharfarm.co.nz

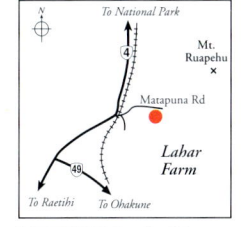

| 5 bdrm | 1 enst | 2 prbth | House rate $210 for 2 persons Extra adults $60 each, children $20 each | *Breakfast basket & dinner extra* Specials rates available | *Self-catering* |

DIRECTIONS: From Raetihi or Ohakune, travel north to Horopito. Turn right into Matapuna Rd & cross railway. Turn left & continue for 2km. Lahar Farm on right.

Dominated by Mt Ruapehu, the North Island's highest volcanic peak, Lahar Lodge and Cabin are alpine retreats within a 600-hectare sheep, cattle and deer farm, overlooking the wilderness of Tongariro National Park. Both the Lodge and Cabin are quality full log-style houses, featuring hand-scribed craftmanship throughout. Lahar Cabin is single level, while Lahar Lodge is two storey, a solid log stairway leading to the two bedrooms from where the balcony provides uninterrupted views of Mt Ruapehu. Single-party bookings ensure peace and seclusion, with both Cabin and Lodge at a distance from each other and the hosts. A detailed farm map leads to Lahar Lake, a wild fowl habitat stocked with rainbow trout, and fishing licences are available.

Facilities

- self-contained log cabin & lodge; single-party bookings
- Lodge: 1 queen/twin & 1 double/twin bedroom, 1 fold-away bed, 1 bathroom
- Cabin: 1 queen ensuite bedroom, 1 queen bedroom & 1 twin with extra bunks; bathroom & toilet
- cotton bed linen, electric blankets; toiletries, hair dryers
- full kitchens for self-catering
- breakfast basket including farm fresh eggs, $7 pp
- 4-course à la carte dinner delivered to lodge or cabin, $25–$50 pp
- open-plan dining & lounge rooms; log-fires, TV/video/CD
- pure spring water; full laundry
- gumboots supplied
- children welcome

Activities available

On-site activities:

- native bush or farm walks
- farm animals & pets
- Lahar Lake; canoeing, trout fishing
- 4WD adventures
- Black Forest safari park, wild deer to view or stalk
- guided bird-watching
- mountain bike trails

Off-site activities:

- restaurants, shops & après ski
- Tongariro World Heritage Park
- Whanganui River: jet boat, canoe
- hot mineral pools at Tokaanu
- Turoa & Whakapapa ski-fields; Mt Ruapehu chairlifts in summer
- Waimarino golf course
- army museum at Waiouru
- Horopito vintage cars

Rangataua, Ohakune
Whare Ora Lodge

Hosts Diana and Tiri Sotiri

1 Kaha Street, Rangataua, Ohakune, Central Plateau
Phone 0-6-385 9385 *Email* whareora@xtra.co.nz
Fax 0-6-385 9385 *Website* www.whareoralodge.co.nz

Suite rate $195–$225   Includes breakfast   Lunch & dinner extra
Extra persons $60 each   Seasonal rates available

2 bdrm / 2 enst

DIRECTIONS: From Waiouru, turn off SH 1 into SH 49. Travel 21km to Rangataua. Turn right into Piwari St, left into Kaha St. Whare Ora at end on right. From Taumarunui, take SH 4 to SH 49A to Ohakune. Continue 5km.

Maori for "place of well-being", Whare Ora Lodge is located 20 minutes from the Turoa Ski-field and only five minutes from an entrance to the Tongariro World Heritage Site where much of the filming of *The Lord of the Rings* was shot. Originally built in 1910, Whare Ora Lodge was architecturally redesigned in 1997, blending the existing home with contemporary accommodation facilities. Two guest suites are now available. The quietness is enhanced by the garden setting, framing views of Mt Ruapehu in its varied moods, with Mt Taranaki also visible to the west. Tiri and Diana have a large library and wide music selection. Their New Zealand art collection includes hand-blown glass. New Himalayan Persian cats are in residence.

Facilities
- 1 upstairs queen suite with lounge, ensuite & 2 extra single beds
- 1 downstairs queen suite with ensuite & spa bath, lounge & undercarpet heating
- demist mirror & heated towel rail in downstairs ensuite
- fresh flowers, hair dryer, TV, radio & toiletries in both rooms
- cotton bed linen & goosedown duvets on all beds in winter
- 3-course dinner with wine, by request, $70 pp
- lunch by arrangement
- tea/coffee available
- phone, fax & email
- complimentary laundry
- children by arrangement
- lock-up ski cupboard & drying room
- garaging; cats on site

Activities available
- pétanque & croquet lawn
- native bird-watching
- native bat colony
- 2 ski-fields in winter
- Tongariro World Heritage site
- Mt Ruapehu walks
- Waimarino Golf Course, 10 mins
- squash courts, 5-min drive
- scenic flights over volcanoes
- cafés & restaurants
- night club in winter
- Ohakune, 5-min drive
- snow-boarding
- NZ beech forest walks
- trout fishing; horse treks
- Karioi Lake
- garden visits
- Waiouru Army Museum, 20-min drive away

WANGANUI
ARLES B & B

Hosts Sue and Tom Day

50 Riverbank Road, State Highway 4, R D 3, Wanganui
Phone 0-6-343 6557   *Mobile* 021 257 8257   *Fax* 0-6-343 6557
Email sue.day@clear.net.nz   *Website* babs.co.nz/arles

| 6 bdrm | 2 enst | 2 prbth | 1 pdrm |

Room rate $120–$160
Apartment rate $120–$240

Includes breakfast
Self-catering in apartment

DIRECTIONS: Take SH 3 to City. Travel north on Anzac Pde, to SH 4. Travel 4km from Dublin St bridge to Arles B&B on right. Or from National Park, take SH 4 towards Wanganui to B&B on left.

Arles is a large comfortable country home originally built in the 1880s on 400 hectares (over 1,000 acres) of farmland, less than one hectare of gardens now remaining. The spacious grounds feature many mature native and exotic trees, wisteria softens the front of the house and an indoor grapevine in the conservatory bears grapes in summer. The original kauri staircase takes guests to their upstairs bedrooms. Downstairs, guests can relax in the rimu-panelled guest lounge with a complimentary glass of wine and a book, game or puzzle from the library. There is a fully equipped guest kitchen/laundry and a barbecue and swimming pool for the summer months. Treetops is a separate two-bedroom apartment with kitchen, living/dining room and balcony.

Facilities
- 1 king with private balcony & 1 queen ensuite bedroom
- 1 double & 1 twin bedroom family suite, with 1 bathroom, claw-foot bath & bathrobes
- Treetops: self-catering apartment with 1 queen & 1 twin bedroom; sofa bed in lounge & 1 bathroom
- conference room & guest laundry in house
- full breakfast includes home-made bread, jams & baking
- tea/coffee in bedrooms & both guest kitchens
- TV & CD-player in both guest lounges
- phone, fax & email available
- families welcome; cot & highchair available
- secure garaging for guests on river trips; on-site parking

Activities available
- swimming pool & BBQ on site
- garden ramble & bird watching on site
- historic *Waimarie* paddle steamer on river
- art galleries & museums
- scenic drive along Whanganui River across road
- river & beaches nearby
- Cooks Gardens & Splash Centre
- restaurants, shops & historic buildings, 6-min drive
- renowned children's play area at Kowhai Park, 4km – bumper boats, mini-golf, train rides & go carts
- Virginia & Westmere lakes
- jet boating, 2 hour to full day trips; canoeing on river
- 3 golf courses within 15km
- ski-fields, 1½-hr drive north

229

© Friars' Guide to New Zealand Accommodation for the Discerning Traveller

WANGANUI CITY
THE RUTLAND ARMS INN

Hosts Peter and Judy Jefferson   *Phone* 0-6-347 7677

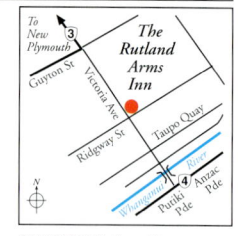

48–52 Ridgway Street, Wanganui   *Postal* P O Box 499, Wanganui
Freephone 0800 RUTLAND   *Mobile* 021 331 338   *Fax* 0-6-347 7345
Email enquiries@rutland-arms.co.nz   *Website* www.rutland-arms.co.nz

8 bdrm | 8 enst | 1 pdrm

Room rate $115–$160

Continental breakfast included
Cooked breakfast, lunch & dinner extra

DIRECTIONS: From New Plymouth, take SH 3 to Victoria Ave. Turn left into Ridgway St. Inn on corner. From Wellington take SH 3, or from Ohakune take SH 4 to Victoria Ave. Turn right into Ridgway St.

Named after the Rutland Stockade which was erected in 1847 on the hill in the centre of Wanganui, the original Rutland Hotel was built in 1849. A colourful history includes two fires destroying the wooden building, which was first rebuilt in 1869, then the present brick building in 1904. This central city hotel has been totally restored and refurbished, retaining the Edwardian architectural features with an old English-style pub downstairs. Imported English beers are offered with à la carte meals, served by the open fire or in the courtyard café which includes the original well. The upstairs guest accommodation comprises eight bedrooms carefully finished in early-colonial design with ensuite bathrooms and Victorian-style mahogany furniture throughout.

Facilities

- 6 queen & 2 queen/twin ensuite bedrooms, 4 with spa baths
- special suite includes double spa bath, twin basins & bidet
- tea/coffee, writing desk, Sky TV, minibar, direct-dial phone, fax & ISDN lines in all guestrooms
- 100% cotton bed linen
- laundry & dry cleaning service, extra
- private guest entrance
- licensed restaurant & bar, with open fire
- à la carte dinner, extra
- à la carte lunch, extra
- full cooked breakfast, extra
- continental breakfast served in suite or restaurant
- powder room downstairs
- central heating
- off-street carpark

Activities available

- licensed restaurant on site
- wishing well on site
- historic riverboat cruise
- historic opera house
- unique Durie Hill elevator
- art gallery & museum, 500m
- library, 500m away
- Central City shopping
- Kowhai Park
- Wanganui in Bloom, Dec.–Feb.
- Belmont Golf Course
- Virginia Lake Reserve & Bason Botanic Gardens
- private gardens to visit
- Whanganui River walks; canoeing
- Cooks Gardens
- Kai-iwi beach
- historic Bushy Park homestead
- Mt Ruapehu ski-field, 1½-hr drive

WESTMERE, WANGANUI
ARLESFORD HOUSE

Hosts June and George Loibl

202 State Highway 3, R D 4, Westmere, Wanganui
Phone 0-6-347 7751   *Mobile* 025 852 922   *Fax* 0-6-347 7561
Email arlesford.house@xtra.co.nz   *Website* arlesfordhouse.co.nz

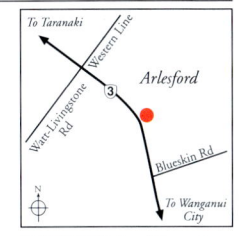

4 bdrm | 2 enst | 2 prbth   Double $160–$220   Single $120–$140   *Includes breakfast*

DIRECTIONS: From Wanganui City, take SH 3 towards New Plymouth. Travel for 8km to Arlesford on right.

Designed by Wanganui architect Bob Talboys and built from native heart rimu by Joseph Gopperth in 1934, Arlesford House is located just eight kilometres north of the city. Set in established landscaped gardens with mature trees, Arlesford is furnished with antiques and original New Zealand artwork. This two-storey Georgian-style homestead now offers accommodation comprising four guestrooms, each with its own bathroom and rural or garden views. Open fires warm the lounge and drawing room with an adjacent sunroom. A leisurely breakfast is served downstairs in the dining room or alfresco beside the swimming pool in the park-like gardens. There is a new three-bedroom, two-bathroom self-contained cottage available on site.

Facilities

- Regency Room: 1 super-king ensuite bedroom & spa bath
- Victoria Room: 1 super-king/twin ensuite bedroom & bath
- Ruapehu & Anne Rooms: each with queen/twin or king/twin bedroom & private bathroom
- hair dryer, toiletries, heated towel rails & bathrobes; baths in Anne & Victoria bathrooms
- children welcome
- full cooked or continental breakfast buffet; afternoon tea on arrival
- cotton bed linen, tea/coffee, desk & TV in bedrooms
- guest lounge with open fire, tea/coffee, TV, video, phone & writing desk
- complimentary laundry service
- on-site parking
- courtesy passenger transfer

Activities available

- swimming pool on site
- flood-lit tennis court
- pétanque
- barbecue available
- small conference room
- Westmere Lake Wildlife Reserve, 2-min drive
- Bason Botanical Gardens
- Virginia Lake
- Mowhanau Beach
- Wanganui restaurants, cafés & shops, 10-min drive
- canoeing
- jet boating
- paddle steamer on river
- museum
- Sarjeant Art Gallery
- 4 golf courses nearby
- gardens open to visit
- New Plymouth, 2 hrs north

MANGAWEKA, RANGITIKEI
MAIRENUI RURAL RETREAT

Hosts Sue and David Sweet

Ruahine Road, Mangaweka
Phone 0-6-382 5564   *Mobile* 025 517 545   *Fax* 0-6-382 5564
Email mairenui@xtra.co.nz   *Website* www.mairenui.co.nz

| 10 bdrm | 2 enst | 3 shbth |

The Homestead: *Includes breakfast*
Double $130–$280, Single $95–$140

The Retreat: *Meals extra*
Double $150, Extras $50

The Villa: *Meals extra*
Double $70, Extras $35

DIRECTIONS: From Mangaweka, take SH 1 north. Turn right into Ruahine Rd. Cross the Rangitikei River, travel 11km to Mairenui Rural Retreat on left, halfway up 1st hill.

The century-old farm homestead has been in the Sweet family for four generations. David and Sue chose a Comesky design from the Athfield architectural school for their 1970s self-contained Retreat, built among a stand of 700-year-old native trees, apart from the homestead. The multi-storey Retreat features an open-plan design around a circular staircase, with polished floors, brickwork, 'seventies furnishing, memorabilia and refurbished interiors. The original homestead, built in 1896, has been totally restored as a self-contained colonial villa, also set in the expansive park-like grounds featuring ponds, rhododendrons, camellias and old roses. The spacious lounge in The Villa includes a small pool table, plenty of games and books and a wind-up gramophone. Guests enjoy relaxing on the large sunny verandah with its rural outlook. Both The Retreat and The Villa are self-catering, but meals are also available at the homestead, which is hung with original artwork by New Zealand and European artists. Its furniture in native timbers is hand-crafted by a German craftsman who lived on the 310-hectare sheep and cattle farm.

Facilities

- The Homestead: 1 double & 1 twin bedroom with ensuites, 1 including sunken bath, sitting area & verandah
- The Retreat: 1 twin & 2 double bedrooms with 1 shared bathroom & 2 toilets
- The Villa: 3 double & 2 twin bedrooms, with 2 guest-share bathrooms, & 1 original claw-foot bath
- cotton bed linen, duvets &/or blankets in Homestead
- single-party bookings for The Retreat & The Villa
- Retreat & Villa self-contained with full kitchens for self-catering
- Retreat & Villa breakfast, served at Homestead, $10–$15 pp
- 3-course dinner served at Homestead, $40 pp; wine extra
- lunch on request $12.50 pp
- lounge facilities in Homestead bedrooms, with tea/coffee
- spacious lounges in Homestead, Retreat & Villa, with open fires
- pool table & gramophone in Villa
- French & German spoken
- on-site parking

Activities available

- barbecues at each house
- pétanque court at Villa
- croquet on Homestead & Villa lawns
- concrete tennis court
- Homestead garden, 1.6ha
- farm & bush walks
- four-wheel-drive farm tours
- horses for experienced riders
- river swimming
- Rangitikei private garden visits
- Rangitikei historic home tour
- bird-watching
- white water & float rafting
- bungy jumping & flying fox
- on-farm catch & release trout fishing
- 4 scenic golf courses
- wool warehouse, craft shops
- café & restaurants, 30km away
- Waiouru Army Museum, 45km
- Ohakea Airforce Museum, 80km
- Rugby Museum, PN, 80km
- winter ski areas, 90 mins away
- Wellington or Rotorua, 3-hour easy drive away

HUNTERVILLE, RANGITIKEI
RATHMOY GARDEN COTTAGE

Hosts Susanna and Christopher Grace

Rangatira Road, Hunterville *Postal* Rathmoy, R D 6, Hunterville
Phone 0-6-322 8334 *Email* sgrace.rathmoy@xtra.co.nz
Fax 0-6-322 8380 *Website* www.rathmoy.co.nz

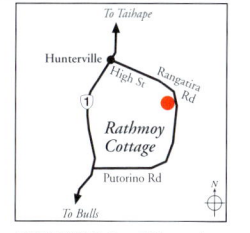

Room rate $275–$330
Extra persons $60 each

Includes breakfast provisions
Self-catering Dinner extra

2 bdrm 1 prbth

DIRECTIONS: From Taihape, take SH 1 to Hunterville. Turn left into High St & then Rangatira Rd. Travel 4km to Rathmoy on right. Or from Bulls, take SH 1 north. Turn right into Putorino Rd. Travel 12km to Rathmoy on left.

Set in the well-known Rathmoy Garden in the Rangitikei, this self-contained cottage is located on the far side of the lake, ensuring guest privacy and peaceful garden views. Built in 1990, Rathmoy Cottage provides two guest bedrooms and wheelchair access bathroom for private-party bookings. A fully equipped kitchen with well-stocked pantry enables guests to self-cater, although breakfast provisions are supplied and country-style dinners are available by arrangement. Guests also enjoy using the gas barbecue for alfresco dining beside the lake, which is home to waterfowl. Other on-site activities include bird-watching, feeding the friendly farm animals and pets, wandering in the 2.4-hectare garden, and farm and bush walks for all fitness levels.

Facilities
- single-party bookings only
- 1 super-king/twin & 1 twin bedroom
- 1 wheelchair access bathroom
- quality linen, hair dryer, bathrobes & heated towel rails
- antiques, books & flowers
- log fire, TV, CD, tape-player, writing desk & guest phone
- underfloor heating
- breakfast provisions supplied; bread-making machine
- dinner, by arrangement, extra
- complimentary beverages
- fully equipped kitchen for self-catering including microwave & dishwasher
- fax & email available
- guest laundry; garaging
- helipad; private airstrip

Activities available
- multiple-night rate available
- established garden on site
- farm & bush walks for all fitness levels
- farming activities
- friendly farm animals & pets
- Rangitikei River access on farm for swimming, picnicking & trout fishing
- mountain bikes & dinghy available
- bird-watching & waterfowl
- restaurants, 5-min drive
- antiques & crafts shops
- white water & float rafting
- historic house tours
- private gardens to visit
- golf courses 10-min drive, clubs available
- bungy jumping; jet boat rides
- snow skiing, 1½-hour drive

KIMBOLTON, MANAWATU
WOODLAND GRANGE

Hosts Juanita and Scott Curry

13 Grammar Street, Kimbolton   *Postal* P O Box 71, Kimbolton
Phone 0-6-328 9667   *Mobile* 021 142 9570   *Fax* 0-6-328 9614
Email hotcurry@xtra.co.nz   *Website* friars.co.nz/hosts/woodland.html

| 1 bdrm | 1 enst | Cottage rate $180 for 2 persons
Extra persons $30 each | *Includes continental breakfast provisions*
Self-catering |

DIRECTIONS: From Feilding, take Kimbolton Rd north for 28km to Kimbolton village. Turn left into Grammar St & travel 100m to Woodland Grange on right. Follow driveway to cottage.

Set in a rambling woodland garden of almost two hectares (four acres), the self-contained cottage at Woodland Grange provides a quiet retreat for honeymooners and garden lovers. Located in the upper Manawatu, on the outskirts of Kimbolton village, Woodland Grange is just minutes from the renowned Cross Hills Gardens and the Heritage Park of the Rhododendron Association. The cottage includes a queen-size bedroom, with an extra sofa-bed in the living room. Provisions for self-catering are supplied. Juanita and Scott, who live adjacent, also cater for weddings in their chapel on site and guests are welcome to play the organ. Originally designed as a nursery, the garden now features mature trees and ponds with seating areas.

Facilities
- single-party bookings only
- 1 queen ensuite bedroom in self-contained cottage
- bathrobes, hair dryer, toiletries & heated towel rails
- dressing room
- phone jack in bedroom
- night-store heater
- lounge with open fire, TV, CD-player, games & books
- continental breakfast provisions supplied
- small kitchen with basic provisions for self-catering
- fresh flowers; confectionery
- fax available in house
- self-serve laundry in cottage
- iron & ironing board
- extensive garden setting
- on-site parking

Activities available
- guest BBQ in secluded cottage courtyard
- 2ha (4-acre) woodland garden ramble on site
- chapel on site for weddings
- organ in chapel for guest use
- heated outdoor shower & bath
- swimming; trout fishing
- rhododendron gardens nearby: Cross Hills & Heritage Park, 3–5-min drive north
- historical café & wine bar, 3-min walk away
- dinner at Cheltenham Hotel, 10-min drive
- Kimbolton village, 3-min walk
- walkways; picnic areas
- gardens open to visit
- Feilding, 20-min drive
- Palmerston North City, 35-min drive south

© Friars' Guide to New Zealand Accommodation for the Discerning Traveller

Palmerston North
Hiwinui Country Estate

Hosts Jan and Dave Stewart

465 Ashhurst-Bunnythorpe Road, Hiwinui, R D 11, Palmerston North
Phone 0-6-329 2838   *Mobile* 025 268 0173   *Fax* 0-6-329 2828
Email jan@hiwinui.co.nz   *Website* www.hiwinui.co.nz

3 bdrm | 3 enst

Double $250–$300
Single $180

Includes breakfast & apéritifs
Dinner extra

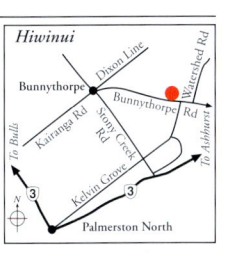

DIRECTIONS: From Palmerston North, take Tremaine Ave north. Continue into Kelvin Grove Rd. At "T" junction, turn left into Ashhurst-Bunnythorpe Rd. Hiwinui Country Estate on right (15 mins from city).

Hiwinui Country Estate is set on 450-hectares (1,100 acres) of the Stewart family's farming properties on the northern outskirts of Palmerston North. Guests can choose from three bedrooms with ensuites. A large schist fireplace opens both to the lounge and the dining room. The underground cellar offers an extensive range of wines from New Zealand's leading vineyards. Nestled close to the lodge, in a secret garden for privacy, is an outdoor spa pool and open log fireplace for guests seeking relaxation. Hiwinui Country Estate has its own in-house beauty therapist who offers body treatments. Guests can also enjoy one of New Zealand's renowned river trips through the dramatic Manawatu Gorge, aboard the Lodge's private jet boat.

Facilities

- 1 super-king ensuite bedroom with spa bath & double basin
- 1 king ensuite bedroom with double shower & 1 queen ensuite bedroom
- cotton bed linen, fresh flowers, phone, tea/coffee, mineral water & TV in bedrooms
- hair dryers, toiletries, bathrobes & heated flooring
- children over 8 yrs welcome
- cooked or continental breakfast
- formal dinner on request, $70 pp; complimentary apéritifs & hors d'oeuvres; licensed
- phone, fax & email
- lounge with open fire, Sky TV, video, CDs, piano & artwork
- laundry; wheelchair access
- courtesy airport transfer
- on-site parking; helipad

Activities available

- BBQ & outdoor spa pool on site
- pets welcome, kennels supplied
- guided tours of farm
- feeding calves & lambs in season
- in-house massage & beauty therapy
- private hosted jet boat
- pétanque court
- golf-driving pad
- duck shooting parties
- restaurants in Palmerston North, 15-min drive
- helicopter flights arranged
- trip to windfarm
- Manfield Autocourse
- walks in Ruahine Ranges
- Feilding saleyards
- Victoria Esplanade gardens
- fly fishing
- airport, 10-min drive

235

© Friars' Guide to New Zealand Accommodation for the Discerning Traveller

WOODVILLE
OTAWA LODGE

Hosts Del and Sue Trew

132 Otawhao Road, Kumeroa, R D 1, Woodville
Phone 0-6-376 4603 *Mobiles* 021 175 4727 or 025 230 1327
Fax 0-6-376 5042 *Email* otawa.lodge@xtra.co.nz *Website* otawalodge.co.nz

Room rate $215–$265   Includes breakfast   Lunch & dinner extra

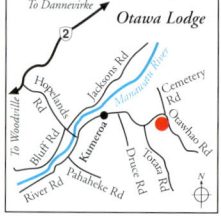

2 bdrm 2 prbth

DIRECTIONS: From Woodville take SH 2 north for 4.1km. Turn right into Hopelands Rd, travel 6.1km & cross river. Turn left into Kumeroa Rd & travel 6.7km through Kumeroa. Continue into Otawhao Rd to Lodge.

Set on 32 hectares, in the rolling hills at the head of the Otawhao Valley, Otawa Lodge is an original example of Art Nouveau architecture. Built in 1914, this single-storey Edwardian homestead features a Marseilles tiled roof and stained glass leadlight windows. The intricate plasterwork of the ceilings and walls in the entrance hall and sitting room are complemented by native rimu dados and panelling. Guests dine on fresh organic produce and speciality fish dishes. The Queen Anne-style turret serves as an octagonal guest library with views of the surrounding garden. Guests enjoy the six hectares of native bush with tui, bellbirds and native pigeons. The house is heated by hot water radiators and both of the two guestrooms have private bathrooms.

Facilities

- 1 super-king/twin & 1 queen bedroom with cotton bed linen & mineral water
- 2 private bathrooms with hair dryer, bathrobes, heated towel rails & toiletries
- guest sitting & dining room with piano & writing desk
- library; TV on request
- laundry available
- email, fax & phone available
- choice of full cooked or continental breakfast
- 4-course dinner with apéritifs & coffee, $70 pp
- selected NZ wine list
- fresh flowers
- central heating
- private guest entrance
- on-site parking; garaging
- courtesy passenger transfer

Activities available

- conferences, honeymoons & formal dinners catered for
- pétanque & croquet on site
- hill & bush walks on site
- 1ha (2-acre) garden, 26ha (64-acre) farmland & 6ha (14-acre) native bush & creek on site
- farm visits; tennis courts nearby
- golf course; horse riding
- fishing; swimming
- antiques shopping
- sky diving; quad-bike trips
- tramping; hunting
- Lindauer Memorial Gallery
- lavender farm
- Mt Bruce Wildlife Centre
- Wind Farm visits
- Manawatu Gorge – for jet boats, abseiling & kayaking

MASTERTON, WAIRARAPA
FRESH EGG RETREAT

Hosts Daniel Clenott and Randall Cobb

Bute Road, R D 9, Masterton, Wairarapa
Phone 0-6-372 3506 *Email* freshegg@hotmail.com
Fax 0-6-372 3505 *Website* www.freshegg.co.nz

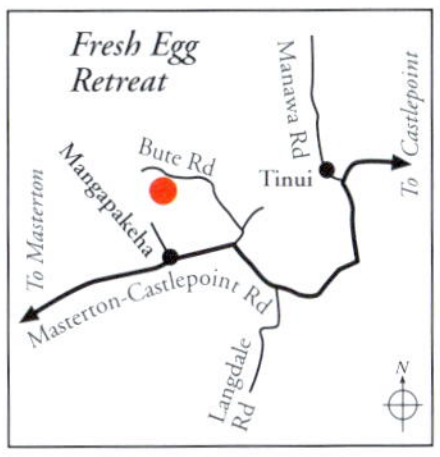

2 bdrm | 2 enst | 1 prbth
Double $195
Single $110

Includes breakfast & dinner
Lunch extra

DIRECTIONS: Take SH 2 to Masterton. Turn east into Te Ore Ore Rd & travel 37km towards Castlepoint. Turn left into Bute Rd & travel 3.7km to Fresh Egg Retreat on the left.

Set in an established garden on over two hectares (six acres), surrounded by bush, Fresh Egg Retreat provides a genuine secluded retreat of peace and quiet for up to four guests. Although there are no chickens at Fresh Egg Retreat, all the meals are home-made such as waffles, blintzes, bagels, omelettes, or cinnamon buns for breakfast. A gourmet five-course dinner is included in the tariff and can include home-made pasta and ice-cream, with Cajun and Italian cuisine a speciality. Lunch of sandwiches, salads, light soups and fresh fruits is also available. Daniel and Randall emigrated from the United States and totally renovated this 1948 farm homestead to provide guests with two ensuite queen bedrooms and an additional private bathroom with tub.

Facilities
- 2 ensuite queen bedrooms
- additional private bathroom with tub for guest use
- hair dryers, toiletries, & high-pressure instant-hot showers in all 3 bathrooms
- cotton bed linen
- laundry available, $5
- gift vouchers available
- phone, fax, email available
- tea/coffee available
- tariff includes gourmet 5-course dinner
- International cuisine
- hearty home-made breakfast served in dining room, or alfresco on verandah
- lunch, $15 pp
- open fire & satellite TV in guest lounge
- extensive video library
- on-site parking

Activities available
- home gym
- sauna on site
- swimming pool
- hiking
- Castlepoint & Riversdale Beaches
- local crafts in Tinui
- vineyards
- gardens to visit
- shopping, 37km
- Masterton, 30-min drive
- hot air ballooning
- horse riding
- plant nurseries
- fishing
- golf
- walks
- wine trail
- caving
- Mt Bruce Wildlife Centre

MASTERTON, WAIRARAPA
CAMELLIA ESTATE

Hosts Ray and Liz Piper

39 Renall Street, Masterton, Wairarapa   *Fax* 0-6-370 9055
Phone 0-6-370 9088   *Mobiles* 027 488 8921 *and* 025 888 922
Email camellia@wise.net.nz   *Website* friars.co.nz/hosts/camellia.html

| 4 bdrm | 2 prbth | Double $160
Cottage rate $160 | Single $90 | *Includes breakfast*
Self-catering in cottage | *Dinner extra* |

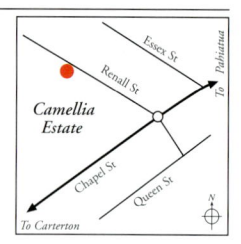

DIRECTIONS: From north, take SH 2 to Masterton. Continue into Chapel St. Turn right into Renall St. Camellia Estate on left. From south, take SH 2 to Masterton. Continue into High St, veer left into Chapel St.

This historic villa, built in 1903, still features the original finials, high ceilings, stained-glass doors and tiled fireplace. Camellia Estate is set in a half-hectare woodland garden, which features a stream running through it and a fountain on the lawn. Accommodation in the villa comprises three bedrooms, including a king-size four-poster bed, and spa bath in the guest bathroom, with single-party bookings ensuring privacy. A full breakfast is served either indoors or alfresco overlooking the swimming pool and tennis pavilion. Dinner with wine is available by prior request, or a barbecue can be arranged in the summer months. Then, in winter, guests can enjoy the log fire in the sitting room. A new self-catering cottage is also available.

Facilities
- private-party bookings
- 1 king, 1 queen & 1 twin bedroom & 1 private bathroom
- 1 self-catering cottage with 1 queen bedroom
- cotton bed linen & bathrobes
- hair dryer, toiletries, heated towel rails & spa bath
- fresh flowers in rooms
- central heating
- 11am checkout time
- continental/cooked breakfast
- dinner with wine, $35 pp
- log fire, Sky/Digital TV, DVD, video & music in guest lounge
- grand piano in lounge
- phone, fax & email facilities
- complimentary tea/coffee
- children over 10 years welcome
- complimentary laundry
- off-street parking

Activities available
- 0.5ha garden with stream
- barbecue on site
- tennis court & pavilion
- pétanque/boules court
- swimming pool
- hot air ballooning, adjacent
- antique shops
- historic town tours
- vineyards
- town centre, 5-min walk
- restaurants, 5-min walk
- beaches
- gardens open to visit
- horse riding
- bush walks
- golf
- fishing
- caving
- Mt Bruce Wildlife Centre
- Wellington City, 2-hr drive

Masterton, Wairarapa
Natusch House

Hosts Anne and Alan Bohm

55 Lincoln Road, Masterton   *Postal* P O Box 469 Masterton
Phone 0-6-378 9252   *Mobile* 027 436 3732   *Fax* 0-6-378 9330
Email anne@natusch.co.nz   *Website* www.natusch.co.nz

| 4 bdrm | 1 prbth | 1 shbth | House rate $160 for up to 2 persons
Extra persons $60 each | *Self-catering*
Includes basic provisions |

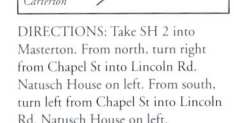

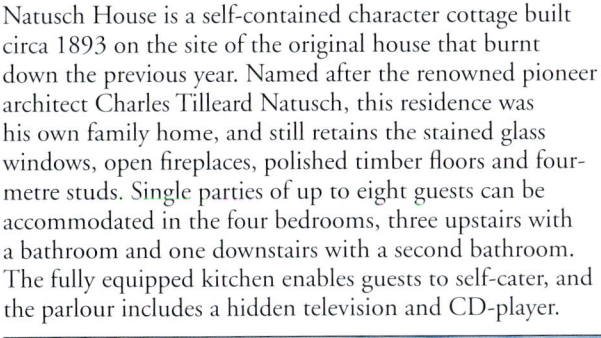

DIRECTIONS: Take SH 2 into Masterton. From north, turn right from Chapel St into Lincoln Rd. Natusch House on left. From south, turn left from Chapel St into Lincoln Rd. Natusch House on left.

Natusch House is a self-contained character cottage built circa 1893 on the site of the original house that burnt down the previous year. Named after the renowned pioneer architect Charles Tilleard Natusch, this residence was his own family home, and still retains the stained glass windows, open fireplaces, polished timber floors and four-metre studs. Single parties of up to eight guests can be accommodated in the four bedrooms, three upstairs with a bathroom and one downstairs with a second bathroom. The fully equipped kitchen enables guests to self-cater, and the parlour includes a hidden television and CD-player.

Facilities
- private-party bookings only
- self-contained historic house
- 4 queen bedrooms
- 2 private bathrooms
- cotton bed linen; fresh flowers
- hair dryer, toiletries & heated towel rails
- full kitchen for self-catering
- home-made jams, marmalade, breads, biscuits, muffins, fruit bowl, free-range eggs supplied
- complimentary wine, beer & frozen meals in fridge
- dining alfresco or in dining room
- email, fax & phone available
- oil-filled heaters in every room
- parlour with historic artwork, writing desk, TV & CD-player
- children under 2 & over 11 yrs
- hosts live off-site
- courtesy passenger transfer
- off-street parking; carport

Activities available
- books, magazines & games
- weddings & honeymoons catered for
- restaurant, walking distance
- 4WD tours
- historic town tours
- museum; arts studio
- antique shops
- Martinborough wineries
- bush walks; caving
- gardens open to visit; herb & lavender gardens
- hot air ballooning
- bush walking, 20-min drive
- Mt Bruce National Bird Reserve & endangered species refuge
- Castlepoint beach & lighthouse, 45 mins
- Palliser lighthouse & seal colony, 1½-hour drive
- Wellington airport, 1½ hrs

MASTERTON, WAIRARAPA
RIDDLESWORTH ESTATE

Hosts Roger and Sonya Steeby

61 Masterton-Gladstone Road, R D 4, Masterton
Phone 0-6-378 0130   *Mobile* 021 705 007   *Fax* 0-6-378 0131
Email rsteeby@xtra.co.nz   *Website* www.riddlesworth.com

| 3 bdrm | 3 enst | Double $165 / Cottage rate $285 | Single $130 / 2-night minimum stay | Includes breakfast for all guests / Self-catering for lunch & dinner |

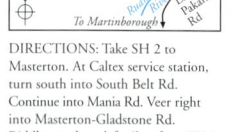

DIRECTIONS: Take SH 2 to Masterton. At Caltex service station, turn south into South Belt Rd. Continue into Mania Rd. Veer right into Masterton-Gladstone Rd. Riddlesworth on left, 6km from SH 2.

Bounded on two sides by the Ruamahanga River, Riddlesworth is a 24-hectare farm offering fly fishing on site. With views of the Tararua Range, this 24-hectare (60-acre) property was a former thoroughbred stud farm, named after an early racehorse imported from England. Built in 2001 in American southern colonial style, the house provides two queen-size ensuite guestrooms with rural views. A separate self-contained cottage also has a queen-size bedroom, as well as a fully equipped kitchen for self-catering if desired. A three-course gourmet breakfast is served in the house dining room, or alfresco on the patio. Restaurants are only six kilometres away in Masterton, and winery tours are popular with guests.

Facilities
- House: 2 queen bedrooms, both with baths in ensuites
- Cottage: 1 queen bedroom, with spa bath in ensuite
- hair dryers, demist mirror, bathrobes & heated towel rails
- central heating & air conditioning in house
- afternoon tea & coffee
- fresh flowers
- email, fax & phone facilities
- 3-course gourmet breakfast
- full kitchen for self-catering in cottage
- billiards/snooker room
- lounge with open fire & tea/coffee in house
- media room with big-screen Sky TV, DVD & video
- courtesy passenger transfer from railway station
- on-site parking

Activities available
- swimming pool
- barbecue available for guest use
- tennis court on site
- 24ha (60 acres) on site with mature trees, orchard, vegetable garden & river
- fly fishing for trout on site or guided fishing on local rivers
- bird-watching on site
- river walks & bicycling on site
- restaurants, 6km
- antique shops, 6km
- laundry, 6km
- mountain hiking
- river rafting
- golf
- hot air ballooning
- gardens open to visit
- horse riding
- wine tasting & wine tours

Above: The Ruamahanga River flows adjacent to Riddlesworth Estate, providing popular spots for fly-fishing for trout.
Below: One of the two queen-size guest bedrooms in the main house, looking into the ensuite which includes a bath.
Opposite top: The exterior of the main house at Riddlesworth Estate, built in southern colonial American style in 2001.
Opposite bottom left: The separate self-contained guest cottage at Riddlesworth, where guests can self-cater in the full kitchen.
Opposite bottom right: The queen-size bedroom in the guest cottage opens into an ensuite bathroom with a spa bath.

CARTERTON, WAIRARAPA
GLADSTONE VINEYARD APARTMENT

Hosts Christine and David Kernohan

20 Gladstone Road, R D 2, Carterton
Phone 0-6-379 8563 *Email* info@gladstone.co.nz
Fax 0-6-379 8564 *Website* www.gladstone.co.nz

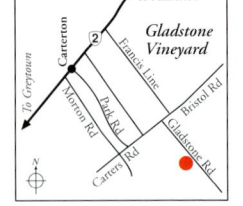

1 bdrm | 1 enst | Apartment rate $215 | *Includes breakfast provisions* | *Self-catering*

DIRECTIONS: From Greytown or Masterton, take SH 2 to Carterton. Turn east into Park Rd. At "T" junction turn left into Carters Rd. Take 1st right into Gladstone Rd. Travel 3 mins to Vineyard on right.

Set in the thriving wine-growing area of the Wairarapa, Gladstone Vineyard Apartment is situated above the Gladstone winery. The apartment offers a queen-size bed with double settee for additional guests. The lounge area is warmed by a wood burner and a spacious deck is popular for alfresco dining in the summer. Guests enjoy the views over the vineyard to the hills beyond, or for the more active walks around the vineyard and pond or through the native bush adjacent. Country breakfast supplies and a bottle of wine are provided and dinner can be delivered by arrangement. A lunchtime café operates on site from October to March, on Friday, Saturday and Sunday. The hosts live in a separate Victorian house about 200 metres from the winery.

Facilities
- private-party bookings only
- 1 queen ensuite bedroom
- phone, TV & tea/coffee in bedroom; fresh flowers
- hair dryer, heated towel rails, bathrobes, bath & toiletries
- double bed settee for extras
- email, fax & phone available
- laundry by arrangement
- complimentary bottle of wine
- full kitchen for self-catering
- provisions – mushrooms, eggs, bacon, fruit, cereal, fresh bread/croissants & tea/coffee
- café on site, Oct–Easter
- delivered dinners if required
- wine for sale
- private guest lounge with wood burner, nibbles, TV & CD-player
- on-site parking; helipad

Activities available
- pétanque court on site
- vineyard, wine tastings & winery tours on site
- pond & garden walks
- small dogs welcome
- honeymoons catered for
- Carters Reserve with board walk through native bush next door
- ostrich farm
- adventure activities
- wheelwright
- cheesemaker
- restaurants nearby
- museum
- arts studio
- antique shops
- wineries
- bush walks
- gardens open to visit

CARTERTON, WAIRARAPA
CARRINGTON COTTAGES AND GARDENS

Hosts Shirley and John Cameron

High Street North, Carterton
Phone 0-6-379 7039 *Mobile* 027 445 6409 *Fax* 0-6-379 7039
Email cameron@wise.net.nz *Website* www.carringtoncottages.co.nz

3 bdrm | 2 enst

Cottage rate $150 for 2 persons
Extra persons $45 each

Includes breakfast provisions
Self-catering

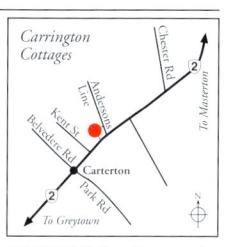

DIRECTIONS: From Greytown take take SH 2 north through Carterton. Turn left into Carrington House on corner of Andersons Line. From Masterton take SH2 south towards Carterton. Carrington on right

Carrington Cottages are set in eight hectares (20 acres) of park-like grounds and gardens designed by the renowned New Zealand landscape architect, Alfred Buxton, in the early 1900s. Original features can still be seen including the lake and the driveway that winds through mature exotic trees to arrive at the house. Accommodation is offered in two separate self-contained cottages tucked away on the northern sunny side of the property. Carrington Farm Cottage (*above*) was originally built in 1860 and is now restored and refurbished with colonial furniture to provide two double bedrooms, a bathroom, laundry and full kitchen. Carrington House Cottage (*below*) was relocated in the 1970s and furnished in Italian designer style. This cottage comprises one queen-size bedroom and ensuite, with laundry facilities, a full kitchen and mountain views. Guests can self-cater in both cottages, and dine beside the open fire or alfresco looking out to the daffodil fields and garden.

Facilities
- 2 self-contained cottages
- single party bookings per cottage
- House Cottage: 1 queen bedroom, 1 ensuite with shub, video & mountain views
- Farm cottage: 2 double bedrooms, 1 bathroom with heated towel rails & wheelchair access
- hair dryer, toiletries & bathrobes in both cottage bathrooms
- fresh flowers
- lounge with open fire, TV, books & artwork in both cottages
- phone jacks in cottages for laptop computer connection
- full kitchen for self-catering in both cottages
- breakfast provisions supplied
- laundry facilities in both cottages
- views of mountain ranges or garden
- colonial furniture in Farm Cottage
- Italian designer furnishings in House Cottage
- pet sheep, cats & dogs on site
- children by arrangement
- historic garden setting
- private location
- off-street parking

Activities available
- garden seats on site
- garden walks on site
- vineyards, 10-min drive
- wine trails
- sports ground
- Clareville showground
- antiques shop, 2-min drive
- antiques trail
- local crafts
- museum
- arts studio
- historic town tours
- restaurants nearby
- gardens open to visit
- plant nurseries
- cheesemaker to visit
- east coast beaches
- fishing
- swimming
- bush walks
- Tararua Forest Park
- caving
- adventure activities
- Mt Bruce Wildlife Centre
- hot air ballooning
- Carterton township, within walking distance
- Masterton, 7-min drive
- Greytown, 5 mins south
- Wellington City, 1½ hrs

GREYTOWN, WAIRARAPA
BRIARWOOD

Host Liz Kennedy

21 Main Street, Greytown
Phone 0-6-304 8336 *Mobile* 027 252 4902 *Fax* 0-6-304 8316
Email briarwood@xtra.co.nz *Website* www.briarwood.biz

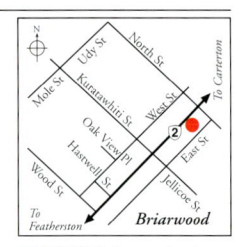

2 bdrm | 2 enst | Double $185–$235 | Single $120–$165 | Includes breakfast | Self-catering | Lunch & dinner extra

DIRECTIONS: From north, take SH 2 to Greytown. Continue on Main St to Briarwood on left. From south, take SH 2 to Greytown. Continue on Main St through centre of town to Briarwood on right.

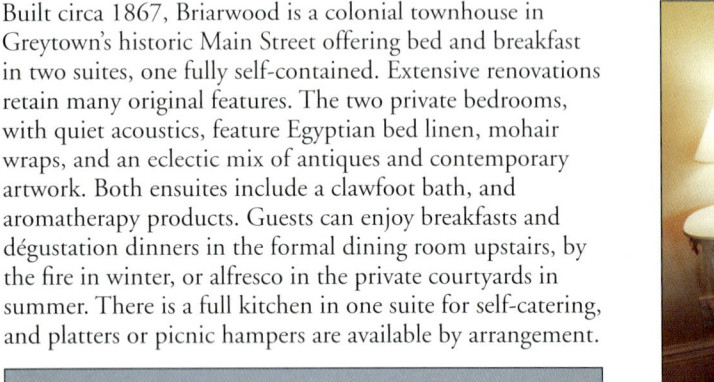

Built circa 1867, Briarwood is a colonial townhouse in Greytown's historic Main Street offering bed and breakfast in two suites, one fully self-contained. Extensive renovations retain many original features. The two private bedrooms, with quiet acoustics, feature Egyptian bed linen, mohair wraps, and an eclectic mix of antiques and contemporary artwork. Both ensuites include a clawfoot bath, and aromatherapy products. Guests can enjoy breakfasts and dégustation dinners in the formal dining room upstairs, by the fire in winter, or alfresco in the private courtyards in summer. There is a full kitchen in one suite for self-catering, and platters or picnic hampers are available by arrangement.

Facilities
- 1 super-king/twin & 1 queen suite, each with ensuite, private courtyard, lounge & dining area
- bathrobes, clawfoot bath, double shower, hair dryer, toiletries, heated floor & towel rails in both ensuites
- Egyptian cotton bed linen
- wheelchair access
- keypad entry to each suite
- fresh flowers; fax & phone
- complimentary laundry
- café-style breakfast menu
- lunch or picnic hamper by arrangement, $35 pp; dinner with wine, $65 pp
- full self-catering kitchen
- tea/coffee, nibbles, bar, Sky TV, video, DVDs, CDs, desk, artwork, books & internet access in both suites
- courtesy passenger transfer
- off-street parking

Activities available
- pétanque/boules & BBQ on site
- vineyard tours
- paua factory
- golf courses
- tennis courts
- adventure sports
- hot air ballooning
- mountain hiking
- horse trekking
- gardens open to visit
- beaches & scenic coastal tours
- award-wining restaurants
- museums & historic buildings
- antique shops & galleries
- colonial heritage walks
- hunting & fishing, guides available
- spectacular river gorge
- Martinborough, 15 mins
- Masterton, 20 mins
- Wellington City, 1 hour

GREYTOWN, WAIRARAPA
WESTWOOD COUNTRY HOUSE

Host Jill Kemp

82 West Street, Greytown *Postal* P O Box 34, Greytown
Phone 0-6-304 8510   *Mobile* 027 471 6466   *Fax* 0-6-304 8610
Email westwood.kemp@xtra.co.nz   *Website* westwood.greytown.co.nz

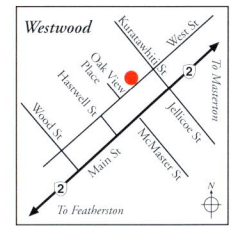

| 4 bdrm | 3 enst | 1 prbth | Double $195–$250 | Single $175–$225 | *Includes breakfast* |

DIRECTIONS: From Featherston, take SH 2 north to Greytown. Turn left into Wood St, then right into West St. Westwood on left. From Carterton, take SH 2 south to Greytown. Turn right into Kuratawhiti St, then left.

A top category award winner in New Zealand House of the Year, Westwood has been designed to blend with the surrounding trees, stream and mountain views. The guest wing provides spacious bedrooms for up to seven guests, with dressing rooms, large ensuites or private bathrooms and adjoining verandahs opening into the garden. Each bedroom also includes tea and coffee-making facilities, a fridge and Sky television. Breakfast is served alfresco by the pool in summer, in the dining room in winter, or in the guests' rooms if preferred. Guests enjoy the formal Italian-inspired herb garden and landscaping, playing croquet and pétanque, swimming in the pool, picking raspberries in season, or viewing the animals on the four-hectare (nine-acre) site.

Facilities
- 3 super-king/twin & 1 single bedroom
- 3 ensuites & 1 private bathroom
- hair dryers, bathrobes & wheelchair access
- heated towel rails & heated floors
- 1 bath & double basin
- 2 dressing rooms
- fresh flowers in rooms
- breakfast served in dining room, bedrooms, or by pool
- tea/coffee, fridge & Sky TV in all 3 bedrooms
- guest lounge with open fire
- phone, fax & email facilities
- laundry available
- private guest entrance
- off-street parking
- barbecue available

Activities available
- swimming pool on site
- in-ground croquet lawn
- pétanque/boules on site
- exclusive garden tours on site
- raspberry picking in season
- nearly 4ha (9 acres) with formal herb garden on site
- sheep & hens on site
- golf courses & tennis courts
- gardens open to visit
- restaurants, 3-min stroll
- antique shops, nearby
- hiking on mountain & river walks
- horse trekking
- adventure sports
- Greytown shops, 3-min walk
- Martinborough's world renowned vineyards, 20 mins
- Wellington City, 1-hour drive

Martinborough, Wairarapa
Margrain Vineyard Villas

Hosts Daryl and Graham Margrain

Ponatahi Road, Martinborough *Postal* P O Box 97, Martinborough
Phone 0-6-306 9292 *Email* margrain@xtra.co.nz
Fax 0-6-306 9297 *Website* www.margrainvineyard.co.nz

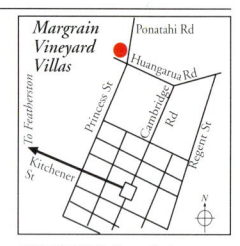

15 bdrm | 15 enst | Room rate $160–$300 *Includes continental breakfast provisions*

DIRECTIONS: From Featherston, travel towards Martinborough. On edge of township turn left into Princess St. Continue to Huangarua Rd. Cross intersection to Margrain driveway, 200m past left corner of Ponatahi Rd.

The four-hectare Margrain Vineyard was first planted in 1992. Three years later the first wines from the estate were produced, coinciding with the opening of the first eight of the 15 Margrain Vineyard Villas, sited adjacent to the terraced vineyard. The architecture was designed by Roger Walker, with interior design by Decor Trends. Each villa comprises a king/twin or queen-size bed, ensuite bathroom with wheelchair access, and lounge area (one separate suite), with French doors opening to a spacious balcony overlooking the rural pastureland of the Huangarua River valley, to the Tararua Range beyond. This is a favourite spot for watching pukeko. Facilities are available for small conferences adjacent to the wineshop and winery with its three-vault cellars.

Facilities

- 15 separate villas
- single-party bookings for each villa
- each villa comprises 1 bedroom, 1 spacious bathroom, sitting area & extensive private balcony
- 9 king/twins & 6 queen bedrooms, all with ensuites
- 15 ensuite bathrooms with heated towel rails
- continental breakfast provisions
- tea/coffee-making facilities
- TV in each villa
- iron & board in each villa
- cotton bed linen
- wheelchair access to 1 villa
- balconies overlook river valley
- children by arrangement
- off-street parking
- developing garden

Activities available

- wine tasting, winery & vineyard
- Old Winery Café on site
- pukeko watching on site
- pétanque/boules on site
- trout fishing in adjacent river
- good restaurants, 5-min drive
- Wairarapa wine trail
- tennis & squash courts
- 18-hole golf course
- private gardens to visit
- antiques & craft shops
- colonial museum
- glow-worm caves
- horse trekking
- canoeing; caving
- chasm walkway; seal colony
- abseiling, rafting
- Putangirua Pinnacles
- Ngawi fishing village
- Palliser Bay coast

© Friars' Guide to New Zealand Accommodation for the Discerning Traveller

MARTINBOROUGH, WAIRARAPA
AYLSTONE BOUTIQUE HOTEL

Hosts Roger and Jill Fraser

Huangarua Road, Martinborough
Phone 0-6-306 9505   Mobile 021 329 335   Fax 0-6-306 8066
Email bookings@aylstone.co.nz   Website www.aylstone.co.nz

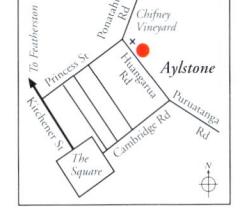

| 6 bdrm | 6 enst | 1 prbth | Double $275–$295   Single $250–$270 | Includes breakfast   Picnic baskets & dinner extra |

DIRECTIONS: From Featherston, travel towards Martinborough. On edge of township, at church, turn left into Princess St. Turn 4th right into Huangarua Rd. Aylstone is 2nd property on left, past vineyard.

Aylstone Boutique Hotel is located among the renowned vineyards of Martinborough, on the outskirts of the village. Surrounded by vineyards, Aylstone is popular with wine aficionados and the new owner, Roger, offers guided tours to selected vineyards, including his own Murdoch James Estate. Set in relaxing gardens, the homestead at Aylstone hosts up to 12 guests in six ensuite bedrooms, served by an in-house restaurant. Wine connoisseurs can personally select their wines from the collection of local and international labels in the bar, to accompany their table d'hôte meal, or Roger can assist. The professionally trained chef provides seasonal menus to complement the chosen wines. Small conferences can also be catered at Aylstone.

Facilities
- 1 king/twin, 3 queen & 2 twin ensuite bedrooms, all with mountain & vineyard views
- fruit bowl, tea/coffee, phone, fresh flowers & TV in rooms
- bathrobes, hair dryers, toiletries & heated towel rails & floors
- phone, fax, email available
- complimentary laundry
- conference room & facilities
- wheelchair access
- full breakfast served in dining room, or alfresco in gazebo in garden
- picnic baskets, extra
- restaurant open Fri.–Sat. or by arrangement, $60 pp
- fully licensed wine bar
- sunset drinks in belvedere
- on-site parking
- transfers by limousine or helicopter, extra

Activities available
- viewing vineyards from belvedere on site
- pétanque court on site
- bicycles & helmets available
- Basil, the Jack Russell & other pets on site
- boutique wineries nearby
- guided vineyard tours & activities in season
- walking tour itineraries
- Martinborough Square, 1km
- local gardens to visit; tramping
- golf course, 5-min drive
- fishing; jet boating; hunting
- white water rafting; canoeing
- horse treks; 4WD bike riding
- clay bird shooting arranged
- glow-worm caves; tennis
- seal colony at Cape Palliser, 1 hr
- Mt Bruce Wildlife Centre, 2 hrs

MARTINBOROUGH, WAIRARAPA
Petit Hotel

Hosts Des and Susan Vize

3 Kitchener Street, Martinborough   *Phone* 0-6-306 8086
Postal P O Box 169, Martinborough   *Fax* 0-6-306 8087
Email bookings@petithotel.co.nz   *Website* www.petithotel.co.nz

4 bdrm   4 enst   Room rate $200–$250   *Breakfast, picnic hamper & dinner extra*

DIRECTIONS: From Featherston, take SH 53 to Martinborough. Continue into Kitchener St to Memorial Square. Travel clockwise around square back to Kitchener St. Petit Hotel 1st on left.

Originally built in 1907 by Adam Wright, Petit Hotel was fully restored in 2001. Renovated to retain its historic character, with wooden shutters and balconies, this boutique hotel offers four ensuite bedrooms, these bedrooms each themed and featuring artwork, Sky television, DVD-player and a bookcase of books. Tea and coffee facilities are provided in each bedroom, as well as a fridge, distilled water, cake, truffles and complimentary port and sherry. Three of the ensuites include claw-foot baths and two bedrooms open to private balconies. Adjacent to The Square in Martinborough, there are three cafés within walking distance where guests can breakfast, and à la carte dinner room service is available. Picnic hampers are available.

Facilities
- 4 queen ensuite bedrooms
- hair dryer, toiletries, bathrobes, heated towel rails & floors
- claw-foot bath in 3 ensuites
- cotton bed linen
- Sky TV & DVD in bedrooms
- tea/coffee, fridge, mineral water, port, sherry, cake, truffles, writing desk & bookcase of books in all guestrooms
- phone & laundry facilities
- continental breakfast or breakfast vouchers, extra
- picnic hamper on request, extra
- à la carte dinner available
- artwork & fresh flowers throughout
- courtesy passenger transfer
- off-street parking
- honeymoons & weddings catered for

Activities available
- 3 cafés within walking distance for breakfast/brunch or lunch
- vineyard tours nearby
- local touring packages
- Martinborough shops
- jet boating
- kayaking
- golf courses
- tennis courts
- gardens open to visit
- restaurants, walking distance
- scenic coastal tours
- mountain hiking
- river walks
- horse trekking
- adventure sports
- windmills, 20-min drive
- Featherston, 15-min drive
- Greytown, 15-min drive
- Wellington City, 1-hour drive

© Friars' Guide to New Zealand Accommodation for the Discerning Traveller

MARTINBOROUGH, WAIRARAPA
SAGE AND PAVILION COTTAGES

Hosts James and Ann Brodie

129A Dublin Street, Martinborough   *Postal* 142 Dublin Street, Martinborough
Phone 0-6-306 8835   *Mobile* 027 444 6648   *Fax* 0-6-306 8871
Email j.brodie@paradise.net.nz   *Website* www.sagecottage.co.nz

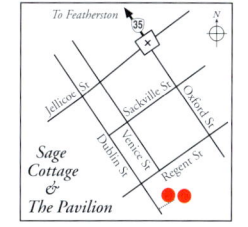

Cottage rate $140	Extra persons $40 each
Pavilion rate $170	Extra persons $40 each

Includes continental breakfast provisions
Self-catering in both cottages

5 bdrm / 2 prbth

DIRECTIONS: From Martinborough Square, take Jellicoe St & travel south-west. Turn left into Dublin St. Travel 300m to Sage & Pavilion Cottages along driveway on left.

Located in a one-hectare rural setting, surrounded by orchards and a wildflower meadow, with vistas to the Orongorongo and Tararua mountain ranges, Sage Cottage (*see above*) and Pavilion Cottage (*see below*) offer peaceful retreats for travellers or weary Wellingtonians. These two cottages are both secluded, with single-party bookings ensuring privacy, yet within walking distance of Martinborough's cafés, restaurants, craftshops and vineyards. Sage Cottage is built in the style of early Wairarapa cottages and was completely renovated in 1998 to provide accommodation for up to two couples. Pavilion Cottage is a spacious character villa, fully renovated in 1999 to provide three bedrooms and a log fire in the lounge, as well as a barbecue. Both cottages feature deep verandahs opening to individual gardens with rural outlooks, for alfresco dining and enjoying the sunsets. Guests can self-cater using the fully equipped kitchens, and continental breakfast provisions are supplied.

Facilities
- single-party bookings only, for each cottage
- 2 self-contained cottages
- Pavilion Cottage: 1 double & 2 queen bedrooms, 1 spacious private bathroom including bath & wall heater
- Sage Cottage: 1 queen & 1 double bedroom, & 1 private bathroom
- hair dryers & heated towel rails in both bathrooms
- tea/coffee facilities, TV & music in both cottages
- children welcome
- spacious verandahs for alfresco dining
- continental breakfast provisions to both cottages include cereal, fruit juice, toast, eggs, fruit, teas & coffee
- fully equipped kitchens for self-catering in both cottages
- BBQ for Pavilion Cottage
- log fire in Pavilion Cottage lounge only
- private garden for each cottage
- mountain views
- rural setting
- off-street parking

Activities available
- walks in 1ha orchards, among trees & wildflowers on site
- wine sampling at Martinborough vineyards
- craft shops, 10-min walk
- Hau Nui Wind Farm
- private gardens open to visit
- horse riding
- golf courses
- tennis courts
- squash courts
- rafting & canoeing
- gliding
- trout fishing
- hunting
- 5 restaurants, 10-min walk
- walks through limestone chasm
- hot air ballooning
- sky diving
- Fell Engine Museum
- bush walking
- tramping in Tararua Range
- seal colony
- Kupe's sail at Cape Palliser
- Mt Bruce Wildlife Centre
- Martinborough Square, 10-min walk away
- Featherston, 15km
- Masterton, 40km
- Wellington City, 65-min drive

PALLISER BAY, WAIRARAPA
POUNUI HOMESTEAD

Hosts Ju and Nick Allen

2110 Western Lake Road, R D 3, Featherston
Phone 0-6-307 7687   Email pounui@xtra.co.nz
Fax 0-6-307 7686   Website www.pounuihomestead.co.nz

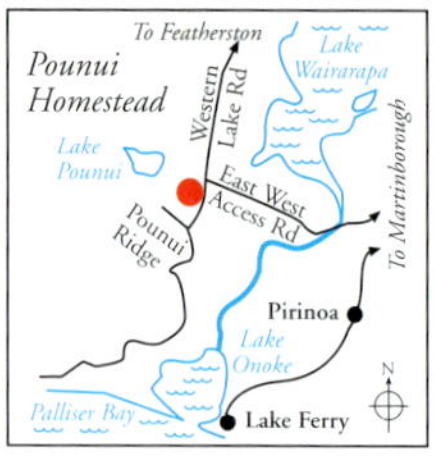

| 4 bdrm | 2 enst | 1 shbth | 1 pdrm |

House rate $250–$350 for 2 persons   Multiple-night rates available
Extra persons $50 each   Children under 10 years $30 each   *Self-catering*

DIRECTIONS: From Wellington take SH 2 over Rimutaka hill to Featherston. Take Western Lake Rd & travel 33km to Pounui on right. Homestead at top of drive. (Pounui is 1½-hour drive from Wellington.)

Located in a rural setting with lake and sea views, Pounui Homestead is a self-contained house set in 13 hectares (33 acres) of mature gardens, lawns and covenanted first-generation native bush. The hosts live on site in an adjacent historic cottage and welcome the opportunity to provide guests with information about activities, the property and local history. Pounui Homestead offers four bedrooms, a bunkroom and three bathrooms, as well as two lounges and a fully equipped kitchen for self-catering. Two bedrooms and both lounges access private garden and lawn areas from separate verandahs. Breakfast provisions for the first morning are supplied and further provisions can be arranged. A chef is available for catered meals if required.

Facilities
- private-party bookings only
- 1 king & 1 king/twin bedroom
- 2 ensuites with claw-foot baths
- 1 queen & 1 queen/twin bedroom share 1 bathroom
- cotton bed linen, hair dryers, heated towel rails; fresh flowers
- children welcome; cots available
- self-serve laundry
- 1 powder room
- full kitchen for self-catering
- 1st morning breakfast supplies
- chef by arrangement, extra
- 2 lounges with open fireplace & woodburner
- Sky TV, CD & video players, books, magazines & artwork
- phone, email & fax available
- private tree-lined guest entrance
- on-site parking, garaging; helipad

Activities available
- farm/bush walks on neighbouring Pounui farm by arrangement
- in-season feeding lambs/calves
- garden & native bush walks
- croquet & pétanque/boules
- 4WD vehicle & ATV/quad bike tours, extra charge:
  – Lake Pounui & bushland tours
  – sheep/dairy farm guided tours
- Cape Palliser seal colony & lighthouse
- jet boat tours, extra charge:
  – Lake Onoke/Lake Ferry
  – Ruamahanga River
- Putangirua Pinnacles
- surfing, fishing & diving at Ocean Beach
- Martinborough vineyards
- tramping & hunting in 2 forest parks in area
- spit walk at Lake Onoke
- canoeing; horse trekking

PALLISER BAY, WAIRARAPA
WHAREKAUHAU COUNTRY ESTATE

General Manager Bruce Garrett

Western Lake Road, R D 3, Featherston
Phone 0-6-307 7581   *Email* reservations@wharekauhau.co.nz
Fax 0-6-307 7799   *Website* www.wharekauhau.co.nz

12 bdrm | 12 enst | 1 pdrm

Double $1,340–$1,725
Single $895–$1,120

*Includes breakfast & dinner
Lunch & activities extra*

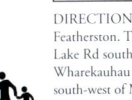

DIRECTIONS: Take SH 2 to Featherston. Then take Western Lake Rd south & travel for 40km. Wharekauhau at end of road. (50km south-west of Martinborough also.) Or 10 mins by helicopter from Wellington.

Wharekauhau is a luxury lodge, set on 2,200 hectares of farmland overlooking the rugged coastline of Palliser Bay on the southern tip of the North Island, providing uninterrupted panoramic ocean views from every guestroom. Opened in 1998, the Edwardian-style main lodge is within walking distance of 12 cottage suites, each comprising a king/twin bedroom, lounge area featuring an open fireplace, walk-in dressing room, ensuite bathroom, mini-bar and fridge. A full buffet and à la carte cooked breakfast is served in the country kitchen. Pre-dinner drinks and a four-course table d'hôte dinner are included in the tariff and served in the licensed lodge dining room. Private dining is also available in the Drawing Room or Palliser Room, by request.

Facilities
- 12 cottage suites, each with 1 king/twin ensuite bedroom
- 1 bath, dual basins, hair dryer, toiletries, heated floor, heated towel rails & demist mirror in each ensuite bathroom
- phone, open fireplace, walk-in dressing room, tea/coffee, mini-bar & fridge in each cottage suite
- Egyptian cotton bed linen
- fresh fruit
- tariff includes full buffet & à la carte breakfast, apéritifs & 4-course dinner
- fully licensed
- à la carte light lunch, extra
- modem & fax line in suites
- TV available on request
- laundry charged per item
- children welcome
- on-site parking

Activities available

On site complimentary:
- health facility:
  – all-weather tennis court,
  – indoor heated pool,
  – outdoor spa pool,
  – gym
- helipad for heli-tours
- pétanque/boules & croquet
- mountain biking
- hiking

On site charged:
- massages; 4WD safaris; ATV bike tours
- sheep farm tours; jet boating
- sporting clay-field; hunting
- surf-casting; horse riding

Off site:
- seal colony; wine tasting
- golf; gardens to visit
- Martinborough vineyards

228 — Te Horo, Kapiti Coast
The Kilns Pottery and Station B&B

Hosts Helen and John Wi Neera

990 State Highway 1, Te Horo, Kapiti Coast   *Mobile* 021-152 6898
Postal P O Box 85, Te Horo, Kapiti Coast   *Phone* 0-6-364 3646
Website www.thestation.net.nz   *Email* stay@thestation.net.nz

1 bdrm   1 prbth

Cottage rate $150–$185 for two persons   Includes breakfast or provisions / Self-catering

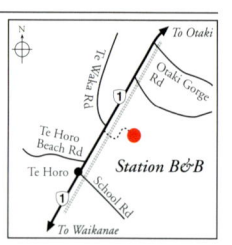

DIRECTIONS: Take SH 1 & travel 5km south from Otaki or 10km north from Waikanae to Te Horo. Turn east at "Pottery" sign over private rail crossing with caution. Continue to The Kilns Pottery & Station B&B.

Set amid mature trees in the established gardens of a working pottery, this heritage building was originally a New Zealand Railway station. Built in the 1940s, a kilometre south on the main trunk line, the station has been converted into a self-catering cottage featuring a railways theme. The former public waiting room is now the lounge, complete with ticket hatch, kauri counter, train seats and New Zealand rail memorabilia. The adjoining queen-size bedroom was the station master's office, and the kitchen, once the ladies' waiting room, is now stocked with John's pots and home-made breakfast provisions. Guests can purchase John's salt-glazed pottery, and observe him working in the studio adjacent to the historic beehive kilns.

Facilities
- one-party bookings only
- self-contained heritage building
- 1 queen bedroom
- dressing room with 1 single bed
- cotton bed linen; fresh flowers
- private bathroom with clawfoot bath, hair dryer, toiletries & heated towel rails
- woodburner in lounge opening to guest garden
- breakfast served or breakfast provisions supplied
- self-catering kitchen with home-made preserves
- TV, CD-player, books on local & rail history
- John's salt-glazed pottery
- NZ railways memorabilia
- views of Tararua Range
- parking at door

Activities available
- on-site 2ha (5-acre) garden with 1 acre protected totara trees
- John's salt-glazed pots for sale in garden gallery
- guests welcome in studio; potting by arrangement
- observing salt firings
- historic kilns on site
- local bush walks
- Kapiti Coast beaches
- restaurants at Waikanae, 10km
- river rafting; golf courses
- local museum & galleries; Kapiti arts trail
- lavender farm & winery
- Kapiti Island excursions, prior bookings necessary
- Nga Manu bird sanctuary
- private gardens to visit
- Wellington City, 1 hour south

© Friars' Guide to New Zealand Accommodation for the Discerning Traveller   252

TE HORO, KAPITI COAST
TE HORO LODGE

Host Craig Garner

109 Arcus Road, Te Horo *Postal* P O Box 43, Te Horo *Mobile* 027 430 6009
Freephone 0800 483 467 *Phone* 0-6-364 3393 *Fax* 0-6-364 3323
Email reservations@tehorolodge.co.nz *Website* www.tehorolodge.co.nz

Double $195–$280 *Includes breakfast*
Single $150–$190 *Dinner extra*

4 bdrm 4 enst 1 pdrm

DIRECTIONS: From Otaki, take SH 1 for 8km south. At Te Horo, turn left across railway into School Rd. Turn left again into Arcus Rd. Te Horo Lodge at end of road on left. Or from Waikanae, take SH 1 for 9km north.

Designed by architect Gary Cullen and purpose-built in 1998, Te Horo Lodge offers four ensuite guestrooms with a conservatory, private lounge and boutique conference room. A roaring open fire in the stone fireplace in the lounge in winter and the spa and swimming pool in summer make Te Horo a suitable get-away for Wellingtonians all year round. Set in two hectares (five acres) of gardens and developing orchard, and surrounded by another two hectares of native bush, Te Horo provides peace and tranquillity for rest and recreation. A full breakfast is served in the dining room and dinner is also offered in this fully licensed Lodge. Alfresco barbecues in the gazebo are popular or, alternatively, restaurants are just a 10-minute drive away at Waikanae.

Facilities
- 1 wheelchair access guestroom
- 3 super-king/twin bedrooms with ensuites & verandahs
- 1 super-king/twin upstairs suite with ensuite & bush views
- hair dryers, toiletries, heated towel rails, demist mirror, bathrobes & heated floor
- carafe of port, chocolates & fresh flowers in bedrooms
- laundry available, $5
- 3-course dinner, by arrangement only, $55 pp
- conservatory, BBQ & gazebo
- guests' tea/coffee facilities
- business & conference room for up to 12 people
- lounge with open fire, TV, video, CD-player, books
- phone & fax available
- on-site parking
- courtesy passenger transfer

Activities available
- conferences for 12–15 people
- outdoor swimming & spa pools
- pétanque court on site
- 2ha-gardens & orchard with tamarillos & olives on site
- 2ha native bush on site
- Ruth Pretty's cooking classes, booking essential
- 5 golf courses within 30 mins
- Te Horo Beach, 10 mins
- Waikanae restaurants, 10 mins
- 4WD adventures, 20 mins
- garden visiting; biking; fishing
- Nga Manu Nature Reserve
- Southwards Car Museum
- Lindale Centre, including Kapiti cheeses & Kapiti ice cream
- Kapiti Island excursions
- Wellington, 1 hour south

WAIKANAE, KAPITI COAST
CAMELLIA COTTAGE @ SUDBURY

Hosts Glenys and Brian Daw

39 Manu Grove, Waikanae, Kapiti Coast
Phone 0-4-902 8530   Mobile 021 129 6970   Fax 0-4-902 8531
Email stay@sudbury.co.nz   *Website* www.sudbury.co.nz

1 bdrm | 1 prbth

Cottage rate $150–$195   *Includes breakfast Dinner extra*   *Self-catering*

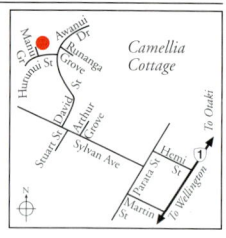

DIRECTIONS: From Wellington or Otaki, take SH 1 to Waikanae. Turn west into Ngaio Rd, right into Parata St, left into Sylvan Ave, right into David St, left into Hurunui St, right into Manu Gr. Cottage at end.

Set in a hectare of landscaped gardens, Camellia Cottage at Sudbury provides self-contained accommodation for two guests. Situated in a quiet location on the Kapiti Coast, less than an hour north of Wellington, Sudbury is adjacent to a nature reserve, and attracts native birds into its large gardens. The queen-size bedroom in the cottage opens directly into a private camellia-edged courtyard. A full continental breakfast is provided, served either in the cottage or with the hosts in the house, and dinner with wine from the cellar is also offered. Alternatively, guests can dine at the restaurants in Waikanae village, just five minutes' drive away. An extra guestroom is available in the main house, and there are bicycles for guest use.

Facilities
- 1 self-contained cottage
- single party bookings only
- 1 queen bedroom with direct access to private courtyard
- hair dryer, toiletries & heated towel rails in private bathroom
- spa bath in Sudbury house
- bathrobes & cotton bed linen
- lounge with phone, TV, CD-player, games, artwork & books
- babies welcome
- full continental breakfast served in cottage, house, or alfresco in garden
- 3-course dinner with wine, $50 pp, in house with hosts
- self-catering kitchen with nibbles & some provisions
- fax & email available
- laundry available, $10
- off-street parking
- courtesy passenger transfer

Activities available
- BBQ for guest use
- complimentary bicycles available
- itinerary assistance
- nature reserve adjacent
- car & motorcycle museum
- 4 golf courses
- safe beaches
- bush walks
- horse riding
- Fly-by-Wire
- Waikanae village restaurants, 1km away
- art galleries
- antique shops
- gardens open to visit
- wildlife sanctuary
- adventure activities
- Kapiti Island visits
- Wellington City, 50-min drive south

© Friars' Guide to New Zealand Accommodation for the Discerning Traveller

WAIKANAE, KAPITI COAST
HURUNUI HOMESTEAD BOUTIQUE LODGE

Hosts Erica and Geoff Lineham

15 Hurunui Street, Waikanae   *Postal* P O Box 81, Waikanae
Phone 0-4-902 8571   *Email* relax@hurunuihomestead.co.nz
Fax 0-4-902 8572   *Website* www.hurunuihomestead.co.nz

2 bdrm | 2 enst | 1 pdrm
Double $175–$225
Single $155–$205

Includes breakfast
Bridal & honeymoon packages available

DIRECTIONS: From Wellington or Otaki, take SH 1 to Waikanae. Turn west into Ngaio Rd, then 1st right into Parata St. Turn left into Sylvan Ave, then right into David St. Turn left into Hurunui St to Lodge at end.

Hurunui Homestead is set in peaceful park-like gardens, with a bushwalk where guests enjoy the native birdlife. Accommodation comprises two ensuite guestrooms upstairs with a mezzanine sitting room. Two downstairs living rooms furnished with antiques and comfortable furniture open to a large sun-drenched courtyard. Breakfast is served in the dining room with different fine china each morning. The emphasis is on seasonal fruits, freshly baked breads and pastries, cheeses, antipasto and yoghurts. The extensive grounds include a summer house and feature a collection of contemporary garden art and pottery. Guests enjoy the heated outdoor swimming pool in summer, aromatherapy spa pool, hard-surface tennis court and pétanque piste.

Facilities
- 2 queen ensuite bedrooms upstairs, 1 with dressing room
- cotton bed linen; bathrobes
- TV, ironing board & iron in rooms
- hair dryer, toiletries, heated towel rails & heating in ensuites
- 2 open fires in guest lounges
- cable TV, video, CD-player, piano
- tea/coffee, nibbles, filtered water, fridge with beer & sodas
- breakfast served
- artwork & fresh flowers
- garden views from rooms
- large courtyard
- email & fax available
- laundry service, extra
- garden wedding ceremonies (no catering) & honeymoons
- off-street parking

Activities available
- heated pool (summer), on site
- private spa pool/jacuzzi room
- on-site art quilt studio gallery
- all-weather tennis court on site
- pétanque court; bird-watching
- 0.8ha native bush walk on site
- Nga Manu Nature Reserve & nocturnal house, 5-min drive
- safe swimming, sand beaches, 5-min drive
- restaurants & cafés, 2 mins
- Waikanae shops, 2-min drive
- Lindale Tourist Centre – Kapiti cheeses, specialty shopping, farm walk & demonstrations
- Paraparaumu Beach golf course
- antiques, arts & craft stores
- Wellington-Picton interisland ferries, 50-min drive south
- Wellington City, 50 mins south

WAIKANAE, KAPITI COAST
TE NIKAU FOREST RETREAT

Owners Noel and Helen Trustrum *Local hosts* Patricia and Murray Cardie

Kakariki Grove, Waikanae *Postal* 42 Mortimer Terrace, Brooklyn, Wellington
Owners' Phone 0-4-938 7774 *and Fax* 0-4-938 9994 *Email* info@tenikau.co.nz
Hosts' Phone and Fax 0-4-293 5737 *Website* www.tenikau.co.nz

2 bdrm | 1 prbth | House rate $245–$295 for 2 persons *Includes breakfast provisions* *Self-catering or catering arranged*
Extra persons $45 each 2-night minimum for weekends/high season/public holidays Long-stay rates available

DIRECTIONS: From Wellington, take SH 1 to Waikanae. Turn right at traffic lights into Elizabeth St, then left into Winara Ave. Turn right into Kakariki Grove, then left at "T" junction. Travel 100m to Te Nikau.

Set in a clearing of a native coastal forest, on a terrace above a mountain stream, Te Nikau Forest Retreat offers total self-contained privacy. The seclusion of Te Nikau makes it suitable for honeymooners and romantic weekends. Local hosts, Patricia and Murray, welcome guests to Te Nikau. The chef from Rumours, a well-known Waikanae restaurant, will tailor dinner requirements to suit individual needs, or guests may choose to self-cater using the well-equipped kitchen. Built in 1997, Te Nikau borders Hemi Matenga Nature Reserve, which features abundant birdlife and the largest remnant stand of kohekohe forest in New Zealand. Guests enjoy relaxing in the spa pool on the deck, surrounded by the native forest.

Facilities
- self-contained forest retreat
- single-party bookings only
- 1 king & 1 single bedroom, & double sofa-bed in study
- 1 private bathroom
- large open fire, TV & video
- hair dryer, toiletries, heated towel rails & bathrobes
- guest balcony & decks
- clothes dryer
- fully equipped kitchen for self-catering
- continental & cooked breakfast provisions
- catered dinner tailored to needs of guests, extra
- complimentary bottle wine
- unsuitable for young children
- native forest setting
- off-street parking

Activities available
- tree house spa pool on site
- bird-watching on site
- native forest walks & mountain stream on 0.5ha site
- Nature Reserve adjacent, with native forest walks
- wildlife reserves; horse riding
- Kapiti coast beaches & rivers
- restaurants & cafés, 5 mins
- Paraparaumu Beach golf course
- Waikanae shops, 5-min drive
- Lindale tourist complex
- Southwards Motor Museum
- pottery & craft shops
- Kapiti Island bird sanctuary, prior bookings necessary
- Wellington-Picton interisland ferries, 45-min drive
- Wellington City, 45-min drive
- babs.co.nz/tenikau

… 233

WAIKANAE, KAPITI COAST
NGARARA BED AND BREAKFAST

Hosts Decima and John Gambitsis

389 Te Moana Road, Waikanae, Kapiti Coast
Phone 0-4-293 2088   *Email* gambitsis@xtra.co.nz
Fax 0-4-293 2088   *Website* friars.co.nz/hosts/ngarara.html

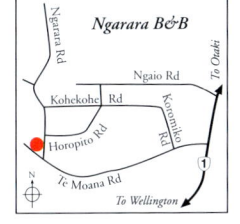

2 bdrm   1 prbth

Double $150   Single $100   *Includes breakfast*

DIRECTIONS: From Wellington, take SH 1 to Waikanae. Just past Waikanae Bridge, turn left at traffic lights into Te Moana Rd. Travel 1.1km to corner of Ngarara Rd. Ngarara B&B on right.

Ngarara is a renovated 1940s bungalow set in a large garden with established trees including a sycamore, ginkgo, maples, beech trees and natives. The accommodation overlooks the garden, with guests having exclusive use of the upstairs floor. This comprises one king and one queen-size bedroom and a private bathroom. Decima has used her skills as interior designer to tastefully furnish Ngarara. She serves a full breakfast downstairs in the family room, or in the spacious formal lounge, and there is new decking for alfresco dining in the garden. Licensed restaurants in Waikanae township are within walking distance. Single-party bookings ensure privacy, with children and pets welcome. There is a resident cat, Vinnie, on site.

Facilities

- single-party bookings only
- 1 king & 1 queen bedroom upstairs; cotton bed linen
- private upstairs bathroom with bath, hair dryer & toiletries; separate toilet
- family room with tea/coffee, video, CDs, books & desk
- spacious formal lounge with gas fire, wide-screen Sky TV & DVD
- full breakfast, served alfresco on patio or indoors
- children by arrangement
- fresh flowers
- pets welcome; cat on site
- phones in king bedroom & family room; email & fax available
- courtesy passenger transfer
- off-street parking/garaging

Activities available

- large garden on site with mature trees
- gymnasium & swimming pool, 5-min walk
- river & bush walks nearby
- Waikanae River within walking distance – fishing, swimming & whitebaiting
- golf course, 5-min drive
- gardens open to visit
- licensed restaurants, within 1km walking distance
- Southwards Motor Museum, 5-min drive south
- Waikanae shops, 1km
- Lindale Tourist Centre
- Kapiti Coast beaches for watching sunsets
- interisland ferries
- Wellington City, 45-min south

WAIKANAE, KAPITI COAST
BROADEAVES

Hosts Liz and Andrew Kirkland

24 Ngarara Road, Waikanae, Kapiti Coast, Wellington
Phone 0-4-293 1483   *Mobile* 021 545 175   *Fax* 0-4-293 1583
Email stay@broadeaves.co.nz   *Website* www.broadeaves.co.nz

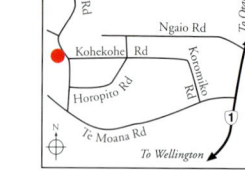

| 3 bdrm | 1 enst | 1 prbth | 1 pdrm | Room rate $120–$180 Children $50 each | Includes breakfast Family package available | Dinner extra |

DIRECTIONS: From Wellington, take SH 1 to Waikanae. Turn left at 1st traffic lights into Te Moana Rd. Turn right into Ngarara Rd. Travel past T-junction to Broadeaves on left.

Located in a quiet neighbourhood, in a peaceful garden setting, Broadeaves provides child-friendly, family-oriented accommodation. With a maximum of two parties, the accommodation includes a main bedroom opening to a private spa pool deck surrounded by trees. Continental and cooked breakfast is served in the dining room, or alfresco on the verandah looking out to the garden. A complimentary platter and wine are offered before dinner. Liz is happy to baby-sit children while their parents dine in the village close by, or dinner is available at Broadeaves by arrangement. Liz and Andrew have two school-age children themselves, as well as two retriever dogs and a cat. Broadeaves is less than an hour north of Wellington.

Facilities

- 1 queen bedroom with ensuite, dressing room & tea/coffee opens to private spa pool
- 1 super-king/twin opening to verandah & 1 queen bedroom share 1 private bathroom, in single-party bookings only
- bathrobes, double basins, hair dryer, toiletries, heated floor & towel rails in bathrooms
- cotton bed linen; fresh flowers
- full breakfast; complimentary pre-dinner wine & platter
- 3-course dinner in dining room, $35 pp; wine extra
- games, artwork, books & Sky TV/video/DVD/CD, tea/coffee & fresh baking in lounge
- complimentary laundry
- basic German spoken
- off-street parking

Activities available

- garden, pétanque court & gym equipment on site
- children's play area with toys
- swimming pool, gym & park, all 3-min walk
- Kapiti coast beach, 4-min drive
- river walks & whitebaiting, 3-min drive
- native birds at Nga Manu Nature Reserve, 5-min drive
- restaurants, 5-min drive, or courtesy transfer available
- golf, bowls, croquet, 4–5 mins
- horse riding, 5-min drive
- Waikanae village, 5-min drive
- art galleries; gardens to visit
- Southwards Motor Museum, 7-min drive
- Lindale tourist centre, 8 mins
- Wellington City, 45 mins south

© Friars' Guide to New Zealand Accommodation for the Discerning Traveller

Raumati Beach, Kapiti Coast
Hill House Lodge

Hosts Fraser and Anne McDougall

69 Matatua Road, Raumati Beach *Phone* 0-4-299 2027
Postal P O Box 1570, Paraparaumu Beach *Fax* 0-4-299 2784
Email info@hillhouselodge.co.nz *Website* friars.co.nz/hosts/hillhouse.html

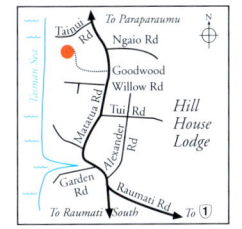

Room rate $250 *Includes breakfast & apéritifs*

DIRECTIONS: From Paraparaumu, take SH 1 towards Raumati. Turn right at Raumati Beach sign into Raumati Rd. At "T" junction turn right into Matatua Rd. Take 4th turn on left into Goodwood to Hill House.

Hill House Lodge is set in a woodland garden with views of the surrounding Maungakotukutuku hills from the guest lounge and terrace. The Empire Room, adjoining the main house, comprises a canopied king-size bed, ensuite including a bath, and a large private sundeck. The Nautilus Cottage (*right*) is self-contained with a queen-size bed, galley-style kitchenette, sitting area and large verandah with table and chairs. A speciality breakfast is served in the dining area, or alfresco on the terrace. After complimentary apéritifs in the lounge or garden, dinner is available at a range of restaurants and cafés at Raumati village, a 10-minute walk away. Guests enjoy the secluded ozone-purified spa pool backed by the woodland. The beach is five minutes' walk.

Facilities

- The Nautilus: 1 self-contained cottage with 1 queen ensuite room, kitchenette, sitting area & verandah
- The Empire: 1 king bedroom in Lodge, with bath in ensuite, private entrance & deck
- cotton bed linen; fresh flowers
- TV, CDs, fridge, tea/coffee & mineral water in both rooms
- hair dryers, toiletries, spa towels & bathrobes; turn-down service
- breakfast indoors or alfresco
- complimentary pre-dinner drinks in Lodge; licensed
- email, phone & fax in office
- wood burner, DVD, CDs, TV, video in Lodge lounge; artwork; 1 powder room
- complimentary laundry use
- 1 cat, Crumble, on site
- off-street parking

Activities available

- BBQ available on site
- pétanque court on site
- spa pool & birdlife on site
- beach, 5-min walk
- Kapiti Island Nature Reserve & bird sanctuary, prior bookings necessary
- Kapiti Island ferry, 5 mins
- native forest walks nearby
- Paraparaumu Beach golf links
- restaurants & shops, 10-min stroll to village
- Lindale Agricultural Centre
- pottery & craft shops
- Southwards car museum
- 4WD motorbike treks
- gliding & scenic flights
- Wellington-Picton interisland ferries, 45-min drive south
- Wellington City, 45 mins

Raumati South, Kapiti Coast
Sea Spirit Boutique Accommodation

Hosts Debbie Young and Campbell Thomson

1 Forest Lane, Raumati South, Kapiti Coast   *Phone* 04-902 3114
Postal 1 Karekare Road, Raumati South, Kapiti Coast   *Mobile* 029 902 3114
Email debbie@seaspirit.co.nz   *Website* www.seaspirit.co.nz   *Fax* 04-902 3114

House rate $295 for 2 persons
Extra persons $45 each

Self-catering
Includes breakfast provisions

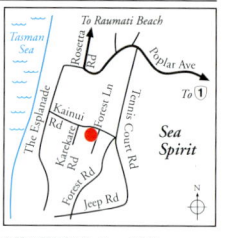

2 bdrm | 1 prbth

DIRECTIONS: From Wellington, take SH 1 towards Paraparaumu. Turn left at Raumati South turn-off into Poplar Ave. At "T" junction, turn left into Kaunui Rd, then 2nd right into Forest Lane. Sea Spirit is 1st on right.

Sea Spirit offers self-contained contemporary boutique accommodation with sea views. Using timber lining and with careful attention to detail, Sea Spirit was purpose built in 2004. Featuring views to Kapiti Island, the upstairs floor comprises a spacious king-size bedroom opening to a balcony with café-style table and chairs. There is a massage table and professional massage therapists can be arranged. Downstairs is an extra single bedroom, bathroom, and full kitchen with high-quality appliances. There is also a separate office including a guest computer, and a laundry. The dining room opens to a courtyard with South-East Asian influence, where from an outdoor bathtub guests can view the sea through a courtyard wall window.

Facilities
- single-party bookings only
- 1 king bedroom upstairs with foot massager, massage table & oils; opens to balcony
- 1 single bedroom downstairs
- 1 bathroom with spa bath, hair dryer, toiletries, heated floor, mirror & towel rail; slippers
- cotton bed linen; bathrobes
- office with computer, fax & phone
- full breakfast supplies
- complimentary wine & Kapiti cheese platter on arrival
- full self-catering kitchen
- lounge with wide-screen TV, DVDs, CDs & local artwork
- self-service laundry; beach bag
- off-street parking
- outdoor bathtub in courtyard; 3-flame gas fire, grasses, native flax & hammock

Activities available
- professional massage therapist by arrangement, extra
- tarot-card & clairvoyant readings on site, extra
- beach, a short walk, for: swimming, surf, sea kayaking, sunsets; kayaks, surfboards & mountain bikes available
- Kapiti Island tour bookings
- international golf course
- Southwards Motor Museum
- restaurants & cafés
- shopping centre; Raumati village boutique shops
- 4WD tours; 4WD quad
- Fly-by-wire; horse trekking; mountain biking; river kayaking, fishing
- Queen Elizabeth Park
- Lindale farm complex
- Wellington, 45 mins south

© Friars' Guide to New Zealand Accommodation for the Discerning Traveller

Pauatahanui, Wellington
Arawa Homestead

Hosts Julie and Rob McLagan

280 Paekakariki Hill Road, Pauatahanui, R D 1, Porirua
Phone 0-4-237 9022   *Mobile* 021 425 872   *Fax* 0-4-237 6614
Email contactus@arawahomestead.co.nz   *Website* www.arawahomestead.co.nz

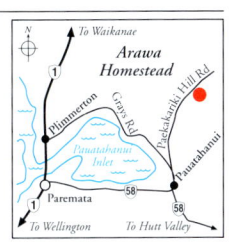

3 bdrm | 1 enst | 1 prbth
Double $500
Single $250
Includes breakfast
Lunch & dinner extra

DIRECTIONS: From north take SH 1 across Paremata Bridge & turn left into SH 58. Travel 5km to round-about & turn left through village into Paekakariki Hill Rd. Travel 2.8km to Arawa on right. From south, turn right into SH 58.

Built in the early 1850s for a pioneering family, Arawa Homestead is still the hub of a 24-hectare (60-acre) farm. The architecture, typical of early colonial New Zealand, has been faithfully restored, featuring leadlights and New Zealand native timbers, complemented by antique furnishings. Nestled in a large woodland garden surrounded by hills, with views of the Pauatahanui countryside, Arawa Homestead offers guests a peaceful stay and is popular as a wedding venue. The guest wing comprises a spacious super-king ensuite bedroom, and a twin and single bedroom which share a private spa bathroom. Guests enjoy wandering across the lawns and lunching in the dell beside the reflecting pond, or in the shade of the patio or the gazebo.

Facilities

- 1 super-king ensuite bedroom
- 1 twin & 1 single bedroom with private spa bathroom
- crisp linen, hair dryers, toiletries, heated towel rails, bathrobes & fresh flowers
- 2 lounges, both with wood fires, Sky TV, video, CD library, tea/coffee & freshly baked cookies
- honeymoon cottage available
- extensive library with open fire
- continental or cooked breakfast, indoors or alfresco
- lunch/picnic hamper, $25 pp
- 4-course country dinner, or BBQ, with NZ wine, $50 pp
- babies catered for
- phone, fax & email facilities
- complimentary laundry
- garaging available
- helipad

Activities available

- pétanque/boules on site
- tennis court; billiards
- antique pedal organ
- grand piano in lounge
- barbecue available
- farm walks on site
- skeet-shooting by arrangement
- golf course next door
- wetlands; bird sanctuary
- personalised tours arranged
- restaurants/shopping nearby
- charter flights
- Maori & historic sites
- windsurfing; waterskiing
- Fly By Wire; bungy jumping
- art galleries; bush walks
- fishing; sailing
- Te Papa Museum
- live theatre; concerts
- Wellington City, just 30km

Pauatahanui, Wellington
Huntaway Lodge

Hosts Dianne and Paul Boyack

168 Flightys Road, R D 1, Pauatahanui, Porirua, Wellington
Phone 0-4-234 1428 *Email* enquiries@huntawaylodge.co.nz
Fax 0-4-234 1429 *Website* www.huntawaylodge.co.nz

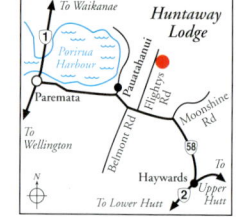

3 bdrm | 1 prbth | 1 pdrm Room rate $120–$150 *Includes breakfast* *Dinner extra*

DIRECTIONS: From Wellington, take SH 1 to Paremata. Turn right into SH 58 for 8km to Flightys Rd. Lodge 1.68km on right. Or take SH 2 for 20km. Turn left into SH 58 & travel 8km. Turn right into Flightys Rd.

This New Zealand log home was designed by architect Lloyd Dalton and built in 1998. The macrocarpa ceilings and doors complement the Douglas fir logs, creating a warm ambience. Sited on a hilltop in Pauatahanui, Huntaway Lodge offers 360-degree rural views over the inlet and Cook Strait to the Marlborough Sounds in the South Island. Huntaway is a unique log home in that it is large and spacious with a mezzanine overlooking the sunken lounge and log fire. Two guest bedrooms and bathroom are located upstairs with a private balcony extending the vistas over the surrounding countryside. The lodge features American Indian artefacts and memorabilia, but the cuisine is Kiwi style. Alpacas, cattle, goats and sheep add interest.

Facilities
- private-party bookings only
- 2 queen bedrooms upstairs & 1 twin bedroom downstairs
- clawfoot bath in bathroom
- hair dryer, heated towel rails, bathrobes & toiletries
- balcony from 2 bedrooms
- laundry services, $5
- email, fax & phone available
- powder room downstairs
- full cooked breakfast, served in dining room downstairs
- 3-course dinner, Kiwi cuisine with wine, $40 pp
- lounge with open fire, Sky TV, video, books & laser disk player
- children welcome
- alpaca & sheep farm setting
- pets on site
- on-site parking

Activities available
- Alpaca Gift Shop on site
- barbecue available
- feeding alpaca on site
- farm tour, walks & tramps on site
- pamper weekends including masseuse & pedicures
- hunting packages
- tramping packages
- beaches nearby
- golf
- restaurants nearby
- garden tours
- Porirua, 12km
- Lower Hutt, 13km
- Upper Hutt, 13km
- Wellington City, 25-min drive south
- interisland ferries, 15–20-min drive
- airport, 45-min drive

OHARIU VALLEY, WELLINGTON
TIKARA COUNTRY LODGE AND GARDENS

Hosts Mary and Bruce McCallum

995–997 Ohariu Valley Road, R D, Johnsonville, Wellington
Phone 0-4-473 4086   Mobile 021 223 6405   Fax 0-4-473 4084
Email tikaralodge@xtra.co.nz   Website www.tikaralodge.co.nz

5 bdrm	3 enst	1 prbth	Lodge rate $550	*Includes breakfast & dinner*		
			Cottage rate $240–$265 for 2 persons	Extra adults $40 each, children $20	*Self-catering*	

DIRECTIONS: From Wellington, take motorway to Johnsonville exit. At 2nd roundabout turn left into Ironside Rd. Continue into Ohariu Valley Rd for 5km. At cross-roads turn right & travel 5km to Tikara.

Located at the end of Ohariu Valley, Tikara Country Lodge is set in a secluded garden of more than two hectares (six acres). Accommodation comprises a self-contained cottage, as well as a suite in the homestead. Guests can relax in the peace and quiet of this rural retreat with views over the 148-hectare farm (370 acres) down the valley to the hills beyond. The pond area is popular for picnic lunches, and garden weddings are held in the rose area at Tikara. Walkways are established through the woodland and down to the stream. The gardens are open to visit by arrangement. Guests in the two cottage suites can self-cater in the fully equipped kitchen, while Lodge guests are served a full country breakfast and à la carte dinner.

Facilities

- Lodge suite: 1 super-king/twin bedroom with spacious ensuite
- hair dryer, toiletries, heated floor, heated towel rails & bathrobes in large ensuite
- guest lounge with open fire, Sky TV, video, CDs, tea/coffee, bar, artwork & library in Lodge
- full country breakfast included
- 4-course dinner included; licensed
- on-site parking; courtesy transfer
- 1 self-contained cottage:
  – Valley View suite:
  1 queen & 1 twin bedroom,
  1 bathroom including bath
  & separate shower room,
  & lounge with open fire,
  – Garden View suite: 1 queen
  & 1 double ensuite bedroom
- TV, games, magazines, books
- kitchen for self-catering; provisions can be supplied
- continental breakfast, extra

Activities available

- BBQ on site
- guided off-road 4WD tour
- garden walks on site
- farm & bush walks
- clay bird shooting on site
- golf courses
- horse-riding
- garden opens to vist
- sculpture garden to visit
- walking & hiking
- restaurants, 10km
- fishing
- east coast beaches
- swimming
- Staglands animal park
- Te Papa; Botanical Gardens
- interisland ferries, 35 mins
- Wellington City attractions, 35-min drive
- airport, 40-min drive

263

OHARIU VALLEY, WELLINGTON
WOODHAVEN

Hosts Anne and James Conder

20 Riflerange Road, Ohariu Valley, Wellington
Phone 0-4-477 4047 *Email* anne@woodhaven.co.nz
Fax 0-4-477 4047 *Website* www.woodhaven.co.nz

| 5 bdrm | 3 enst | 2 prbth | 1 pdrm |

Room rate $180–$275 Extra adults, $50 pp, children $25 *Includes breakfast* Lunch & dinner extra
Studio rate $180 Cottage rate $225 *Includes breakfast provisions* *Self-catering*

DIRECTIONS: From Wellington take motorway to Johnsonville exit. At 2nd roundabout turn left into Ironside Rd. Continue into Ohariu Valley for 5km. At cross-roads turn left into Rifle Range Rd. Woodhaven 200m on right.

Woodhaven is set in a two-hectare (four and a half-acre) garden, featuring a pond with birdlife, in the rural location of Ohariu Valley, just 20 minutes from Wellington City. In the homestead, designed and built in French Farmhouse style in 1999, guests are offered the king-size Mt Kaukau Room, with a backdrop of Mount Kaukau, the spacious Chateau Suite including a lounge, balcony and French antiques, the Rose Room with spa bath, or the self-contained Studio with full kitchen and breakfast provisions. Features include Egyptian cotton bed linen and furniture from native timbers. Organic vegetables grown in the potager and fresh produce are included in the cuisine. A self-catering cottage with king-size bedroom is a new addition.

Facilities
- 1 king & 2 queen ensuite bedrooms with dressing rooms, 1 spa bath, 1 lounge with open fire
- 1 self-catering studio: 1 queen bedroom with bathroom, kitchen & continental breakfast provisions
- 1 self-catering cottage: 1 king/twin bedroom, kitchen, claw-foot bath, log fire, deck & sofa-bed in lounge
- hair dryers, toiletries, heated towel rails, heated floors & bathrobes
- continental or full breakfast
- lunch/picnic by request, extra
- 3-course dinner & wine, $60 pp, or formal dinner by chef, by prior arrangement
- lounge with open fire, Sky TV, video, CDs & artwork
- email, phone & fax in office
- children welcome
- fresh flowers; on-site parking

Activities available
- BBQ & pétanque on site
- Riley, the labrador, Oscar, the cat & Doris, the pet sheep, on site
- 1.6ha of gardens to explore
- pond with birdlife on site
- horse trekking stables, 2-min walk
- 9-hole golf course, 3-min drive
- Old Coach Road heritage trail walk
- local gardens open to visit
- Karori wildlife reserve
- restaurants, 10–15 mins
- valley café, 2-min walk
- farm visits
- mountain biking
- fishing
- snorkelling
- bush walks
- Te Papa
- Botanic Gardens
- Wellington City, 20 mins

LOWER HUTT, WELLINGTON
COOPERS MANOR

Hosts Shirley and Alan Davis

132 Woburn Road, Lower Hutt, Wellington
Phone 0-4-566 2272   Fax 0-4-569 2426
Website friars.co.nz/hosts/coopersmanor.html

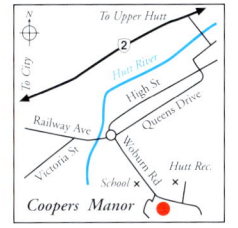

Double $285
Single $200

Includes breakfast
Dinner extra

2 bdrm   2 prbth

DIRECTIONS: From Wellington, take SH 2 motorway. Take Petone exit & cross overbridge into Hutt Rd. Turn right into Railway Ave. At roundabout, turn right into Woburn Rd. Coopers Manor on right.

Built in 1921 as a residence for English seed merchant Fred Cooper, this English-style manor was totally restored in the 1990s to accommodate guests. Original features such as the timber panelling and 2.8-metre stud have been retained, including the polished matai floor and oak panelling in the entrance hall. Guests have the choice of a queen or twin room upstairs, with an adjacent private bathroom, or a super-king-size bedroom downstairs also with a private bathroom. The ground floor also includes the formal lounge, sunroom and dining room. Coopers Manor is set in English-style gardens featuring oak trees, roses and spacious lawns where guests can relax or alternatively enjoy the tennis court, swimming pool, and sauna.

Facilities

- 1 super-king bedroom downstairs with private bathroom
- 1 queen or twin bedroom upstairs with private bathroom, bath & heated towel rails
- hair dryers & toiletries in both bathrooms
- cotton bed linen
- fresh flowers
- children by arrangement
- continental/cooked breakfast, served in dining room
- dinner by request, extra
- tea & coffee available
- Sky TV & video available
- central heating
- open fireplaces
- laundry available, extra
- quiet garden setting
- off-street parking

Activities available

- in-house sauna room
- in-ground swimming pool
- tennis court on site
- bars & restaurant 1-min walk
- art gallery, 5-min walk
- bowling club, 5-min walk
- Riddiford Gardens, 5-min walk
- shopping centre, 5-min drive
- Settler's Museum, 5-min drive
- charter clubs, 5-min drive
- 4 golf courses, 5-min drive
- watersports, 10-min drive
- trout & sea fishing
- Hutt recreation ground opposite
- Te Papa Museum of NZ, 15 mins
- Trentham Racecourse, 20 mins
- Heretaunga Golf Course, 20 mins
- Wellington City, 20-min drive
- interisland ferries, 15-min drive
- airport, 25-min drive

© Friars' Guide to New Zealand Accommodation for the Discerning Traveller

Khandallah, Wellington
Homebush House

Hosts Judy and Peter Devane

75 Homebush Road, Khandallah   *Phone* 0-4-479 1810   *Mobile* 027 416 3155
Postal 22 Woodmancote Road, Khandallah, Wellington   *Fax* 0-4-479 1812
Email surgjw@xtra.co.nz   *Website* friars.co.nz/hosts/homebush.html

4 bdrm	2 prbth	House rate $330 for 2 persons	*Includes continental breakfast provisions*
		Extra adults $30 each Extra children $15 each	*Self-catering*

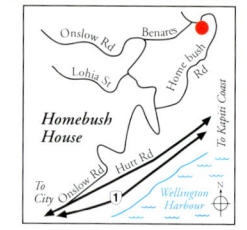

DIRECTIONS: From SH 1 motorway towards Wellington, take Ferry exit to Hutt Rd. Travel 2km & turn right into Onslow Rd. Travel 1km uphill & turn right into Homebush Rd. Travel 1km to Homebush House.

High on the hills above Wellington Harbour, Homebush House features unobstructed panoramic views of Wellington City and the surrounding hills. This newly refurbished house offers self-contained accommodation for single-party bookings of up to eight guests. Sea views are captured from every angle throughout the house which includes spacious living areas, hardwood floors, French doors, Italian-tiled bathrooms and gas fireplaces. Guest privacy and security are ensured by electric gates, and an extensive deck and tiled courtyards are designed for alfresco entertaining. A large fully equipped kitchen enables self-catering, and continental breakfast supplies are provided. There are restaurants and shops nearby, and a bus service can take guests to the city.

Facilities
- single-party bookings only
- 1 king, 1 queen & 2 single bedrooms
- 2 private bathrooms with hair dryers, toiletries & heated towel rails; spa bath in 1 bathroom
- bottle NZ wine, tea/coffee, fruit bowl & chocolates
- cotton bed linen; fresh flowers
- full laundry; central heating
- continental breakfast supplies
- full kitchen for self-catering
- Sky TV, DVD, videos, CDs, artwork, books, desk, phones
- 2 large living rooms, each with gas fireplace; sofa bed; separate dining room & study
- large deck around ground level
- double garage, 4 off-street carparks, electric gates & security system

Activities available
- courtyards for alfresco dining
- harbour & hillside walks
- Khandallah village, 2km
- Te Papa Museum of NZ
- Embassy theatre, home of *The Lord of the Rings*
- Westpac Trust Stadium, 5 mins
- cable car; golf courses
- regular bus service to city, 50m
- City Centre, 10-min drive
- restaurants & shops nearby
- fishing; cycling; waterfront
- sandy beach & swimming at Oriental Bay; harbour cruises
- Courtenay Place – cinemas, concerts, live theatre, ballet, galleries, national orchestra
- private & Botanic Gardens; zoo; Karori Wildlife Sanctuary
- ferry terminal, 5-min drive; airport, 20-min drive

Khandallah, Wellington
Khandallah Bed and Breakfast

Hosts Margaret and Tim Fairhall

50 Clark Street, Khandallah, Wellington
Phone 0-4-479 5578   *Email* fairhall@paradise.net.nz
Website friars.co.nz/hosts/khandallah.html

2 bdrm | 1 enst | 1 prbth   Room rate $180–$210   Includes breakfast

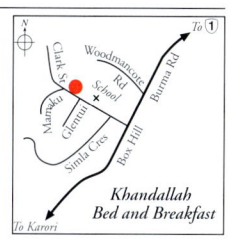

DIRECTIONS: From SH 1 Motorway, take Johnsonville exit & follow signs towards Khandallah & Karori. Turn right off Box Hill into Clark St. Khandallah B&B on right. (4km from SH 1.)

Khandallah Bed and Breakfast is set in large grounds with formal rose gardens and box hedging, with views over Wellington and the bush-clad Mount Kaukau that guests often enjoy climbing. The heated swimming pool and tennis court are also popular and Tim is happy to arrange a round of golf with guests. The house was built in 1926 in double brick and has weatherboard additions. Both rooms have french doors opening on to a balcony where guests can watch the sunset. Margaret provides fresh home baking and serves full breakfasts including fresh muffins and croissants in the formal dining room using antique silver and chinaware. Tim runs a large model railway, set in southern Germany in the 1930s to 1950s.

Facilities
- 1 twin ensuite bedroom & 1 queen bedroom with private bathroom; cotton bed linen
- TV, tea/coffee & home baking in both bedrooms
- hair dryer, heated towel rail & bathrobes in both bathrooms
- balcony opening from ensuite bedroom, with table & chairs
- laundry available
- email, fax & phone available
- full or continental breakfast including home-made jams, preserved fruit & fresh baking, served in formal dining room
- lounge with open fire, tea/coffee, baking, Sky TV, video, CDs & writing desk
- central heating; fresh flowers
- antiques & NZ paintings
- friendly cat, Samantha
- off-street parking

Activities available
- tennis court on site, tennis racquets & balls provided
- heated swimming pool, towels provided
- formal garden with roses & box hedging on site
- watching sunset from balcony
- native bush walk to top of Mt Kaukau, 1 hour return
- regular bus & rail service, 5-min walk away
- restaurants, 5-min walk
- golf courses nearby, rounds arranged
- Otari Native Botanic Garden
- Wellington Botanic Gardens
- Te Papa Museum, 15 mins
- Karori Wildlife Sanctuary
- sports stadium, 10-min drive
- interisland ferry, 7-min drive
- airport, 25-min drive

THORNDON, WELLINGTON
KAURI TREES HOUSE

Hosts Daniel McKeown and Gerard Walsh

35 Hobson Street, Thorndon, Wellington
Phone 0-4-472 5675   Email enquiries@kauritrees.com
Mobile 021 171 8897   Website www.kauritrees.com

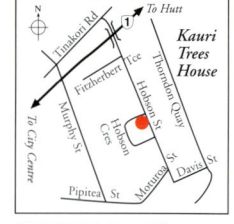

2 bdrm | 2 enst   Room rate $200–$300   Includes breakfast

DIRECTIONS: From Wellington, take Motorway (SH 1) towards the Hutt. Take Tinakori Rd exit & turn right into Hobson St to Kauri Trees House, just past first Hobson Cres turn-off.

Kauri Trees is a colonial villa, built circa 1901 as a private residence, in what is now a leafy inner city area of ambassadors' residences and embassies. Wellington City is right on the doorstep. The central location enables guests to walk to restaurants and Parliament. Kauri Trees offers two ensuite guestrooms and a spacious lounge featuring Gerard's grand piano, which guests can enjoy listening to or playing. Gerard also speaks French. Danny serves a full breakfast in the dining room, where small conferences can be held. Named because of the native kauri trees recently planted in the street-front garden, this accommodation includes New Zealand artwork, and an elderly dachshund named Skippy is also in residence.

Facilities
- 1 king & 1 twin bedroom, both with ensuite bathrooms
- Sky TV, phone jacks & tea/coffee in both bedrooms
- hair dryers & toiletries in both ensuites
- 1 bath & 1 double basin
- open fire, grand piano, artwork & books in lounge
- quiet central city location
- cooked/continental breakfast served in dining room
- central heating
- phone available
- children welcome
- French spoken by Gerard
- complimentary laundry
- secure off-street parking
- courtesy passenger transfer

Activities available
- playing or listening to grand piano in lounge
- small conference room
- elderly dachshund on site
- Parliament, within walking distance
- art galleries
- concerts
- embassies nearby
- City shops, 5-min walk
- cafés & restaurants
- historic buildings in Thorndon, short walk
- sandy beaches
- private gardens open to visit
- Botanic Gardens
- Westpac Stadium, 5-min walk away
- interisland ferry, 5-min drive
- airport, 25-min drive

© Friars' Guide to New Zealand Accommodation for the Discerning Traveller

KELBURN, WELLINGTON
SOMMERVILLE HOUSE

Hosts Lynda and Wally Sommerville

30 Clermont Terrace, Kelburn, Wellington
Phone 0-4-973 0094   *Email* info@sommervillehouse.com
Mobile 021 121 5272   *Website* www.sommervillehouse.com

| 2 bdrm | 2 enst | Suite Rate $275 / Room Rate $180 | Includes breakfast / Long-term rates available | Self-catering in suite |

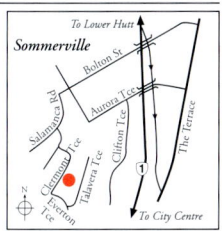

DIRECTIONS: From SH 1 Motorway take Terrace/Kelburn exit, turn left into The Terrace at lights & left into Bolton St. Clermont Tce is 2nd on left & Sommerville House has sign on garage at number 30.

Within walking distance of downtown Wellington, Sommerville House provides a spacious, fully self-contained suite that occupies the top floor, including a conservatory with panoramic views over the city and harbour. Downstairs is a queen-size ensuite bedroom opening to a private courtyard garden. Built circa 1900, this Victorian villa was renovated in the mid 1980s, retaining original features such as the high ceiling. Guests are served a full breakfast downstairs in the dining room, or upstairs by request. Basic cooking ingredients are supplied in the suite, which has a full kitchen for self-catering, making it suitable for longer stays. Both lounges include Sky television, DVD and CD-players, with a piano for guest use in the downstairs lounge.

Facilities

- 1 self-contained super-king suite upstairs with dressing room, desk, phone, kitchen, lounge, TV, conservatory, deck
- 1 queen ensuite bedroom downstairs with walk-in wardrobe, fridge, tea/coffee
- hair dryers, toiletries, heated towel rails & bathrobes
- cotton bed linen; fresh flowers
- email & phone available
- breakfast served in downstairs dining room, or in suite
- complimentary bar, tea/coffee, nibbles, Sky TV, DVD, CDs, piano, games, artwork, books & writing desk in lounge
- children welcome in suite; extra beds available
- central heating; complimentary laundry
- off-street parking; garaging

Activities available

- courtyard garden with BBQ
- panoramic city & harbour views
- cable car to city, 2-min walk
- Botanic Gardens, 3-min walk
- Wellington Stadium & Te Papa Museum of NZ, 15-min walks
- Wellington Carter Observatory, 5-min walk
- concerts; art galleries
- beaches; bush walks
- Wellington shops, restaurants, night life & Victoria University, all 5-min walks away
- private gardens open to visit
- Karori Wildlife Sanctuary, 5-min drive
- interisland ferry terminal, 3km
- railway station, 1½km
- airport, 10km away

Kelburn, Wellington
Rawhiti Boutique Bed and Breakfast

Host Annabel Leask

40 Rawhiti Terrace, Kelburn, Wellington
Phone 0-4-934 4859   *Fax* 0-4-972 4859
Email rawhiti@paradise.net.nz   *Website* www.rawhiti.co.nz

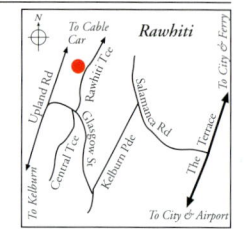

2 bdrm | 2 enst

Room rate $150–$230   Includes breakfast

DIRECTIONS: From City, take The Terrace & turn north into Salamanca Rd. Turn left into Kelburn Pde, right into Glasgow St, then right again into Rawhiti Tce. Rawhiti on left. Or take Cable Car from City to Rawhiti Tce.

Meaning "the rising sun" in Maori, Rawhiti faces east so that both guest bedrooms are warmed by the morning sun. Both bedrooms have views over the city and harbour by day and city lights at night, as does the sunny breakfast room. This historical home, built in the early 1900s, has been refurbished to retain original features such as the sash windows and open fireplace. Sited high above the university, Rawhiti is within walking distance of the city, yet provides a peaceful retreat, with a private garden overlooking the city and harbour vistas. Annabel is a born and bred Wellingtonian, having lived in Kelburn most of her life, but with many years overseas as well. She speaks French and her oil paintings feature on the walls of Rawhiti.

Facilities
- 1 king ensuite bedroom with bath, writing desk, TV, fridge, iron & small balcony with night views of city lights
- 1 super-king/twin ensuite bedroom with TV & views
- bath, hair dryer, demist mirror, heated towel rails, bathrobes & toiletries
- tea/coffee, filtered water, glass of wine & cotton bed linen in both bedrooms
- full cooked breakfast, served in dining room upstairs
- upstairs lounge with open fire, piano, artwork, library & views
- NZ artwork; French spoken
- children by arrangement
- central heating
- laundry available
- phone, fax & email available
- garage space available

Activities available
- garden with harbour views on site
- walking track to Upland Rd & village
- 2-min walk to Cable Car to city
- 5-min walk to restaurants, cafés, bars & shopping
- 5-min walk to Botanic Gardens & Observatory
- 2-min walk to Victoria University
- Central Business District
- restaurants, 5-min walk
- beaches
- art galleries; concerts
- Te Papa Museum of NZ
- historic buildings
- private gardens to visit
- railway, 5-min drive
- airport, 20-min drive
- interisland ferries, 5-min drive away

KELBURN, WELLINGTON
RUBY HOUSE

Host Elizabeth Barbalich   *Phone* 0-4-934 7930

14B Kelburn Parade, Kelburn, Wellington   *Fax* 0-4-934 7935
Postal 35 Rawhiti Terrace, Kelburn, Wellington   *Mobile* 021 483 980
Email elizabeth@rubyhouse.co.nz   *Website* www.rubyhouse.co.nz

3 bdrm   3 enst   Room rate $185–$230   Includes continental breakfast

DIRECTIONS: From City, take The Terrace & turn north into Salamanca Rd. Turn left into Kelburn Pde. Narrow Lane between #10 & 14 to Ruby House. Drive down narrow lane to unload bags. Sign high on lamppost.

Nestled among native trees, Ruby House offers guests comfort and privacy in a central location. A self-contained villa-style guesthouse provides three spacious bedrooms with antique furniture, ensuite bathrooms, television, and phone and modem lines. The guesthouse has been purpose-built for maximum privacy, with entry via a security keypad at the front door. Guests may choose a country-style bathroom complete with claw-foot bath and French doors opening to a private courtyard, a sunny loft bedroom overlooking the garden, or an elegant room with sash windows and stained glass.

Facilities
- 1 super-king/twin, 1 queen & 1 king ensuite bedroom
- toiletries & heated towel rails in all 3 ensuites
- 1 claw-foot bath
- quality cotton bed linen & down duvets on all beds
- antique furniture, writing desk, phone, TV & iron in all 3 bedrooms
- kitchenette in central living area
- healthy continental breakfast buffet provided
- quiet acoustics
- fax facility available
- children by arrangement
- 1 bedroom opens onto private courtyard
- sundecks & balcony
- private guest entrance
- off-street site with garaging

Activities available
- rear garden with lavender, roses & kowhai trees on site
- Cable Car, 3-min walk
- Victoria University, 2-min walk
- Italian, Mediterranean & Indian restaurants in local Kelburn village
- Club Kelburn for gym, squash & tennis courts, 3-min walk
- Kelburn village with cafés & restaurants, 10-min walk
- botanical gardens, 3-min walk
- Carter Observatory, 6-min walk
- CBD, 5 mins by Cable Car
- private gardens open to visit
- art galleries
- Te Papa Museum of NZ, 10-min walk away
- native botanic garden, 5 mins
- harbour cruises
- interisland ferries, 7-min drive
- airport, 15-min drive

MOUNT VICTORIA, WELLINGTON
VILLA VITTORIO

Hosts Annette and Logan Russell

6 Hawker Street, Mount Victoria, Wellington
Phone 0-4-801 5761   *Mobile* 027 432 1267   *Fax* 0-4-801 5762
Email l&a@villavittorio.co.nz   *Website* friars.co.nz/hosts/vittorio.html

Double $150–$180
Single $120–$135

Includes breakfast
Lunch & dinner xtra

DIRECTIONS: From City Centre, take Courtenay Pl & continue along Majoribanks St. Turn left into Hawker St. Villa Vittorio on right. From airport, take Cambridge Tce. Turn right into Majoribanks St, then as above.

Centrally located in the heart of the capital city, Villa Vittorio is a late 1890s character cottage featuring the original native kauri floors, and now offering one bedroom with private bathroom for accommodation. Annette delights in preparing gourmet dishes, and serves breakfast in their Italian-style dining room that has been painted by a local artist. The Mediterranean-style courtyard catches the morning sun, making it a favourite spot for alfresco breakfasts. Picnic hampers are available by arrangement, and three-course dinner accompanied by a bottle of New Zealand wine can be served in the dining room. Views over the city including the carillon tower can be enjoyed from the house and the private garden with its outdoor furniture.

Facilities

- 1 double bedroom & 1 private bathroom including bath
- hair dryer, heated towel rails, demist mirror, robes & toiletries
- cotton bed linen & fresh flowers
- guest sitting room with gas fire, TV, radio, music system, tea/coffee, bar & balcony
- complimentary port & sherry in guest sitting room
- phone, fax & email available
- full breakfast served in Italian-style dining room, or alfresco in private courtyard
- picnic hampers by arrangement, $25 pp
- 3-course gourmet dinner & bottle NZ wine, $50 pp
- laundry available, extra
- garaging, extra
- courtesy passenger transfer

Activities available

- personally escorted tours arranged
- Te Papa Museum, 5-min walk
- Wellington shops, 5-min walk
- conference & civic centres
- concerts, theatres, ballet, national orchestra & cinemas
- Oriental Bay & waterfront
- parliament; old St Paul's
- Wellington Sports Stadium
- Basin Reserve
- restaurants close by
- Wellington Arts Festival
- several golf courses nearby
- Cable Car
- Botanic Gardens
- Wairarapa vineyards, 1-hour drive away
- railway station, 5-min drive
- airport, 8-min drive
- interisland ferries, 7 mins

© Friars' Guide to New Zealand Accommodation for the Discerning Traveller

ORIENTAL BAY, WELLINGTON
298 ORIENTAL PARADE

Hosts Susan Bilbie and family

298 Oriental Parade, Oriental Bay, Wellington
Phone 0-4-384 4990   Mobile 021 113 5960   Fax 0-4-384 4990
Email 298@298.co.nz   Website www.298.co.nz

2 bdrm 2 enst 1 pdrm

Double $500
Single $450

Includes breakfast & apéritifs
Lunch & dinner extra

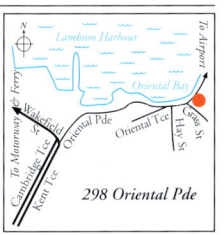

DIRECTIONS: From Motorway, take Aotea exit. Keep left along waterfront to Oriental Bay, to 298 on right. From airport, follow signs towards City. Continue along waterfront to 298 Oriental Pde on left.

Built in 1928 in the style of a Parisian townhouse, 298 Oriental Parade was the Japanese Embassy for about 30 years. It has been in the Bilbie family since 1980. It now offers 2 ensuite guestrooms – the Summer House with open fire and the Forget Me Not Room. Set in a private walled garden featuring a pond and fountain, 298 provides water's edge, harbour and city views and guests can enjoy watching sunsets from the balconies. Original ornate plaster ceilings, stained glass windows and wood panelling feature throughout. Complimentary wine and hors d'oeuvres are offered in the evening, and a full breakfast is served each morning. Lunch and dinner are also available. The airport is 10 minutes' drive away and City Centre just two minutes.

Facilities
- Summer House: 1 queen ensuite bedroom with open fire
- Forget Me Not Room: 1 king ensuite bedroom with balcony
- cotton bed linen, dressing room & stereo in bedrooms
- hair dryers, toiletries & bathrobes in both ensuites
- 3 lounges include open fire, Sky TV, video, library, writing desk, CD-player & piano
- continental or cooked breakfasts, served anywhere
- lunch, $25 pp
- 3–4-course dinner with wine, $75 pp
- complimentary laundry
- children by arrangement
- central heating; garaging
- private guest entrance
- courtesy passenger transfer

Activities available
- in-house billiards table
- gym equipment on site
- garden with pond & fountain
- beach, across road
- jogging & roller blading
- swimming pool & gym, within walking distance
- Oriental Bay Marina
- live theatre, walking distance
- Te Papa, walking distance
- City Centre for shopping, cafés & bars, nearby
- harbour cruises
- town belt scenic walks
- golf course, 10-min drive
- Opera House
- Maritime Museum
- harbour activities, eg: kayaking, sailing
- airport, 10-min drive

SEATOUN, WELLINGTON
EDGEWATER WELLINGTON

Hosts Stella and Colin Lovering

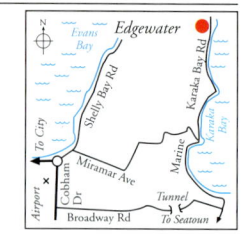

459 Karaka Bay Road, Karaka Bay, Seatoun, Wellington *Phone* 0-4-388 4446
Faxes 0-4-388 4446 *and* 0-4-388 4649 *Email* edgewaterwellington@xtra.co.nz
Mobile 021 613 357 *Website* www.edgewaterwellington.co.nz

4 bdrm / 4 enst
Double $190–$290
Single $150
Includes breakfast
Lunch & dinner extra

DIRECTIONS: From City, follow signs towards Airport & Seatoun. Turn left into Broadway Rd. Travel through Tunnel to Seatoun. Continue to waterfront. Turn left & follow water's edge to Edgewater on left.

Seatoun is a historic seaside village where waterfront houses were originally built as holiday homes. Located at the water's edge in Karaka Bay, Edgewater was used for accommodation during the filming of *The Lord of the Rings*. This Mediterranean-style home was built to an award-winning design in 1976. Featuring expansive ocean views, Edgewater offers four ensuite bedrooms with peaked cedar ceilings beneath separate roofs. Stella serves fresh fruits, home-made breads, pancakes and egg dishes for breakfast in the dining room or alfresco in the inner courtyard or on the guest balcony. Dinner is also offered, specialising in premium quality meats, seafood and game. As ex-owner/chef of an award-winning Wellington restaurant, Stella's motto is "fresh is best".

Facilities
- 1 queen, 1 king/twin & 2 super-king bedrooms, all with ensuite bathrooms
- hair dryers, toiletries, heated towel rails & heated floor
- cotton bed linen; fresh flowers
- tea/coffee & Sky TV in all 4 bedrooms
- 4 private guest entrances
- laundry available, $10
- children welcome
- gourmet breakfast
- lunch, $30 pp
- à la carte dinner, $80 pp
- comprehensive wine selection
- meals served in dining room, or alfresco in courtyard or balcony
- phone & fax available
- central heating
- guest balcony
- off-street parking

Activities available
- restaurant nearby
- seashore strolls
- fishing
- swimming
- snorkelling
- diving by arrangement
- historic seaside village, within walking distance
- cycling
- walks
- Te Papa Museum of NZ
- golf club, 10-min drive
- harbour cruises
- shopping, 10-min drive
- NZ's only cable car
- parks & gardens to visit
- galleries
- City Centre, 10-min drive
- airport, 5-min drive
- interisland ferries, 15 mins

© Friars' Guide to New Zealand Accommodation for the Discerning Traveller

SEATOUN, WELLINGTON
VILLA KARAKA BAY

Hosts Stella and Colin Lovering

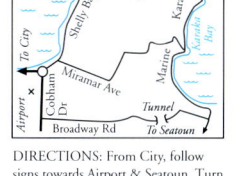

387 Karaka Bay Road, Karaka Bay, Seatoun, Wellington
Phone 0-4-388 4446   *Mobile* 021 613 357   *Fax* 0-4-388 4446
Email edgewaterwellington@xtra.co.nz   *Website* www.villakarakabay.co.nz

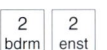

Villa rate $270–$300 for 2 persons
Extra persons $100 each

Self-catering
Dinner extra

DIRECTIONS: From City, follow signs towards Airport & Seatoun. Turn left into Broadway Rd. Travel through Tunnel to Seatoun. Continue to waterfront. Turn left & follow water's edge to Villa Karaka Bay on left.

Located on the sea front at Karaka Bay, this French-style villa was originally built in 1898 as a holiday and convalscent home beside the sea. Featuring twin bay windows with sash panes and stained glass sky-lights, Villa Karaka Bay has a distinctive colonial gabled roofline topped by finials, and has been carefully restored to provide self-contained accommodation. Guests have two bedrooms, each with its own ensuite bathroom including a bath, and a separate lounge. A fully equipped kitchen enables guests to self-cater, and dinner is available by arrangement at Edgewater (*see opposite page 276*), a short stroll along the road. With panoramic harbour views, the villa's courtyard and balcony are popular spots for alfresco breakfast in the sun.

Facilities
- self-contained cottage; one-party bookings only
- 1 king & 1 twin bedroom, each with ensuite bathroom
- hair dryer, toiletries, bath & bathrobes in both ensuites
- cotton bed linen
- tea/coffee, nibbles, bar, phone, Sky TV, CD-player & books in lounge
- children welcome
- full self-catering kitchen
- à la carte dinner on request at Edgewater, $80 pp (*see p. 276*)
- alfresco dining
- balcony & courtyard
- fresh flowers
- ocean views
- email & laundry available
- hosts live off-site nearby
- on-site parking

Activities available
- seaside strolls from site
- historic seaside village nearby
- homes of *The Lord of the Rings* directors nearby
- swimming beaches
- snorkling
- cycling
- fishing
- art galleries
- golf club, 10-min drive
- restaurant within short stroll
- shopping, 10-min drive
- Te Papa Museum of NZ
- parks & botanic gardens
- private gardens to visit
- harbour cruises
- NZ's only cable car
- City Centre, 10-min drive
- airport, 5-min drive
- interisland ferries, 15 mins

FRIARS' GUIDE TO NEW ZEALAND ACCOMMODATION FOR THE DISCERNING TRAVELLER

SOUTH ISLAND

Ulva Island bird sanctuary, adjacent to Stewart Island – for accommodation see pages 502–504.

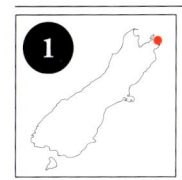

Kenepuru Sound
Raetihi Lodge

Hosts Mandy Leung and Christoph Szymanski

Kenepuru Road, Double Bay, Kenepuru Sound   *Phone* 0-3-573 4300
Postal Kenepuru Road, R D 2, Picton   *Fax* 0-3-573 4323
Email hotel@raetihi.co.nz   *Website* www.raetihi.co.nz

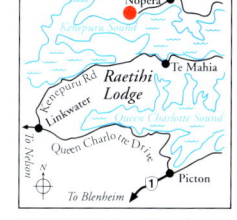

Room rate $195–$305   *All meals extra*
Seasonal rates & special packages available

14 bdrm | 14 enst | 1 pdrm

DIRECTIONS: From Picton ferry, take water taxi, if pre-arranged. Or take Queen Charlotte Dr to Linkwater. Turn right & travel to Te Mahia. Take water taxi to Double Bay. Raetihi Lodge adjacent to jetty. Moorings.

Raetihi Lodge was redesigned and rebuilt in 2000, to provide relaxation in a tranquil environment. Nestled in native bush on the waterfront, it offers 14 ensuite guestrooms, each opening to a private deck, with nine of the bedrooms featuring views out to Kenepuru Sound. Raetihi is an isolated retreat which can be reached by water taxi, air, or road. The Lodge also incorporates conference facilities and is available for secluded weddings. Meals are served in the dining room, with a selection of regional and international wines to complement the chef's cuisine. The on-site sauna, spa pool and aromatherapy massages are popular, after a day exploring the Sounds. Guests also enjoy walking beside the seashore and on the hillsides, or fishing in Kenepuru Sound.

Facilities

- 9 sea view rooms, 2 garden view rooms & 3 hillside rooms, each with super-king, king, queen or twin beds
- all 14 rooms open to sundecks
- 14 ensuites with fluffy towels, bathrobes, heated towel rails, hair dryers & toiletries
- mini-bar, tea & coffee-making facilities in 11 bedrooms
- individual heating in bedrooms
- fully licensed bar & restaurant
- continental or gourmet breakfasts, extra
- daily gourmet lunch & dinner menus, extra
- guest lounge with open fireplace & library
- conference room & business centre with email facilities
- German, Cantonese & Mandarin spoken by hosts

Activities available

- gymnasium, sauna & spa pool
- aromatherapy massage on site
- courtesy use of fishing tackle, mountain bikes, kayaks & dinghies
- scenic walks from Lodge
- mooring available
- fishing trips; yachting
- 9-hole golf course, 4km
- local garden tours
- visits to local artist
- scenic boat cruises & mussel farm visits
- water skiing; sea kayaking
- dolphin watching
- snapper fishing trips
- scenic flights to/from Picton or Wellington
- Picton by water taxi, 45 mins; by air, 10 mins; by road, 2½-hour drive

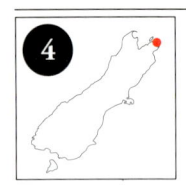

Queen Charlotte Sound
Bay of Many Coves Resort

Hosts Lisa Bardebes and Mark Jensen

Bay of Many Coves, Queen Charlotte Sound, Picton   *Postal* Private Bag, Picton
Freephone 0800 579 977   *Email* enquiries@bayofmanycovesresort.co.nz
Phone 0-3-579 9771   *Fax* 0-3-579 9777   *Website* www.bayofmanycovesresort.co.nz

17 bdrm   15 enst   1 prbth   Apartment rate $300–$700   *All meals extra*

DIRECTIONS: Water or air access only. From Picton, depart from main commercial wharf. Arrangements for transfers made with hosts at time of booking. All guests met at Resort.

Bay of Many Coves Resort, located in the heart of the Marlborough Sounds, can be accessed by a 12-minute scenic helicopter flight or 30-minute cruise by boat. Architecturally designed by Marshall Cook, the apartments have been strategically placed to optimise the panoramic views across the bay. Emphasis has been placed on utilising materials such as cedar and copper that blend naturally into the environment. Each apartment includes a kitchenette for self-catering if desired although the Resort offers an all-day café with bakery, as well as a fine cuisine restaurant for evening dining. Also provided for the guests' convenience and enjoyment are massage therapy facilities, a hot tub, an all-seasons swimming pool and a small shop.

Facilities
- 1 apartment with 3 bedrooms, ensuite & private bathroom
- 4 apartments with 2 ensuite bedrooms
- 6 apartments with 1 ensuite bedroom
- hair dryers, local toiletries & heated towel rails
- cotton bed linen, phone, safe, bathrobes & slippers in rooms
- children welcome; balconies
- full breakfast & lunch at on-site licensed café, bakery, or room service, all extra
- 2–3-course dinner at licensed restaurant on site, $55–$70 pp
- kitchenette in each apartment, & on-site shop for provisions
- Sky TV, CD-player, games & books in all apartments
- laundry, email, fax & phones
- helipad; safe boat moorings

Activities available
- heated swimming pool & hot tub
- sailing, sea kayaking, fishing & walking from site
- private jetty; fuel, LPG & dive fills
- Queen Charlotte Track access from site, 2 hrs–5 days round trip, or boat transfer service
- guided walking & kayaking
- Salmon Farm at nearby bay
- eco cruises
- heli-fishing & fly fishing
- scenic flights
- personalised wine tours
- art & craft trails
- seals, dolphins & native birdlife to view
- safe swimming beaches
- Ship Cove – site of Captain Cook's arrival
- Picton, 30 mins by sea

© Friars' Guide to New Zealand Accommodation for the Discerning Traveller

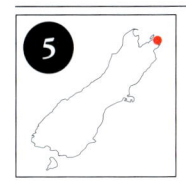

Queen Charlotte Sound
The Lazy Fish Retreat

Host Chris Warren

Kahikatea East Bay, Marlborough Sounds   *Phone* 0-3-573 5291
Postal Private Bag 429, Picton   *Fax* 0-3-573 5291
Email relax@lazyfish.co.nz   *Website* www.lazyfish.co.nz

4 bdrm   4 prbth   1 pdrm

Double $395–$495
Single $345–$395

Includes all meals
Water taxi extra

DIRECTIONS: Boat service leaves from Picton wharf or ferry terminal twice daily or by arrangement. From south, take SH 1 to Picton wharf.

The Lazy Fish has been upgraded to provide quality accommodation, located right on the water's edge, in the remote and secluded setting of a private bay in the Marlborough Sounds, reached only by boat from Picton. The land around The Lazy Fish Guest House was farmed for 20 years until the late 1950s, and is now garden surrounded by rejuvenating bush. Guests are offered the choice of four bungalows, all with verandahs and hammocks. The bungalows each have a private terrace, outside bath, and sea or garden views. A chef provides all the meals, and small conferences and weddings can be catered for. Row boats and kayaks, as well as windsurfing, snorkelling and fishing equipment are available on site for guest use.

Facilities

- 4 bungalows: each including queen bedroom, private bathroom, outdoor bath & private terrace
- cotton bed linen; fresh flowers
- toiletries & bathrobes
- 2 lounges, tea/coffee, CDs, piano, library, games & artwork
- open fires in lounge
- self-serve laundry
- tariff includes all meals
- continental or cooked breakfast served
- buffet-style lunch
- dinner served in main dining area, or alfresco
- vegetarians catered for
- small weddings, honeymoons & conferences catered for
- email & phone available

Activities available

- water taxi fares extra
- well stocked library
- BBQ on site
- kayaks & row boat available
- swimming & snorkelling
- windsurfing from site
- fishing from site
- Queen Charlotte Track day walks
- hiking & tramping
- Marlborough Sounds scenic cruises
- sailing charters on request
- eco tours
- nature tours to Motuara Island – birdlife, seals, & dolphins to view
- Ship Cove – site of Captain Cook's arrival
- Picton, 12km by sea

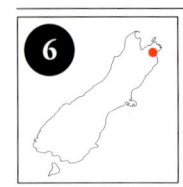

PICTON
SENNEN HOUSE

Hosts Imogen and Richard Fawcett

9 Oxford Street, Picton   *Mobile* 021 359 956
Phone 0-3-573 5216   *Email* enquiries@sennenhouse.co.nz
Fax 0-3-573 5216   *Website* www.sennenhouse.co.nz

3 bdrm | 3 enst

Apartment rate $245–$325
Extra persons $50 each

Includes breakfast hamper
Self-catering

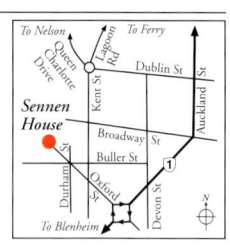

DIRECTIONS: From Picton ferries, travel into Kent St. Turn right into Buller St, right into Durham St & left into Oxford St. Sennen House at end. From Blenheim, turn left into Kent St & 2nd left into Oxford St.

Sennen House was built in 1886 by Englishman George Smith, a local timber merchant. Rescued from demolition in 1965, and restored to its former glory in 2002, this colonial villa now offers three self-contained apartments. Original features include the grand kauri staircase, ornate woodwork and verandahs. The Victoria, Banks' and Cooks' apartments open to balconies with views of sheep on the native bush-clad hills, gardens or Picton and the sea beyond. Continental breakfast hampers are provided in the apartments each morning where guests can self-cater using the fully equipped kitchens, or enjoy the range of nearby restaurants. Complimentary transfers are available from the Picton airport, interisland ferry or the train.

Facilities

- Cooks' apartment: 1 king/twin ensuite bedroom with lounge, open fire, full kitchen, balcony, hills & sea view
- Banks' apartment: 1 queen/twin ensuite bedroom with lounge, full kitchen, balcony, hills & native bush view
- Victoria apartment: 1 queen ensuite bedroom with sitting area, kitchenette, balcony & view to Picton & sea
- breakfast hamper & daily newspaper supplied
- pure cotton bed linen; Sky TV, tea/coffee & phone in all 3 apartments
- hair dryer, toiletries, bathrobes & heated towel rails in all 3 ensuites
- children welcome by request
- laundry, $5; email facility
- courtesy passenger transfer

Activities available

- native bush & birds on site
- cats & sheep on site
- strolling on foreshore nearby
- local shops nearby
- kayaking; sailing; fishing
- local walks to lookouts
- Edwin Fox & Picton museums
- boat trips in Sounds
- Picton restaurants within walking distance
- wine tours of Marlborough vineyards
- dolphin & bird watching
- Queen Charlotte track
- Picton ferries, 10-min walk
- horse trekking in Blenheim & Pelorus
- Blenheim, 20-min drive
- Rainbow ski-field, 1 hour
- Nelson City, 2-hour drive

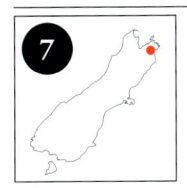

WAIKAWA BAY, PICTON
VUE POINTE

Hosts Elaine and John Roberts   *Phone* 0-3-573 7621

236 Port Underwood Road, Waikawa Bay, Picton   *Mobile* 025 205 1664
Postal P O Box 12, Waikawa Bay, Picton   *Fax* 0-3-573 7621
Email j_roberts@xtra.co.nz   *Website* friars.co.nz/hosts/vuepointe.html

1 bdrm   1 enst   Room rate $275
Multiple-night rate available   *Includes continental breakfast basket*

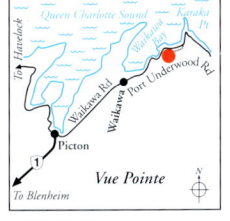

DIRECTIONS: From Picton, take Waikawa Rd for 5km. Continue on Port Underwood Rd for 2.5km & turn right into Sunshine Heights private road. Travel up steep hill for 0.5km to Vue Pointe at top left.

Purpose-built in 1996 to maximise sea views, Vue Pointe is set in an elevated position in native bush overlooking the Marlborough Sounds. Named after the Vue Pointe area in the Caribbean Island of Montserrat where the hosts lived with their dog Gus, this self-contained accommodation opens to extensive deck areas with 180-degree views of both bush and sea. The guest suite features temperature control, king-size ensuite bedroom, lounge and dining/kitchenette area. A continental breakfast basket is provided daily, and Picton's restaurants, cafés and shops are just 10 minutes' drive away. Guests enjoy watching the boat traffic below and the native birdlife. Further afield the dolphin watching and Marlborough's vineyards are popular activities.

Facilities
- 1 self-contained suite
- 1 king bedroom with ensuite, lounge & dining area
- cotton bed linen; bathrobes
- hair dryer, toiletries, heated towel rails, heated floor & bidet
- private guest entrance & sundeck
- TV, CDs, books, nibbles, tea/coffee & mineral water
- complimentary laundry available
- continental breakfast basket daily
- guest kitchenette for preparing light meals
- fresh flowers
- email, fax & phone available in main house
- central heating
- honeymoons catered for
- on-site parking

Activities available
- barbecue on site
- boat watching from site
- bush walks
- bird-watching from site
- yachting; fishing
- sea kayaking
- boat trips in Sounds
- sailing; diving
- walking; hiking; trekking
- restaurants in Picton, 8km
- Marlborough Vineyard restaurants & wine tasting
- golf course
- dolphin watching
- scenic flights
- Queen Charlotte Track
- Picton ferries, 10 mins
- Blenheim, 45-min drive
- Nelson City, 2-hour drive

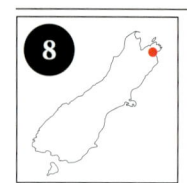

WHATAMANGO BAY, PICTON
A SEA VIEW

Hosts Christine and Dave Grigg   *Phone* 0-3-573 8815

424 Port Underwood Road, Whatamango Bay Heights, Picton
Postal P O Box 71, Waikawa Bay, Picton   *Fax* 0-3-573 8815
Email aseaview@paradise.net.nz   *Website* www.aseaview.co.nz

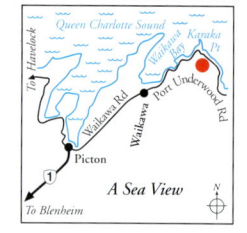

3 bdrm | 3 enst   Room rate $115–$199   Includes breakfast   Lunch & dinner extra   Self-catering

DIRECTIONS: From Picton, take Waikawa Rd for 8km to Karaka Point. Continue 1km on Port Underwood Rd to sign *Sea View* on right (about 15-min drive from Picton). Turn right into driveway to A Sea View.

Set on the slopes above Whatamango Bay, A Sea View offers expansive views over Queen Charlotte Sound from the deck and guestrooms. The large terraced garden features native plants which attract abundant birdlife. The three ensuite guestrooms have sea views and private entrances, and two offer self-catering facilities. Guests are served a continental or full cooked breakfast including bacon, eggs, tomatoes, mushrooms, fruit, home-made jams, yoghurt, muesli and bread, in the main house, or alfresco while enjoying the view from the deck. Christine and David welcome the opportunity to help guests with their holiday plans and arrange activities in the Marlborough Sounds. An evening meal and lunch are available by prior arrangement.

Facilities
- 2 king ensuite bedrooms
- 1 queen ensuite bedroom
- toiletries & hair dryers
- cotton bed linen, TV, tea/coffee & mineral water in bedrooms
- sea & garden views
- laundry available
- email, fax & phone available in main house
- 2-tonne registered boat mooring
- continental or full cooked breakfast served in main house or alfresco on deck
- lunch, $10 pp on request
- 3-course dinner with wine, $65 pp, by arrangement
- full kitchen or kitchenette for self-catering in 2 rooms
- courtesy passenger transfer from Picton airport or ferry; on-site parking

Activities available
- winery tours
- boat trips in Sounds
- dolphin & penguin watching
- fishing
- kayaking; sailing
- diving
- restaurants, nearby
- hiking to nearby Maori pa site
- golf course
- swimming
- Queen Charlotte Track
- trekking
- day trips to Kaikoura & Nelson Lakes
- Picton ferries, 15-min drive
- Blenheim, ½-hour drive
- Nelson City, 2-hour drive

© Friars' Guide to New Zealand Accommodation for the Discerning Traveller

Picton
Koro Park Lodge

Hosts Diane Purkis and Brian Martin

779 State Highway 1, Koromiko, R D 3, Blenheim
Phone 0-3-573 5542   *Email* koropark@actrix.co.nz
Fax 0-3-573 5548   *Website* friars.co.nz/hosts/koro.html

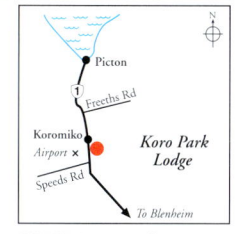

2 bdrm | 1 enst | 1 prbth   Double $120–$180   Single $90–$145   *Includes breakfast*

DIRECTIONS: From the Picton ferry terminal, take SH 1 south for 9km to Koromiko. Koro Park Lodge on left, sign at gate. From Blenheim, take SH 1 north for 19km. Koro Park Lodge on right.

Situated in the Koromiko Valley, nine kilometres south of Picton on State Highway One, Koro Park Lodge is centrally located for guests to visit the many wineries, arts and crafts, restaurants, shopping facilities, golfing, and scenic and fishing boat trips available in the Marlborough region. Not far from the Picton ferry terminal or airport, Koro Park Lodge is set on a hectare of park-like grounds, with mature trees and sweeping lawns surrounded by rural views of the valley and bush-clad hills beyond. A full continental or cooked breakfast is served downstairs in the guest lounge or breakfast room, by the new hosts at Koro Park Lodge, Diane and Brian. Guests are offered either a queen-size guestroom and bathroom upstairs or a full suite downstairs.

Facilities

- 1 queen/twin bedroom upstairs, with bath in private bathroom
- 1 queen suite downstairs, with spa bath in ensuite & lounge opening to private courtyard
- hair dryer, toiletries & heated towel rails in both bathrooms
- TV, music, & tea/coffee facilities in both guestrooms
- complimentary laundry
- fresh flowers
- full continental or cooked breakfast served in guest guestrooms, dining room, or alfresco
- phone, fax & email available on request
- garden setting
- rural views
- courtesy passenger transfer
- on-site parking

Activities available

- Picton Airport close by
- golf course, 1km away
- fishing & cruising trips in Marlborough Sounds
- wine trail & wine tasting
- arts & crafts trail
- private gardens to visit
- alpaca & llama farm
- Brayshaw Museum Park
- Blenheim, 19km
- licensed restaurants nearby
- white water rafting
- yacht & launch charter
- Marlborough Sounds Adventures, 15-min drive
- Old Beaver Town, 15-min drive to Blenheim
- dolphin-watching eco tours
- Rainbow Ski-field, 1 hour
- Picton interisland ferries, 9km

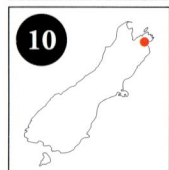

Blenheim
Old St Mary's Convent

Hosts Wilfried and Mieke Holtrop

Rapaura Road, R D 3, Blenheim
Phone 0-3-570 5700 *Email* retreat@convent.co.nz
Fax 0-3-570 5703 *Website* www.convent.co.nz

5 bdrm | 5 enst | Room rate $350–$450 | *Includes breakfast*

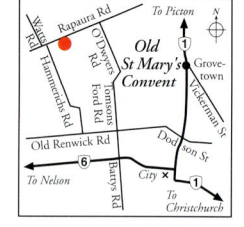

DIRECTIONS: From the Picton ferry, take SH 1 south towards Blenheim. Turn right at Spring Creek into Rapaura Rd. Travel 5km to Convent on left. Or from Blenheim, take SH 1 north 3km to Spring Creek.

In 1994 the Old St Mary's Convent was relocated on its eight-hectare (20-acre) setting in the heart of Marlborough's wine district. Built in 1901, the Convent is now restored to its former glory with the ground floor interiors replicating the century-old layout. The upstairs former chapel has now been transformed into an apartment-size honeymoon suite, retaining the original arched, stained-glass windows and cathedral ceilings. Four of the five ensuite bathrooms include claw-foot baths, and all five guestrooms are spacious and airy, with balconies overlooking the gardens to the surrounding hills. A separate historic chapel, complete with original pews, pulpit and organ, is set in the gardens for a peaceful retreat and is available for small weddings.

Facilities
- 1 super-king/twin, 1 super-king, 1 king & 2 queen bedrooms
- 5 ensuite bathrooms, all with toiletries & hair dryers; 4 baths
- honeymoon suite in old chapel
- 2 room family suite
- guest balconies & verandahs
- fresh flowers
- air-conditioning
- internet terminal for guests
- breakfast served in formal dining room, or alfresco on verandah
- billiards room with antique full-size table
- guest library with ornate kauri fireplace
- 19th & 20th century European & NZ paintings
- German, Dutch & basic French spoken

Activities available
- 8-ha garden & birdlife on site
- spring-fed stream & trout on site
- complimentary bicycles
- grass tennis courts next door
- golf courses close by
- wineries tours nearby
- arts & crafts trail
- private gardens to visit
- trout fishing, guide available
- restaurants nearby
- sailing
- horse trekking
- mountain biking
- Marlborough Sounds fishing trips & kayaking
- scenic walks in Marlborough Sounds
- Rainbow Ski-field, 1½-hour scenic drive

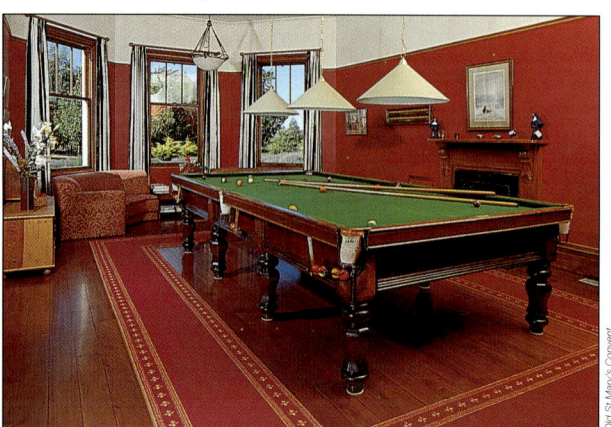

© Friars' Guide to New Zealand Accommodation for the Discerning Traveller

Above: The private lounge in the honeymoon suite, formerly the chapel, looking through the arched doorway to the bedroom.
Below: The historic Old St Mary's Convent set in eight hectares of grounds, with a separate chapel for garden weddings.
Opposite top: Black swans frequent the stream and water features in the gardens at the Old St Mary's Convent in Marlborough.
Opposite bottom left: The billiards room featuring an antique full-size billiards table and bay window with views to the garden.
Opposite bottom right: One of the spacious ensuite bathrooms looking through to the former Mother Superior's Room.

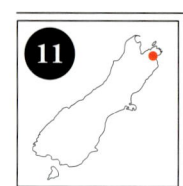

BLENHEIM
OPAWA LODGE

Hosts Lesley Tuckett and Ross Connochie

143A Budge Street, Blenheim
Phone 0-3-577 9989   *Mobile* 025 411 214   *Fax* 0-3-577 9949
Email opawalodge@xtra.co.nz   *Website* www.marlborough.co.nz/opawa

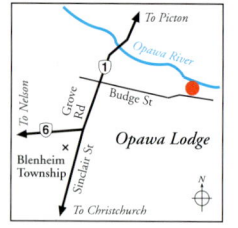

Double $140–$180
Single $100–$125   *Includes breakfast*   *Dinner extra*

DIRECTIONS: Take SH 1 to Blenheim. On the northern outskirts, just south of Opawa River bridge, turn east into Budge St. Travel 1.1km to Opawa Lodge on left.

Set on the outskirts of Blenheim, Opawa Lodge is close to Marlborough vineyards, yet within minutes of the township. This riverside accommodation comprises three guest bedrooms and two bathrooms, with views of the Opawa River even from the ensuite! Adjacent is the guest conservatory, where a continental or full cooked breakfast is served overlooking the garden that slopes down to the river, with rural vistas to the fields and Richmond Range beyond. Lesley and Ross specialise in local cuisine, offering informal dining in the evening by prior arrangement. Guests enjoy the on-site access to the Opawa River, with fishing rods and rowboat available and there is also an in-ground pool for summer swimming.

Facilities
- 1 queen bedroom with ensuite & spa bath
- 1 queen & 1 twin bedroom with private bathroom
- bathrobes, hair dryers, toiletries & heated towel rails
- TV & video in queen bedroom & conservatory
- complimentary laundry
- luggage/vehicle storage for overnight trips away
- full breakfast in conservatory
- 3-course dinner & wine, $65 pp, served in conservatory
- tea/coffee in conservatory
- powder room; fresh flowers
- phone, fax & email available
- children over 10 yrs welcome
- rail & airport courtesy passenger transfers
- ample off-street parking

Activities available
- swimming pool on site
- river fishing access on site, fishing rods available
- barbecue on site
- fresh & saltwater fishing trips
- row boat & canoes available
- arts & crafts trail
- personal wine tours arranged
- restaurants, only minutes away
- adventure activities in Sounds
- Blenheim town for shopping
- private garden tours
- golf courses
- white water rafting
- Queen Charlotte Walkway
- Kaikoura whale watching
- Marlborough Sounds, 30km
- Nelson Lakes National Park for winter skiing
- interisland ferries, 25 mins

© Friars' Guide to New Zealand Accommodation for the Discerning Traveller

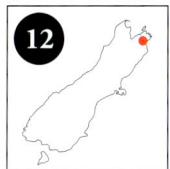

BLENHEIM
THE PEPPERTREE
LUXURY ACCOMMODATION

Hosts Heidi and Werner Plüss

3284 State Highway 1, Riverlands, Blenheim   *Postal* P O Box 279, Blenheim
Phone 0-3-520 9200   *Email* info@thepeppertree.co.nz
Fax 0-3-520 9222   *Website* www.thepeppertree.co.nz

| 5 bdrm | 3 enst | 2 prbth | Double $350 Single $310 | Includes breakfast Dinner extra |

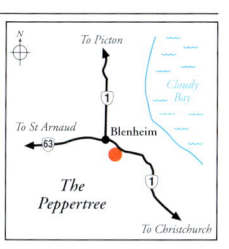

DIRECTIONS: 25 mins from the Picton ferry. Take SH 1 south to Blenheim. Continue for another 5km to Cob Cottage, on the right. The Peppertree is next door on the south side.

The Peppertree takes its name from the pepper-trees (*Schinus molle*) lining the driveway. Built as a farmhouse in 1901 for Adam Bell, this Edwardian villa was converted into a restaurant in 1984. Then, in late 1994, The Peppertree was transformed into boutique accommodation. Constructed from the native timbers rimu, kauri and matai, the interior has been refurbished in sympathy with the era of the home. The five bedrooms are individually designed, three with private balconies or verandahs. Alfresco country breakfasts or in the evening local wines – some of the world's finest – can be enjoyed on the verandah, which opens to almost a hectare of mature garden, surrounded by Peppertree's own boutique vineyard and the newly established olive grove.

Facilities

- 1 king, & 2 king/twin & 2 queen bedrooms, 3 with private balcony or verandah
- 5 bathrooms, 1 with spa bath
- toiletries, hair dryers & central heating
- fresh flowers, chocolates & coffee/tea facilities in rooms
- phone & TV in bedrooms
- open fires in guest lounge, dining room & bedrooms
- country breakfast in dining room or alfresco on verandah
- fax & email available
- complimentary port & sherry in lounge or verandah
- fully licensed, with NZ wines
- walnut pillars, kauri archway, stained glass in entrance hall
- small conference venue
- on-site parking; helipad

Activities available

- croquet lawn & pétanque/boules
- in-ground swimming pool
- Cob Cottage colonial museum adjacent
- Marlborough wine trails & tasting, with lunches available
- historic Brayshaw Park
- golf courses nearby
- visiting private gardens
- freshwater & sea fishing
- restaurants, 5-min drive
- walking; horse riding
- summer sailing
- Blenheim Airport, 10-min drive, transport if required
- Marlborough Sounds, 30km
- interisland ferries, 25 mins
- winter skiing, 1½-hour drive
- whale watching at Kaikoura, 1½-hour drive south

291

© Friars' Guide to New Zealand Accommodation for the Discerning Traveller

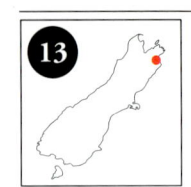

SEDDON, BLENHEIM
UGBROOKE COUNTRY HOUSE

Hosts Teresa and Guido Bertogg

Ugbrooke Road, Redwood Pass, Dashwood, Seddon   *Postal* R D 4, Blenheim
Phone 0-3-575 7988   *Mobile* 025 601 1991   *Fax* 0-3-575 7970
Email ugbrooke@xtra.co.nz   *Website* www.ugbrooke.co.nz

| 3 bdrm | 2 enst | 1 prbth | 1 pdrm |

Double $240
Single $200

Includes continental breakfast
Dinner extra

DIRECTIONS: From Christchurch, take SH 1 north to Seddon. Travel 5 mins north to Dashwood. Turn right into Redwood Pass Rd. Take 2nd left into Ugbrooke Rd. Travel to Ugbrooke Country House at end.

Set on park-like grounds with sea views, sweeping lawns and gardens bordered with mature trees, Ugbrooke Country House is the original farm homestead built in 1885 by William Clifford using bricks fired on the property. The Vasavour family bought Ugbrooke and completed the 890-square metre (10,000-square foot) single-storey house in 1904. Now restored and offering accommodation, Ugbrooke retains many of its historic features such as the high ornate zinc-pressed ceilings, timber panelling, crafted fireplace surrounds and mantelpieces, arched doorways, polished rimu floors and bay windows. The guestrooms are spacious with four-poster beds, and the formal dining room is available for dinner prepared by Guido, the resident Swiss chef.

Facilities
- Vavasour: 1 super-king ensuite bedroom with 4-poster bed, writing desk, wheelchair access & opens to verandah
- Clifford: 1 queen bedroom with canopy bed & double spa bath in ensuite
- 1 twin bedroom & private bathroom
- hair dryer & toiletries in all 3 bathrooms
- continental breakfast served
- dinner by arrangement, extra
- drawing room with open fire, nibbles, Sky TV, CD-player, piano & games; powder room
- fresh flowers; laundry available
- email, fax & phone available
- children welcome
- Swiss German spoken
- on-site parking

Activities available
- small dog, cat, pet sheep & pony on site
- swimming pool, croquet, lawn boules & BBQ on site
- 28ha grounds with lawn, gardens & historic trees
- 9-hole golf course
- horse riding; local beaches
- heritage trail
- private gardens open to visit
- dining at local wineries
- restaurants, 20-min drive
- freshwater & sea fishing
- scenic walking & hiking
- wilderness tours; dolphins, Kaikoura whale watching
- Blenheim Airport, 30-min drive
- Marlborough Sounds, 45 mins
- interisland ferries, 50-min drive
- winter skiing, 2-hour drive

© Friars' Guide to New Zealand Accommodation for the Discerning Traveller

BLENHEIM
ANTRIA BOUTIQUE LODGE

Hosts Phil Sowman and Kathryne Fleming

276 Old Renwick Road, R D 2, Blenheim
Phone 0-3-579 2191 *Mobile* 025 207 6947 *Fax* 0-3-579 2192
Email stay@antria.co.nz *Website* www.antria.co.nz

2 bdrm | 2 enst | 1 prbth

Double $335–$375   **Single $295**   *Includes breakfast or brunch*

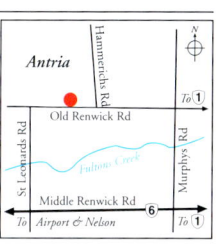

DIRECTIONS: Take SH 1 from Picton or Christchurch to Blenheim. Turn west into SH 6 (Middle Renwick Rd) towards Nelson. Turn right into Murphys Rd & left into Old Renwick Rd. Antria on right down long drive.

Set in an orchard in the heart of Marlborough wine country, Antria, meaning "a new beginning", is within walking and biking distance of many vineyards and restaurants. Phil and Kathryne designed their boutique lodge in 2000, in the style of a contemporary European castle with metre-thick concrete walls for guest privacy and quiet. Purpose-built to provide two guest suites, Antria features Greek-style recesses and archways, with French doors from every room opening to the three-metre deep verandahs for relaxing around the fountain. Quality fabrics have been chosen for the bedrooms, with Italian fittings in the ensuites. Original New Zealand art is displayed and leisurely breakfast or brunch at hand-painted stone Italian tables is a speciality.

Facilities
- 1 super-king/twin & 1 king bedroom with ensuites
- cotton bed linen, writing desk & mineral water in bedrooms
- double showers, hair dryers, toiletries, bathrobes, heated floors, towel rails; 1 dual basin
- complimentary laundry
- full office facilities available
- guest lounge with open fire, Sky TV, DVD & music centre
- full cooked gourmet breakfast/brunch
- guest pantry with complimentary beverages
- individual security system per room; security lights
- hand-made soaps & shampoos
- bedrooms open onto verandahs
- guest garaging
- courtesy passenger transfer

Activities available
- eco tours available
- cat & collie dog, Fly, on site
- tailored wine tours
- masseur/trainer by arrangement
- children's room for 2, with Xbox, & TV; trampoline outdoors
- 1.3ha (3.5 acres) plum, apple & olive trees for picking in season
- loungers & hammocks on verandahs around fountain
- private dinner/gourmet BBQ, chef by arrangement
- local vineyards with restaurants, close by
- Maori guide & carver available
- Blenheim town, 3-min drive
- airport, 2-min drive
- Marlborough Sounds fishing trips & diving
- Picton ferries, 25-min drive

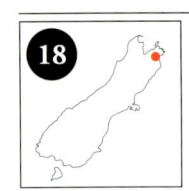

OMAKA VALLEY, BLENHEIM
THE BELL TOWER

Hosts Maria and Eric Deane

95 Brookby Road, Omaka Valley, R D 2, Blenheim, Marlborough
Phone 0-3-572 8831   *Mobile* 021 440 351   *Fax* 0-3-572 8831
Email thebelltower@paradise.net.nz   *Website* www.thebelltower.co.nz

| 5 bdrm | 3 enst | 1 prbth | Double $450 Single $300 | *Includes breakfast, brunch or lunch & pre-dinner drinks* Extra persons $75 each   *Dinner extra* |

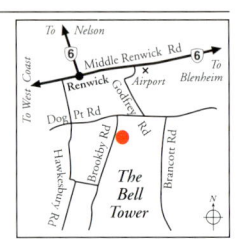

DIRECTIONS: Take SH 1 to Blenheim. Turn west into Middle Renwick Rd (SH 6). After airport, turn left into Godfrey Rd & right into Dog Point Rd. Turn left into Brookby Rd. Travel 1km to The Bell Tower on left 200m up drive.

Purpose-built in 2001 in French country style, to accommodate four guestrooms, The Bell Tower comprises a main lodge with separate Barn adjacent. A bell tower mounted on the roof holds a replica of the East India Company's bell high above the walled garden on the 5-hectare (12-acre) property. Panoramic views extend over the vineyards and Marlborough countryside to the Richmond Range and Cloudy Bay. Guests can choose between two spacious ensuite rooms within the lodge, each opening to private courtyards, or the separate two-bedroom Barn for total privacy. Breakfast, brunch or lunch are served inside or alfresco in the courtyard. A four-course dinner with wine is also available by prior arrangement.

Facilities
- 3 super-king suites in house with private courtyards
- Barn: 1 super-king/twin & 1 double bedroom share private bathroom & kitchenette with provisions; children welcome
- TV & tea/coffee in bedrooms
- bath, hair dryer, toiletries, bathrobes, heated towel rails & heated floor in each bathroom
- complimentary laundry
- full cooked traditional breakfast or brunch or lunch to guests' preferences
- 4-course dinner, $75 pp, wine extra
- email, fax & phone available
- private guest lounge with open fire, tea/coffee, bar, nibbles, Sky TV & video
- courtesy passenger transfer; on-site parking; helipad

Activities available
- pétanque court on site
- small-bore shooting
- bicycles for guest use
- barbecue available
- honeymoons catered for
- Marlborough Golf Club, 2-min drive
- surrounded by vineyards & wineries with restaurants
- 4WD off-road driving
- Blenheim restaurants, cafés & shops, 12km
- sea fishing & cruises in Marlborough Sounds
- lake & river trout fishing
- deer hunting
- scenic walking tracks
- Marlborough wine trail
- arts & crafts
- winter skiing

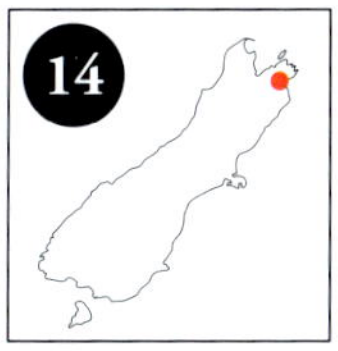

BLENHEIM
ANTRIA BOUTIQUE LODGE

Hosts Phil Sowman and Kathryne Fleming

276 Old Renwick Road, R D 2, Blenheim
Phone 0-3-579 2191   *Mobile* 025 207 6947   *Fax* 0-3-579 2192
Email stay@antria.co.nz   *Website* www.antria.co.nz

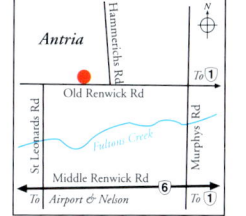

Double $335–$375   Single $295   *Includes breakfast or brunch*

DIRECTIONS: Take SH 1 from Picton or Christchurch to Blenheim. Turn west into SH 6 (Middle Renwick Rd) towards Nelson. Turn right into Murphys Rd & left into Old Renwick Rd. Antria on right down long drive.

Set in an orchard in the heart of Marlborough wine country, Antria, meaning "a new beginning", is within walking and biking distance of many vineyards and restaurants. Phil and Kathryne designed their boutique lodge in 2000, in the style of a contemporary European castle with metre-thick concrete walls for guest privacy and quiet. Purpose-built to provide two guest suites, Antria features Greek-style recesses and archways, with French doors from every room opening to the three-metre deep verandahs for relaxing around the fountain. Quality fabrics have been chosen for the bedrooms, with Italian fittings in the ensuites. Original New Zealand art is displayed and leisurely breakfast or brunch at hand-painted stone Italian tables is a speciality.

Facilities
- 1 super-king/twin & 1 king bedroom with ensuites
- cotton bed linen, writing desk & mineral water in bedrooms
- double showers, hair dryers, toiletries, bathrobes, heated floors, towel rails; 1 dual basin
- complimentary laundry
- full office facilities available
- guest lounge with open fire, Sky TV, DVD & music centre
- full cooked gourmet breakfast/brunch
- guest pantry with complimentary beverages
- individual security system per room; security lights
- hand-made soaps & shampoos
- bedrooms open onto verandahs
- guest garaging
- courtesy passenger transfer

Activities available
- eco tours available
- cat & collie dog, Fly, on site
- tailored wine tours
- masseur/trainer by arrangement
- children's room for 2, with Xbox, & TV; trampoline outdoors
- 1.3ha (3.5 acres) plum, apple & olive trees for picking in season
- loungers & hammocks on verandahs around fountain
- private dinner/gourmet BBQ, chef by arrangement
- local vineyards with restaurants, close by
- Maori guide & carver available
- Blenheim town, 3-min drive
- airport, 2-min drive
- Marlborough Sounds fishing trips & diving
- Picton ferries, 25-min drive

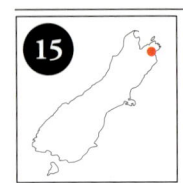

BLENHEIM
Uno Più

Hosts Gino and Heather Rocco

75 Murphys Road, Blenheim
Phone 0-3-578 2235   *Mobile* 021 174 4257   *Fax* 0-3-578 2235
Email stay@unopiu.co.nz   *Website* www.unopiu.co.nz

2 bdrm / 2 enst

Double $210–$290
Single $150–$230

Includes breakfast
Dinner extra

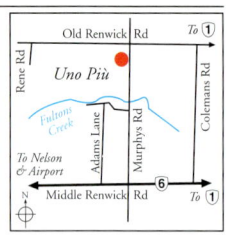

DIRECTIONS: Take SH 1 from Picton or Christchurch to Blenheim. Turn west into SH 6 (Middle Renwick Rd) towards Nelson. Turn right into Murphys Rd. Uno Più on left. (3km from town centre.)

Uno Più, meaning "One Plus" in Italian, provides Italian-style hospitality set on a farmlet of almost two hectares, where horses and sheep graze in the paddocks surrounding the historic homestead. Built in 1917, this private residence has been renovated to offer guest accommodation comprising two king bedrooms with ensuites. The swimming pool is enclosed with roses and a predominantly white garden. Special features include the baby grand piano in the guest lounge, a sauna, a guest office with broadband internet access, Luca the friendly collie and, of course, the Italian cuisine. Gino's home-made pasta is as popular as his Italian breakfast platter with hot rolls, to complement his pancakes with maple syrup, strawberries and cream.

Facilities
- 1 super-king/twin & 1 king bedroom, each with ensuite
- claw-foot bath in 1 ensuite
- Sky TV, iron, tea/coffee, fridge with complimentary drinks & fresh flowers
- hair dryers, toiletries, demist mirrors, heated floors & heated towel rails
- bathrobes
- high-speed internet access
- breakfast served in dining room or alfresco
- 3-course Italian dinner with wine by arrangement, $70 pp
- guest lounge with open fire & baby grand piano
- complimentary laundry; phone, fax & email available
- off-street parking
- established trees & gardens

Activities available
- Marshall & Rose baby grand piano for guest use
- in-house sauna room
- 10m swimming pool on site
- 1.5ha farmlet with horses, Luca the collie dog & Oswald the sheep
- private gardens to visit
- arts & crafts
- walks & tramping
- Rocco's Restaurant, 2km
- wine trail, 5-min drive away
- tennis courts nearby & croquet, 1.5km away
- Blenheim township, 3km
- shopping
- river & sea fishing
- Queen Charlotte walkway
- Marlborough Sounds
- 30 mins from Picton ferry

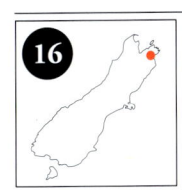

Blenheim
Ancora Uno Più

Hosts Gino and Heather Rocco

75 Murphys Road, Blenheim
Phone 0-3-578 2235   *Mobile* 021 174 4257   *Fax* 0-3-578 2235
Email stay@unopiu.co.nz   *Website* www.unopiu.co.nz

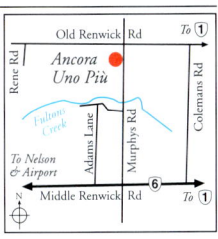

2 bdrm | 1 prbth | Cottage rate $240–$350 for 2 persons
Extra persons $60 each
Self-catering
Includes breakfast
Dinner extra

DIRECTIONS: Take SH 1 from Picton or Christchurch to Blenheim. Turn west into SH 6 (Middle Renwick Rd) towards Nelson. Turn right into Murphys Rd. Uno Più on left. (3km from town centre.)

Ancora Uno Più, meaning "Yet Another One Plus" in Italian, is a self-contained cottage set among olive trees in the garden of Uno Più homestead. This mud-block cottage features a cathedral ceiling and restored native kauri doors and surrounds which complement the natural mud-block interiors. The cottage provides two bedrooms, a super-king size and a queen/twin, and private bathroom with a 1920 claw-foot bath. A fully equipped kitchen allows for self-catering, the lounge features a Victorian fireplace and French doors open to a sunny patio where a barbecue is located. Breakfast is delivered to the cottage, or guests are welcome to breakfast in the homestead (*see opposite page 294*), and Gino's Italian dinners are also available by request.

Facilities

- single-party bookings only
- 1 super-king & 1 queen/twin bedroom & 1 private bathroom
- clawfoot bath in bathroom
- bathrobes, hair dryer, toiletries, heated floor & towel rails
- open fire & Sky TV in lounge
- fresh flowers & complimentary drinks; self-serve laundry
- children by arrangement
- full kitchen for self-catering
- breakfast supplied
- 3-course Italian dinner with wine, $70 pp, by arrangement
- BBQ on verandah
- phone, fax & email available
- high-speed internet access
- serviced daily
- garden views
- off-street parking

Activities available

- sauna room on site
- 10m swimming pool on site
- 1.5ha farmlet, horses, sheep
- friendly sheep (Oswald), 1 cat & collie dog (Luca) on site
- tennis courts nearby
- croquet, 1.5km away
- private gardens open to visit
- public gardens & parks
- arts & crafts
- Rocco's Restaurant, 2km
- wine trail, 5-min drive away
- walks & tramping
- Blenheim township, 3km
- shopping
- river & sea fishing
- Queen Charlotte walkway
- Marlborough Sounds
- Picton ferry, 30 mins north

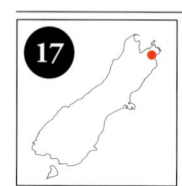

BLENHEIM
ST LEONARDS VINEYARD COTTAGES

Hosts Jeanette and Steve Parker

18 St Leonards Road, R D 1, Blenheim
Phone 0-3-577 8328   *Mobile* 025 686 1636   *Fax* 0-3-577 8329
Email stay@stleonards.co.nz   *Website* friars.co.nz/hosts/stleonards.html

| 5 bdrm | 2 enst | 2 prbth |

Room rate $90–$250
Extra persons $35–$50 each

Includes continental breakfast provisions
Self-catering

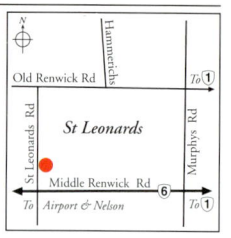

DIRECTIONS: Take SH 1 from Picton or Christchurch to Blenheim. Turn west into SH 6 (Middle Renwick Rd) towards Nelson. Travel 4km & turn right into St Leonards Rd. Vineyard Cottages 2nd on right.

The four St Leonards Vineyard Cottages are set in two hectares (approximately five acres) surrounding the original homestead of the area, circa 1884. The hosts, the Parker family, occupy the homestead. The Stables is converted into a self-contained cottage overlooking the lemon grove and animal paddocks, to the distant Wither Hills. A barbecue can be enjoyed in a private garden and a pot-belly stove provides added warmth in winter. The architecturally restored Woolshed overlooking the vineyards sleeps five guests and features rustic recycled materials, an open fire in the lounge area opening to decking with a barbecue and an outdoor bath. A smaller annexe adjacent to the house, separated by the carport, is also self-contained with a kitchenette for self-catering. The newest addition is a character one-bedroom cottage reminiscent of colonial New Zealand, with extra beds, full kitchen, pot-belly stove, verandah and barbecue. Guests enjoy the tennis, pétanque and swimming pool on site.

Facilities
- Woolshed: 1 queen & 1 twin bedroom, private bathroom, extra toilet, lounge with divan & open fire, deck & outdoor bath
- Stables: 1 queen ensuite bedroom, lounge, pot-belly & patio
- Cottage: 1 queen bed, 2 foldaway beds, divan bed in lounge, bathroom, pot-belly & verandah
- Annexe: 1 double bedroom with ensuite bathroom
- all 4 cottages include TV, microwave & BBQ
- hair dryers, heated towel rails & toiletries in all bathrooms
- children & pets welcome

- breakfast provisions in all 4 cottages, including home-made preserves
- wine in guest fridges, extra
- full kitchens in Woolshed & Cottage for self-catering
- kitchenettes in Stables & Annex for self-catering
- email, fax & phone available in main house
- self-serve laundry
- orchard & gardens
- local artwork
- on-site parking
- courtesy airport transfer

Activities available
- in-ground lawn tennis court
- farmyard animals to pet
- pétanque & croquet on site
- swimming pool on site
- 2ha (5-acre) garden on site
- picking fruit & walnuts from trees in season, on site
- surrounded by vineyards
- wineries, 3-min drive
- shopping, 5-min drive
- trout fishing nearby
- bush walks
- horse trekking
- fishing in Marlborough Sounds, 30-min drive

- restaurants, 5-min drive
- golf courses
- gardens open to visit
- airport, 3-min drive
- Blenheim township, 5 mins
- scenic flights
- boat trip through Malborough Sounds
- Picton ferries, 25-min drive
- Rainbow Ski-field, 1 hour
- Nelson, 1 hr 20-min drive
- dolphin swimming in Kaikoura, 2-hour drive
- whale watching in Kaikoura, 2-hour drive

© Friars' Guide to New Zealand Accommodation for the Discerning Traveller

Opposite top far left: Inside The Stables, showing dining and lounge area with queen-size bedroom in the background. The lounge opens to a private patio. An ensuite bathroom and kitchenette completes this self-contained accommodation option.

Opposite top right: The exterior of The Stables showing the garden setting. Each of the four accommodation options is quite private and located separately from the others.

Above: Inside The Annexe, showing the double bedroom and kitchenette beyond. An ensuite bathroom completes this self-contained accommodation option.

Below: The exterior of the newest self-contained character cottage. Guests can look out to borrowed views of the neighbouring vineyards.

Opposite bottom far left: The Woolshed interior shows the open-plan dining and living area with open firelace. There is a full kitchen for self-catering, two bedrooms and a bathroom. The lounge opens onto a sundeck.

Opposite bottom right: The exterior of The Woolshed, surrounded by vineyards in the heart of the Marlborough wine area.

Above: The on-site swimming pool is a popular spot with guests in the hot Marlborough summers.

Below: The separate lounge room in the newest self-contained cottage featuring a pot-belly fire. There is a full kitchen for self-catering, a queen-size bedroom and bathroom. The lounge opens to a private verandah.

Below: The queen-size bedroom in the newest cottage, with vineyard views. There is a bathroom, and further fold-away beds and divan bed in the lounge for family groups.

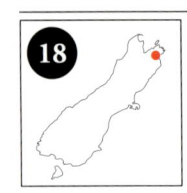

Omaka Valley, Blenheim
The Bell Tower

Hosts Maria and Eric Deane

95 Brookby Road, Omaka Valley, R D 2, Blenheim, Marlborough
Phone 0-3-572 8831   Mobile 021 440 351   Fax 0-3-572 8831
Email thebelltower@paradise.net.nz   *Website* www.thebelltower.co.nz

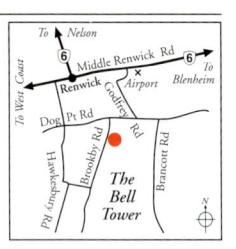

| 5 bdrm | 3 enst | 1 prbth |

Double $450
Single $300

Includes breakfast, brunch or lunch & pre-dinner drinks
Extra persons $75 each   *Dinner extra*

DIRECTIONS: Take SH 1 to Blenheim. Turn west into Middle Renwick Rd (SH 6). After airport, turn left into Godfrey Rd & right into Dog Point Rd. Turn left into Brookby Rd. Travel 1km to The Bell Tower on left 200m up drive.

Purpose-built in 2001 in French country style, to accommodate four guestrooms, The Bell Tower comprises a main lodge with separate Barn adjacent. A bell tower mounted on the roof holds a replica of the East India Company's bell high above the walled garden on the 5-hectare (12-acre) property. Panoramic views extend over the vineyards and Marlborough countryside to the Richmond Range and Cloudy Bay. Guests can choose between two spacious ensuite rooms within the lodge, each opening to private courtyards, or the separate two-bedroom Barn for total privacy. Breakfast, brunch or lunch are served inside or alfresco in the courtyard. A four-course dinner with wine is also available by prior arrangement.

Facilities
- 3 super-king suites in house with private courtyards
- Barn: 1 super-king/twin & 1 double bedroom share private bathroom & kitchenette with provisions; children welcome
- TV & tea/coffee in bedrooms
- bath, hair dryer, toiletries, bathrobes, heated towel rails & heated floor in each bathroom
- complimentary laundry
- full cooked traditional breakfast or brunch or lunch to guests' preferences
- 4-course dinner, $75 pp, wine extra
- email, fax & phone available
- private guest lounge with open fire, tea/coffee, bar, nibbles, Sky TV & video
- courtesy passenger transfer; on-site parking; helipad

Activities available
- pétanque court on site
- small-bore shooting
- bicycles for guest use
- barbecue available
- honeymoons catered for
- Marlborough Golf Club, 2-min drive
- surrounded by vineyards & wineries with restaurants
- 4WD off-road driving
- Blenheim restaurants, cafés & shops, 12km
- sea fishing & cruises in Marlborough Sounds
- lake & river trout fishing
- deer hunting
- scenic walking tracks
- Marlborough wine trail
- arts & crafts
- winter skiing

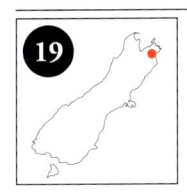

Wairau Valley, Blenheim
Straw Lodge

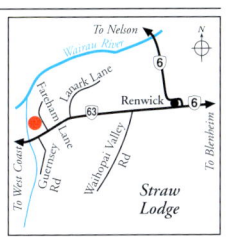

Hosts Nettie Barrow and Jane Craighead

17 Fareham Lane, R D 1, Blenheim
Phone 0-3-572 9767   *Email* strawlodge@xtra.co.nz
Fax 0-3-572 9769   *Website* www.trailsofmarlborough.co.nz

| 3 bdrm | 3 enst | Double $195–$245
Single $145–$195 | *Includes breakfast*
Extra persons $50 each | *Dinner extra*
Self-catering |

DIRECTIONS: From Blenheim, take SH 6 towards Nelson. Pass airport then turn left into SH 63 towards West Coast. Travel 7km & turn right into Fareham Lane. Straw Lodge 200m on left.

Set in a private vineyard with rural views to the ranges, the Straw Lodge was purpose built in 2002, with a guest spa pool set among the vines. Separate from the main home, the accommodation is a carefully designed straw-bale construction, furnished with hand-crafted furniture. All guestrooms have a private entrance and courtyard, ensuite bathroom, fridge and tea and coffee facilities. Two of the guestrooms also have a lounge area each with double sofa bed. There is a communal guest lounge with open fire and adjoining kitchen. A full breakfast includes home-grown produce in season. Nettie and Jane are wine growers and accredited Department of Conservation guides who will host or advise guests on Marlborough's wine, water and wilderness trails.

Facilities
- 2 super-king/twin vineyard suites each with ensuite bathroom, double sofa-bed & fridge
- 1 super-king/twin guestroom with ensuite bathroom & fridge
- hair dryers, toiletries, heated towel rails & spa pool towels
- tea/coffee, organic juices, phone jack & writing desk in bedrooms
- wine tasting on arrival
- children by arrangement
- full breakfast in dining room, on verandah, or room service
- dinner with wine, $65 pp; light meals, $25 pp, wine extra
- guest lounge with open fire, teas/coffee, nibbles, Sky TV, video, books; guest kitchen
- phone, fax & email in office
- laundry; pets on site
- on-site parking; courtesy transfer

Activities available
- vineyard tour on site
- badminton, pétanque, BBQs & outdoor spa pool on site
- bicycles & golf clubs for guest use
- tour advice or hosted guiding service
- airport, 8-min drive
- Blenheim, 15-min drive
- Picton ferries, 30 mins
- restaurants, gourmet to casual, 5–15-min drive away
- day trips:
  – wine & art & craft trails
  – Marlborough Sounds
  – Queen Charlotte walkway
  – Nelson Lakes National Park
  – Kaikoura whale watching & swimming with dolphins
  – kayaking Pelorus Sound
  – Nelson's WOW museum
  – fly or sea fishing

299

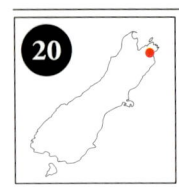

Wairau Valley, Blenheim
Glenavy Vineyard Apartment

Hosts Jackie and Trevor McGarry

1046 State Highway 63, R D 1, Wairau Valley, Blenheim
Phone 0-3-572 9562 *Email* glenavy@mlb.planet.gen.nz
Fax 0-3-572 9567 *Website* glenavy-vineyard.co.nz

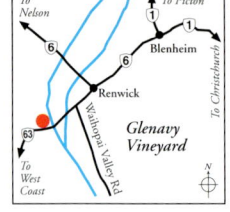

1 bdrm / 1 enst

Apartment rate $195–$215   Includes continental breakfast hamper   Self-catering

DIRECTIONS: From Blenheim, take SH 6 towards Nelson. Turn left onto SH 63 towards West Coast. Travel 10.46km, crossing Waihopai River bridge to Glenavy on right. Turn sharp right & travel along drive 1.2km.

Set on a working vineyard, Glenavy provides a self-contained upstairs apartment which is detached from the main house to ensure guest privacy. Located in the Wairau Valley, just 20 minutes from the township of Blenheim, Glenavy is a peaceful retreat set in a garden on 16 hectares (40 acres) beside the Wairau River, with rural views to the Wither Hills and the Richmond Range. The hot dry climate is ideal for growing grapes, and Trevor enjoys taking guests on a vineyard tour of Glenavy and answering their enquiries about grape growing. Jackie provides a continental breakfast hamper to the apartment each morning and a fully equipped kitchen enables guests to self-cater. Restaurants and shops are only a 10-minute drive away.

Facilities
- 1 upstairs apartment with 1 queen ensuite bedroom
- hair dryer & toiletries in ensuite bathroom
- quality bed linen
- phone jack
- guest balcony opening from lounge
- fresh flowers
- quiet vineyard setting
- continental breakfast hamper provided
- fully equipped kitchen for self-catering
- Sky TV, video & CD-player
- fax & email available
- complimentary laundry
- rural views
- hosts in main house
- on-site parking

Activities available
- guided tour of 8ha (20-acre) vineyard on site, by Trevor
- extensive garden on site
- Wairau River access on site
- trout fishing from site
- swimming in river
- winery tours & tastings
- 5 golf courses, 10-min drive
- boating
- bush walks
- restaurants, 10-min drive
- Renwick, 10-min drive
- Blenheim, 20-min drive
- boating in Marlborough Sounds, 40-min drive
- whale watching, 1½-hr drive
- skiing, 2-hour drive away
- Picton ferries, 40-min drive
- airport, 15-min drive
- Nelson, 1½-hour drive

© Friars' Guide to New Zealand Accommodation for the Discerning Traveller

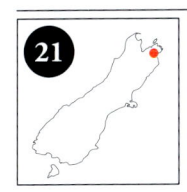

RENWICK, BLENHEIM
LeGrys Vineyard Stay

Hosts Jennifer and John Joslin

Conders Bend Road, Renwick, Blenheim   *Postal* P O Box 65, Renwick
Phone 0-3-572 9490   *Mobile* 021 313 208   *Fax* 0-3-572 9491
Email stay@legrys.co.nz   *Website* friars.co.nz/hosts/legrys.html

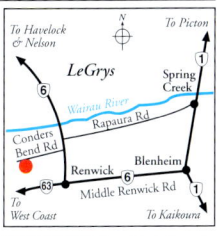

| 3 bdrm | 2 prbth | Cottage rate $225 for 2 persons
Extra persons $45 each | *Includes breakfast or hamper*
House room rate $140 | *Self-catering in cottage* |

DIRECTIONS: From Blenheim, take SH 6 towards Nelson. Travel through Renwick & continue 1.5km. Turn left into Conders Bend Rd. Travel 1km to LeGrys on left. From Nelson take SH 6, cross Wairau River & turn right.

Set in a private vineyard, with rural views to the Richmond Range, the accommodation at LeGrys was purpose-built in 1993. Both the main house and adjacent cottage are constructed from mudbricks, complemented by contemporary interiors. The self-contained cottage features a cathedral ceiling and provides two guest bedrooms, a bathroom and kitchenette for self-catering. The main house includes another guest bedroom and bathroom. All guests are offered a complimentary platter and tasting of LeGrys and Mudhouse wine on arrival. The vineyard setting, with backdrop of hills, ensures quietness, and a stream runs past the cottage door. On-site activities include swimming in the solar-heated indoor pool and touring LeGrys Vineyard.

Facilities
- single-party bookings for self-contained cottage only
- 1 queen & 1 twin bedroom, with 1 bathroom in cottage
- 1 queen bedroom & private bathroom with bath in house
- hair dryers, heated towel rails, bathrobes & toiletries
- cotton bed linen; fresh flowers
- verandah opening from queen bedroom in main house
- full breakfast in main house or alfresco; hamper to cottage
- kitchenette in cottage
- house lounge with open fire, music, tea/coffee, TV & CDs
- central heating in house
- log burner in cottage
- children welcome in cottage
- email, fax & phone available
- Springer spaniel & Airedale dogs

Activities available
- indoor solar-heated swimming pool on site
- pétanque/boules on site
- Mudhouse wines in tasting room
- vineyard tour on site
- day tours/activities, with transport to & from LeGrys
- winery visits
- 6 golf courses
- restaurants, 5–10-min drive
- pony-&-trap winery trail
- sailing
- bush walks in hills
- guided trout fishing
- horse trekking
- garden visits
- mailboat trips at Kenepuru & Marlborough Sounds
- Rainbow Ski Field, 1½ hours

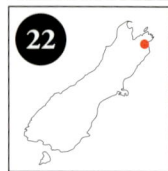

RENWICK, BLENHEIM
VINTNERS RETREAT

General Manager Stewart Milne

55 Rapaura Road, Blenheim   *Postal* P O Box 109, Renwick
Freephone 0800 484 686   Phone 0-3-572 7420   Fax 0-3-572 7421
Email info@vintnersretreat.co.nz   *Website* www.vintnersretreat.co.nz

30 bdrm | 28 prbth
Villa rate $200–$360 for 2 persons
Extra persons $35 each
Self-catering
Breakfast extra

DIRECTIONS: From Picton take SH 1 towards Blenheim. At Spring Creek turn right into Rapaura Rd. Travel 5.5km to Vintners Retreat on left. From Nelson take SH 6 towards Blenheim & turn left into Rapaura Rd.

Located in the heart of Marlborough's renowned wine region, Vintners Retreat is set in nearly two hectares (four acres) of park-like grounds surrounded by vineyards. The accommodation comprises 14 individual European-style villas separate from each other, each with two or three bedrooms and two bathrooms. Catering for a maximum of 60 guests, Vintners Retreat provides full self-catering facilities, with a well equipped kitchen in each villa and barbecue on each patio. Breakfast can be provided by arrangement and there are many restaurants in the surrounding area. Guests enjoy the on-site activities such as pétanque, tennis, and swimming in the pool. Bicycles are available for hire and wine trails nearby are popular with guests.

Facilities

- 14 separate self-contained villas
- 4 Stables & 4 Lodges: each with 2 bedrooms & 2 bathrooms
- 2 Lodges: 3 bedrooms & 2 bathrooms in each
- 4 Manors: 2 bedrooms & 2 bathrooms & balcony in each
- cotton bed linen & phone in all villas & 1 spa bath per villa
- hair dryer, toiletries & heated towel rails in all 28 bathrooms
- fully equipped kitchen for self-catering in all 14 villas
- continental or cooked breakfast by request, extra
- barbecue on private patio area of each villa
- laundry facilities in each
- lounge area in each villa
- internal garaging per villa
- courtesy passenger transfer

Activities available

- nearly 2ha park-like grounds on site
- vineyards adjacent
- swimming pool on site
- pétanque/boules on site
- tennis court on site
- bike hire available
- wine trails in vicinity
- golf courses
- fishing
- restaurants, nearby
- sailing in Sounds
- guided trout fishing
- horse trekking
- gardens open to visit
- Kenepuru & Marlborough Sounds day trips
- airport, 10-min drive
- Blenheim, 20-min drive
- Rainbow Ski Field, 1½ hours

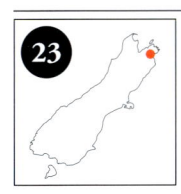

RENWICK, MARLBOROUGH SOUNDS
JEFFERSWOOD

Hosts Sandra and Jeff Sewell

Camerons Road, R D 1, Havelock, Marlborough
Phone 0-3-572 8081   *Email* jefferswood.sewell@xtra.co.nz
Fax 0-3-572 8091   *Website* www.jefferswood.co.nz

2 bdrm | 2 enst

Double $180–$215
Single $145–$175

Includes breakfast
Picnic hampers, BBQ & dinner extra

DIRECTIONS: From Blenheim, take SH 6 towards Nelson. Travel through Renwick & cross Wairau River bridge to Kaituna Valley. Turn left into Camerons Rd to Jefferswood, 300m on right.

Jefferswood is an eco-friendly adobe mudbrick, timber and schist homestead, opened in 2003. A verandah surrounds the homestead, and the two guestrooms open to a gallery with bi-fold windows providing a rural outlook to the foothills of Mt Riley. The environmentally sustainable property includes a two-hectare developing arboretum and a pond to attract the birdlife. Jefferswood offers peaceful accommodation 20 minutes from Blenheim. Sandra serves a gourmet breakfast in the dining room or alfresco on the verandah, and will provide picnic hampers and barbecues by arrangement. Pre-dinner wine and nibbles are served in the evening, and restaurants are 15 minutes' drive away. Guest enjoy picnicking under the native totara trees or beside the pond.

Facilities
- 1 super-king/twin & 1 queen ensuite bedroom
- double showers, hair dryers, heated towel rails, demist mirrors, toiletries, bathrobes
- cotton bed linen; fresh flowers
- underfloor heating
- wheelchair access; wake-up calls
- complimentary laundry
- solar-heated hot water
- gourmet breakfast
- picnic hampers, BBQ & dinner on request
- complimentary wine & nibbles
- home baking; kitchen available
- lounge with gas fire, daily newspaper, music centre, tea/coffee, books & games
- email, fax & phone available
- garaging; courtesy transfer

Activities available
- picnicking, bird-watching & 2ha arboretum, on site
- jogging local trails with host; local bush walks
- private farms, wineries, gardens & scenic day tours; guide available
- landing strip nearby; airport, 15-min drive
- arts & crafts; horse riding
- Havelock marina; golf
- restaurants, cafés & shopping in Havelock/Blenheim, 15–20 mins
- Marlborough Sounds for fishing, walks, boating, touring, kayaking
- trout fishing; guide available
- Gold-mining at Wakamarina
- Queen Charolotte Track
- whale watching arranged
- Picton, 50-min drive; Nelson City, 1¼-hour drive

303

© Friars' Guide to New Zealand Accommodation for the Discerning Traveller

HAVELOCK, MARLBOROUGH SOUNDS
PELORUS LODGE

General Manager Tim Smith

Clive Street, Havelock, Marlborough Sounds *Phone* 0-3-574 2999
Postal P O Box 9304, Wellington *Fax* 0-4-385 3175
Email service@peloruslodge.com *Website* www.peloruslodge.com

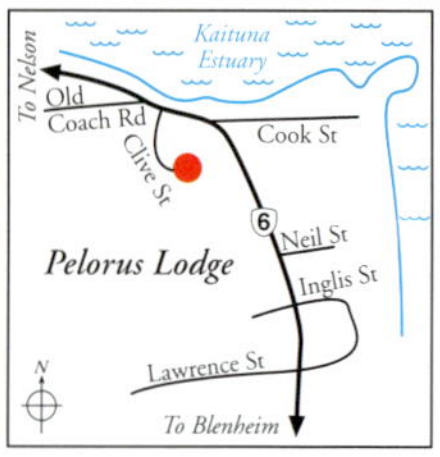

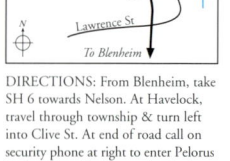

| 4 bdrm | 4 enst | **Room rate** $2,250–$2,700 **Lodge rate** $6,750 | *Includes breakfast, apéritifs, dinner & luncheon cruise* |

DIRECTIONS: From Blenheim, take SH 6 towards Nelson. At Havelock, travel through township & turn left into Clive St. At end of road call on security phone at right to enter Pelorus Lodge. Cross ford & travel to Lodge.

Ensconced within 12 hectares (30 acres) of grounds, overlooking Havelock Marina and the Marlborough Sounds, is Pelorus Lodge, completed in 2002. A Mercedes ML320 will transport guests to the entrance, through the security gates, across the waterfall to the seclusion of the lodge. Inside, the focal point of the spacious conservatory is a ceiling height waterfall, tumbling over rocks. Personally designed five-course dinner, with Pacific Rim cuisine, is served in the adjacent dining room with panoramic views of the Sounds. Downstairs is a separate guest lounge separating two of the ensuite bedrooms. A luncheon cruise on the 14-metre (42-foot) *Lady Karita*, built in 1939, is included in the tariff. Exclusive use of the Lodge is available.

Facilities
- Pelorus: king ensuite bedroom, spa bath, dressing room, TV
- Forest: super-king bedroom, ensuite & hydrotherapy spa bath
- Rewarewa: queen bedroom, ensuite includes spa bath
- Rata: queen bedroom with TV & private bathroom
- Egyptian cotton bed linen, safe, phone, fridge & tea/coffee; toiletries, heated towel rails & bathrobes
- breakfast served in conservatory
- 5-course gourmet dinner
- complimentary cocktail hour
- luncheon included on cruise
- 2 guest lounges with open fire, tea/coffee, Sky TV & video
- business centre available
- complimentary laundry
- courtesy transfer; security system
- on-site parking; helipad nearby

Activities available
- sauna on site
- 2ha of native planting on site with waterfall
- garden walks
- complimentary 5-hr launch cruise & seafood luncheon
- honeymoons catered for
- barbecue available
- fishing tours
- gold-mining
- cafés for lunch within walking distance
- scenic drives
- museum; wineries
- Havelock shops & township, within walking distance
- airport, 20-min drive
- Blenheim, 25-min drive
- Picton ferries, 45-min drive
- Nelson, 45-min drive

Above: The waterfall tumbles down the garden, over the driveway and into the pool, in the peaceful two-hectare setting.
Below: Pelorus Lodge overlooks the marina where *Lady Karita* is moored, awaiting guests for their luncheon cruise in the Sounds.
Opposite top: The spacious dining room and upstairs guest lounge provide panoramic views of the Marlborough Sounds.
Opposite bottom left: The upstairs Pelorus guestroom includes a king-size bed, with dressing room, ensuite and sea views.
Opposite bottom right: Dining is a highlight at Pelorus Lodge with resident chef providing Pacific Rim cuisine and fine wine.

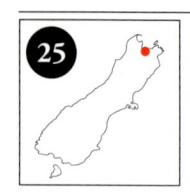

RAI VALLEY, MARLBOROUGH SOUNDS
MUDBRICK LODGE

Hosts Tania and Shorty Shand

150 Rimu Gully Road, Rai Valley   *Postal* P O Box 92, Rai Valley, Marlborough
Phone 0-3-571 6147   *Mobile* 027 251 3867   *Fax* 0-3-571 6147
Email tania@mudbricklodge.co.nz   *Website* www.mudbricklodge.co.nz

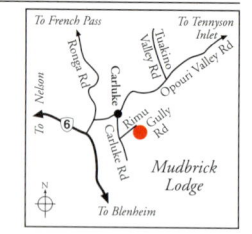

3 bdrm | 3 enst | 1 pdrm
Double $195–$250
Single $150
Includes breakfast
Lunch & dinner extra

DIRECTIONS: From Blenheim, take SH 6 towards Nelson. Turn right towards French Pass. Take 1st right over bridge, then right into Carluke Rd. Take 1st left into Rimu Gully Rd. Travel to end to Mudbrick Lodge.

Constructed from mudbricks and macrocarpa in 1996, Mudbrick Lodge is located in a secluded 400-hectare (1,000-acre) valley. Set in almost two hectares (four acres) of landscaped gardens, the separate guest accommodation comprises two ensuite bedrooms upstairs and a deluxe guestroom downstairs opening to a verandah. Guests are welcome to relax in the garden or become actively involved in personally guided experiences with Shorty, hunting, fishing, diving, horse trekking or following wine and art trails. Tania is a professional chef who serves full cooked breakfasts, including home-made preserves, in the conservatory, homestead, garden or room service. She is happy to prepare lunch and dinner to a personalised menu too.

Facilities
- 2 super-king/twin ensuite bedrooms upstairs
- 1 super-king/twin ensuite bedroom with bath, wheelchair access & verandah downstairs
- percale bed linen, Egyptian cotton towels & down duvets
- tea/coffee, mineral water, phone & writing desk in bedrooms
- hair dryers & toiletries
- wheelchair access
- full breakfast indoors, in conservatory or alfresco
- picnic or light lunch, $25 pp
- 3-course dinner, $50 pp
- licensed; fresh flowers
- lounge with open fire, Sky TV, DVD, CDs & bar
- children welcome
- phone, fax, email; laundry
- on-site parking; helipad

Activities available
- BBQ on site
- pet dog, cats, pigs & chickens on site
- fly fishing at end of driveway
- native bush walks
- guided hunting
- fly & salt-water fishing
- scuba & free diving
- sea kayaking
- wine trails
- horse treks; golf courses
- historic gold trails
- art & craft trails
- guided tramping
- Queen Charlotte track
- Abel Tasman National Park
- Havelock, 20-min drive
- Okiwi Bay & Duncan Bay, 20-min drive
- Blenheim & Nelson, 40 mins

© Friars' Guide to New Zealand Accommodation for the Discerning Traveller

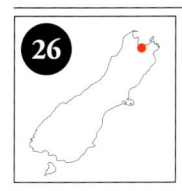

NELSON
RETIRO FARM LODGE

Hosts Robbert de Jongh and Victor Flores

152 Teal Valley, R D 1, Nelson
Phone 0-3-545 0118 *Email* info@retirofarmlodge.co.nz
Website www.retirofarmlodge.co.nz

3 bdrm | 2 enst | 1 prbth

Double $195–$275
Single $135

Includes breakfast
Lunch & dinner extra

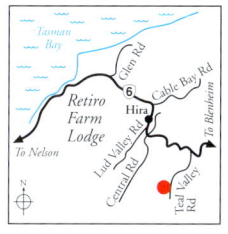

DIRECTIONS: Take SH 6 from Picton or Blenheim towards Nelson, or from city, travel 14km north. Turn south into Teal Valley Rd. Travel 1.4km to private road & continue 200m to Retiro Farm Lodge on right.

Set in a peaceful valley 15 minutes from Nelson City, Retiro Farm Lodge (*see centre of photo above*) offers guests a quiet get-away with rural views. Spanish for "retreat", Retiro Farm Lodge provides a spacious converted barn as well as accommodation in the Lodge. Victor, a trained chef, serves breakfast in the dining room, or alfresco in the vine-clad courtyard opening to the large garden, and he will also provide a picnic basket and dinner by arrangement. Guests can enjoy relaxing in the extensive garden setting and view the resident llamas and donkeys. There are walking tracks throughout the almond and olive groves on site to the new vineyard. Cable Bay, a popular attraction, is just 12 kilometres away for kayaking and visiting local crafts and artists.

Facilities

- 1 queen ensuite bedroom & 1 double bedroom with 1 private bathroom in Lodge
- 1 queen ensuite bedroom & kitchenette in converted barn
- toiletries & heated towel rails in all 3 bathrooms; 2 baths
- bathrobes, cotton bed linen & fresh flowers in bedrooms
- fridge & tea/coffee in bedrooms, opening to balconies

- English/continental breakfast
- lunch or lunch baskets, extra
- 3-course à la carte dinner with wine, $50–$60 pp; licensed
- kitchenette in Lodge & lounge with open fire, bar, Sky TV, CD-player, artwork & books
- phone, email & laundry
- Dutch & Spanish spoken
- courtesy transfer; parking

Activities available

- swimming pool & BBQ on site
- pets, donkeys & llamas on site
- walks on site through olive & almond groves & boutique vineyard
- Nina Davis & Living Earth potteries, short drive
- Happy Valley 4WD adventures & flying fox, 6km
- horse treks

- restaurants, 14km
- Cable Bay, 12km
  – kayaking
  – local artists
  – scenic & estuary walks
  – David Haig Furniture
- gardens open to visit
- Nelson City, 15-mins south
- Picton ferries, 1¾-hr drive
- Nelson Lakes, Kahurangi & Abel Tasman national parks

307

© Friars' Guide to New Zealand Accommodation for *the Discerning Traveller*

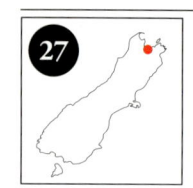

NELSON CITY
MURITAI MANOR

Hosts Jan and Stan Holt

48 Wakapuaka Road, Wakapuaka, R D 1, Nelson *Mobile* 025 370 622
Freephone 0800 260 662 *Phone* 0-3-545 1189 *Fax* 0-3-545 0740
Email muritai.manor@xtra.co.nz *Website* www.muritaimanor.co.nz

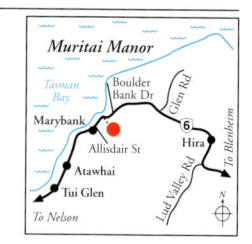

| 5 bdrm | 5 enst | Double $190–$230
Single $150–$195 | *Includes breakfast*
Off-peak rates available | *Dinner extra* |

DIRECTIONS: Take SH 6 from Picton or Blenheim towards Nelson. At Wakapuaka, 5 mins north of city, Muritai Manor well signposted on left. (Signs illuminated at night.) From Nelson, take SH 6 past Atawhai.

This Edwardian colonial house, built in 1903 for the local archdeacon, was renovated by Jan and Stan in 1997, the new extensions blending with the original style. Muritai means "sea breeze" in Maori, referring to its setting above the ocean. Sited just five minutes north of Nelson on a north-west facing elevation, Muritai Manor looks across Tasman Bay to Abel Tasman National Park in the distance. Guests have the choice of five ensuite bedrooms furnished with antiques, and can enjoy the outdoor facilities, including the heated swimming pool, spa and croquet lawn. Flower beds line the driveway and mature English oaks and lime trees provide summer shade and autumn colour. Jess, Gennie, Dande and Flora are the four canine family members.

Facilities
- 2 king/twin, 1 king & 2 queen ensuite bedrooms
- 5 ensuites, 2 with baths
- toiletries & heated towel rails
- cotton bed linen & electric blankets
- antiques; fresh flowers
- all rooms serviced daily
- guest balconies; sea views
- laundry available
- cooked or continental breakfast in dining room
- lunch or dinner by request, $30–$75 pp
- tea/coffee facilities & TV
- guest lounge with open fire
- children by arrangement
- phone, fax & email available
- guest parking for 5 cars
- airport or bus depot transfer

Activities available
- solar-heated swimming pool
- Nelson restaurants 5-min drive
- spa pool, robes provided
- BBQ available
- croquet lawn on site
- pétanque/boules on site
- public Japanese stroll garden, 5-min drive away
- vineyards
- arts & crafts
- Nelson City, 5-min drive
- horse riding; golf
- gardens open to visit
- fishing
- Nelson Lakes
- skiing in winter
- 3 National Parks – Abel Tasman, Kahurangi & Nelson Lakes
- Picton ferry, 2-hour drive

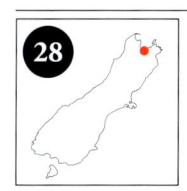

Nelson City
California House Inn

Hosts Janice and Ray Evans

29 Collingwood Street, Nelson
Phone 0-3-548 4173   *Email* info@californiahouse.co.nz
Fax 0-3-548 4184   *Website* www.californiahouse.co.nz

Room rate $185–$260   *Includes breakfast*
Packed lunches & dinner extra

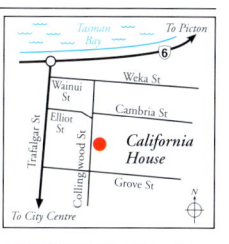

| 6 bdrm | 6 enst |

DIRECTIONS: Take SH 6 to Nelson roundabout & turn into Trafalgar St towards City Centre. Turn 1st left into Wainui St, then 1st right into Collingwood St. California House Inn on left. (1-min drive from City Centre.)

Built as a large family home in 1893, for Albert Everett, this Victorian villa has been recently renovated and refurbished. Original features include the impressive English oak-panelled entrance hall, open fireplaces with carved kauri surrounds, and 24 stained-glass windows including the central skylight that gives a sense of spaciousness to the house. Native timbers, colonial furnishings and fine English antiques feature throughout, with books and photographs from the early 1900s. Sunny verandahs offer relaxation in the quiet garden setting. Janice's speciality breakfasts are a highlight and may include home-made Bircher muesli, smoked salmon crepes, mushroom and spinach frittata or French toast with manuka dry-cured bacon, bananas and maple syrup.

Facilities

- 1 king, 1 twin & 4 queen bedrooms, each with ensuite, 2 with baths
- heated towel rails, hair dryers, locally hand-made toiletries
- winter heating & electric blankets; quality bed linen
- hi-speed internet access, tea/coffee, chocolates & fresh flowers in bedrooms
- fluent French spoken
- full breakfast served; gourmet packed lunches & dinner, extra
- guest sitting room with wood-burning stove, desk, grand piano, library & wine
- computer, fax, TV/DVD/VCR & laundry service available
- guest fridge; guest parking
- activity planning assistance
- all trips collect from door

Activities available

- short walk from house to:
  – City Centre, cinema
  – restaurants, cafés, shops
  – arts & crafts galleries
  – WOW Trafalgar Centre
  – geographical centre of NZ
- running, walking or biking on Matai riverside path
- Saturday morning market
- 3 golf courses; gear hire
- river & ocean fishing
- vineyard & Macs Brewery tours
- Abel Tasman kayaking & walks
- yacht cruising & sail racing
- public parks & gardens
- Tahunanui Beach, 5-min drive
- scuba diving base, 5-min drive
- airport, 15-min drive
- interisland ferries, 1¾ hours
- 3 National Parks, within 1½-hour drive away

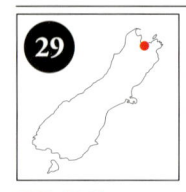

Nelson City
Riverside Apartment

Hosts Alison Phillips and Robin White

Riverside, Nelson   *Postal* 45 Collingwood Street, Nelson
Phone 0-3-548 9418   *Mobile* 025 678 1170   *Fax* 0-3-548 9418
Email waimarie.motel@xtra.co.nz   *Website* friars.co.nz/hosts/riverside.html

2 bdrm	1 prbth	1 pdrm	Apartment rate $150–$200 for 2 persons	*Self-catering*	*Breakfast extra*
			Extra persons $25 each	Corporate & long-stay rates available	

DIRECTIONS: From SH 6, turn left into Trafalgar St. Turn left into Halifax St & continue into Riverside. Apartment 1st on left. From airport take Wakefield Quay into Haven Rd. Turn left into Halifax St.

Overlooking the Maitai River, Riverside Apartment provides peace and quiet, just one block from the City Centre. This self-contained apartment includes a full kitchen for self-catering, with a terrace opening from the lounge where guests enjoy alfresco dining above the river, close enough to see trout jumping! Native birds such as the tui, heron and kingfisher feed on the river, and there is a formed walkway along the riverside. Upstairs in the apartment is a queen-size bedroom and bathroom, and downstairs are a twin bedroom and powder room. There are many restaurants a few minutes' walk away, and a heated swimming pool, sauna and gym are a 200-metre walk along Riverside.

Facilities
- 1 self-contained apartment for one-party bookings only
- 1 queen bedroom upstairs & 1 twin bedroom downstairs share upstairs bathroom
- bath, hair dryer & toiletries
- TV & phone in queen bedroom, opens to balcony
- cotton bed linen
- double sofa-bed & TV in downstairs lounge opening to verandah
- continental breakfast on request, extra, in 6-seater dining room or alfresco on terrace overlooking river
- full self-catering kitchen with phone
- fresh flowers; powder room
- laundry available
- children under 10 years, by arrangement
- off-street parking; 1-car garage

Activities available
- bird-watching from site
- Maitai River access from site for fishing, walkway, native birds
- heated swimming pool, sauna & gym, 200m walk
- Within 5–10-min walk:
  – pottery, craft & art galleries
  – Nelson Cathedral
  – Nelson School of Music
  – restaurants, cafés & shopping
  – Queens Gardens
  – Suter Art Gallery
  – Saturday craft & produce market
  – movie theatre
  – Maitai River walkway
  – track to centre of NZ lookout
- 3 golf courses, 10–20-min drive
- sailing, kayaking
- wineries, beaches, fishing
- airport, 15-min drive
- Abel Tasman National Park, 1hr
- interisland ferries, 2-hr drive

© Friars' Guide to New Zealand Accommodation for the Discerning Traveller

NELSON CITY
SUSSEX HOUSE BED & BREAKFAST

Hosts Vikki and David Los

238 Bridge Street, Nelson   *Phone* 0-3-548 9972
Freephone 0800 868 687   *Mobile* 027 478 4846   *Fax* 0-3-548 9975
Email reservations@sussex.co.nz   *Website* www.sussex.co.nz

| 5 bdrm | 4 enst | 1 prbth |

Double $120–$150
Single $100–$130

Includes continental breakfast

DIRECTIONS: Take SH 6 to Nelson roundabout & turn into Trafalgar St towards City Centre. Turn left into Bridge St, to Sussex House on right. From Richmond, follow sign "City via Hospital" & turn right into Bridge St.

Built circa 1880, Sussex House is one of Nelson's original homes, which was retained in the same family for three generations. Now fully restored, this historic home offers three sunny ensuite rooms, Strauss, Mozart, and Brahms upstairs and Beethoven with a private bathroom. Downstairs is Schubert with its wheelchair access ensuite, as well as the guest lounge/dining room where breakfast is served. The continental buffet includes fresh fruit, cereals, yoghurts, croissants, muffins and cheeses. All rooms have access to the sunny verandahs, and tea and coffee facilities are provided on both floors. Sussex House is set in an English-style garden adjacent to the Maitai River, yet within walking distance of the centre of Nelson and its restaurants.

Facilities

- 1 queen/twin & 2 queen ensuite bedrooms
- 1 queen/twin bedroom with private bathroom & robes
- 1 queen/twin ensuite bedroom with wheelchair access
- cotton bed linen, writing desk, TV & iron in bedrooms
- hair dryers, toiletries & heated towel rails
- tea/coffee on landing
- continental breakfast buffet with muffins, croissants, yoghurts, cheeses, fruit
- guest lounge with open fire, tea/coffee, port, phone, CDs, piano, books & writing desk
- upstairs guest balcony
- laundry available, $5
- email, & fax, $5
- marmalade cat Riley on site

Activities available

- piano for guest use
- swimming in river holes
- river, bush & hill walks
- river & ocean fishing
- kayaking
- arts & crafts trail
- vineyard trail
- Saturday markets
- golf course, 6km away
- local concerts
- restaurants, 5-min walk
- glass-blowing studios
- gardens open to visit
- Tahunanui Beach, 7 mins
- Abel Tasman walks
- Nelson Centre, 500 metres
- airport, 15-min drive
- National Parks
- interisland ferries at Picton, 1¾-hour drive away

311

© Friars' Guide to New Zealand Accommodation for the Discerning Traveller

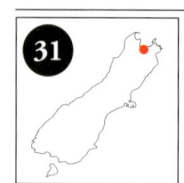

NELSON CITY
THE BAYWICK INN

Hosts Janet Southwick and Tim Bayley

51 Domett Street, Nelson
Phone 0-3-545 6514   Mobile 027 454 5823   Fax 0-3-545 6517
Email baywicks@iconz.co.nz   Website www.baywicks.com

| 3 bdrm | 2 enst | 1 prbth |

Double $135–$155
Single $105–$120

Includes breakfast
Dinner extra

DIRECTIONS: From Picton or Christchurch, take SH 6 to Nelson. Turn left into Trafalgar St. Turn left again into Hardy St & continue to river. Turn right into Domett St. The Baywick Inn on right.

Overlooking Maitai River and bordering Brook Stream, this restored Victorian villa was built in 1885 and features native rimu panelling and tiled carved fireplaces. Guest accommodation comprises three spacious upstairs bedrooms: Parkdale, named after Janet's Toronto neighbourhood, includes a sunroom; Burnside, the original name of the house, has its own balcony; and Greenwood with river views. Guests enjoy the private garden beside the Brook where they can feed eels, trout and ducks. Janet, a chef by profession, serves gourmet breakfasts in the sunny dining room, and her menu includes fresh fruit salad, toasted pecan muesli, and smoked salmon or other speciality omelettes. The Baywick is also home to Mombozzie, the wire-haired fox terrier.

Facilities

- Parkdale: 1 queen bedroom with ensuite including claw-foot bath, & sunroom
- Burnside: 1 queen/twin ensuite bedroom with private balcony
- Greenwood: 1 queen bedroom with private bathroom
- bathrobes, toiletries & hair dryer in all 3 bathrooms
- turn-down service, chocolates
- tea/coffee/cappuccino downstairs
- House Special breakfast
- 3-course dinner, with wine, by arrangement, $40–$50 pp
- open fire & complimentary sherry & port in guest lounge
- TV, fresh flowers in bedrooms
- high-speed internet
- off-street parking
- peaceful residential setting
- Canadian/NZ hospitality

Activities available

- City Centre, 5-min walk
- pétanque/boules on site
- feeding wildlife in the Brook
- Tim's classic MGs to view
- Baywick's Wine Cellars showroom on site
- Maitai River walkway
- Polytechnic, walking distance
- wine & arts & crafts trails
- art gallery & gardens
- restaurants & shopping within walking distance
- golf links, 5-min drive
- cathedral; beaches nearby
- sailing & kayaking
- Founders Park
- Centre of NZ trail
- Japanese gardens
- Abel Tasman National Park day trips

© Friars' Guide to New Zealand Accommodation for the Discerning Traveller

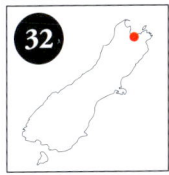

Nelson City
The Little Manor

Hosts Angela Higgins and Christopher Geen

12 Nile Street West, Nelson *Postal* P O Box 767, Nelson
Phone 0-3-545 1411 *Mobile* 021 247 1891 *Fax* 0-3-545 1417
Email the.little.manor@xtra.co.nz *Website* friars.co.nz/hosts/littlemanor.html

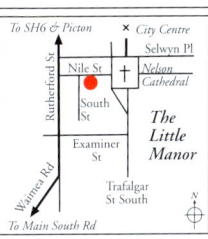

2 bdrm 1 prbth
Cottage rate $195–$240 for 2 persons
Extra persons $45 each
Self-catering
Includes breakfast basket

DIRECTIONS: From SH 6, turn left into Trafalgar St, then right into Halifax St. Turn left into Rutherford St, then left again into Nile St West. The Little Manor is on the right.

The Little Manor is self-contained accommodation set in the historic precinct of inner Nelson. Built in 1863, this colonial Victorian home has been elegantly renovated to provide two upstairs bedrooms, sundeck, and extra sofa-bed in the reading room. The bathroom features a claw-foot bath downstairs. The breakfast basket comprises a fruit bowl, cereals, eggs, bagels, croissants or other fresh breads, home-made jams and sauces. Other meals can be self-catered in the fully equipped kitchen. A dining room, lounge, and full laundry are also downstairs and the spacious entrance hall includes a writing desk. Antiques enhance the quiet old-world ambience.

Facilities
- fully self-contained house
- single-party bookings only
- 1 king & 1 queen bedroom with bathrobes
- 1 bathroom, claw-foot bath, toiletries & hair dryer
- 100% cotton bed linen
- double sofa-bed, magazines in reading room upstairs
- 2 TVs, video & CD-player
- fresh flowers
- private sundeck balcony
- full kitchen for self-catering
- selection of teas & coffees
- breakfast basket & pantry
- open fire & central heating
- phone, fax & writing desk
- complimentary guest laundry, or valet service
- masseuse & hairdresser available, by arrangement

Activities available
- City Centre, 2-min walk
- Nelson Cathedral, 2-min walk
- award-winning restaurants & cafés, 2–3-min walk
- shopping, 3-min walk
- golf courses, 10–20-min drive
- harbour cruises & watersports
- art galleries & pottery studios
- local markets
- parks & public gardens to visit
- private gardens open to visit
- wineries
- 4WD biking in native NZ forest
- trout & sea fishing
- Tahunanui & Kaiteriteri Beaches
- Golden Bay cruises
- Nelson Lakes – walks, skiing
- Abel Tasman & Kahurangi National Parks
- airport, 12-min drive

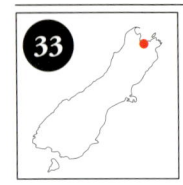

NELSON CITY
SouthHaven

Hosts Jeanette and Peter Hancock   *Mobile* 025 363 858

2B South Street, Nelson   *Email* info@cottageaccommodation.co.nz
Postal Pomona Road, Ruby Bay, R D 1, Upper Moutere, Nelson
Phone 0-3-540 2769   *Fax* 0-3-540 2769   *Website* www.cottageaccommodation.co.nz

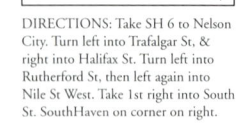

| 2 bdrm | 1 enst | 1 prbth | Apartment rate $190–$210
Extra persons $35 each | *Includes breakfast provisions*
2-night minimum stay on weekends & public holidays | *Self-catering* |

DIRECTIONS: Take SH 6 to Nelson City. Turn left into Trafalgar St, & right into Halifax St. Turn left into Rutherford St, then left again into Nile St West. Take 1st right into South St. SouthHaven on corner on right.

SouthHaven was built in 1998 atop the corner of historic South Street, the oldest fully preserved street in New Zealand. This two-storey self-contained townhouse is sited overlooking the street, with French doors opening from the lounge on to the spacious garden balcony for alfresco dining. From here the spire of Trafalgar Cathedral can be seen and its carillon bells enjoyed. The well-equipped rimu kitchen is designed for self-catering for single-party bookings. The spacious main bedroom is upstairs, with queen-size bed, ensuite, television and chaise longue. A second double bedroom below has a separate toilet. Within minutes of SouthHaven, guests can wander through art and craft galleries or dine at award-winning restaurants and cafés.

Facilities
- single-party bookings only
- 1 queen ensuite bedroom
- 1 double bedroom & toilet
- TV, phone & chaise longue in upstairs queen bedroom
- cotton bed linen, hair dryers, bathrobes, toiletries
- fresh flowers
- self-serve laundry
- secure garaging
- breakfast provisions, including cereals, eggs, bread, home-made jams, teas & plunger coffee
- full kitchen for self-catering
- balcony suitable for alfresco dining overlooking street
- living room with gas fire, Sky TV, video, CD-player, music, games, phone, fax & writing table

Activities available
- relaxing on spacious balcony
- award-winning restaurants, cafés & wine bars, 2-min walk
- pottery & craft galleries
- shopping; theatres
- Nelson Cathedral
- golf courses; trout fishing
- mountain climbing; hiking
- Miyazu Japanese Gardens
- Queens Gardens
- City Centre, 3-min walk
- private garden tours
- Maitai River walks
- wine tours; glass blowing
- golden beaches; safe swimming
- sailing; kayaking; windsurfing
- heritage trail; Nelson Lakes
- 3 National Parks, 1-hr drive
- Nelson airport, 10-min drive
- interisland ferries, 1¾ hours

© Friars' Guide to New Zealand Accommodation for the Discerning Traveller

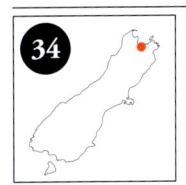

NELSON CITY
SOUTH STREET COTTAGES

Hosts Jeanette and Peter Hancock   *Mobile* 025 363 858

1, 3 and 12 South Street, Nelson   *Website* cottageaccommodation.co.nz
Postal Pomona Road, Ruby Bay, R D 1, Upper Moutere   *Fax* 0-3-540 2769
Phone 0-3-540 2769   *Email* info@cottageaccommodation.co.nz

6 bdrm 3 enst   Cottage rate $160–$175 for 2 persons   *Includes breakfast provisions*   *Self-catering*
Extra adults $30 each   Children $15 each   2-night minimum stay on weekends

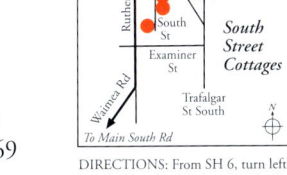

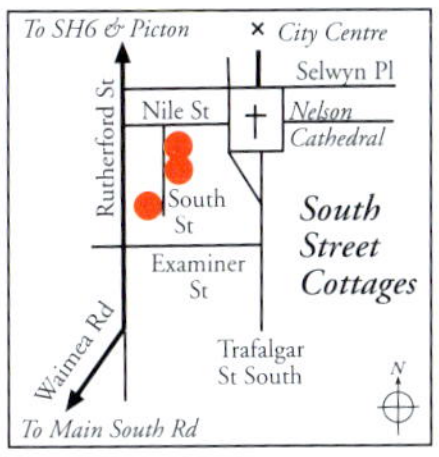

DIRECTIONS: From SH 6, turn left into Trafalgar St, right into Halifax St, then left into Rutherford St. Turn left into Nile St West, then 1st right into South St. Biddle & Dillon Cottages on left, & Briar Cottage at end on right.

Biddle, Dillon and Briar Cottages are three of the restored residences in historic South Street, the oldest preserved precinct in New Zealand. These cottages were built around 1864 and are now available for single-party bookings, being self-contained and private, with two double bedrooms in each. Biddle Cottage *(see photographs above)* was named after a local pharmacist who began the restoration work in the 1980s, which Peter and Jeanette completed. Dillon Cottage *(see right below)* is named after Constantine Augustus Dillon who in 1851 bought the town acre which now includes South Street. Briar Cottage *(see left below)* is larger, although it was originally only a two-room cottage, before being transformed briefly into a gallery in the 1970s. Each cottage is designed for guests' independence, with dining room, lounge, fully equipped kitchen and paved garden seating area. Jeanette supplies breakfast provisions, including fresh fruit, home-made jams, bread and eggs, for guests' use.

Facilities
- 3 self-contained cottages:
  – Biddle Cottage (no. 1)
  – Dillon Cottage (no. 3)
  – Briar Cottage (no. 12)
- single-party bookings only in each cottage
- 2-night minimum stay on weekends & public holidays
- fully fenced – children & pets welcome in all 3 cottages
- 2 double bedrooms & fold-down sofa in each cottage
- cotton bed linen
- 1 private bathroom with heater, hair dryer & toiletries in each cottage
- full laundry in each cottage
- breakfast provisions supplied
- full-sized fully equipped kitchen including microwave in each cottage, for self-catering & entertaining
- guest phone, log burner, & dining room in each cottage
- lounge with books, TV, stereo, CDs & tapes in each cottage
- fresh flowers & window boxes in each cottage
- garden courtyard with outdoor furniture & BBQ per cottage
- private independent locations
- historic setting
- quiet cul-de-sac location

Activities available
- relaxing in private cottage garden at each cottage
- restaurants, cafés & wine bars, 2-min walk away
- City Centre, 3-min walk
- pottery & craft galleries in South Street & region
- historic buildings/precinct
- shopping
- theatres
- golf links
- trout-fishing rivers
- private gardens to visit
- Miyazu Japanese Stroll Gardens
- mountains & skiing in winter
- wine trails
- Heritage Trail
- Maitai Valley walks
- Queens Gardens
- swimming; beaches
- sailing; sea kayaking
- skydiving
- caving
- mountain biking
- glass blowing
- arts & crafts trails
- Nelson Lakes
- Abel Tasman National Park day trips

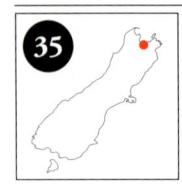

Nelson City
Cathedral Inn

Hosts Judith Nicholas and Joy Nimmo

369 Trafalgar Street South, Nelson
Freephone 0800 883 377   Phone 0-3-548 7369   Fax 0-3-548 0369
Email info@cathedralinn.co.nz   *Website* cathedralinn.co.nz

Double $190–$240
Single $165–$180

Includes breakfast
House rate available

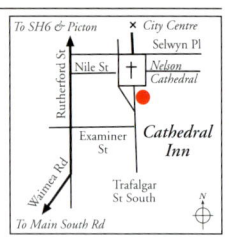

7 bdrm   7 enst

DIRECTIONS: From Picton, travel into City. Take Rutherford St, then turn left into Examiner St. Turn left into Trafalgar St. Cathedral Inn up driveway on right. From south, turn right into Examiner St, then as above.

Set on a rise at the edge of the Cathedral gardens, the Cathedral Inn was once the home of Bishop Andrew Suter, founder of the City's art gallery. Located in the quiet residential heart of the City, the 130-year-old building has been sensitively restored. The broad staircase takes guests to seven sunny bedrooms upstairs, each with fresh flowers, writing desk and ensuite. Refreshments and ironing facilities are provided. Below are the living areas, including the spacious dining and living room with open fireplace, drinks cabinet and writing desk. This opens to a covered terrace and sunny courtyard where guests enjoy socialising in summer. Full breakfasts feature fresh local produce, home-made baking and a cooked speciality daily, with dietary requests catered for.

Facilities

- Superior: 4 king/twin, 1 queen
  Standard: 1 queen, 1 twin
  all ensuite bedrooms
- 7 ensuite bathrooms – bathrobes, toiletries, heated towel rails
- desk, TV, direct dial phone, tea/coffee, electric blankets, hair dryer, fresh flowers & home-made chocolates in all bedrooms
- under-carpet heating, open fires
- books, magazines, periodicals
- full breakfast options
- complimentary sherry, port, chocolates, cookies & tea/coffee-making facilities
- fax & email facilities, & computer ports available
- guest luggage elevator; all rooms fully serviced daily
- covered terrace & private courtyard with table & chairs
- 6 guest carparks

Activities available

- outdoor spa pool/hot tub for guest use on site
- Nelson City, easy 4-min walk
- art galleries, cinemas, shopping, restaurants & cafés within walking distance
- Saturday craft/produce market
- public Japanese stroll gardens, 5-min drive away
- wine trail
- arts & crafts trails
- trout fishing; hunting
- range of adventure activities
- horse trekking
- kayaking; beaches
- watersports
- private gardens open to visit
- 3 golf courses, 10–20-min drive
- 3 National Parks, 1-hr drive
- winter skiing, 1½-hour drive

© Friars' Guide to New Zealand Accommodation for the Discerning Traveller

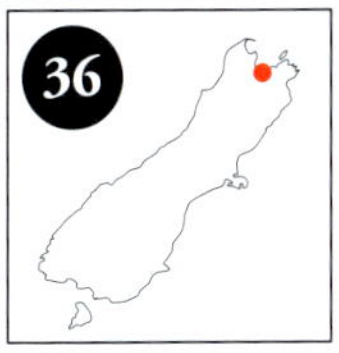

Nelson City
Shelbourne Villa

Hosts Val and Wayne Ballantyne

21 Shelbourne Street, Nelson
Phone 0-3-545 9059   *Email* beds@shelbournevilla.co.nz
Fax 0-3-546 7248   *Website* www.shelbournevilla.co.nz

| 4 bdrm | 4 enst | Double $195–$250 Single $175–$230 | *Includes breakfast* *Self-catering apartment* |

DIRECTIONS: Take SH 6 to Nelson. Turn into Trafalgar St. At "T" junction, turn left into Selwyn Pl. Take 1st right into Trafalgar Sq. Turn 1st left into Nile St East & 1st right into Shelbourne St. Villa on left.

Shelbourne Villa is in a quiet suburban location, yet within five minutes' walk of the City Centre. Originally built in 1929, this classic villa has been refurbished, still in New Zealand style, and is set in an English-style garden with separate seating areas including a terrace with small pond and waterfall. Accommodation comprises four guestrooms: the Master Suite, Newby Suite, Super-king Loft, and self-contained apartment with patio seating. The continental breakfast menu includes European pastries, cereals, yoghurt, sliced fresh fruit, and freshly squeezed fruit juice blends. Cooked breakfast options are also available by request. Coffees, teas and baked goodies are available in the guest lounge, and the apartment has a kitchenette for self-catering.

Facilities
- 1 king-size ensuite apartment with full kitchenette for self-catering
- 2 king ensuite bedrooms
- 1 super-king ensuite loft with deck
- hair dryers, curling irons, heated towel rails, toiletries, 2 double basins
- phone, writing desk, cotton bed linen & bathrobes in all bedrooms
- TV in all bedrooms; fresh flowers
- 2 verandahs overlooking garden
- continental breakfast, or cooked by request
- tea/coffee & baking available
- complimentary apéritifs
- TV, VCR & CDs in lounge
- heating & air-conditioning
- laundry, fax/email available
- off-street parking
- children over 11 yrs in aptmt.
- courtesy passenger transfer

Activities available
- seating areas in gardens for reading, lounging & relaxing
- craft studios
- cinemas in walking distance
- cafés & restaurants, short walk
- city shopping, 5-min walk
- Cathedral & churches
- Nelson School of Music
- Queens Gardens
- Suter Art Gallery
- Maitai River walks close by
- Grampian Trail nearby
- trail to centre of New Zealand within 5-min walk
- full exercise facility, 5 mins
- Tahuna Beach
- Stonehurst Farm horse treks
- Höglund glass blowing
- wineries
- tour planning, extra charge

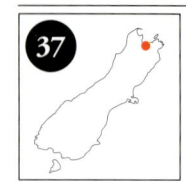

Nelson City
Grampian Villa

Hosts Jo and John Fitzwater

209 Collingwood Street, Nelson *Mobile* 021 459 736
Phone 0-3-545 8209   *Email* stayinnelson@grampianvilla.co.nz
Fax 0-3-548 5783   *Website* www.grampianvilla.co.nz

| 4 bdrm | 4 enst |

Double $195–$295
Single $150–$275

Includes breakfast
Dinner extra

DIRECTIONS: Take SH 6 to Nelson roundabout & turn into Trafalgar St. Turn 1st left into Wainui St, then 1st right into Collingwood St. Cross bridge & continue to Grampian Villa on left, on corner of Bronte St.

Originally built in 1895 for a pioneer family, this two-storey Victorian villa was the home of Frederick G. Gibbs, Nelson botanist and arts supporter. Located on a tree-lined street on the lower slopes of The Grampian hills, the villa is five minutes' walk to the City Centre. The spacious guestrooms have French doors opening to verandahs with views to the city and sea. An open fire warms the guest lounge during winter evenings. Native timbers are used extensively in panelled doors, polished floors, carved fireplaces, stair bannister and entranceway. John and Jo serve a healthy gourmet breakfast of freshly baked croissants and local produce on the verandah or in the guest dining room overlooking the English garden. Dinner is also available by arrangement.

Facilities

- 2 super-king ensuite bedrooms upstairs, each with twin shower-heads & walk-in wardrobe; 1 with bidet & balcony
- 1 super-king ensuite bedroom downstairs with verandah
- 1 queen ensuite bedroom downstairs with claw-foot bath
- bathrobes, toiletries & hair dryers in all bathrooms
- tea/coffee, port & cookies
- gourmet breakfasts in dining room or alfresco on verandah
- dinner by arrangement, extra
- Sky TV, VCR, DVD, CDs, movies & open fire in lounge
- quality linen, phone, TV & writing desk in bedrooms
- fax & computer available; wireless broadband internet access thoughout house
- off-street under-cover

Activities available

- garden on site
- City Centre, 5-min walk
- range of restaurants, cafés & wine bars, easy walk
- Grampian, Centre of NZ & Maitai Walkways nearby
- Fairfield Park/Melrose House
- arts & crafts galleries within walking distance
- wine tours of Nelson
- Saturday market
- Höglund glass blowing studio
- World of Wearable Arts
- range of motorcycles to hire
- horse trekking; kayaking
- cathedral, churches & School of Music, within 5-min walk
- full exercise facility, 5 mins
- 3 golf courses; polytechnic
- airport, 12-min drive

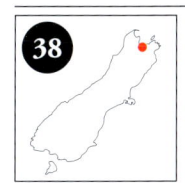

NELSON CITY
WARWICK HOUSE

Hosts Jenny and Nick Ferrier

64 Brougham Street, Nelson *Mobile* 021 688 243
Freephone 0800 022 233 *Phone* 0-3-548 3164 *Fax* 0-3-548 3215
Email enquiries@warwickhouse.co.nz *Website* www.warwickhouse.co.nz

Room rate $180–$350
Guest wing rate $1,200

Includes breakfast
Lunch & dinner extra

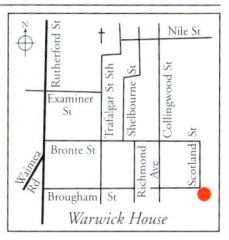

3 bdrm | 2 enst | 1 prbth

DIRECTIONS: Take SH 6 to Nelson roundabout & turn into Trafalgar St. Turn 1st left into Wainui St, then 1st right into Collingwood St. Continue to Brougham St & turn left to Warwick House at end on right.

Designed in Gothic Revivalist style and built in the mid 1800s for Alfred Fell and his family, Warwick House was named after Warwickshire in England, where the Fells emigrated from in 1842. Recently restored to offer guest accommodation in the former ballroom wing, Warwick House retains many original features such as the castle-like four-storey tower and the polished native matai flooring throughout including the sprung dancing floor in the ballroom where meals are now served. Wild game, seafood or Thai specialities are available for evening dining by arrangement, for groups of four or more guests. Set in traditional rose gardens with heritage trees, Warwick House provides garden, rural and city views that extend to the Tasman Sea.

Facilities

- Tower Suite: queen bedroom, ensuite with claw-foot bath, 2-storey octagonal lounge in upper tower & rural views
- Bayview Suite: queen bedroom with private bathroom, large lounge & city & sea views
- Peacock Garden Room: super-king bedroom ensuite with claw-foot bath, rural views & opens to garden
- 2 cooked breakfast options in ballroom, verandah or rooms
- TV, CDs, DVD & open fire in ballroom; lunch & dinner extra
- cotton bed linen, TV, writing desk, fridge, tea/coffee in rooms
- extra single bed for both suites
- bathrobes, toiletries & hair dryers & heated towel rails
- phone, fax & email available
- fresh flowers; verandahs

Activities available

- piano in ballroom for guest use
- BBQ & gardens on site
- bicycles available for guest use
- aromatherapy, massage & reflexology, by arrangement
- walking labrador, Victoria
- Brook & Maitai river walks, 5–10-min walk from site
- Nelson Cathedral, 5-min walk
- bush walks; golf
- Nelson City, 5–10-min walk via riverside "Willowwalk"
- wine tours & art tours
- pottery; galleries
- weekend markets
- sailing; kayaking
- skiing; caving
- trout fishing & fishing tours
- private scenic flights
- Centre of NZ walk

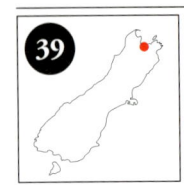

Nelson City
Sunnybank Homestead

Hosts Margaret and Robbie Johnston

156 Nile Street, Nelson
Phone 0-3-548 1971 *Email* relax@sunnybank.co.nz
Fax 0-3-548 1973 *Website* www.sunnybank.co.nz

| 3 bdrm | 2 enst | 1 prbth | Room rate $325 | Includes breakfast | Lunch & dinner extra |

DIRECTIONS: Take SH 6 to Nelson roundabout & turn into Trafalgar St. Turn 1st left into Wainui St, then 1st right into Collingwood St. Continue & turn left into Nile St. Sunnybank on left on corner of Mayroyd Tce.

Located in the heart of Nelson City, Sunnybank Homestead is one of Nelson's protected heritage homes. Originally built circa 1856 and now restored to its Victorian grandeur, Sunnybank offers guests three spacious bedrooms and bathrooms. Sunnybank features original imported marble and slate fireplaces, gilt mirrors and ornate plaster cornices. Margaret is a working artist and her paintings and sculptures are displayed at Sunnybank, along with many antiques and other New Zealand artworks. Set in large gardens, restored and developed, the Homestead provides quality accommodation in a central location, with city shops only 10 minutes' walk away. Margaret serves a leisurely breakfast using fresh local produce.

Facilities

- Annies Room: 1 super-king/twin bedroom with private bathroom & clawfoot bath
- Magnolia & Milner Suites: 1 queen ensuite bedroom in each
- cotton bed linen, phone, TV, tea/coffee & mineral water
- hair dryer, heated towel rails, toiletries & bathrobes
- laundry available, extra
- email & fax facilities available
- continental or cooked breakfast served
- lunch by arrangement, extra
- 3-course dinner with wine, by arrangement, extra
- sitting room upstairs with tea/coffee, fridge & port
- family lounge with Sky TV, video, CD-player & books
- courtesy airport transfer; off-street parking

Activities available

- large gardens & grounds featuring mature trees
- BBQ on sundeck
- honeymoons & small weddings catered for
- walking/running tracks nearby
- Abel Tasman National Park, 1 hr
- local wineries, 15 mins
- many galleries, arts & crafts
- gardens open to visit
- city restaurants & cafés, 10-min walk
- World of Wearable Art museum; Tahuna Beach
- Rainbow Ski-field
- trout fishing
- mountain biking
- City Centre for shopping & cafés, 10-min walk
- airport, 10-min drive

© Friars' Guide to New Zealand Accommodation for the Discerning Traveller

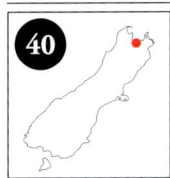

Nelson City
Manuka Cottage

Hosts Alison Phillips and Robin White

3 Manuka Street, Nelson *Postal* 45 Collingwood Street, Nelson
Phone 0-3-548 9418 *Mobile* 025 678 1170 *Email* manukacottage@xtra.co.nz
Fax 0-3-548 9418 *Website* friars.co.nz/hosts/manuka.html

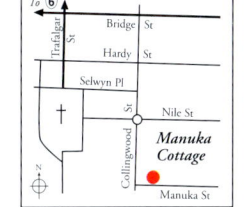

2 bdrm | 1 prbth

Cottage rate $190–$220
Extra persons $30–$40 each

Includes continental breakfast provisions
Corporate & long-stay rates available

Self-catering

DIRECTIONS: Take SH 6 to Nelson roundabout & turn south into Trafalgar St. Travel to cathedral steps & turn left into Selwyn Place. Take 2nd right into Collingwood St & turn left into Manuka St. Cottage on left.

Originally built circa 1890, Manuka Cottage has been restored to provide accommodation in the heart of Nelson City. This historic self-contained cottage still retains the native totara and kauri flooring and now offers a king-size bedroom and private bathroom featuring a claw-foot bath downstairs. Up the spiral staircase is a loft with queen and single beds. A separate living area includes a wood burner and opens to a sundeck and bricked courtyard bordered by a small private cottage garden. A continental breakfast basket is provided for the first morning, and guests enjoy alfresco dining in the sunny courtyard where a gas barbecue is available. A full kitchen enables guests to self-cater, with shops and restaurants just a short walk away.

Facilities
- one-party bookings
- 1 king bedroom downstairs with phone & TV
- 1 queen & 1 single bed in upstairs loft bedroom, access via spiral staircase
- 1 bathroom downstairs including claw-foot bath
- toiletries, hair dryer & heated towel rails in bathroom
- bathrobes; cotton bed linen
- continental breakfast basket supplied for 1st morning
- full kitchen for self-catering
- TV, DVD, CD-player, music, books, nibbles & wood burner in lounge, opening to deck
- phones & fax; self-service laundry
- children under 10 years by arrangement
- bicycle & kayak storage

Activities available
- gas BBQ area in bricked courtyard bordered by private cottage garden
- Within 5–10-min walk:
  – pottery, craft & art galleries
  – Cathedral & School of Music
  – restaurants, cafés & shopping
  – Queens Gardens
  – Suter Art Gallery
  – Saturday craft & produce market
  – movie theatre
  – Maitai River walkway
  – track to centre of NZ lookout
- wineries
- gardens open to visit
- 3 golf courses, 10–20-min drive
- sailing; kayaking
- beaches; fishing
- airport, 15-min drive
- Abel Tasman National Park, 1-hour drive
- interisland ferries, 2 hrs

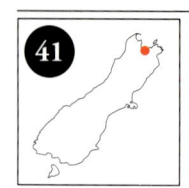

NELSON CITY
LONG LOOKOUT GARDENS

Hosts Yvonne and David Trathen

60 Cleveland Terrace, Nelson
Phone 0-3-548 3617 · Mobile 021 152 3321 · Fax 0-3-548 3127
Email enjoy@longlookoutgardens.co.nz · *Website* www.longlookoutgardens.co.nz

2 bdrm · 2 enst · Room rate $295–$350 · Includes breakfast · Dinner extra

DIRECTIONS: Take SH 6 to Nelson, turn into Trafalgar St, 1st left into Wainui St & 1st right into Collingwood St. Turn left into Nile St. Turn right into Mayroyd Tce & right into Cleveland Tce. Long Lookout on left.

Named in 1866 because of the extensive views across the landscaped garden to Tasman Bay in the distance, Long Lookout Gardens is located in the foothills overlooking Nelson City. This English two-storey residence was originally built in 1864, for J.C. Richmond, a local politician and engineer. The house was rebuilt in 1936 and now offers two ensuite guestrooms, a queen-size downstairs and a super-king/twin upstairs. The classic English interiors include richly coloured fabrics and under-carpet heating. An English-style breakfast is served in the formal dining room, in the kitchen, or alfresco on the patio, and dinner is also available, by prior arrangement. There are many restaurants and cafés within walking distance.

Facilities
- 1 queen ensuite bedroom with bath, downstairs
- 1 super-king/twin ensuite bedroom, upstairs
- cotton bed linen, tea/coffee, mineral water, nibbles, fridge, wine, port & chocolates
- bathrobes, hair dryer, toiletries, heated floor & towel rails
- iron, ironing board & security safe available to guests
- English-style full cooked or continental breakfast
- dinner by request, extra
- vegetarians catered for
- laundry service, $15
- fresh flowers; email, fax & phone available
- private guest entrance
- courtesy passenger transfer
- off-street parking

Activities available
- large (over 0.5ha) garden on site for walking & relaxing
- Nelson City, 10-min walk
- golf course, 5-min drive
- Maitai River walks
- Centre of NZ walk
- fishing charters to Abel Tasman
- wine tours
- private gardens open to visit
- public gardens & parks
- many restaurants, cafés & bars, 10-min walk
- horse trekking
- trout fishing
- sailing
- sea kayaking
- skydiving
- mountain biking
- ski-field, 1½-hour drive
- Picton ferries, 1¾ hours

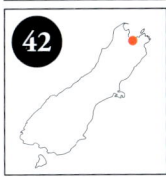

MAITAI VALLEY, NELSON
MAITAI RIVER LODGE

Hosts Cathie and Bob Bowley

14 Ralphine Way, Maitai Valley, Nelson *Phone* 0-3-548 8999
Freephone 0800 MAITAI *Mobile* 021 548 899 *Fax* 0-3-548 3830
Email enquiries@maitai.co.nz *Website* www.maitai.co.nz

5 bdrm 5 enst Room rate $220–$320 Includes breakfast Supper platter extra

DIRECTIONS: Take SH 6 towards Nelson. Turn left into Atawhai Drive. Continue into Milton St. Turn right into Bridge St, left into Tasman St, left into Nile St East & left into Maitai Rd. Turn left into Ralphine Way.

Set in almost a hectare in the Maitai Valley, surrounded by farmland, river flats and native bush, Maitai River Lodge is only three kilometres from Nelson City Centre. There are two spacious bedrooms upstairs opening to the verandah with river views, and three bedrooms downstairs with garden access. Guest safes are provided and separate conference facilities are available. The Lodge is fully hosted and features clay art, paintings and glass art throughout. A breakfast selection is served in the upstairs dining room or alfresco on the verandah, where guests can relax with a glass of wine or supper platter as the sun sets. Guests enjoy soaking under the stars in the therapeutic spa pool. The Newfoundland, Shade, and cat, Pepper, complete the scene.

Facilities

- 3 super-king/twin ensuite bedrooms downstairs, 2 with private garden entrances
- 2 super-king/twin bedrooms upstairs with bathrobes, port, sherry, safe & verandah
- cotton bed linen, writing desk, phone, tea/coffee & mineral water in rooms
- hair dryer, heated towel rails & toiletries in all 5 ensuites
- continental & cooked breakfast
- bottle of wine & nibbles
- supper platter by request, extra
- formal guest lounge downstairs with open log fire, bar, video, TV, DVD, CDs & artwork
- informal lounge upstairs
- email, fax & phone available
- laundry available, extra
- on-site parking

Activities available

- 2 BBQs; 2 mountain bikes
- small conference & wedding venue; honeymoons catered for
- pétanque & croquet
- therapeutic spa pool
- feeding pet lambs & goat
- swimming in river hole opposite
- golf courses; boating
- sea & fly fishing
- 2 National Parks; walking tracks
- restaurants & cafés, 3km
- vineyards & wine tours
- potters & glass blowing
- Wearable Arts festival
- Centre of NZ
- arts & crafts
- 2 ski-fields; 2 lakes
- Nelson Beaches; kayaking
- helicopter scenic tours

323

© Friars' Guide to New Zealand Accommodation for the Discerning Traveller

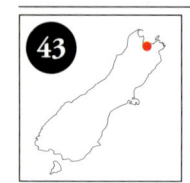

NELSON CITY
HAVEN GUEST HOUSE

Host Mike Gepp

89 Haven Road, Nelson *Phone* 0-3-545 9321
Freephone 0800 446 783   *Mobile* 021 521 501   *Fax* 0-3-545 9320
Email havengh@xtra.co.nz   *Website* www.havenguesthouse.co.nz

9 bdrm | 9 enst

Double $89–$160
Single $75–$95

Includes continental breakfast

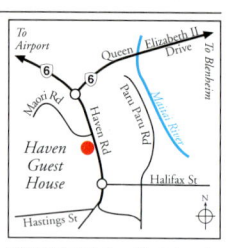

DIRECTIONS: From Blenheim, take SH 6 to Nelson. At 2nd roundabout turn left into Haven Rd. Haven Guest House on right. From south, travel thru Richmond & take SH 6 along waterfront. Veer right into Haven Rd.

Haven Guest House was one of Nelson's earliest homes, built circa 1860 for David Prouting Johnston, the first collector of customs. Originally part of Nelson Haven, the first port in New Zealand, Haven Guest House is located opposite Trafalgar Park where the Wearable Art awards are held. It is just a five-minute walk to the City Centre and also to the beach. Extensive renovations to the two-storey house were undertaken in 2002, which resulted in the provision of nine guestrooms all with ensuite bathrooms. A full continental breakfast buffet is available downstairs in the separate guest dining room each morning, and restaurants and cafés are just a short stroll for lunch and dinner, while a corner pub is just 100 metres away.

Facilities
- 2 king, 4 queen, 2 twin bedrooms & 1 family room
- 9 ensuite bathrooms
- hair dryer, heated towel rails & toiletries in each ensuite
- cotton bed linen
- lockable bedrooms
- writing desk, phone, Sky TV in each bedroom
- children welcome
- full continental buffet breakfast in separate dining room downstairs
- tea/coffee in dining room
- email & fax available
- laundry available
- wheelchair access
- private guest entrance
- historic architecture
- off-street parking

Activities available
- Wearable Art awards opposite
- Saturday market
- arts & crafts
- wineries
- Nelson beaches
- parks; rivers
- golf
- gardens open to visit
- watersports
- restaurants & cafés in City Centre, 5-min walk away
- shopping in City Centre
- Cathedral, 5-min walk
- Centre of NZ, 15-min walk away
- Abel Tasman National Park
- airport, 10-min drive
- Picton ferries, 1¾ hours
- Farewell Spit, 2½ hours

© Friars' Guide to New Zealand Accommodation for the Discerning Traveller

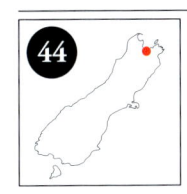

Port Hills, Nelson
Harbour View Apartments

Hosts Penny Adams and John Rowburrey

5 Harbour Terrace, Nelson   *Phone* 0-3-545 7044
Mobile 021 299 4307   *Email* hva@paradise.net.nz
Fax 0-3-548 8420   *Website* www.HarbourViewApartments.co.nz

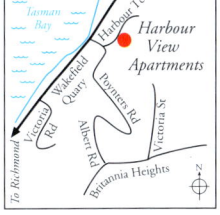

3 bdrm | 2 prbth

Apartment rate $200–$250 for 2 persons
Extra adults $40 each   Children over 5 years $20 each

Self-catering
No meals available

DIRECTIONS: From Nelson City, take Haven Rd (SH 6) into Wakefield Quay. Turn left into Poynters Cres. Turn sharp left into Harbour Tce. Turn right up steep drive to Harbour View Apartments.

Opened in 2003, Harbour View Apartments offer uninterrupted views of Nelson's harbour entrance, known as "The Cut", to Tasman Bay and the Western Ranges beyond. Harbour View comprises two self-contained apartments, the first with one bedroom and the second with two. Both apartments include spacious living areas which open onto large decks edged with glass balustrades. Guests can also enjoy the views from the private outdoor spa pool beneath a maple tree. Contemporary furnishings and Persian rugs complement the native rimu hardwood flooring. The fully equipped kitchen in each apartment enables guests to self-cater, or they can dine at restaurants only a few minutes' walk along Nelson's waterfront.

Facilities
- single-party bookings
- 2 self-contained apartments
- 1st apartment: 1 queen bedroom
- 2nd apartment: 1 queen & 1 king/twin bedroom
- cotton bed linen
- fresh flowers
- 1 bathroom per apartment
- hair dryer & toiletries in bathrooms
- full kitchen per apartment for self-catering
- biscuits & fresh fruit
- living room per apartment with queen bed-settee, TV, video, CD-player, music, phone, artwork & magazines
- spacious decks; sea views
- laundry available
- off-street parking

Activities available
- private outdoor spa pool on site
- alfresco dining on deck
- watching ships & yachts from site
- arts & crafts trail
- cinema
- sailing; rafting
- 3 national parks
- fishing; hunting
- hiking; kayaking
- beaches
- restaurants, bars & cafés, within walking distance
- live music in Nelson City, 5-min drive
- wineries
- golf courses
- mountain biking
- horse trekking
- winter skiing
- Picton ferries, 2-hr drive

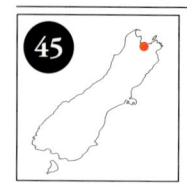

PORT HILLS, NELSON
KIMBERLEY HOUSE NELSON

Hosts Jenny Wilson and Chris North

25 Victoria Road, Nelson   *Postal* P O Box 26–126, Epsom, Auckland
Office phone 0-9-623 1551   *Phone* 0-3-546 8965   *Fax* 0-9-630 1048
Email j-wilson@clear.net.nz   *Website* www.kimberley.co.nz

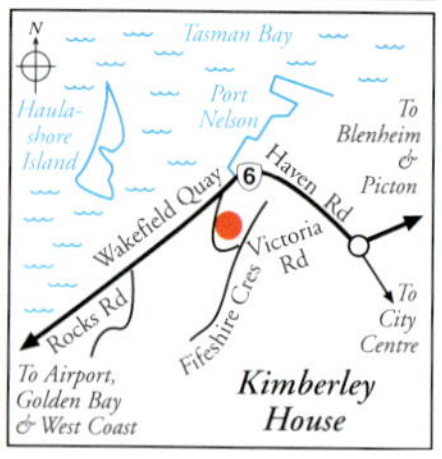

| 6 bdrm | 5 enst | 1 prbth |

Apartment rate $180–$300
Extra persons $50 each
Low-season rates available
Includes continental breakfast provisions
Self-catering

DIRECTIONS: From Nelson City, take Haven Rd (SH 6) to Port. Turn left up Victoria Rd. Kimberley House 400m on left – 2 entrances. From airport, take Rocks Rd towards city. Turn right up Victoria Rd.

Overlooking "The Cut" in Nelson Harbour, Kimberley House features panoramic sea views and endless hours of interest for guests watching the boats and ships below and the sunsets each evening. Originally built in 1964 and extensively renovated in 2001 to offer guest accommodation, Kimberley House now provides three self-contained apartments, a three-bedroom upstairs and a two and one-bedroom apartment downstairs. Each apartment features native timber furniture, an outside deck with barbecue, and a private entrance. Guests can self-cater in the fully equipped kitchen in each apartment, and continental breakfast provisions are supplied daily. A 400-metre walk down the hill takes guests to top seaside restaurants.

Facilities
- 2 downstairs apartments with 1 or 2 super-king/twin ensuite bedrooms; 1 large bathtub
- 1 upstairs apartment with 3 king/twin bedrooms, phone, fax, writing desk, 2 ensuites & 1 bathroom with bidet & bath
- hair dryer, heated towel rails & toiletries in all bathrooms
- cotton bed linen
- children welcome – steep site
- continental breakfast provisions per apartment
- self-contained kitchen per apartment for self-catering
- lounge in each with Sky digital TV, video & music
- central heating & air-conditioning per apartment
- serviced daily if required
- private guest entrances & decks; off-street parking

Activities available
- spa pool & 3 barbecues on site
- viewing sunsets over harbour
- bird & boat watching from site
- Tahunanui Beach
- swimming; sailing
- windsurfing; water skiing
- sea & white water rafting
- golfing; roller blading
- mountain biking; hiking
- wineries trail
- Boat Shed Café & 3 top restaurants, short walk
- central Nelson restaurants, cafés & bars, 5-min drive
- wilderness park walks
- arts & crafts; art galleries
- Nelson's weekend market
- winter snowboarding & skiing at Nelson Lakes National Park & Rainbow ski-fields

© Friars' Guide to New Zealand Accommodation for the Discerning Traveller   326

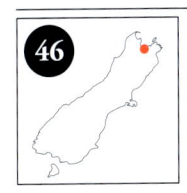

Port Hills, Nelson
Abel Tasman Villa

Host Nicola Clinton

31A Fifeshire Crescent, Nelson
Phone 0-3-548 8533 *Mobile* 025-289 8982 *Fax* 0-3-548 8533
Email clinton@abeltasmanvilla.co.nz *Website* www.abeltasmanvilla.co.nz

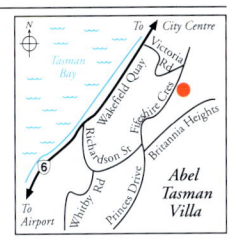

| 2 bdrm | 1 enst | 1 prbth |

Villa rate $275–$445
Extra persons $45 each

Includes breakfast provisions
Multiple-night & corporate rates available

Self-catering

DIRECTIONS: From City, take Wakefield Quay & turn left into Victoria Rd. Turn right into Fifeshire Cres. Villa on left. From airport, take Rocks Rd towards City. Turn right up into Richardson St. Turn left into Fifeshire.

Abel Tasman Villa is self-contained accommodation set high above the harbour with panoramic sea views. This architecturally designed purpose-built apartment provides privacy and independence for guests and is suited to long-term stays. Breakfast provisions are supplied according to a previously chosen menu, and a fully equipped open-plan kitchen enables guests to self-cater. Single parties of up to four guests can be accommodated in two bedrooms each with its own bathroom. A lock-up garage is available for roadside parking, then a stairway leads up to the villa, which is unsuitable for children. Overlooking "The Cut", guests can enjoy viewing the setting sun across Tasman Bay, while ships and pleasure craft provide endless interest.

Facilities
- private-party bookings only
- 1 queen bedroom with ensuite including bath
- 1 queen bedroom & bathroom
- cotton bed linen
- hair dryer & toiletries
- phone jacks; phone available
- fax & email in office
- complimentary fruit bowl & bottle of wine
- breakfast provisions, pre-faxed or emailed choices
- self-contained with full kitchen for self-catering
- lounge with open fire, Sky TV, video, CD-player & music
- fresh flowers; garaging
- self-serve laundry
- unsuitable for children
- decking surrounding villa

Activities available
- patio area for entertaining
- special packages available
- boat watching with binoculars
- walks
- Abel Tasman day boat trips
- wine tours
- arts & crafts
- gardens open to visit
- Haulashore Island
- waterfront restaurants, cafés & bars, within 5-min walking distance
- ferry trips; water skiing
- watersports
- yachting; sailing
- Nelson City Centre, 5-min drive away
- airport, 10-min drive
- Picton ferries, 1¾ hrs

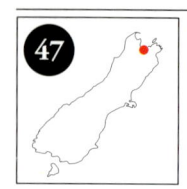

47

PORT HILLS, NELSON
WATERFRONT PENTHOUSE

Hosts Alison Phillips and Robin White

14/311 Wakefield Quay, Nelson   *Postal* 45 Collingwood Street, Nelson
Phone 0-3-548 9418   *Mobile* 025 678 1170   *Fax* 0-3-548 9418
Email water.front@xtra.co.nz   *Website* friars.co.nz/hosts/waterfrontpent.html

3 bdrm | 2 enst | 1 prbth   Apartment rate $290–$350 for 2 persons   *Includes breakfast basket*
Extra persons $40–$50 each   Long stay & winter rates available   *Self-catering*

DIRECTIONS: From Nelson City, take Haven Rd towards airport. Continue into Wakefield Quay. Penthouse is on left, opposite Yacht Club. From airport, take Rocks Rd towards city & continue into Wakefield Quay.

Maximising the extensive harbour views from every room, Waterfront Penthouse is the largest apartment of the complex that was opened in 2003. With secure garaging beneath, the spacious living areas on the first floor open to a balcony, across the road from the yacht club, providing guests with continual boating activities to watch. Fully self-contained, the Waterfront Penthouse has a well-equipped kitchen for self-catering and large living room with telescope for watching ships coming through The Cut. As well as the main ensuite bedroom on the first floor, there are two further bedrooms and bathrooms upstairs, with an office too. Restaurants are within walking distance along the waterfront, and the city is just a short drive away.

Facilities

- private-party bookings only
- 2 super-king/twin ensuite bedrooms, 1 with bath
- 1 twin bedroom & private bathroom on top floor
- hair dryers, toiletries, heated floor & heated towel rails
- study/office with writing desk
- bathrobes; cotton bed linen
- fresh flowers; nibbles; phone
- full self-catering kitchen
- continental breakfast basket provided for 1st morning
- lounge with TV/DVD/CD, NZ artwork & magazines
- air-conditioning/heat pump in each room
- self-serve laundry
- children welcome
- secure garaging

Activities available

- small conference/meeting venue
- alfresco dining, bird-watching, harbour sunset & yacht race viewing from balcony
- fishing opposite site, or tours
- swimming beach, easy walk
- Trafalgar Centre, 15-min walk
- helicopter rides; art tours
- walking tracks; wineries
- adventure activities
- award-winning waterfront restaurants & cafés, 2-min walk
- 3 golf courses, 10–20 mins
- boating; sailing
- Abel Tasman National Park, 1-hour drive
- City Centre, 5-min drive
- airport, 10-min drive
- interisland ferries, 1¾ hours

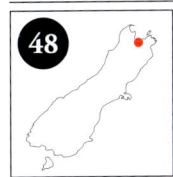

Port Hills, Nelson
Te Puna Wai

Hosts Richard Hewetson and James Taylor

24 Richardson Street, Port Hills, Nelson
Phone 0-3-548 7621   *Mobile* 021 679 795   *Fax* 03 548 7645
Email stay@tepunawai.co.nz   *Website* www.tepunawai.co.nz

3 bdrm | 3 enst

Double $160–$260
Single $120–$195

Includes breakfast
Self-catering in 1 suite

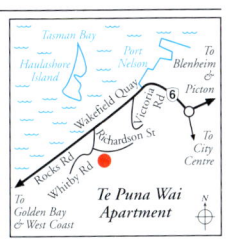

DIRECTIONS: From Nelson City, take Wakefield Quay towards airport. Opposite Haulashore Island, turn left uphill into Richardson St. Continue left. Te Puna Wai is 2nd drive on right. From airport, take Rocks Rd.

Te Puna Wai offers boutique accommodation, with panoramic sea and mountain views from Nelson's Port Hills. This restored 1857 three-storey villa offers three different accommodation options. At ground level are the Haulashore apartment and Wakatu room, with marble-tiled bathrooms. Haulashore has a designer kitchen, includes laundry and opens to a verandah and courtyard. The Fifeshire suite occupies the top floor, and comprises a spacious queen-size bedroom with picture window, anteroom with extra double bed and large bathroom. All rooms have fridges and tea/coffee facilities. Guest areas include lounge, verandah and elevated lawn. High-speed internet access and computer are available. Nelson City Centre is a three-minute drive.

Facilities
- 1 self-contained apartment with queen ensuite bedroom
- 1 upstairs suite with queen & double beds & ensuite
- 1 queen ensuite bedroom
- heated floor, mirrors & towel rails downstairs
- TV, phone, fridge & tea/coffee in all bedrooms
- central heating & open fireplaces; art collection
- full breakfast, served alfresco, weather permitting
- high-speed internet access, computer available
- children & well-behaved pets welcome
- Richard speaks Portuguese, French, German, Spanish & Danish
- off-street parking
- friendly pets on site

Activities available
- foreshore walks to beach
- 7-mins walk to waterfront restaurants, cafés, bars
- 10-min drive to airport
- 3-min drive to Nelson City
- swimming at bottom of Richardson St & nearby at Tahunanui Beach
- local arts community
- gardens & parks to visit
- Nelson Saturday morning market
- Wearable Arts centre
- wineries; quad biking
- walks, hiking, bike hire & scenic flights
- mountain climbing & hiking
- sailing & fishing charters; kayaking
- kayaking at Cable Bay & Abel Tasman National Park
- Picton train or ferry, 1½ hours

49

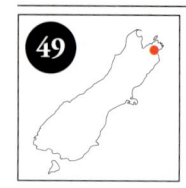

PORT HILLS, NELSON
THE WHEELHOUSE INN
AND CAPTAIN'S QUARTERS

Hosts Ralph and Sally Hetzel
41 Whitby Road, Port Hills, Nelson
Phone 0-3-546 8391   *Mobile* 025 493 380   *Fax* 0-3-546 8391
Email wheelhouse@ts.co.nz   *Website* wheelhouse.nelson.co.nz

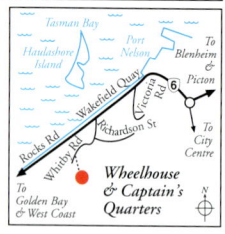

3 bdrm	2 prbth	1 prbth	Apartment rate $120–$175 for 2 persons	*Self-catering*
			Extra persons $15 each	*Breakfast extra*

DIRECTIONS: From Nelson City, take Haven Rd & continue along the waterfront. Turn left up Richardson St & veer right into Whitby Rd. Take drive to left at end of road up to The Wheelhouse Inn & Captain's Quarters.

Overlooking the harbour entrance and Tasman Bay are these two totally separate self-contained apartments. The Wheelhouse Inn was built first in 1997, followed by the Captain's Quarters two years later. The nautical theme harmonises with the seascapes and the enthusiasm of the hosts who sailed to New Zealand in 1974. North-facing, the apartments enjoy all-day sun and the seaward windows and decking afford wonderful views of not only the boating activites below, but also the sunsets. The bedrooms in these two multi-level apartments are located upstairs, with the living areas below. Full kitchens provide for self-catering, although meals can be served by prior arrangement. Restaurants are on the waterfront within walking distance.

Facilities

- 2 self-contained apartments
- Wheelhouse Inn: 1 queen bedroom with private bathroom
- Captains Quarters: 1 queen bedroom & 1 bunkroom, with private bathroom
- children welcome
- basic Spanish spoken
- off-street parking

In both apartments:
- single-party bookings only
- breakfast on request, $15 pp
- full kitchen for self-catering
- lounge with TV, CDs, stereo, DVD, phone & writing desk
- extra fold-out sofa beds
- hair dryer & toiletries
- guest laundry
- sea views

Activities available

- binoculars for enjoying sea views from apartments
- dining available on request
- barbecue available
- mountain bikes available
- viewing sunsets
- watersports
- arts & crafts
- wineries
- beaches; fishing

- restaurants nearby
- waterfront, 2-min drive
- cultural events
- gardens open to visit
- walking
- National Parks
- Nelson City, 5-min drive
- Marlborough Sounds, 1 hour
- airport, 5-min drive
- Picton ferries, 1¾-hour drive

© Friars' Guide to New Zealand Accommodation for the Discerning Traveller

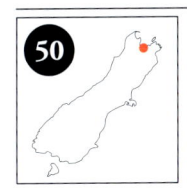

RICHMOND, NELSON
ALTHORPE

Hosts Jenny and Bob Worley

13 Dorset Street, Richmond, Nelson
Phone 0-3-544 8117   *Email* stay@althorpe.co.nz
Fax 0-3-544 8117   *Website* friars.co.nz/hosts/althorpe.html

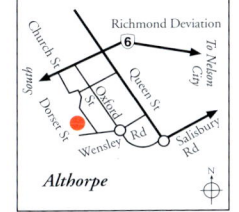

| 2 bdrm | 1 enst | 1 prbth |

Double $140–$160
Single $110–$130

Includes breakfast

DIRECTIONS: From Nelson City, or from Motueka or West Coast, take SH 6 to Richmond, via deviation. Turn south into Church St & then continue into Dorset St. Althorpe on right.

Althorpe was built circa 1887 for Richard Weston Dyson and remained in his family for over 70 years. The Worleys began restoration in 1982, original features retained including spacious entrance hallways, high ceilings, native rimu woodwork, open fireplaces and the kitchen coal range. The two guest bedrooms and the private lounge have been designed with guest privacy in mind, verandahs opening to secluded gardens with the mature trees framing a distant sea view. French doors open to the private swimming pool. Jenny serves her special breakfast selection in the informal dining area in the large kitchen. Period and antique furniture complement the warm atmosphere of this colonial homestead. Restaurants are within walking distance.

Facilities
- 1 double bedroom with writing desk & ensuite bathroom
- 1 king/twin bedroom with private bathroom
- cotton bed linen, down duvets & electric blankets
- laundry, for multiple nights
- children over 12 yrs welcome
- central heating
- open fireplaces
- special breakfast with fresh fruit platter, omelettes, crêpes, croissants, muffins, pastries, etc
- tea/coffee selection in lounge
- guest lounge with open fire & piano, opens to verandahs
- computer facilities available including email in sunroom
- large quiet garden with mature trees & rose beds
- off-street parking

Activities available
- swimming & spa pools on site
- restaurants nearby
- Richmond Tavern, 5-min walk
- shopping centre, including antique shops, 5-min walk
- arts & crafts trails
- wine trails
- golf links, 10-min drive
- beaches, 10km
- trout fishing
- pottery, 5-min walk away
- glass blowing, 5-min drive
- public parks & gardens
- caving, horse trekking
- sailing, sea kayaking
- private gardens to visit
- Abel Tasman National Park
- Nelson Lakes National Park 40–50-min drive away
- Nelson City, 15-min drive

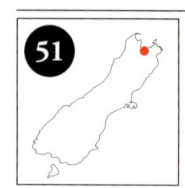

RICHMOND, NELSON
KERSHAW HOUSE

Hosts Nicky Watson and Ian Hannell

10 Wensley Road, Richmond, Nelson
Phone 0-3-544 0957 *Email* info@kershawhouse.co.nz
Fax 0-3-544 0950 *Website* www.kershawhouse.co.nz

4 bdrm | 4 enst | Room rate $150-$275 | *Includes breakfast*

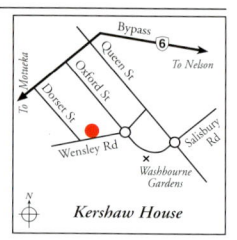

DIRECTIONS: From Nelson City, take SH 6 south to Richmond. Turn left at Mobil Service Station into Oxford St. Then turn right at roundabout into Wensley Rd. Kershaw House on right.

Kershaw House is a character home built in 1929 and has a Historic Places Trust Category Two classification. Historic features include the oak-panelled entrance hall, its wooden staircase ascending to the gallery with the original Art Deco leadlight window. Providing accommodation for up to eight guests, Kershaw House offers four ensuite guestrooms. Located close to local beaches, golf courses and Nelson City, Kershaw House is a convenient base for excursions to Abel Tasman and Nelson Lakes National Parks, award-winning vineyards and restaurants, and the region's many artisan galleries. Nicky and Ian serve breakfast, the menu changing daily, either in the dining room or alfresco in the garden. The new cat, Dougal, is in residence.

Facilities

- 1 super-king, 1 double & 2 king air-conditioned ensuite bedrooms
- 4 ensuites, each including toiletries & hair dryer
- tea & coffee making facilities, ports & sherries in all bedrooms
- private garden & relaxation area
- guest lounge with well-stocked library & satellite TV
- unsuitable for children
- full continental or cooked breakfast served in dining room or alfresco in garden
- complimentary email & internet workstation for guest use
- Nicky speaks German
- young cat, Dougal, on site
- courtesy airport transfer
- secure off-street parking

Activities available

- boutique vineyards nearby
- local pottery, handicraft & glass-blowing studio nearby
- hiking trails & nature walks
- parks & gardens to visit
- horse trekking
- sailing & fishing charters
- fishing/hunting guides available
- adventure sports – skydiving, kayaking, white water rafting
- award-winning restaurant & café, 5-min walk
- 2 local beaches 10-min drive
- tour bus stops, 2-min walk
- Nelson Airport, 10-min drive
- Nelson City, 15-min drive
- Abel Tasman National Park, 40-min drive
- Nelson Lakes, 1-hour drive
- interisland ferries, 2-hr drive

© Friars' Guide to New Zealand Accommodation for the Discerning Traveller

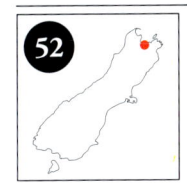

RICHMOND, NELSON
MAPLEDURHAM

Host Deborah Grigg

8 Edward Street, Richmond, Nelson
Phone 0-3-544 4210   *Email* deborah@mapledurham.co.nz
Fax 0-3-544 4210   *Website* www.mapledurham.co.nz

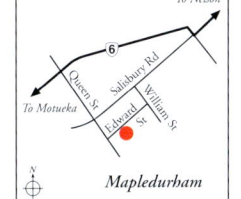

| 3 bdrm | 2 enst | 1 prbth | Double $225–$245 | Single $185–$215 | *Includes breakfast* |

DIRECTIONS: Travel 15 mins south of Nelson City to Richmond. Turn left off Salisbury Rd into William St. Then turn 1st right into Edward St. Mapledurham on left.

Guests are warmly welcomed into this colonial villa, built in 1910 and restored 80 years later when the ensuites were sympathetically added. The historic ambience is created by the external detail, wood-panelled ceilings, fireplaces with carved mantels, and deep verandahs which look out on the quiet tree-lined garden. Hospitality at Mapledurham extends from the welcoming drink to fresh fruit and flowers in the guest bedrooms. A healthy and satisfying breakfast comprises fresh hand-squeezed juice, fruit, and a cooked option, as well as traditional home-made bread and preserves, finishing with a choice of teas and coffee blends. Richmond also includes two top award-winning restaurants, within 10 minutes' walk of Mapledurham.

Facilities

- 2 queen ensuite bedrooms
- 1 queen/twin & private bathroom with original claw-foot bath & bathrobes
- fruit bowl, fresh flowers & tea/coffee tray with biscuits in each bedroom
- fleecy electric blankets on beds
- all 3 bedrooms open to wide verandahs
- historic architecture
- gourmet breakfast served in dining room
- guest lounge with open fireplace & piano
- local & original artwork
- quiet secluded garden setting with seating beneath pergola draped in grapevines
- pétanque/boules & croquet on front lawn
- off-street parking

Activities available

- licensed restaurants within walking distance
- glass blowing & arts & crafts trails
- Nelson City, 15-min drive north
- golden sandy beaches
- swimming at Rabbit Island
- sailing in Nelson Harbour
- private & public gardens to visit
- Abel Tasman & Kahurangi National Park day-trips
- wine trails
- sea kayaking
- trout fishing rivers
- horse trekking
- tandem skydiving
- white water rafting
- caving; paragliding
- bungy jumping
- 4WD motorbike tours

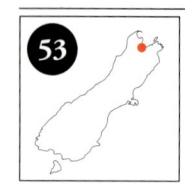

TASMAN BAY, NELSON
ISTANA COASTAL COTTAGE

Hosts Sara and Bernard Isherwood

Coastal Highway, R D 1, Richmond
Phone 0-3-544 1979   *Mobile* 021 255 1555   *Fax* 0-3-544 1979
Email info@istana.co.nz   *Website* friars.co.nz/hosts/istana.html

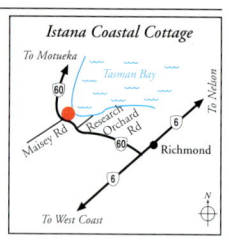

1 bdrm | 1 prbth

Cottage rate $150–$175
Extra persons $25 each

Includes continental breakfast provisions
Self-catering

DIRECTIONS: From Nelson, take SH 6 south to Richmond. Continue & turn right into SH 60. Travel on this Coastal Highway 9.6km to Istana Coastal Cottage on right.

Istana Coastal Cottage is located on the Waimea Estuary. The name Istana is the Malay word for "palace" as the hosts lived for some years in Malaysia. Designed in 1985 by Graham Postles, the cottage was built with rammed earth and New Zealand native rimu and matai, then furnished with Asian furniture. Accommodation comprises one queen-size bedroom and a separate alcove with double sofa bed. A full kitchen allows guests to self-cater, and continental breakfast provisions are supplied. The estuary provides guests with the opportunity for kayaking, sailing and bird-watching. Rabbit Island beach and a choice of golf courses are nearby. Istana Coastal Cottage is set in the heart of the Nelson wine and café area and Nelson City is only 20 minutes away.

Facilities

- private-party bookings only
- 1 self-contained cottage
- 1 queen bedroom
- double sofa bed in alcove
- writing desk in bedroom
- private bathroom with hair dryer, toiletries, heated towel rails & bathrobes
- phone & fresh flowers
- self-serve laundry
- continental breakfast provisions supplied
- full kitchen for self-catering
- TV, stereo, books & games
- smoking area outside on terrace
- French spoken by hosts
- on-site parking
- garaging
- www.istana.co.nz

Activities available

- almost 2ha (4 acres) on site, with estuary access
- bird-watching
- swimming pool on site
- tennis court on site
- pétanque/boules on site
- kayaking & sailing from site
- Rabbit Island beach, 10-min drive away
- bush & beach walks
- award-winning cafés to visit, 2-min drive away
- 5 golf courses within 30-min drive; courtesy clubs
- wine trails; arts & crafts
- sea kayaking
- trout fishing
- Abel Tasman National Park, 40-min drive
- Nelson City, 20-min drive

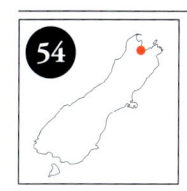

Tasman Bay, Nelson
Kimeret Place

Hosts Clare and Peter Jones

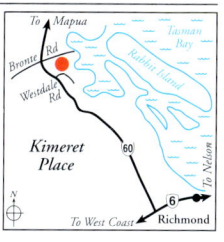

Bronte Road East, Near Mapua, Nelson *Phone* 0-3-540 2727
Postal Bronte Road East, R D 1, Upper Moutere, Nelson *Fax* 0-3-540 2726
Email stay@kimeretplace.co.nz *Website* www.kimeretplace.co.nz

4 bdrm	4 enst	Double $175–$340 Single $135–$275 *Includes breakfast*
		Cottage rate $240–$320 *Self-catering in cottage*

DIRECTIONS: From Nelson City, take SH 6 past Richmond, & turn right into SH 60. Travel 12km towards Motueka & turn right at top of hill into Bronte Rd East. Travel 750m to Kimeret Place on right.

Kimeret Place is set on two hectares (five acres) of sloping land overlooking the Waimea Inlet to the Richmond Range beyond. The upper guest floor in the main house comprises the spacious Edwin and Alexander suites, both opening to a balcony with views over the garden and inlet to the mountains. Native rimu timber and leadlights feature throughout the house. Located separately from the house are a studio and adjoining one-bedroom apartment, which can also be booked as a two-bedroom cottage. Each has an ensuite and private deck. The apartment includes cooking facilities for self-catering. A full breakfast is served for all guests in the house, or alfresco on the large main deck overlooking the heated swimming and spa pools.

Facilities

- Alexander Suite: 1 California king/twin bedroom with Sky TV & DVD; Edwin Suite: 1 king/twin bedroom
- ensuite with spa bath, bathrobes, sitting area, desk, TV, video, hi-fi, dressing room, fridge, mini-bar & balcony in both suites
- 1 apartment with self-catering kitchen & 1 studio – each with 1 king/twin ensuite bedroom, sitting area, TV, hi-fi & fridge
- continental or cooked breakfast in house lounge or on deck; daytime snack menu
- hair dryers, toiletries, heated towel rails, cotton bed linen & tea/coffee in all bedrooms
- laundry available, $5
- email, fax & phone available
- airport/bus station/restaurant transfer service, from $5
- on-site parking

Activities available

- heated swimming pool
- spa pool & pétanque on site
- paintings, by Clare, for sale
- large deck area with BBQ for guest use
- Abel Tasman & Kahurangi National Parks; sandy beaches
- sea & fly fishing
- kayaking; walking tracks
- arts & crafts
- 5 restaurants nearby
- winery & gallery, 500m
- Seifried Vineyard, 4km
- 20 wineries within 10km
- olive groves to visit
- gardens open to visit
- Mapua, 4km north
- 4 golf courses, 10–20 mins
- Golden Bay or Marlborough Sounds, 2-hour drive away

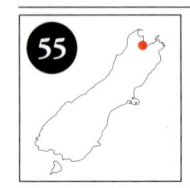

TASMAN BAY, NELSON
BRONTË LODGE

Hosts Margaret and Bruce Fraser

Bronte Road East, off Coastal Highway 60, near Mapua, Nelson
Phone 0-3-540 2422   *Email* margaret@brontelodge.co.nz
Fax 0-3-540 2637   *Website* brontelodge.co.nz

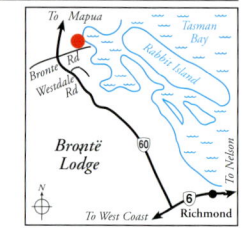

Double $440–$540   Single $425–$525   *Includes breakfast*

DIRECTIONS: From Nelson City, take SH 6 south past Richmond. Turn right into SH 60. Continue 10 mins to Bronte Rd East on right. Travel 1.5km to end of road. Brontë on left. Helicopter site available.

The homestead at Brontë is set in mature gardens adjacent to the boutique vineyard and orchards. Garden pathways lead to the shores of the Waimea Estuary, where the two adjoining guest suites are sited, with the two guest villas nearby. Here, in the quiet of the inlet, white herons, royal spoonbills and oystercatchers can be observed. Each suite or villa is tastefully decorated and includes king-size bed, quality bed linen, lounge area with sofa, writing desk, commissioned New Zealand artworks, dressing room and ensuite. À la carte breakfast is served at the homestead, alfresco in warm weather on the decks overlooking the garden to the estuary, or in the Edwardian dining room with its polished wood, leadlights and open fire.

Facilities

- 2 separate suites & 2 villas, with king & king/twin beds
- each suite & villa includes 1 dressing room & 1 private bathroom with spa bath
- separate lounge facilities in suites/villas with Sky TV & phone; kitchenette with fridge, tea/coffee & microwave
- portable BBQ on request
- original local artwork
- full breakfast at homestead or continental breakfast in suites & villas, by arrangement
- complimentary beverages & home-baking in suites & villas
- phone/fax & CD in villas; wheelchair access to 1 villa
- binoculars for viewing birdlife
- native & villa watergardens
- private driveways to villas & suites; helipad available

Activities available

- pétanque/boules on site
- heated swimming pool & all-weather tennis court
- relaxing in homestead garden
- boutique vineyard on site
- walks through orchard along estuary shoreline; swimming
- Canadian canoeing, sailing & windsurfing from site
- hunting & fishing guides
- restaurants 5–10-min drive
- 5 award-winning wineries
- 3 golf links, 7–15-min drive
- sea kayaking; golden beaches
- swimming at Rabbit Island
- craft trail; skiing in winter
- hiking in Abel Tasman National Park, 45-min drive
- Nelson Airport, 20-min drive
- Picton ferry, 2½ hours away

Above: The two villas are purpose-built for estuary views, with a driveway for easy access. The two suites have a similar vista.
Below: Bi-fold windows of the villas open to the lawn overlooking Waimea Estuary, for indoor/outdor living and alfresco dining.
Opposite top: In summertime, breakfast is served alfresco on the deck of the homestead at Brontë Lodge overlooking the garden.
Opposite bottom left: Guests are welcome to relax in the exclusive lounge in the homestead overlooking the garden at any time.
Opposite bottom right: Guests enjoy the new heated swimming pool at Brontë Lodge, where they can also relax on deckchairs.

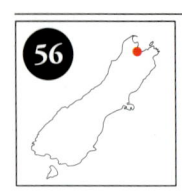

TASMAN BAY, NELSON
ATHOLWOOD COUNTRY ACCOMMODATION

Hosts Robyn and Grahame Williams

Bronte Road East, R D 1, Upper Moutere
Phone 0-3-540 2925   *Mobile* 025 310 309   *Fax* 0-3-540 3258
Email atholwood@xtra.co.nz   *Website* www.atholwood.co.nz

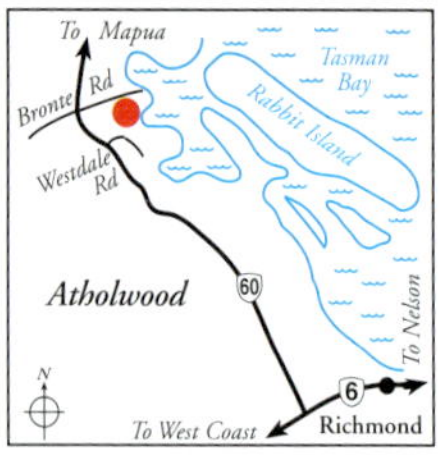

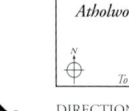

3 bdrm	3 enst	Double $180–$200 Single $150 *Includes breakfast* *Lunch & dinner extra*
		Extra adult $50, children $30 each Weekly rate available *Self-catering in apartment*

DIRECTIONS: From Nelson City, take SH 6 south past Richmond. Turn right into SH 60. Continue 10 mins to Bronte Rd East on right. Travel 1km to Atholwood Country Accommodation on right.

Atholwood offers two accommodation options – The Gatehouse, a separate self-contained apartment (*see below right*), and an upstairs guest wing in the main house overlooking Waimea Inlet. The Gatehouse is the converted ground floor of the original pottery, built at the driveway entrance. It includes a spacious bedroom, bathroom, lounge, a full kitchen for self-catering, and indoor and alfresco dining areas. Built in 1982, the contemporary-style timbered house features high ceilings and native rimu interiors. Set in almost one hectare of landscaped gardens on the edge of the inlet, Atholwood affords water views across the surrounding orchards and olive groves to the mountains beyond. Guests enjoy the hidden walks in the garden and watching the tides ebb and flow from the gazebo. Both accommodation options provide guests with privacy and seclusion. Within the house, breakfast, at a time to suit, is served in the dining room, upstairs in the guest lounge, or on the deck. Home-made muesli and fruit, or a special cooked selection, are offered. Picnic lunches and a three-course dinner with local wine can be arranged.

Facilities
- The Gatehouse: 1 king/twin bedroom with single trundler, 1 bathroom with wheelchair access, laundry, full kitchen, dining/lounge & outdoor area
- 1 guest wing upstairs in house:
  – opens to balcony
  – 1 queen & 1 queen/twin bedroom, each with ensuite
  – bath in 1 ensuite
- open fire, organ & Sky TV in downstairs lounge in house
- cotton bed linen; fresh flowers
- hair dryers, toiletries, heated towel rails & bathrobes
- breakfast selection in house
- picnic lunches, $12 pp
- 3-course à la carte dinner with local wine, $50 pp
- fruit, teas/coffee & home baking in both guest lounges
- self-service laundry both in house & in Gatehouse
- children/pets by arrangement
- Carlos, the cat, in residence
- basic German spoken
- email, fax & cordless phone
- courtesy car available
- on-site parking

Activities available
- spa pool & swimming pool
- croquet lawn on site
- BBQ available on site
- canoe available for Inlet
- sea & native bird-watching
- garden walks on site
- Mapua Village, nearby
- watersports
- swimming
- fishing
- boating
- kayaking
- walking
- selection of restaurants
- award-winning wineries
- golf club, 10-min drive
- charter boats
- dolphins
- arts & crafts trail
- gardens open to visit
- Richmond, 10-min drive
- Motueka, 20-min drive
- Abel Tasman National Park, 40-min drive away
- day tours arranged
- skiing in winter, 1½ hrs

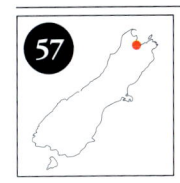

UPPER MOUTERE
MAPLE GROVE COTTAGE

Hosts Judy Straford and George Page

72 Flaxmore Road, R D 2, Upper Moutere, Nelson
Phone 0-3-543 2267   Mobile 025 623 8631   Fax 0-3-543 2267
Email george1judy@xtra.co.nz   Website www.maplegrove.co.nz

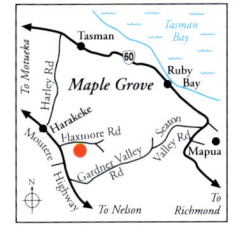

| 2 bdrm | 1 prbth | Double $160 Single $150 | *Includes breakfast hamper Cooked breakfast extra* | *Self-catering* |

DIRECTIONS: From Richmond take SH 60 towards Mapua. Turn west into Seaton Valley Rd. Continue into Gardner Valley Rd. Turn right into Moutere Highway. Take 1st right into Flaxmore Rd to Maple Grove on right.

Located in rural seclusion in the countryside of Upper Moutere, Maple Grove Cottage is set in nearly two hectares (four acres) of landscaped grounds featuring a mature acer grove. Purpose built in 2002 in pioneer style, Maple Grove Cottage provides self-contained accommodation for up to four guests in one party. The cottage comprises two bedrooms, a bathroom, kitchenette and lounge, with a colonial-style verandah overlooking the pond, and views to Mt Arthur and the western ranges. A breakfast hamper is supplied daily and cooked breakfast is also available. Guests can self-cater in the kitchenette and a gas barbecue is popular for alfresco dining by the brook under the trees. Restaurants, cafés and vineyards are a short drive away.

Facilities
- single-party bookings only
- 1 self-contained cottage with 1 queen & 1 twin bedroom
- 1 bathroom with double shower, hair dryer, toiletries & bathrobes
- cotton bed linen; fresh flowers
- Sky TV, video, CD-player, music, games, artwork, books, writing desk & nibbles in lounge
- breakfast hamper includes continental, fresh farm eggs, home-made bread & jams
- cooked breakfast, extra
- kitchenette for self-catering
- hosts live in main house
- self-service laundry
- phone, fax & email in cottage
- verandah; garaging
- courtesy passenger transfer

Activities available
- nearly 2ha (4 acres) land with gas BBQ, mature trees, garden walks, pond & farm animals
- tramping on Mt Arthur & at Kahurangi National Park
- Abel Tasman National Park walkways & sea kayaking
- jet boating
- mountain biking
- golf; fishing
- award-winning restaurants & cafés at Mapua, 5-min drive
- Kaiteriteri & Tahunanui beaches
- vineyards, wine tasting & olive groves
- arts, crafts & galleries
- local potters
- Motueka, 10-min drive north
- Nelson, 30-min drive

339

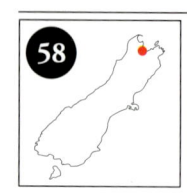

Upper Moutere, Nelson
Mahana Escape

Hosts Gloria Eggeling and Steven Edwards

750 Old Coach Road, R D 1, Upper Moutere, Nelson
Phone 0-3-540 3090   *Mobile* 025 289 0060   *Fax* 0-3-540 3090
Email gloria@mahanaescape.co.nz   *Website* www.mahanaescape.co.nz

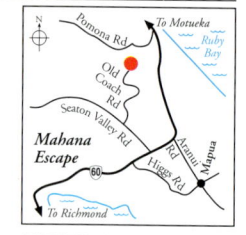

5 bdrm	1 enst	2 prbth	Room rate $160–$210	Includes breakfast	Lunch & dinner extra
			Apartment rate $310	Self-catering in apartment	

DIRECTIONS: From Richmond, take SH 60 towards Motueka. Turn left into Seaton Valley Rd, then right into Old Coach Rd. Mahana Escape at end of road (6 mins from SH 60 turn-off).

Set on two hectares (five acres) of developing land, Mahana Escape features panoramic views overlooking the Tasman Sea. Mahana is Maori for "a warm place to rest", and provides accommodation with a Mediterranean ambience, comprising three upstairs guestrooms and a downstairs two-bedroom apartment. Gloria serves a full breakfast in the dining room, or alfresco on the deck, and she offers picnic lunch by arrangement. She will also prepare two or three-course dinners, with whitebait a speciality, and wheat-free or gluten-free meals can be arranged. Guests enjoy the Abel Tasman National Park nearby, and Gloria offers a luggage-minding service for her guests. The cafés and art studios at Mapua village are just a short drive away.

Facilities

- 1 king bedroom upstairs, with dressing room, spa bath & dual basin in ensuite, TV, phone jack
- 1 queen & 1 twin bedroom upstairs, with bath in bathroom
- 1 apartment downstairs, with 1 queen & 1 twin bedroom, 1 bathroom, kitchenette, lounge, TV & phone jack
- bathrobes, hair dryers, toiletries, heated floor & heated towel rails
- full breakfast choice
- 2–3 course à la carte dinner with wine, $35–$60 pp; lunch/picnic by request, extra
- open fire, Sky TV/video/DVD CDs, & art in upstairs lounge
- nibbles & home-made cookies
- phone, fax & email available
- children welcome; fresh flowers
- courtesy laundry; parking

Activities available

- guest BBQ on site, with salads by request
- small weddings catered
- courtesy passenger transfer
- pétanque/boules on site
- garden walks on site
- neighbouring alpaca farm
- golf courses
- local potteries & artists
- award-winning wineries
- Mapua village restaurants, cafés & art studios, 6-min drive
- horse riding, 15-min drive
- walking/trekking in Abel Tasman National Park & Kahurangi National Park, 30 mins; transport arranged & luggage minded
- gardens open to visit
- Motueka, 16-min drive
- Nelson City, 45-min drive

© Friars' Guide to New Zealand Accommodation for the Discerning Traveller

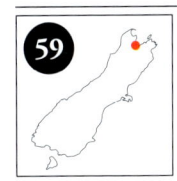

Ruby Bay
SANDSTONE HOUSE

Hosts Jenny and John Marchbanks

30 Korepo Road, Ruby Bay, Nelson *Phone* 0-3-540 3251
Postal Korepo Road, R D 1, Upper Moutere, Nelson *Fax* 0-3-540 3251
Email sandstone@rubybay.net.nz *Website* rubybay.net.nz

Double $190 Single $170 *Includes breakfast*

DIRECTIONS: From Nelson take SH 6 past Richmond & turn right into SH 60. Travel past Mapua turn-off. Turn left into Pomona Rd & then 1st right into Korepo Rd. Travel 300m to Sandstone House on right.

Purpose built from imported Australian sandstone in 2001, Sandstone House is located above Ruby Bay with panoramic views over the Tasman Sea. The Australian ambience is enhanced by the deep verandahs surrounding the house, the high ceilings and clay-tiled roof. Guests can enjoy the privacy of their own wing, with private verandahs opening from both bedrooms, each including a writing desk, tea and coffee-making facilities and fridge. Breakfast is prepared according to guests' wishes and is served in the dining room or on the decking overlooking the sea. The guests have a private entrance, and upstairs are the hosts, who have lived in the area since 1970. Restaurants are only five minutes' drive away at the village of Mapua.

Facilities

- 2 queen ensuite bedrooms
- bedrooms open to verandah
- hair dryer, toiletries, bathrobes, demist mirror & heated towel rails in both bathrooms
- writing desk, phone, TV, tea/coffee, fridge, fruit, mineral water & juice in each bedroom
- Sky TV, video & CD in lounge
- open fire in lounge
- continental or cooked breakfast in dining room or alfresco on verandah
- guest barbecue
- 1 powder room
- fresh flowers
- central heating
- fax & email available
- on-site parking
- private guest entrance

Activities available

- self-serve BBQ
- track to beach, 5-min walk
- flat-bottomed scenic boat
- jet boating
- watersports; swimming
- fishing; aquarium
- gardens open to visit
- award-winning wineries, 10-min drive away
- Mapua village, 5-min drive
- restaurants, 2km away
- horse riding, 5-min drive
- arts & crafts
- Motueka, 15-min drive away
- sea kayaking
- trout fishing rivers, 30-min drive
- Abel Tasman & Kahurangi National Parks, 30–50 mins
- Nelson City, 30-min drive

341

© Friars' Guide to New Zealand Accommodation for the Discerning Traveller

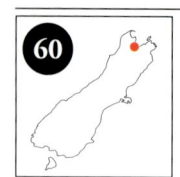

Ruby Bay
Tasman View

Hosts Jenny and Gerald Allsopp

106 Brabant Drive, Pine Hill Heights, Ruby Bay, Nelson
Phone 0-3-540 2966   *Mobile* 027 439 0041   *Fax* 0-3-540 2965
Email relax@tasmanview.co.nz   *Website* www.tasmanview.co.nz

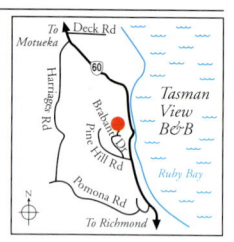

Double $195–$225   Single $175   *Includes breakfast*

DIRECTIONS: From Nelson, take SH 6 past Richmond & turn right into SH 60. Travel through Ruby Bay & turn left to Pine Hill Heights subdivision. Turn right into Brabant Dr & travel 1km to Tasman View at end.

With panoramic views over Tasman Bay, north of Nelson, Tasman View Bed and Breakfast was purpose built on Pine Hill Heights in 2001. The indoor/outdoor living design reveals a Mediterranean influence, with a walled courtyard featuring a spa pool and dining area overlooking the ocean. Guests enjoy the privacy of the upper floor which is booked for private parties only, comprising two spacious bedrooms which share a bathroom and guest sitting room. Breakfast is served downstairs in the dining room or alfresco in the courtyard or on the patio, with vistas extending over Ruby Bay to D'Urville Island. Four restaurants and a lunch café are just five minutes' drive away in Mapua village, and Nelson City is half an hour drive.

Facilities

- single-party bookings
- 1 super-king/twin & 1 king bedroom with 1 private bathroom upstairs in guest wing
- 1 bathroom downstairs
- cotton bed linen, hair dryer, bathrobes, toiletries, heated towel rails & heated floor
- complimentary laundry available
- fresh flowers
- continental or full cooked breakfast
- light refreshments on request
- guest sitting room upstairs with TV, video, phone & writing desk
- lounge downstairs
- office facilities
- private guest entrance
- on-site parking

Activities available

- native bush walk on site to beach; glow-worms
- 2 mountain bikes available
- outdoor spa pool; pétanque, table tennis; sand bunker for experienced golfers on site
- 4 golf courses, 10–25-min drive
- arts & crafts; wine trails
- Mapua village & restaurants 5km
- eco tours; watersports
- swimming beaches
- sea kayaking; jet boat rides
- bush walks in native reserve
- Motueka, 15-min drive
- Nelson City, 30 mins
- tramping at Abel Tasman National Park, 30 mins
- trout rivers, 30-min drive
- alpine flowers at Kahurangi National Park, 50-min drive

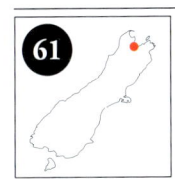

TASMAN BAY
APORO PONDSIDERS

Hosts Marian and Mike Day

Permin Road, Tasman   *Postal* R D 1, Upper Moutere, Nelson
Phone 0-3-526 6858   Mobile 025 240 3757   Fax 0-3-526 6258
Email marian@aporo.co.nz   *Website* aporo.co.nz

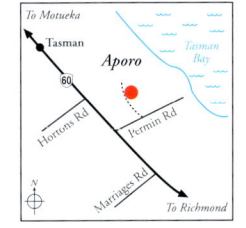

4 bdrm | 2 enst | 1 prbth
Double $300   Single $280   Extra persons $50 each
Self-catering   *Includes continental or cooked breakfast in hamper*

DIRECTIONS: Take scenic coastal highway, SH 60, from Nelson & travel about 40km towards Motueka. Turn right into Permin Rd. Travel 200m to Aporo Pondsiders, 1st driveway on left. Continue to Aporo on right.

Inspired by historic boat sheds, these three cottages were purpose-built in 2002 in contemporary New Zealand design perched over a large rural pond. The cottages have been staggered for privacy with cantilevered decks over the ornamental pond and views to the farmland and mountains beyond. Each cottage features original art, timber ceilings, spacious living area and bedroom opening to individual decks over the pond. The east cottage is the largest with two bedrooms and wheelchair access. Gourmet breakfast hampers, cooked or continental, are provided. Full kitchens for self-catering and barbecues make alfresco dining popular on the decks or by the jetty. Aporo is located close to Tasman village and within easy access to the attractions of the Nelson region.

Facilities

- 2 cottages with 1 king ensuite bedroom in each, 1 with bath
- 1 cottage with 1 king bedroom, 1 twin bedroom & private bathroom
- cotton bed linen, hair dryer, bathrobes, heated towel rails & toiletries in all 3 cottages
- laundry available
- heated floor in bedrooms & bathroom in each cottage
- kitchen in each cottage for self-catering; continental or cooked breakfast hamper
- lounge in each cottage with Sky TV, CDs, fruit bowl, flowers, port, chocolates & laptop jack
- cantilevered decks opening over pond from each cottage
- private guest entrance
- on-site parking
- children welcome by arrangement

Activities available

- guest barbecue
- rowing boat available
- pétanque/boules
- farm & woodland walk
- bird-watching
- 3 golf courses nearby
- swimming beaches
- gardens open to visit
- award-winning wineries, 5-min drive away
- restaurants 5km away
- horse riding, 5-min drive
- arts & crafts
- Motueka, 10km away
- Nelson Airport, 30 mins
- sea kayaking at Abel Tasman National Park, 30 mins
- trout rivers, 30-min drive
- alpine flowers at Kahurangi National Park, 50-min drive

343

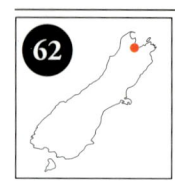

KINA PENINSULA, TASMAN BAY
KINA COLADA HOLIDAY & HEALTH RETREAT

Hosts Christine and Franz Lieber

Kina Peninsula, Tasman *Postal* R D 1, Upper Moutere, Nelson
Phone 0-3-540 3915 *Email* info@kinacolada.co.nz
Fax 0-3-540 3916 *Website* www.kinacolada.co.nz

3 bdrm 3 enst
Double $180–$495
Single $110–$180
Includes continental breakfast
Lunch, dinner & treatments extra

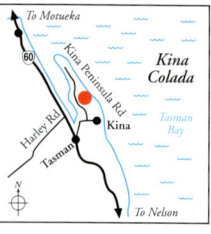

DIRECTIONS: Take scenic coastal highway, SH 60, from Nelson & travel 40km towards Motueka. At Tasman, turn right into Kina Rd. Travel 1km & turn left. Kina Colada is 1st driveway on right.

Kina Colada is a European-style holiday and health retreat sited on eight hectares on a cliff-top on Kina Peninsula overlooking Tasman Bay. Built in 1997 with Mediterranean architecture complemented by timber floors and ceilings, ensuites with heated tile floors, and double-glazed windows, Kina Colada combines relaxation with the opportunity for spa treatments. The uniquely designed health treatment rooms offer a choice of beauty treatments, massages, marine bodyworks, antique mud room, oxygen therapy and marine baths. Guest facilities include European sauna, and large salt-water swimming pool with ha-ha blending into the bay vista. As well as healthy continental breakfasts, Franz serves Mediterranean-style lunch or dinner, by arrangement.

Facilities
- 1 king & 2 king/twin upstairs suites
- 3 ensuites with heated floors
- tea/coffee, fridge, TV & phone in all 3 bedrooms
- health treatment rooms
- double glazing
- sea & mountain views
- guest lounge
- laundry available
- healthy continental breakfast, in breakfast room or alfresco
- lunch of salads & bread, $12 pp
- Mediterranean-style 3-course dinner, by request, $45–$65 pp
- children over 10 years welcome
- German spoken by hosts
- massages & treatments, extra
- salt-water swimming pool
- on-site parking

Activities available
- therapeutic massage, $120/1 hr or $150 for 1½ hours
- exfoliating body scrub, $140/1 hr
- body wraps & masks, $180/1½ hrs
- manicure or pedicure, $120/1 hr
- Indian scalp massage, $120/1 hr
- slimming wrap, $240 for 2 hrs
- re-mineralising wraps, $180
- facial treatments, $160/1½ hrs
- Swedish sauna, $20
- swimming pool on site, complimentary
- wineries; restaurants
- walkways & beachwalks
- tidal inlet for motor boating
- 9-hole golf course, 1.5km
- swimming beaches
- arts & crafts; gardens to visit
- kayaking; fishing
- 3 National Parks, hiking

© Friars' Guide to New Zealand Accommodation for the Discerning Traveller

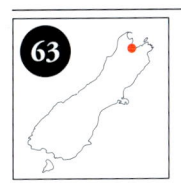

KINA BEACH, TASMAN BAY
OLD SCHOOLHOUSE VINEYARD COTTAGE

Hosts Dave Birt and Pam Robert

Dee Road, Kina Beach, R D 1, Upper Moutere, Nelson
Phone 0-3-526 6252   Mobile 025 281 2425   Fax 0-3-526 6252
Email kinabeach@xtra.co.nz   *Website* www.kinabeach.com

Cottage rate $150–$200
Extra persons $25 each

*Includes continental breakfast provisions
Self-catering*

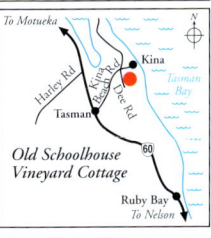

1 bdrm   1 prbth

DIRECTIONS: Take scenic coastal highway, SH 60, from Nelson & travel 40km towards Motueka. At Tasman, turn right into Kina Beach Rd. Take 1st right into Dee Rd. Kina Beach Vineyard 1st on left to Cottage.

Sited on Kina Beach Vineyard Estate, the Old Schoolhouse Vineyard Cottage has been carefully restored and transformed into self-contained accommodation. Originally built in 1934, the Redwoods Valley Schoolhouse was moved to the vineyard in 1999 and retains the native heart matai floors, tongue and groove walls and ceilings. Guests enjoy the panoramic views over Tasman Bay, the sunrises and sunsets being especially popular. Vineyard tours are also available to guests. Breakfast provisions are supplied, sufficient for two days and a fully equipped kitchen enables guests to self-cater. A barbecue is also available for alfresco dining, and restaurants are not far away. The cottage can accommodate honeymoon couples and a sunroom provides an extra single divan.

Facilities
- single-party bookings only
- self-contained cottage
- 1 queen bedroom
- sunroom with single daybed
- toiletries, hair dryer & heated towel rail in bathroom
- cotton bed linen
- fresh flowers
- babies or children over 14 years welcome
- continental breakfast provisions for 2 mornings
- full kitchen, including dishwasher, for self-catering
- open fire, bar, writing desk, books & CDs in lounge
- guest laundry
- wrap-around decks
- fax & phone in main house
- outdoor furniture & BBQ

Activities available
- vineyard tours on site
- relaxing in NZ native & cottage garden on site
- Kina Beach, 200m walk
- Tasman Golf Course, 5 mins
- craft shops nearby
- Rabbit Island; gardens to visit
- safe swimming beaches
- watersports
- winery tours, by arrangement
- restaurants nearby
- Mapua village, 10-min drive
- Kaiteriteri Beach, 30-min drive
- Tahunanui Beach, 30-min drive
- kayaking, 40-min drive
- Abel Tasman walks, 40-min drive
- Rainbow Ski-field, 2-hour drive
- Motueka, 10-min drive
- Nelson City & airport, 30 mins

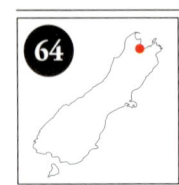

TASMAN
WAIREPO HOUSE

Hosts Joyanne and Richard Easton

Weka Road, Mariri, Coastal Highway, Nelson
Phone 0-3-526 6865 *Mobile* 027 435 7902 *Fax* 0-3-526 6101
Email joyanne@wairepohouse.co.nz *Website* www.wairepohouse.co.nz

5 bdrm | 3 enst | 1 prbth
Double $295–$550
Single $265–$520
Includes breakfast

DIRECTIONS: From Nelson City, travel on SH 60 towards Motueka for 45km. Continue 3km past Tasman township, then turn left at Weka Rd. Wairepo House is the stone entrance 1st on the right.

Wairepo House is a three-storey colonial homestead with views towards Tasman Bay. The rural setting is complemented by Wairepo's fourth-generation apple and pear orchard and the 7,000 peonies grown for export. Wairepo House features warm native timbers, chapel ceilings, and sundecks. Four suites have been designed and furnished for guest comfort and privacy with rich-coloured fabrics, antiques and local artwork. Flexi-time gourmet breakfast or brunch can be served on the sundeck overlooking the heated pool. Almost a hectare (two acres) of woodland garden is planted for all seasons with established trees and rambling perennial borders. Guests can enjoy the grass tennis court, pétanque lawn, and refreshments in the summer house.

Facilities

- 1 upstairs suite: 1 super-king/twin & 1 super-king bedroom, desk & balcony, ensuite with double spa bath & bidet, kitchenette, lounge, open fire, TV & private balcony
- 1 downstairs suite: 1 super-king bedroom, private bathroom, sun-room with TV, tea/coffee, desk
- 1 downstairs suite: 1 super-king bedroom, spa bath in ensuite, lounge, kitchenette, wheelchair access
- full flexi-time breakfast
- complimentary drinks, alcohol, nibbles & platters
- heated tiled floors & demist mirrors in all bathrooms
- 1 extra suite available with ensuite & private lounge
- CDs, cassettes, radios, hair dryers, flowers & chocolates
- original NZ art, leadlights, rimu panelling, throughout
- fax, email, laundry available

Activities available

- heated swimming pool; tennis court
- chess set in garden, pond, summer house & peony garden walk
- croquet & pétanque/boules
- orchard & packhouse tour
- vineyard next door
- good restaurants nearby
- wine trails & craft trails
- Motueka, 6km north
- Nelson City, less than 50km
- windsurfing & water skiing according to tides
- trout fishing guides available
- golden beaches; kayaking
- golf courses at Tasman & Motueka, 4-min drive away
- lakes & mountains; walks
- Abel Tasman & Kahurangi National Parks
- winter snow skiing & Picton, 2-hour drive

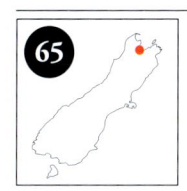

MOTUEKA
COPPER BEECH GALLERY

Hosts John and Carol Gatenby

240 Thorp Street, Motueka, Nelson
Phone 0-3-528 7456   *Fax* 0-3-528 7456   *Mobile* 021 256 0053
Email copper.beech.gallery@xtra.co.nz   *Website* www.copperbeechgallery.co.nz

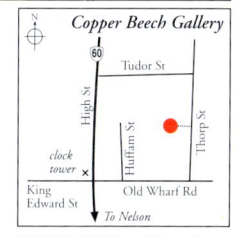

Double $220–$280   Single $180–$230   *Includes breakfast*

DIRECTIONS: From Nelson City, travel on SH 60 towards Motueka for about 45 mins. At clock tower corner, turn right into Old Wharf Rd. Then turn 2nd left into Thorp St. Copper Beech Gallery is 100m on left.

Copper Beech Gallery is the home of landscape artist John R Gatenby. His paintings are exhibited throughout the house and in his adjacent studio and gallery. The rooms in this contemporary home open onto extensive patios and a hectare of park-like gardens. Nelson's fresh fruit and seafood feature on the breakfast menu and are served alfresco beneath a pergola, in the courtyard, or more formally in the sunlit dining area. Copper Beech Gallery is a semi-rural retreat offering mountain views, peace, relaxation and recreation, just 10 minutes' drive from Motueka River's renowned trout fishing. Located on the outskirts of Motueka township, it is 20 minutes to Kaiteriteri's golden beaches and half an hour to Abel Tasman or Kahurangi National Park.

Facilities

- 1 queen & 1 twin bedroom, each with ensuite bathroom
- hair dryers, toiletries, heaters, heated towel rails & bathrobes
- bedrooms open to sundecks
- private guest lounge
- phone & fax facilities
- TV in the Snug
- fresh flowers & chocolates in both bedrooms
- full breakfast with selection of fresh local produce – fruit platters & seafood
- tea/coffee & guest fridge with quality refreshments
- original NZ paintings – tuition available on request
- tranquil garden overlooking bird & water fowl sanctuary & estuary
- level access – no stairs
- off-street parking beside door

Activities available

- art gallery; summer house in garden & outdoor golden labrador, Abbi, on site
- beach, 5-min walk
- golf course, 2-min drive
- restaurants/shops, 2 mins
- scenic flights, tandem skydiving, 5-min drive
- wineries, 20-min drive
- arts & crafts trails, pottery, woodwork available
- golden sandy beaches & coastal tracks, 20-min drive
- marine reserve & helicopter fishing trips, guide available
- kayaking/walks/tramps/boat trips into Abel Tasman & Kahurangi National Parks, 30-min drive
- Marble Mountain – extensive limestone cave systems, 40 mins
- Nelson City, 45-min drive
- Picton interisland ferry, 2½ hours

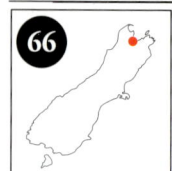

ABEL TASMAN NATIONAL PARK, NELSON
KANUKA HILL LODGE

Manager Jo Sherlaw

The Anchorage, Abel Tasman National Park, Nelson   Phone 0-3-548 2863
Postal P O Box 1349, Nelson   Mobile 027 242 4052   Fax 0-3-548 2869
Email stay@kanukalodge.co.nz   Website www.kanukalodge.co.nz

| 3 bdrm | 3 enst | 1 pdrm |

Double $345–$500
Single $205–$300

Includes breakfast & dinner
Low-season rates available

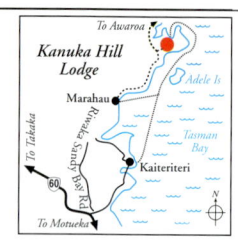

Lunch or picnic extra

DIRECTIONS: From Kaiteriteri or Marahau, take water taxi or sea kayak to The Anchorage, to Kanuka Hill Lodge. Or from Marahau, take Abel Tasman National Park coastal track to Kanuka Hill Lodge.

Accessible by water taxi or sea kayak, or by walking the Abel Tasman National Park coastal track from Marahau, Kanuka Hill Lodge is sited at The Anchorage overlooking Anchorage Beach. (*See Lodge above centre at bottom of frame.*) Built in 1993 this open plan Lodge is split-level on the hillside surrounded by native bush including kanuka trees, with panoramic views of the Abel Tasman coastline. Accommodation comprises three ensuite guestrooms. Meals are offered in the dining room or alfresco on the deck overlooking the ocean. Breakfast is continental or cooked, three-course dinner is served, and lunches or picnics are available by arrangement. Kanuka Hill Lodge is closed from May until September, except for multiple-night group bookings.

Facilities
- 2 king/twin ensuite bedrooms
- 1 queen ensuite bedroom
- toiletries
- guest lounge with tea/coffee, herbal teas, games & library
- fresh flowers
- children welcome if booking entire lodge
- small weddings & honeymoons catered for
- continental or cooked breakfast, served in dining room or on deck
- light lunch or packed lunch available, extra
- 3-course dinner, served in dining room or deck
- private guest entrance
- boat, sea kayak or walking access only
- ocean views

Activities available
- barbecue available
- private functions catered
- full-day sea-kayaking trip
- dinghy available
- bush walks from site
- glow-worm visits
- pétanque/boules on site
- swimming from site
- direct access to Abel Tasman National Park from site
- boat trips
- swimming with seals
- sailing; diving
- Marahau via Abel Tasman walking track, 3 hours
- Awaroa, 6-hour walk
- Kaiteriteri/Marahau, 30 mins by water taxi
- Marahau, 3 hrs by sea kayak
- Nelson, 2 hours away

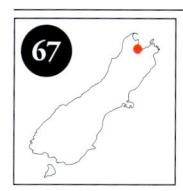

KAITERITERI, MOTUEKA
THE HAVEN

Hosts Alison and Tom Rowling

Bay View Road, Kaiteriteri   *Postal* Kaiteriteri, R D 2, Motueka
Phone 0-3-527 8085   *Email* thehaven@internet.co.nz
Fax 0-3-527 8065   *Website* friars.co.nz/hosts/thehaven.html

2 bdrm	1 enst	1 prbth	House rate $150	Extra couple $50	*Includes breakfast provisions*
			2-night minimum stay	Winter rates available	*Self-catering*

DIRECTIONS: Take SH 60 to Motueka. Continue through Riwaka, turn right & travel 6km to Kaiteriteri. Travel 0.5km up hill & turn left into Rowling Heights, then left into Bay View Rd. The Haven is 1st on left.

The Haven was designed in nautical style in 2000, reflecting Tom's seafaring career as captain of many vessels. Tom's great-great-grandfather was the first European to land in Kaiteriteri. With panoramic views over Tasman Bay, The Haven provides self-contained accommodation for four guests in the ensuite Captain's Cabin and Crews Quarters with private bathroom. The fully equipped "galley" for self-catering includes breakfast provisions, local produce and home baking. A barbecue and two decks make alfresco dining popular with guests. The hosts live adjacent, their house set in a large garden with a swimming pool for guest use, and a woodland track leading down to Kaiteriteri Beach where a dinghy is available for the more adventurous.

Facilities
- private-party bookings only
- 1 king ensuite bedroom
- 1 twin bedroom with private bathroom
- cotton bed linen; fresh flowers
- hair dryer, toiletries, heated towel rail & bathrobes
- self-service laundry
- lounge with pellet fire, TV, video & phone
- breakfast provisions
- fully self-contained kitchen for self-catering
- complimentary wine, nibbles, home-baking & organic local produce
- fax & email available
- 2 sundecks; on-site parking
- unsuitable for children
- courtesy passenger transfer

Activities available
- swimming pool on site
- Oscar, the elusive cat, on site
- barbecue available
- private bush walk to beach
- dinghy available
- line fishing from rocks
- sea kayaking
- ocean swimming
- snorkelling; horse trekking
- water taxis & tourist launches
- restaurants, 10-min drive
- wine trails
- bush walks; tramping
- potters; arts & crafts trail
- gardens open to visit
- Abel Tasman National Park gateway
- Kahurangi National Park tours
- Motueka, 30-min drive
- Nelson City, 1-hour drive

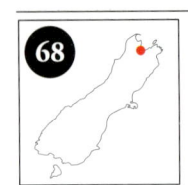

KAITERITERI, MOTUEKA
BELLBIRD LODGE KAITERITERI

Hosts Anthea and Brian Harvey

Sandy Bay Road, Kaiteriteri **Postal** Kaiteriteri, R D 2, Motueka
Phone 0-3-527 8555 *Mobile* 025 678 8441 *Fax* 0-3-527 8556
Email stay@bellbirdlodge.com *Website* www.bellbirdlodge.com

| 3 bdrm | 1 enst | 1 prbth | 1 pdrm | Double $150–$225 Single $100–$150 | Includes breakfast |

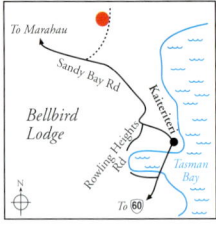

DIRECTIONS: Take SH 60 to Motueka. Continue through Riwaka, turn right & travel 6km to Kaiteriteri. Continue uphill towards Marahau. After 1.5km turn right into private road. Lodge is 3rd house on left.

Bellbirds sing in the garden and native bush behind the Lodge above Tasman Bay. Built in 1998, the house was remodelled in 2001 for ground-floor accommodation. Set on a quiet hillside just minutes' drive from Kaiteriteri Beach, Bellbird Lodge features sea or bush views from the spacious Magnolia Room, and both bedrooms in the Rosewood Suite. Anthea and Brian offer home baking with complimentary afternoon tea, and are happy to book local activities for their guests. The continental breakfast buffet is complemented by a hot speciality, such as grilled local nectarines with mascarpone served on toasted fruit bread in the dining room, or alfresco overlooking the ocean. Quality local restaurants offer lunch and dinner.

Facilities
- 1 super-king/twin ensuite bedroom
- 1 queen & 1 twin bedroom with private bathroom & spa bath
- hair dryer, toiletries & bathrobes
- tea/coffee & mineral water in all 3 bedrooms
- TV, video, books, games, music, CD-player & piano in lounge
- fresh flowers; guest fridge
- children over 10 yrs welcome
- continental breakfast buffet & cooked course each day
- complimentary afternoon tea provided; home baking
- 3-course dinner with wine, $50 pp by prior arrangement, May – Oct.
- phone fax & email available; complimentary laundry
- courtesy passenger transfer; on-site parking

Activities available
- gas barbecue on sun terrace
- golden beaches; swimming
- water taxis; yacht charter & launch cruises
- skydiving; flying fox
- scenic helicopter flights
- tramping, bush & coastal walks
- horse trekking; caves, 25 mins
- sea kayaking; sailing; snorkelling & river or sea fishing
- 4 restaurants 3–10-min drive
- potters; arts & crafts trail
- golf courses; mini golf
- wineries; gardens to visit
- gateway to Abel Tasman National Park
- Kahurangi National Park tours, 35-min drive
- Motueka, 20-min drive
- Nelson 1-hour drive away

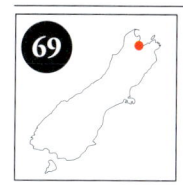

Riwaka Valley, Motueka
The Resurgence

Hosts Clare de Carteret-Bisson and Peter Adams

574 Riwaka Valley Road, R D 3, Motueka
Phone 0-3-528 4664 *Email* info@resurgence.co.nz
Fax 0-3-528 4605 *Website* www.resurgence.co.nz

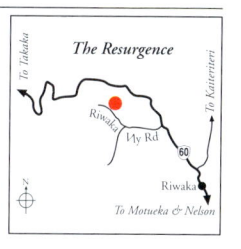

6 bdrm	6 enst	2 pdrm	Room rate $225–$320	Includes breakfast, apéritifs & dinner	Lunch extra
			Cabin rate $175–$245	Self-catering in cabins	Dinner & provisions extra

DIRECTIONS: From Nelson, take SH 60 north-west through Motueka, towards Takaka. Turn left into Riwaka Valley Rd & travel 5.7km, taking North Branch on right to The Resurgence on right.

Located in the Riwaka River valley, The Resurgence offers tranquillity enhanced by 20 hectares of the surrounding native bush, with walking tracks and views to the Kahurangi National Park. With architect-designed renovations, The Resurgence was opened in 2003, providing guests with four ensuite queen-size bedrooms upstairs, and two separate self-contained cabins. Clare and Peter, both trained in French cuisine, serve a full breakfast in the dining room, or alfresco on the verandah. They also offer lunch as required, and four-course dégustation dinner matched with fine Nelson wines. Guests enjoy the swimming pool, spa pool, and the walk to the crystal pools at the Riwaka Resurgence, where the river emerges from a marble cave.

Facilities
- 4 queen ensuite bedrooms upstairs in main house
- 2 self-contained cabins, with 1 queen ensuite bedroom & self-catering kitchen each
- all rooms with writing desk & private balcony/verandah
- massage showers, hair dryers, toiletries, demist mirrors, heated floor & towel rails
- cooked & continental breakfast
- lunch, $15 pp; 4-course table d'hôte dinner, $50 pp; wine extra
- open fire, tea/coffee, nibbles, bar, CDs, games, artwork, books & guides in lounge & maproom
- TV, videos, phone, fax, email, BBQ & laundry available
- cotton bed linen; French spoken
- wheelchair access; garaging & on-site parking

Activities available
- spa pool, swimming pool & hammocks on site
- 20ha (50 acres) native bush walks on site; bikes for hire
- picnicking, swimming hole, native bush walks & fishing at Riwaka Resurgence, 2 mins
- kayaking, walking & sailing in Abel Tasman National Park, 20 mins away
- eco tours
- walking, fishing, horse riding, & river canoeing in Kahurangi National Park
- restaurants & shops at Motueka, 20 mins drive
- local wineries, artists & markets
- safe swimming beaches
- golf at Motueka & Tasman
- Nelson airport, 50-min drive

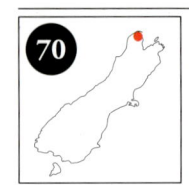

Takaka Hill, Motueka
Kairuru Farm Cottages

Hosts Wendy and David Henderson *Phone* 0-3-528 8091

SH 60, Takaka Hill, Motueka *Postal* Private Bag, Motueka
Freephone 0800 KAIRURU *Mobile* 027 433 7457 *Fax* 0-3-528 8091
Email kairuru@xtra.co.nz *Website* www.kairurufarmstay.co.nz

5 bdrm	3 prbth	Cottage rate $120 for 2 persons	Self-catering	Breakfast provisions & dinner extra
		Extra persons $15 each	Long-stay rates available in low season	

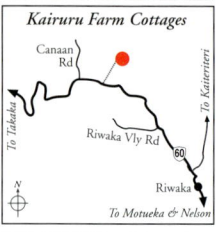

DIRECTIONS: From Nelson, take SH 60 north-west to Motueka. Continue 17 km towards Takaka. Driveway to Kairuru on right. (About 25 mins from Motueka, 1 hour from Nelson, or 3 hours from Picton ferries.)

Kairuru is a working hill-country sheep and cattle farm of 1,600 hectares (4,000 acres), between Golden Bay and the Abel Tasman National Park. Set in an established country garden with views over the Tasman Sea, the three cottages provide privacy, peace and quiet. Guests enjoy the paddock of pet sheep and goats, with a pig for variety. Kea Cottage includes two bedrooms and a loft, sleeping up to six guests. Pipit Cottage has two bedrooms. Canaan Cottage is a one-bedroom pioneer cottage. All three cottages are constructed from timber in rustic colonial style, with French doors opening from the living rooms on to sunny verandahs which offer extensive rural and sea views. Fully equipped kitchens in all three cottages enable guests to self-cater.

Facilities
- private-party bookings
- Pipit Cottage: 1 queen & 1 twin bedroom, with 1 private bathroom
- Kea Cottage: 1 queen & 1 super-king/twin bedroom, with 1 private bathroom
- Canaan Cottage: 1 double bedroom & private bathroom
- hair dryers, toiletries, heated towel rails & bathrobes
- breakfast provisions, $15 pp
- dinner & wine, $45 pp, served in house or cottage
- full kitchens for self-catering
- children welcome
- phone, TV, tea/coffee & guest laundry in each cottage
- open fire in 2 cottages
- 3 sunny verandahs
- on-site parking; helipad

Activities available
- BBQ on site
- walks on 1600ha working sheep & cattle farm on site
- daily farming activities
- in-ground swimming pool
- games court on site
- historic marble quarry on site
- walking tracks on site
- limestone caves on site
- Ngarua caves, nearby
- café, 11km drive away
- wineries; local potters
- safe swimming beaches
- kayaking; boating
- horse riding; Golden Bay
- Kaiteriteri, 20-min drive
- Abel Tasman National Park
- Motueka township, 17km
- Nelson City, 1 hour south

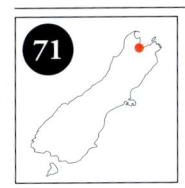

POHARA, GOLDEN BAY
BAY VISTA HOUSE

Hosts Sue and Ian McCracken

Paradise Way, Pohara   *Postal* Paradise Way, R D 1, Golden Bay
Phone 0-3-525 9772   *Mobile* 021 378 736   *Fax* 0-3-525 9772
Email hosts@bayvistahouse.co.nz   *Website* www.bayvistahouse.co.nz

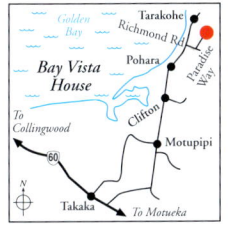

3 bdrm | 3 enst

Double $185–$250   Single $165–$220   *Includes continental breakfast*

DIRECTIONS: Take SH 60 to Takaka. Turn right into Motupipi St. At roundabout turn right into Abel Tasman Dr. At "T" junction, turn left to Pohara. Turn right into Richmond Rd, then left into Paradise Way to end.

Bay Vista House is situated on the hillside above Pohara Beach, one and a half hours' drive from Nelson City. The setting takes advantage of the sun and the views across Golden Bay to Collingwood and Farewell Spit. The activities and scenic sites of Golden Bay are within easy reach, and Abel Tasman National Park is just 20 minutes' drive away through Wainui Bay. All three guestrooms enjoy panoramic views of Golden Bay and open to the terrace where Sue and Ian serve continental breakfast alfresco, while guests enjoy the native birds from the adjacent nature reserve. The spa pool in the garden is popular with guests in the evenings, for relaxing and watching the sun set over the mountains of Kahurangi National Park.

Facilities

- 1 king suite & 2 queen bedrooms
- 3 ensuite bathrooms
- hair dryers, toiletries, heated towel rails, iron & ironing board in all 3 guestrooms
- guest fridge, TV & tea/coffee
- beach towels available
- all bedrooms open to terrace
- phone, fax & email available
- fresh, healthy continental breakfast served
- outdoor spa pool with view
- landscaped gardens with views & native birdlife
- native bush reserve adjacent
- day tours/activities arranged
- courtesy passenger transfers from/to buses & shuttles
- on-site parking

Activities available

- 3 restaurants within 5-min walk for evening meals
- Pohara beach, 5-min walk
- Pohara tennis court, 2 mins
- Pohara golf course, 5-min drive
- Tarakohe boat harbour, 5 mins
- Takaka township, 10-min drive
- arts & crafts of Golden Bay
- Te Waikoropupu Springs, 20-min drive away
- Farewell Spit 4WD tours from Collingwood, 30 mins
- Abel Tasman National Park, 20-min drive; Kahurangi National Park access
- golden sand swimming beaches; horse trekking
- sea kayaking & fishing; bird-watching
- bush walks; coastal walkways
- Nelson Airport, 1½ hours

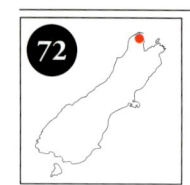

COLLINGWOOD, GOLDEN BAY
COLLINGWOOD HOMESTEAD

Hosts Maggie and Adrian Veenvliet

Elizabeth Street, Collingwood, Golden Bay
Phone 0-3-524 8079 *Email* maggie@collingwoodhomestead.co.nz
Fax 0-3-524 8979 *Website* www.collingwoodhomestead.co.nz

4 bdrm | 3 enst | 1 prbth   Double $265   Single $245   *Includes breakfast*   *Dinner extra*

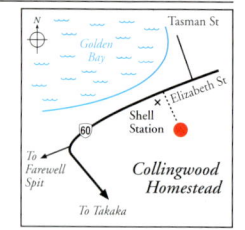

DIRECTIONS: From Nelson City, take SH 60 south over Takaka Hill to Golden Bay. At Collingwood village, turn right at beginning of Elizabeth St into driveway at sign, to Collingwood Homestead.

This turn-of-the-century colonial home was built as a private residence when Collingwood was a thriving gold town of three thousand people. Adrian extended the drawing room and added decking using the original verandah posts. The leadlight windows, polished matai floors, high ceilings and open fire are also original features. Sited across the road from the beach, Collingwood Homestead overlooks the Aorere River Estuary, with a backdrop of mountain ranges. The house is set in a cottage garden with climbing roses and native tree ferns. Maggie enjoys serving elaborate breakfasts and, by prior arrangement, three-course European-style dinners using Golden Bay salmon for entrées, farm meat and organic vegetables.

Facilities
- 1 queen & 2 king ensuite bedrooms
- 1 twin bedroom with spacious private bathroom
- drawing room with antiques, piano, open fire & verandah
- laundry available, charged
- Dutch & some German spoken
- courtesy passenger transfer
- old china & glass collection
- children over 11 yrs welcome
- gourmet breakfasts
- 3-course dinner, including pre-dinner drinks & wine, $65 pp
- vegetarian option provided
- Boris, the ginger cat & Poppy, the tortoise-shell
- phone, fax & email available
- off-street parking

Activities available
- relax on decking, opposite beach
- swimming beach, only 300m away across road
- fishing boat trips
- Farewell Spit trip
- guided walks on tracks
- bungy jumping
- squash & tennis courts
- Pupu Springs
- Settlers' Museum
- guided trout fishing
- surf-casting
- shellfishing
- Te Anaroa caves
- Begonia House
- scenic tour to West Coast & Westhaven Inlet
- Cob Valley tour to glacial north range
- Takaka, 27km away

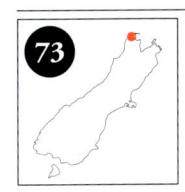

WHANGANUI INLET
WESTHAVEN RETREAT

Hosts Monika and Bruno Stompe

Te Hapu Road, Westhaven Inlet, Collingwood, Golden Bay
Phone 0-3-524 8354 Email westhave@ihug.co.nz
Fax 0-3-524 8354 Website www.westhavenretreat.com

| 7 bdrm | 3 enst | 2 prbth | Double $175–$255 Single $155–$235 | *Includes breakfast* *Lunch & dinner extra* | Cottage rate $280 for 1–2 persons Extra persons $22 each | *Self-catering* |

DIRECTIONS: From Collingwood, travel towards Farewell Spit. Turn right to Pakawau & continue 12km. Turn left towards Westhaven Inlet. 2km before Mangarakau turn right to Westhaven Retreat at end of road.

The drive from Collingwood takes guests off the beaten track through the Scenic Reserve of forests, streams and lakes to the untouched wilderness at Westhaven *(see above)*. Panoramic views are captured from both the octagonal dining and living room windows in the house overlooking the ocean, and from the self-contained cottage below. Set on a 500-hectare peninsula, Westhaven includes private beaches, caves, eye-catching rock formations, rainforest, hundreds of native nikau palms and 55 llamas for guests to feed and trek with. A new highlight is the two-kilometre track through native bush to the western beach. Breakfast in the house is guests' choice of cooked or buffet breakfast. Picnic lunches and Austrian dinner menus are also available.

Facilities
- self-catering cottage with 1 king & 1 twin bedroom & sofa bed
- 1 twin, 1 super-king/twin & 3 king bedrooms in house
- 3 ensuites & 1 private bathroom in house, 1 with dual basins
- hair dryers, toiletries & bathrobes
- laundry available
- phone, fax, email & computer
- German spoken

- European breakfast
- lunch by arrangement
- 3-course dinner, with NZ wine selection, $45 pp
- tea/coffee, juice & soft drinks available
- crayfish, crabs, mussels
- TV in both lounges
- panoramic ocean views
- passenger transfer; helipad

Activities available
- 500 ha (1,250 acres) with private beaches & secluded swimming pool
- 55 friendly llamas on site to feed, groom & for trekking
- fishing for snapper & blue jackfish
- bush walks through rainforest & natural nikau palm groves on site
- seals & penguins in season
- complimentary 4WD tour
- charter boat for fishing/sightseeing

- swimming & surfing
- private caves on site
- hiking & diving
- bird-watching
- photography
- rock climbing
- horse riding arranged
- Cape Farewell, 45 mins
- Collingwood, 1 hour
- Nelson, 3-hour drive

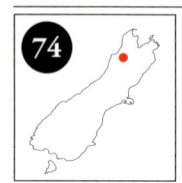

Nelson Lakes
St Arnaud House

Hosts Debbie and Justin Murphy

Corner Bridge Street and Lake Roads, St Arnaud *Phone* 0-3-521 1028
Postal P O Box 88, St Arnaud, Nelson Lakes *Fax* 0-3-521 1208
Email enquiries@st-arnaudhouse.co.nz *Website* www.st-arnaudhouse.co.nz

| 4 bdrm | 3 enst | 1 prbth |

Room rate $125–$215
House rate available

Includes breakfast
Dinner extra

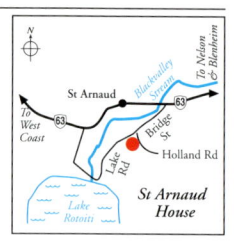

DIRECTIONS: From Blenheim, Nelson or West Coast, take SH 63 to St Arnaud. At Blackvalley Stream bridge, turn south into Bridge St. St Arnaud House on left, on corner of Holland Rd.

St Arnaud House provides secluded, subalpine accommodation adjacent to the native beech forest of Nelson Lakes National Park boundary. Lake Rotoiti, the national park and the internationally renowned Mainland Island recovery programme are all only a few minutes' stroll from the doorstep, as are the forest, lake and alpine walks which are suited to all fitness levels. Accommodation comprises three ensuite guestrooms, and a twin bedroom with private bathroom. Breakfast is served either in the dining room or alfresco on the sun decks, and dinner is available by arrangement. St Arnaud House offers guests total privacy, with the new hosts, Debbie and Justin, living in a separate dwelling adjacent to the main house.

Facilities

- 1 king & 2 queen ensuite bedrooms
- 1 twin bedroom with private bathroom
- toiletries & hair dryers in all rooms
- cotton bed linen
- forest & alpine views
- guest library
- laundry service available

- full breakfast options
- dinner by arrangement, extra
- tea/coffee & BBQ available
- fully stocked bar
- spacious, sunny decks for breakfast, relaxing & reading
- insect screens on all windows
- hosts live adjacent, on site
- on-site parking
- direct native forest access

Activities available

- Nelson Lakes National Park
- 5-min walk to Lake Rotoiti
- forest & birdlife recovery area, short walks
- kiwi re-introduction zone
- Peninsula, St Arnaud Range & lake circuit walks
- bush & alpine walks from 1 hour to 10 days
- wine trails; art & craft trails

- local restaurant, bar & store
- Mt Robert day walk
- hunting; world-class trout fishing, guide available
- golf courses; DOC information
- local Rainbow Ski Field
- Nelson City, Blenheim, or Motueka, 1-hour drive north
- West Coast, 2-hour drive
- Franz Josef Glacier, 5 hrs south

© Friars' Guide to New Zealand Accommodation for the Discerning Traveller

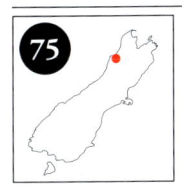

WESTPORT
RIVER VIEW LODGE

Host Noeline Biddulph

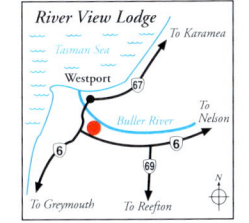

State Highway 6, Buller Gorge Road, Westport   Postal P O Box 229, Westport
Freephone 0800 184 656   Phone 0-3-789 6037   Fax 0-3-789 6037
Email info@rurallodge.co.nz   Website www.rurallodge.co.nz

| 4 bdrm | 4 enst |

Double $190
Single $170

Includes breakfast
Lunch & dinner extra

DIRECTIONS: From Nelson City, take SH 6 south towards Westport. Travel through the Buller Gorge almost to Westport. River View Lodge on the right.

Overlooking the Buller River, seven kilometres from Westport, River View Lodge is located in the Lower Buller gorge, off the Nelson/Picton highway. With picturesque views of the large garden and over the river to the surrounding mountains, the contemporary guest wing comprises three king-size ensuite bedrooms, one with wheelchair access, and all opening to a verandah. There is also one queen-size bedroom in the house with a small lounge which looks onto a private courtyard. Guests are offered both buffet and cooked breakfasts, and all meals are served in the lounge/dining room in the house, with panoramic views of the river and garden. A three-course table d'hôte dinner with New Zealand wine is available, by arrangement.

Facilities

- 1 king/twin & 2 king ensuite bedrooms in guest wing
- 1 queen bedroom with 1 ensuite bathroom in suite in house
- hair dryer, toiletries, heated towel rails, bathrobes & heater in all 4 ensuite bathrooms
- 1 wheelchair access bathroom
- TV, radio/clock, tea/coffee, sweets, fresh flowers, electric blankets & seating area in all 4 bedrooms
- breakfast by room service
- lunch available, $10–$15 pp
- 3-course dinner & wine, $45 pp, by arrangement
- laundry, $5 per load
- phone & fax available
- children by arrangement
- panoramic river views
- barbecue available
- on-site parking; helipad

Activities available

- established English-style garden
- grass tennis court on site
- therapeutic massage by arrangement, extra
- Buller River adjacent
- bush walks; golf course
- fishing
- gardens to visit
- jet boating
- heated swimming pool, 7km
- restaurants nearby
- picture theatre
- underwater & white water rafting
- beaches; seal colony
- coaltown museum
- horse trekking
- Westport, 7km away
- pancake rocks
- sightseeing by arrangement

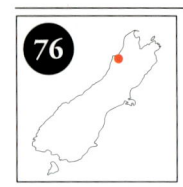

WESTPORT
ARCHER HOUSE

Host Kerrie Fairhall

75 Queen Street, Westport   *Phone* 0-3-789 8778
Freephone 0800 789 877   *Mobile* 025 260 3677   *Fax* 0-3-789 8763
Email accom@archerhouse.co.nz   *Website* www.archerhouse.co.nz

3 bdrm | 2 enst | 1 prbth   Double $150   Single $140   *Includes breakfast*

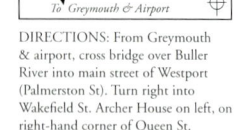

DIRECTIONS: From Greymouth & airport, cross bridge over Buller River into main street of Westport (Palmerston St). Turn right into Wakefield St. Archer House on left, on right-hand corner of Queen St.

Archer House is a Category 1 New Zealand Heritage Home, built in 1890 as an Italianate villa for Robert Taylor, a prosperous Westport grocer. It was used by the Sisters of Mercy from 1947 for 34 years, until Paul Archer bought and renovated it for accommodation. Now offering three queen-size guestrooms, with bathrooms and original open fireplaces, Archer House also retains leadlighting throughout and is furnished with antiques and artwork. A full cooked breakfast is served in the dining room or the conservatory with views to the mature garden. The spaciousness of Archer House makes it suitable for weddings, private functions, and small business conferences, or the entire house can be booked for privacy. Kerrie, the host, lives off-site.

Facilities

- 1 queen bedroom with private bathroom
- 2 queen/twin bedrooms with ensuite bathrooms
- cotton bed linen, TV & tea/coffee in bedrooms
- hair dryer, toiletries, heated floor & heated towel rails
- open fires in 1 lounge & 2 bedrooms
- email, fax & phone
- full cooked breakfast, with daily specials, served in dining room or conservatory
- 2 lounges with TV & piano & conservatory with verandah opening to garden
- fresh flowers; artwork
- laundry available
- children welcome
- off-street parking
- host lives off-site

Activities available

- weddings, functions & conferences catered for
- large mature garden on site
- Tauranga Bay
- heated swimming pool nearby
- town centre, short stroll away
- walkways & tracks
- Coaltown Museum
- beach & bush walks
- Kawatiri Golf Links
- Bay House & other restaurants nearby
- seal colony; jet boating
- Underworld Rafting
- white water rafting
- horse trekking
- fishing; whitebaiting
- Hector Pottery
- Karamea Limestone Caves
- Pancake Rocks

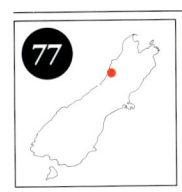

PUNAKAIKI, WESTLAND
HYDRANGEA COTTAGES

Hosts Karen Dickson and Neil Mouat

4224 Main Road, Punakaiki *Postal* P O Box 47, Punakaiki, Westland
Phone 0-3-731 1839 *Email* punakaiki@xtra.co.nz
Fax 0-3-731 1838 *Website* www.pancake-rocks.co.nz

Cottage rate $175–$275 for 2 persons
Extra persons $20–$30 each

Self-catering
No meals available

5 bdrm / 4 prbth

DIRECTIONS: From Greymouth, take SH 6 north towards Punakaiki. Travel 300m north of Punakaiki Bridge to Hydrangea Cottages on right. From Westport, take SH 6 to 700m south of Pancake Rocks on left.

Just a short walk from the Pancake Rocks and Blowholes, the Hydrangea Cottages enjoy panoramic views overlooking the Tasman Sea. Built among limestone outcrops surrounded by native bush and wild hydrangeas, the four self-contained cottages comprise a two-bedroom cottage, one-bedroom studio, and two-storey house with two apartments. Each cottage is individually designed and carefully created using native timber, and sited for privacy as well as sea views. Kitchens enable self-catering in each cottage, and there is a restaurant and café just minutes walk away. Located on the rugged west coast at Punakaiki, the Hydrangea Cottages provide a peaceful escape from city life; the nearest shop is half an hour south at Greymouth.

Facilities
- single-party bookings per cottage
- 4 cottages, each with 1 or 2 queen bedrooms & 1 bathroom:
  – Rata: upstairs apartment & bath
  – Mamaku: downstairs apartment
  – Rimu: 1-bedroom studio
  – Nikau: 2-bedroom cottage
- hair dryers & toiletries
- Nikau includes CDs, bathrobes, heated towel rails & mirror
- fresh flowers; decks with sea views
- kitchenette for self-catering in all 4 cottages
- lounge in each cottage, with TV, artwork & books
- guest laundry; dryer, $2
- on-site parking
- courtesy coach to gate
- phone & internet café, 700m walk away
- hosts live adjacent

Activities available
- horse trekking on site, novice to experienced; 19 horses & dog
- swimming in river mouth, 150m
- Pancake Rocks at beach opposite
- glass blowing & craft gallery within walking distance
- dolphin swimming nearby
- canoeing, 2km north; caving
- golf courses, 30 mins – 1 hour
- west coast gardens open to visit
- restaurants, 200m – 1.5km
- greenstone/jade carving, 30 mins – 1 hour south
- tramping/hiking in Paparoa National Park
- seal colony, 1-hour drive
- Greymouth, 30 mins south
- Hokitika or Westport, 1 hr
- Franz Josef Glacier, 3 hours
- Nelson, 3½-hour drive

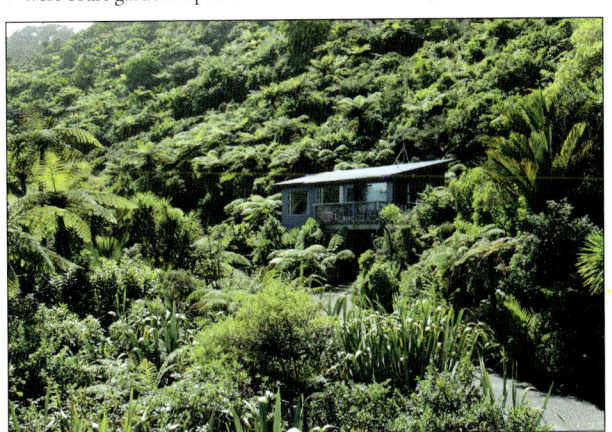

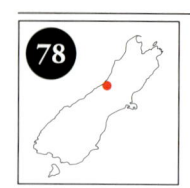

NINE MILE CREEK, GREYMOUTH
THE BREAKERS

Hosts pending

Nine Mile Creek, State Highway 6, Greymouth *Postal* P O Box 188, Greymouth
Freephone 0800 350 590 Phone 0-3-762 7743 Fax 0-3-762 7733
Email stay@breakers.co.nz *Website* www.breakers.co.nz

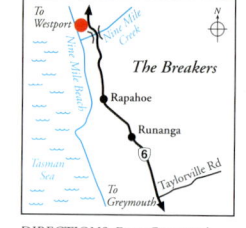

4 bdrm 4 enst Double $150–$235 Single $125–$175 *Includes breakfast*

DIRECTIONS: From Greymouth, take SH 6 north 10.5km to Rapahoe. Continue 4km over Nine Mile Creek to The Breakers on left. (29km south of Pancake Rocks at Punakaiki.)

Designed to maximise the panoramic views over the Tasman Sea and Paparoa National Park, The Breakers provides direct access to a secluded West Coast beach. Recently refurbished, The Breakers offers two ensuite guestrooms upstairs in the main house and two new ensuite guestrooms in the garden annex, all with ocean views. Guests enjoy falling asleep to the sound of waves on the beach below. Cooked or buffet breakfast is served in the dining room downstairs in the main house. Located in a quiet setting on almost a hectare (two acres) of land on the rugged unspoiled West Coast, The Breakers is only 14 minutes north of the township of Greymouth, and close to many tourist activities. The Pancake Rocks at Punakaiki are 30 kilometres north.

Facilities

- 2 queen ensuite bedrooms upstairs in main house
- 2 queen ensuite bedrooms in garden annex
- hair dryers & toiletries
- cotton bed linen, TV & tea/coffee in bedrooms
- all rooms opening to balcony or deck area overlooking the ocean
- cooked or buffet breakfast available in dining room
- lunch & picnic hampers by arrangement
- guest lounge with tea/coffee, library & magazines
- internet, fax & phone on request
- laundry available, extra
- ocean views from every room
- on-site parking

Activities available

- private beach access for beach walks
- 0.8ha (2-acre) coastal garden
- surfing & surf-casting
- black water rafting
- caving
- sea kayaking
- seal colony
- quad-bike bush tours
- Croesus Track
- restaurants, 14km south
- Shanty Town
- Lake Brunner
- gardens open to visit
- Jade Trail at Jade Boulder gallery
- Pancake Rocks & blowholes at Punakaiki, 30km north
- Paparoa National Park
- Greymouth township, 14km south, for shopping

WESTLAND
LAKE BRUNNER LODGE

Hosts Janice and Gary Hopper

Mitchells, Lake Brunner   *Postal* Mitchells, R D 1, Kumara, Westland
Phone 0-3-738 0163   *Email* lodge@brunner.co.nz
Fax 0-3-738 0163   *Website* www.lakebrunner.com

11 bdrm | 11 enst
Double $533–$700
Single $295–$420

Includes breakfast & dinner
Long-term & off-season rates available

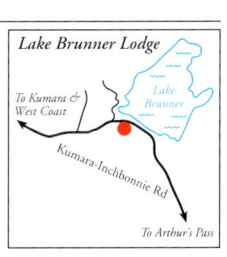

DIRECTIONS: Take SH 73 to the West Coast. From Greymouth, turn off at Kumara, & travel 22km to Mitchells & Lake Brunner Lodge. From Christchurch turn off at Jacksons & travel 17km to Lodge.

Lake Brunner Lodge offers peace and seclusion on the shores of Lake Brunner amid temperate rainforest. Constructed from local rimu, this 1930s bungalow still generates its own hydro power and reticulates its own water. Original native timber panelling features throughout the Lodge, which has recently been refurbished. The villa behind has been built in harmony with the existing Lodge. Lake Brunner Lodge provides professional fishing and conservation expertise, with brown trout fishing a speciality and guided environmental explorations. The chef prepares a daily changing menu using fresh meat, fish and produce, which is served table d'hôte to guests on the large dining-room table with premium New Zealand wines.

Facilities

- 7 ensuite bedrooms in Lodge, 4 in villa – doubles & twins; lounges in 2, verandahs on 5
- views of Lake Brunner
- separate library with trophies
- guest drawing room with open fire, separate bar & wine list
- fishing & environmental guides available for discussions, by request
- landscaped garden
- professional chef in house
- tariff includes table d'hôte dinner of NZ meat & fish, classic sauces & fresh produce, premium NZ wines, extra
- continental/cooked breakfast
- separate dining room
- Donna, the boxer dog, a playful extra
- float plane & boat charter service available on site

Activities available

- qualified guide services available
- fly & spin fishing – qualified guides available
- guided botanical photography
- guided bird-watching
- walking tracks
- mountain biking; golf
- canoeing; horse trekking
- trophy brown trout & salmon
- black water rafting
- visits to skilled craftspeople – woodturners, jade sculptor & spinners
- kiwi nesting sanctuary
- black petrel nesting sanctuary
- Hector's dolphin, spotted shag & seal colonies
- duck shooting in autumn
- close to Arthur's Pass & Paparoa National Parks

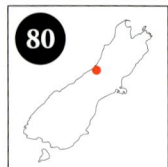

KUMARA, WESTLAND
WINDSOR FARM HOMESTEAD

Hosts Rhonda and Geoff Stewart

Kumara Junction, R D 1, State Highway 6, via Westland
Phone 0-3-736 9222   Mobile 021 736 922   Fax 0-3-736 9205
Email windsorfarm@xtra.co.nz   *Website* friars.co.nz/hosts/windsor.html

1 bdrm   1 enst   Room rate $275–$320   Includes breakfast   Dinner extra

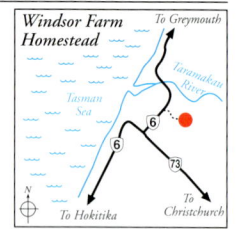

DIRECTIONS: From Greymouth, take SH 6 south for 16km. Cross historic Taramakau road & rail bridge & travel 800m. Turn left into private driveway & travel 500m to Windsor Farm Homestead.

Architecturally designed to blend into the native surroundings, Windsor Farm Homestead was built in 1992, on a plateau overlooking the Taramakau River. Located on the West Coast, between Greymouth and Hokitika, Windsor Farm is just south of the historic Taramakau road and rail bridge. Guests enjoy the tranquil setting with access to bush walks, native birds, a waterfall and fishing from the site. Windsor Farm Homestead offers one king-size ensuite guestroom opening onto a private patio with views over the cottage garden to the native bush beyond. Breakfast of seasonal fruits, hot scones and home-made jams, with two cooked options, is served in the dining room or alfresco. A three-course dinner with wine is also available.

Facilities

- 1 king bedroom
- 1 ensuite bathroom with spa bath, hair dryer, heated towel rails, bathrobes & toiletries
- cotton bed linen,
- writing desk, TV, tea/coffee, mineral water, port, chocolates & cookies in bedroom
- shared lounge with tea/coffee, bar, Sky TV, video, CD-player, piano & books
- continental or choice of cooked breakfasts
- 3-course dinner with complimentary wine, served in dining room, $65 pp
- email, fax & phone available
- fresh flowers
- laundry available
- honeymoons catered for
- on-site parking

Activities available

- large grounds with cottage garden on site
- fishing on site
- bush walks to waterfall on site
- native bird-watching on site
- local beach access
- native bush & beach walks
- Shantytown
- scenic flights to glaciers
- hunting
- restaurants, 20-min drive
- greenstone, gold & pottery artists
- historic buildings & sites
- gardens open to visit
- Kumara, 10-min drive
- Pancake rocks at Punakaiki
- Greymouth, 20-min drive
- Hokitika, 20-min drive
- skiing in winter

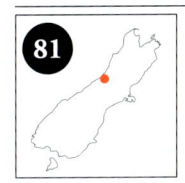

GREYMOUTH–HOKITIKA
KAPITEA RIDGE

Hosts Trixie and Murray Montagu

Chesterfield Road, Kapitea Creek, R D 2, Hokitika
Phone 0-3-755 6805   *Fax* 0-3-755 6895
Email stay@kapitea.co.nz   *Website* www.kapitea.co.nz

| 7 bdrm | 7 enst | 1 pdrm |

Room rate $250–$495   Includes breakfast & interpreted coastal walk
Dinner extra

DIRECTIONS: From Greymouth, take SH 6 south for 23km. Turn left into Chesterfield Rd. Cross railway line & take 1st driveway on left, signposted to Kapitea Ridge. From Hokitika, take SH 6 for 17km.

Overlooking the Tasman Sea, Kapitea Ridge is nestled into the coastal landscape, with native bush and rural farmland, and provides easy access to West Coast activities. The curved roofline of each guestroom enhances the panoramic views of the ocean and mountains. The furnishings reflect New Zealand landscape colours, and one ensuite features paua shell and tiles. Guests can relax in front of the log fire, the bay window or within the large native garden. Pacific Rim cuisine, focusing on seasonal fresh local fare and fine wine, is served alfresco or in the conservatory. Early evening is a favourite time for guests to stroll on the deserted beach with Bella, a young sheep dog, to unwind in the hot tub, enjoy a reflexology treatment, or apéritifs.

Facilities

- 1 suite sleeps 3 guests
- 4 super-king/twin, 1 double & 2 queen bedrooms
- 7 ensuites with hair dryers, heaters, demist mirrors, toiletries, 1 with bath & 1 with claw-foot bath
- bathrobes, fresh flowers, phone, chocolates, tea/coffee, port, TV & seating area in each bedroom
- balconies/patio with sea views
- children over 12 years welcome
- gourmet breakfast buffet
- 3-course dinner by prior arrangement, $65 pp
- alfresco fireside BBQ; wine cellar & liquor licence
- NZ art & gift gallery
- hydrotherapy hot tub
- native birds in coastal garden
- on-site car park
- helipad

Activities available

- weddings catered, with Murray, a marriage celebrant
- reflexology treatments, extra
- mountain bikes, gold panning, pétanque/boules & clay-bird shooting on site
- fishing guide available
- 2 golf courses, complimentary fee
- dolphins & seal colonies
- Shanty town & Punakaiki Pancake Rocks tours
- restaurants, 15-min drive
- white heron sanctuary
- coastal fauna & flora walk; historic gold tunnel walk
- alpine & coastal national parks
- local artisans – in wood, greenstone/jade, gold, fibre
- scenic flights to Franz Josef & Fox Glacier tours
- white water & cave rafting

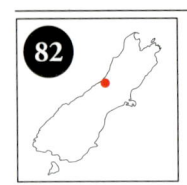

AWATUNA, WESTLAND
AWATUNA HOMESTEAD

Hosts Pauline and Hemi Te Rakau *Phone* 0-3-755 6834

Stafford Road, Awatuna, Westland   *Postal* P O Box 25, Hokitika, Westland
Freephone 0800 006 888   Mobile 025 260 3171   Fax 0-3-755 6876
Email rest@awatunahomestead.co.nz   *Website* www.awatunahomestead.co.nz

| 5 bdrm | 3 enst | 1 prbth | 1 pdrm | **Double** $175–$285 **Apartment rate** $185 | **Single** $110 **Extra persons** $25 each | *Includes breakfast, dinner extra* *Self-catering* |

DIRECTIONS: From Greymouth, take SH 6 south for 25km. Cross Waimea Creek bridge at Awatuna & turn left into Stafford Rd. Travel 100m to Homestead on left. Or from Hokitika, take SH 6 north for 15km.

Awatuna Homestead is a peaceful private coastal retreat with river frontage. It is set in extensive gardens featuring natives and conservation planting including traditional harakeke or flax gardens. Pauline and Hemi are happy to share the Maori and European cultural heritage of the site and surrounding area with their guests. Timber is used throughout the colonial homestead and the wood stove provides heating and cooking facilities. Accommodation comprises three ensuite bedrooms in the house as well as a separate self-contained apartment with a further two guestrooms. French doors open from all bedrooms onto the verandahs. Farmhouse-style dining is available using home-grown produce in season. Self-catering is optional for apartment guests.

Facilities

- 1 super-king/twin, 1 queen & 1 twin bedroom, with 3 ensuite bathrooms, in homestead
- self-contained apartment: 1 queen & 1 twin bedroom, with 1 bathroom & full kitchen
- TV, clock-radio, seating & electric blankets in bedrooms
- hair dryers, bathrobes, toiletries, heated tiled floors & towel rails
- 1 spa bath & heated mirror
- continental or special breakfast served
- 3-course table d'hôte dinner, $55 pp, by prior arrangement
- private hot tub/spa pool in bush setting
- guest laundry, fax & phone, extra
- parking & helipad on site; flights arranged

Activities available

- cultural interpretative talks by Hemi
- garden walks; bird-watching
- farm animals, 2 small friendly dogs, 2 cats, horses & pony
- canoes available on site
- vintage car ride on site
- evening glow-worm tour
- beachcombing, walking distance
- whitebaiting in season
- fishing, hunting, eco tours
- award-winning cafés
- greenstone, gold, wood, pottery & fibre artists
- golf course; garden tours
- paddle boat; gold panning
- historic walking tracks
- Shantytown; Pancake rocks
- sailing on Lake Kaniere
- scenic flights; lakes; glaciers; National Parks; white herons

© Friars' Guide to New Zealand Accommodation for the Discerning Traveller

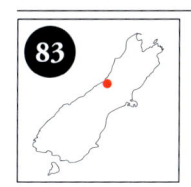

HOKITIKA, WESTLAND
VILLA POLENZA BOUTIQUE LODGE

Hosts Trina and Russell Diedrichs

143 Brickfield Road, R D 2, Hokitika   *Phone* 0-3-755 7801
Freephone 0800 241 801   *Mobile* 021 2477 123   *Fax* 0-3-755 7901
Email villapolenza@xtra.co.nz   *Website* www.villapolenza.co.nz

| 3 bdrm | 2 enst | 1 prbth | **Room rate $400–$550** Low-season rates available | *Includes breakfast* *Dinner extra* |

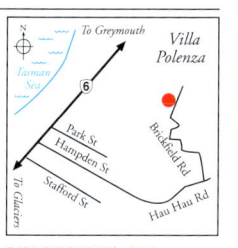

DIRECTIONS: Take SH 6 to Hokitika. 3 streets north of bridge, turn east into Hampden St. Travel 2km & continue into Hau Hau Rd. Turn left into Brickfield Rd & travel to Villa Polenza on left.

This Italian-style villa was purpose-built on the hill overlooking Hokitika, with panoramic views of the ocean framed by the Southern Alps. The native bush setting ensures peace and quiet for guests at Villa Polenza, which is a suitable venue for exploring the untamed beauty of the West Coast. The bright Mediterranean colours of the interiors of the Lodge complement the architecture, and outdoors guests can enjoy "*Il Bagno*" – two heated lime-green porcelain baths, discreetly placed on the edge of the hill surrounded by native bush. Dining is available under the chandelier by prior arrangement, featuring a choice of lamb, beef, chicken or salmon fillets and fresh garden salads, accompanied by pinot noir and other top-rated wines.

Facilities

- 1 queen/twin & 2 king bedrooms, 2 with walk-in wardrobes
- fresh flowers & Egyptian cotton bed linen in all bedrooms
- French doors from bedrooms
- 2 ensuites & 1 private bathroom, each with hair dryer, heated towel rails, demisting mirror, heated tile floor & bathrobes; 2 with bidets
- children over 13 yrs welcome
- dinner by request, $90 pp
- full breakfast options
- guest lounge with telescope & open fire
- laundry & guest email, extra
- Ruby the boxer dog & Oscar the Persian cat on site
- courtesy passenger transfer
- on-site parking
- helipad available

Activities available

- gardens to visit adjacent
- scenic flights to glaciers & Milford Sound
- white heron sanctuary
- glow-worm dell
- birdlife in native bush
- Pancake Rocks
- fishing guides available
- horse-trekking
- Water World
- Lake Kaniere & Hokitika Gorge rainforest walks
- local artisans: wood, jade, ruby rock, glass, gold, paua & merino-possum fibre
- water skiing
- microlighting
- canoeing
- snow skiing, 1½-hour drive
- 3 National Parks

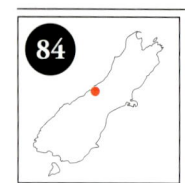

HARIHARI, SOUTH WESTLAND
WAPITI PARK HOMESTEAD

Hosts Bev and Grant Muir   *Mobile* 021 385 252

State Highway 6, R D 1, Harihari, South Westland
Freephone 0800 WAPITI   *Phone* 0-3-753 3074   *Fax* 0-3-753 3024
Email wapitipark@xtra.co.nz   *Website* www.wapitipark.co.nz

| 5 bdrm | 4 enst | 1 prbth | Double $465 Single $325 | Includes breakfast & dinner B&B rates available | Lunch extra |

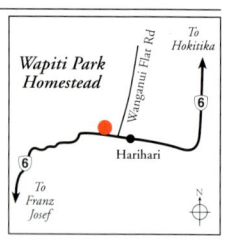

DIRECTIONS: 50 mins south of Hokitika, or north of Franz Josef. Take SH 6 to Harihari. Wapiti Park Homestead is on the southern edge of Harihari, on the west side of the state highway.

Kiwi Hosts Bev and Grant provide rural accommodation set in the remote south of Westland, at the gateway to the Franz Josef Glacier, 68km south. Their spacious country homestead overlooks their deer farm which specialises in the breeding of wapiti (Rocky Mountain elk), and is near the renowned brown trout fishery, Lafontaine Stream. The award-winning landscaped garden includes native ferns and flora, azaleas, rhododendrons, camellias and old roses, and a pond with an island is home to duck, swans and native birds. A convenient West Coast stop-over between Queenstown and Christchurch or Picton, this neo-colonial homestead was built in 1978 on the site of the original 1908 boarding house, coach stop and post office.

Facilities
- 4 king/twin ensuite bedrooms
- 1 king/twin bedroom with bathroom & wheelchair access
- fridge, fan, TV, tea/coffee, fruit basket, electric blankets, wool underlays & hair dryer
- phone, fax, email & complimentary laundry
- 2 guest lounges & trophy/games room with pool table
- off-season rates available
- full cooked or continental breakfast; B&B available
- 5-course table d'hôte dinner included in tariff
- unsuitable for young children
- award-winning garden with stone patios, pond & fountain
- 6pm Elk farm tour
- on-site parking; helipad & light aircraft landing facility

Activities available
- guided hunting safaris
- guided fishing for brown trout, salmon & saltwater surf-casting
- treks & nature tours arranged
- glow-worm walk; horse treks
- bush/rainforest walks
- white heron sanctuary
- historic goldfields
- community tennis & squash court; golf course, 25 mins
- mountain climbing
- National Park tracks
- photographic opportunities
- glacier walks
- scenic flights
- heliskiing in winter
- canoeing; white water rafting
- National Park attractions
- greenstone crafts, 78km north in Hokitika

© Friars' Guide to New Zealand Accommodation for the Discerning Traveller

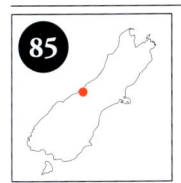

Franz Josef
GLENFERN VILLAS

Hosts Wendy and Marcel Fekkes

State Highway 6, Franz Josef **Postal** P O Box 85, Franz Josef
Freephone 0800 453 633   *Phone* 0-3-752 0054   *Fax* 0-3-752 0174
Email host@glenfern.co.nz   *Website* www.glenfern.co.nz

18 villas | 18 prbth

1-bedroom villa rate $135–$180
2-bedroom villa rate $170–$230

Self-catering
Continental breakfast provisions extra

DIRECTIONS: From Hokitika, take SH 6 south towards Franz Josef. 3km north of township, turn left into Glenfern Villas. Or from Wanaka take SH 6 north to Franz Josef village. Continue 3km to Glenfern on right.

With views of the snow-capped Southern Alps, Glenfern Villas were purpose built in 2000 to provide fully self-contained accommodation just north of Franz Josef village. The villas are family friendly with children's activities available on site. The 18 villas are designed in contemporary chalet style with cedar and Colorsteel. Each villa includes one or two bedrooms, a bathroom, separate lounge area and well equipped kitchen for self-catering. Breakfast can be delivered to the villas the previous evening, by arrangement. Restaurants and cafés are just three minutes south in the village. Franz Josef Glacier is a popular attraction. Glenfern Villas are easily accessible, yet surrounded by rural farmland, native bush and mountains beyond.

Facilities

- 4 villas with 1 queen & 1 twin bedroom in each
- 4 villas with 2 queen bedrooms
- 10 villas with 1 queen bedroom in each, 3 with extra sofa bed
- 1 private bathroom per villa, with hair dryer & toiletries
- cotton bed linen
- guest lounge with Sky TV in all 18 villas
- children welcome
- continental breakfast, to villas in evenings, $12.50 pp
- full kitchens for self-catering
- phone in each villa; fax available at reception
- wheelchair access to 2 villas
- laundry available $2.00
- conferences; weddings; & honeymoons catered for
- carport parking on site

Activities available

- portable BBQ available
- trampoline for children on site
- swing ball on site
- glacier & rainforest walks
- kayaking
- fishing in river
- helicopter flights
- White Heron Sanctuary tours
- 3 craft shops at Franz Josef
- restaurants, at Franz Josef, 3km south
- Maori carving studio at Whataroa, 30-min drive
- Fox Glacier, 35 mins south
- Hokitika, 1¾ hours north
- Greymouth, 2 hours north
- Christchurch City, 4-hr drive
- Lake Wanaka, 4 hours south
- Queenstown, 5 hours south

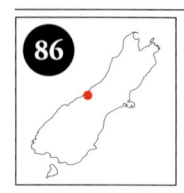

Franz Josef
Westwood Lodge

Hosts Janet and Bill Gawn

State Highway 6, Franz Josef   Postal P O Box 37, Franz Josef
Phone 0-3-752 0112   Email westwood@xtra.co.nz
Fax 0-3-752 0111   Website www.westwood-lodge.co.nz

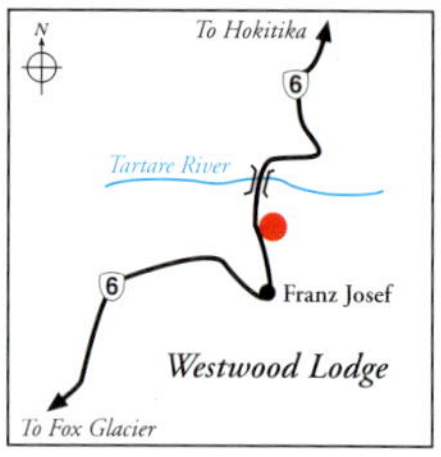

| 8 bdrm | 8 enst | 1 pdrm | Double $900–$1,125 Single $500–$787 | Includes breakfast & dinner Package available   Lunch extra |

DIRECTIONS: From Hokitika, take SH 6 south 150km towards Franz Josef. Cross bridge over Tartare River to Westwood Lodge on left. Or from south, take SH 6 to Franz Josef. Continue 2km to Westwood on right.

Westwood Lodge has been renovated with eight spacious suites and a guest lounge featuring a picture window with alpine views. Located on one hectare in a rural setting on the outskirts of Franz Josef village, Westwood is close to the glaciers. A full breakfast and four-course table d'hôte dinner are served from the chef's menu in the licensed dining room. There is a bar in the guest lounge and a full-size snooker table in the billiards room. The suites each have a super-king/twin bed, ensuite bathroom and include tea and coffee facilities, television, writing desk, and lounge area opening to a verandah with outdoor seating. Six suites have mountain views and two look on to a courtyard. Two-day packages with tours are also available.

Facilities

- 8 suites, each with super-king/twin bed, bath in ensuite, TV, phone, writing desk, tea/coffee, dual basin & demist mirror
- hair dryer, toiletries, heated floor & wheelchair access in ensuites
- guest lounge with mountain views, open fire & writing desk
- conservatory area with mountain view & private dining by request
- fax available; 2 cats on site
- continental or cooked breakfast in dining room
- light lunch on request
- 4-course table d'hôte dinner, from chef's menu included
- bar in guest lounge
- complimentary laundry service
- children over 12 yrs welcome
- on-site parking
- courtesy passenger transfer

Activities available

- 2-night package includes jet boat river, lagoon & rainforest tour, & view southern & white heron breeding colony in season
- white water rafting, grade 2 – grade 5 rivers
- glacier walks
- heli-hiking; kayaking
- bush walks; guided bush hikes
- lake, river & sea fishing
- lunch cafés in Franz Josef village, 1-min drive south
- bird-watching
- Franz Josef Glacier, 10 mins
- Fox Glacier, 30 mins south
- scenic flights
- rugged West Coast scenic route
- lake paddle-boat cruises
- Hokitika, 150km north
- tandem sky diving

© Friars' Guide to New Zealand Accommodation for the Discerning Traveller

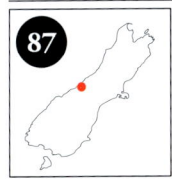

Fox Glacier
Te Weheka Inn

Host Guy Sanders

State Highway 6, Fox Glacier *Postal* P O Box 90, Fox Glacier
Freephone 0800 313 414 *Phone* 0-3-751 0730 *Fax* 0-3-751 0731
Email stay@teweheka.co.nz *Website* www.teweheka.co.nz

20 bdrm | 20 enst | 1 pdrm
Double $295
Single $275
Includes breakfast
Dinner extra

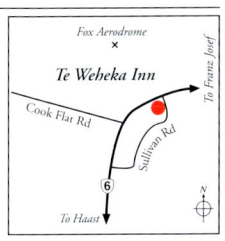

DIRECTIONS: From Franz Josef, travel south on SH 6 for 23km to Fox Glacier village. Te Weheka on left, opposite Department of Conservation Information Centre.

Purpose-built in November 2001 at Fox Glacier township, Te Weheka Inn provides accommodation in 20 super-king/twin-size ensuite guestrooms. Each bedroom features full amenities including phone, Sky television, tea and coffee-making facilities, writing desk, ironing facilities and easy chairs. All 20 bedrooms and the upstairs guest lounge open to individual balconies, some with views over the Lower Fox and Cook River Valley. A full breakfast is included in the tariff and served in the dining room downstairs. There is a breakfast buffet as well as a variety of cooked dishes. Packed lunches are available by request, and dinner is offered during the summer season only. Guests enjoy exploring Fox Glacier and the nearby walking tracks.

Facilities
- 20 king/twin ensuite bedrooms
- 2 sets of interconnecting rooms
- cotton bed linen, writing desk, phone, Sky TV, tea/coffee & balcony from each bedroom
- baths, hair dryers, toiletries
- wheelchair access
- self-serve laundry facilities
- underfloor heating
- fax & email available
- self-serve continental or full cooked breakfast; vegetarians catered for
- dinner available from November to April, extra
- guest lounge upstairs with music, artwork, library, magazines, writing desk, internet access & balcony
- internal elevator/lift
- on-site under-cover parking

Activities available
- guided glacier walks
- local day & half-day walks
- Lake Matheson walks
- Gillespies Beach walks
- ice climbing instruction
- scenic flights
- Fox Glacier & walks, 5-min south of village
- Franz Josef Glacier & village, 30-min drive north
- restaurants, gift shop & viewing Mt Cook, 2-min walk
- West Coast scenic route
- fishing; hunting
- bush walks; bird-watching
- heli-hikes; mountain trekking
- art & crafts at Franz Josef
- Hokitika, 2-hour drive north
- Haast, 1½-hour drive south
- Wanaka, 3-hour drive south

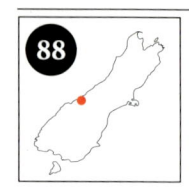

Haast
WILDERNESS LODGE LAKE MOERAKI

Hosts Dorothy Piper and Malcolm Edwards

State Highway 6, Haast   *Postal* Private Bag 772, Hokitika
Phone 0-3-750 0881   *Email* lakemoeraki@wildernesslodge.co.nz
Fax 0-3-750 0882   *Website* www.wildernesslodge.co.nz

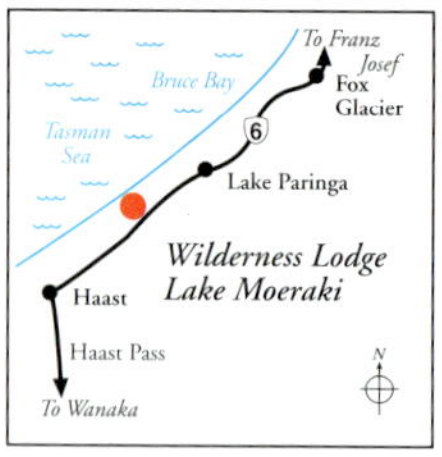

28 bdrm | 28 enst
Double $500–$700
Single $320–$395

Includes breakfast, dinner & guided activity programme
Low-season rates available

DIRECTIONS: From Haast, take SH 6 north for 30km. Wilderness Lodge on left of highway. From Fox Glacier, take SH 6 south for 90km. Wilderness Lodge on right of highway.

This Wilderness Lodge is located on the southern West Coast, on the banks of the Moeraki River where it flows from Lake Moeraki, only two kilometres from the Tasman Sea. Its very remoteness is its prime feature, giving access to a pristine area of New Zealand including 1,000-year-old native trees, rare Fiordland crested penguins and elephant seals in season, or fur seals year round. This was the original road camp site in the 1960s when the Haast Road was built. In 1989 Dr Gerry McSweeney and Anne Saunders developed it into a premier nature lodge. The surrounding wilderness can be explored on foot, by vehicle or by canoe. Guided group walks and tours for a minimum of four people are offered daily at extra cost, as below.

Facilities

- the Wilderness Lodge mission is "to combine quality hospitality with nature discovery & conservation"
- 4ha grounds set in rainforest World Heritage Park
- 18 Lodge & 10 Garden bedrooms, all with ensuites
- spacious guest lounge, with open log fire, overlooking river
- wine cellar, liquor licence
- continental buffet of cereals, yoghurts, fruit & home-style cooked breakfast served in Riverside Restaurant
- 4-course dinner with choices
- vegetarian option on request
- restaurant or picnic lunch available for guests, extra
- guest laundry
- Lodge shop with local souvenirs

Activities available

- complimentary daily naturalist-guided programme of 2 activities eg rainforest & bird discovery walks, lake canoeing, giant eel feeding & glow-worm/night sky walks
- network of forest, lake & sea-coast short to full-day walks, penguin walks & canoe trips; kayaks & canoes for guest use
- DOC Guiding Licence RCT 0122

Optional guided adventures extra:
- guided 4–5 hr seal & penguin walks
- guided 4-hr sea-coast, rainforest, Hector's dolphin & historic goldminers walk
- guided ½-day canoe safaris
- trout fishing gear hire
- Fox Glacier & Lake Matheson, 1-hour drive north

Westland and Central Canterbury
Wilderness Lodges
Lake Moeraki and Arthur's Pass

(See pages 370 and 372)

New Zealand's only two Wilderness Lodges, established and owned by biologists Anne Saunders and Dr Gerry McSweeney, are a day's drive apart in dramatically contrasting natural settings. Guided activities explore the forests, rivers and wildlife around both Lodges. West of the Southern Alps, Wilderness Lodge Lake Moeraki features towering rainforest, pristine seacoast, Fiordland crested penguins and fur seals. The Lodge lies on the lake shore, 30 minutes' forest walk from the Tasman Sea. Wilderness Lodge Arthur's Pass is in the heart of the Southern Alps amid a landscape of wild rivers, tawny tussock, snow-capped peaks, beech forest, kea parrots and alpine flowers. This Lodge is located on a 2,400-hectare (6,000-acre) sheep station and nature reserve.

Above: Upper Otira Valley in Arthur's Pass National Park. Daily guided walks from both Lodges take guests into the mountains, forests, rivers & coast to discover unique native flora and fauna.

Right top: Moeraki seacoast – just 30 minutes easy walk from the Wilderness Lodge. Fiordland crested penguins, elephant seals, fur seals, Hector's dolphins and marine life are found on this coast.

Right centre: Tawaki – Fiordland crested penguins on the Moeraki coastline. Only 6,000 of these rare penguins remain in the entire world. They breed at Moeraki from July to early December.

Right bottom: Kea – the world's only mountain parrot. Cheeky and intelligent, they have little fear of humans and feed on fruit, insects and worms at Arthur's Pass, and flax nectar at Moeraki.

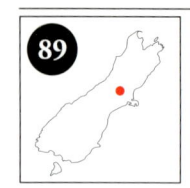

ARTHUR'S PASS
WILDERNESS LODGE ARTHUR'S PASS

Hosts Anne Saunders and Dr Gerry McSweeney

State Highway 73, Arthur's Pass *Postal* P O Box 33, Arthur's Pass
Phone 0-3-318 9246 *Email* arthurspass@wildernesslodge.co.nz
Fax 0-3-318 9245 *Website* www.wildernesslodge.co.nz

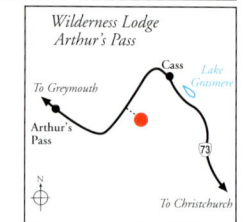

24 bdrm | 24 enst
Double $590–$980
Single $395–$690

Includes breakfast, dinner & guided activity programme
Low-season rates available

Wilderness Lodge Arthur's Pass

DIRECTIONS: From Christchurch, take SH 73 for 130km west. 16km before Arthur's Pass, turn left into the Wilderness Lodge driveway. Travel 1km to Lodge. Well signposted. From Greymouth travel 130km to driveway.

Built in 1996, this Wilderness Lodge lies between Arthur's Pass National Park and Craigieburn Forest Park, surrounded by 2,000 hectares of native beech forest, tussock grasslands and a small lake. The Lodge is sited on the historic 2,400-hectare high-country Cora-Lynn Station, farmed since 1860, and invites guests to experience high-country nature and merino sheep farming. A network of mountain, forest, river and farm walks and complimentary guided activities introduce visitors to high-country ecology and wildlife in a wilderness setting. Day walks, and canoe and fishing trips, are optional extras. Wilderness Lodge Arthur's Pass nestles into the natural landscape and every room enjoys sunshine and alpine views.

Facilities

- the Wilderness Lodge mission is "to combine quality hospitality with nature discovery & conservation"
- 20 queen/twin bedrooms, each with ensuite shower & bath
- 4 king-size lodges, each with spa
- spacious mountain view lounge with fireplaces, library of NZ books
- historic David McLeod library
- 4-course dinner choices; vegetarian by arrangement
- continental or home-style cooked country breakfast
- picnics & lunches, $18–$32 pp
- Black Range conference room
- children 2–12 yrs, half rates when sharing with 2 adults
- passenger transfers from Tranz Alpine Train available

Activities available

- 30km of mountain, forest & farm self-guided nature walks
- complimentary daily guided programme of 2 activities eg bird-watching, forest, wetlands, tussockland walks, shearing & spinning; night sky walks
- DOC Guiding Licence CA 215
- picnic areas & lookouts
- trout fishing, guided by prior arrangement

Optional guided adventures extra:
- Southern Alps Otira Glacier & wildflower expedition
- Limestone Castles & lake canoeing
- Torlesse Tussockland Park traverse
- West Coast rainforests & Granite Island canoe safari
- Southern Alps waterfalls, pygmy forest & giant buttercup walk

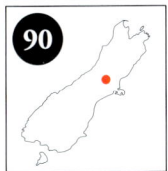

ARTHUR'S PASS
GRASMERE LODGE

Hosts Oliver and Vicki Newbegin

State Highway 73, Cass   *Postal* Private Bag 55 009, Christchurch
Phone 0-3-318 8407   *Email* retreat@grasmere.co.nz
Fax 0-3-318 8263   *Website* grasmere.co.nz

13 bdrm | 13 enst

Double $1,350–$1,800
Single $1,070–$1,520

*Includes breakfast & dinner
Lunch extra*

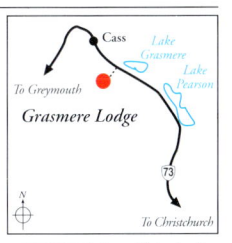

DIRECTIONS: From Christchurch take SH 73 towards Arthur's Pass. Travel past Lake Pearson for 5km. Follow Grasmere Lodge sign on left.

Surrounded by snowcapped mountains and alpine lakes, Grasmere Lodge is a high-country retreat, not far from Arthur's Pass, sited on a merino sheep station 700 metres above sea level. The Lodge now combines the old station homestead built in 1858, with new buildings which feature 13 luxurious guest bedrooms, each with a tiled ensuite including a spa bath. Before dinner, guests gather around the log fires in the spacious panelled lounge or the library and sample wines from Oliver's extensive underground cellar. The resident chefs offer a daily five-course table d'hôte menu, serving candlelit dinner to guests in the formal dining room. Breakfast and lunch are served in the conservatory or Verandah Restaurant looking out to the garden.

Facilities

- 13 king/twin bedrooms, each with ensuite bathroom
- all 13 ensuite bathrooms include spa bath, heated mirror, underfloor heating, hair dryer & quality toiletries
- 1 spa studio, with resident therapist, available
- cotton bed linen, bathrobes & slippers in each bedroom
- laundry available
- spacious lounge & bar with stone fireplace, billiards table, grand piano & original artwork
- library with stone fireplace
- French & German spoken
- children welcome, by arrangement
- covered garage parking
- helipad
- small conference boardroom

Activities available

- outdoor heated swimming pool
- relaxing & enjoying views from loungers on private guest patios opening from each guestroom
- 3 pianos for guests' use
- picnicking – lunch available, extra charge
- 2ha garden & lawns
- tennis on site
- guided horse trekking
- pétanque/boules on site
- clay pigeon shooting on site
- fly fishing
- kayaks available
- mountain bikes available
- nearby lakes
- tramping in Arthur's Pass National Park
- Arthur's Pass, 30km away
- Christchurch, 1½ hours away

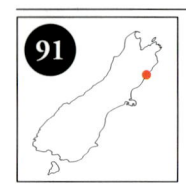

Kaikoura
Kaikoura Lodge

Managers Liane and Richard Rumble

Corner Hapuku Road and State Highway 1, R D 1, Kaikoura
Freephone 0800 KAIKOURA *Phone* 0-3-319 6559 *Fax* 0-3-319 6557
Email kaikouralodge@paradise.net.nz *Website* www.kaikouralodge.com

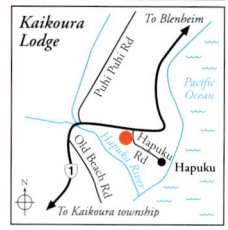

| 7 bdrm | 7 enst | 1 pdrm | Room rate $255–$350 | Includes breakfast | Lunch & dinner extra |
| | | | Apartment rate $350 | Self-catering in apartment | |

DIRECTIONS: From Kaikoura, take SH 1 north for 12km. Cross Hapuku River & turn right into Hapuku Rd. Kaikoura Lodge immediately on right. From Picton, take SH 1 towards Kaikoura. Turn left into Hapuku Rd.

Purpose-built in 2003, Kaikoura Lodge provides contemporary accommodation in six spacious ensuite guestrooms and a separate fully self-contained apartment. Designed as eco-friendly accommodation, Kaikoura Lodge features a spacious guest lounge with double-glazed windows and an open double fire. Meals are available at the on-site Hapuku Café which specialises in organic food. Guests can also dine alfresco on the second-storey lookout of the Lodge, and enjoy the ocean views from upstairs with the backdrop of snow-capped mountains. Set on a deer farm with a landscaped organic wind garden and olive grove, Kaikoura Lodge is just 10 minutes north of Kaikoura township. Children are welcome in the apartment by arrangement.

Facilities

- 1 king & 5 queen ensuite bedrooms in Lodge
- 1 separate self-contained upstairs apartment including spa bath
- desk, Sky TV, phone, tea/coffee & fridge in all 7 bedrooms
- hair dryers, toiletries, bathrobes, heated towel rails, heated floors
- fresh flowers; fax & email
- open double fire, CDs, artwork, books & desk in guest lounge
- full breakfast in café
- complimentary refreshments
- lunch & dinner in apartment or Lodge, or at adjacent café & licensed restaurant, extra
- basic provisions in self-catering kitchen in apartment
- laundry available, extra
- courtesy transfer; helipad
- on-site parking/garaging

Activities available

- guests' pets by arrangement; cat, chickens, goat, deer on site
- BBQ on site
- bicycles & picnics available
- entertainment in Hapuka Café on occasions, on site
- diving, kayaking & fishing in ocean
- swimming with dolphins
- horse riding
- shopping & art galleries in Kaikoura township, 12km
- whale watching; bird-watching
- golf course
- 4WD tours; scenic flights
- gardens open to visit
- tramping in Arthur's Pass National Park
- interisland ferry, 2 hours north
- Christchurch, 2 hours south

© Friars' Guide to New Zealand Accommodation for the Discerning Traveller

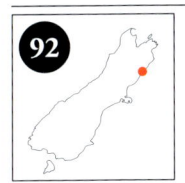

KAIKOURA
KINCAID LODGE

Hosts Helen and Judith Costley

611 Main North Road, State Highway 1, Hapuku, R D 1, Kaikoura
Phone 0-3-319 6851   *Mobile* 025 686 1820   *Fax* 0-3-319 6801
Email helen@kincaidlodge.co.nz   *Website* www.kincaidlodge.co.nz

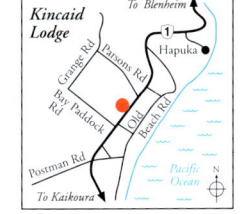

4 bdrm / 4 enst   Room rate $395–$480   Includes breakfast   Dinner extra

DIRECTIONS: From Kaikoura, take SH 1 north towards Blenheim for 6km. Pass Hapuku School on right of main road. Driveway to Kincaid Lodge immediately on left of main highway.

After a century in one family, the historic homestead of the original farm, Kincaid Downs, has been totally renovated to provide accommodation. Mother and daughter team, Judith and Helen, born and bred New Zealanders, welcome guests to Kincaid Lodge, set in a large garden, with bush walks and mountain views. The four ensuite bedrooms each open to a private verandah, with garden outlooks. Helen gives sheepdog displays with Bonnie rounding up the coloured sheep, and Foalie the horse is a favourite with guests. Just five minutes north of Kaikoura township, Hector dolphins can be seen swimming most mornings, 20 mintues' walk away, and whale-watching can be booked. Formal dinners and barbecues are available by prior arrangement.

Facilities
- 2 super-king & 2 queen ensuite bedrooms
- hair dryers, toiletries, heated towel rails & demist mirrors
- bathrobes & slippers; cotton bed linen; fresh flowers
- spa bath in honeymoon room
- TV, sofa, tea/coffee & fridge in all 4 bedrooms
- children over 12 yrs welcome
- full breakfast served indoors or alfresco on verandah
- formal or BBQ dinner by arrangement, extra
- 2 open fires, nibbles, bar, CDs, piano, guitar, artwork & books in lounge
- complimentary laundry
- courtesy passenger transfer
- on-site parking; helipad

Activities available
- all-weather tennis court, pétanque, badminton, croquet & clay-bird shooting on site
- garden, bush & farm on site with cattle & old horse, Foalie
- sheepdog displays with Bonnie & coloured sheep on site
- mountain bikes & golf clubs available for guest use
- hunting; quad biking
- whale watching tour bookings
- restaurants within 6km
- beach, 20-min walk or 5-min drive, to view Hector dolphins
- diving; kayaking; surfing
- bush walks; Mt Fyffe walks
- art galleries; winery
- Mt Lyford ski-field, 1 hour
- scenic & whale flights
- Kaikoura, 5-min drive south
- Christchurch, 2 hours south

375

© Friars' Guide to New Zealand Accommodation for the Discerning Traveller

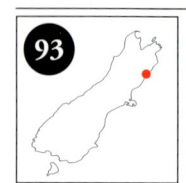

Kaikoura
Miharotia House

Hosts Polly and Trevor Ruawai

274 Scarborough Street, Kaikoura
Phone 0-3-319 7497 *Email* bestviewsmiharotia@xtra.co.nz
Fax 0-3-319 7498 *Website* www.miharotia.co.nz

4 bdrm / 4 enst Room rate $150–$240 *Includes continental breakfast / Cooked breakfast extra*

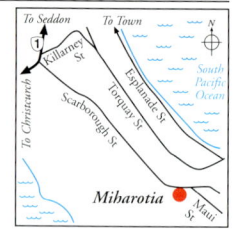

DIRECTIONS: From Blenheim take SH 1 to Kaikoura. Travel 1.75km past Caltex & turn left then right into Scarborough St. Miharotia on right. From Christchurch, take SH 1 north. Turn 1st right past Southbay Pde.

Miharotia is Maori for to admire, or to wonder at, with panoramic views over the Pacific Ocean and Kaikoura township to the Southern Alps beyond. Set in a landscaped garden, Miharotia offers four individually designed ensuite guestrooms with individual temperature control, opening to a private balcony. Continental breakfast includes home-made yoghurt, a platter of seasonal fruits and muffins, or cooked options are available such as fresh locally farmed eggs and local fish. Breakfast is served in the upstairs dining room, alfresco on the balcony, or room service if desired. Whale and bird watching by boat or air are popular, and guests enjoy swimming with dolphins and seals. Polly has Ngai Tahu ancestry and is happy to arrange Maori tours.

Facilities
- 1 super-king/twin & 3 queen ensuite bedrooms, each opening to private balcony
- cotton bed linen; fresh flowers
- phone, TV & tea/coffee in rooms
- hair dryer, toiletries, heated floor, heated towel rails & bathrobes
- wheelchair access
- phone & fax available
- laundry, $5; 1 powder room
- continental breakfast served in dining room, on balcony, or room service
- full cooked breakfast, $10 pp
- lounge with tea/coffee, Sky TV, video, CDs, books & writing desk
- email, phone & fax available
- courtesy passenger transfer
- private guest entrance; on-site parking

Activities available
- spa pool on site
- native bird-watching
- swimming with dolphins or seals
- whale watching by boat or air
- paeony garden flowering November/December
- conservational walkway
- groper or crayfishing trips
- art galleries
- Maori tours
- restaurants & cafés, 2 mins
- fur seal colony
- mountain climbing; hiking
- swimming; scuba diving
- golf course
- horse trekking
- skiing in winter
- Kaikoura township, 2 mins
- Christchurch, 2 hours south

© Friars' Guide to New Zealand Accommodation for the Discerning Traveller

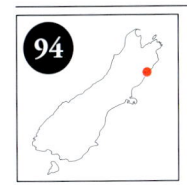

Kaikoura
Kahutara Homestead

Hosts Nikki and John Smith

Dairy Farm Road, Kaikoura Postal P O Box 9, Kaikoura
Phone 0-3-319 5580 *Freephone* 0800 273 351 *Fax* 0-3-319 5580
Email kahutarahomestead@xtra.co.nz *Website* friars.co.nz/hosts/kahutara.html

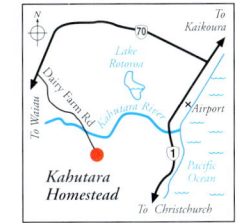

| 2 bdrm | 1 enst | 1 prbth |

Double $210–$230
Single $180

*Includes breakfast
Dinner extra*

DIRECTIONS: From Kaikoura, take SH 1 south for 5km. Turn right into SH 70 & travel 11km. Turn left into Dairy Farm Rd & travel nearly 6km, crossing bridge over Kahutara River to Kahutara Homestead at end of road.

Kahutara Homestead was built in 1910 on the 1,100-hectare (2,600-acre) farm that runs Corriedale sheep and Angus cattle. Named after the Australasian harriers (kahu) that live among the rocky outcrops (tara), Kahutara Homestead affords views to the Seaward Kaikoura Range and out to sea towards Christchurch. John enjoys taking guests on the 1880s horse mail route to a lookout point 500 metres above sea level, and farm activities can be viewed in season. The homestead features native rimu panelling and offers two guestrooms – a queen/twin with ensuite, and a queen/twin with a private bathroom including a claw-foot bath. Nikki serves meals in the country kitchen, with fresh New Zealand lobster a speciality.

Facilities

- 1 queen/twin bedroom with ensuite bathroom
- 1 queen/twin bedroom with private bathroom, claw-foot bath & bathrobes
- toiletries & heated towel rails
- hair dryers available
- fresh flowers
- phone & fax available
- complimentary laundry
- full cooked breakfast served in country kitchen
- 3-course dinner, apéritifs & NZ wine with hosts, $50–$70 pp; NZ lobster/crayfish or venison by arrangement
- tea & coffee available
- Sky TV & open fire in private guest lounge
- on-site parking
- helipad

Activities available

- native birds in extensive garden
- viewing seasonal farm activities
- farm walks on almost 1,100ha hill country, includes extensive areas of native bush
- peony garden flowering November/December
- horse stud on site
- bookings for whale watching, dolphin swimming, ocean wings & albatross tours
- bookings for horse trekking
- located on scenic Alpine Pacific Triangle Route, linking to Hanmer Springs
- sea fishing trips for crayfish/lobster & groper
- trout fishing
- seal colony
- Kaikoura, 20-min drive
- Christchurch, 2 hours south

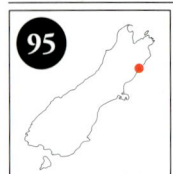

KAIKOURA
FYFFE COUNTRY LODGE

Hosts Christine Rye and Colin Ashworth

State Highway 1, R D 2, Kaikoura
Phone 0-3-319 6869 *Fax* 0-3-319 6865
Email fyffe@xtra.co.nz *Website* fyffecountrylodge.com

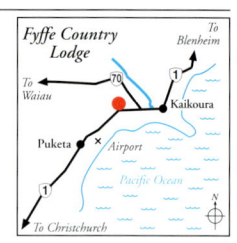

| 6 bdrm | 6 enst | 1 pdrm |

Double $495–$867
Single $250–$475

Includes breakfast, dinner & drinks
Lunch extra

DIRECTIONS: From Blenheim, take SH 1 south to Kaikoura. Continue for 5km on SH 1. Fyffe Lodge on right of SH 1. From Christchurch, take SH 1 north towards Kaikoura. Pass airport on right, to Fyffe Country Lodge on left.

This adobe country lodge was built in 1994 from rammed earth bricks and roofed with hand-split Canadian cedar shakes. Set in an English-style cottage garden beneath the snow-capped mountains of the rugged Kaikoura coastline, Fyffe Country Lodge provides uninterrupted rural views of Mt Fyffe. Only five minutes south of Kaikoura on the main highway, the Lodge offers two executive suites and four ensuite bedrooms, all with mountain vistas. Breakfast can be served in the guestrooms, and meals are available in the licensed award-winning restaurant downstairs or alfresco in the north-facing courtyard that captures the all-day sun. Seafood is a favourite, with fresh crayfish and local produce complemented by Marlborough wines.

Facilities

- 2 king suites with ensuite, 1 with jacuzzi, video & library
- 2 king & 2 queen ensuite bedrooms with tea/coffee
- chauffeur's ensuite bedroom
- hair dryer, cotton bed linen, robes, toiletries, TV in rooms
- laundry & dryer available
- pure artesian bore water
- tea/coffee; video library
- award-winning licensed gourmet restaurant serving fresh crayfish/lobster daily with "Fyffe" brand Seafood Chowder
- à la carte dinner, licensed bar
- complimentary pre-dinner drinks
- continental breakfast in guestrooms, dining room, courtyard
- phone, fax, email & photocopying available
- courtesy car; helipad

Activities available

- 100-guest functions – garden parties, family reunions, weddings, small conferences catered for
- courtesy mountain bikes
- barbecue on site
- beach walks, 200m away
- arts & crafts; seal colonies
- 4WD treks; hunting deer
- swimming with dolphins
- Kaikoura shops, 5-min drive
- quad bikes for famland tours, 20-min drive south
- hiking & mountain climbing
- scenic helicopter flights; golf
- horse trekking; whale watching
- ski-field in winter, 1-hour drive to Mt Lyford
- Blenheim, 1½-hour drive north
- Christchurch, 2-hr drive south

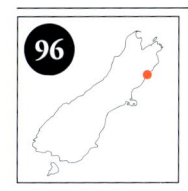

KAIKOURA
GREYSTONES

Hosts Jane and Tony Henderson

Boat Harbour, State Highway 1, Oaro, R D 2, Kaikoura
Phone 0-3-319 5299   *Mobile* 025 640 5110   *Fax* 0-3-319 5049
Email hendersons@greystones.co.nz   *Website* www.greystones.co.nz

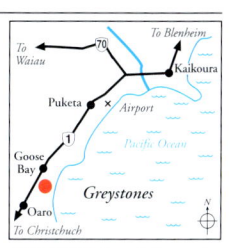

Double $845   *Includes breakfast, dinner & drinks*
Single $570   *Lunch extra*

2 bdrm / 2 enst

DIRECTIONS: From Kaikoura, take SH 1 south for 20km. Greystones on left. Or from Christchurch, take SH 1 north towards Kaikoura. Travel through Oaro & continue past Oceanview Restaurant for 100m to Greystones.

Uniquely located on the seaward side of State Highway One, just 20 kilometres south of Kaikoura, is Greystones, overlooking the South Pacific Ocean. Purpose-built in 1999 and true to its name, the ground floor at Greystones is clad in grey riverstone, with the upper storey in rough-sawn board and batten, roofed in slate. A spacious deck overlooks the sea, just 20 metres away at high tide, where breakfast with home-made bread is served alfresco, weather permitting. Guests can choose from an in-house dinner menu which includes New Zealand crayfish, accompanied by New Zealand cheeses, fresh fruit and vegetables, apéritifs and wine. Fur seals can be observed on the rocks in front of the house and dolphins swim by for seven months of the year.

Facilities

- 1 queen/twin & 1 queen ensuite bedroom
- hair dryers & heated towel rails
- cotton bed linen; fresh flowers
- lounge with open fire, tea/coffee, TV, video, CDs, writing desk & billiards room
- air-conditioning; central heating & double glazing
- email, fax & phone in office
- continental/cooked breakfast served in dining room or alfresco on decking
- 3-course dinner with NZ wine & apéritifs, in tariff
- lunch by arrangement, extra
- rooms overlooking ocean
- large deck & rock garden
- unsuitable for children
- on-site parking

Activities available

- in-house billiards room
- relaxing on deck; enclosed courtyard garden
- watching sunrise over ocean
- fur seals adjacent
- ocean, 20 metres below
- whale-watching
- dolphin-watching in season from site (7 months/year)
- 4WD quad bike treks
- swimming with dolphins
- sea kayaking
- fishing; scuba diving
- 18-hole golf course
- scenic flights
- horse riding & trekking
- Kaikoura township, shops & activities, 20km north
- Christchurch City, 1½-hour drive south

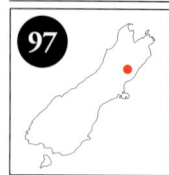

Hanmer Springs
Cheltenham House

Hosts Maree and Len Earl

13 Cheltenham Street, Hanmer Springs
Phone 0-3-315 7545 Email cheltenham@xtra.co.nz
Fax 0-3-315 7645 Website www.cheltenham.co.nz

Includes breakfast

| 6 bdrm | 5 enst | 1 prbth | Double $160–$200 Single $130–$170 |

DIRECTIONS: From Christchurch, take SH 7 to Hanmer Springs turn-off on right. Continue 9km to Hanmer village. Turn right into Cheltenham St. Cheltenham House on right. From north take Lewis Pass to Hanmer.

In a quiet setting in the heart of Hanmer Springs alpine village is Cheltenham House, with its extensive garden of spacious lawns, flower beds and mature trees which attract native birdlife. This double-gabled, bungalow-style residence, built in the 1930s, has been restored by the Earls since 1996. Constructed from native heart rimu, Cheltenham House features the original billiards room with rimu timber panelling, open fireplace, piano and full-size billiards table. Guests are accommodated in six spacious bedrooms with seating and dining areas, and all house rooms can be configured as twin facilities. Two bedrooms open to private sunrooms, and two are located in the garden. A full range of breakfasts is served in the guests' private rooms.

Facilities
- 2 queen ensuite garden rooms
- 1 queen/twin ensuite bedroom upstairs under eaves
- 2 super-king/twin ensuite bedrooms downstairs with private sunrooms
- 1 queen/twin bedroom & private bathroom with wheelchair access
- each bedroom features breakfast area with table & chairs, couch, TV, coffee/tea & electric blanket
- friars.co.nz/hosts/cheltenham.co.nz
- room service – large choice of cooked breakfasts
- open fireplace & piano in lounge; central heating
- lounge/billiards room
- laundry available
- local wine shared with hosts each evening
- off-street parking
- Labrador, Jessie, & siamese cat, Phoebe, on site

Activities available
- full-size billiards table
- pétanque/boules on site
- high country station tours
- restaurants, 1-min walk away
- 2-min stroll to thermal pools
- shops, an easy walk away
- 18-hole golf course, 3-min drive
- tennis courts; horse trekking
- historic home & garden tours
- Christchurch, 1½ hours south
- salmon & trout fishing
- helicopter scenic flights
- kayaking; paragliding
- bungy jumping
- river rafting; jet boating
- massage & beauty therapy
- mountain bike rides
- 2 ski-fields, within 1 hour
- extensive range of forest walking & tramping

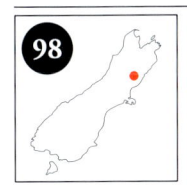

HANMER SPRINGS
RIPPINVALE RETREAT

Hosts Helen and John Beattie

68 Rippingale Road, Hanmer Springs
Phone 0-3-315 7139   *Email* rippinvale123@xtra.co.nz
Fax 0-3-315 7139   *Website* www.hanmersprings.net.nz

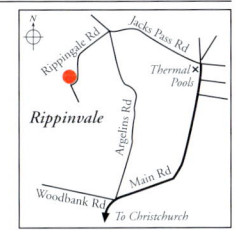

2 bdrm | 2 enst   Suite rate $195–$285   *Includes breakfast*   *Picnic hampers & massage extra*

DIRECTIONS: From Christchurch, take SH 7 to Hanmer Springs turn-off on right. Continue 9km towards Hanmer village. Turn left into Argelins Rd, then left again into Rippingale Rd. Rippinvale on right.

Nestled in a secluded one-hectare wooded garden in a 20-hectare (50-acre) lifestyle block adjacent to the Hanmer Springs golf course, Rippinvale Retreat is located two minutes' drive from the village with its thermal springs. This country lodge was built in 2000 in traditional New Zealand colonial style with mudbrick and boasts uninterrupted alpine views. A separate guest wing provides total privacy with two cosy apartment-style queen suites. Each centrally heated suite has French doors opening to a private courtyard garden. A gourmet breakfast menu of the freshest produce can be served in the guest suites, or alfresco. Helen, who is a massage therapist, can provide in-house therapeutic massages. John can arrange free chase hunting/fishing trips.

Facilities
- 2 cottage-style suites: each with 1 queen bedroom, ensuite & sitting room
- cotton bed linen
- hair dryer, heated towel rails & toiletries in ensuites
- bathrobes
- TV, phone, games & ironing facilities in both suites; all suites open to verandahs
- laundry service available
- full gourmet breakfast in suite or alfresco in garden
- kitchenettes with teas, percolator coffee, iced water, nibbles, fruit
- fresh flowers
- fax & email available
- private guest entrances
- on-site parking
- courtesy passenger transfer

Activities available
- in-house therapeutic massage, by Helen, massage therapist
- black labrador, Meg, & Burmese cat, Lilly, on site
- tennis court & pétanque on site
- picnicking, hampers available
- hunting, hiking & 4WD treks, with John (professional hunting guide)
- winter pamper package, extra
- restaurants nearby
- thermal springs
- mountain biking
- bungy jumping
- jet boating; golf
- horse riding
- camera treks
- kayaking; rafting
- fishing; hunting
- winter skiing

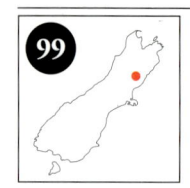

Hanmer Springs
Albergo Hanmer Lodge

Hosts Bascha and Beat Blattner

88 Rippingale Road, Hanmer Springs   *Postal* P O Box 79, Hanmer Springs
Freephone 0800 342 313   Phone 0-3-315 7428   Fax 0-3-315 7428
Email albergo@paradise.net.nz   *Website* www.albergohanmer.com

3 bdrm   3 enst   1 pdrm

Double $140–$280   *Includes breakfast*   *Dinner extra*
Single $100–$220   **Off-peak & house rates available**   *Self-catering*

DIRECTIONS: From Christchurch, take SH 7 to Hanmer Springs turn-off on right. Continue 9km towards Hanmer village. Turn left into Argelins Rd, then left again into Rippingale Rd. Albergo Hanmer is 900m on right.

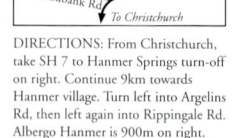

With uninterrupted mountain views, Albergo Hanmer & Alpine Villa are set in almost a hectare of alpine gardens, two minutes' drive from the centre of Hanmer. Italian for "boutique hotel", Albergo Hanmer was purpose-built in Hacienda style to catch all-day sun and features an eclectic interior design. Constructed from Oamaru stone, the Lodge and Villa include double-glazing, underfloor heating and quality fittings. Bascha and Beat specialise in designer breakfasts, providing over 10 choices to start the day: Swiss Birchermuesli, Spanish Summer Frittata, wafer-thin sweet or savoury French crêpes, or a full English breakfast. Cuisine du Marché dinners offer a blend of European and Pacific Rim cuisine, with Swiss Surprise Desserts.

Facilities

- 3 super-king/twin ensuite bedrooms; 1 double spa bath
- in-room tea/coffee, wine list, TV, fridge & electric blankets
- alpine views from all windows, sunsets & stars over Lewis Pass
- 3 living areas: formal lounge, sunny conservatory, chat-lounge with internet & coffee
- Feng shui sunken courtyard, BBQ area, waterfall & love swing
- flexitime 3-course gourmet breakfast, extensive menu
- 3–7-course tailored silver service dinner by arrangement, extra
- full kitchen for guest use
- phone, fax & email available
- Swiss/German, French, Italian & Spanish spoken by hosts
- courtesy passenger transfer

Activities available

- healing retreats available
- on-site motivational workshops, exclusive "Soul for Women" retreats
- pamper packages & gift vouchers
- massage & beauty treatments on site
- honeymoons & events catered
- 18-hole golf course, adjacent
- squash & tennis courts nearby
- Hanmer thermal pools & day spa
- fishing/hunting, guides available
- restaurants, cafés, boutique shops & gym
- family maze & mini golf
- mountain bike & hiking trails; bungy jumping; jet boating; scenic flights
- guided forest/nature walks
- Kaikoura: whale watching, dolphins, kayaking & paragliding, 1½-hour drive
- 2 ski-fields, within 1 hour

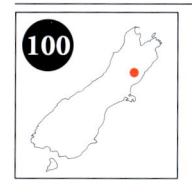

HANMER SPRINGS
ALBERGO HANMER ALPINE VILLA

Hosts Bascha and Beat Blattner

88 Rippingale Road, Hanmer Springs *Postal* P O Box 79, Hanmer Springs
Freephone 0800 342 313 *Phone* 0-3-315 7428 *Fax* 0-3-315 7428
Email albergo@paradise.net.nz *Website* www.albergohanmer.com

1 bdrm	1 enst	Villa Rate $280–$525 for 2 persons *Includes breakfast* *Dinner extra*
		Extra persons $80 each Off-peak rates available *Self-catering*

DIRECTIONS: From Christchurch, take SH 7 to Hanmer Springs turn-off on right. Continue 9km towards Hanmer village. Turn left into Argelins Rd, then left again into Rippingale Rd. Albergo Hanmer is 900m on right.

The new stand-alone Alpine Villa has been built in Oamaru stone to complement Albergo Lodge (*see opposite page 382*). The villa includes a full apartment-style kitchen with double doors leading to the spacious bedroom featuring an American king bed, raised ceiling, in-room DVD/cinema system and suspended cupid sculptures created by Bascha. The large marble ensuite has a dedicated wet area and a high panorama window for uninterupted mountain views while showering. Guests have private access to the split-level courtyard featuring a jacuzzi, which is popular on starry nights. Bascha and Beat's three-course designer breakfast is served in either the privacy of the suite, alfresco, or in the main lodge at a time to suit guests.

Facilities

- all facilities at Albergo main Lodge (*page 382*) available for Villa guests' use also
- 1 American king/twin bedroom with ensuite bathroom
- dual basins, bidet, heated towel rail, demist mirrors & heated floor in marble ensuite
- hair dryer, toiletries, bathrobes
- double glazing, insect screens, heated floors & air-conditioning
- flexi-time 3-course gourmet breakfast, extensive menu
- in-room tea/coffee, wine list, Albergo Special Tinto drink
- dining room & lounge with double sofa-bed
- in-room DVD/cinema
- split-level courtyard with tables, sun loungers & private jacuzzi
- phone, fax & email available

Activities available

- honeymoons & events catered
- in-house massage & beauty treatments; aromatherapy
- 18-hole golf course, adjacent; 'hole-in-one' golf challenge
- village cruisers & quad bikes
- argo (8WD) & 4WD tours
- back-country Molesworth farm 4WD tours
- adventure activities
- cafés, boutique shops, art galleries & museum, nearby
- night spot, bar & dancing, 10-min walk
- horse trekking
- river rafting & jet boating
- heli-tours: scenic & skiing
- local taxi service, all hours
- Maruia Springs Japanese bathhouse & restaurant, 50-min drive

383

© Friars' Guide to New Zealand Accommodation for the Discerning Traveller

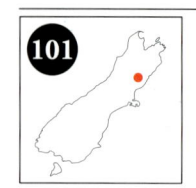

WAIPARA GORGE, WAIPARA
CLAREMONT COUNTRY ESTATE

Hosts Richard and Rosie Goord

828 Ram Paddock Road, Waipara Gorge, Amberley, R D 2, North Canterbury
Phone 0-3-314 7559   Email relax@claremont-estate.com
Fax 0-3-314 7065   Website www.claremont-estate.com

5 bdrm	3 enst	2 prbth

Double $625–$980
Single $515–$755

Includes breakfast & dinner
Includes tour for 2-night stays

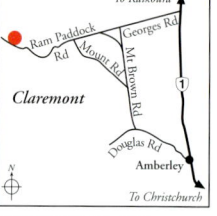

DIRECTIONS: Take SH 1 to Amberley. Take Douglas Rd west for 5km. Take right fork into Mt Brown Rd & travel 5km. Veer left into Ram Paddock Rd. Travel 8.28km to Claremont on right.

Claremont Country Estate is located on the spectacular Waipara Gorge, close to the Waipara wineries, 45 minutes north of Christchurch Airport. Set on a 700-hectare farm that runs deer, sheep and cattle, the 1866 homestead was carefully restored in 2000 as a Lodge, and is now furnished with antiques. Guests enjoy two living rooms, a pavilion dining room, vine-clad verandahs and five bedrooms, each with a spacious bathroom. Family accommodation is available within a separate three-bedroom self-contained cottage. The Estate features a limestone escarpment and unique rock formations, including the giant sculptural "Bishop's Head" rock (*see opposite*) and ancient "God's marbles" – one-metre spheres found within the river bank.

Facilities
- 1 super-king/twin ensuite bedroom downstairs with dressing room
- 3 queen bedrooms upstairs, 2 with ensuites & 1 with private bathroom, all 3 with baths
- 1 twin bedroom with private bathroom & spa bath
- family accommodation in 3-bedroom, 2-bathroom self-contained cottage
- hosted apéritifs & fine dining
- hair dryers, toiletries, demist mirrors & heated towel rails
- bathrobes & slippers; cotton bed linen
- 2 guest living rooms with open fires, library, vine-clad verandahs & stone-walled courtyard
- Sky TV, video, DVD & CD-player; multi-room audio

Activities available
- guided 4WD tour of estate, Waipara gorge & limestone cliffs; complimentary for 2-night stay
- scenic walks through 700ha farm with 10km of river
- hard tennis court, badminton, lawn croquet & garden spa pool
- corporate retreats & small conferences catered for
- golf course at Amberley Beach
- Amberley award-winning restaurant & shops, 12 mins
- Waipara vineyards, wine tasting & café lunches, 10–15 mins
- guided fishing – ocean & river; guided horse trekking trips
- Christchurch City, 1 hr south
- Hanmer Springs thermal pools, 1-hr drive
- Kaikoura whale watching, 1½-hour drive north

© Friars' Guide to New Zealand Accommodation for the Discerning Traveller

Above left: Claremont offers a four-wheel-drive safari of the Estate with its natural rock formations, such as the "Bishop's Head".
Above right: The dramatic Waipara gorge is on site with its natural clear water swimming pool in the river.
Below: Claremont enjoys 10 kilometres of direct river frontage, with scenic walks and colourful autumn foliage.
Opposite top: The Claremont Country Estate historic homestead was built in 1886 from locally handcut limestone blocks.
Opposite bottom left: The guestrooms are individually themed, and three of the adjoining bathrooms include claw-foot baths.
Opposite bottom right: Four-course dinner is offered, including home-produced venison, lamb and garden-fresh vegetables.

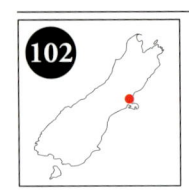

RANGIORA, CHRISTCHURCH
OAKLEIGH

Hosts Leon Mary Russell-White and Philip Holden

148 King Street, Rangiora, North Canterbury
Phone 0-3-313 0420   *Mobile* 025 750 169   *Fax* 0-3-313 0421
Email leonmrussell@xtra.co.nz   *Website* www.oakleigh.co.nz

| 2 bdrm | 1 enst |

Room rate $180 for 2 persons
Extra persons $60 each

Includes breakfast
Lunch & dinner extra

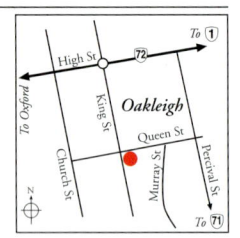

DIRECTIONS: From Christchurch, take SH 1 north & exit to Rangiora. Travel north on Linesman Rd & continue into Percival St. Turn left into Queen St & travel to corner King St. Turn left into carpark at Oakleigh.

Set in a landscaped garden in Rangiora, Oakleigh is a colonial villa built in 1885 and now upgraded for comfortable contemporary living. Oakleigh offers guests a spacious bedroom with ensuite, and French doors leading to verandah and garden. A smaller twin room is also available for extra guests in the same party, or children. Guests enjoy relaxing in two living rooms, both with open fires. Philip is a prolific author on New Zealand country life, and Leon enjoys entertaining. Meals are provided according to guests' requirements. A full breakfast is served and lunch or dinner with wine are also offered. Rangiora is a small friendly New Zealand rural town, located on scenic highway 72, less than half an hour's drive north of Christchurch City.

Facilities

- one-party bookings only
- 1 king ensuite bedroom with TV, phone & desk, opens to verandah; 1 twin bedroom
- bath, toiletries, heated towel rails & demist mirror
- bathrobes; cotton bed linen
- 2 lounges with open fire, tea/coffee, nibbles, Sky TV, video, CDs, games, artwork, books & writing desk
- continental or cooked breakfast served in dining room
- lunch, $20 pp, in dining room or alfresco in garden
- 3-course dinner & wine, $50 pp
- children welcome; fresh flowers
- 1 small Westhighland terrier
- fax, email & laundry available
- garaging
- passenger transfer, extra

Activities available

- Philip Holden's books in-house
- landscaped garden on site
- farm tours
- golf; fishing
- wineries; art galleries
- Maori pa; Orana Park
- Willowbank Wildlife Reserve & kiwi house
- gardens open to visit
- hiking & mountain bike trails
- restaurants & shops nearby
- within 25-min drive:
  – Christchurch City
  – airport; Antarctic Centre
  – university
  – Botanic Gardens
  – Hagley Park; Avon River
- safe swimming beaches
- river & adventure activities
- Tranz Alpine scenic day trip

© Friars' Guide to New Zealand Accommodation for the Discerning Traveller

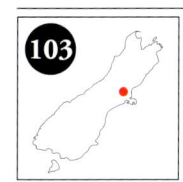

OXFORD
WAIMAKARIRI LODGE

Hosts Sharon and Ian Moore

45 Depot Gorge Road, R D 1, Oxford, North Canterbury
Phone 0-3-312 3662 • *Mobile* 027 437 1096 • *Fax* 0-3-312 3662
Email sharonian@xtra.co.nz • *Website* www.waimakaririlodge.co.nz

3 bdrm | 2 enst | 1 prbth
Double $175–$225
Single $130

Includes breakfast
Dinner extra

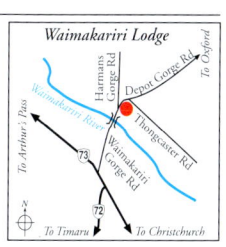

DIRECTIONS: From Christchurch, take SH 73 towards Arthur's Pass. Turn right into Waimakariri Gorge Rd. Cross Waimakariri River bridge & continue on Depot Gorge Rd to Waimakariri Lodge on right.

This home was purpose-built in 2000 in the Waimakariri Gorge, with sweeping rural and mountain views to the Southern Alps. The spacious grounds enhance the peaceful location and guests can enjoy viewing the vintage cars on site, playing golf on the adjacent course or fishing for trout and salmon nearby. Three guestrooms open to verandahs and the turret offers panoramic views. Each bedroom has its own bathroom as well as tea and coffee making facilities. A hearty full breakfast is served in the dining room and a three-course dinner with wine featuring country fare is available by arrangement. An open fire warms the guest lounge in winter and there is a home gymnasium and spa pool for guest use. Christchurch City is half an hour south.

Facilities
- 1 super-king/twin bedroom with ensuite bathroom
- 1 queen ensuite bedroom
- 1 king & 1 twin bedroom with private bathrooms
- cotton bed linen & tea/coffee
- hair dryer, toiletries & bathrobes
- private guest lounge with open fire, games, TV & music
- children over 12 yrs welcome
- continental or cooked breakfast in dining room
- lunch by request, extra
- 3-course dinner with wine, $45 pp
- phone, fax & email
- fresh flowers
- complimentary laundry
- private guest entrance
- on-site parking

Activities available
- barbecue available
- honeymoons catered for
- spa pool on site
- home gymnasium on site
- large grounds & garden with private courtyard
- trout & salmon fishing; guide
- 18-hole golf course adjacent to property, golf clubs for hire
- horse trekking; bush walks
- restaurants, nearby
- Tranz Alpine Rail stop, 5 km
- farm tours by arrangement
- museum; heritage trail
- jet boat rides
- private gardens open to visit
- mountain bike trails; wagon adventures
- wine tasting
- ski-fields, 30-min drive

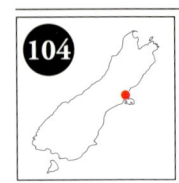

Rangiora, Christchurch
Frantoio Cottage

Host Barbara Smith

94 Isaac Road, Eyrewell, R D 1, Rangiora, Christchurch
Phone 0-3-310 6144   *Mobile* 027 251 1959   *Fax* 0-3-310 6133
Email bvtaylor@xtra.co.nz   *Website* friars.co.nz/hosts/frantoio.html

1 bdrm   1 enst   Cottage rate $195

Includes breakfast basket
Lunch hamper & dinner extra

Self-catering

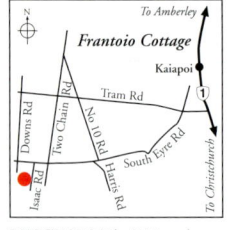

DIRECTIONS: Take SH 1 north over Waimakariri bridge. Take Tram Rd exit. Travel 0.5km & turn left into South Eyre Rd. Travel 12–15 mins & turn left into Isaac Rd. Turn right into driveway. Frantoio Cottage at end.

Located on a 20-hectare (50-acre) olive grove and nut orchard, Frantoio Cottage provides self-contained accommodation for one couple in a rural setting, 30 minutes north of Christchurch City. Purpose built in 2003, this contemporary cottage is named after an Italian variety of olives grown on the property. Adjacent are vineyards and there are many other activities within half an hour's drive. The cottage comprises one super-king/twin bedroom opening to private decking, an ensuite including a bath, a lounge which also opens to the deck, and a fully equipped kitchen complete with dishwasher. Breakfast supplies are delivered to the guests each evening, and dinner can be served at the cottage by arrangement. Restaurants are a short drive away.

Facilities
- 1 self-contained cottage with 1 super-king/twin bedroom
- 1 ensuite bathroom includes bath, hair dryer & toiletries
- cotton bed linen; bathrobes
- fresh flowers
- original artwork
- sundeck from lounge & bedroom
- log fire, TV, CD, DVD in lounge
- Italian & basic Japanese spoken
- breakfast basket delivered
- lunch hamper, extra
- dinner, $25–$40 pp
- full kitchen for self-catering
- basic provisions, nibbles, wine & mineral water supplied
- email, fax & phone available
- laundry service available
- pets on site
- on-site parking

Activities available
- wildlife reserve nearby
- Clydesdale wagon trips
- gardens & nurseries to visit
- 3 safe swimming beaches
- trout & salmon fishing
- horse riding & trekking
- jet-boating
- hot air ballooning
- wine trails, 40-min drive
- Antarctic Centre, 25 mins
- vineyard restaurant, 7 mins
- Kaiapoi/Rangiora/Oxford, 15 mins
- golf courses including Clearwater Resort International, 20 mins
- Christchurch & airport, 30 mins
- Port of Lyttelton cruises, 45 mins
- Hanmer Springs thermal alpine village; Akaroa, each 80 mins
- Tranz Alpine scenic train day trip
- 4 ski-fields, 1-hour drive

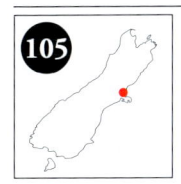

BELFAST, CHRISTCHURCH
DEVONDALE HOUSE

Hosts Sue and Stuart Fox   *Phone* 0-3-323 6616

66 Johns Road, Belfast, Christchurch
Freephone 0800 167 735   *Mobile* 025 200 7236   *Fax* 0-3-323 8723
Email info@devondalehouse.co.nz   *Website* www.devondalehouse.co.nz

Room rate $210–$250   Includes breakfast   Dinner extra

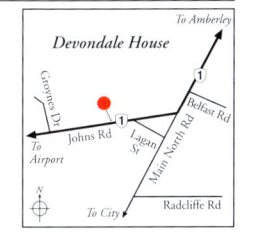

DIRECTIONS: From north take SH 1 right into Johns Rd. Devondale House on right by statue. Take private road towards security gate. Intercom on right, 3m before gate. Press Fox button. From airport, take Johns Rd for 6km.

Devondale House is a rural retreat, just minutes from the city, yet in a quiet location behind security gates adjacent to a peaceful walkway through farmland. Set in extensive gardens, complete with tennis court, Devondale offers guests spacious ensuite bedrooms with views to the Southern Alps, quality linen, tea and coffee-making facilities, writing desks and fresh flowers. A traditional English breakfast is served in the sunny breakfast room or alfresco on the terrace. Popular activities with guests include a fireside evening meal at Willowbank wildlife restaurant, with deer outside the window, followed by a guided night tour to see live kiwi. Clearwater Golf Resort nearby also offers fine dining. Molly, a West Highland terrier, is a friendly extra.

Facilities
- East Room: spacious queen bedroom & spa bath in ensuite
- West Room: spacious king/twin bedroom with colonial bed & mist-free mirrors in ensuite
- hair dryers, toiletries & heated towel rails in both ensuites
- TV, phone, writing desk, fresh flowers, chocolates & tea/coffee in both bedrooms
- quality bed linen; fresh flowers
- breakfast served in dining room or alfresco on terrace
- dinner by request, extra
- complimentary sherry or port
- views to Southern Alps
- private guest lounge
- security gate
- statue marks entrance
- secure off-street parking

Activities available
- tennis court on site
- Clearwater Golf Course & restaurant adjacent
- Willowbank restaurant & wildlife reserve, includes kiwi
- Groynes recreation/picnic area with fish & birdlife, nearby
- Antarctic Centre, 6-min drive
- Orana Park
- jet boating on Waimakariri River
- Rosebank winery & restaurant, 2-min drive
- Russley Golf Course
- seasonal trout fishing
- guided salmon fishing
- Botanic Gardens, 12 mins
- private gardens to visit
- airport 7–8-min drive
- City Centre, 15-min drive
- local ski-field, 1¼ hours

106

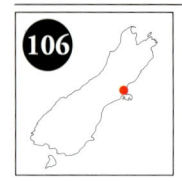

HAREWOOD, CHRISTCHURCH
CLEARVIEW LODGE

Hosts Sue and Robin Clements

8 Clearwater Avenue, Christchurch
Phone 0-3-359 5797 *Mobile* 021 727 883 *Fax* 0-3-358 9131
Email robin@clements.net.nz *Website* www.clearview.net.nz

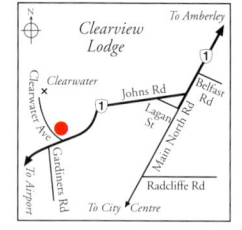

| 3 bdrm | 3 enst | Room rate $225–$325 | Includes breakfast Lunch & dinner extra |

DIRECTIONS: From north, follow SH 1 right into Johns Rd. Turn right into Clearwater Ave. After 50m turn right into Clearview driveway. From airport, take Russley Rd/Johns Rd (SH 1) for 6km to Clearwater Ave.

Set in four hectares (10 acres), surrounded by an olive grove, vineyard and apple orchard, at the entrance to Clearwater Golf Resort, Clearview Lodge was built in 2001 in French chateau-style. With views to the Port Hills and Southern Alps beyond, Clearview offers three ensuite guestrooms. The Pinot and Frantoio Rooms are upstairs adjacent to the guest lounge opening to a large balcony. Downstairs is the Braeburn Room with wheelchair access and the guest dining room. The Pinot and Braeburn ensuites include a bath and the showers have massage nozzles. A full breakfast including home baking and home-made jams is served in the conservatory, dining room or alfresco on the patio in summer. Lunch and dinner are available by arrangement.

Facilities

- Pinot Room: 1 super-king/twin ensuite bedroom & bath upstairs
- Braeburn Room: 1 super-king/twin ensuite bedroom with bath & wheelchair access downstairs
- Frantoio Room: 1 super-king/twin ensuite bedroom upstairs
- cotton bed linen, phone & TV
- hair dryers, heated floors & bathrobes in all 3 ensuites
- fresh flowers
- continental & cooked breakfast served
- lunch & dinner, by prior arrangement, extra
- email & fax available
- guest lounge with open fireplace, opens to balcony
- guestrooms serviced daily
- private guest entrance
- on-site parking

Activities available

- 8-seater spa pool
- pétanque on site
- barbecue available
- honeymoons, weddings & conferences catered for
- Clearwater Golf Resort, 2-min drive away
- Groynes park & picnic area
- Willowbank Wildlife Reserve with kiwi house
- restaurants, nearby
- seasonal trout/salmon fishing
- St Helena Vineyard
- wineries; berry farm
- Orana Park
- International Airport & Antarctic Centre, 10 mins
- City Centre, 15-min drive
- Waimakariri River jet boating
- ski-fields, 1 hr 15-min drive

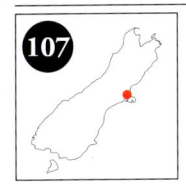

Papanui, Christchurch
HEATHERSTON

Hosts Jan and Murray Binnie

46 Searells Road, Papanui, Christchurch
Phone 0-3-355 3239 *Email* enquiries@heatherston.co.nz
Fax 0-3-355 3259 *Website* www.heatherston.co.nz

3 bdrm 3 enst

Double $180–$220 Single $120–$160 *Includes breakfast*

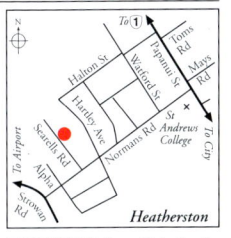

DIRECTIONS: From Christchurch airport, take Memorial Ave. Turn left into Glandovey Rd, thru roundabout, then left into Strowan Rd. Turn left into Normans Rd & 2nd left into Searells Rd, to Heatherston on right.

Set in a quiet suburban street in Christchurch, Heatherston was purpose-built in 2003 to offer boutique accommodation. Professionally designed, Heatherston provides an upstairs guest floor with three ensuite bedrooms, separated by a relaxing area with a balcony. Peace and quiet is ensured by the double-glazed windows, and quality furnishings include a claw-foot bath in the queen ensuite. Breakfast is served downstairs, at separate tables in the dining room, with a continental buffet and cooked options. The front garden at Heatherston features a fountain that is lit at night. Just 10 minutes' drive from the City Centre, and 15 minutes from the airport, guests at Heatherston are within walking distance of restaurants and close to bus routes.

Facilities
- upstairs guest floor
- 1 queen ensuite bedroom upstairs, with claw-foot bath
- 2 king/twin ensuite bedrooms upstairs, 1 with extra single bed
- hair dryer, toiletries, demist mirror, heated towel rails & heated floor in all 3 ensuites
- TV & tea/coffee in bedrooms
- cotton bed linen; fresh flowers
- continental/cooked breakfast served in dining room
- relaxing upstairs area with fridge, books, games, phone & opens to small balcony
- piano in lounge downstairs
- powder room; central heating
- basic French spoken
- fax & email available
- 2 off-street car parks

Activities available
- Merivale Mall, 2 blocks away
- local bars, cafés & restaurants
- small boutique local shops
- City Centre, 10-min drive
- Cathedral Square, 10 mins
- Arts Centre, 5 mins
- weekend markets
- Avon River & Hagley Park
- Christchurch Botanic Gardens
- wineries; Orana Park
- private gardens open to visit
- gondola rides with city views
- Antarctic Centre, 15 mins
- airport, 15-min drive
- Tranz Alpine express
- Akaroa day trips
- ski-fields, 1 hour away
- Hanmer Springs, 1½ hours

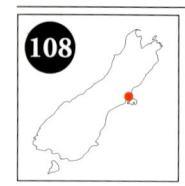

MERIVALE, CHRISTCHURCH
ELM TREE HOUSE

Hosts Karen and Allan Scott

236 Papanui Road, Merivale, Christchurch
Phone 0-3-355 9731   *Mobile* 025 232 5058   *Fax* 0-3-355 9753
Email stay@elmtreehouse.co.nz   *Website* www.elmtreehouse.co.nz

6 bdrm   6 enst
Room rate $235–$325 for 2 persons
Seasonal rates available   *Includes breakfast*

DIRECTIONS: From the City, take Victoria St or Bealey Ave north. Turn right into Papanui Rd. Elm Tree House on right on corner Murray Pl. From airport, take Harewood Rd to Papanui Rd. Elm Tree House on left.

Elm Tree House, named after the large weeping elm on the front lawn, has a Historic Places classification. Built in 1920 by the England Brothers, this home was later owned by a former Canterbury Member of Parliament. Native timbers and leadlight windows are used throughout both storeys. Set in a large Merivale garden, this large English colonial-style house is only 15 minutes' walk from the City Centre, or 15 minutes' drive from the airport and Tranz Alpine rail station. A continental or cooked breakfast is served in the dining room, where French doors open to the lawn. Licensed restaurants and cafés are 200 metres away in Merivale Village. Complimentary tea and coffee are available in guests' bedrooms and the spacious guest lounge.

Facilities
- 2 king/twin & 2 queen ensuite bedrooms upstairs
- 1 king/twin & 1 queen ensuite bedroom downstairs
- hair dryer & heated towel rails in all 6 ensuite bathrooms
- electric blankets & hypo-allergenic pillows on all beds
- laundry & dry cleaning available
- fresh flowers & direct-dial phones in all bedrooms
- breakfast in dining room
- outdoor dining area
- complimentary tea/coffee, port & sherry in bedrooms & lounge
- spacious lounge with gas fire, TV & Wurlitzer
- double glazing
- fax, email & internet
- off-street parking

Activities available
- walled garden on site
- Merivale Mall, 200m walk
- antique shops
- 6 licensed restaurants
- turn-of-century large timber homes in area
- Hagley Park, 15-min walk
- City Centre, 15-min walk
- Tranz Alpine express, 15-min drive
- airport, 15-min drive
- private gardens open to visit
- golf
- Arts Centre
- Cathedral Square
- Botanic Gardens
- Christchurch Casino
- Avon River
- assistance with South Island itineraries

Above: On summer evenings, wine and apéritifs are offered to guests in the conservatory or in the walled rose garden outside.
Below: Featuring an old weeping elm on the front lawn, Elm Tree House is a spacious English colonial-style house built in 1920.
Opposite top: The guest lounge features a Wurlitzer and includes a gas fire, television, and complimentary port and sherry.
Opposite bottom left: The honeymoon suite upstairs features timber panelling and is one of the six ensuite guestrooms available.
Opposite bottom right: A continental or cooked breakfast is served in the dining room, with French doors opening to the garden.

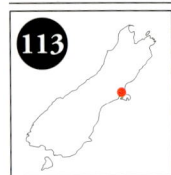

… 113

CHRISTCHURCH CITY
BISHOPS MANOR

Host Andrea Richards

14 Bishop Street, St Albans, Christchurch
Phone 0-3-379 7990   *Mobile* 021 453 248   *Fax* 0-3-379 7990
Email info@bishopsmanor.co.nz   *Website* www.bishopsmanor.co.nz

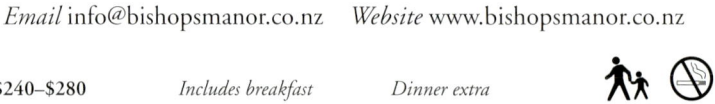

4 bdrm   4 enst   1 pdrm   **Room rate** $240–$280   *Includes breakfast*   *Dinner extra*

DIRECTIONS: From City, take Colombo St north to Bealey Ave & turn right. Travel to Bishop St & turn left. Bishops Manor is on the right. From airport turn left into Bealey Ave.

Bishops Manor was built in the 1890s to an England Brothers' design, and now offers four spacious guestrooms upstairs, each with an ensuite including a bath. All bedrooms feature cable television, a phone and refrigerator. Downstairs is the guest lounge and dining room, where a continental breakfast buffet is served, or room service is available if preferred. Dinner, platters, picnic hampers, small wedding and corporate functions can be catered for by prior arrangement. Within walking distance of the City Centre, Bishops Manor is situated on a quiet tree-lined street in a tranquil garden setting. Recently refurbished, it retains the original ornate plaster ceilings and stained glass windows, creating an atmosphere reminiscent of an earlier era.

Facilities

- 1 king/twin, 1 king & 2 queen bedrooms, each with ensuite
- 2 dressing rooms
- cotton bed linen; fresh flowers
- bath, bathrobes, hair dryer, demist mirror, toiletries & heated floor in all 4 ensuite bathrooms
- tea/coffee, fridge, cable TV, phone & internet port in all bedrooms
- children welcome
- continental breakfast buffet in dining room, or room service available
- wedding lunches & dinners catered for by arrangement
- beauty salon; powder room
- fax & email available
- 2 guest lounges with artwork, Sky TV, CDs, video
- off-street parking

Activities available

- tennis, boating, golf course & fitness track at Hagley Park
- Arts Centre; art galleries
- Court Theatre; Cathedral Square
- gondola; golf courses
- boutique shopping
- Botanic Gardens & Mona Vale
- private gardens open to visit
- Avon River; punting
- Boulevard trams; antiques trail
- restaurants in City Centre & in Merivale Mall
- Christchurch Casino
- hot air ballooning
- Ferrymead historic park
- Lyttelton Harbour
- Tranz Alpine day trip
- Antarctic Centre, 20 mins
- airport, 20-min drive
- ski-fields, 1½ hours away

© Friars' Guide to New Zealand Accommodation for the Discerning Traveller

CHRISTCHURCH CITY
RIVERVIEW LODGE

Hosts Ernst Wipperfuerth and Sabine Rogge

361 Cambridge Terrace, Christchurch
Phone 0-3-365 2860   Fax 0-3-365 2845   Mobile 025 394 017
Email riverview.lodge@xtra.co.nz   *Website* www.moacottages.co.nz

| 6 bdrm | 5 enst | 1 prbth |

Double $160–$225
Single $100–$160

Includes breakfast for Lodge & Suites
Self-catering in cottages

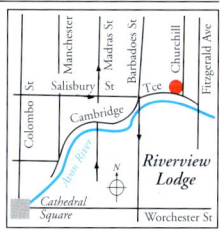

DIRECTIONS: From Cathedral Square, take Colombo St north. Turn right into Salisbury St. Continue into Cambridge Tce. Riverview Lodge on left. From Bealey Ave, turn right into Churchill, then right into Cambridge.

Set on the banks of the Avon River, this restored Edwardian villa, built in 1903, features the original Queen Anne-style turret, carved kauri and rimu fireplaces and stairs, and stained-glass windows. Next door to Riverview Lodge is an Edwardian townhouse with two self-contained Churchill Suites. Downstairs is a queen bedroom, spacious lounge with French doors opening into a formal courtyard, kitchen and bathroom. Upstairs are two bedrooms, a lounge, kitchen and bathroom. Another four guestrooms and bathrooms are available in the Lodge. For longer stays, there are two historic cottages nearby that are self-contained and have been carefully restored. The 10-minute Avon River walk, past the weeping willows and ducks, takes guests into the City Centre.

Facilities
- 1 queen, 1 double/twin, 1 double & 1 single bedroom in house
- 3 ensuites in house & 1 private bathroom for Turret Room
- 2 self-contained Churchill Suites next door: 1 queen downstairs, 1 queen & 1 single upstairs
- flowers, TV, cotton bed linen & hair dryers in all bedrooms
- lounge with open fire, tea/coffee, Sky TV, CD-player & library
- breakfast choice served in turret dining room
- email/fax/phone available; phones in both suites
- balconies open from all double bedrooms
- river views from windows & all verandahs
- German, French, Spanish & Dutch spoken
- off-street parking

Activities available
- 2 cottages available nearby
- bicycles available
- kayaks & canoes available for guests' use on river
- golf clubs available
- river walk, 10 mins to City
- punting on Avon River
- Cathedral Square
- Hagley Park
- private gardens to visit
- restaurants, 5-min walk
- Christchurch City shops
- Arts Centre & Botanic Gardens, 20-min river walk
- theatre & concerts
- art galleries
- craft shops
- museum
- Antarctic Centre, 15 mins
- airport, 15-min drive

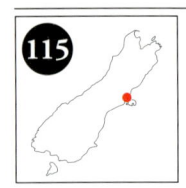

CHRISTCHURCH CITY
THE WESTON HOUSE

Hosts Stephanie and Len May

62 Park Terrace, Christchurch
Phone 0-3-366 0234   *Email* enquiries@westonhouse.co.nz
Fax 0-3-366 5254   *Website* www.westonhouse.co.nz

2 bdrm | 2 enst | 1 pdrm   Room rate $325   Includes breakfast
Picnic hampers extra

DIRECTIONS: From the airport, take Memorial Ave. Turn left into Harper Ave. Then turn right into Park Tce. The Weston House is on the left, on the corner of Peterborough St.

The Weston House was built for Christchurch lawyer, George Weston, from 1923 to 1924 to a neo-Georgian design by architect Cecil Woods. The former servants' quarters have been converted into guest accommodation, comprising an upstairs queen ensuite bedroom and a super-king/twin ensuite bedroom downstairs. Original features include the triple-brick walls with false street window, polished oak floors, and the mature trees in the guest courtyard. Stephanie serves fresh fruit, home-made muesli, bacon and eggs, and whitebait fritters in season, in the breakfast room, and picnic hampers are also available on request. The Weston House is centrally located on a direct route from the airport, yet quiet, opposite the Avon River and North Hagley Park.

Facilities

- Peterborough: 1 downstairs super-king/twin bedroom, walk-in wardrobe & ensuite bathroom
- Hagley: 1 upstairs queen bedroom, seating area & ensuite
- toiletries, hair dryers, heated floor, bathrobes in both ensuites
- TV, writing desk, fridge, fresh fruit, home baking & tea/coffee in suites
- complimentary fine NZ wine served each evening before dinner
- continental or traditional English cooked breakfast
- picnic hampers by request
- fresh flowers; central heating
- phone, fax & email
- private guest entrance, staircase & courtyard
- courtesy vehicle on request from airport/railway station
- off-street parking

Activities available

- guest courtyard & garden
- croquet lawn on site
- personal guided tours on request
- bus-stop at door; trams
- golf course in Hagley Park
- fitness track in Hagley Park
- licensed restaurants nearby
- punting on the Avon
- casino, 5-min walk
- City Centre, 10-min walk
- Botanic Gardens
- Arts Centre; museum
- art gallery
- gondola
- gardens open to visit
- Sumner Beach, 20 mins
- Lyttelton Harbour, 20-min drive away
- airport, 15-min drive

© Friars' Guide to New Zealand Accommodation for the Discerning Traveller

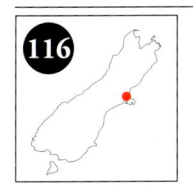

CHRISTCHURCH CITY
ORARI BED AND BREAKFAST

Host Ashton Owen

42 Gloucester Street, Christchurch City   *Postal* P O Box 1685, Christchurch
Phone 0-3-365 6569   *Fax* 0-3-365 2525   *Mobile* 025 344 110
Email orari.bb@xtra.co.nz   *Website* friars.co.nz/hosts/orari.html

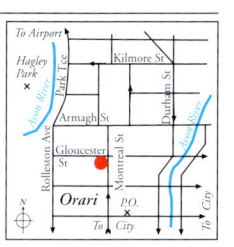

Double $160–$190
Single $130–$150

Includes breakfast

10 bdrm 8 enst 2 prbth 1 pdrm

DIRECTIONS: From airport, take Memorial Ave into Fendalton Rd. Turn left into Harper Ave, then right into Park Tce. Turn left into Gloucester St. Orari on corner of Montreal St on right.

Built in 1893 by the renowned England Brothers, Orari was the private townhouse of Annie Macdonald, widow of one of Canterbury's earliest landholders. Restored and refurbished in 1999, retaining the original native kauri construction, Orari now offers 10 guestrooms, each with a bathroom. Each bedroom includes television, phone, and tea or coffee facilities, making it suitable for the entire house to be booked for small conferences or weddings. The living rooms open to verandahs looking out to the garden pool. Orari is located opposite the new Christchurch art gallery, within comfortable walking distance of coffee houses and restaurants, the Arts Centre, Botanic Gardens, Museum, Hagley Park and golf course, and the City Centre.

Facilities

- 6 queen, 3 queen/twin & 1 bedroom with 3 singles
- 8 ensuite bathrooms
- 2 private bathrooms with bathrobes & wheelchair access
- hair dryers, heated towel rails & toiletries in all 10 bathrooms
- cotton bed linen
- phone, TV & tea/coffee in all 10 bedrooms
- full cooked breakfast, daily special, in dining room
- complimentary sherry/wine served in sitting room
- fresh flowers
- fax available
- children welcome
- local artwork throughout
- verandahs open to garden
- off-street parking

Activities available

- coffee houses & restaurants within walking distance
- central City shopping area
- Christchurch Museum
- Christchurch Convention Centre
- Christchurch Botanic Gardens
- private gardens to visit
- punting on Avon River
- airport, 15-min drive away
- Christchurch Art Gallery, opposite
- Hagley Park
- golf course
- Art Centre
- casino
- town hall
- public library
- public hospital
- Cathedral Square
- CBD, short walk

CHRISTCHURCH CITY
THE WORCESTER OF CHRISTCHURCH B&B

Hosts Maree Ritchie and Tony Taylor

15 Worcester Boulevard, Christchurch
Freephone 0800 365 015   *Phone* 0-3-365 0936   *Fax* 0-3-364 6299
Email info@worcester.co.nz   *Website* www.worcester.co.nz

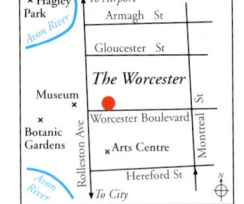

2 bdrm | 2 enst | Room rate $380 | *Includes breakfast*

DIRECTIONS: From airport, take main route to City. Follow Park Tce into Rolleston Ave. Turn left into Worcester Boulevard to The Worcester of Christchurch on left.

Sited on the inner-city recreated Worcester Boulevard with its restored trams, this 1893 colonial house was originally built for the Chief Constable of Lyttelton. The Worcester of Christchurch is now richly decorated in classical Victorian style, featuring antiques, artworks and leadlight windows. Maree runs her exclusive art business from the house, specialising in major New Zealand and European works. Upstairs are two super-king guest bedrooms with ensuite bathrooms; one includes a private lounge, and the other a dressing room. A full choice of continental and cooked breakfast is served in the dining room downstairs. The house is complemented by a peaceful garden featuring a reflection pond, gazebo and New Zealand sculpture.

Facilities

- 1 super-king/twin bedroom upstairs with lounge & ensuite
- 1 super-king ensuite bedroom upstairs with dressing room
- Les Floralies toiletries & hair dryers in each ensuite
- tea/coffee-making facilities, ironing board, iron, direct-dial phone & writing desk in both bedrooms
- pure cotton bed linen
- full choice of continental & cooked breakfasts served in dining room downstairs
- complimentary pre-dinner drinks & tea/coffee
- fresh flowers
- antiques, art & leadlight windows throughout
- baggage elevator
- inner city site; off-street parking court

Activities available

- personalised hosted tours of Christchurch & surrounding area, wine trails & whale watch tours, by arrangement
- in-house New Zealand & European artworks for sale
- tourist tram stop opposite
- Court Theatre close by
- Arts Centre close by
- Cathedral Square, 5 mins
- cafés & restaurants, 5-min walk
- central city shopping, 5-min walk
- Christchurch Art Gallery
- Botanic Gardens, walking distance
- Christchurch Casino & Town Hall
- Information Centre
- Christchurch Art Gallery
- Hagley Park sports: bowls, golf, tennis, boating, croquet, pétanque
- Christchurch Airport, 20 mins

Christchurch City
West Fitzroy Apartments

Hosts Maree Ritchie and Tony Taylor

Armagh Street, Christchurch   *Postal* 15 Worcester Boulevard, Christchurch
Freephone 0800 365 015   *Phone* 0-3-365 0936   *Fax* 0-3-364 6299
Email info@worcester.co.nz   *Website* www.westfitzroy.co.nz

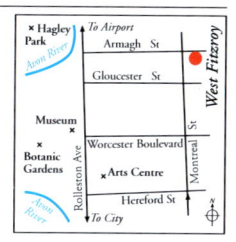

4 bdrm | **1** enst | **2** prbth

Apartment rate $275 for two persons
Multiple-night rates available

Extra persons $50 each

Self-catering
Includes continental breakfast provisions

DIRECTIONS: From airport, take main route to City. Follow Park Tce. Turn left into Armagh St to West Fitzroy on right. Carpark on top level.

The Worcester at West Fitzroy comprises three self-contained apartments on the historic tram route on Armagh Street. The award-winning West Fitzroy building is centrally located, five minutes' walk from Worcester Boulevard and Cathedral Square. The apartments are designed in contemporary style and complemented with original artworks. Each apartment has a comfortable lounge which opens onto a private full-length tiled balcony with outdoor seating. There is a well equipped kitchen in each apartment which enables self-catering, and continental breakfast provisions are supplied daily. Cafés, restaurants and shops are just a short walk away. There is a guest laundry in each apartment as well as a small gymnasium on site.

Facilities

- single-party bookings per apartment
- 1 apartment with 1 king & 1 twin bedroom & 1 ensuite
- 2 apartments, each with 1 super-king/twin bedroom & 1 private bathroom
- apartments serviced daily
- pure cotton bed linen; bathrobes & toiletries
- children welcome, cot available
- continental breakfast provisions
- 1 fully equipped kitchen, lounge & laundry per apartment
- lounges open to tiled balconies with outdoor furniture & smoking area
- TV, stereo & sofa bed in all 3 lounges; TV in each bedroom
- secure carpark
- full security system

Activities available

- on-site gymnasium
- personalised hosted tours of Christchurch & surrounding area, wine trails & whale watch tours, by arrangement
- tourist tram stop opposite
- cafés & restaurants, 5-min walk
- central city shopping, 5-min walk
- Cathedral Square, 5-min walk
- Botanic Gardens, walking distance
- Arts Centre close by
- Court Theatre close by
- Christchurch Casino
- Christchurch Art Gallery
- Christchurch Town Hall
- Hagley Park sports
- private gardens to visit
- punting on Avon River
- Christchurch Airport, 20-min drive away

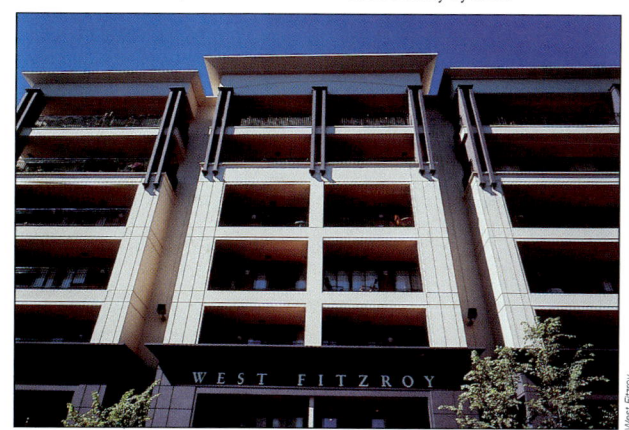

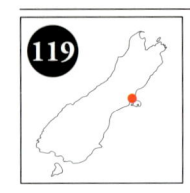

CHRISTCHURCH CITY
DOROTHY'S BOUTIQUE HOTEL

Host Stu McDougall

2 Latimer Square, Christchurch   Phone 0-3-365 6034
Postal P O Box 13 608, Christchurch   Fax 0-3-365 6035
Email dorothys@xtra.co.nz   *Website* www.dorothys.co.nz

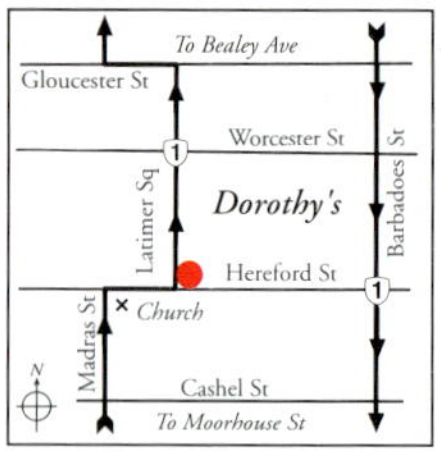

| 10 bdrm | 6 enst | 2 prbth | 1 pdrm |

Room rate $180–$250
Apartment rate $250   *All meals extra*

DIRECTIONS: From north, take SH 1 to City. Turn right into Hereford St. Dorothy's on right at corner of Latimer Sq. From Cathedral Sq, take Worcester St to Latimer Sq. Turn right, then left into Hereford St.

Dorothy's Boutique Hotel and Restaurant is situated in the heart of Christchurch overlooking leafy Latimer Square. Built in 1916 but restored in recent years, the house offers six ensuite guestrooms including the Queens Suite with its private lounge, as well as two separate purpose-built apartments on the boundary. The boutique hotel features the original Gothic-style doorways, red brick and Banks Peninsula volcanic rock and high quality antiques and artworks, mainly Japanese and Art Nouveau. The restaurant is a popular Christchurch venue for top cuisine, and guests are provided with fresh Canterbury produce each day. The fully licensed Rainbow Bar features the Wizard of Oz theme from which Dorothy's takes its name.

Facilities

- 6 queen ensuites bedrooms
- 2 separate apartments, each with 1 queen & 1 single bedroom & 1 private bathroom
- toiletries & hair dryers
- cotton bed linen
- fresh flowers
- children welcome
- TV & tea/coffee facilities
- guest laundry, extra
- breakfast served, extra
- à la carte lunch & dinner, extra
- private dining room, seats 12
- fully licensed bar & in-house restaurant
- antique furniture
- phone/fax & email available
- inner city site
- off-street parking

Activities available

- cafés, wine bars & restaurants, within walking distance
- central City shopping
- Christchurch Cathedral
- Christchurch Convention Centre
- Christchurch Symphony Orchestra
- Centre of Contemporary Art
- Hagley Theatre Company
- Robert McDougall Art Gallery
- punting on Avon River
- Arts Centre
- Christchurch Casino
- Canterbury opera
- Botanic Gardens
- Canterbury Museum
- Visitor Centre
- Court Theatre
- Cathedral Square
- Hagley Park

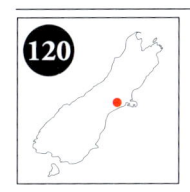

West Melton, Christchurch
Tresillian

Hosts Heather Anderson and Graeme Lindsay   *Mobile* 021-897 283

45 Johnson Road, West Melton, Christchurch   *Phone* 0-3-347 4103
Postal P O Box 6221, Upper Riccarton, Christchurch   *Fax* 0-3-347 4104
Email stay@tresillian.co.nz   *Website* www.tresillian.co.nz

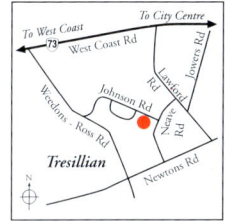

3 bdrm | 1 enst | 1 prbth   Room rate $200–$300   *Includes breakfast*   *Dinner extra*

DIRECTIONS: From Christchurch, take SH 73 towards West Coast. Travel about 13km & turn left into Weedons-Ross Rd. Travel 2km & turn left into Johnson Rd. Travel 1.2km to Tresillian on right.

Set in an eight-hectare vineyard, Tresillian offers contemporary accommodation half an hour west of Christchurch City. Purpose-built in 2002, Tresillian was inspired by Frank Lloyd Wright prairie house designs, all three bedrooms opening to verandahs with vineyard views. Breakfast is served in the dining room, guestrooms, or alfresco on the private verandahs, using home-grown produce in season. Dinner is also available by arrangement, accompanied by wine from the cellar. There are restaurants nearby, and the airport is just 20 minutes' drive east. Tresillian offers a peaceful quiet location on part of the original sheep run that was established in 1851. Grousie, the dog, and the two cats, Pinot and Gris, complete the family.

Facilities

- 1 super-king/twin ensuite bedroom with private entrance
- 2 queen bedrooms share private bathroom; 1-party booking only
- TV, CD-player, phone, tea/coffee, fridge in all 3 bedrooms, opening to private verandahs
- spa bath, hair dryer, toiletries, demist mirror, heated floor & towel rails in both bathrooms
- cotton bed linen; bathrobes
- breakfast including home-grown eggs & home baking served in dining room, bedrooms, or alfresco on private verandah
- 3-course dinner & wine, by arrangement, $50 pp
- central heating
- email & fax available
- on-site parking
- helicopter access

Activities available

- pool table
- pétanque & croquet, on site
- walking or jogging in vineyard
- golf courses nearby
- jet boating at Waimakariri & Rakaia rivers
- aero club, 5km
- motor racing at Ruapuna Park, 7km
- local lavender farm
- Trans Alpine express train
- restaurants, 10–20 mins
- gardens open to visit
- punting on Avon River
- Hagley Park sports
- Antarctic Centre, 20 mins
- International Airport, 20-min drive away
- Christchurch City, ½ hr
- 5 ski-fields within 1½-hour drive

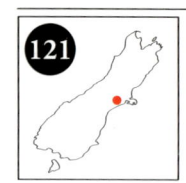

121

ROLLESTON–LINCOLN, CHRISTCHURCH
LINSTON BED AND BREAKFAST

Hosts Jane Allan and Wayne Mclaren

Springston-Rolleston Road, R D 4, Christchurch
Phone 0-3-347 4200   Mobiles 027 420 0265 and 027 432 1523
Fax 0-3-347 4201   Email jane@linston.co.nz   Website www.linston.co.nz

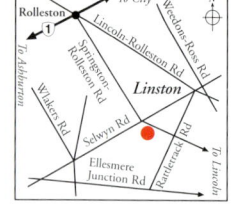

| 3 bdrm | 2 enst | 1 prbth | Room rate $220–$300 Apartment rate $300 | Includes breakfast Self-catering in apartment | Dinner extra |

DIRECTIONS: From Christchurch City take SH 1 south to Rolleston. Turn left into Tennyson St & continue into Springston-Rolleston Rd. Travel 4.2km to Linston B&B on right.

Linston is set in two hectares (five acres) of landscaped gardens featuring mature trees and an extensive lawn. The homestead offers two guestrooms opening onto verandahs, as well as an apartment including a spa bath and a kitchenette for self-catering. Breakfast with a selection of fresh fruit, home-made jams, ground bean coffee, and continental and cooked options is served in the formal dining room, and dinner is offered by arrangement. Hereford cattle can be viewed on the working stud on site. Located in 12 hectares of lush Canterbury farmland, Linston is only 20 minutes from Christchurch International Airport and 30 minutes from the City Centre. Day trips by shuttle to Akaroa, Kaikoura and local wineries are popular.

Facilities
- 2 queen bedrooms & bathrooms
- 1 apartment with queen ensuite bedroom & spa bath
- cotton bed linen; fresh flowers
- bathrobes, demist mirror, hair dryers, toiletries & heated towel rails
- TV & phone in bedrooms on request; 2 verandahs
- central heating; wheelchair access
- full breakfast in dining room
- dinner by arrangement, extra
- kitchenette in apartment
- guest lounge with open fire, tea/coffee, mineral water, CD-player, books & artwork
- email, fax, phone in guest office
- laundry, $25; pets welcome
- private guest entrance; garaging
- on-site parking; helipad

Activities available
- landscaped gardens on site
- restaurants 5-min drive
- famous Lincoln bakery
- Lincoln University close by
- local wine trails
- guided hunting trips
- gardens open to visit
- golf course
- fishing
- tennis
- Avon River punting, 25 mins
- Hagley Park activities
- theatre in Christchurch
- Christchurch Casino
- day trips to Akaroa
- whale watching in Kaikoura
- winter skiing
- Christchurch International Airport, 20-min drive
- Christchurch City, 30 mins

© Friars' Guide to New Zealand Accommodation for the Discerning Traveller

Tai Tapu, Christchurch
Chatterley Manor

Host Isabella Hockey

433 Old Tai Tapu Road, R D 2, Christchurch
Phone 0-3-329 6658 *Mobile* 025 310 773 *Fax* 0-3-329 6827
Email enquiries@ladychatterley.co.nz *Website* www.ladychatterley.co.nz

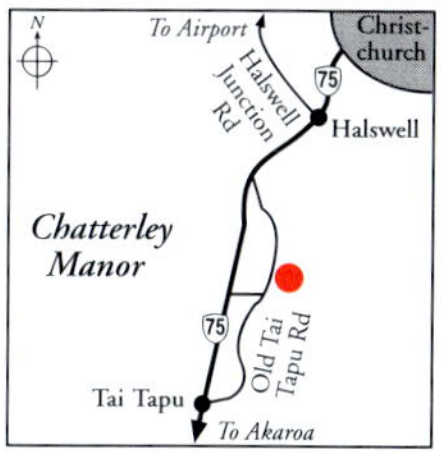

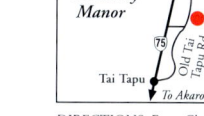

Double $175–$240
Single $150–$190

Includes breakfast
Lunch & dinner extra

8 bdrm / 7 enst

DIRECTIONS: From Christchurch, take SH 75 south. After Halswell pass 100km sign, then turn left into Old Tai Tapu Rd. Travel 3.5km to Chatterley Manor on left. From airport, take Halswell Junction Rd to meet SH 75.

Set in extensive gardens, Chatterley Manor is easily accessible from the city and airport, yet it is totally rural – suitable for weekend get-aways for Christchurch residents. The cuisine caters for individual needs, with menus designed for all tastes, by prior arrangement. The separate guest wing comprises four executive suites with a queen and two single beds in each, and a family suite of two rooms, a double and a twin. The executive suites incorporate a mezzanine floor and a lounge area opening directly on to the extensive lawn and formal gardens. A spacious guest lounge offers conviviality for guests, as does the billiards room which is adjacent to the sauna and large indoor 16-seater spa pool.

Facilities

- 4 queen/twin suites, with ensuites including baths
- family suite with 1 double & 1 twin bedroom, & 1 ensuite
- 1 twin & 1 single, & 1 ensuite
- toiletries, bathrobes, hair dryers, tea/coffee & CD-player in each guest suite
- mezzanine in 4 queen suites
- phone, fax, internet access & email available
- country-style breakfast choice
- 3-course gourmet dinner, with fresh local food, extra
- licensed dining room, seats 18
- picnic/lunch, extra
- special diets catered for
- guest lounge with open fire
- complimentary laundry
- courtesy airport transfer
- on-site parking

Activities available

- alfresco barbecues on site
- guided tours with picnic lunches
- in-house ¾-size billiards table
- sauna & 16-seater spa pool
- extensive gardens & pond on site
- pétanque/boules on site
- croquet on site
- swimming pool on site
- hard-surface tennis court
- local wineries, 5-min drive
- winery trail
- horse riding & trekking
- fishing
- jet boating
- golf course, 3-min drive
- shopping in Christchurch
- theatre in Christchurch
- Christchurch Casino
- skiing in winter
- Akaroa, 45-min drive

407

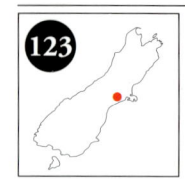

Tai Tapu, Christchurch
Otahuna Lodge

Hosts Greg and Julie Leniston

Rhodes Road, R D 2, Christchurch
Phone 0-3-329 6333   *Mobile* 027 585 0888   *Fax* 0-3-329 6336
Email enquiries@otahuna.co.nz   *Website* www.otahuna.co.nz

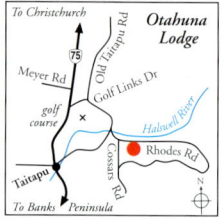

| 9 bdrm | 9 enst | Double $700–$1,800 Single $500–$1,050 | Includes breakfast & dinner Lunch extra |

DIRECTIONS: From Christchurch take SH 1 south. At Hornby turn left into Halswell Junction Rd. At end turn right into SH 75, travel 6km & turn left into Golf Links Dr. Turn right, then left into Rhodes Rd. Lodge on right.

Of historical significance, Otahuna is the largest, best-preserved homestead in New Zealand. Set in 12 hectares of mature garden, surrounded by 800 hectares of native bush, to which guests have exclusive access, Otahuna was originally built in 1895 for Sir Heaton Rhodes, a Canterbury pioneer. Completely renovated to offer nine spacious bedrooms and huge bathrooms, the guestrooms feature open fireplaces and balconies overlooking the garden. A chef provides creative individual cuisine, the guests dining with their hosts. On-site activities at this gourmet retreat include natural horsemanship clinics, cooking schools, and the day spa. Otahuna's private, tranquil, park-like setting is only 20 minutes south of Christchurch City.

Facilities

- 5 California-king & 4 super-king/twin bedrooms
- 9 ensuites: 2 with spa baths, 6 with baths & all with bathrobes, hair dryers, toiletries, demist mirrors & heated towel rails
- TV, phone, desk, fridge in all 9 bedrooms & 9 open fires
- 2 dressing rooms; 3 balconies
- children/pets by arrangement
- Egyptian linen; fresh flowers

- full breakfast; in-house chef
- lunch or packed picnic, extra
- 5-course table d'hôte dinner
- lounge with open fire, Sky TV, video, DVD, CDs, piano & artwork; central heating
- library; email/fax available
- complimentary laundry
- security gates; helipad
- courtesy passenger transfer

Activities available

- gourmet cooking classes; day spa facilities; spa pool & sauna
- tennis, croquet, gymnasium, BBQ area & swimming pool on site
- 12ha garden, orchard & historic stables on site for walks, bird-watching & mountain biking
- natural horsemanship clinics
- pony trap rides on site
- sheep shearing in season; farm tours on site

- exclusive use of 800ha native bush adjacent for hunting, claybird shooting, hiking, horse riding & trekking
- gardens open to visit
- wineries; golf courses
- hot air ballooning
- salmon & trout river fishing
- surf beaches, 40-min drive
- Christchurch City & airport, 20-min drive

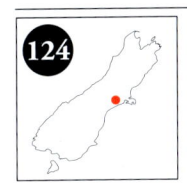

Tai Tapu, Christchurch
Ballymoney Farmstay and Garden

Hosts Merrilies and Peter Rebbeck

Wardstay Road, Tai Tapu *Phone* 0-3-329 6706
Postal Wardstay Road, R D 2, Christchurch *Fax* 0-3-329 6709
Email info@ballymoney.co.nz *Website* www.ballymoney.co.nz

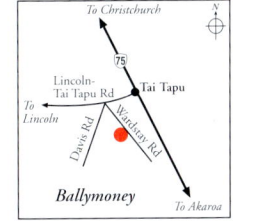

3 bdrm	2 enst	1 prbth

Suite rate $160–$280
Farm package: Double $270

Includes breakfast
Single $170

Lunch & dinner extra
Includes breakfast, dinner & tour

DIRECTIONS: From Christchurch City, take SH 75 to Tai Tapu. Turn right towards Lincoln. Travel 2 km then turn into Wardstay Rd. Travel 800 metres to Ballymoney on right.

Ballymoney is a century-old farm cottage with new additions including a conservatory and sitting room opening to the large private garden and pond. The 14-hectare (35-acre) farm is home to many rare breeds of animals and birds such as white peacocks, water fowl, Dorset horn sheep, Dexter cattle, donkeys and Saddleback pigs. The historic part of the farm homestead features native timber, polished floors, open fireplaces, period furniture and original artwork. Named after the family farm in Ireland, Ballymoney offers "slow food" country cuisine prepared from home-grown spray-free produce and local wine with Kiwi/Irish hospitality. The Ballymoney farm package includes breakfast, dinner and a farm tour. The city and airport are easily accessible.

Facilities
- Manuka Suite: 1 super-king/twin bedroom with ensuite & private verandah & 1 double bedroom adjoining, with private bathroom & bath
- Kowhai Garden Suite: 1 queen bedroom with extra single bed, ensuite & private courtyard; suite detached from house
- hair dryers, toiletries, heated towel rails & bathrobes
- children welcome
- full breakfast served in country kitchen/conservatory
- Mediterranean BBQ area with Italian pizza oven
- dinner & wine, $40–$50 pp formal, casual or BBQ
- TV, tea/coffee in all bedrooms & fridge in both suites
- 2 sitting rooms with open fires, TV, video & piano in house
- phone, fax & email available

Activities available
- farm package includes breakfast, dinner, farm tour & animal feeding
- golden retriever & fox terrier in residence
- pétanque & croquet on site
- courtesy bicycles available
- garden lunches & weddings catered for on site
- garden & chestnut orchard walks, feeding rare animals & birds, & seasonal farm activities on site
- restaurants nearby
- golf course, 5km
- gardens & parks to visit
- horse riding; wine trails
- Lincoln University, 5km
- day trips to Akaroa, 1 hour
- Christchurch City, 20 mins
- airport, 20-min drive
- shuttle bus available from airport & city

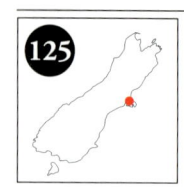

LYTTELTON
CAVENDISH HOUSE

Hosts Jenny and Graham Sorell

10 Ross Terrace, Lyttelton
Phone 0-3-328 9505 *Email* cavendish@clear.net.nz
Fax 0-3-328 9502 *Website* www.cavendish.co.nz

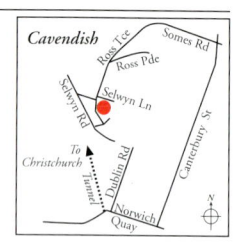

Double $170–$200
Single $150–$170

Includes breakfast
Multiple-night rates available

2 bdrm 2 enst

DIRECTIONS: From tunnel, bear left into Norwich Quay towards Lyttelton. Turn left up Canterbury St. At top, take left fork into Somes Rd. Continue past Ross Pde & 50m past Cavendish House sign to gate on left.

Nestled on Mt Cavendish overlooking the Port of Lyttelton is Cavendish House, built in 1910. This Edwardian villa is set in a terraced garden of perfumed vines, old roses, olive, fig and other fruit trees. Historic features of Cavendish House include the stained glass leadlights, large bay windows, return verandah, and the rare Tasmanian antiques in the Chart Room and former Ballroom. A breakfast selection including free range eggs and fresh garden produce is served in the dining room, or alfresco on the verandah with its Port views to Diamond Harbour and the mountains beyond. Guests can wander down the stepped laneways to the cafés, restaurants and the Port below, then call their hosts to collect them for the homeward journey.

Facilities

- Venice Room: 1 spacious queen ensuite bedroom with spa bath & writing desk
- Tasman Room: 1 super-king/twin ensuite bedroom
- cotton bed linen; fresh flowers
- hair dryer, heated towel rails, toiletries & bathrobes
- children by arrangement
- return verandah opening from both lounges
- full breakfast served in former Ballroom or alfresco
- apéritifs, port, teas, coffee, nibbles, writing desk, TV, video & DVD in Chart Room
- French spoken; art collection
- phone, fax & email available
- private guest entrance
- off-street parking
- outdoors cat

Activities available

- wedding & honeymoon packages
- barbecue available
- relaxing in extensive garden
- watching boats/ships/yachts
- historic Lyttelton buildings
- Diamond Harbour Ferry
- Major Hornbrook Track & other Port Hills walks
- Maritime Museum
- Time-Ball, 15-min walk
- restaurants, cafés, bars, shops, 0.5 km downhill in village
- Port, 10-min walk downhill
- Sumner Beach, 10-min drive
- 1½-hr trip on historic steam tug *Lyttelton* on Sundays
- *Black Cat* wildlife tour
- gardens open to visit at Governor's Bay & in City
- Christchurch City, 15-min drive

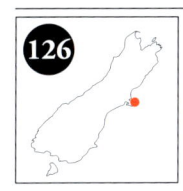

OKAINS BAY, BANKS PENINSULA
KAWATEA FARMSTAY

Hosts Judy and Kerry Thacker

Kawatea, Okains Bay, Banks Peninsula
Phone 0-3-304 8621   *Email* kawatea@xtra.co.nz
Fax 0-3-304 8621   *Website* friars.co.nz/hosts/kawatea.html

3 bdrm | 1 enst | 1 prbth
Double $110–$130
Single $75–$95
Includes breakfast
Lunch & dinner extra

DIRECTIONS: From Christchurch, take SH 75 to Hilltop Hotel. Continue down to Duvauchelle, then take 2nd turning to left. Climb to Okains Bay summit. Continue downhill for 6km. Kawatea on right.

Kerry and Judy are the third generation of Thackers to live at Kawatea, built in 1900. This spacious Edwardian villa was designed by Hurst Seager and built from native timbers with 3.6-metre rimu studs. Historic features include stained-glass windows, plaster ceiling roses, a carved fireplace and polished kauri floors. Judy and Kerry have recently refurbished all rooms in keeping with the period of the house. French doors open from the bedrooms on to the deep verandahs that surround the house, set in an established garden with mature trees, camellias and rhododendrons planted early last century. Kawatea is a working farm, its elevated site, bounded by five kilometres of pristine coastline, providing panoramic rural views.

Facilities
- 1 queen & 1 queen/twin bedroom share bathroom with bath & separate toilet
- 1 private upstairs queen/twin bedroom with ensuite, suitable for families or honeymooners
- New Zealand artwork includes woodwork, pottery, glassware & photography
- expansive verandahs opening to established garden
- full breakfast selection, served in conservatory
- dinner & NZ wine with hosts, $30–$35 pp; local seafood
- alfresco dining on verandah in summer, by fireside in winter
- 2 lounges with fireplaces, library of NZ books, piano, TV, stereo & eclectic music
- complimentary laundry
- 540-ha sheep & cattle farm

Activities available
- seasonal farm activities, such as moving stock, lambing, calving & shearing
- horse for experienced riders
- feeding pet sheep; large aviary & pond on site
- scenic farm walk to seal colony
- pétanque & badminton on site
- swimming at Okains Bay; birdlife on estuary
- Maori & Colonial Museum
- tennis 2-min drive
- golf course, 15-min drive
- arts & crafts, shops & cafés at historic township of Akaroa, 20-min drive
- Akaroa Harbour cruises
- swimming with Hector's dolphins; private garden tours
- sea kayaking; fishing trips
- traditional cheese-making & local wineries

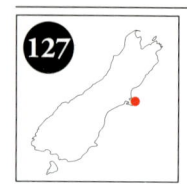

Akaroa, Banks Peninsula
Wilderness House

Hosts Liz and Jim Coubrough

42 Rue Grehan, Akaroa, Banks Peninsula
Phone 0-3-304 7517   *Mobile* 021 669 381   *Fax* 0-3-304 7518
Email info@wildernesshouse.co.nz   *Website* www.wildernesshouse.co.nz

| 4 bdrm | 3 enst | 1 prbth |

Double $195–$220
Single $160–$180

Includes breakfast
Dinner extra

DIRECTIONS: From Christchurch, take SH 75 & travel 80km to Akaroa. From Rue Lavaud, turn left into Rue Grehan. Travel 200m to Wilderness House on right.

This English colonial-designed homestead was built in 1878 in the French-style village of Akaroa on Banks Peninsula. Set in a large traditional garden featuring protected trees, rare camellias, roses and a small private vineyard, Wilderness House provides views of Akaroa Harbour and Grehan Valley. Restored and refurbished in English country-style to provide accommodation, this historic house retains many original features. Wilderness House offers four bedrooms, each with its own bathroom, and guests are given a choice of breakfasts served in the dining room, or alfresco on the verandahs or in the garden. A range of restaurants are only a 500-metre walk away in Akaroa village. Two cats named Beethoven and Harry complete the household.

Facilities
- 3 queen ensuite bedrooms, 1 including bath
- 1 king/twin bedroom with private bathroom & bath
- cotton bed linen, wool duvets & feather pillows
- fresh flowers, tea/coffee & home baking in bedrooms
- hair dryers, toiletries, heated towel rails & bathrobes
- email, fax & phone available
- full breakfast served
- complimentary glass of house wine with hosts every evening
- dinner by arrangement, $50 pp
- guest lounge with open fire, tea/coffee, TV & writing desk
- guest fridge
- spacious sunny guest verandah
- 2 friendly cats in residence
- off-street parking

Activities available
- relaxing in large traditional garden with protected trees, rare camellias & roses on site
- private vineyard on site
- village centre for restaurants, cafés, bars & shops, 500m
- horse riding
- charter fishing trips
- gardens open to visit
- French history museum
- wineries
- harbour cruises
- swimming with dolphins
- tramping & walks
- historic buildings
- boating & diving
- kayaking
- tennis court
- Christchurch, 80km

© Friars' Guide to New Zealand Accommodation for the Discerning Traveller

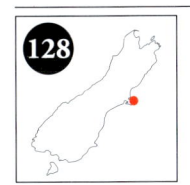

AKAROA, BANKS PENINSULA
MILL COTTAGE

Hosts Louisa and Cliff Hobson-Corry

81 Rue Grehan, Akaroa, Banks Peninsula
Phone 0-3-304 8007   *Mobile* 027 494 9062   *Fax* 0-3-304 8007
Email millcottage@xtra.co.nz   *Website* www.akaroa.gen.nz

3 bdrm   2 prbth   Cottage rate $275   Extra persons $50 each

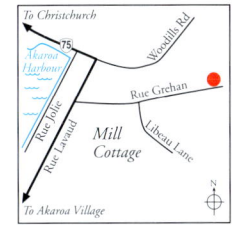

DIRECTIONS: From Christchurch, take SH 75 & travel 80km to Akaroa. From Rue Lavaud, turn left into Rue Grehan. Travel 300m to Mill Cottage on left.

Located on the outskirts of the historic township of Akaroa, Mill Cottage was built in 1850 and has been carefully restored to provide self-contained accommodation. This English-style cottage is set in almost a hectare (two acres) of park-like gardens featuring mature trees, a gazebo and summer house. Mill Cottage was named after Canterbury's first water-driven flour mill that was originally on the site. Guests are offered a queen bedroom downstairs, and two single bedrooms with dormer windows in the attic. French doors open to a sunny verandah with garden views. There is a kitchenette with microwave, and restaurants are a 10-minute walk away. The hosts live separately in the adjacent house, ensuring guest privacy.

Facilities
- single-party bookings only
- restored historic cottage
- 1 queen with private bathroom; 2 single attic bedrooms share 1 private bathroom
- cotton bed linen
- hair dryers, toiletries, & bathrobes
- lounge with tea/coffee, nibbles, CD-player, books & artwork
- kitchenette
- pot-belly in historic kitchen area
- fresh flowers
- weddings & honeymoons catered for
- private guest entrance
- guest verandah; gazebo & summer house
- off-street parking

Activities available
- 1ha park garden on site
- croquet
- historic township
- harbour trips
- tramping & walking tracks
- gardens open to visit
- swimming with dolphins
- local cheese factory
- kayaking
- scenic drives
- restaurants, cafés, bars & shops, 10-min walk
- vineyards & wineries
- historic museum with restored French cottage
- historic homes
- local craft shops
- fishing trips
- horse riding
- Christchurch City, 80km

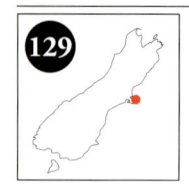

AKAROA, BANKS PENINSULA
MAISON DE LA MER

Hosts Laurice and Alan Bradford

1 Rue Benoit, Akaroa, Banks Peninsula
Phone 0-3-304 8907   Mobile 025 376 982   Fax 0-3-304 8907
Email maisondelamer@xtra.co.nz   Website www.maisondelamer.co.nz

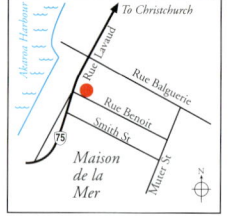

| 4 bdrm | 4 enst | Double $150–$200 Apartment rate $220 | Single $130 2-night minimum stay | Includes breakfast or provisions Self-catering |

DIRECTIONS: From Christchurch, take SH 75 & travel 80km to Akaroa. Continue along Rue Lavaud to Maison de la Mer on left, on corner of Rue Benoit.

Maison de la Mer is French for "House by the Sea", aptly named for its location on the edge of the historic French-style Akaroa village set on the harbour. This classic two-storey villa was built in 1910 for local merchant T.E. Taylor. Completely refurbished to provide three guestrooms, Maison de la Mer has retained its original leadlight windows, complemented by hand-made furniture, ceramics, artwork and designer fabrics. A self-catering loft apartment is also available. Set in an established garden with roses, trees and lawn, the house features wide harbour views to the surrounding hills beyond. Continental or cooked breakfast, including home baking and seasonal fruits, is served in the dining room or alfresco on the verandah with sea views.

Facilities
- 2 queen ensuite bedrooms, 1 with double spa bath
- 1 queen/twin ensuite bedroom with private sunroom
- The Loft: separate self-contained apartment with 1 queen ensuite bedroom & kitchenette
- cotton bed linen, fans, fridges, TV & tea/coffee in bedrooms
- hair dryer, heated towel rails & toiletries
- full breakfast; or provisions for self-catering apartment
- lounge with open fire, TV & writing desk
- golf clubs available
- email, fax & phone available
- fresh flowers; central heating
- laundry available
- off-street parking

Activities available
- mountain bikes available
- dinghy available on site
- garden with mature trees & roses for walking & relaxing
- swimming beach opposite
- seal & penguin colony
- swimming with dolphins
- historic French architecture
- harbour cruises
- cruises on vintage ketch
- restaurants & cafés nearby
- garden tours
- 4 wheel bike safaris
- horse trekking
- fishing trips
- Banks Peninsula track, 3–4 days' tramp
- historic museum
- wineries & golf course
- Christchurch, 80km

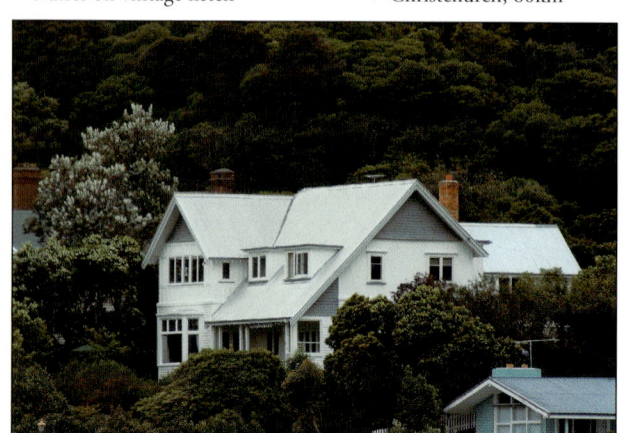

© Friars' Guide to New Zealand Accommodation for the Discerning Traveller

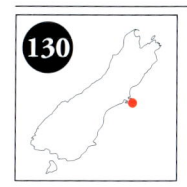

Akaroa, Banks Peninsula
Maison des Fleurs

Hosts Margy and Dai Morris

6 Church Street, Akaroa, Banks Peninsula
Phone 0-3-304 7804   *Email* fire.and.ice@xtra.co.nz
Fax 0-3-304 7804   *Website* friars.co.nz/hosts/maison.html

1 bdrm   1 enst   Cottage rate $250   *Self-catering*

DIRECTIONS: From Christchurch, take SH 75 to Akaroa. Travel along Rue Lavaud, past the beach into Rue Jolie. Then turn right into Church St. Travel 10m to Maison des Fleurs on left.

Located just 100 metres from Akaroa Harbour, Maison des Fleurs is a two-storey self-contained cottage, built in 1999. This colonial-style cottage, handcrafted in New Zealand native timbers with natural finishes, is complemented by antique and contemporary furnishings, including a historic open fireplace in the lounge upstairs. The sunny afternoon balcony is a favourite spot for watching sunsets, and the secluded garden courtyard has a swing seat for two. Designed as a romantic retreat, Maison des Fleurs (meaning the House of Flowers) features fresh flowers and extras including aromatherapy oils, chocolates and port.

Facilities
- self-contained cottage
- single-party bookings only
- 1 queen bedroom with ensuite
- Pro-natura designed bed (handmade) & cotton bed linen
- king-size spa bath, bidet, demist mirror & heated towel rails
- bathrobes, hair dryer, toiletries, bubble bath & aromatherapy oils
- open fire, CD-player, magazines, guitar & games
- kitchenette for self-catering
- organic teas, coffees, juices, purified water, port & chocolates
- complimentary champagne for 2-night stay
- fresh flowers
- upstairs lounge with antique open fireplace, opens to balcony
- central heating
- honeymoon retreat

Activities available
- swing seat in secluded garden courtyard
- watching sunsets
- historic village walk
- restaurants, cafés & boutique shopping in historic town, 100m walk
- French history museum
- walking; tramping
- local winery
- local cheese factory
- Banks Peninsula track, 2–4 days' tramp
- seal colony tours
- charter fishing trips
- watching & swimming with dolphins
- harbour cruises
- private garden tours
- tennis courts
- golf course
- Christchurch City, 1½ hrs

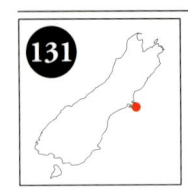

Akaroa, Banks Peninsula
Aylmer House

Hosts Bob Parker and Joanna Nicholls

7 Percy Street, Akaroa, Banks Peninsula *Postal* P O Box 53, Akaroa
Phone 0-3-304 7008 *Mobile* 027 597 8373 *Fax* 0-3-304 7008
Email accommodation@aylmer.co.nz *Website* friars.co.nz/hosts/aylmer.html

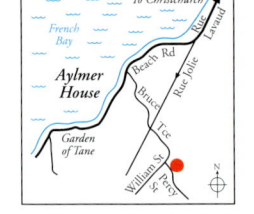

2 bdrm | 2 enst Room rate $395 *Includes breakfast*

DIRECTIONS: From Christchurch, take SH 75 to Akaroa. Travel along Rue Lavaud & continue into Rue Jolie. Turn left into Bruce Tce & left again into Percy St. Aylmer House 1st on left.

Aylmer House is a French colonial home built in 1852 for the first Anglican vicar on Banks Peninsula, Reverend Aylmer. It has been restored by Bob, the current Mayor of Banks Peninsula, and now offers two king-size ensuite guestrooms, Misty Peaks and Harbour View. Both bedrooms, which open to a sunny balcony, are named after their views. Aylmer House is set in a large garden with native trees, a pond and a stream featuring a historic waterwheel and mill. There is also a swimming pool for the guests' enjoyment. Joanna graduated from the New Zealand School of Food and Wine and also offers aroma-massage. She serves a full breakfast sourced from organic supplies, in the French country kitchen, and restaurants are within walking distance.

Facilities
- 2 king ensuite bedrooms, each opening to the balcony
- hair dryer, toiletries, bidet, heated floor, heated towel rails & bathrobes in both ensuites
- bath in Misty Peaks ensuite
- cotton bed linen; fresh flowers
- tea/coffee, CDs & phone in bedrooms
- guest fridge adjacent to bedrooms
- breakfast with organic muesli, nuts, seasonal fruit, muffins, yoghurt, French soufflé
- open fire, nibbles, Sky TV, video, DVD, CD-player, piano, artwork, books, phone & writing desk in lounge
- complimentary house wine
- email, fax & laundry available
- private guest entrance
- off-street parking

Activities available
- heated swimming pool on site
- in-house aroma-massage, extra
- walking in large garden with pond, native trees, water wheel & mill
- Akaroa village shops, cafés & restaurants, 5-min walk
- Within 10–15-min walk:
  – swimming with dolphins in Akaroa Harbour
  – herb gardens to visit
  – hiking trails within the volcanic basin
  – tennis courts
  – fishing; kayaking
  – Maori cultural activities
  – artists' galleries; museum
  – selection of walking tracks
- Banks Peninsula 2–4-day tramp
- Christchurch City, 1½ hours

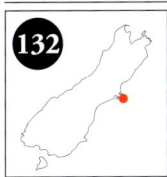

Akaroa, Banks Peninsula
Oinako Lodge

Hosts Teresa and Greg Miller

99 Beach Road, Akaroa, Banks Peninsula
Phone 0-3-304 8787   *Fax* 0-3-304 8787
Email bookings@oinako.co.nz   *Website* www.oinako.co.nz

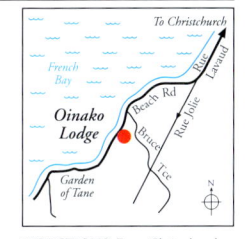

Room rate $165–$220   *Includes breakfast*

6 bdrm / 6 enst

DIRECTIONS: From Christchurch, take SH 75 to Akaroa. From Rue Lavaud continue into Beach Rd. Follow 1-way system into Rue Jolie, turn right into Bruce Tce & left into Beach Rd. Continue to Oinako on left.

Originally built in 1865 as the official residence for an English magistrate, Oinako was rebuilt by a French settler after a fire in 1895. Historic features include the spacious entrance hall with open fire and sweeping French staircase, marble fireplaces, and the ornate plaster ceilings and cornices. Furnished in keeping with the architecture, Oinako now incorporates modern amenities and luxurious contemporary touches such as spa baths in four of the ensuite bathrooms. The king-size Jade room is pictured below. The Amethyst, Jasmine and Napoleon rooms each similarly include a spa bath in the ensuite. All six bedrooms feature garden or harbour views. Gourmet breakfasts are served in the original dining room looking out to the rose garden.

Facilities
- 1 twin, 2 queen & 3 king upstairs bedrooms, all with ensuite bathrooms
- spa bath in 4 ensuites
- freshly cut flowers in all guestrooms
- serviced daily
- tranquil rose garden
- open fire in spacious entrance hall
- gourmet breakfast served in downstairs dining room
- tea/coffee buffet
- guest fridge
- guest lounge with TV
- balcony overlooking garden & Akaroa Harbour
- weddings, receptions & meetings catered
- off-street parking

Activities available
- relaxing in peaceful garden
- fishing trips
- horse trekking
- beach, 2 mins away
- Hector's dolphins
- cheese factory
- winery
- walking & tramping
- tennis; badminton
- restaurants, shops nearby
- Akaroa Harbour & sail cruises
- catamaran trips
- seaside swimming
- historic Akaroa township
- cycling
- mini-golf
- golf course
- heritage trail

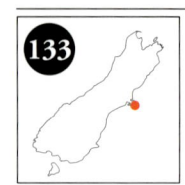

Akaroa, Banks Peninsula
Onuku Heights

Host Eckhard Keppler

166 Haylocks Road, R D 1, Akaroa, Banks Peninsula
Email onuku.heights@paradise.net.nz   *Phone* 0-3-304 7112
Website www.onuku-heights.co.nz   *Fax* 0-3-304 7116

3 bdrm / 3 enst   Room rate $140–$240   *Includes breakfast*   *Dinner extra*

DIRECTIONS: From Christchurch, take SH 75 to Akaroa. Travel through village & turn left at bakery into Rue Jolie. Follow signs to Onuku Marae. Continue into Haylocks Rd & travel up to Onuku Heights at end.

Set high overlooking Akaroa Harbour is the historic farm at Onuku Heights. Built in the 1860s, the homestead has been carefully restored and is furnished with antiques and period furniture. With an abundance of birdlife, Onuku Heights is nestled in gardens and orchard, and surrounded by native bush reserves, streams and waterfalls on a 309-hectare working sheep farm. There are two ensuite guestrooms upstairs in the homestead, with a separate ensuite guestroom in a cottage adjacent to the homestead. A full breakfast with home-made bread and jams is served in the downstairs guest lounge or alfresco on the terrace with panoramic sea views. Candlelit dinners by the open fire are available by prior arrangement.

Facilities
- 2 king ensuite bedrooms upstairs in homestead
- 1 separate guestroom with king bed & ensuite bathroom
- embroidered bed linen
- hair dryer & toiletries
- fresh flowers
- rose garden with fountain
- laundry available
- sunny guest verandah
- cooked or continental breakfast with home baking
- 3-course candlelit dinner by prior arrangement, $40–$60 pp
- private guest lounge with open fire, tea/coffee & sea vistas
- large terrace with sea views
- seats in orchard & garden
- private guest entrance
- courtesy passenger transfer

Activities available
- heated swimming pool & sauna on site
- 300ha sheep farm on site, farm activities & tours
- walking tracks to 700m altitude with views over harbour & ocean to Alps
- bush walks & waterfall
- pétanque court on site
- pet lambs & hens on site
- wineries
- swimming with dolphins
- kayaking
- horse riding
- Akaroa cafés, restaurants, bars & shops, 5km away
- golf course
- Akaroa Harbour trips
- gardens open to visit
- arts & crafts; museum
- Onuku Marae

© Friars' Guide to New Zealand Accommodation for the Discerning Traveller

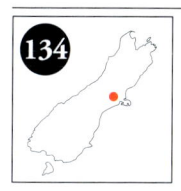

DARFIELD
BANGOR COUNTRY ESTATE

Hosts Cliff and Biba Baker

Bangor Road, Darfield, Canterbury
Phone 0-3-318 7588 *Mobile* 021 284 4125 *Fax* 0-3-318 8485
Email sales@bangor.co.nz *Website* www.bangor.co.nz

Double $950–$1,350
Single $625–$875

*Includes breakfast & dinner
Lunch extra*

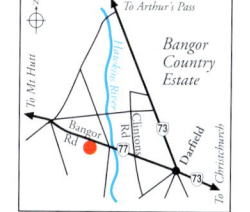

DIRECTIONS: From Christchurch, take SH 73 to Darfield. Continue through Darfield and take Bangor Rd (SH 77) towards Methven & Mt Hutt. Travel 5 mins to Bangor Country Estate on left.

6 bdrm / 6 enst

Founded in 1854 by the Ward brothers and named in honour of their uncle, the Viscount Bangor of Ireland, Bangor Country Estate today comprises a 13-hectare (33-acre) setting of lush lawns, gardens and woodlands for the finely detailed and restored Victorian colonial mansion. At the foothills of the Southern Alps, yet only half an hour from Christchurch, Bangor provides a luxury escape for the discerning traveller, or newly-wed, and an exclusive executive retreat. The six guest suites are individually furnished with antiques and art from around the world. The cuisine, prepared by the resident chef, includes five-course evening meals, full country breakfasts, and lunches on request. The wine cellar features a range of vintages from the Southern Hemisphere.

Facilities

- 1 super-king, 4 queen & 1 twin bedroom, all with ensuites
- 1 claw-foot bath, 1 spa bath & double basins in 2 ensuites
- hair dryer, heated floor, heated towel rails, demist mirror, wall heater & toiletries in each
- bathrobes, cotton bed linen, phones & TV in premium suite
- 2 lounges with open fires, Sky TV, video, DVD & CDs
- full breakfast in dining room or alfresco on garden patio
- light lunch or picnic basket available on request, extra
- 5-course dinner served with gourmet/seasonal specialities & selection of wine
- tea/coffee, fax, email & laundry available on request
- limousine transfers
- ample parking; helipad

Activities available

- pond & garden gazebo
- tennis court & croquet lawn
- in-ground swimming pool
- archery & bicycles available
- pétanque/boules on site
- guided hunting arranged
- 4WD tours arranged
- working farm visits
- horse riding
- Darfield, 5-min drive
- wineries & golf courses nearby
- Waimakariri & Rakaia Rivers
- trout fishing
- garden tours; hiking; walking
- jet boats on river
- hot air balloon trips
- winter heli-skiing & skiing at Canterbury ski-fields
- Christchurch City, 30-min drive
- International Airport, 25 mins

135

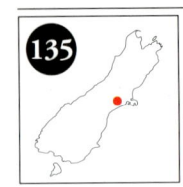

MOUNT HUTT–METHVEN
GREEN GABLES DEER FARM

Hosts Colleen and Roger Mehrtens

185 Waimarama Road, Methven   *Postal* R D 12, Rakaia
Freephone 0800 466 093   *Phone* 0-3-302 8308   *Fax* 0-3-302 8309
Email greengables@xtra.co.nz   *Website* www.nzfarmstay.com

| 3 bdrm | 2 enst | 1 prbth |

Double $140–$180
Single $110–$140

Includes breakfast
Dinner extra

DIRECTIONS: From Christchurch, take SH 1 to Rakaia. Turn right & travel to Methven. Turn right again into SH 77. Continue into Waimarama Rd, veering left. Travel 4km to Green Gables Farm on left.

Green Gables is a working deer farm, where guests can hand-feed Lucy the pet deer and other friendly deer including the Royal Danish white deer. This centrally located farm is one hour south of Christchurch City and its International Airport. Rural views from every room in the homestead extend to the nearby Mount Hutt ski area. The three guest bedrooms open on to a private verandah, with adjacent parking. Colleen enjoys preparing New Zealand cuisine for guests, and serves meals in the dining room, in front of the log fire in winter. Breakfast includes hot muffins or croissants, yoghurt, and a cooked English-style selection. Dinner featuring the freshest local produce can be provided by arrangement, or restaurants are nearby.

Facilities

- 2 super-king ensuite bedrooms
- 1 super-king/twin bedroom with private bathroom, including bath
- toiletries & hair dryers
- oil-filled heater, clock-radio, tea/coffee, bathrobes, iron & ironing board in each bedroom
- private entrance, decking & mountain views from all 3 bedrooms
- tea/coffee upon arrival
- full breakfast in dining room
- dinner by request, $45 pp; vegetarians catered for
- dining room with log fire
- open fire & TV in sitting room
- double glazing
- phone, fax & internet jack
- golden labrador, Max
- on-site parking

Activities available

- hand-feed pet deer Lucy & her family
- 2 golf courses – Methven & Terrace Downs; golf club & cart hire
- hot air ballooning
- jet boating
- salmon & trout fishing – guides by arrangement
- bush & mountain walks nearby
- licensed restaurants nearby at Mt Hutt/Methven village
- Mt Somers sub-alpine walkway
- private gardens open to visit
- horse riding
- skiing at Mt Hutt – transport from gate (closest accommodation)
- Christchurch International Airport, 1 hour north
- Christchurch City, 1¼ hours

© Friars' Guide to New Zealand Accommodation for the Discerning Traveller

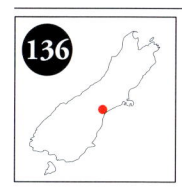

ASHBURTON
CONISTON HOMESTEAD

Hosts Carolyn and Donald Williamson

30 Methven Highway, R D 6, Ashburton
Phone 0-3-307 8189   *Mobile* 027 435 4705   *Fax* 0-3-307 8179
Email coniston@xtra.co.nz   *Website* www.coniston.co.nz

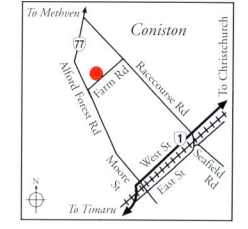

4 bdrm | 3 enst | 1 prbth

Double $180–$220
Single $140

Includes breakfast
Lunch & dinner extra

DIRECTIONS: From south end of Ashburton, turn west off SH 1 into Moore St, then continue on Alford Forest Rd (SH 77) for 3km to Coniston on right.

A tree-lined driveway leads to the homestead at Coniston, built in 1918, when the extensive woodland gardens were planted. Recently renovated to provide four guestrooms, Coniston is located on a farm offering sheep, cropping and seed farm tours and activities to guests. The garden attracts birdlife and includes many rare and mature trees, with one planted to commemorate the visit of Queen Elizabeth II in 1981. The rhododendrons, azaleas and camellias feature in the springtime, the blossom reflected in the lake, where guests enjoy rowing. Meals are served in the formal dining room or alfresco on the guest verandahs, looking out into the garden. Country cuisine dinner is available by arrangement, and Ashburton restaurants are nearby.

Facilities

- 1 super-king & 1 queen ensuite bedroom with TV & phone; queen room opens to verandah
- 2 twin bedrooms share 1 bathroom with spa bath
- hair dryers, toiletries, heated floors & towel rails, demist mirrors & bathrobes
- cotton bed linen; fresh flowers
- children over 10 yrs welcome
- phone, fax & email available
- full breakfast served
- lunch by request, extra
- dinner, $45 pp
- guest kitchenette
- guest lounge with open fire, TV, video, CDs, games, books & writing desk
- laundry available, $5
- on-site parking
- helicopter access

Activities available

- 2ha (5-acre) gardens on site
- lake rowing & canal walk, on site
- marquee garden weddings on site; two vintage cars available
- sheep, cropping & seed farm tours & activities on site
- salmon/trout river fishing/guides
- 5 golf courses; horse trekking
- *Lord of the Rings* sight-seeing
- jet boating; hot air ballooning
- Mt Somers subalpine walkway; garden tours
- Lake Hood recreational lake, 10-min drive
- historic plains village & railway museum, 5 mins
- vintage car & farm machinery museum, 5 mins
- art gallery, tennis & indoor swimming, 3-min drive
- Mt Hutt ski-field, 30 mins

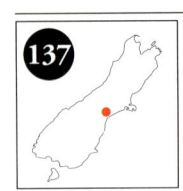

Geraldine
The Crossing Guest Lodge

Manager Patti Epp

124 Woodbury Road, R D 21, Geraldine, South Canterbury
Phone 0-3-693 9689   Email srelax@xtra.co.nz
Fax 0-3-693 9789   Website friars.co.nz/hosts/crossing.html

Double $160–$190
Single $140–$170

Includes breakfast
Dinner extra

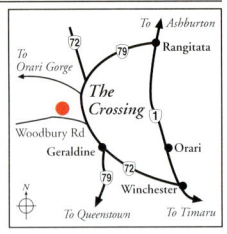

3 bdrm | 3 enst

DIRECTIONS: Take SH 79 south until 200m past "Welcome" sign. Turn right into Woodbury Rd. Travel 1.5km to The Crossing on right. From Geraldine, take SH 72 north for 3km. Turn left into Woodbury Rd.

The Crossing is an English-style manor house, incorporating a fully licensed restaurant. Named after the original Waihi River crossing on the property, The Crossing was built as a banker's retirement estate in 1908. The lounge still features the panelled dado, open fireplace and grand piano, and with the dining room, opens on to a shady verandah where wisteria frames the expansive garden, rural pastureland and mountains beyond. Upstairs are the three renovated guestrooms, comprising the Sinclair-Thompson Suite with queen bed, bay window sitting area and ensuite, Catherine's Suite with queen and single beds, sitting area and ensuite, and the Sally Barker Suite with queen and single beds, sitting area and ensuite bathroom.

Facilities

- 1 queen & 2 queen/twin bedrooms, each with ensuite
- toiletries, hair dryers
- cotton bed linen
- children over 12 years welcome
- board games available
- separate TV lounge
- spacious reading lounges
- dining room with open fire
- peaceful garden for relaxing
- breakfast choice, served in dining room
- à la carte dinner by prior arrangement, extra
- fully licensed in-house restaurant
- guest lounge with open fireplace & grand piano
- bar opens to verandah & established garden
- on-site parking

Activities available

- croquet & pétanque on site
- in-ground garden walks
- 14.8ha pasture for strolling
- trekking in Peel Forest & Talbot Forest
- white water rafting at Rangitata
- hunting, guides available
- 18 golf courses, 10-min to 1-hour drive away
- restaurants, 3km south
- salmon & trout fishing, guides available
- vintage car museum
- scenic walks
- private garden visits
- Geraldine, 3km away
- Timaru, 30 mins south
- Christchurch, 1¾ hrs north
- www.thecrossingbnb.co.nz

GERALDINE
FOUR PEAKS LODGE

Hosts Ineke and Ashley Pierce

414 Four Peaks Road, R D 21, Geraldine
Phone 0-3-693 8587 *Email* info@fourpeakslodge.co.nz
Fax 0-3-693 8572 *Website* www.fourpeakslodge.co.nz

4 bdrm | 4 enst | Double $450–$900 | Single $360–$720

*Includes breakfast, apéritifs & dinner
Lunch extra for single-night stays*

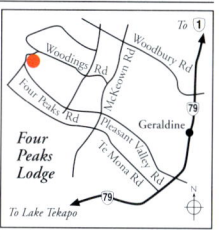

DIRECTIONS: From Geraldine, turn into Woodbury Rd. Travel to Woodbury & turn left into McKeown Rd. Follow signs to Four Peaks Lodge. Or from SH 79, turn into Pleasant Valley Rd & follow signs to Lodge.

Designed by Heathcote Helmore in 1924, Four Peaks Lodge is a Georgian-style homestead set in formal gardens bounded by woodlands and native bush. Recently renovated, the Lodge offers four ensuite guestrooms upstairs, which include a suite with a private lounge that opens onto a deep balcony overlooking the garden. A chef provides dinner, the meals being served in the formal dining room, or alfresco on the terrace. Guests enjoy the seclusion of Four Peaks with its deer farm and extensive bush and woodland walks where bird-watching is popular. The landscaped gardens can also be viewed from the warmth of a jacuzzi within the gazebo. The Lodge is close to the Inland Scenic Route at Geraldine, en route to Tekapo, Queenstown or Christchurch.

Facilities

- 1 queen & 3 super-king/twin ensuite bedrooms upstairs
- hair dryers, toiletries, heated towel rails & demist mirror
- bath, dual basin & double shower in suite with balcony
- cotton bed linen; bathrobes
- open fire & phone in drawing room opening to verandah
- fax & email available; Dutch spoken by hosts
- full breakfast, apéritifs, à la carte dinner & wine served
- light lunch included in tariff for multiple-night stays
- open fire, bar, Sky TV, CDs, games, artwork, books & writing desk in guest lounge, opening to terrace
- central heating; fresh flowers
- complimentary laundry
- on-site parking

Activities available

- jacuzzi in formal gardens
- bush, woodland walks & deer farm on site
- golf courses nearby
- gardens open to visit
- high country wilderness tours
- tramping & hiking
- native bird-watching
- white water rafting at Rangitata
- kayaking; mountain biking
- trout & salmon fishing
- glass blowing, 5-min drive
- Geraldine township, 10 mins
- vintage car museum, 10 mins
- local chocolate factory & cheese factory to visit, 10 mins
- quality local arts & crafts
- ski-fields & heli-skiing within 1-hour drive away
- Christchurch, 1¾ hrs north

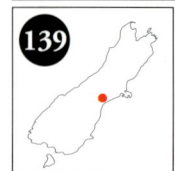

WINCHESTER
KAVANAGH HOUSE

Hosts Juliearna and Killian Kavanagh

State Highway 1, Winchester   *Postal* P O Box 33, Winchester
Phone 0-3-615 6150   *Email* kavanaghhouse@kavanaghhouse.co.nz
Fax 0-3-615 9694   *Website* www.kavanaghhouse.co.nz

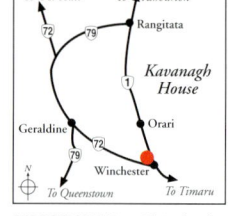

| 3 bdrm | 3 enst | 1 pdrm | Room rate $195–$295 | Includes breakfast | Lunch & dinner extra |

DIRECTIONS: From Christchurch, take SH 1 south to Winchester. Kavanagh House on right in Winchester. From Timaru, take SH 1 north to Winchester. Kavanagh House on the left in Winchester.

Kavanagh House is a restored two-storey character home built in neo-Tudor style in 1907 in the rural setting of Winchester. Furnished with flair, Kavanagh House now provides accommodation comprising three ensuite bedrooms, two with private verandahs overlooking the rose garden, pastureland and mountains beyond. Features include the high hand-painted ceilings & carved bannisters. Guests are greeted with a complimentary glass of champagne on arrival and a licensed restaurant serves café-style food during the day and country cuisine in the evening. Gourmet breakfast, including cooked options such as Eggs Benedict and French toast, is served each morning and à la carte lunch and five-course dinner are also available.

Facilities
- 1 queen & 2 king bedrooms, 2 with verandahs
- 3 ensuite bathrooms with toiletries, bathrobes, 1 spa bath & 2 claw-foot baths
- direct-dial phone, CD-player & fruit platter in bedrooms
- cotton bed linen; fresh flowers
- TV on request
- after 3pm check-in & 12-noon check-out
- gourmet breakfast, served in café downstairs
- fully licensed in-house restaurant for lunch/dinner
- complimentary glass of champagne on arrival
- living room with open fire; central heating
- courtesy passenger transfer
- off-street parking
- unsuitable for children

Activities available
- garden walks on site
- salmon & trout fishing; guides available
- trekking in Peel Forest
- golf courses
- white water rafting at Rangitata
- horse riding
- vintage car museum
- private gardens to visit
- hunting
- Winchester, short stroll
- scenic walks & tramping/hiking
- public parks & gardens
- ski-fields, 1-hour drive
- Geraldine, 8km
- Timaru, 30km south
- Lake Tekapo, 96km
- Christchurch, 147km
- Mt Cook, 195km

© Friars' Guide to New Zealand Accommodation for the Discerning Traveller

Timaru
Tighnafeile House

Hosts Bev and Robin Jenkins

62 Wai-iti Road, Timaru   *Postal* P O Box 685, Timaru
Phone 0-3-684 3333   *Mobile* 025 386 272   *Fax* 0-3-684 3328
Email tighnafeile-house@timaru.co.nz   *Website* www.tighnafeile.com

| 4 bdrm | 3 enst | 1 prbth | **Double $325** | **Single $295** | *Includes breakfast* |

DIRECTIONS: Take SH 1 towards Timaru. On north edge of town, opposite entrance to Caroline Bay, turn right into Wai-iti Rd. Travel 4 blocks to Tighnafeile House on left.

Tighnafeile (pronounced "Tine-a-fay-lee") is Gaelic for "House of Welcome". This Dutch Jacobean mansion was designed by Timaru architect Walter Panton and built in 1911 originally for John Matheson, a station owner in the Mackenzie Country, and his wife and six children. After a varied history, the house has been restored and converted for accommodation, now offering two upstairs honeymoon suites, one with four-poster bed, twin bedroom with private bathroom, and single ensuite bedroom. Breakfast is served in the formal dining room downstairs and guests can relax in the private lounge, reading room and balcony, or on the extensive verandah opening to the spacious lawns and landscaped gardens. Caroline Bay is a five-minute walk away.

Facilities

- 1 king honeymoon suite
- 1 queen honeymoon suite
- 1 twin bedroom with private bathroom, heated towel rail & bath
- 1 single ensuite bedroom
- cotton bed linen
- TV available for bedrooms
- fresh flowers in bedrooms
- verandah opens to garden
- full breakfast in dining room
- tea/coffee in reading room, balcony overlooking garden
- phone, fax & email available
- TV, video & gas fire in private guest lounge
- laundry available, $5
- children over 12 yrs welcome
- courtesy passenger transfer
- off-street parking

Activities available

- gardens & lawn on site
- art gallery, across road
- restaurants & bars nearby
- swimming pool nearby
- Caroline Bay, 5-min walk
- golf course nearby
- tennis stadium
- shopping, 1km
- private gardens open to visit
- Centennial Park, 5-min drive
- Timaru township, 1km
- Timaru Botanic Gardens, 10-min drive
- fishing trips arranged
- sightseeing trips arranged
- winter skiing, 95km
- Lake Tekapo, 105km
- Christchurch, 164km north
- Oamaru, 80km south
- Dunedin, 200km south

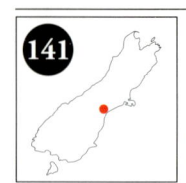

TOTARA VALLEY, PLEASANT POINT
CENTRE HILL COTTAGE

Host Ian Blakemore *Mobile* 027 420 1120

59 Howell Road, Pleasant Point   *Postal* Totara Valley, R D 12, Pleasant Point
Freephone 0800 203 473   *Phone* 0-3-614 7385   *Fax* 0-3-614 7380
Email centre.hill@paradise.net.nz   *Website* www.centrehillcottage.com

2 bdrm | 1 prbth

Cottage rate $250 for 2 persons
Extra persons $50 each

Includes continental breakfast provisions
Dinner extra   *Self-catering*

DIRECTIONS: From Timaru, take SH 8 to Pleasant Point. At hotel turn right into Tengawai Rd. Cross bridge, turn left into Totara Valley, then left into Howell Rd. Centre Hill Cottage 1st on left, 5.2km from SH 8 turn-off.

Centre Hill Cottage is located on an organic farm where organic produce including meat is available for sampling. The cottage is self-contained with a full kitchen for self-catering. Continental breakfast provisions are supplied, and a chef can provide dinner by prior arrangement. Alternatively, restaurants are just five minutes away at Pleasant Point. Guests are offered two bedrooms, for single-party bookings only, with a large deck opening from the main bedroom and living area. From the outdoor bathtub, guests can enjoy the rural views over farmland to the Southern Alps. Centre Hill is two hours from Christchurch International Airport, 15 minutes from Timaru airport, and one hour from winter ski-fields and Lake Tekapo.

Facilities
- 1 single-party bookings
- 1 self-contained cottage
- 1 queen & 1 twin bedroom
- 1 private bathroom & spa bath
- cotton bed linen; phone jack
- bathrobes, hair dryer, toiletries, heated towel rails, demist mirror & heated floor
- outdoor bath
- children welcome
- full kitchen for self-catering
- continental breakfast provisions
- organic venison, beef, lamb & some vegetables available
- chef available for dinner, by prior arrangement only
- tea/coffee, nibbles, TV, CDs, books, artwork & log fire
- laundry available
- on-site parking; garaging

Activities available
- BBQ & outdoor bathtub
- swimming pool & tennis court (Oct.–March) on site
- organic farm walks on site
- Pleasant Point restaurants, shops, museum & steam railway, 5-min drive
- lake & river fishing
- Opihi vineyard
- Maori rock drawings
- walks; hiking; trekking
- gardens to visit; photography
- sketching; painting
- artisan gallery; taxidermist
- Timaru airport, 15 mins
- Timaru botanic gardens & beach, 20-min drive
- Lake Tekapo, 1-hour drive
- winter ski-fields, 1-hr drive
- Christchurch City, 2 hours

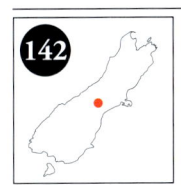

Lake Tekapo
Creel House Bed and Breakfast

Hosts Rosemary and Grant Brown

36 Murray Place, Lake Tekapo *Postal* P O Box 39, Lake Tekapo
Phone 0-3-680 6516 *Email* creelhouse.l.tek@xtra.co.nz
Fax 0-3-680 6659 *Website* friars.co.nz/hosts/creel.html

3 bdrm | 2 prbth | 1 enst

Double $140–$150
Single $70–$80

Includes continental breakfast

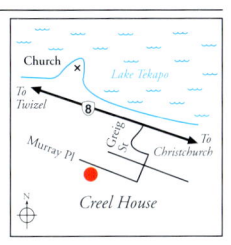

DIRECTIONS: From Christchurch or Queenstown, take SH 8 to Lake Tekapo. East of church, turn south into Greig Street. At top of hill turn right into Murray Place. Creel House on the left.

Creel House was named after the angler's fishing basket, Grant's guided fly fishing trips being a highlight for many visitors to Lake Tekapo. Creel House overlooks the lake with alpine views of the Southern Alps beyond. Guests can enjoy the panorama from the expansive balconies and the queen bedroom upstairs. Grant has built Creel House over the past 20 years in Norwegian chalet style, with the family living quarters separate below. Guests have private entrance stairs and a guest lounge featuring raised rimu ceilings and mounted trout. The Browns designed the colour scheme to blend with the Mackenzie Country environment. Rosemary has developed a New Zealand native garden around the house, with many hebes and native grasses.

Facilities
- 1 upstairs queen bedroom, with private bathroom & balcony overlooking Lake Tekapo
- 1 twin upstairs ensuite bedroom
- 1 downstairs queen bedroom, with private bathroom & bath
- feather duvets & electric blankets on all beds
- hair dryers & heaters in rooms
- expansive balcony with lake view, opening from lounge
- full continental breakfast with fresh fruit in season, home-made muffins & croissants
- separate guest lounge
- fishing trophies
- private guest entrance
- native garden
- alpine views of alps & lake
- laundry available
- well-behaved children welcome

Activities available
- guided fly fishing for brown & rainbow trout with Grant, a member of NZ Professional Fishing Guide Association
- guided salmon excursions
- horse trekking; hunting
- golf course; water skiing
- summer lake swimming
- lakeside & alpine walks
- www.laketekapoflyfishing.co.nz
- scenic flights
- walks up Mt John
- restaurants nearby
- local craft shops
- historic Church of the Good Shepherd
- Mt Cook region
- ski-fields; ice skating
- guided mountaineering
- scenic drives & walks

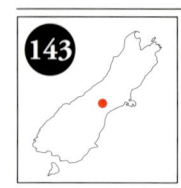

Lake Tekapo
Lake Tekapo Grandview

Hosts Leon and Rosemary O'Sullivan

32 Hamilton Drive, Lake Tekapo   *Postal* P O Box 14, Lake Tekapo
Phone 0-3-680 6910   *Mobile* 021 111 3393   *Fax* 0-3-680 6912
Email lerose@xtra.co.nz   *Website* www.laketekapograndview.co.nz

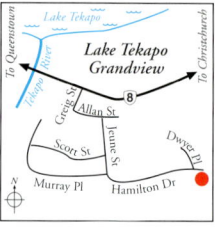

4 bdrm   4 enst   1 pdrm   Room rate $220–$270   *Includes breakfast*

DIRECTIONS: From Christchurch or Queenstown, take SH 8 to Lake Tekapo. East of church, turn south into Greig Street. At top of hill turn left into Hamilton Drive. Lake Tekapo Grandview at bottom of hill on right.

Lake Tekapo Grandview was built on an elevated site in 2001 to provide unobstructed lake and alpine views. The interior design complements the surrounding landscape and the four ensuite guestrooms feature hand-embroidered bed linen. Three of the bedrooms open to verandahs with panoramic lake views, and the fourth bedroom has views of the snow-capped mountains. A gourmet breakfast menu is provided and served in the dining room. A hospitality hour is popular with guests before dining at the local restaurants nearby. Lake Tekapo Grandview is set in a newly landscaped garden featuring roses and rocks. Guests enjoy the local golf, boating, fishing, climbing, historic sites and exploring Mount Cook National Park.

Facilities
- 2 super-king/twin & 2 king bedrooms, each with ensuite
- cotton bed linen, writing desk, phone, TV & tea/coffee
- spa bath in 2 bathrooms
- hair dryer, toiletries, heated mirror, floor & towel rails
- complimentary laundry
- phone, fax & email available
- fresh flowers
- continental & cooked breakfast menus
- private guest lounge with CD-player, artwork & book exchange
- children welcome
- 1 powder room
- central heating
- private guest entrance
- off-street parking

Activities available
- honeymoons & weddings catered for
- newly landscaped garden on site with rocks & roses
- star watching
- scenic walks
- golf courses
- boating; fishing
- climbing; hunting
- salmon farm
- restaurants, walking distance
- historic stone church & collie dog monument at lake edge
- horse trekking
- sightseeing tours
- hydro canals
- scenic flights
- skiing in winter
- Mt Cook National Park
- Timaru, 1¼-hour drive

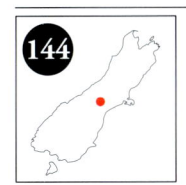

… 144

LAKE TEKAPO
LAKE TEKAPO LODGE

Hosts Lynda and John van Beek *Mobile* 021 129 9439

24 Aorangi Crescent, Lake Tekapo *Postal* P O Box 123, Lake Tekapo
Freephone 0800 LAKE TEKAPO *Phone* 0-3-680 6566 *Fax* 0-3-680 6599
Email lake.tekapo.lodge@xtra.co.nz *Website* www.laketekapolodge.co.nz

4 bdrm | 4 enst | 1 pdrm | Room rate $200–$335 | *Includes breakfast* *Lunch & dinner extra*

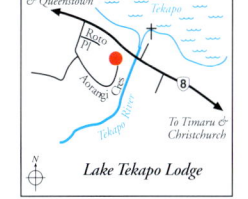

DIRECTIONS: From Christchurch, take SH 1 south to Rangitata. Turn right into SH 79 to Fairlie. Then turn right into SH 8 to Lake Tekapo. Take 2nd turn on left into Aorangi Cres. Lake Tekapo Lodge at end.

Opened in 1998, Lake Tekapo Lodge is built with adobe earth block cladding, with Gothic-style antique church doors from England at the entrance. The dining room and three of the four guest ensuite bedrooms open to the decking with panoramic lake views. The guest lounge also features a star-watching window for star gazing in the clear night sky. The guestrooms are all fire-rated and have underfloor heating, with 100% wool carpets and bed covers ensuring year-round comfort. Meals are served in the dining room beside the open fire, or alfresco on the deck in the sun. The adjacent walkway takes guests directly down to the town amenities. From there it is an easy drive east to Timaru, or west past Lake Pukaki to Mt Cook and Twizel.

Facilities
- 2 queen/twin & 2 super-king ensuite fire-rated bedrooms, with phones
- hair dryers, toiletries, heated flooring, heated towel rails, bathrobes & slippers; 1 spa bath
- cotton bed linen; fresh flowers
- 3 bedrooms open to decking
- TV, fridge, tea/coffee, gas fire & star-watch window in guest lounge
- laundry available, $10 per load
- 3-course dinner, $70 pp, BYO, by arrangement
- lunch or picnic hampers, $20 pp, by arrangement
- open fire in dining room
- TV, fax, email available
- private guest entrance
- John speaks Dutch
- courtesy passenger transfer
- off-street parking

Activities available
- pétanque, golf putting on lawn
- fishing gear, tennis racquets & mountain bikes available
- spinning demonstrations & lessons, by arrangement
- fishing in rivers & lake; guide available by arrangement
- star watching with guide
- horse treks; shooting
- bird-watching reserve, 10 mins
- 4 restaurants across road
- historic stone church
- sheepdog monument
- golf, 4km; canoeing
- watersports
- walking & hiking tracks
- ice skating & skiing, 30 mins
- scenic flights over Mt Cook, lakes, Fox & Franz Josef glaciers
- Timaru, 1¼-hour drive

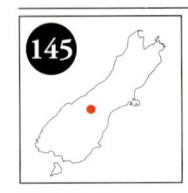

TWIZEL, MT COOK
MATUKA LODGE

Hosts Rosalie and Russell Smith

Old Station Road, Twizel   *Postal* P O Box 63, Twizel
Phone 0-3-435 0144   *Mobile* 027 426 1213   *Fax* 0-3-435 0149
Email info@matukalodge.co.nz   *Website* www.matukalodge.co.nz

| 4 bdrm | 4 enst | 1 pdrm |

Double $410–$490
Single $275–$325

Includes all meals

DIRECTIONS: From Lake Tekapo, take SH 8 south towards Twizel. Cross Twizel River, then turn right into Glen Lyon Rd. After 3km, turn left into Old Station Rd. Matuka Lodge is on the left.

Opened in 2004, Matuka Lodge provides purpose-built contemporary accommodation, in the countryside just north of Twizel. Set on nearly two hectares of tussock land, with uninterrupted views to the Ben Ohau Range, and the Southern Alps beyond, Matuka Lodge is located beside a natural pond, with itinerant trout. Overlooking the pond are the two guest wings, each with two bedrooms, spacious ensuites and quality fittings. All meals and wine are included in the tariff. Breakfast and dinner using fresh New Zealand produce, such as salmon and venison, are served in the dining room. Picnic lunches are also available. The lounge opens to the sunroom with decking extending over the pond, and there is a separate den and guest area.

Facilities

- 2 super-king/twin bedrooms, each with spa bath in ensuite
- 2 king ensuite bedrooms
- dressing room, phone, iron, heat pump/air-conditioner & verandah from each bedroom
- hair dryer, toiletries, heated floors & towel rails in ensuites
- guest lounge with log fire, music, magazines & artwork
- fresh flowers
- cooked & continental breakfast in dining room
- picnic lunch available
- 4-course dinner with wine
- guest area with fridge, tea/coffee, nibbles & computer
- den with Sky TV, videos, DVDs & library
- self-service laundry
- on-site parking; helipad

Activities available

- 2ha (4 acres) land with BBQ
- helicopter tours from Lodge to Mt Cook & glaciers
- fishing in rivers, streams or lakes, within 30-min drive
- tours to High Country Station
- site of climactic battle in *Rings* movie, *Return of the King*
- alpine walks
- Twizel township, 3km south
- tours to black stilt (world's most endangered wading bird) breeding programme
- golf cross; heli-biking
- tramping & hiking
- tours to Aoraki/Mt Cook, 45-min drive
- mountain climbing
- Christchurch, 3 hours north
- Queenstown, 3 hours south

© Friars' Guide to New Zealand Accommodation for the Discerning Traveller

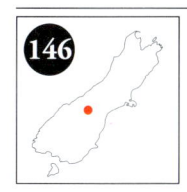

Twizel, Mt Cook
Aoraki Lodge

Hosts Oksana and Vlad Fomin

32 Mackenzie Drive, Twizel
Phone 0-3-435 0300   *Email* aorakilodge@xtra.co.nz
Fax 0-3-435 0305   *Website* friars.co.nz/hosts/aoraki.html

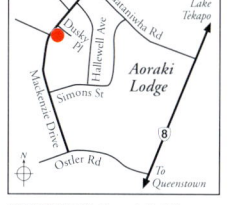

4 bdrm · 4 enst
Double $130–$140
Single $100
Includes breakfast
Multiple-night rates available
Dinner extra

DIRECTIONS: From Lake Tekapo, take SH 8 to Twizel. Turn right into Ruataniwha Rd. At "T" junction, at service station, turn left into Mackenzie Drive. Travel 100m to Aoraki Lodge on left.

Aoraki Lodge is located in Twizel, the nearest town to Mount Cook, which is 40 minutes' drive away. The Lodge is also conveniently situated half-way between Christchurch City and Queenstown. Oksana and Vlad operate a tour company, *Rock Wolf*, which provides specialist guided tours including boat trips, fishing, tramping and weekend family boat trips. Guests enjoy staying several days at Aoraki Lodge to take in the activities of the high country region. The four ensuite guestrooms open to a sunny verandah. A leisurely breakfast, either continental or cooked, includes Oksana's home-made specialities and local produce, and dinner is also offered. A variety of restaurants in the town centre are only a two-minute walk away.

Facilities

- 1 queen/twin, 1 double/twin, 1 double & 1 twin bedroom
- 4 ensuite bathrooms with toiletries, heated towel rails, hair dryers & 1 bath
- TV, oil-filled heaters & electric blankets in all 4 bedrooms
- wheelchair access to 2 ensuite bedrooms
- fresh flowers; smoking outside
- children welcome
- continental/cooked breakfast
- 3-course dinner specialising in local produce, salmon, lamb, $40 pp, BYO
- Sky TV, video, tea/coffee & open fire in guest lounge
- phone, fax & email available
- complimentary laundry
- hosts live off site
- off-street parking

Activities available

- guided tours, boat trips, tramping, fishing & weekend family boat trips with hosts
- star gazing
- restaurants in walking distance
- Mt Cook National Park, 40 mins
- alpine walks; tramping
- fishing safaris; hunting
- golf course
- farm tours
- Twizel shops, 2-min walk
- mountain biking
- horse trekking
- mountain climbing
- 4WD safaris
- scenic flights
- winter skiing
- Christchurch, 3 hrs north
- Queenstown, 3 hrs south

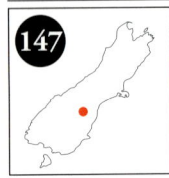

TOKARAHI, DUNTROON
TOKARAHI HOMESTEAD

Hosts Lyn and Mike Gray

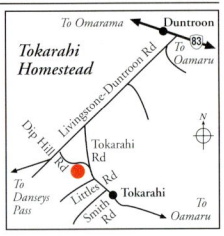

47 Dip Hill Road, Tokarahi *Postal* R D 12C, Oamaru
Phone 0-3-431 2500 *Email* tokarahi@xtra.co.nz
Fax 0-3-431 2551 *Website* www.homestead.co.nz

Room rate $190–$290 *Includes breakfast*
Lunch, picnic hampers & dinner extra

4 bdrm | 4 enst

DIRECTIONS: From SH 1, turn inland into SH 83 & travel 35km towards Duntroon. Turn left towards Danseys Pass. Travel 11km, then turn left again into Dip Hill Rd. Travel 2km to Tokarahi Homestead on right.

Tokarahi is located in unique limestone country, close to the historic Danseys Pass gold trail, Maori rock drawings and fossil sites. This heritage country homestead was built out of limestone in 1878, with the grand entrance hall and living areas added, as a wedding present, in the 1890s. The homestead has been carefully restored and is authentically furnished in classical Victorian style, featuring imported period wallpapers and fabrics, antiques and New Zealand artworks. Candlelit dinners are served in the elegant formal dining room by the open fire, while country breakfasts are enjoyed in the sunny morning room or alfresco in the courtyard. The four character bedrooms are furnished in colonial style, each with an ensuite bathroom.

Facilities
- 1 super-king/twin & 3 queen bedrooms with guest phones
- 4 ensuite bathrooms with hair dryers & toiletries
- wool duvets & quality bed linen
- 2 antique ball & claw baths
- original NZ art; baby grand piano
- Lyn's award-winning individually sculptured contemporary porcelain dolls
- flexi-time continental & cooked breakfast in morning room
- lunch/picnic hampers by request
- 3-course dinner in formal dining room, $50 pp; wine list available
- central heating & open fires
- TV, fax & computer available
- Premier Award winner in Whitestone Waitaki Tourism Awards, 2003–2004

Activities available
- star gazing with telescope
- pétanque & croquet on site
- horse trekking, novice–advanced
- working historic farm buildings
- Maori rock drawings on private limestone caves & cliffs
- Elephant Rocks in amphitheatre
- local blacksmith shop
- historic Oamaru precinct, 35 mins
- little blue penguins, 35-min drive
- 9-hole golf course nearby
- trout & salmon fishing – guide available
- "Vanished World" fossil centre & trail
- gardens to visit
- historic gold-mining sites
- Waitaki Lakes, 43km
- Danseys Pass, 30 mins
- Mt Cook, 180km

PALMERSTON
CENTREWOOD HISTORIC HOMESTEAD

Hosts Drs Jane and David Loten

Bobby's Head Road, Goodwood, R D 1, Palmerston
Phone 0-3-465 1977 *Email* centrewood@xtra.co.nz
Fax 0-3-465 1977 *Website* www.ecostay.co.nz

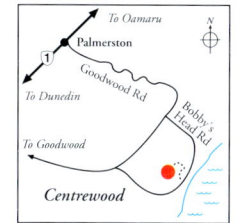

Room rate $200–$400   Includes breakfast   Dinner extra

DIRECTIONS: Take SH 1 to Palmerston. Turn east at Warren's Garage into Goodwood Rd. Travel about 10 mins, then turn left into Bobby's Head Rd. Travel 1.5km to Centrewood on right.

Centrewood is a large heritage country homestead set in 20 hectares of farmland and native bush, conveniently situated mid-way between Christchurch and Queenstown. It is adjacent to rugged cliffs, unpopulated sandy beaches, and yellow-eyed penguins and seals. Original features include ornate plaster ceilings, marble fireplaces and spacious rooms. Guests enjoy a separate private wing, containing two bedrooms, bathroom and guest living room with billiards, piano and classical music. Exclusive bookings in the guest wing ensure privacy. Pre-dinner drinks are served in the living room around the open fire, with dinner in the dining room. As Ernest, Lord Rutherford's great-granddaughter, Jane has set up a corner of Rutherford scientific and family memorabilia.

Facilities

- single-party bookings only for private guest wing
- 1 king & 1 queen/twin bedroom
- 1 large private bathroom with bath, hair dryer & toiletries
- private guest living room with CD-player, TV, video, billiards table, piano, desk, fridge & tea/coffee
- private guest entrance
- laundry, phone & email
- breakfast – fresh fruit, home-made bread, croissants & cooked option
- lunch, picnic hampers & afternoon tea by arrangement
- dinner – garden-fresh produce & country cuisine, $40–$60 pp
- spacious verandahs
- daffodils, rhododendrons & roses in extensive gardens

Activities available

- cliff walk adjacent, to view seals, yellow-eyed penguins, seabirds
- ocean & sandy beach, adjacent to property, in walking distance
- native bird-watching on site
- guided wildlife tours & horse riding by arrangement
- farm activities & tame animals eg horse, goat, calves & cattle
- 2 local golf courses; tennis court on site; bicycles available
- restaurants, 10-min drive
- Rutherford memorabilia
- in-house billiards & piano
- books on natural history & early settlers
- Moeraki Boulders, 20 mins
- Oamaru, 45-min drive north
- Dunedin City, 40 mins south
- Christchurch, 300km north
- Queenstown, 300km west

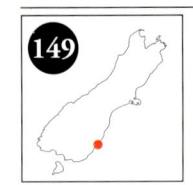

DUNEDIN
MANDENO HOUSE

Host Phillipa Connolly

667 George Street, Dunedin   *Postal* P O Box 6002, Dunedin
Phone 0-3-471 9595   *Email* mandeno.house@xtra.co.nz
Fax 0-3-474 5056   *Website* www.mandenohouse.com

3 bdrm   3 enst   Double $285   Single $225   Includes breakfast

DIRECTIONS: From north, take SH 1 into Cumberland St. Turn right into St David St & left into George St. Mandeno on right. From south take SH 1 into Gt King St & turn left into Union St, then right into George St.

Set in formal green and white gardens, featuring over 100 white roses, Mandeno House has been restored to provide quality accommodation in the heart of Dunedin. Designed by Harry Mandeno in 1936, the architecture of this home is complemented by the interiors, with design elements influenced by Scottish designer Charles Rennie Macintosh. With careful attention to detail, the understated design of Mandeno House provides a sophisticated ambience for guests to relax in. Three ensuite bedrooms are offered upstairs, with a guest lounge and separate dining room downstairs, where a full breakfast is served including fresh fruit in season, home-baked muesli, home-made bread and cooked options, or room service if preferred.

Facilities

- 1 twin & 2 queen bedrooms
- 3 ensuites, each with toiletries, hair dryer, demist mirror & bathrobes
- cotton bed linen; fresh flowers
- writing desk, phone & Sky TV in all 3 bedrooms
- guest lounge includes tea/coffee facilities, nibbles, CD-player, games, library & artwork
- extensive music library

- full breakfast served in dining room, or room service available
- supper by request, extra
- central heating
- fax & email available
- fresh flowers
- self-serve laundry
- private guest entrance
- off-street parking

Activities available

- BBQ on site
- weddings/honeymoons catered
- tours/dining arranged
- bus passes door
- Dunedin CBD, 5-min easy walk away
- Otago University adjacent
- parks & botanic garden
- private gardens open to visit
- museum

- large variety restaurants, bars cafés & shops in George Street
- steepest street in the world
- wildlife harbour cruises
- Otago Peninsula
- penguin colony
- Larnach Castle & Scottish heritage sites
- Taieri Gorge Railway
- Dunedin airport, 30-min drive

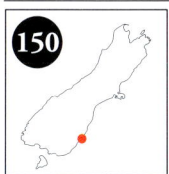

Roslyn, Dunedin
Mahara

Host Rosie Creighton

2 Fifield Street, Roslyn, Dunedin
Phone 0-3-467 5811   *Mobile* 021 217 2438   *Fax* 0-3-467 5587
Email reservations@mahara.co.nz   *Website* www.mahara.co.nz

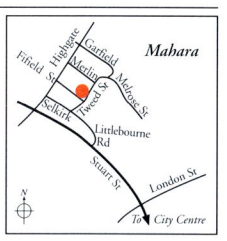

2 bdrm   2 enst   Double $160–$350   Single $130–$285   *Includes breakfast*

DIRECTIONS: From the Octagon, turn up Stuart St. Turn right into Littlebourne Rd. Turn left into Tweed St. Take 2nd left into Fifield St. Mahara immediately on right, on corner of Tweed St.

Designed by architect E.W. Waldron for retailer Andrew Lee's daughters, Mahara is one of two adjacent Edwardian homes built in 1905. Still retaining its Queen Anne revival features, Mahara now offers two guestrooms upstairs. The carved staircase ascends to a cathedral-size stained-glass window created by R.H. Fraser, and other historic features include the ornate plaster ceilings, carved archways, open fireplaces and bay windows in original sash style with leadlights. Teas, freshly ground coffee, and hot chocolate with marshmallows are available anytime in the drawing room and there is also a billiards room. Annie Lee's Room has antique beds, television area and harbour views, while the Leebank Room has garden views and local artwork.

Facilities
- 1 queen ensuite bedroom
- 1 queen/twin with ensuite & claw-foot bath
- cotton bed linen, phone, TV, writing desk, port & mineral water, chocolates, ironing facilities & fresh flowers
- hair dryers, heated towel rails, toiletries, bathrobes & slippers
- photocopier, fax & email
- laundry available, $8
- continental & cooked breakfast in drawing room
- open fire, teas, coffee, hot chocolate, biscuits, books & magazines in drawing room
- children by arrangement; baby's cot available
- central heating
- harbour & city views
- private guest entrance

Activities available
- billiards room with full-size table
- landscaped gardens on site with mature trees & rhododendron dell
- Olveston historic home tours
- golf links nearby; beach & bush walks
- royal albatross colony; yellow-eyed penguin adventure tours
- guided heritage tours; NZ's 1st university
- NZ's 1st Botanic Garden
- Central City restaurants, cafés & shops, 3-min drive
- Moana swimming pool
- Larnach Castle; horse treks
- museums; Carisbrook Oval
- Scottish heritage, Victorian architecture; art galleries
- harbour cruises; wildlife tours
- private gardens open to visit
- Taieri Gorge railway trips

Dunedin City
Fletcher Lodge

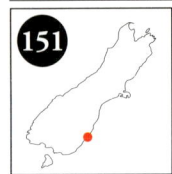

Hosts Keith and Ewa Rozecki-Pollard

276 High Street, Dunedin
Freephone 0800 THELODGE *Phone* 0-3-477 5552 *Fax* 0-3-474 5551
Email admin@fletcherlodge.co.nz *Website* www.fletcherlodge.co.nz

Double $225–$550
Single $175–$400
Includes breakfast

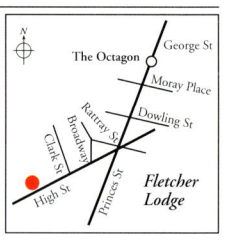

6 bdrm / 6 enst

DIRECTIONS: Central Dunedin. From The Octagon, travel south along Princes St. Turn right into Rattray St, then left into Broadway. Turn right up High St. Fletcher Lodge is 100m up the hill on the right.

Fletcher Lodge was built in 1923 by Sir James Fletcher to serve as his private residence while he was overseeing the construction of the New Zealand and South Seas Exhibition. Set in a secluded garden with mature trees, this Dutch colonial-style house features decorative brick and plaster work, extensive oak panelling, ornate plaster ceilings and leadlight windows with stained-glass inserts. The Lodge is richly furnished with antique period furniture. Guests are offered complimentary port in the panelled oak lounge which features a marble fireplace and overlooks a sunken garden. The carved staircase with elaborate newel posts leads to the six upstairs bedrooms featuring antique French beds and embroidered cotton bed linen.

Facilities

- 1 super-king, 1 queen/twin, 1 king, 1 twin & 2 queen bedrooms, all with ensuites
- antique French beds
- embroidered cotton bed linen
- direct-dial phone, internet access & TV in all 6 bedrooms
- guests' coffee/tea facilities
- fax & photocopier available
- formal Wedgewood dining room
- full breakfast served, including fresh orange juice, fresh fruit, cereals, yoghurt, croissants, home-made conserves & cooked option
- complimentary port in lounge
- private guest oak-panelled lounge with marble fireplace
- laundry available, $20
- historic architecture
- off-street parking

Activities available

- many restaurants, within walking distance
- Victorian architecture in city
- Olveston historic home
- Dunedin Botanic Gardens
- rhododendron festival
- Glenfalloch Woodland Garden
- Larnach Castle
- Royal Albatross Colony
- yellow-eyed penguin tours
- Dunedin City shops, 5-min walk downhill
- Speights brewery tours
- museums & art galleries
- Underwater World Aquarium
- golf courses
- Cadbury's tours
- wildlife harbour cruises
- Taieri Gorge Railway
- scenic flights

© Friars' Guide to New Zealand Accommodation for the Discerning Traveller

Caversham, Dunedin
Lisburn House

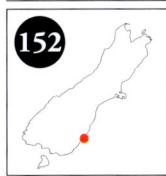

Hosts Olivia and Alan Johnston

15 Lisburn Avenue, Caversham, Dunedin
Phone 0-3-455 8888   *Email* stay@lisburnhouse.co.nz
Fax 0-3-455 6788   *Website* friars.co.nz/hosts/lisburnhouse.html

| 3 bdrm | 1 enst | 2 prbth |

Double $195–$260   *Includes breakfast*   *Dinner extra*
Single $170   **Extra person** $60

DIRECTIONS: From Queenstown, take SH 1 into Dunedin. Turn right at 1st lights at Caversham into South Rd. Lisburn Ave is 5th street on left. Lisburn House is on the left.

Lisburn House was built in 1865 as a townhouse for an Outram farming family. Set in a mature garden, this two-storey Gothic-style townhouse still features the original exterior, with decorative polychrome brickwork walls, lattice-work slate roof and stained glass. The interior includes a marble-floor entrance hall with sweeping carved staircase, panelled dining room, tall arched windows, high ceilings, cornices and spindles. Guests enjoy the blend of Irish and Kiwi hospitality, sharing port with Olivia and Alan in front of the oval open fire in the entrance hall, or tiled fireplace in the lounge. Each bedroom has its own style: "Blue", "Rose" and "Victorian" with four-poster beds. Bookings are essential for the in-house boutique à la carte restaurant.

Facilities
- 3 queen bedrooms upstairs, 2 with private bathrooms, 1 with bath in ensuite
- 4-poster beds in all 3 bedrooms, with extra single bed in "Rose"
- quality bed linen; fresh flowers
- fresh fruit, chilled mineral water, pot-pourri & towelling bathrobes in all 3 bedrooms
- Historic Places Trust category 1
- children welcome
- à la carte dinner, extra, served in boutique restaurant, in-house, booking essential
- continental & full cooked breakfast choices
- coffee/tea offered on arrival
- open fireplaces in panelled hall, dining & drawing rooms
- laundry available
- off-street parking

Activities available
- NZ's 1st Botanic Gardens
- albatross & penguin colonies
- peninsula wildlife tours
- museums & art galleries
- guided heritage tours
- beach & clifftop walks
- historic gold trail train trips
- Carisbrook Sports Park
- restaurants, within walking distance
- Edwardian/Victorian architecture
- St Clair beach; golf courses
- Larnach Castle; Olveston House
- private & public garden visits
- heated fresh- & salt-water pools
- harbour salmon fishing & cruises
- inland guided trout fishing
- City Centre, 5-min drive
- airport, 25-min direct drive
- gateway to Southern Scenic Route

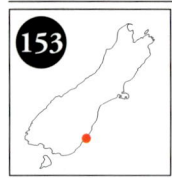

CORSTORPHINE, DUNEDIN
CORSTORPHINE HOUSE

Hosts Irina and Nico Francken

23A Milburn Street, Corstorphine, Dunedin   *Phone* 0-3-487 1000
Postal P O Box 3058, Dunedin   *Fax* 0-3-487 6672
Email info@corstorphine.co.nz   *Website* corstorphine.co.nz

| 7 bdrm | 7 enst | 1 pdrm | Double $595 Single $545 | *Includes breakfast Lunch & dinner extra* |

DIRECTIONS: From Dunedin City, take SH 1 south. Take Caversham turn-off, then left into South Rd. Turn right into Playfair St. Continue into Corstorphine Rd. Turn left into Milburn St. Corstorphine House on left.

Built in 1863 on a hill overlooking Dunedin with views of the harbour and surrounding mountains, Corstorphine House was extended in 1905 by the original family, who lived there for 100 years. This Edwardian mansion has now been fully restored and converted to provide accommodation. Irina, who hails from Russia, and Nico, from the Netherlands, have totally renovated and re-furnished Corstorphine as a luxury private hotel. Seven guestrooms are decorated in individual themes with quality bathroom fittings and great attention to detail. A full breakfast is served in the main dining room or alfresco in the garden or gazebo, while à la carte dinner is served in the Conservatory Restaurant, or private dining is available in the house.

Facilities
- 1 queen/twin & 6 super-king ensuite bedrooms
- cotton bed linen; fresh flowers
- toiletries, bidets, heated towel rails, heated floor, hair dryers, demist mirrors & bathrobes
- phone, fax & email available
- laundry available
- German, French, Spanish, Russian & Dutch spoken
- full breakfast served in dining room or alfresco
- à la carte lunch & dinner served in Conservatory Restaurant or in private dining room, extra
- fully licensed
- room service
- wheelchair access to 4 rooms
- small conference facilities
- on-site parking

Activities available
- formal gardens, organic vegetables, fruits, herbs & nuts, chickens, native trees & birds, goat, pond & streams on site
- eco-tours on scenic peninsula or Catlins to view albatrosses, penguins & seals – selfdrive, group, boat or private tour
- gardens to visit – botanic, private, public & historic
- sparsely populated beaches with white sand, surf, wildlife & cliffs
- City – art galleries, museums & university, 10-min drive away
- royal albatross colony
- 13 golf courses
- heritage architecture – Olverston House, Larnach Castle & Railway Station
- harbour cruises & fishing
- Taieri Gorge railway & 4WD tours

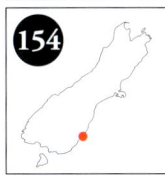

ST CLAIR, DUNEDIN
AVERLEIGH COTTAGE

Host Joanne O'Carroll-McKellar

7 Coughtrey Street, St Clair, Dunedin
Phone 0-3-455 8829   *Mobile* 027 563 1725   *Fax* 0-3-455 6380
Email joanne@averleigh.co.nz   *Website* www.averleigh.co.nz

Room rate $260–$295   *Includes breakfast*

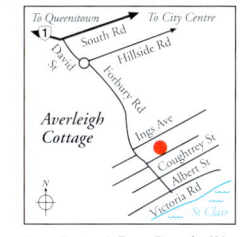

DIRECTIONS: From City, take SH 1 south to Andersons Bay Rd. Turn right into Hillside Rd. At roundabout, turn left into Forbury Rd. Turn left again into Coughtrey St. Averleigh Cottage is on left (5 mins from City).

Built in 1910, Averleigh is still in original condition with native timber, ornate plaster ceilings and open fires. This Edwardian villa has been in the McKellar family since 1936. Accommodation comprises the ensuite queen Tarlton Room and king/twin Watson Room with open fire and an antique bath in its private bathroom. A guest drawing room provides a piano for musical guests, and the dining room leads into the morning room which opens through French doors into the courtyard and garden rooms. Joanne serves a gourmet continental breakfast in the dining room, guests' bedrooms, or courtyard. Averleigh is designed for art, antique, animal and garden lovers, and is only five minutes' walk from St Clair beach and its waterfront cafés.

Facilities
- 1 queen ensuite bedroom
- 1 king/twin bedroom & private bathroom with bath
- fresh flowers, bathrobes & cotton bed linen
- phone, radio/alarm clock, TV & video in both bedrooms
- hair dryer, toiletries, & heated towel rails, in both bathrooms
- check-in after 4 pm, or by prior arrangement
- full continental breakfast choices
- complimentary beverages
- central heating; fax available
- open fires in all guest areas
- local artists' works displayed
- laundry available, extra charge
- 2 curly-coated retrievers, Brodie & Flynn, & 1 marmalade tabby cat, Rupert, in residence
- unsuitable for children

Activities available
- piano for guest use; music, book, & video library in-house
- croquet, pétanque/boules & relaxing in spacious garden
- hot salt-water pool, 5-min walk
- St Clair surf beach, 5-min walk
- Forbury Park Raceway, 5 mins
- Carisbrook Park, 10-min walk
- St Clair Golf Course, 10 mins
- gateway to southern scenic route
- licensed St Clair restaurants
- City Centre, 5-min drive
- regular bus route to City
- art galleries & museums
- Dunedin fashion designers
- guided heritage tours
- Glenfalloch Woodland Gardens, 15-min drive
- Larnach Castle, 20 mins
- royal albatross colony

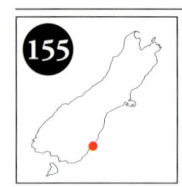

Shiel Hill, Dunedin
Nature Guides Otago / Nisbet Cottage

Hosts Hildegard and Ralf Lübcke

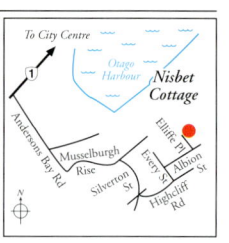

6A Elliffe Place, Shiel Hill, Dunedin   *Postal* P O Box 8058, Dunedin
Phone 0-3-454 5169   *Email* stay@nznatureguides.com
Fax 0-3-454 5369   *Website* www.nznatureguides.com

2 bdrm   2 enst   Nature Dunedin package $495 per person
Room rate $175–$195   *Includes breakfast*

DIRECTIONS: From SH 1 turn into Andersons Bay Rd. Continue into Musselburgh Rise, then Silverton St. Turn left into Highcliff Rd. Turn left again into Every St, right into Albion St, then left into Elliffe Pl to Cottage.

Nisbet Cottage is the base for Hildegard's eco-tourism venture *Nature Guides Otago*, which is designed to give guests first-hand experience of New Zealand wildlife. Situated in a quiet area on the hills to Otago Peninsula, Nisbet Cottage offers a super-king bedroom and a queen-size bedroom with an extra single bed. Breakfast is served in the private guest lounge with open fireplace and French doors leading to a spacious semi-circular sundeck, with panoramic views of the city and surrounding hills. A *Nature Dunedin* package of two nights' bed and breakfast, Sunrise Penguin Walk, and a full-day guided wildlife tour is available, with the option of extending it to three nights' bed and breakfast with a full-day guided tour to the Catlins.

Facilities
- 1 super-king ensuite bedroom
- 1 queen/twin ensuite bedroom
- hair dryer, toiletries & heated towel rails in both ensuites
- TV, phone & coffee/tea in both guest bedrooms
- children by arrangement
- guest lounge with open fireplace & breakfast table
- large sundeck overlooking city
- continental breakfast & cooked on request, served in guest lounge
- fax & email available
- German spoken
- courtesy passenger transfer
- regular bus route close by
- off-street parking
- Basil, the grey fluffy cat, an optional extra

Activities available
- Nisbet Cottage caters exclusively for guests participating in nature tours
- scenic lookout, easy walk
- restaurants, within walking distance & 5–10-min drive
- Larnach Castle
- Glenfalloch Gardens
- royal albatross colony
- Rhododendron Week, in Oct.
- Nature Dunedin package: 2 nights B&B, Sunrise Penguin Walk (view yellow-eyed penguins) & full-day tour of Dunedin & Otago Peninsula wildlife
- extension tour to 3 nights B&B with full-day tour to Catlins
- *Nature Guides Otago* offers nature-based packages & day tours in the Dunedin area
- Dunedin City, 8-min drive

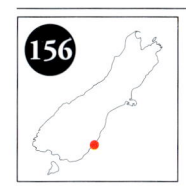

MOSGIEL, DUNEDIN
HIGHLAND PEAKS

Hosts Dr Peter and Di Espie

333 Chain Hills Road, R D 1, Dunedin
Phone 0-3-489 6936   *Mobile* 021 162 9489   *Fax* 0-3-489 6924
Email highlandpeaks@clear.net.nz   *Website* friars.co.nz/hosts/highland.html

Room rate $185–$275   Includes breakfast   Dinner extra

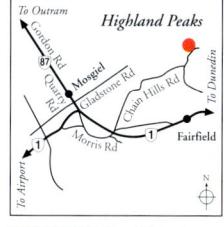

DIRECTIONS: From SH 1 take Mosgiel exit, then turn south into Quarry Rd. Continue left on Morris Rd over motorway. Turn 1st left into Chain Hills Rd. Take left fork to Highland Peaks on left at road end.

Purpose built in 2004, Highland Peaks provides quality accommodation with panoramic mountain and sea views. Located 15 minutes from Dunedin City and the airport, and set in 8.5 hectares (18 acres) of country grounds, guests enjoy the tranquillity, native birdsong and walks. Designed to catch the sun, Highland Peaks features extensive views and energy conservation, the private guest wing comprising two comfortable bedrooms and bathrooms. A separate lounge is warmed by a large fire in winter, and dinner is served by arrangement, with quality home cuisine complemented by the wine cellar. Peter guides personalised tours and is well qualified, as an ecologist and former director of the National Trust, to advise about New Zealand's natural heritage.

Facilities
- 1 king bedroom with ensuite & dressing room
- 1 king bedroom with private bathroom & spa bath
- hair dryer, toiletries, bathrobes, heated towel rails & demist mirror in both bathrooms
- cotton bed linen; electric blankets; kauri furniture
- fresh flowers
- laundry available
- breakfast served in dining room or alfresco; gluten-free option available
- dinner by arrangement, extra
- phone jack in bedrooms; CD-writer, internet, email & fax
- log burner, tea/coffee, video & CD-players & books in guest lounge; wine cellar
- private sundeck & BBQ
- on-site parking

Activities available
- cat, Jasper, pet sheep, & other pet farm animals on site
- in-house library; private areas for reading & relaxing
- 8.5ha (18 acres) grounds
- mountain bikes & tracks on site
- pétanque; on-site & local nature & beach walks
- guided personalised eco-tours, 4WD tussock grassland & wildflowers in season
- restaurants & cafés, 10 mins
- scenic Taieri Gorge Railway
- museums
- art galleries
- royal albatross, penguin, seal & sea lion colonies
- launch trips on Otago Harbour
- local golf courses; fishing
- Dunedin heritage architecture

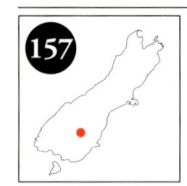

ALEXANDRA, CENTRAL OTAGO
ROCKY RANGE LODGE

Hosts Lisa and Colin Strang   *Mobile* 027 445 0695

The Half Mile, Alexandra   *Postal* P O Box 323, Alexandra
Freephone 0800 153 293   *Phone* 0-3-448 6150   *Fax* 0-3-448 6150
Email relax@rockyrange.co.nz   *Website* friars.co.nz/hosts/rockyrange.html

| 4 bdrm | 4 enst | 1 pdrm | Double $400 | Single $325 | Includes breakfast |

DIRECTIONS: From Cromwell, take SH 8 to Alexandra. Continue south, cross Clutha Bridge & travel 1.5km. Rocky Range Lodge on left, up driveway. From Dunedin, take SH 8 towards Alexandra. Lodge on right.

Located on 40 hectares set amid wild thyme and schist rock formations, Rocky Range is a custom-built Lodge on the outskirts of Alexandra. Designed in French Provincial style, Rocky Range offers 360-degree views of Central Otago's rugged beauty. In summer the deep verandahs provide shade, while in winter an open fire in the spacious guest lounge ensures comfort. All four ensuite bedrooms in the Lodge are well appointed, each one planned with individual character. Juliet balconies open from the bedrooms to panoramic views of the surrounding mountain ranges and river valleys. Rocky Range is a private hideaway, where guests can relax, or use the Lodge as a base to explore the myriad activities that the region offers.

Facilities
- 1 king, 1 king/twin & 2 queen bedrooms
- 4 ensuite bathrooms
- bathrobes, toiletries, hair dryers & heated towel rails in all 4 ensuite bathrooms
- tea/coffee, TV in bedrooms
- quality cotton bed linen & electric blankets on beds
- private Juliet balconies
- full breakfast served in dining room
- complimentary apéritifs & snacks
- guest lounge with home theatre (TV, DVD, video) & open fire
- double glazing; underfloor heating
- phone, fax & email available
- spacious outdoor patio
- outdoor spa pool set in rocks
- ample private parking on site
- www.rockyrange.co.nz

Activities available
- mountain bikes available
- walking on 40-ha site
- Alexandra & Clyde restaurants
- trout fishing; professional guide
- kayaking, guided trips available
- autumn foliage, in April/May; spring blossom festival, in Sept.
- summer stone fruit orchards
- safari excursions with local guide
- eco experience on Lake Dunstan
- wine trail & tasting
- golf course, 5-min drive
- historic gold trail
- Lake Dunstan boat cruises
- scenic & garden tours
- biking & walking Otago Central Rail Trail
- Cromwell, 20-min drive
- Queenstown/Wanaka, 1 hr
- Dunedin, 2-hour drive

WANAKA
PARKLANDS LODGE

Hosts The Carwardine Family

Ballantyne Road, R D 2, Wanaka
Phone 0-3-443 7305   *Mobile* 021 529 118   *Fax* 0-3-443 7345
Email parklandslodge@xtra.co.nz   *Website* www.parklandswanaka.co.nz

Room rate $250–$295   *Includes breakfast*
Picnic hampers & gourmet BBQ extra

6 bdrm | 6 enst | 1 prbth

DIRECTIONS: From Wanaka, take SH 6 & travel 6km to Parklands Lodge on right, on corner Ballantyne Rd. From Cromwell, take SH 6 towards Wanaka. Parklands Lodge on left, on corner Ballantyne Rd.

Parklands Lodge is nestled on four hectares (10 acres) of farmland, featuring uninterupted alpine views. Just six kilometres south of Lake Wanaka, Parklands offers guests two spacious suites and four large bedrooms, each with fine linen, an ensuite and verandah. An open log fire warms the comfortable, open-plan lounge and dining room, with French doors opening out to an expansive verandah and barbecue area. Adjacent is the swimming pool which is popular in summer, spa pool and a five-hole putting course. A full breakfast, with buffet and cooked options, is served in the dining room or alfresco in the garden. Restaurants are within an eight-minute drive of Parklands Lodge, and three ski-fields are 35 to 45 minutes away.

Facilities

- 2 super-king/twin ensuite bedrooms; wheelchair access
- 1 king & 1 queen bedroom, each with ensuite
- 2 king suites; 1 with private lounge & log fire
- hair dryers, fine toiletries, bathrobes & heated tiled floors
- verandah opening from each bedroom to garden
- fresh flowers; cotton bed linen
- traditional cooked or continental breakfast
- picnic hampers & gourmet BBQ, extra
- apéritifs on arrival
- 1 lounge with open fire, tea/coffee, Sky TV, video, CD-player & library
- internet & business facilities
- ski storage & drying facilities; laundry; parking & helipad

Activities available

- spa pool & swimming pool
- BBQ area on site
- 5-hole pitch & putt golf on site
- golf course nearby
- fishing; horseback treks
- rock climbing; tramping
- mountain biking
- snow-boarding, skiing & heli-skiing, June–October
- parapenting; tandem skydiving
- restaurants, 8-min drive
- Wanaka airport, 5-min drive
- Lake Wanaka, 8-min drive
- wine tasting at local vineyards
- private gardens to visit
- jet boating
- scenic flights
- motorcycle safaris
- Fighter Pilots Museum
- Great Maze Puzzling World

443

© Friars' Guide to New Zealand Accommodation for the Discerning Traveller

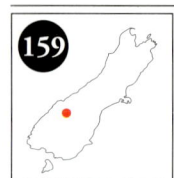

WANAKA
RIVER RUN

Hosts Meg Taylor and John Pawson

Halliday Road, R D 2, Wanaka
Phone 0-3-443 9049 *Email* riverrun@xtra.co.nz
Fax 03-443 8454 *Website* www.riverrun.co.nz

5 bdrm | 5 enst

Double $320–$460
Single $260–$420

Includes breakfast
Picnic hampers & dinner extra

DIRECTIONS: 5km from Wanaka, on SH 6. Turn left into Halliday Rd. Continue to end of road, to River Run stone entrance. From Cromwell, take SH 6 towards Wanaka. Turn right into Halliday Rd. River Run at end.

Set on an escarpment with sweeping 180-degree views towards the Southern Alps, River Run offers guests a private, relaxed and comfortable retreat from which to explore the region. River Run's 183-hectare (460-acre) property, bordering the Cardrona and Clutha Rivers, provides on-site walks, picnics, fishing, kayaking, jet boating or rafting. Wanaka township is only six minutes away by car, with Mount Aspiring National Park beyond. The lodge is an imaginative composition in recycled materials including kauri doors, bridge and railway timbers, hardwood floors and hand-crafted iron balustrades. A generous breakfast is served with buffet and cooked options. River Run also offers fine cuisine for dinner, with an extensive wine list.

Facilities

- 4 king/twin ensuite bedrooms
- 1 queen ensuite bedroom
- cotton bed linen, phone, TV or TV/video in all 5 bedrooms
- 5 spacious ensuites, with power showers, fine toiletries, hair dryers & wrap towels
- baths in 2 ensuite bathrooms
- deep verandahs
- book, video & CD library
- 3-4-course dinner, $90 pp
- fully licensed – local wine list
- picnic hampers, extra
- buffet & à la carte breakfasts
- 2 guest lounges with log fires
- fax & email available
- laundry & drying room
- private outdoor spa pool & entertainment area with alpine views

Activities available

- 183ha riverside farmland with walks & picnic spots
- mountain bikes available
- access to fishing, kayaking, rafting, jet boating
- restaurants, 5-min drive
- guided fly-fishing for brown & rainbow trout
- canyoning; paragliding
- heli-hiking; horse trekking
- Lake Wanaka resort, 5-min drive
- wine tasting at local vineyards
- golf course; aircraft museum
- private gardens to visit
- 3 ski-fields, 35–45-min drive
- skiing & heli-skiing, June–Oct.
- scenic flights to Milford Sound, Mt Aspiring & Mt Cook
- walks & day hikes in Mt Aspiring National Park

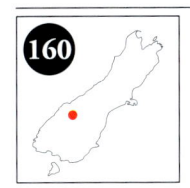

Dublin Bay, Wanaka
The Stone Cottage

Host Belinda Wilson

Dublin Bay, R D 2, Wanaka
Phone 0-3-443 1878   *Email* stonecottage@xtra.co.nz
Fax 0-3-443 1276   *Website* www.stonecottage.co.nz

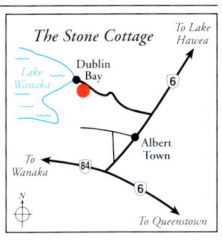

Double $230–$260
Single $210

Includes breakfast provisions
Self-catering, or dinner extra

DIRECTIONS: Take SH 6 to or from Wanaka & turn north towards Lake Hawea (& West Coast). Travel 5km, then turn left to Dublin Bay. Travel 3km to The Stone Cottage on left. (10-min drive from Wanaka township.)

Originally built in 1977 from local schist, and furnished with antique oak furniture, The Stone Cottage at Dublin Bay now features a loft comprising two separate self-contained suites. Dormer windows and private balconies overlook the waters of Lake Wanaka to the Treble Cone ski-field beyond. Each suite has an external staircase providing a private entrance. Both kitchens are well stocked, with fridge, microwave or stove, enabling guests to self-cater, or if preferred, dine with their host, Bindy, downstairs. The Stone Cottage is set in a tranquil lakeside garden featuring spring bulbs and blossom, through to summer roses, followed by dramatic autumn colouring, just 10 minutes' drive from Wanaka township.

Facilities

- 1 super-king suite & 1 queen/twin self-contained suite
- electric blankets, bathrobes, heated towel rails, hair dryers & toiletries in both suites
- 2 private guest entrances
- single-party bookings per suite, or 1 party can use interconnecting door
- phone, fax & email available
- television & video
- breakfast ingredients & basics provided in both kitchens
- 3-course dinner with wine, pre-dinner drinks & savouries, by arrangement, $65 pp
- complimentary sherry & port
- lake views; fresh flowers
- laundry available, extra
- courtesy passenger transfer
- established garden

Activities available

- BBQ on site
- croquet, boules on site
- mountain bikes available
- local walks
- Lake Wanaka, 4-min walk
- fishing guide available
- vineyards; wine-tasting
- private garden visiting
- trout fishing; boating
- restaurants, 10-min drive
- arts & crafts trail
- 18-hole golf course
- horse trekking
- hiking; tramping
- jet boating; scenic flights
- adventure activities
- skiing, from June to Sept.
- 3 ski-fields – Treble Cone, Cardrona & Nordic ski area

DUBLIN BAY, WANAKA
DUBLIN BAY LODGE

Hosts Neil Farrin and Emily Wong

Dublin Bay, R D 2, Wanaka
Phone 0-3-443 8833   *Mobile* 021 185 3181   *Fax* 0-3-443 7880
Email info@dublinbaylodge.com   *Website* www.dublinbaylodge.com

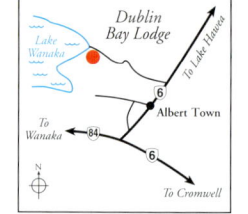

1 bdrm   1 enst   Room rate $250–$295   *Includes continental breakfast provisions*   *Self-catering*

DIRECTIONS: Take SH 6 to or from Wanaka & turn north towards Lake Hawea (& West Coast). Travel 4.1km, then turn left to Dublin Bay. Travel 2.7km to Dublin Bay Lodge on left. (10-min drive from Wanaka.)

Set in a picturesque garden only three minutes' walk from Lake Wanaka, Dublin Bay Lodge was built from New Zealand larch and oregon in 1950 and recently renovated to retain the extensive use of timber and adzed beams. The self-catering studio has panoramic views of the lake and mountains beyond, with trout fishing and kayaking only 200 metres away. The studio features a photographic theme which reflects the main interest of the new host, Neil, an internationally published photographer whose work has appeared in magazines such as *Time* and *Geo*. Neil offers guests to Dublin Bay Lodge a photographic adventure called "Shadowcatcher", individually tailored to each photography enthusiast. Each venture is guided by Neil, through Central Otago.

Facilities

- 1 king ensuite studio
- spa bath, hair dryer, toiletries, & heated towel rails in ensuite
- bathrobes; cotton bed linen
- Sky TV, video, DVD, CD-player, games, books & writing desk in living area
- artwork & fresh flowers
- studio opens to verandah with lake & mountain views
- continental breakfast provisions
- guest fridge, mineral water, tea/coffee facilities & nibbles
- central heating
- email, phone & laundry available
- Cantonese/Mandarin spoken by host
- on-site parking

Activities available

- pétanque & full grass tennis court on site
- established grounds with private access to Lake Wanaka
- 2 mountain bikes & kayaks available for guest use
- photographic adventures
- trout fishing; boating
- hiking & tramping
- art & craft tours
- restaurants, 10-min drive
- 18-hole golf course, 10 mins
- scenic flights
- horse trekking
- vineyard & garden tours
- Fighter Pilots Museum
- 4-wheel motor biking
- 3 international ski-fields
- Wanaka town, 10-min drive

© Friars' Guide to New Zealand Accommodation for the Discerning Traveller

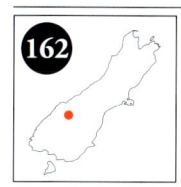

LAKE WANAKA
ATHERTON HOUSE

Hosts Kate and Roy Summers

3 Atherton Place, Wanaka
Phone 0-3-443 8343   *Mobile* 025 228 1982   *Fax* 0-3-443 8343
Email roy.kate@xtra.co.nz   *Website* www.atherton.co.nz

| 2 bdrm | 2 enst | 1 pdrm | Double $175–$235 Single $150 | *Includes breakfast & apéritifs Dinner extra* |

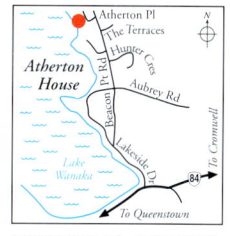

DIRECTIONS: Take SH 6 & SH 84 to Wanaka. Continue on Ardmore St towards lake. Turn right into Lakeside Drive. Turn right into Beacon Pt Rd. Travel 1.5km then turn left into Atherton Pl. Atherton House on left.

Located at the fringe of Wanaka, Atherton House was built on the shore of the lake in 2001. Set in half a hectare of lawns and gardens, surrounded by trees, this contemporary home in classic design enjoys unimpeded views across the lake to the mountains beyond. Furnished with New Zealand and English antiques and featuring contemporary New Zealand art, Atherton House providess two ensuite guestrooms. A full breakfast with home-made bread, jams, preserves and cooked options is served in the dining room or alfresco in the courtyard. Complimentary pre-dinner drinks and hors d'oeuvres are offered, and dinner served with wine is available by arrangement. Guests enjoy the lakefront walk from Atherton House to Wanaka village.

Facilities
- 1 king/twin ensuite bedroom
- 1 queen ensuite bedroom
- hair dryer, demist mirror, heated floor & towel rails in both ensuite bathrooms
- cotton bed linen, tea/coffee & fresh flowers
- central heating; guest fridge
- email & fax available
- laundry available
- full cooked & continental breakfast, served in dining room or courtyard
- apéritifs & nibbles
- 3-course dinner with wine, $65 pp, by arrangement
- private guest lounge with open fire, tea/coffee, Sky TV, video, library & writing desk
- guest entrance & verandahs
- on-site parking

Activities available
- barbecue available
- lakefront access from site
- nearly 0.5ha (1 acre) lawn, trees & gardens on site
- walks
- vineyards
- wine tasting
- private garden visits
- horse trekking
- hiking
- restaurants, 20-min walk
- Wanaka shops, 3-min drive
- 18-hole golf course
- scenic flights
- fishing guides available
- skiing, June to September
- airport, 10-min drive
- watersports
- Queenstown, 45-min drive

447

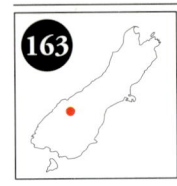

LAKE WANAKA
BREMNER BAY LODGE

Hosts Deborah and Gavin Humphrey

17 Waimana Place, Wanaka *Postal* 19 Brighton Terrace, Mairangi Bay, Auckland
Phone 0-9-476 7297 *Mobile* 021 333 455 *Fax* 0-9-478 3521
Email info@bremnerbay.co.nz *Website* www.bremnerbay.co.nz

| 4 bdrm | 4 enst | 1 pdrm |

Lodge rate $2,800–$3,600
2-night minimum stay

*Includes breakfast
Self-catering, or dinner extra*

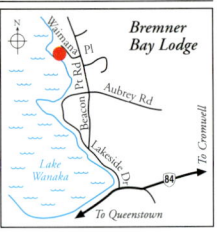

DIRECTIONS: Take SH 84 to Wanaka township. At lake turn north into Lakeside Drive. Turn right into Beacon Pt Rd. Travel 1km then turn left into Waimana Place. Bremner Bay Lodge on left. (3km from township.)

Built on the edge of Lake Wanaka in 2003, just three kilometres from the township, Bremner Bay Lodge offers self-contained accommodation for single-party bookings. Completely constructed out of schist, the Lodge includes three ensuite bedrooms and a separate two-storey self-contained apartment. Bordered by roadside schist walls and lawns sweeping down to the lake, Bremner Bay Lodge is located in a peaceful lakefront development. The Lodge features designer Italian bathrooms and vaulted ceilings with recycled old hardwood beams in the living rooms and Great Room. A large internal courtyard with heated pool and open fireplace is popular for alfresco dining. A chef supplies gourmet breakfasts each morning and dinner by arrangement.

Facilities
- one-party bookings only
- 2 super-king & 2 queen ensuite bedrooms, 1 in apartment
- hair dryer, toiletries, heated floor, heated towel rails, demist mirror & bathrobes in ensuites
- 2 baths, 2 double showers & 1 double basin
- cotton bed linen, TV & phone in all 4 bedrooms
- fresh flowers; email & fax
- gourmet breakfast by chef
- dinner by arrangement, extra
- 2 full kitchens for self-catering with basic pantry provisions
- complimentary nibbles, drinks fridge; self-serve laundry
- 3 living rooms
- Sky TV, video, DVD, CDs, games, artwork, books & desk
- serviced daily; garaging

Activities available
- home theatre with 254cm rear-projection screen
- BBQ, outdoor open fire & heated swimming pool on site
- canoes available for guest use
- jet ski & 6m (18-foot) Bayliner launch, by arrangement
- lakefront walkways & fly fishing from site
- hunting; fishing
- restaurants & shops in Wanaka township, 3km
- vineyards
- lake activities
- scenic flights to Milford Sound & glaciers
- Mt Aspiring National Park walks & hikes
- heli-skiing
- 3 ski-fields nearby

Above: The Great Room in the Lodge, featuring a schist fireplace, vaulted ceiling, exposed beams and deer antler chandeliers.
Below: Bremner Bay Lodge, built in 2003 from local schist, is bordered by schist walls on the roadside and has direct lake access.
Opposite top: With lawns sweeping down to the edge of Lake Wanaka, Bremner Bay Lodge is set in a peaceful private location.
Opposite bottom left: All four ensuites and the powder room are designer Italian bathrooms featuring glass mosaic work.
Opposite bottom right: The internal courtyard is popular for alfresco dining with its outdoor fireplace and heated swimming pool.

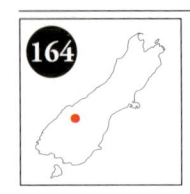

Lake Wanaka
MINARET LODGE

Hosts Fran and Gary Tate

34 Eely Point Road, Wanaka   *Postal* P O Box 352, Wanaka
Phone 0-3-443 1856   *Mobile* 021 644 406   *Fax* 0-3-443 1846
Email relax@minaretlodge.co.nz   *Website* www.minaretlodge.co.nz

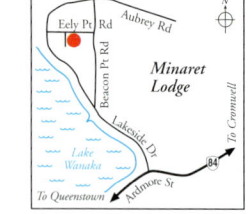

| 5 bdrm | 4 enst | 1 prbth | Double $350 Single $330 | Includes breakfast Dinner extra |

DIRECTIONS: From Cromwell or Haast, take SH 6 towards Wanaka. Continue on SH 84 & Ardmore St towards Lake Wanaka. Turn right into Lakeside Drive. Turn right into Eely Pt Rd. Minaret Lodge on right.

With views of the Minaret Mountains, after which the Lodge is named, Minaret Lodge is set in almost a hectare of spacious grounds with well established trees. The mudbrick construction, with plastered finish, was built in the 1950s for the Ellis family, then in 2001 the guestrooms were added. The three guest chalets all have one or two super-king/twin bedrooms, each with bathroom, tea and coffee-making facilities, fridge with refreshments, and a verandah opening to the garden. One chalet features a special *Lord of the Rings* theme in a guestroom called "Barlimans". Breakfast includes daily specialities and dinner with wine is also available. A short stroll takes guests to the lake, and it is a 10-minute walk to Wanaka's town centre.

Facilities
- 2 chalets: 2 super-king/twin ensuite bedrooms in each
- 1 chalet: 1 super-king/twin bedroom, bathroom & lounge with queen-size sofa bed
- tea/coffee, mineral water, TV & phone in all 5 bedrooms
- toiletries, bathrobes, hair dryers, heated floor & towel rails in all 5 bathrooms
- wheelchair access in suite
- traditional cooked or continental breakfast
- 3-course dinner with wine, seasonal menu, $80 pp
- verandah opening from each bedroom to garden
- laundry service available
- email & fax available
- courtesy passenger transfer
- private guest entrance; on-site parking

Activities available
- weddings, honeymoons & conferences catered for
- ski storage & drying room
- barbecue available on site
- sauna & spa pool on site
- tennis court on site
- mountain bikes available
- pétanque/boules on site
- pool table on site
- golf course nearby
- many restaurants in Wanaka, 10-min walk
- gymnasium, 5-min drive
- lake activities
- fishing & hiking
- horse trekking
- Fighter Pilots Museum
- scenic flights
- snow boarding & skiing, June to September

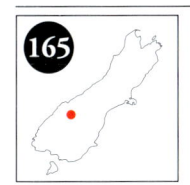

Lake Wanaka
Lakeside Apartments

Manager Sandra Peat

9 Lakeside Road, Wanaka   *Postal* P O Box 609, Wanaka
Phone 0-3-443 0188   *Email* info@lakesidewanaka.co.nz
Fax 0-3-443 0189   *Website* www.lakesidewanaka.co.nz

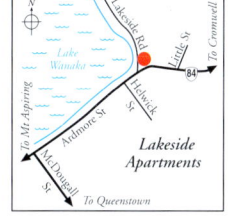

3 bdrm per apartment | 2 bthrm per apartment | **Apartment rate $295–$795** Extra persons $45 each | *Self-catering Breakfast extra*

DIRECTIONS: From Cromwell or Haast, take SH 6 towards Wanaka. Continue on SH 84, then into Ardmore St towards Lake Wanaka. Turn right into Lakeside Rd. Lakeside Apartments on immediate right.

Lakeside Apartments comprise 21 self-contained apartments each with three bedrooms and two bathrooms, available as one, two, or three-bedroom apartments. Located beside Lake Wanaka, the apartments provide uninterrupted vistas across the lake to the snow-capped mountains beyond. The grounds include a heated swimming pool and spa pool, as well as rock and water features, lawns and extensive landscaping. The architecturally designed apartments feature schist and recycled hardwood beams which blend with steel and glass to give a rustic but contemporary feel. Each apartment includes a full kitchen with quality fittings and a living area that opens to its own spacious lakefront balcony, with cedar shutters ensuring maximum privacy.

Facilities

- 5 Superior Apartments on pool & garden level
- 10 Deluxe Apartments on higher level
- 3 Premier Apartments on larger &/or higher level
- 3 Penthouse Apartments, each with spa bath, bidet, BBQ on larger deck, spa pool & seating
- toiletries, bath/spa bath, hair dryers & double basins
- fully equipped kitchen for self-catering per apartment
- all lounges with Sky TV, DVD & CD-player
- underfloor heating in tiled areas & double glazing
- large balconies & laundry facilities in each apartment
- drying room & ski storage
- lock-up garaging
- guest lift to all levels

Activities available

- room service from local cafés
- BBQs available
- heated swimming pool on site (for 6-month summer season)
- children's & spa pools on site
- water gardens on site
- extensive decking with loungers & tables on site
- transfer to & from Dunedin & Queenstown airports, extra
- variety of restaurants, short walk away
- aquatic sports
- Wanaka Town Centre, walking distance
- trekking; cycling
- golf course; wineries
- arts & crafts trail
- gardens open to visit
- skiing & heli-skiing

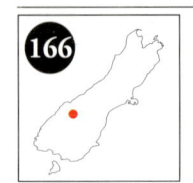

Lake Wanaka
Wanaka Springs Boutique Lodge

Hosts Lyn and Murray Finn

21 Warren Street, Wanaka   Postal P O Box 25, Wanaka
Phone 0-3-443 8421   Mobile 027 241 4113   Fax 0-3-443 8429
Email relax@wanakasprings.com   Website www.wanakasprings.com

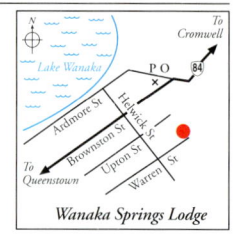

8 bdrm   8 enst   Room rate $250–$330   Includes breakfast

DIRECTIONS: Take SH 6 towards Wanaka & continue on SH 84. Turn left into Brownston St. Take 3rd left into Helwick St, then 2nd left again into Warren St. Wanaka Springs Lodge at end of cul-de-sac on left.

Wanaka Springs was opened in 2000 and reflects traditional Central Otago styles. This in-town retreat is a central base for countless activities and only a three-minute stroll from Wanaka's shops, restaurants and bars. "Wanaka Springs" refers to the natural springs that surface around the Lodge and which form the central water features in the native landscaped gardens. The interior furnishings complement the scenic views of the surrounding mountains and Lake Wanaka. The eight ensuite guestrooms are individually designed, with private deck or courtyard. Guests can enjoy the vistas from the sunny dining room where breakfast is served, relax in the guest lounge with its open log fire, or rejuvenate alfresco in the eight-seater hot tub.

Facilities
- 1 twin, 5 queen & 2 super-king/twin bedrooms; wheelchair access to 1 room
- 8 ensuites, each with heated towel rails, hair dryer, heat lamp, toiletries & bathrobes
- imported quality bed linen
- private decks or courtyards
- guest lounge with open log fire & book collection
- laundry service
- special full breakfast
- complimentary afternoon tea, nightcaps & hosted pre-dinner drinks
- Sky TV, DVD & music system
- recycled native timber furniture
- fax & email facilities
- outdoor 8-seater hot tub
- ski gear storage & drying rooms
- off-street parking

Activities available
- fishing & hunting – guiding service available
- wine-tasting at local vineyards
- 18-hole golf course
- scenic flights
- garden tours
- jet boating; kayaking; rafting
- sailing; canyoning; paragliding
- mountain biking; 4WD safaris
- horse trekking
- restaurants, cafés, shopping & lake, 5-min stroll
- walks & hikes in Mt Aspiring National Park
- NZ Fighter Pilots & Warbirds Museum
- rock climbing; mountaineering
- heli-hiking
- skiing, heli-skiing, June – Oct; 3 ski areas, 35–45-min drive

© Friars' Guide to New Zealand Accommodation for the Discerning Traveller

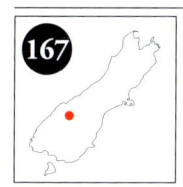

WANAKA
RENMORE HOUSE

Hosts Rosie and Blair Burridge

44 Upton Street, Wanaka
Phone 0-3-443 6566   Email rosie@renmore-house.co.nz
Fax 0-3-443 6567   Website www.renmore-house.com

Room rate $135–$215   Includes breakfast

DIRECTIONS: Take SH 6 towards Wanaka & continue on SH 84. Turn left into Brownston St. Take 3rd left into Helwick St, then 1st left again into Upton St. Renmore House on corner site on right.

3 bdrm   3 enst

Located in the heart of Wanaka, in a quiet cul-de-sac, Renmore House is just 200 metres from lakefront cafés, restaurants, bars and shops, where the long twilight of the south makes it easy to walk to the evening dining venues. Purpose-built in 1999, Renmore House offers three super-king/twin ensuite bedrooms with all guest facilities on the ground floor, separate from the hosts who live upstairs. Landscaped gardens along the banks of the Bullock Creek that runs through the site provide outdoor relaxation for guests. Continental or cooked breakfast is served in the guests' dining area or upstairs with the hosts. Watersports on Lake Wanaka are popular with guests during the summer months, and snow sports are the main attractions in winter.

Facilities
- 3 super-king/twin bedrooms
- 3 ensuites with toiletries
- cotton bed linen
- Sky TV in all 3 bedrooms
- guest lounge with tea/coffee, music, games & magazines
- additional single beds available
- fresh flowers
- phone, fax & email available
- central heating throughout
- continental/cooked breakfast
- laundry available $5
- complimentary tea/coffee
- minibar fridge for guests
- quiet cul-de-sac setting
- children welcome
- hosts live upstairs
- gardens with creek on site
- off-street parking

Activities available
- BBQ available in summer
- 200 metres to Wanaka shops
- walking distance to 20 restaurants, cafés & bars
- Lake Wanaka, 3-min walk
- golf
- jet boating
- kayaking; rafting
- windsurfing; water skiing
- tramping & climbing
- fishing & sailing on lake
- mountaineering
- gardens open to visit
- "Warbirds over Wanaka"
- skiing & snowboarding
- heli-skiing; paragliding
- horse riding
- scenic flights over glaciers, Mt Aspiring, Mt Cook & Milford Sound

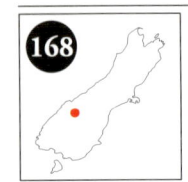

Lake Wanaka
Te Wanaka Lodge

Hosts Andy and Graeme Oxley

23 Brownston Street, Wanaka
Freephone 0800 WANAKA Phone 0-3-443 9224 Fax 0-3-443 9246
Email tewanakalodge@xtra.co.nz Website www.tewanaka.co.nz

13 bdrm | 13 enst
Double $160–$200
Single $150–$190
Includes breakfast

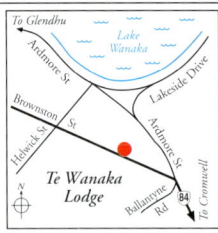

DIRECTIONS: Take SH 6 north of Cromwell towards Wanaka. Continue on SH 84 to Wanaka. At the Caltex service station turn left into Brownston St. Continue 100m to Te Wanaka Lodge on right.

Designed by architects Kurt Lehmann and Walter Heron, Te Wanaka Lodge is a contemporary European-style chalet constructed from New Zealand native timber and corrugated iron. Te Wanaka is an easy walk to the golf course, lake, and township with its restaurants and shops. Decorated with fishing and skiing memorabilia, the lodge has an alpine ambience. On a hot summer's day, guests can relax under the walnut tree or in the private courtyard garden with a cool drink from the house bar. In winter, skiers can enjoy the log fires in the guest lounge areas, and also the cedar hot tub. Breakfast is served around the huge antique dining table and features full cooked options and gourmet buffet from a menu that changes daily.

Facilities

- 1 king, 8 queen & 3 twin bedrooms, each with ensuite & private balcony
- 1 self-contained garden cottage for up to 3 persons
- bathrobes, hair dryers, heated towel rails, toiletries & mist-free mirrors in all ensuites
- TV lounge, log fire, library lounge, bar lounge, dining room & private courtyard garden
- full gourmet breakfast
- house bar, Sky TV, book, video & CD-library
- gear storage, drying room & guest laundry
- therapeutic massage service
- catering for functions & groups by arrangement
- off-street parking
- fax, internet & business facilities available

Activities available

- secluded cedar hot tub on site
- booking service for flights/tours; in-house therapeutic massage
- on-site native & deciduous trees, rhododendrons & roses
- lake-front restaurants, cafés & shopping, 2-min walk
- trout fishing & hunting, guides available by request
- scenic flights over Mt Aspiring, Mt Cook & to Milford Sound
- kayaking; swimming
- horse trekking
- bush walking; golf
- jet boating; sailing
- local crafts
- paragliding
- mountain bike hire
- Lake Wanaka
- skiing & heliskiing in winter

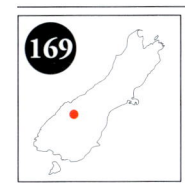

WANAKA
WILLOWRIDGE HOUSE

Hosts Lorraine and Wayne Thorpe

52 Willowridge, Wanaka
Phone 0-3-443 1330   *Email* stay@willowridgehouse.co.nz
Fax 0-3-443 1338   *Website* www.willowridgehouse.co.nz

| 4 bdrm | 1 enst | 1 prbth | Room rate $200–$300 Apartment $180 for 2 persons | *Includes breakfast* Extra persons $50 each | Lunch & dinner extra Self-catering in apartment |

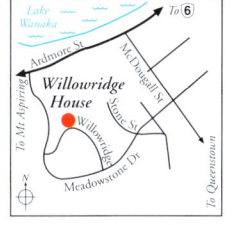

DIRECTIONS: From Wanaka township, turn left into Ardmore St & travel round lake front. Turn left into Meadowstone Drive. Then take 2nd left into Willowridge. Willowridge House is on left.

Providing both self-contained and hosted options, Willowridge House is popular year round. Summer watersports in Lake Wanaka are just a 500-metre walk away, and the snow-capped mountains above the lake are attractive on the crisp clear sunny days in winter. Built in 2000, Willowridge is designed in three levels with the self-contained apartment opening to the garden. Hosted accommodation on the top level comprises two bedrooms and a bathroom, private lounge and tea/coffee facilities on the landing. Meals are served on street level in the formal dining room or alfresco on one of the tiled deck areas. Lunch and dinner are provided by request and a barbecue is also available on site. Restaurants are just two kilometres away in the town.

Facilities

- two single-party bookings
- 1 self-contained apartment downstairs, with 1 queen & 1 twin bedroom; 1 bathroom
- 2 queen bedrooms upstairs, 1 ensuite; 2 dressing rooms
- extra bedroom available
- hair dryers, toiletries, heated towel rails & demist mirrors
- email facilities available
- fresh flowers; laundry
- full self-catering kitchen in apartment for all meals
- continental breakfast upstairs
- lunch $20 pp, by request
- 2–3 course dinner $50 pp, BYO
- upstairs meals in formal dining room or alfresco on 2 tiled decks
- wood burner, Sky TV, video, CD-player & piano in upstairs guest lounge
- off-street parking

Activities available

- BBQ on site
- 500m walk to lake
- 10-min walk to township
- Wanaka golf course 5 mins
- 6 golf courses within 1 hour
- guided fishing
- swimming in summer
- vineyard, 10-min walk
- scenic flights over glaciers, Mt Cook & Milford Sound
- Wanaka restaurants & shops
- art galleries
- paragliding; heli-skiing
- boating; kayaking; rafting
- jet boating; sailing
- tramping, mountaineering
- Warbirds over Wanaka
- 3 ski-fields, 30-min drive
- Queenstown, 50 mins south

Wanaka
Villa South Pacific

Hosts Sue Barltrop and Michael Hughes

155 Stone Street, Wanaka   *Postal* P O Box 614, Wanaka
Freephone 0800 484 437   *Mobile* 021 484 437   *Fax* 0-3-443 9508
Email stay@villasouthpacific.com   *Website* www.villasouthpacific.com

| 4 bdrm | 3 enst | 1 prbth |

Room rate $995–$1,560
Villa rate $2,700–$4,000

Includes breakfast, dinner & beverages
Self-catering   Chef extra

DIRECTIONS: Take SH 84 to Wanaka. Continue into Ardmore St, & travel along lake front. Turn left into MacDougall St, then right into Tenby St. Turn left into Stone St. Villa South Pacific on right, at end of drive.

Single-party bookings at Villa South Pacific ensure total guest privacy. Designed in Mediterranean style, the Villa includes security gates and is suitable for honeymooners and small parties. Sue has drawn upon her years in Europe to design the indoor/outdoor living spaces, including a verandah bed for summer sleeping. Broad views of Lake Wanaka and the mountains beyond make alfresco dining popular on the verandah, with its wood-fired pizza oven and barbecue. The heated swimming and spa pools overlook the floodlit tennis court. The Villa option allows guests to self-cater in the fully equipped kitchen, or a qualified chef is available by prior arrangement. In addition to the four guest bedrooms there is a studio with a double bed.

Facilities
- 2 super-king/twin & 1 twin bedroom & 2 ensuites upstairs
- 1 super-king/twin ensuite bedroom downstairs with spa bath, dressing room, wheelchair access
- cotton bed linen; writing desks
- hair dryer, toiletries, bathrobes, heated floor & towel rails
- laundry, email & fax available
- open fire, wine cellar, Sky TV, video, CDs, books in lounge
- gourmet breakfast
- champagne, cheese, whitebait & fruit platter on arrival
- 3-course dinner served; chef on request, extra
- complimentary wine, beverages & nibbles fridge
- children welcome
- central heating; serviced daily; off-street parking

Activities available
- heated swimming pool
- spa pool on site
- tennis court on site
- wood-fired pizza oven on site
- barbecue on site
- golf course, 100 metres away
- 3 ski-fields, 20-min drive
- scenic flights
- Milford Sound, 30-min flight
- town centre, 3-min drive
- restaurants nearby
- Lake Wanaka, within walking distance
- guided fishing
- watersports
- gardens open to visit
- walking; tramping
- climbing; mountaineering
- vineyards
- Queenstown, 50-min drive

Above: The view from an upstairs bedroom of Villa South Pacific looking over Wanaka and the lake to the mountains beyond.
Below: Guests can open the wooden shutters from the honeymoon room to admire the lake and alpine views.
Opposite top: The outdoor living and dining areas of the villa overlook the tennis court, which can be floodlit at night.
Opposite bottom left: The heated swimming and spa pools, wood-fired pizza oven and barbecue are popular with guests.
Opposite bottom right: The downstairs living room showing the Mediterranean influence in the interior design and furnishings.

Lake Wanaka
WANAKA HOMESTEAD

Hosts Shonagh and Roger North

1 Homestead Close, Wanaka
Phone 0-3-443 5022   Email stay@wanakahomestead.co.nz
Fax 0-3-443 5023   Website www.wanakahomestead.co.nz

| 10 bdrm | 7 enst | 2 prbth | 1 pdrm |

Double $225–$255   **Single** $180–$230   *Includes breakfast & apéritifs*
Cottage rate $310–$395   *Self-catering*

DIRECTIONS: From Christchurch, travel through town centre & continue 1.5km to Wanaka Homestead on right. From Queenstown, turn left at "T" junction & travel 900m to Wanaka Homestead on right.

Wanaka Homestead offers 10 king-size bedrooms in either the main lodge or the two self-contained cottages. Crafted with environmental sensitivity, using solar technology, Wanaka Homestead has access to Lake Wanaka via the historic Wanaka Station Park, which features century-old redwoods. Purpose-built on an original homestead out-building site, using recycled red beech timber and rimu, Wanaka Homestead is within walking distance of the town centre. Cottage guests can self-cater using the fully equipped kitchens and lodge guests are served a full breakfast in the dining room downstairs. Guests have use of the hot tub, barbecue, and outdoor fireplaces on site, and the in-house Fly Fishing Academy is a special attraction.

Facilities
- 1 California king ensuite bedroom upstairs with double shower & double basins
- 4 super-king/twin ensuite bedrooms, 1 with wheelchair access
- 3-bedroom, 2-bathroom cottage
- 2-bedroom, 2-bathroom cottage with wheelchair access
- children welcome in cottages
- ski storage & drying room
- full breakfast, apéritifs & evening nibbles for lodge guests
- full kitchen in each cottage for self-catering
- bathrobes, hair dryer, toiletries & heated floor in all bathrooms
- open fire in homestead
- TV, VCR, DVD, CDs, books & local artwork
- phones, fax, computer & fast internet access; laundry

Activities available
- in-house Fly Fishing Academy
- outside fires, 2 BBQs & hot tub; Jess, a child-friendly collie, on site
- direct park access; 200m to lake
- 18-hole golf course, winery & vineyards, 1km; wine tours
- town centre, 1.5km; art galleries & museum
- skiing, heli-skiing & snowboarding June – Oct.
- Warbirds over Wanaka air show
- restaurants, cafés & shopping, 15-min walk
- kayaking; white water rafting & sledging; jet boating; canyoning; fly & boat fishing
- 4WD safaris; rock climbing; mountain biking
- walking trails; horse trekking
- tramping & mountaineering
- scenic flights to Milford Sound; skydiving; paragliding

© Friars' Guide to New Zealand Accommodation for the Discerning Traveller

Wanaka
Wanaka Stonehouse Boutique Lodge

Hosts Susanne and Bruce Bussell

21 Sargood Drive, Wanaka
Phone 0-3-443 1933   *Email* indulge@wanakastonehouse.co.nz
Fax 0-3-443 1929   *Website* www.wanakastonehouse.co.nz

4 bdrm / 4 enst

Room rate $320–$395   Includes breakfast

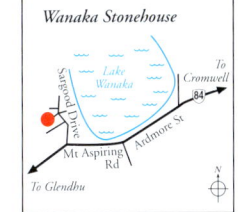

DIRECTIONS: From Wanaka township, take Ardmore St along lake front into Mt Aspiring Rd. Turn right into Sargood Drive. Wanaka Stonehouse is 300m on left.

Wanaka Stonehouse has been refurbished and upgraded. This alpine-style retreat is set in secluded landscaped gardens in Wanaka, close to the lake front, within half an hour of the local ski areas. The Lodge is built of local stone with exposed beams and oak panelling creating the ambience of a traditional hunting and fishing lodge. Four spacious ensuite guestrooms are individually designed with contemporary furnishings. Guests enjoy the exclusive use of all Lodge facilities, as the hosts live in a separate cottage in the grounds. Guests can relax in the large open lounge with exposed beams and open fireplace, the private reading room, peaceful garden, and in the conservatory. The spa pool and sauna complex is also popular with guests.

Facilities

- 2 spacious super-king/twin & 2 queen ensuite bedrooms
- bathrobes, wrap towels, heated towel rails, aromatherapy toiletries, hair dryers in ensuites
- TV, phone, tea/coffee, cotton linen, electric blankets, seating areas, ironing facilities, iced water, cookies & chocolates in each bedroom; central heating
- full business facilities
- full cooked/continental breakfast served in dining room
- NZ wines & beers; guest fridges
- lounge with log fire; library room; music system; writing desk
- spa pool, sauna & massage
- laundry facilities
- ski storage & drying room
- courtesy passenger transfer
- off-street parking

Activities available

- full itinerary booking service
- lakefront, vineyard, shops & restaurants, short stroll
- private mature gardens on site
- BBQ on site
- sauna & spa pool on site
- in-house massage & reflexology
- golfing
- walking & climbing
- hunting/fishing guides on request
- boating
- sailing
- swimming
- horse trekking
- winter skiing
- heli-skiing
- snowboarding
- scenic flights to Milford Sound, Mt Aspiring, Mt Cook, glaciers & West Coast

Wanaka
Whare Kea Lodge

Host Kelly Delahunt

Mount Aspiring Road, Lake Wanaka *Postal* P O Box 115, Wanaka
Phone 0-3-443 1400 *Mobile* 027 243 3253 *Fax* 0-3-443 9200
Email admin@wharekealodge.com *Website* www.wharekealodge.com

| 6 bdrm | 6 enst | 1 pdrm |

Double $1,000
Single $580

Includes breakfast & dinner
Lunch extra

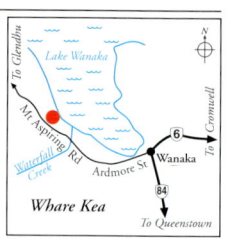

DIRECTIONS: Take SH 6 or SH 84 to Wanaka. From town centre, take Ardmore St along lake edge towards Glendhu. Continue into Mt Aspiring Rd. Turn right into driveway to Whare Kea Lodge at end, 7km from township.

Set on the edge of Lake Wanaka, Whare Kea was designed by John Mayne and built in 1996 in contemporary-style featuring timber, steel and glass, maximising the lake views. The spacious rooms provide six guest bedrooms all with ensuite bathrooms including baths. Buffet and cooked breakfasts, as well as three-course dinners, are served in the large dining room overlooking Lake Wanaka, with views to the Southern Alps beyond. Whare Kea Lodge is fully licensed, and picnic lunches are also available on request. Set on farmland planted with native grasses and trees, Whare Kea is just seven kilometres from Wanaka township. Guests enjoy watersports in the lake during the hot summer season, and skiing or heli-skiing in the winter.

Facilities
- 6 spacious ensuite guestrooms
- cotton bed linen, dressing room & writing desk in all 6 bedrooms/suites
- double showers, deep baths, hair dryer, heated floor, toiletries & wheelchair access
- phone, fax & email
- guest lounge with open fire, tea/coffee, nibbles, bar, TV, video & library
- buffet cooked breakfast
- light lunch/picnic, extra
- 3-course dinner, served in dining room
- fresh flowers
- laundry available
- central heating
- lake views
- garaging; helipad
- on-site parking

Activities available
- billiards & table tennis
- walking track on site
- honeymoons & conferences catered for
- barbecue available on site
- helicopter & helipad available on site for scenic flights
- vineyards
- golf
- hiking; fishing
- Wanaka's shops & cafés, 7km
- watersports on Lake Wanaka
- climbing
- garden tours
- bungy jumping; jet boating
- boat trips
- National Parks
- winter skiing & heli-skiing
- Queenstown, 50-min drive south, via the Crown Range

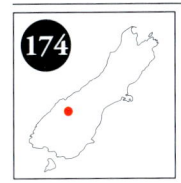

Wanaka
Mountain Range

Hosts Lindsey and Matthew Brady

Heritage Park, State Highway 89, Wanaka
Postal P O Box 451, Wanaka   *Phone* 0-3-443 7400   *Fax* 0-3-443 7450
Email stay@mountainrange.co.nz   *Website* www.mountainrange.co.nz

Double $225–$280
Single $195–$235

Includes breakfast
Picnic lunch extra

7 bdrm / 7 enst

DIRECTIONS: Take SH 84 towards Wanaka. Turn left into Ballantyne Rd, then right into Golf Course Rd. Turn left into SH 89. Travel 500m & turn left into Heritage Park. Mountain Range is 40m on left.

Located in Heritage Park estate, Mountain Range draws its inspiration from the surrounding mountain views. Purpose built in 2002, this ranch-style lodge features local timbers, exposed beams, wooden floors and schist. Mountain Range provides seven guest bedrooms, all with 180-degree mountain views, six opening to private verandahs, and the honeymoon ensuite including a candlelit spa bath. Afternoon tea and evening apéritifs are offered daily. A full breakfast is served in the dining room, or alfresco on the verandah opening onto the landscaped gardens. The private parkland beyond ensures a quiet peaceful stay. Restaurants are situated two kilometres north in Wanaka township, and the lake is within walking distance.

Facilities

- 2 super-king/twin & 4 queen ensuite bedrooms
- 1 honeymoon king bedroom with candlelit spa bath in ensuite
- cotton bed linen & direct dial phone in each bedroom
- hair dryers, toiletries, bathrobes, heated towel rails/mirrors/floors
- guest lounge with log fire & entertainment system
- laundry service; fresh flowers
- fresh breakfast with hot option
- complimentary afternoon tea & apéritifs
- guest kitchen includes cookies
- fax & email available in office
- drying room for ski storage
- honeymoons, small weddings & corporate retreats catered
- courtesy passenger transfer
- on-site parking

Activities available

- pétanque court on site
- 18-hole golf course
- vineyards; 4WD safaris
- fly fishing tours
- paragliding & skydiving
- walking & hiking
- horse trekking; scenic flights
- Fighter Pilot Museum
- tramping & mountaineering
- restaurants, 10-min walk
- Lake Wanaka, 3-min drive
- kayaking; canoeing
- sailing; jet boating
- windsurfing; swimming
- white water rafting
- wake boarding
- skiing & snow boarding
- heli-biking & heli-skiing

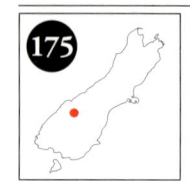

WANAKA
OAKRIDGE LODGE

Manager Patrick Waser

Corner Cardrona Valley and Studholme Roads, Wanaka   Phone 0-3-443 7707
Postal P O Box 390, Wanaka   *Fax* 0-3-443 7750   *Email* info@oakridge.co.nz
Freephone 0800 869 262   *Website* www.oakridge.co.nz

Room rate $120–$220   *Includes continental breakfast*   *Cooked breakfast & dinner extra*

12 bdrm / 12 enst

DIRECTIONS: Take SH 84 towards Wanaka. Turn left into Ballantyne Rd, then right into Golf Course Rd. Turn left into SH 89, & right into Studholme Rd. Oakridge 1st on right. Or from Wanaka, turn left into MacDougall St.

With 180-degree views of snow-capped mountains of the Southern Alps, this purpose-built Lodge is set on one and a half hectares of tree-studded lawns and gardens. Contemporary guest wings were added to the original hunting and fishing lodge in 2000, providing a total of 12 super-king/twin guestrooms. The eight new suites each includes a seating area and ensuite bathroom, six with spa baths and two with wheelchair access. A continental breakfast buffet in the dining room features juices, fresh fruit, yoghurt, cereals and breads. Cooked breakfast is available by request. Oakridge also offers evening dining in its popular and fully licensed restaurant and bar. Guests enjoy mingling with the locals while enjoying the food, wine, ambience and alpine views.

Facilities
- 12 super-king/twin ensuite bedrooms, 8 with seating areas
- bathrobes, demist mirrors, heated towel rails, hair dryers & toiletries in all 12 ensuites
- spa baths in 6 ensuites
- phone, writing desk, Sky TV & tea/coffee in bedrooms
- cotton bed linen
- open fire, Sky TV, video, CDs & writing desk in lounge
- continental buffet breakfast
- cooked breakfast, $15 pp
- fully licensed restaurant & bar for evening dining
- computer, email & fax
- children welcome
- laundry, $10 for wash/dry
- wheelchair access to 2 ensuites
- courtesy minibus transfer
- on-site parking

Activities available
- outdoor spa pool
- outdoor swimming pool
- lawn tennis court on site
- croquet & pétanque on site
- golf practice area on site
- scenic flights; paragliding
- walking; tramping
- kayaking; canoeing
- mountain biking; golf
- restaurants, 1-min drive
- sailing; skydiving
- windsurfing; swimming
- trout fishing; jet boating
- white water rafting; white water sledging
- horse trekking
- rock climbing; archery
- clay pigeon shooting
- winter skiing

© Friars' Guide to New Zealand Accommodation for the Discerning Traveller

CARDRONA, WANAKA
HOT TODDY LODGE

Hosts Sean and Christine Colbourne

2206 Crown Range Road, Cardrona, R D 1, Wanaka
Phone 0-3-443 1225 *Mobile* 027 233 0868
Email stay@thehottoddy.co.nz *Website* www.thehottoddy.co.nz

Guest wing rate $200–$400   *Includes breakfast provisions*   *Self-catering*

DIRECTIONS: From Wanaka take MacDougall St (SH 89) towards Queenstown. Continue on Crown Range Rd 22km to Hot Toddy Lodge on right. From Queenstown, take SH 89 & travel 30 mins to Lodge on left.

Located in Cardrona, in the heart of the southern lakes district, Hot Toddy Lodge is situated at the foot of Mt Cardrona. Hot Toddy offers a self-contained private guest wing for single-party bookings, comprising two queen ensuite bedrooms, a spacious lounge and fully equipped kitchen. Breakfast provisions are supplied, as well as the basics for self-catering. An open fireplace adds atmosphere to the guest lounge, with views to the surrounding countryside and mountains beyond. The lounge opens to a deck adjacent to the six-seater outdoor spa pool from where guests enjoy star gazing. Built in 2002 on an early settlers' house site, Hot Toddy Lodge is set in an extensive garden bordered by mature poplar trees planted in the 1860s.

Facilities
- one-party bookings only
- self-contained guest wing
- 2 queen ensuite bedrooms
- hair dryers, toiletries, heated towel rails & bathrobes
- cotton bed linen
- open fire, video, CDs, DVD & phone in guest lounge
- mountain views
- guest deck opens from lounge
- breakfast provisions
- full kitchen with basic supplies for self-catering
- chef available by arrangement
- fresh flowers
- guest laundry, drying room
- central gas heating
- babysitting service available
- adjacent to Cardrona Hotel
- on-site parking

Activities available
- garden spa pool on site
- full guiding service available
- heli-skiing from site
- facials, skin-care & massage therapist by appointment
- walking & tramping trails
- mountain biking
- closest accommodation to Cardrona & Snow Farm ski-fields, 5-min walk
- wine trail
- rally driving
- high country farm tour
- southern lakes
- 6 ski-fields within 1 hour
- gardens open to visit
- Lake Wanaka, 15-20 mins
- Arrowtown, 25 mins south
- Queenstown, 45 mins south

Arrowtown
Skyview Magic

Hosts Robina Bodle and Jef Desbecker

44 Jeffery Road, Crown Terrace, R D 1, Arrowtown
Phone 0-3-442 9405   Mobile 027 433 7232   Fax 0-3-442 9405
Email info@skyview.co.nz   *Website* www.skyview.co.nz

| 4 bdrm | 3 enst | 1 prbth |

Lodge rate $400 for 2 persons
Extra persons $75 each

Self-catering
2-night minimum stay

DIRECTIONS: Take SH 6 towards Queenstown. Turn right into Crown Range Rd (SH 89) towards Wanaka. Turn right into Jeffery Rd. Travel 500m, turn right into driveway & take left fork to Skyview Magic.

Located on 68 hectares (168 acres) on the Crown Range, Skyview is a self-contained lodge built in a unique rustic architectural style with spacious rooms. Totally renovated in 2003, Skyview includes quality fittings and timber feature walls. Providing panoramic mountain views, quiet seclusion and secure privacy, Skyview offers four guestrooms and a spacious lounge which is heated by a wood burner. Living areas open onto a large sundeck and there is a fully equipped kitchen for self-catering. The lodge can sleep up to 12 guests in one-party bookings only, and the hosts live separately, 300 metres away. Guests enjoy the indoor climbing wall, 25-metre solar-heated summer swimming pool, and three kilometres of jogging track around the property.

Facilities
- single-party bookings only
- 1 king & 1 queen bedroom upstairs, both with ensuites
- 1 king/twin bedroom downstairs with ensuite
- 1 queen bedroom upstairs with separate access & toilet
- 1 double bed on sundeck with private bathroom, double bath & wheelchair access
- children welcome
- full kitchen for self-catering
- 1 bottle champagne in fridge
- wood burner, Sky TV, DVD, CDs, games, books, phone & writing desk in lounge
- cotton bed linen; hair dryers, toiletries, heated floor
- self-service laundry
- fax on request; central heating
- garaging; on-site parking

Activities available
- outdoor bath; BBQ on sundeck
- indoor solar-heated chlorine-free 25m swimming pool (not available winter); indoor climbing wall; trampoline
- 3km of tracks for walking & mountain biking on 68ha site
- kayaking; wind surfing; canoeing; watersports
- bungy jumping; rafting; sailing; jet boating
- local restaurants, bars, boutique shops & wineries
- 4 golf courses; fishing
- horse trekking; 4WD touring
- hang gliding; parapenting; hot air ballooning
- wilderness tramping & walks; mountain & rock climbing
- alpine & Nordic skiing; snowboarding; heli-skiing & heli-boarding in winter

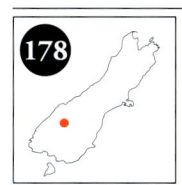

QUEENSTOWN
RIVERBANK COTTAGE

Hosts Sheila and Lex Emslie

1350 State Highway 6, R D 1, Queenstown   *Mobile* 021 347 804
Postal P O Box 1093, Queenstown   *Email* cottage@riverbank.co.nz
Phone 0-3-442 1518   *Fax* 0-3-442 1519   *Website* www.riverbank.co.nz

3 bdrm   3 enst   Double $215–$265   Single $195   Includes breakfast

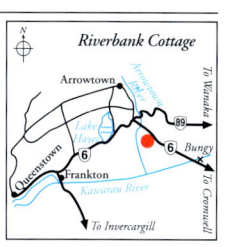

DIRECTIONS: From Cromwell, take SH 6 towards Queenstown. Pass Kawarau bungy bridge on right & continue 4km to Riverbank Cottage on left, signposted 400m before cottage. (Queenstown 15km away.)

Riverbank Cottage provides country-style accommodation set in almost a hectare (two acres) of established cottage gardens above the banks of the Arrow River. With 360-degree views of the surrounding mountains – Coronet Peak and the Remarkables – Riverbank Cottage is adjacent to deer farms, yet only 15 minutes' drive to Queenstown centre. Built in 1992, the Cottage offers three ensuite guestrooms and a full choice of breakfast served in the quilt gallery. Sheila's quilts adorn the walls and are available for sale. Lex is a classic car enthusiast, happy to share his pastime with interested guests. The historic village of Arrowtown is just five minutes' drive away, where guests can enjoy dining at the many restaurants and cafés.

Facilities

- 1 super-king & 1 king bedroom, both with ensuite bathrooms
- 1 king/twin ensuite bedroom
- hair dryers, bathrobes, heated towel rails & toiletries
- cotton bed linen & TV in both bedrooms
- verandah opens from bedrooms
- guest lounge with open fire, tea/coffee, nibbles, Sky TV, video, CD-player & writing desk
- continental or full cooked breakfast, served in gallery
- fresh flowers; central heating
- children welcome
- complimentary laundry
- email, fax & phone
- mountain views
- private guest entrance
- on-site parking
- courtesy passenger transfer

Activities available

- pétanque/boules on site
- 1ha (2-acre) cottage garden
- viewing Sheila's quilts
- viewing Lex's classic cars
- garden & mountain walks
- fishing, rods provided
- golf courses
- visiting deer farms
- lake cruises
- wineries
- restaurants in Arrowtown, 5-min drive away
- bungy jumping
- jet boating
- horse riding
- garden tours
- Botanic Gardens
- restaurants, cafés, bars, shops in Queenstown, 15 mins
- 4 winter ski-fields nearby

465

© Friars' Guide to New Zealand Accommodation for the Discerning Traveller

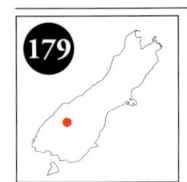

ARROWTOWN
ARROWTOWN OLD NICK

Hosts Marie and Steve Waterhouse

70 Buckingham Street, Arrowtown   *Postal* P O Box 36, Arrowtown
Freephone 0800 OLD NIC   *Phone* 0-3-442 0066   *Mobile* 021 258 5545
Fax 0-3-442 0066   *Email* host@oldnick.co.nz   *Website* www.oldnick.co.nz

4 bdrm | 3 enst | 1 prbth   Double $150–$220   Single $130–$175   *Includes breakfast*

DIRECTIONS: From Queenstown, take SH 6A to Arrowtown. Take Berkshire St to township & turn right into Buckingham St. Continue 200m through intersection to Arrowtown Old Nick on right.

Arrowtown Old Nick was built in the early 1900s with 45-centimetre (18-inch) thick schist walls and high ceilings. As part of the original Police Camp, it was designed as the jailer's home, with the historic jail still next door. The front of the homestead was preserved and additions made in 1995, which include a spacious country kitchen with Aga heating system and three-metre long table, where breakfast is served, and lounge with open fireplace. The double schist garage was converted to provide three semi-detached ensuite bedrooms. In the homestead is one further bedroom with king-size bed and a private bathroom with spa bath. The guestrooms look on to the established garden surrounded by 25-metre high trees, with views to the mountain backdrop.

Facilities

- 3 detached super-king/twin ensuite bedrooms
- 1 king bedroom with private bathroom & spa bath
- cotton bed linen
- hair dryer, heated towel rails, toiletries & wheelchair access
- lounge with open fire, tea/coffee, nibbles, mineral water, TV, video & CD-player
- children welcome
- continental & cooked breakfast, served in kitchen/dining area or room service
- central heating
- phone, fax & email available
- complimentary laundry
- pets welcome
- courtesy passenger transfer
- BBQ available
- off-street parking

Activities available

- garden with mature trees & outdoor furniture on site for relaxing & reading
- historic Arrowtown, restaurants, cafés, movies, museum, Chinese goldminers' site, short walk
- Queenstown shops, restaurants & activities, 15-min drive
- 4 golf courses nearby, including Millbrook
- ski-fields, 15–40-min drive
- gold panning
- river walks; horse riding
- rafting; hang gliding
- bungy jumping
- jet boating; parapenting
- 4WD tours to historic Macetown & Skippers
- wineries; art trails
- fishing; hunting
- helicopter tours

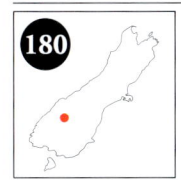

Arrowtown
ARROWTOWN HOUSE

Hosts Caroline Hickin and Philip Hickin

10 Caernarvon Street, Arrowtown
Phone 0-3-442 0025 *Email* gold@arrowtownhouse.co.nz
Fax 0-3-442 0051 *Website* www.arrowtownhouse.co.nz

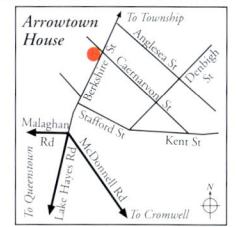

5 bdrm 5 enst Double $350–$395 Single $225 *Includes breakfast*

DIRECTIONS: From Queenstown, take SH 6A to Lake Hayes. Turn left and travel to Arrowtown. Continue on Berkshire St to Caernarvon St. Arrowtown House on corner on left.

Arrowtown House is located on a tree-lined avenue in Arrowtown's historic precinct. Set in landscaped gardens, featuring a large *Catalpa bignonioides* (Indian bean tree) which flowers in January, rhododendrons in November, and autumn colours, Arrowtown House offers year-round interest for the garden lover. The accommodation is separate from the house, ensuring guest privacy. Each of the guestrooms includes a lounge area, fridge, microwave, phone, fax and modem and its own washer/dryer. The five spacious guestrooms provide mountain and garden views, and three open to verandahs or private courtyard gardens. Brother and sister, Philip and Caroline, serve breakfast at the long kauri dining table in the house, or in the guestrooms.

Facilities

- 1 queen, 2 king & 2 super-king/twin spacious ensuite bedrooms
- heated tiled floors, heated towel rails, demist mirrors, hair dryers, bathrobes & toiletries in all 5 bathrooms, 2 with double baths
- cotton bed linen; fresh flowers
- phone, fax, modem, writing desk, TV, video, CD-player & seating area in all 5 guestrooms
- guest library; artwork
- breakfast served in house, or continental room service
- washer/dryer, fridge, mineral water, tea/coffee in 5 rooms
- Millbrook Resort/Spa facilities available
- central heating; wheelchair access
- private guest entrance
- off-street parking

Activities available

- relaxing in garden on site
- local historic township, within walking distance
- 5 golf courses; river walks
- mountain biking
- jet boating; fishing
- 4WD excursions
- award-winning museum
- local art-house cinema
- 5 ski-fields, 20–90 mins
- restaurants & cafés, 2-min stroll
- wine bars, wineries & vineyards
- local art tours & galleries
- horse treks; bungy jumping
- gold panning; gardens to visit
- soft adventure tourism options
- Queenstown, 10-min drive
- scenic flights to Milford Sound
- Wanaka, Alexandra, or Cromwell, within 1-hour drive

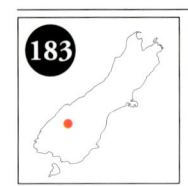

DALEFIELD, QUEENSTOWN
BELLINI'S OF QUEENSTOWN

Hosts John Lapsley and Melinda Hayton

578 Speargrass Flat Road, R D 1, Queenstown
Phone 0-3-442 0771 *Email* holiday@bellinis.co.nz
Fax 0-3-442 0715 *Website* www.bellinis.co.nz

3 bdrm | 3 enst | Suite rate $400–$450 | Includes breakfast | Lunch & dinner extra

DIRECTIONS: From Queenstown take SH 6 & turn left into Lake Hayes-Arrowtown Rd. Travel 3km & turn left into Speargrass Flat Rd. Travel 20m & take 1st driveway on left. Bellini's is 1st on right.

Bellini's is set in large lawns and gardens, surrounded by mountain views. The three suites open to the garden where guests can relax under a willow tree and enjoy alfresco drinks. Bellini's schist and cedar exterior was designed by architect Fred van Brandenburg, with timbered interiors. The lounge ceilings are supported by recycled wooden beams that once braced rural bridges, and the long dining table sits beneath a large iron candelabra which hangs from a high pyramidal ceiling. Bellini's also features a wine cellar, large library, and extensive CD collections in the guest suites which include (of course) Bellini's operas. John and Melinda are happy to help guests choose scenic drives, walks, golfing and fishing venues, as well as restaurants.

Facilities

- 1 super-king/twin suite
- 2 queen suites with lounges
- all 3 suites open to garden
- hair dryer, toiletries, heated towel rails, robes in 3 ensuites
- quality bed linen, tea/coffee, fridge, phone, Sky TV, DVD & CD-player in each suite
- fax & email; fresh flowers
- children welcome; laundry

- full breakfast menus including salmon caviar & pastries
- lunch, picnic, dinner, or BBQ pack, by arrangement, extra
- complimentary cocktails & hors d'oeuvres; bar/wine cellar, extra
- open fireplace, Sky TV, DVDs, games, extensive library of books & CDs
- well-behaved dog on site
- on-site parking

Activities available

- 1ha (2 acres) garden on site
- artists' galleries & coffee shop, short walk away
- Lake Hayes, with sandy beach & summer swimming, 3 mins
- tennis, gym, beauty & spa facilities available nearby
- 5 golf courses, within 30 mins
- specialist NZ wool & outdoor clothing shops in Arrowtown & Queenstown, 5–20-min drive

- restaurants at historic Arrowtown, 5-min drive
- winery tours & tasting
- heritage gold-mining area
- guided trout fishing
- scenic walks & drives – lakes, mountains & wilderness
- gardens open to visit
- extreme sports; horse treks
- 4 ski-fields, from 15 mins

Above: The main lounge at Bellini's features an open schist fireplace and exposed beams recycled from rural bridge supports.
Below: The formal dining room is dominated by a long table lit by an iron candelabra hung from the high pyramidal ceiling.
Opposite top: Bellini's has a schist and cedar exterior, and is set in almost one hectare of gardens and lawns, with mountain views.
Opposite bottom left: The three guest suites each include a spacious bedroom, ensuite and private lounge opening to the garden.
Opposite bottom right: Alfresco breakfast on the terrace is popular at Bellini's of Queenstown, featuring extensive menus.

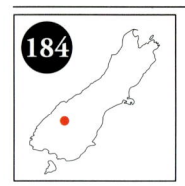

DALEFIELD, QUEENSTOWN
White Shadows Country Inn®

Hosts William Bailey and Michael Harris

58 Hunter Road, R D 1, Queenstown
Phone 0-3-442 0871 *Email* info@whiteshadows.co.nz
Fax 0-3-442 0872 *Website* www.whiteshadows.co.nz

| 2 bdrm | 2 enst | 1 pdrm |

Suite rate $649 *Includes breakfast & pre-dinner hors d'oeuvres with wine*

DIRECTIONS: Take SH 6 towards Queenstown. Pass Lake Hayes, then turn right into Lower Shotover Rd. Continue into Hunter Rd & travel 1.5km uphill to White Shadows driveway on the left.

White Shadows Country Inn was custom-built to the highest of standards with luxury furnishings, traditional and contemporary art and sculpture, and has received a 5-star "Guest & Hosted" Qualmark rating. Separate from the main house is a schist stone cottage with the two guest suites, each including a stone fireplace, lounge area, wood-beamed ceilings, table and chairs. The glass-roofed bathrooms offer views of the overhanging native red beech trees and sky above. Guests also have full use of the ground floor of the main house, where three areas provide relaxation in front of open fires, a grand piano, and window-seat overlooking three cascading garden ponds, with vistas to Coronet Peak.

Facilities

- 1 super king/twin & 1 queen suite each with ensuite bathroom
- quality toiletries, hair dryer, bathrobes, heated floor & heated towel rails in each ensuite
- 100% cotton bed linen, goosedown duvets & pillows
- Sky TV, CDs, DVD, alarm clock, phone, fridge with complimentary drinks, tea/coffee, writing desk, seating area & fireplace in suites
- private guest entrances
- lounge in house with open fire, grand piano, espressos & lattés
- buffet & cooked specialities for breakfast, served in breakfast room or courtyard
- underfloor heating
- guest fax & email available
- fresh flowers
- complimentary guest laundry
- 2 small resident dogs
- courtesy airport transfer

Activities available

On site complimentary:
- in-ground spa pool
- 21-speed bicycles
- pétanque/boules; croquet court
- 5.7-ha (14-acre) grounds
- picnicking in summer house

Off site:
- Queenstown, 12-min drive
- Millbrook golf, swimming pool, gym & massage, 5 mins
- airport & helipad, 10-min drive
- ski-fields, 25-min drive
- bungy jumping; jet boating
- horse riding; vineyard tours
- gardens to visit; trout fishing
- TSS *Earnslaw* steamship cruise
- white water rafting
- parapenting; arts trail
- historic Arrowtown, 10 mins
- tramping; trekking; heliskiing
- Milford Sound day trips

© Friars' Guide to New Zealand Accommodation for the Discerning Traveller

Far left: White Shadows Country Inn as seen from Malaghan Road. Adjacent to the main house is the schist stone cottage with the two separate guest suites.
Left top: The living room in the main house at White Shadows. The ground floor provides three such areas for guests' relaxation in front of open fires, with views over the garden and ponds to Coronet Peak beyond.
Left bottom: One of the two guest suites in the schist cottage at White Shadows. Each suite includes a stone fireplace, lounge area, wood-beamed ceilings, table and chairs. An ensuite bathroom adjoins each bedroom.
Right centre: Walkways lead down the hill past a waterfall and stream, across a bridge to the largest of the three ponds and an open summer house tucked under a large golden weeping willow tree.

Above: Lying just below the main house and guests' stone cottage is a pergola covered sitting area which, in turn, is on a terrace above the croquet lawn.
Left top: On warm sunny mornings guests can enjoy breakfast on the large stone patio overlooking Coronet Peak, or relax during the day on a chaise longue under an umbrella.

Left bottom: Gourmet breakfasts are served indoors in a double height room surrounded by doors and windows and adjacent to a large open fireplace.
Below: Guests can relax year-round at any time of the day or night in the three-level, tiled spa pool, overlooking green pastures to the snowcapped mountains beyond.

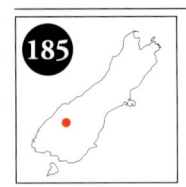

Dalefield, Queenstown
Pear Tree Cottage

Hosts Erina and Terry McLean

51 Mountain View Road, R D 1, Dalefield, Queenstown
Phone 0-3-442 9340   *Mobile* 025 370 935   *Fax* 0-3-442 9349
Email info@peartree.co.nz   *Website* www.peartree.co.nz

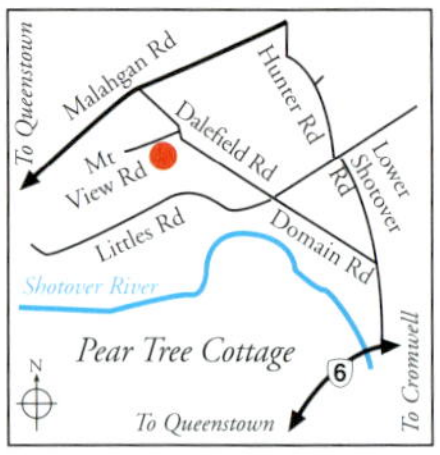

Cottage rate for 2 persons $220–$350
Extra persons $50–$60 each
Self-catering
Includes breakfast
Dinner extra

2 bdrm / 1 prbth

DIRECTIONS: From SH 6, turn north into Lower Shotover Rd, left into Domain Rd & continue into Dalefield Rd. Turn left into Mountain View Rd. Cottage on left. Or from Queenstown, take Gorge Rd (12 mins).

Set in a secluded valley at the foot of Coronet Peak, this rustic colonial cottage, built circa 1870s, has been lovingly restored to provide guests with every comfort, including central heating. Fully self-contained, this historic rural cottage offers total privacy if desired, or guests are welcome to interact with the hosts who live adjacent. Pear Tree Cottage is one of the earliest European buildings in the district, named after the century-old pear tree in the extensive garden. Hanging baskets from the verandah and flower pots add to the summer colour. The cottage is crammed with Kiwi rural memorabilia and bric-à-brac. Breakfast featuring fresh local produce can be served alfresco in the colourful garden, and dinner provided by prior arrangement.

Facilities
- exclusive-party bookings only
- 1 queen & 1 double/twin bedroom
- claw-foot bathtub in bathroom
- hair dryer, & toiletries
- cotton bed linen & goosedown duvets; bathrobes & slippers
- children welcome on request
- open fireplace, TV, VCR, video & CD-library
- phone, fax & email available
- full breakfast, served in cottage or alfresco in garden
- à la carte dinner with wine, $75 pp
- full kitchen with stocked pantry for self-catering
- guest laundry available
- courtesy passenger transfer
- on-site parking
- sunny verandah

Activities available
- back country 4WD tours
- pétanque available
- barbecue available on site
- Coronet Peak ski field
- 3 golf courses, including Millbrook Golf Resort
- arts trail; many walks
- historic Arrowtown & museum
- horse riding/trekking
- helicopter tours arranged
- over 100 restaurants, 12 mins
- fishing arranged
- Shotover jet boating
- white water rafting
- bungy jumping
- garden visits; wineries
- parapenting; sky diving
- *Earnslaw* historic steamship
- Milford & Doubtful Sound day trips arranged

© Friars' Guide to New Zealand Accommodation for the Discerning Traveller

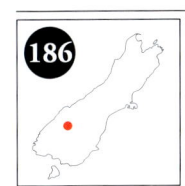

Queenstown
Kahu Rise Bed and Breakfast

Hosts Angela and Bill Dolan

455 Littles Road, R D 1, Queenstown *Mobile* 021 104 0009
Freephone 0800 436 111 *Phone* 0-3-441 2077 *Fax* 0-3-441 2078
Email info@kahurise.co.nz *Website* www.kahurise.co.nz

Room rate $190 for 2 persons
Extra persons $50 each

Includes breakfast
Dinner extra

DIRECTIONS: From Queenstown, take SH 6 towards Cromwell. Cross Shotover River & turn left into Lower Shotover Rd. Turn left into Domain Rd & 1st left into Littles Rd. Travel 900m to Kahu Rise on right.

Opened in 2002, Kahu Rise comprises a cluster of four buildings featuring Colorsteel cladding. With rural views to the mountains, the separate guest wing provides privacy for single-party bookings, the two bedrooms opening to a patio. A full breakfast is served to suit guests' timing in the family kitchen. The living rooms are heated by the central schist fireplace, and the hosts live in a separate wing. Children are welcome by arrangement and there is an additional sleepout available for teenagers. Kahu Rise is named after the Australasian harrier, that flies over the house most days. Sited almost equidistant between Queenstown and Arrowtown, guests can access all the nearby activities, and the airport is just eight minutes' drive away.

Facilities
- single-party bookings only
- 1 queen & 1 twin bedroom in guest wing, open to patio & share 1 private bathroom
- hair dryer, toiletries & heated towel rails
- TV, phone jacks, tea/coffee & fridge in both bedrooms
- ensuite sleepout for teenagers
- 1 powder room; fresh flowers
- continental & cooked breakfast served in kitchen
- dinner by request, $45 pp
- home baking & nibbles
- open-plan lounge with wood fire, TV, artwork & books
- heated floor throughout
- children by arrangement
- self-service laundry
- on-site parking

Activities available
- expansive lawns & garden from guest wing on site
- 4 golf courses
- wineries
- lake cruises
- ski-fields nearby
- Shotover jet boating
- bungy jumping
- garden tours
- 4WD tours
- restaurants & galleries
- horse riding/trekking
- tramping/hiking; nature walks
- parapenting
- Milford & Doubtful Sound day trips
- *Earnslaw* historic steamship
- airport, 8-min drive
- Arrowtown, 10-min drive
- Queenstown, 15-min drive

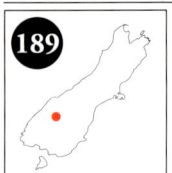

QUEENSTOWN
PENCARROW

Hosts Kari and Bill Moers

678 Frankton Road, Queenstown
Phone 0-3-442 8938   *Fax* 0-3-442 8974
Email info@pencarrow.net   *Website* www.pencarrow.net

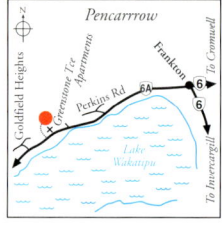

| 4 bdrm | 4 enst | Suite rate $450 | Includes breakfast |

DIRECTIONS: From Cromwell, take SH 6 to Frankton. Continue on Frankton Rd (SH 6A) for 2.4km. At light & dark brown apartments (Greenstone Tce) turn right into gravel drive uphill to Pencarrow at top.

Located on a hillside overlooking Lake Wakatipu to the Remarkables beyond, Pencarrow provides views from every room. Named after New Zealand's first lighthouse, Pencarrow is set in extensive gardens of almost two hectares, with space for guests to relax on the local schist flagstone and timber decks and around the outdoor fireplace. Each of the four spacious guest suites includes a private sitting room and jet spa bath in the ensuite. Guests can play billiards on the full-size historic English snooker table and socialise around the open fireplace in the New River Lounge and Bar. A country breakfast is served in the dining room with its antique fireplace. Guests enjoy sharing their day's adventures over a complimentary drink in the evening.

Facilities

- 2 king suites upstairs
- 2 king suites with extra queen sofa bed downstairs
- writing desk, phone, Sky TV, video & tea/coffee facilities
- jet spa bath, double basin, hair dryer, bathrobes, heated floor & towel rails in all bathrooms
- guest lounge with open fire, nibbles, mineral water, bar, CD-player, artwork & library
- full cooked country breakfast with specials each day
- wine cellar with local & international wines for sale
- videos & fax available
- fresh flowers
- laundry service, $30 per load
- children over 12 yrs welcome
- honeymoons catered for
- on-site parking

Activities available

- outdoor spa pool on site
- ski drying facilities on site
- snooker table & darts
- in-house exercise machine
- table tennis oudoors
- almost 2ha garden & grounds
- golf clubs & gold-mining pans available for guest use
- walks & hiking
- historic Arrowtown
- numerous restaurants nearby
- wineries; botanic gardens
- golf courses; arts trail
- hot air ballooning; gondola
- fishing; white water rafting
- horse riding; jet boating
- skiing, cross-country skiing & heli-skiing; sky diving
- parapenting & hang gliding
- Milford Sound day trips

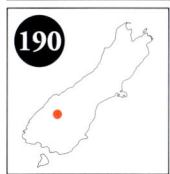

QUEENSTOWN
TWIN PEAKS

Hosts Margaret and Derek Bulman

661 Frankton Road, Queenstown
Phone 0-3-441 8442 *Mobile* 021 685 520 *Fax* 0-3-441 8575
Email bulman@twinpeaks.co.nz *Website* www.twinpeaks.co.nz

Double $300 Single $275 *Includes breakfast*

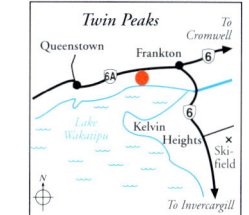

DIRECTIONS: Take SH 6A out of Queenstown. Travel 3km & turn right into Twin Peaks driveway. From Cromwell, take SH 6 towards Queenstown. Continue 2.4km on SH 6A past Frankton to Twin Peaks on left.

Built on the waterfront of the Frankton Arm of Lake Wakatipu, Twin Peaks provides panoramic lake and mountain views. This architecturally designed contemporary home offers two ensuite guestrooms with quality fittings such as the massage shower and marble vanity tops. Both bedrooms include tea and coffee-making facilites, television, fresh flowers and bathrobes. The house is elevated on rock, with schist walls and courtyard garden and is north-facing to catch the all-day sun. Continental or cooked breakfast is served in the dining room at Twin Peaks, with views over the lake to the snowcapped Remarkables. The township of Queenstown is only five minutes' drive away for restaurants, cafés, bars and boutique shopping.

Facilities

- 2 queen ensuite bedrooms
- bathrobes, hair dryers, toiletries, heated floor, heated towel rails, demist mirrors, massage shower rose & marble vanity tops in both ensuite bathrooms
- cotton bed linen
- fresh flowers, tea/coffee facilities & TV in both bedrooms
- phone, fax & email available
- complimentary laundry
- continental or cooked breakfast, in dining room
- complimentary drinks & nibbles
- guest lounge with open fire, TV, video & music
- central heating
- 220º lakefront views
- private guest entrance
- off-street parking

Activities available

- bookings arranged for activities
- mountain bikes available
- walking track to Queenstown
- 4 golf courses, including Millbrook
- TSS *Earnslaw* Steamboat Cruise
- white water rafting
- bungy jumping
- gardens open to visit
- 2 ski-fields within 20-min drive
- Queenstown shops & restaurants, 5-min drive
- jet boating
- parapenting
- wineries
- fishing
- wilderness hikes
- 5-min drive to airport for scenic flights, eg to Milford Sound

QUEENSTOWN
AMOKURA LODGE

Host Jenny Mason

351 Frankton Road, Queenstown
Phone 0-3-441 1175 *Mobile* 027 417 3161 *Fax* 0-3-441 1173
Email enquiries@amokuralodge.co.nz *Website* www.amokuralodge.co.nz

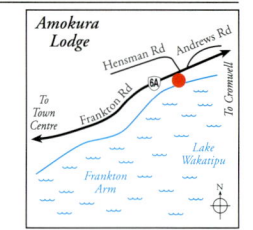

| 4 bdrm | 1 enst | 1 prbth | 1 prbth |

Guest-wing rate $250–$400 *Includes continental breakfast & apéritifs*
Apartment rate $600 *Self-catering in apartment* *Brunch & dinner extra*

DIRECTIONS: From Cromwell, take SH 6 to Frankton. Continue on Frankton Rd (SH 6A) for 7km to Amokura Lodge on left. From Queenstown take SH 6A & travel 2km from PO to Amokura on right.

Overlooking Lake Wakatipu, Amokura Lodge was built in 2003 to provide contemporary accommodation with classically styled interiors. This three-storey home offers a separate guest wing on the middle floor, and a self-contained apartment on the lower floor, both with lake views. There is a home theatre in the guest lounge upstairs, and continental breakfast is served either in the apartment, the upstairs dining room, or alfresco on the terrace. Lunch is available on request, and complimentary pre-dinner wine and cheese are offered, followed by dinner by arrangement. A full kitchen enables apartment guests to self-cater and a barbecue is available in the grassed courtyard. Queenstown restaurants are just a 20-minute lakeside walk away.

Facilities

- 1 self-contained apartment: 2 super-king/twin bedrooms with 1 private bathroom
- 1 guest wing: 1 super-king/twin & 1 twin bedroom share 1 private bathroom
- hair dryers, toiletries, heated towel rails, demist mirrors, heated floors & bathrobes
- cotton bed linen; fresh flowers
- children welcome
- continental breakfast; pre-dinner wine & cheese
- brunch & dinner, extra
- gas fire, Sky TV/video/DVD/CD, artwork, games, books & writing desk in 2 guest lounges
- large sundecks from all levels
- central heating; laundry, email, phone & fax available
- courtesy passenger transfer; off-street parking & garaging

Activities available

- home theatre system
- BBQ; cat on site
- direct access to woodland/lake shore walk to Queenstown, 20-min walk or 10-min bike ride
- scenic & recreational reserves adjacent
- Central Otago wine trails (from door)
- 4 golf courses
- bungy jumping; horse treks
- restaurants, 5 min-drive
- Lake Wakatipu activities from beach access:
  – fishing charters
  – water-skiing
  – jet skiing
  – other watersports
  – picnicking
  – sailing to town
- wilderness hikes; skiing
- scenic flights; parachuting

QUEENSTOWN
BALMORAL LODGE

Hosts Cis and Les Walker

24 York Street, Queenstown *Postal* P O Box 1463, Queenstown
Phone 0-3-442 7209 *Email* balmoral.lodge@xtra.co.nz
Fax 0-3-442 6499 *Website* www.zqnbalmoral.co.nz

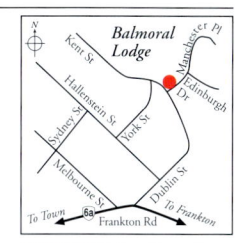

5 bdrm | 5 enst

Room rate $225–$395 *Includes breakfast*

DIRECTIONS: From Cromwell, take SH 6A towards Queenstown. As Frankton Rd approaches township, turn right into Dublin St. At "Give Way" sign, Balmoral Lodge on right.

Balmoral Lodge is situated on Queenstown hill, just 800 metres from the township. The Lodge features panoramic views of the lake, mountains and township from every room. Flowers picked from the rose garden freshen each room. The upstairs honeymoon suite includes a double spa bath and the downstairs family suite opens to the lawn and rose gardens. Guests also enjoy relaxing with complimentary drinks on the sundecks opening from the guest lounge, and the pool room is popular. A full hearty breakfast is served each morning in the dining room, with its picture postcard window overlooking the lake. Balmoral Lodge was designed for guest comfort in 1999 and furnished with antiques. Two friendly cats are in residence.

Facilities

- Honeymoon Suite: 1 king/twin ensuite bedroom & double spa bath
- 1 queen & 1 king ensuite bedroom upstairs; spa bath in king
- Downstairs Suite: 1 queen & 1 twin bedroom, with 2 ensuites
- cotton bed linen, phone jack, TV, tea/coffee & fridge in bedrooms
- hair dryers & toiletries
- phone, fax & email; laundry available
- full hearty breakfast served in dining room
- guest lounge with tea/coffee, Sky TV, video, music, opens to sundecks
- fresh flowers in all rooms
- children welcome
- 2 cats on site
- private guest entrance
- off-street parking

Activities available

- pool room on site
- relaxing in rose garden on site
- luggage storage while guests on walking tracks
- guest activities booked
- boutique shopping, 800m
- walking tracks; tramping
- horse trekking
- fly fishing; jet boating
- gardens open to visit
- restaurants, 800-metre walk
- tandem & single parachuting
- gondola; Fly by Wire
- scenic flights
- bungy jumping
- Lake Wakatipu trips
- kayaking; rafting
- skiing & heliskiing
- Queenstown Gardens

QUEENSTOWN
QUEENSTOWN HOUSE
A SMALL HOTEL

Host Louise Kiely

69 Hallenstein Street, Queenstown
Phone 0-3-442 9043   *Email* queenstown.house@xtra.co.nz
Fax 0-3-442 8755   *Website* www.queenstownhouse.co.nz

14 bdrm   14 enst

Double $250–$595
Single $225

Includes breakfast
Dinner extra

DIRECTIONS: 300 metres from Queenstown P.O. Take Ballarat St north to "T" junction. Turn left into Hallenstein St. Queenstown House is on the right, on the corner of Malaghan St.

Established in 1982, Queenstown House was refurbished in 2002 with the addition of four new rooms plus two suites. Guests have the choice of the original ensuite guestrooms in the main house, or either of the new private suites, each with a fireside sitting room, leather lounge suite, lakeview deck, laundry and kitchenette. A deluxe breakfast menu catering to all tastes is offered in the lakeview dining room. Guests are invited to a pre-dinner social hour each evening, hosted in the fireside sitting room or alfresco in the courtyard, where experiences and restaurant recommendations are shared. Just a four-minute walk to the township, Queenstown House is located in an elevated position overlooking the town and Lake Wakatipu to Walter Peak.

Facilities

- 6 king & 6 queen bedrooms with ensuites
- 2 king suites, 1 honeymoon
- crisp white linen & many fluffy pillows
- TV in each bedroom
- toiletries & hair dryer in each ensuite bathroom
- fireside sitting room
- private oudoor decks
- breakfast in dining room, or room service available
- dinner by prior arrangement
- pre-dinner social hour
- tea & coffee available
- guest laundry or valet service
- email, fax & phone available
- luggage & car storage
- separate guest entrance
- off-street parking

Activities available

- daily excursions planned & arranged by staff
- small weddings & family holidays catered for
- small conference venue
- golf arranged
- 4-min stroll to town for Queenstown shopping
- Queenstown Gardens with tennis & bowling clubs
- restaurants, cafés & bars, 5-min walk
- local & longer walks
- winter ski-fields, transport from door
- landscape painting opportunities
- private gardens to visit
- fishing tours
- winery tours

© Friars' Guide to New Zealand Accommodation for the Discerning Traveller

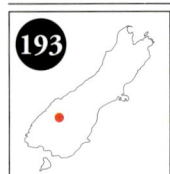

Queenstown
The Glebe

Host Anne Henley

2 Beetham Street, Queenstown   *Phone* 0-3-441 0310
Freephone 0800 484 345   *Fax* 0-3-441 0309
Email stay@theglebe.co.nz   *Website* www.theglebe.co.nz

1, 2, 3 or 4 bdrm   1, 2, 3 or 4 enst   Apartment rate $200–$1,800   *Continental breakfast extra*
Self-catering

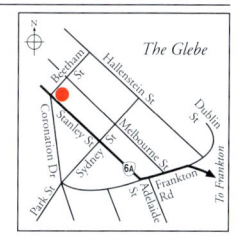

DIRECTIONS: Take SH 6A into Queenstown. Frankton Rd continues into Stanley St. Travel to Beetham St. Glebe on right-hand corner.

The Glebe offers 38 spacious apartments, each containing a fully equipped kitchen, balcony, and a choice of one to four bedrooms, with spa baths in 11 of the ensuites. The 632-square metre penthouse apartment (6,800 square feet) has wide lake views, four ensuite bedrooms, its own gymnasium, sauna, spa pool and home theatre system. Located between two churches, The Glebe features two landscaped courtyards, and its name refers to the church-land where abundant natural produce was raised. Now set in the heart of Queenstown, a wide variety of restaurants are within walking distance, and a continental breakfast can be delivered to the apartments. The Glebe overlooks Lake Wakatipu, with views to Cecil and Walter Peaks.

Facilities
- 38 self-contained apartments
- 2 1-bedroom, 15 2-bedroom 18 3-bedroom & 3 4-bedroom apartments, including penthouse
- 1–4 ensuites per apartment, with hair dryers, toiletries, heated floor, demist mirrors & double basins
- phone, TV, writing desk & tea/coffee in all apartments
- 1 communal guest lounge with open fireplace; fresh flowers
- continental breakfast in apartments, $12 pp
- full kitchen for self-catering per apartment
- balcony, spa bath, double shower, Sky TV, video, CD-player & artwork in most apartments
- email & fax available
- children welcome
- garaging

Activities available
- BBQ available
- boules/pétanque on site
- in-house gymnasium
- walking, hiking & trekking
- native bird-watching
- white water rafting
- fly fishing; hunting
- private gardens to visit
- Queenstown Botanic Gardens
- many restaurants & cafés within walking distance
- golf courses; lake cruises
- steamboat trips on lake
- flightseeing; heliskiing
- bungy jumping
- hot air ballooning
- vineyards & wine tastings
- Queenstown airport, 10-min drive

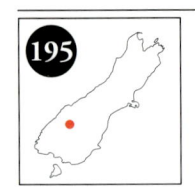

Queenstown
The Chambers Apartment

Manager Steve Lindsay

Level 3, Chambers Suites, 50 Stanley Street, Queenstown
Postal P O Box 2339, Queenstown   *Mobile* 021 454 417   *Fax* 0-3-442 2769
Email service@thechambers.co.nz   *Website* www.thechambers.co.nz

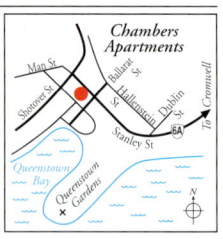

3 bdrm | 1 enst | 1 prbth   Apartment rate $750   Self-catering   Chef extra

DIRECTIONS: Take SH 6A into Queenstown. Frankton Rd continues into Stanley St. Travel through roundabout at Ballarat St. Chambers Suites on left of Stanley St. Take elevator to 3rd floor to Apartment.

Located in the heart of Queenstown, The Chambers Suites were purpose built in 2002. Elevator access takes guests to the third floor where the self-contained unhosted apartment opens to a private balcony overlooking the Queenstown Village Green, Horne Creek and Lake Wakatipu to the snow-capped mountains beyond. The Chambers Apartment features contemporary interior design. Six guests can be accommodated in three bedrooms, complemented by two bathrooms, a spacious lounge, dining area and self-catering kitchen. The pantry can be pre-stocked according to guests' requests and a chef can be provided. Small business meetings, corporate gatherings, weddings and other social functions can be catered.

Facilities
- one-party booking only
- 1 king & 2 super-king/twin bedrooms
- main bedroom includes ensuite, dressing room, writing desk, phone & wheelchair access
- quality bed linen
- hair dryers, toiletries, demist mirrors & heated floors in bathrooms
- spa bath in 1 bathroom
- full kitchen for self-catering
- chef available by request
- guest lounge with Sky TV, DVD, CD-player, email, phone & fax
- balcony opens from lounge
- lake & mountain views
- guest laundry
- children over 9 yrs welcome
- off-street parking

Activities available
- meetings/functions catered
- child-minding services on request
- in-room professional body therapy by arrangement
- restaurant & bar, ground floor
- Queenstown Gardens
- white water rafting; jet-boating
- bungy jumping; scenic flights
- long or short distance tramping & hiking
- many restaurants, cafés, & bars within walking distance
- boutique shopping, theatres, art galleries, short stroll away
- private garden tours
- horse trekking
- winter skiing; snowboarding
- Lake Wakatipu cruises
- Milford & Doubtful Sounds day excursions

© Friars' Guide to New Zealand Accommodation for the Discerning Traveller

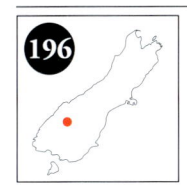

ARTHURS POINT, QUEENSTOWN
SHOTOVER LODGE

Hosts Jeanette and Steve Brough

61 Atley Road, Arthurs Point, R D 1, Queenstown
Phone 0-3-441 8037 *Email* luxury@shotoverlodge.com
Fax 0-3-441 8058 *Website* www.shotoverlodge.com

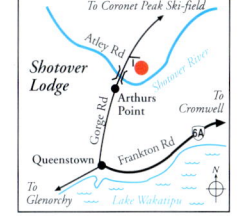

Double $478
Single $433

Includes breakfast
Dinner extra

DIRECTIONS: From Queenstown, take Gorge Rd towards Coronet Peak. Cross historic stone bridge & travel 500m. Turn right into Atley Rd. Take right fork to Shotover Lodge on left.

Steve and Jeanette are past winners of a New Zealand Tourism Award. Guests enjoy the tranquil rural location of Shotover Lodge (*see above right*), which is still only five minutes' drive to Queenstown. The atmosphere is that of an elegant country house on the clifftop above the Shotover River dramatically below. The design of the Lodge as a collection of buildings enhances privacy. Spacious suites, each with a private balcony or coutyard, are detached from the main Lodge where cuisine is a top priority. The Shotover Jet, horse riding, white water rafting and restaurants are within walking distance. Hiking and mountain biking trails lead directly from the Lodge, which is close to Coronet Peak ski resort. Flights to Milford Sound are popular.

Facilities
- 5 suites – king/queen or twin beds, each with ensuite
- hair dryers, bathrobes, heated towel rails & toiletries in ensuites
- private balcony or coutyard opens from all rooms
- quality cotton bed linen & electric blankets on all beds
- tea/coffee, fridge with NZ wines, mineral water & juices, TV, direct-dial phone & fresh flowers
- contemporary dining, extra; espresso coffee
- complimentary pre-dinner drinks & hors d'ouevres
- guest lounge with log fire
- bar & wine cellar
- snooker room & library
- reservations service/advice
- wedding planning service
- drying room

Activities available
- jacuzzi with mountain views; massage/beauty treatments
- helipad, 2-min drive away
- 18-hole golf course, 10-min drive
- walk to Shotover Jet, white-water rafting, horse riding & hiking trails
- scenic flights to Milford Sound
- art & crafts trail near lodge
- day spa, 10-min drive
- ski resort entrance, 2-min drive
- 4 restaurants, short walk
- fly fishing, guides available
- spin-fishing & trolling, boat available
- Lake Wakatipu excursions
- wine tasting & vineyards
- museums; mountain biking
- tours to Skippers Canyon
- special interest tours; Shotover Safaris

ARTHURS POINT, QUEENSTOWN
TRELAWN PLACE

Hosts Nery Howard and Michael Clark

Gorge Rd, Arthurs Point, Queenstown   *Phone* 0-3-442 9160
Postal P O Box 117, Queenstown   *Fax* 0-3-442 9160
Email trelawn@ihug.co.nz   *Website* www.trelawnb-b.co.nz

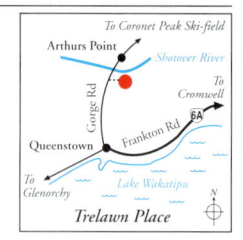

| 7 bdrm | 5 enst | 2 prbth | 1 pdrm | **Room rate** $210–$350 | *Includes breakfast* |

DIRECTIONS: Take SH 6A into Queenstown. At 2nd roundabout turn into Gorge Rd. Travel 4km towards Arthurs Point. Trelawn Place signposted beside gate on right.

Sited dramatically above the Shotover River, Trelawn Place is a secluded rural retreat, yet only four kilometres from Queenstown. Landscaped gardens and lawns sweep to the cliff-edge overlooking the jet boating with views to the mountains beyond. Guests can choose accommodation from five ensuite bedrooms in the house either upstairs or down, three with four-poster beds, including the bridal suite. And the separate honeymoon stone cottage is also available, complete with roses framing the door. The verandahs clad in wisteria, clematis and grape, and the gardens are popular for weddings. Breakfasts are served in cosy homely farmhouse style in the breakfast room in the house looking out to the gardens.

Facilities
- 1 king/twin & 3 king bedrooms, each with ensuite, TV, fridge & tea/coffee
- 1 queen ensuite bedroom
- 1 cottage, with 2 bedrooms, 2 bathrooms & laundry
- hair dryers, toiletries & robes
- quality bed linen, wool or featherdown duvets, underlays & electric blankets
- balconies & patios with views
- hearty cooked English breakfast, with home-grown preserves
- breakfast room with coal range
- tea/coffee always available
- guest lounge with schist fireplace, music & books
- fresh flowers from garden
- guest laundry; guest computer
- ski drying area; guest carparks
- friendly frisbee-playing corgis

Activities available
- seats in 1ha (2-acre) gardens
- Michael, an "Orvis endorsed" guide, available for river fishing
- complete wedding package
- bookings arranged – guests collected from Trelawn
- river access & scenic walks from site
- en route to Coronet Peak ski-field, 6km away
- Botanic Gardens; lake cruises
- Queenstown restaurants, cafés & shops, 5-min drive
- gold panning & jet boating on Shotover River below
- international golf courses
- winery & garden tours
- trout fishing trips
- helicopter transfers from Trelawn's lawn to Milford Sound or heli-skiing fields
- adrenalin adventure activities

QUEENSTOWN
THE DAIRY GUESTHOUSE

Host Elspeth Zemla

10 Isle Street, Queenstown *Postal* P O Box 773, Queenstown
Freephone 0800 333 393 *Phone* 0-3-442 5164 *Mobile* 025 204 2585
Fax 0-3-442 5164 *Email* info@thedairy.co.nz *Website* www.thedairy.co.nz

13 bdrm | 13 enst | 1 pdrm Room rate $265–$355 *Includes breakfast*

DIRECTIONS: Take SH 6A to Queenstown. Continue along Stanley St. Turn left into Memorial St, then right into Camp St. Turn left into Isle St. The Dairy Guesthouse is on the left on corner of Isle St & Brecon St.

The Dairy Guesthouse takes its name from the original 1920s corner store or dairy, where breakfasts are now served. Built around the dairy, the Guest House now offers 13 spacious bedrooms, mostly super-king/twin size. The Dairy Guesthouse was recently upgraded with new beds, quality linen, Italian fittings in the bathrooms, and soft furnishings. There are two private balconies and most guestrooms have views of Lake Wakatipu, Coronet Peak, The Remarkables, or Queenstown township with the mountain range beyond. The new host, Elspeth, welcomes guests with her home-baked afternoon teas. The Dairy Guest House is located centrally, within walking distance of the bars and restaurants in Queenstown.

Facilities
- 13 ensuite bedrooms
- 7 ensuites include bath
- views from all bedrooms
- hair dryers, bathrobes & full-length mirrors in each bedroom
- large guest lounge with open fire
- underfloor heating
- laundry service arranged
- cooked breakfast served
- private library
- guest internet access
- phone & fax available
- 6-seater hydrotherapy spa pool
- ski storage
- off-street parking
- passenger transfer arranged

Activities available
- gondola to Skyline restaurant, adjacent
- many restaurants, cafés, bars & shops within walking distance
- *Earnslaw* steamer on Lake Wakatipu
- local wineries & vineyard tours
- alpine winter sports
- Milford Sounds day trips
- Queenstown Botanic Gardens
- Dart River jet boats
- walks
- fishing
- helicopter flights
- bungy jumping
- garden tours
- sightseeing
- eco-tourism
- golf courses
- winter skiing

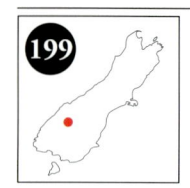

Queenstown
Brown's Boutique Hotel

Hosts Nigel and Bridget Brown

26 Isle Street, Queenstown
Phone 0-3-441 2050   *Mobile* 025 222 0681   *Fax* 0-3-441 2060
Email stay@brownshotel.co.nz   *Website* www.brownshotel.co.nz

10 bdrm   10 enst   1 pdrm
Double $240
Single $200
Includes continental breakfast

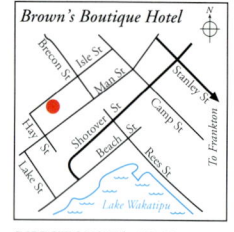

DIRECTIONS: Take SH 6A to Queenstown. Continue along Stanley St. Turn left into Man St, then right into Brecon St. Turn left into Isle St. Brown's Boutique Hotel is on left.

Designed by architect Maurice Orr along traditional European lines, with thick solid walls, this intimate Hotel is sited in the older part of Queenstown above the bay, just a three-minute walk from the centre of town. Brown's Boutique Hotel offers 10 king-size ensuite guestrooms, eight of which include baths, and all rooms have television, phone, and tea and coffee making facilities. The upstairs rooms open to Juliet balconies with views of the Remarkables Mountain Range and Queenstown Bay, and the downstairs rooms open to a paved walled courtyard with outdoor fireplace. A continental buffet breakfast is offered in the dining room downstairs or alfresco in the courtyard, and the adjoining guest lounge features an open fire.

Facilities

- 10 super-king/twin ensuite bedrooms, 8 with baths
- cotton bed linen, phone, TV & tea/coffee in each bedroom
- hair dryer, bathrobes, toiletries
- sunny, private Juliet balcony from each bedroom
- guest lounge with open fire, tea/coffee, TV, video, CD-player, artwork & library
- wheelchair access
- continental breakfast served in dining room
- powder room
- central heating
- email & fax available
- Norman, the cat, on site
- laundry service available
- downstairs living areas open to walled courtyard
- off-street parking

Activities available

- European-style courtyard with outside fireplace on site
- gondola, 1-min walk
- downtown Queenstown shops, 3-min walk downhill
- jet boating
- rafting
- bungy jumping
- horse riding
- garden tours
- large variety of Queenstown bars, cafés & restaurants
- lake cruises
- kayaking
- Botanic Gardens
- historic Arrowtown, 15 mins
- mountain walks
- Remarkables, 45-min drive
- Coronet Peak winter skiing, 20-min drive away

© Friars' Guide to New Zealand Accommodation for the Discerning Traveller   488

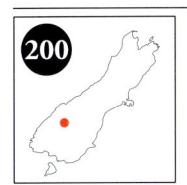

QUEENSTOWN
BRUNSWICK IN QUEENSTOWN
APARTMENT ACCOMMODATION

Manager Julie Edwards

15 Brunswick Street, Queenstown *Phone* 0-9-524 4828
Postal 34C Arney Crescent, Remuera, Auckland *Fax* 0-9-524 4828
Email info@brunswick.co.nz *Website* www.brunswick.co.nz

Apartment rate $630 *Self-catering*
Extra persons $75 each *Breakfast extra*

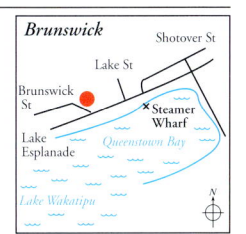

3 bdrm | 3 enst

DIRECTIONS: From The Steamer Wharf Village in central Queenstown, take the Lake Esplanade away from the town. Turn right up Brunswick Street. Apartment on right.

Brunswick is a self-contained, fully serviced apartment nestled in an alpine garden, above Lake Wakatipu, in the heart of Queenstown. This architectural-award winning apartment is offered for single-party bookings to provide privacy, security, comfort and independence. Brunswick's spacious interiors feature liberal use of local stone for the flooring, heavy timbers, original artwork, antique furniture, and a small library. The windows from each room frame spectacular vistas over the lake to the mountain ranges beyond. An outdoor terrace, barbecue area and private spa house enhance the atmosphere of tranquillity and seclusion, yet Brunswick is only five minutes' walk from downtown Queenstown with its busy nightlife and restaurants.

Facilities

- single-party bookings only for 1, 2, or 3-bedroom apartment
- 1 king bedroom with dressing room & ensuite bathroom
- 1 queen ensuite bedroom
- 1 twin bedroom with 3 single beds & ensuite
- hair dryers, toiletries, bathrobes
- quality bed linen
- daily servicing; guest laundry
- breakfast available, extra
- fully equipped kitchen
- spacious dining area for 10
- entertainment system
- underfloor heating; open fire
- lofts & ski drying room
- interior access garage
- electronic security system
- direct-dial phones, fax & modem connections

Activities available

- spa house on site
- barbecue area on site
- over 100 restaurants, cafés & wine bars in walking distance
- private garden tours
- local international ski resorts
- shopping nearby
- tramping
- golf
- adventure activities
- vineyards
- nature walks
- heliskiing
- hunting
- fishing
- tennis
- horse trekking
- botanic gardens
- jet boating

489

© Friars' Guide to New Zealand Accommodation for the Discerning Traveller

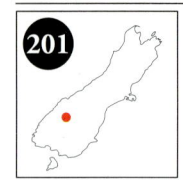

Queenstown
Punatapu

Hosts Dr Patrick and Sue Farry

1113 Glenorchy Road, Queenstown   *Phone* 0-3-442 6624
Postal P O Box 1252, Queenstown   *Fax* 0-3-442 6229
Email info@punatapu.co.nz   *Website* www.punatapu.com

| 7 bdrm | 5 enst | 1 prbth |

Room rate $585–$1,000
Lodge rate $6,500

Includes breakfast & dinner
Self-catering in Studio

DIRECTIONS: From Queenstown, take Lake Esplanade towards Glenorchy. Continue on Glenorchy Rd for 12km to Punatapu. A large rock on left of road with 'Punatapu' in brass lettering marks the entrance.

Set in a pristine alpine landscape surrounded by dramatic mountains, Punatapu, meaning "sacred springs", provides a tranquil retreat in a natural environment. Guests can experience the exclusivity of a private estate, personalised service and New Zealand cuisine prepared by the in-house chef who uses the best local produce served with award-winning wines. Four individually styled guest suites surround a central courtyard with mountain views. Punatapu is owned and operated by New Zealanders, Sue and Pat, who have 30 years' expertise which they are happy to share in co-ordinating activities in and around Queenstown and Fiordland. A scenic 12-kilometre drive from Queenstown along the edge of Lake Wakatipu takes guests to Punatapu.

Facilities

- Punatapu Suite: 1 super-king/twin ensuite bedroom, open fire, sauna & private courtyard; wheelchair access
- Cove Room: 1 king/twin ensuite bedroom upstairs with verandah
- The Stable: 1 small queen bedroom with ensuite upstairs
- The Barn Studio: 1 super-king/twin ensuite bedroom with kitchenette for self-catering
- Family Suite: 2 king/twin & 1 double bedroom with private bathroom & snooker/billiards room
- formal indoor & casual outdoor dining, courtyard kitchen/culinary school
- guest lounge with open fireplace & music
- phone, fax & internet access
- laundry facilities; helipad

Activities available

- in-house books, CDs & video library & art gallery
- artist in residence, Jan.–April
- in-house physiotherapist & doctor; fully equipped gym
- spa pool, heated swimming pool & massage therapy on site
- private hiking trail with mountain & lake views
- 10ha grounds, waterways, native bush, bird & wildlife
- summer: jet boating, fishing, rafting, kayaking, canyoning, hiking, walking, scenic tours, nature excursions, farmtours, horse riding, mountain biking, para-penting, hangliding, ballooning & bungy jumping
- winter: heliskiing, snow boarding, snow-mobiling, downill & cross country skiing
- Queenstown, 12km drive

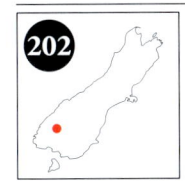

TE ANAU, FIORDLAND
TAKARO LODGE

Hosts Vesna and Tom Thiele

914 Takaro Road, Te Anau   *Postal* P O Box 225, Te Anau
Phone 0-3-249 0083   *Email* contact@takarolodge.com
Fax 0-3-249 0087   *Website* www.takarolodge.com

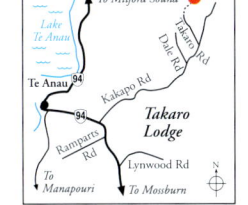

Apartment rate $1,435–$1,660   Includes breakfast & dinner / Lunch extra

DIRECTIONS: From Queenstown or Dunedin, take SH 94 towards Te Anau. 5km before Te Anau, turn right into Kakapo Rd. Travel 15km, then turn left into Takaro Rd. Travel 6.4km to Takaro Lodge gate & driveway.

Takaro Lodge is a peaceful luxury retreat in a *Lord of the Rings* location, with views of the Upukerora River and snow-capped mountains of Fiordland National Park. Offering rejuvenating spa treatments, the masseurs at Takaro Lodge specialise in multi-hands energizing massages. Guests can relax and re-energize in the 10 turf-roofed apartments, individually designed, furnished and coloured according to the Five Chinese Elements – wood, water, fire, metal and earth. Spa facilities include the large indoor heated ozone-purified swimming pool, jacuzzi, steam sauna, fitness room and Energy Clinic spa. The cuisine is prepared by Chinese and Western chefs using mainly organic produce grown on site. Multiple-night stays ensure maximum health benefits.

Facilities
- 10 apartments each with 1 king or 2 queen ensuite bedrooms
- hair dryer, toiletries, heated towel rails, demist mirror & bathrobes in all 10 ensuites
- spa bath or massage showers
- balcony, tea/coffee, nibbles, bar, suround-sound home theatre TV, DVD, CDs, writing desk, 3 phones & high-speed internet access in each apartment
- breakfast & dinner served in dining room or apartment
- lunch menu by arrangement
- children welcome; fresh flowers; central heating
- aquariums in 2 apartments
- open fires in 8 apartments
- German, French, Croatian, Chinese & Slovenian spoken
- car valet

Activities available
- heated swimming & spa pools; steam sauna & fitness centre
- spa treatments; 2–10-hands therapeutic massage
- small conferences, weddings & honeymoons catered
- helipad & airstrip on site
- 1,052-ha grounds with BBQ, surrounded by hills & forest for trekking, mountain biking & horse riding
- native bird-watching & fishing on site
- hiking in Fiordland National Park; Milford, Doubtful Sound, Routeburn & Kepler tracks
- golfing in Te Anau
- scenic flights
- glow-worm caves
- Te Anau township, 30km
- Queenstown, 175km north

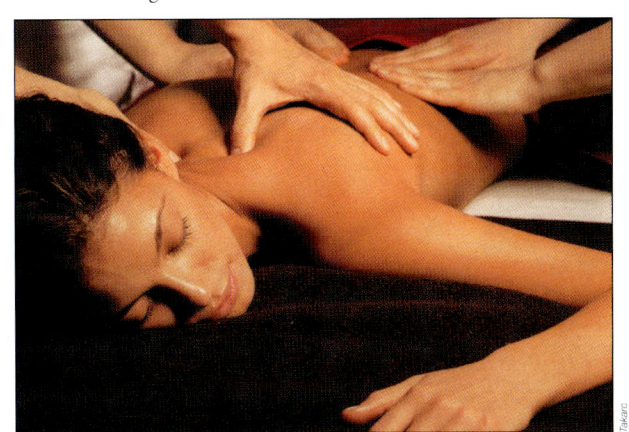

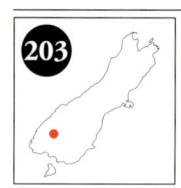

Te Anau, Fiordland
Mt Prospect High Country Homestead

Hosts Joan and Ross Cockburn

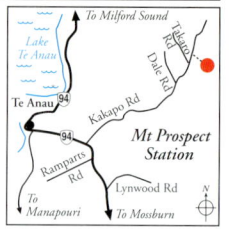

1338 Kakapo Road, Te Anau *Postal* Mt Prospect Station, R D 2, Te Anau
Phone 0-3-249 7082 *Email* prospect@fiordland.net.nz
Fax 0-3-249 7085 *Website* friars.co.nz/hosts/prospect.html

4 bdrm / 4 enst

Room rate $260–$390
Multiple-night rates available

Includes breakfast & farm tour
Lunch & dinner platter extra

DIRECTIONS: From Queenstown or Dunedin, take SH 94 towards Te Anau. 5km before Te Anau, turn right into Kakapo Rd. Travel 16km, then turn right into Mt Prospect Station.

Mt Prospect Station portrays a whole farm experience on a working sheep station of 3,400 hectares (8,500 acres). A guided activity programme with working dogs, sheep and cattle is included in the package. Originally built in 1971, this large country homestead was extensively altered and refurbished to provide guest comfort in 2000. The high-country station has been in the Cockburn family since 1913, and scenic drives are always popular up Mt Prospect on the property to view the Te Anau basin to Lakes Te Anau and Manapouri beyond, from a height of 1,000 metres. In addition guests have superb views of the Murchison mountains and Mt Luxmore from the homestead and expansive garden. Guests enjoy dining at a nearby country restaurant.

Facilities

- private guest wing & entrance
- 4 king ensuite bedrooms
- heated towel rails & hair dryers
- French doors open to private patios from each bedroom
- complimentary laundry
- internet, email & fax available
- children welcome; peaceful secluded setting
- check-in from 4pm
- full breakfast in dining room
- light lunch $15 pp, by request
- light gourmet dinner platter with wine, $35 pp
- vegetarians catered for
- TV, piano & music in lounge
- rural views
- expansive country garden
- passenger transfers to/from Te Anau, $15 pp each way

Activities available

- guided activity programme on Simmental stud cattle farm
- seasonal activities with merino sheep, cattle & working dogs
- drive 1,000m up Mt Prospect on site, for scenic views of Fiordland
- farm & bush walks
- on-site trout fishing in Whitestone River, guide by arrangement
- fishing in Lakes Te Anau & Manapouri
- local country restaurant, 10-min drive
- Lake Te Anau & Te Anau township, 21km
- Milford & Doubtful Sounds day trips
- Milford, Routeburn & Kepler tramping tracks
- Fiordland National Heritage Park; flightseeing
- Queenstown, 170km north

© Friars' Guide to New Zealand Accommodation for the Discerning Traveller

LAKE TE ANAU, FIORDLAND
TE ANAU LODGE

Manager pending

52 Howden Street, Te Anau
Phone 0-3-249 7477 *Mobile* 021 230 7502 *Fax* 0-3-249 7487
Email info@teanaulodge.com *Website* www.teanaulodge.com

Room rate $180–$230
Lodge rate available
Includes breakfast

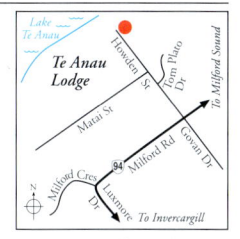

7 bdrm 6 enst 1 prbth

DIRECTIONS: Take SH 94 to Te Anau. Continue on Luxmore Drive towards town centre. Turn right into Milford Rd. Turn left into Howden St. Travel to Te Anau Lodge on right at end.

Set in over two hectares of newly established parkland stretching towards the lake, Te Anau Lodge offers guests seven bedrooms, each with a bathroom. The Lodge is suitable for large-party bookings, and is close to Te Anau township. There are four guestrooms upstairs with mountain views, and a spacious guest lounge with balcony overlooking the lake. Downstairs are three more bedrooms. Built in 1936 as a convent, the Lodge was re-located to Te Anau in 2003, and totally renovated to provide accommodation. The interiors still include the original oak panelling with rimu battening and polished timber floors. A full breakfast selection is served in the dining room, which features the stained glass windows of the original chapel.

Facilities
- 1 super-king/twin & 1 double bedroom upstairs each with ensuite & spa bath
- 1 queen/twin bedroom upstairs, private bathroom & bathrobes
- 1 twin ensuite bedroom upstairs
- 3 queen bedrooms downstairs, each with ensuite
- hair dryers, toiletries, heated towel rails & demist mirrors
- 1 guide's room with ensuite
- full breakfast served in chapel
- open fire, tea/coffee, TV, video, CDs, games & desk in guest lounge/library upstairs
- fresh flowers in rooms
- central heating
- phone, fax & email in office
- phone jacks in guestrooms
- complimentary guest laundry
- on-site parking & garaging

Activities available
- 2.3ha landscaped grounds
- access to Lake Te Anau
- bird-watching
- kayaking
- farm tours
- scenic flights; hunting
- glow-worm caves
- brown & rainbow trout fishing
- Te Anau township, 3 mins
- restaurants, 3-min drive
- 300km walking tracks in Fiordland National Park
- gardens open to visit
- Milford, Routeburn, Kepler & Hollyford hiking tracks
- Doubtful Sound day trips
- Lake Manapouri, 30 mins
- Queenstown, 2 hours north
- Invercargill City, 160km south

© Friars' Guide to New Zealand Accommodation for the Discerning Traveller

LAKE TE ANAU, FIORDLAND
FIORDLAND LODGE

Hosts Robynne and Ron Peacock

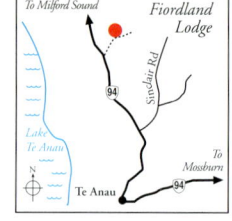

472 Te Anau-Milford Highway, Te Anau *Postal* P O Box 196, Te Anau
Phone 0-3-249 7832 *Email* info@fiordlandlodge.co.nz
Fax 0-3-249 7449 *Website* www.fiordlandlodge.co.nz

14 bdrm | 10 enst | 2 prbth
Lodge room rate $460–$980 Includes breakfast & dinner for Lodge
Cabin rate $240–$340 for 2 persons Includes breakfast for Cabins

DIRECTIONS: Take SH 94 to Te Anau. Continue 4.72km north towards Milford Sound. Turn right into driveway at number 472 & travel uphill to Fiordland Lodge & Log Cabins on left.

Fiordland Lodge and Log Cabins are located at Lake Te Anau in a rural setting ensuring peace and quiet, en route to Milford Sound. With panoramic lake views and mountain backdrops, the Lodge is constructed from Oregon logs and local riverstone, and features a spacious lounge with open log fire and soaring ceilings. The Lodge provides 10 ensuite guestrooms, each opening to a balcony, and the two Log Cabins are also available for single parties. Table d'hôte menus of New Zealand cuisine created by the in-house chef are served in the Lodge. Weddings, functions, corporate retreats and small conferences can be catered. Resident guide, Ron Peacock, offers fishing, walking and bird-watching tours in the adjacent Fiordland National Park.

Facilities
- 10 super-king/twin ensuite bedrooms in Lodge, each with writing desk, phone, TV, bathrobes & balcony
- spa bath & private lounge in executive suite in Lodge
- 2 log cabins each with 1 queen bedroom, twin/triple mezzanine, 1 bathroom & lounge
- hair dryers & toiletries
- heated floors/mirrors in ensuites
- full breakfast served in Lodge dining room with lake views
- 3-course table d'hôte dinner in Lodge tariff; licensed
- wheelchair access to Lodge
- children welcome
- fax & email available
- small conferences & weddings
- on-site parking
- helipad

Activities available
- library in Lodge
- guided fly-tying on site
- Lake Te Anau, across road
- guided fishing trips
- brown & rainbow trout fishing
- nature walks & bird-watching
- glow-worm caves
- kayaking; horse trekking
- Milford, Routeburn, Kepler & Hollyford Tracks
- Fiordland National Park
- golf course
- scenic flights & cruises
- hunting
- Te Anau township, 5 mins
- Milford & Doubtful Sound scenic tours
- Milford Sound, 2-hr drive
- Queenstown, 2 hours north
- Invercargill City, 160km

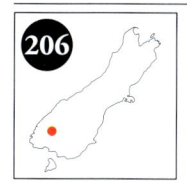

Lake Manapouri, Fiordland
Murrells' Grand View House

Hosts Jack and Klaske Murrell

7 Murrell Avenue, Manapouri   *Phone* 0-3-249 6642
Postal P O Box 7, Manapouri 9660   *Fax* 0-3-249 6966
Email murrell@xtra.co.nz   *Website* www.murrells.co.nz

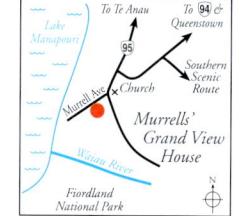

Double $250–$270   Single $230–$250   *Includes breakfast*

3 bdrm   3 enst

DIRECTIONS: Take SH 94 towards Te Anau. Turn left to Manapouri. Opposite the church, turn right into Murrell Ave. Murrells' Grand View House on left.

Built as an accommodation house by Jack's grandparents in 1889, this colonial guesthouse continues to be restored by Jack and Klaske. The nineteenth-century ambience is enhanced by the original oil paintings in the guest library and the historic photographs of the area. Jack is New Zealand's longest operating host, having lived in Murrells' Grand View House since 1934, with Klaske joining him in 1987. Named because of its uninterrupted vistas of Lake Manapouri and the mountains beyond, Murrells' offers three ensuite bedrooms, all with views. Complimentary refreshments are offered on guests' arrival, alfresco on the lawn overlooking the lake, or by the fire in the guest sitting room. Full breakfasts are served in the dining room.

Facilities
- 1 king/twin & 2 queen ensuite bedrooms
- bathrobes, hair dryers, heated towel rails in ensuites
- tea/coffee in bedrooms
- mountain & lake views
- fresh flowers
- phone & fax available
- unsuitable for children
- laundry, $10 per load
- complimentary refreshments on guests' arrival
- full breakfast served in dining room
- open fire in guest lounge
- historic artwork
- Jack speaks basic German & Spanish
- on-site parking
- helipad

Activities available
- reading in library by fire
- relaxing on verandah in sun
- feeding pet deer on site
- swimming in Lake Manapouri, 2-min walk
- kayak & canoe hire
- lake & sea kayaking
- fishing, guides available
- scenic flights by helicopter or fixed-wing
- gateway to Doubtful Sound, reservations essential
- Milford Sound day trips
- Fiordland National Park walking tracks
- day trips on Kepler track & Circle track
- Lake Te Anau, 20km
- Invercargill, 160km south
- Queenstown, 180km north

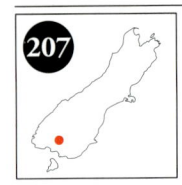

BALFOUR, GORE
BRENTLEIGH HOMESTEAD

Hosts Brian and Mary Dillon   *Mobile* 0274 578 186

1032 Riversdale-Ardlussa Road, Balfour   *Postal* Ardlussa, R D 6, Gore
Freephone 0800 202 018   *Phone* 0-3-201 6166   *Fax* 0-3-201 6168
Email bdillon@esi.co.nz   *Website* www.brentleigh.co.nz

| 3 bdrm | 2 enst | 1 prbth |

Double $265–$325
Single $180–$250

Includes breakfast, cocktail hour, dinner & farm tour
Lunch extra

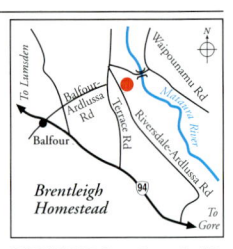

DIRECTIONS: From Gore, take SH 94 towards Balfour. Travel 33km, then turn right into Riversdale-Ardlussa Rd. Travel 10.32km to Brentleigh Homestead on right.

Brentleigh Homestead is located on a 376-hectare (929-acre) mixed farm 30 minutes from Gore. The farm includes 250 hectares of cereal crops such as wheat, barley, oats and peas, and grazing for sheep, dairy heifers, cattle and deer, and diversified into growing paeonies as well. The Mataura River runs through the farm and is famous for its brown trout fishing. There are a further 10 rivers nearby and fishing guides can be arranged. Set in a large country garden with 1,000 paeonies flowering through November and December, Brentleigh Homestead was built in 1950 in the typical brick and rough cast of the era, with verandahs added in 2000. Country kitchen cuisine is provided with varied menus served in the dining room or alfresco on the patio.

Facilities
- 2 detached queen/twin ensuite bedrooms with tea/coffee facilities & verandah
- 1 queen/twin bedroom upstairs, with private bathroom, spa bath & robes
- hair dryer, heated towel rails & toiletries in bathrooms
- cotton bed linen & mineral water in bedrooms
- complimentary laundry
- light/full cooked breakfast
- light lunch, $12 pp
- 2–3-course country kitchen dinner with wine
- guest lounge with open fire, tea/coffee, Sky TV, video & library
- sunroom for reading & TV
- email, fax & phone
- on-site parking

Activities available
- farm tour on site
- large country garden with 1,000 paeonies on site
- Jack Russell dog, Jac, on site
- barbecue available
- fishing on site, in Mataura River
- 9-hole golf courses, 3 courses within 20-min drive
- garden tours
- hiking; winter skiing
- Balfour village, 5-min drive
- trout fishing, guides arranged
- vintage aircraft at Mandeville
- Te Anau, 1-hour drive west
- Invercargill, 1-hr drive south
- The Catlins, 1 hr south-east
- Queenstown, 1½ hrs north
- Dunedin, 2½ hrs north-east
- Milford Sound, 3 hrs north

WINTON, SOUTHLAND
THE LODGE AT TIKANA

Hosts Donna-Maree Day and Dave Lawrence

374 Livingstone Road, Browns, R D 1, Winton
Phone 0-3-236 4117   *Email* info@tikana.co.nz
Fax 0-3-236 4117   *Website* www.tikana.co.nz

2 bdrm / 1 enst

Double $1,400
Single $1,015

Includes breakfast, dinner & drinks
Extra person $600

DIRECTIONS: Take SH 6 to Winton. Turn east to Mataura. Travel 8km to Browns. Turn right into Limeworks Rd. Travel 1.4km to T junction. Turn left into Livingstone Rd. The Lodge is 1st house on right.

Located on a working deer farm in rural Southland, the Lodge at Tikana provides private accommodation separate from the hosts' residence. Built with straw-bale construction, the Lodge features contemporary interiors with inlaid-timber flooring. The dual-level Lodge is set in a private garden with sundeck overlooking the valley to the rolling hills beyond. The main bedroom and spacious ensuite bathroom are on the mezzanine floor. The living area downstairs includes a surround-sound home theatre, wine cellar, built-in espresso machine and deli nibbles. Antipasto platters and meals are served at the Lodge according to guests' tastes, featuring local seasonal produce such as venison, lamb, blue cod, oysters and whitebait.

Facilities
- single-party bookings
- 1 super-king ensuite bedroom
- 1 double bedroom downstairs
- double bath, double basin, hair dryer, toiletries, bidet & demist mirror in ensuite upstairs
- Egyptian cotton bed linen; bathrobes; possum throw
- fresh flowers; artwork
- underfloor heating throughout
- breakfast or brunch served
- dinner with wine in Lodge
- kitchenette; antipasto platter
- wine cellar with NZ wines
- phone, internet access & desk in Snug
- open fire, home theatre system, Sky TV, DVDs, CDs
- laundry, wash & fold service
- on-site parking; helipad

Activities available
- Wapiti deer stud, thoroughbred horses & farm walks on site
- lawn tennis court on site
- outdoor spa pool on site
- 4WD safaris
- eco-tourism/wilderness trips
- heritage/arts day trips
- scenic flightseeing
- guided fly fishing
- day spa available on site
- wilderness jet boating on Wairaurahiri River
- Manderville vintage aircraft restoration museum
- Tiger Moth flights
- Fiordland day trips
- Stewart Island day trips
- Winton 9.5km north-west
- Invercargill, 30 mins south
- Queenstown, 1½ hours north

WINTON, SOUTHLAND
THE OAKS LODGE

Hosts Lynn and John Frew

453 Norman Road, R D 1, Winton
Phone 0-3-236 0646 Mobile 025 362 270 Fax 0-3-236 9664
Email john@southnet.co.nz Website friars.co.nz/hosts/theoaks.html

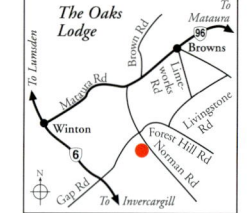

3 bdrm 1 prbth

Room rate $280   Includes breakfast   Lunch extra

DIRECTIONS: From Queenstown or Invercargill, take SH 6 to Winton. Turn east into SH 96 (Mataura Rd) & travel about 5km. Turn right into Norman Rd, & travel 3km to The Oaks Lodge on right.

In a rural setting with views over rolling countryside to the Hokonui hills, The Oaks Lodge is surrounded by two hectares (five acres) of landscaped gardens. Built in 1995, the Lodge has an upper floor for the exclusive use of guests, with two queen bedrooms and an extra bedroom for children. There are three separate lounges, one upstairs and two down, and breakfast is served in the dining room, with French doors opening to the patio. Guests are invited to share pre-dinner drinks and nibbles with the hosts, and restaurants are nearby. A light lunch is available by arrangement. The Oaks Lodge is set on a 10-hectare deer farm, with a walking track through native podocarp forest to a bush reserve nearby. Fly-fishing is also popular with guests.

Facilities
- private-party bookings only
- upstairs guest floor includes 2 queen bedrooms, bathroom, 1 children's room & lounge
- bath, hair dryer, toiletries & demist mirror; separate toilet
- cotton bed linen; bathrobes
- children by arrangement
- phone, tea/coffee & nibbles in upstairs lounge
- continental or cooked breakfast served in dining room
- light lunch, extra
- apéritifs & hors d'oeuvres with hosts in lounge
- open fire, TV, CD-player, artwork & books in 3 lounges
- fax & email; fresh flowers
- self-service laundry
- on-site parking; helicopter access

Activities available
- 2ha landscaped garden walks
- lawn tennis
- 10ha deer farm on site
- Forest Hill Reserve walking track, 5-min drive
- river fishing; guide available
- sea fishing & diving charters
- high country farm tours
- gardens open to visit
- Winton, 5-min drive west
- restaurants within 5-min drive
- 18-hole golf course, 5-min drive away
- Southern Scenic Route, 20 mins away
- Tiger Moth flights, 45 mins
- Invercargill, 30 mins south
- Stewart Island, 20-min flight or 1 hour by ferry
- Queenstown or Te Anau, 1½-hour drive

INVERCARGILL
TUDOR PARK COUNTRY STAY AND GARDEN

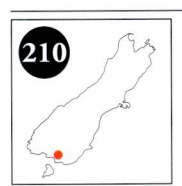

Hosts Joyce and John Robins

21 Lawrence Road, Ryal Bush, R D 6, Invercargill
Phone 0-3-221 7150 *Mobile* 025 310 031 *Fax* 0-3-221 7150
Email tudorparksouth@hotmail.com *Website* www.tudorpark.co.nz

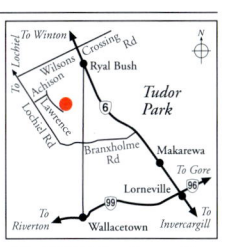

Double $130–$180
Single $100–$120

Includes breakfast
Lunch & dinner extra

DIRECTIONS: From Invercargill, take SH 6 north for 6km. Turn left into Branxholme/Makarewa Rd. Travel 7km & turn right into Achison Rd. Travel 1km & turn right again at "T" junction. Tudor Park 1st on left.

Set in almost two hectares (four acres) of tranquil gardens, Tudor Park is only 15 minutes north of Invercargill City, near the Southern Scenic route. The gardens, featuring two ponds and over 300 old roses, were awarded first prize in the large garden section of the Southern Pride Beautification Competition. This neo-Tudor home has three upstairs bedrooms with garden views, one has a private bathroom with double bath, and the other two have ensuites. Breakfast is served in the dining room downstairs and includes juices, fresh fruit compote, yoghurt, cereals, home-made bread and muffins. Cooked breakfast is also available. Lunch is offered alfresco in the garden in summer, and dinner is available by arrangement, with special diets accommodated.

Facilities
- 1 king/twin ensuite bedroom
- 1 double bedroom with private bathroom including double bath
- hair dryer, bathrobes & toiletries
- cotton bed linen
- fresh flowers in rooms
- supervised children welcome
- lounge with tea/coffee, TV, video, books & artwork
- powder room downstairs
- continental & cooked breakfast served in dining room downstairs
- lunch or picnic, $15 pp
- 3-course dinner with wine, $40–$60 pp
- email, fax & phone available
- laundry available, $5
- off-street parking
- courtesy passenger transfer

Activities available
- 2ha garden walks on site
- viewing horses, dogs, sheep & calves on site
- beef & dairy farm visits
- bush walks
- bird-watching
- private garden visits
- golf nearby
- art gallery featuring NZ art
- museum with NZ tuatara
- restaurants nearby
- fishing nearby
- beaches nearby
- largest old roses planting in NZ
- aluminium smelter
- Winton or Invercargill, 15 mins
- Stewart Island, 20-min flight or 1-hour ferry trip
- Southern Scenic route
- Queenstown or Te Anau, 2 hrs

RIVERTON, SOUTHLAND
NAUTICAL HAVEN

Hosts Gail and Tommy White

9 Ivy Street, Riverton   *Postal* 5 George Street, Riverton, Southland
Phone 0-3-234 8755   *Mobile* 021 159 2758   *Fax* 0-3-234 8755
Email gail.w@ihug.co.nz   *Website* www.harbourviewhouse.biz

House rate $250 for 2 persons
Extra persons $100 each

Self-catering
Breakfast extra

3 bdrm | 1 prbth

DIRECTIONS: From Riverton township take Richard St towards Riverton Rocks. Turn right into Roy St, travel 40m, then turn left into Ivy St. Nautical Haven on left. (Approx. 3km from township.)

Located on the southern coast of New Zealand, Nautical Haven is a fully self-contained house providing single-party bookings for up to six guests. With panoramic views over Foveaux Strait, Nautical Haven has two queen bedrooms opening through French doors to a large deck overlooking the ocean. Originally built circa 1920, Nautical Haven was carefully restored in 2001 to provide self-contained accommodation featuring a nautical theme. There is a fully equipped kitchen for self-catering, or a full breakfast is available by arrangement. A restaurant is within walking distance, and Riverton township is three minutes' drive away. A one-hour historic tour of Riverton, the oldest town in the South Island, is offered in a 1986 classic Mercedes.

Facilities
- private-party bookings only
- 2 queen bedrooms, both with French doors opening to deck & wide ocean views
- 1 twin bedroom
- 1 bathroom with spa bath, hair dryer, toiletries & demist mirror
- bathrobes; cotton bed linen
- marine theme in house & garden
- 180-degree ocean views
- full breakfast available by arrangement, extra
- full kitchen for self-catering
- open fire, TV, CD-player, video, games & books in lounge, opening to deck
- honeymooners welcome
- self-serve laundry
- garaging
- courtesy restaurant transfer

Activities available
- BBQ on site
- 1-hour historic tour in 1986 Mercedes Benz, $50 per trip
- safe swimming beach, 4 mins
- ocean & river watersports
- paua shell factory; art centre
- craft shops; Maori craft studio
- horse trekking, 4km
- scenic walks
- bowling club, 5 mins
- restaurants & cafés, 500m
- heated swimming pool, 5-min drive
- fishing trips; wind surfing
- 9-hole golf course, 5 mins
- heritage trail
- restored working flax mill
- vintage machinery, 6km
- Invercargill, 42-min drive
- Te Anau, 1¾ hour drive

© Friars' Guide to New Zealand Accommodation for the Discerning Traveller

The Catlins
Catlins Farmstay

Hosts June and Murray Stratford

174 Progress Valley Road, South Catlins   *Phone* 0-3-246 8843
Postal R D 1, Tokanui, Southland   *Email* catlinsfarmstay@xtra.co.nz
Fax 0-3-246 8844   *Website* www.catlinsfarmstay.co.nz

3 bdrm | 3 enst

Double $160–$220   *Includes breakfast*   *Dinner extra*
Single $110   Extra persons $50 each

DIRECTIONS: From Balclutha, take coastal route south. Travel 95km & turn left into Progress Valley Rd. Travel 2km to Catlins Farmstay on right. From Invercargill, take inland route, or coastal route via Curio Bay.

Refurbished in 2002, Catlins Farmstay provides hosted accommodation on a genuine working farm. Murray first established the 392-hectare farm (nearly 1,000 acres) in 1966 and has since developed it to run 2,500 sheep, 500 deer and 150 cattle with three sheep dogs. June is locally born and bred and specialises in cooking home-grown meals which she serves in the dining room. Located in the heart of the Catlins, the homestead provides garden views to the surrounding rural forest. Guests enjoy on-site farm tours, brown trout fishing, walking the hills with coastal views, and seasonal farm activities. A 10-minute drive takes guests to the petrified fossil forest at Curio Bay, where dolphins and yellow-eyed penguins can sometimes be seen.

Facilities
- 1 king self-contained suite with writing desk, TV, tea/coffee, kitchenette & sofa bed
- 1 queen & 1 queen/twin bedroom, each with ensuite
- hair dryer & toiletries; heated mirror & floor in 2 bathrooms
- lounge with TV & open fire; piano in dining room
- fresh flowers; central heating
- bedrooms open to gardens
- cooked & continental breakfast in dining room
- 3-course dinner with wine & local produce, $40 pp
- vegetarians catered for
- email, fax & phone, laundry & BBQ available
- children welcome
- on-site parking
- helicopter landing available

Activities available
- large garden on site
- farm tours & seasonal farm activities on site
- tennis court on site
- trout fishing on site
- heritage trail
- Niagara Falls, 2km
- yellow-eyed penguins
- seals & sea lions
- museum, 6km away
- café, 2km drive away
- Hector's dolphins, 10 mins
- petrified fossil forest at Curio Bay, 10-min drive
- McLean & Purakaunui Falls, 20-min drive away
- Cathedral Caves, 25 mins
- Mataura fishing, 30 mins
- Waipapa lighthouse, 30 mins
- Nugget Point, 1½-hour drive

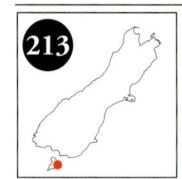

STEWART ISLAND
SAILS ASHORE

Hosts Iris and Peter Tait

11 View Street, Stewart Island   *Phone* 0-3-219 1151
Postal P O Box 66, Stewart Island   *Fax* 0-3-219 1151
Email tait@taliskercharter.co.nz   *Website* www.taliskercharter.co.nz

2 bdrm   2 enst   Suite rate $350   Includes breakfast   Dinner extra

DIRECTIONS: From Bluff, take Foveaux Express catamaran (1hr), or from Invercargill airport take Stewart Island Flights plane (20 mins). Hosts meet guests at wharf or flight depot, with courtesy car to Sails Ashore.

Sails Ashore provides accommodation on remote Stewart Island, a national park featuring native trees, with only 400 residents. To complement their successful charter yacht, Talisker, Iris and Peter have opened accommodation (*see above on right*) with two suites at Sails Ashore. Overlooking Half Moon Bay, Sails Ashore provides easy access to walks and guided tours of the native forest. The bird sanctuary on nearby Ulva Island offers unique opportunities to view native birdlife close at hand, and walk through untouched native bush. Guests enjoy fishing the abundant blue cod, and cruising around inlets and off-shore islands. There are good restaurants within minutes of Sails Ashore, and the mainland is a half-hour flight away, or one hour by sea.

Facilities

- 2 king/twin suites
- hair dryer, toiletries, heated towel rails & demist mirror in 2 ensuites; wheelchair access
- writing desk, phone, fridge & tea/coffee in both suites
- fresh flowers; central heating
- balcony with sea views
- nibbles, TV, video, DVD, CD-player, games, artwork, books & writing desk in lounge
- breakfast served in guest room or conservatory
- lunch by arrangement, extra – local seafood a speciality
- à la carte dinner by prior arrangement, extra
- sunroom
- email, fax & complimentary laundry; children welcome
- courtesy passenger transfer

Activities available

- 3 border terriers on site; mature garden with exotics & natives
- in-house natural history library, local books, videos & photographs
- hosts are Department of Conservation concessioned guides
- *Talisker*, 17m charter yacht
  – sea trips for up to 6 guests
  – 3 double centrally heated cabins
  – raised saloon for all-weather observations
- restaurants nearby
- kayaking & fishing trips, extra
- township centre & main wharf, 5-min walk
- Ulva Island bird sanctuary, 15 mins by boat
- viewing undisturbed birds & marine mammals
- guided diving

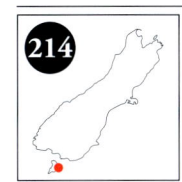

Stewart Island
Stewart Island Lodge

Hosts Margaret and Doug Wright

14 Nichol Road, Stewart Island   *Phone* 0-3-219 1085
Postal P O Box 5, Halfmoon Bay, Stewart Island   *Fax* 0-3-219 1085
Email silodge@xtra.co.nz   *Website* www.StewartIslandLodge.co.nz

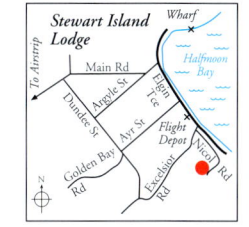

5 bdrm | 5 enst   Double $434   Single $261   *Includes continental breakfast & dinner*

DIRECTIONS: From Invercargill, either take the *Foveaux Express* catamaran to Stewart Island – 1 hour. Or take Stewart Island Flights – 20 mins flying time. Hosts meet all guests, with courtesy car to Lodge.

Stewart Island Lodge is the southernmost lodge in New Zealand. Separated from the South Island by 24 kilometres of the Foveaux Strait, Stewart Island is reached either by catamaran or air. Surrounded by off-shore islets, the island is 750 square kilometres, with extensive walking tracks through temperate podocarp rainforest, rich with native ferns and orchids. Because of its isolation, Stewart Island boasts the largest accessible population of native birds, many of them endangered species, and it is the only place in the world where the brown kiwi can be viewed in its natural habitat. Boat charters are available for cruising, fishing, diving and sightseeing. The licensed Lodge provides gourmet meals with an abundance of seafood and unimpeded ocean views.

Facilities
- 5 king/twin bedrooms, each with ensuite, private patio & ocean views
- baths, hair dryers & toiletries
- tea/coffee, home baking, fresh fruit & flowers in bedrooms
- central heating
- laundry available
- private guest lounge with open fire, tea/coffee, TV & video
- continental breakfast
- packed or served lunch, extra
- 3-course dinner, with local seafood & home-grown veges
- complimentary cocktail hour
- liquor licence
- email, fax & phone available
- weddings, honeymoons & conferences catered for
- courtesy passenger transfer

Activities available
- garden walks on site
- bird-watching on site
- 6-hole golf course
- museum & craft shops
- 230km bush walking tracks
- viewing brown kiwi
- penguin & albatross watching
- endangered NZ native birds
- seals & dolphins in season
- guided nature tours
- sandy beaches
- historical sites
- sightseeing
- skin diving
- 1-hour bus tours
- boat charters & fishing
- offshore islets
- South Island, 1 hour by sea or 20 mins by air

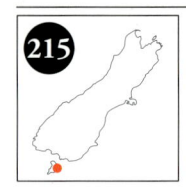

STEWART ISLAND
PORT OF CALL

Hosts Philippa Fraser-Wilson and Ian Wilson

Leask Bay Road, Stewart Island   *Postal* P O Box 143, Stewart Island
Phone 0-3-219 1394   *Mobile* 027 244 4722   *Fax* 0-3-219 1394
Email info@portofcall.co.nz   *Website* www.portofcall.co.nz

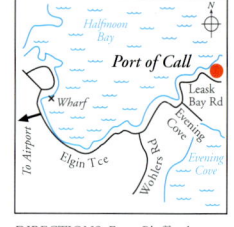

| 2 bdrm | 1 enst | 1 prbth | Double $285 Single $210 | *Includes breakfast Lunch & dinner extra* |

Self-catering in Studio

DIRECTIONS: From Bluff, take Foveaux Express catamaran (1hr), or from Invercargill airport take Stewart Island Flights plane (20 mins flying). Hosts meet guests at wharf or airport, with courtesy car to Port of Call.

Ian and Philippa own and operate eco-tourism businesses on Stewart Island, offering guests a customised trip, tailored from their experience as a sixth generation Island family. Port of Call is surrounded by 20 hectares of tracked native bush stretching from coast to coast, which attracts the birdlife. On site are several historic buildings and farm animals. The 1997 homestead provides one guestroom with ocean views, a guest lounge, deck and courtyard area. Nearby is the secluded self-contained Studio. Its bedroom opens to the lounge which steps down into the kitchen. Alfresco dining is popular on the decking overlooking the sea.

Facilities
- 1 super-king/twin bedroom & private bathroom in house
- Studio: 1 queen/twin ensuite bedroom, full kitchen, lounge area, decking with BBQ
- fresh fruit, flowers, baking, tea/coffee, mineral water & decking opening from rooms
- hair dryer, toiletries, bathrobes & heated towel rails
- central heating
- phone, fax & laundry
- continental breakfast
- lunch & dinner by arrangement, extra
- private guest lounge in house with open fire, tea/coffee, TV, video, artwork, CD-player & library
- private guest entrances
- courtesy passenger transfer; helipad

Activities available
- honeymoons & weddings catered for
- pétanque/boules on site
- 20ha (50 acres) native bush with cottage garden on site
- hosted island eco tours
- bush walks on site
- row boat available
- water taxi run by hosts, Qualmark endorsed
- Ulva Island bird sanctuary, 10 mins by boat
- early 1830s Harrold's Bay Stone House on site, 5-min walk
- coastal track, hiking
- Acker's Pt Lighthouse walk
- fishing, scenic & pelagic trips
- scenic flights
- guided kiwi spotting by night
- kayaking trips
- southernmost golf course in the world

Friars' Guide to New Zealand Accommodation for the Discerning Traveller

This cast bronze plaque graces many accommodation venues recommended by Friars

Evaluation

We appreciate comments from guests who stay at the accommodation included in this special 10th anniversary edition of *Friars' Guide*.

If you would like us to consider any other accommodation for our next annual edition of *Friars' Guide*, please forward the details to us. We begin our next evaluative and photographic trip in spring 2005.

Please send any feedback and suggestions, positive or critical, on any aspect of the accommodation, to the authors:

Jillian and Denis Friar
44 Western Line
R D 1
Wanganui 5021
NEW ZEALAND

Phone ++6-4-6-345 9702
Fax ++6-4-6-345 9703
Mobile ++6-4-21 453 867
Email guidebook@friars.co.nz
Website http://friars.co.nz

Friars' Guide to New Zealand Accommodation for the Discerning Traveller

Accommodation Index

Name of Accommodation	Page
Aachen House	109
Abel Tasman Villa	327
Abri Apartments	37
Acacia Point Lodge	179
Albergo Hanmer	382, 383
Albion Lodge	188
Althorpe	331
Amakaya	186
Amerissit	110, 111
Amokura Lodge	480
Anchorage of Russell	54
Ancora Uno Più	295
Andersons' Alpine Lodge	226
Anlaby Manor	163
Antria Boutique Lodge	293
Aomotu Lodge	49
Aoraki Lodge	431
Aporo Pondsiders	343
Appledore Lodge	36
Arawa Homestead	261
Archer House	358
Ariki Lodge	152
Arles	229
Arlesford House	231
Arrowtown House	467
Arrowtown Old Nick	466
Ashbourne Lodge	94
Atherton House	447
Atholwood	338
Augusta Lodge	140
Averleigh Cottage	439
Awahuri Garden Lodge	172
Awatuna Homestead	364
Aylmer House	416
Aylstone Retreat	247
Ballymoney	409
Balmoral Lodge	481
Bangor Country Estate	419
Bay of Many Coves Resort	282
Bay Vista House	353
35 Bayside	19
Baywick Inn, The	312
Beach Lodge	20
Bell Tower, The	298
Bellbird Lodge	350
Bellini's	470, 471
Beside Lake Taupo	190
Big Tree Hideaway	197
Bishops Manor	398
Boathouse Opua, The	45
Boatshed, The	97
Boscabel Lodge	135
Breakers, The	360
Bremner Bay Lodge	448, 449
Brentleigh Homestead	496
Brenton Lodge	128
Briarwood	244
Broadeaves	258
Brontë Lodge	336, 337

Name of Accommodation	Page
Browns Boutique Hotel	488
Brunswick in Queenstown	489
Buffalo Lodge	121
Bushland Park Lodge	126, 127
Butterfly Bay	23
California House Inn	309
Camellia Cottage @ Sudbury	254
Camellia Estate (*Wairarapa*)	238
Carneval Ocean View	17
Carrington Cottages	243
Casa d'Oro	71
Cassimir	138
Castle Matakana, The	72
Cathedral Inn	316
Catlins Farmstay	501
Cavalli Beach House Retreat	26
Cavendish House	410
Cedar House	196
Centre Hill Cottage	426
Centrewood Historic Homestead	433
Chalet Romantica	41
Chambers Apartment, The	484
Charlotte Jane, The	394
Chatterley Manor	407
Cheltenham House	380
Christopher Brown & Assoc.	10
Claremont Country Estate	384, 385
Clearview Lodge	390
Cliff Edge by the Sea	43
Cliff View	115
Clover Downs	145
Cobden Villa	202
Colleith Lodge	125
Collingwood Homestead	354
Coniston	421
Connells Bay	102, 103
Coopers Beachfront Suites (*Northland*)	18
Coopers Manor (*Wellington*)	265
Copper Beech Gallery	347
Corstorphine House	438
Cotter House	113
Country Villa	146
County Hotel, The	207
Cove, The	183
Creel House	427
Crossing, The	224
Crows Nest, The	42
Dairy Guesthouse, The	487
Devereux Boutique Hotel, The	112
Delamore Lodge	96
Devondale House	389
Dorothy's Boutique Hotel	404
Double Cove Retreat	281
Dream Places	12
Drury Homestead, The	118
Dublin Bay Lodge	446
Duder Homestead	89

Name of Accommodation	Page
Eagles Nest	52, 53
Earnscliff	88
Edgewater Wellington	276
Elm Tree House	392, 393
Emerald Cottage	86
Emerald Villas	87
Endsleigh Cottages	216
Falkirk Cottage	215
Fantail Lodge & Villas	130
Fernbrook	35
Fiordland Lodge & Cabins	494
Fletcher Lodge	436
Four Peaks Lodge	423
Frantoio Cottage	388
Freemans on Clyde	204
Fresh Egg Retreat	237
Fyffe Country Lodge	378
Gatehouse, The	266
Giverny Inn	98
Gladstone Villa (*Napier*)	205
Gladstone Vineyard (*Wairarapa*)	242
Glass House, The	100
Glebe, The	483
Glenavy Vineyard Apartment	300
Glenfern Villas	367
Grampian Villa	318
Grasmere Lodge	373
Great Ponsonby B&B, The	107
Green Gables Deer Farm	420
Greenhills Villa	83
Greenhouse, The	212
Greystones	379
Hambledon	396
Hamurana Country Estate	144
Harbour House Villa	44
Harbour View Apartments	325
Hardinge Cottage	201
Hardings' – Aotearoa Lodge	47
Hastings Hall	105
Haven, The (*Kaiteriteri*)	349
Haven Guest House (*Nelson City*)	324
Heatherston	391
Henwood House	224
Highland Peaks	441
Hill House Lodge	259
Hiwinui Country Estate	235
Hollies	133
Home of Hardy, The	150, 151
Homebush House	268
Hot Toddy Lodge	463
Huka Lodge	171
Hukitawa Country Retreat	162
Huntaway Lodge (*Wellington*)	262
Huntaway Lodge Northland	27
Huntington Stables	166
Hunua Gorge Country House	117
Hurstmere House	73
Hurunui Homestead	255

Friars' Guide to New Zealand Accommodation for the Discerning Traveller

Accommodation Index

Name of Accommodation	Page
Hydrangea Cottages	359
Ika Lodge	193
Island View Lodge	82
Issey Manor	223
Istana Coastal Cottage	334
Jefferswood	303
Kahu Rise	475
Kahutara Homestead	377
Kaikoura Lodge	374
Kairuru Farm Cottages	352
Kamahi Cottage	169
Kanuka Hill Lodge	348
Kapitea Ridge Country Lodge	363
Karaka Cottage	185
Kauri House Lodge	63
Kauri Trees House	270
Kavanagh House	424
Kawaha Point Lodge	156
Kawatea Farmstay	411
Kerikeri Villlage Inn	33
Kershaw House	332
Khandallah Bed & Breakfast	269
Kilns Station B&B, The	252
Kimberley House	326
Kimeret Place	335
Kina Colada Resort	344
Kincaid Lodge	375
Kingfish Lodge	22
Koro Park Lodge	287
La Hacienda	132
La Spa Naturale Day Spa	39
Lahar Farm & Lodge	227
Lake Brunner Lodge	361
Lake Edge Lodge	192
Lake Taupo Lodge	178
Lake Tekapo Grandview	428
Lake Tekapo Lodge	429
Lake View Chalets	68
Lakeside Apartments	451
Lakestay Rotoiti	142
Lazy Fish Retreat, The	283
LeGrys Vineyard Stay	301
Lighthouse Lodge	64
Linston B&B	406
Lisburn House	437
Little Shoal Bay	90
Little Manor, The	313
Lodge at Tikana, The	497
Loft B&B, The	175
Long Lookout Gardens	322
Magic Cottage	28
Mahana Escape	340
Mahara	435
Mairenui Rural Retreat	232
Maison de la Mer	414
Maison des Fleurs	415
Maitai River Lodge	323
Mandeno House	434
Mangawhai Lodge	67
Manor, Christchurch, The	397
Manuka Cottage	321
Maple Grove Cottage	339
Mapledurham	333
Margrain Vineyard Villas	246
Master's Lodge, The	206
Matahui Lodge	131
Matangi Oaks	164
Matarangi Manor	122
Matuka Lodge	430
Maungatautari Lodge	167
Merriwee Country Home	209
Miharotia House	376
Milestone Cottages	66
Milford Lodge, The	85
Mill Bay Haven	21
Mill Cottage	413
Minaret Lodge	450
Moana Vista	106
Moontide Lodge	84
Moorings, The	95
Mornington Private Lodge	203
Motuhora Rise	141
Mountain House Motor Lodge	226
Mountain Range	471
Mt Prospect Station	492
Mudbrick Lodge	306
Mulryans	59
Muritai (*Havelock North*)	217
Muritai Manor (*Nelson*)	308
Murrells' Grand View House	495
Mynthurst Farmstay	220
Natusch House	239
Nautical Haven	500
Netherby Cottage	219
Ngarara B&B	257
Ngongotaha Lakeside Lodge	149
Nicara Lakeside Lodge	147
Nisbet Cottage & Nature Guides	440
NZ Flight Safaris	11
Oak Valley Manor	225
Oakleigh	386
Oakridge Lodge	462
Oaks Lodge, The	498
Oinako Lodge	417
Okareka Lake House	160, 161
Old Schoolhouse Vineyard	345
Old St Mary's Convent	288, 289
Onuku Heights	418
Opawa Lodge	290
Opou – A Country House	198
Ora Ora Resort	34
Oraka Deer Park	168
Orari	401
298 Oriental Parade	275
Orongo Bay Homestead	46
Otahuna Lodge	408
Otawa Lodge	236
Ounuwhao B&B	48
Paihia Beach Resort & Spa	38
Panorama Country Home	143
Paratiho-by-the-Lake	195
Parklands Lodge	443
Parua Bay Cottage	61
Patio Bay	104
Patuha Farm Lodge	221
Pavilion Cottage	249
Pawhaoa Bay Lodge	57
Pear Tree Cottage	474
Pelorus Lodge	304, 305
Pencarrow	478
Peppertree, The	291
Petit Hotel	248
Pillars, The	184
Pinesong Lodge	476
Point Villas, The	181
Poor Knights Lodge	58
Port of Call	504
Portage Resort Hotel, The	280
Pounui Homestead	250
Providencia	214
Pukeko Landing	159
Pukematu Lodge	50
Punatapu	490
Puriri Hills Vineyard & Lodge	116
Quarters, The	200
Queenstown House	482
Raetihi Lodge	279
Rainbow Trout Lodge	194
Rathmoy Garden Cottage	233
Rawhiti	272
Real Estate: CB&A	10
Regal Palms	157
Remarkables Lodge	477
Renmore House	453
Resurgence, The	351
Retiro Farm Lodge	307
Riddlesworth Estate	240, 241
Ridge Contemporary Country Lodge, The	81
Ridge Country Retreat	137
Rippinvale Country Retreat	381
River View Lodge (*Westport*)	357
Riverbank Cottage	465
Riverrun	444
Riverside Apartment	310
Riverview Lodge (*Christchurch*)	399
Rocky Range Lodge	442
Rosemount Homestead	74
Rotorua Country Lodge	153
Royal Palm Lodge	65
Ruby House	273
Rutland Arms Inn, The	230
Sage Cottage	249
Sail Inn	60
Sails Ashore	502
Saltings Estate B&B	76
Sanctuary Palms	40

Friars' Guide to New Zealand Accommodation for the Discerning Traveller

Accommodation Index

Name of Accommodation	Page
Sandpiper Lodge	70
Sandspit Retreat	78
Sandstone House	341
Scenic Heights	174
Sea Breeze	267
Sea Spirit Boutique Accommodation	260
Sea View, A	286
Seaview Heights B&B	114
Sennen House	284
Shanty, The	79
Shaw, The	92, 93
Shearwater	24
Shelbourne Villa	317
Shipwreck Lodge	16
Shotover Lodge	485
Siesta Guest Lodge	15
Silencio Lodge	123
Silverford	208
Skyview Magic	464
Sommerfields Lodge	32
Sommerville House	271
South Street Cottages	315
SouthHaven	314
Spa Naturale Day Spa, La	39
Springfield Cottage	395
St Arnaud House	356
St Georges Bay Lodge	108
St Leonards Vineyard Cottages	296, 297
Stafford Villa	91
Stargate Lodge	75
Steward Island Lodge	503
Stone Cottage, The	445
Stoneridge Lodge	468
Straw Lodge	299
Summer House, The	29
Sunnybank Homestead	320
Sussex House B&B	311
Swiss Lodge Rotorua	154, 155
Taharangi Marie Lodge	14
Takaro Lodge	491
Tapanui Country Home	170
Tasman View B&B	342
Tauhara Sunrise	176
Te Anau Lodge	493
Te Horo Lodge	253
Te Kowhai Landing	187
Te Moenga	173
Te Nikau Forest Retreat	256
Te Puna Wai Lodge	329
Te Puru Coast View Lodge	120
Te Wanaka Lodge	454
Te Weheka Inn	369
Te Whau Lodge	99
Tekau Place	182
Telegraph Hill Villa	213
Tera del Mar	69
Thornton House (*Waikato*)	165
Thornton Lodge (*Bay of Plenty*)	139
Tighnafeile House	425
Tikara Country Lodge	263
Tio Bay Lodge	56
Titore Lodge	51
Tokarahi Homestead	432
Tom's Cottages	218
Top House, The	180
Tours: NZ Flight Safaris	11
Tours: Dream Places	12
Treetops Lodge	158
Trelawn Place	486
Tresillian	405
Tudor Park	499
Tunanui Station Cottages	199
Turret, The	469
Tuscany on Taupo	189
Twin Peaks B&B	479
Ugbrooke Country House	292
Uhuru	80
Umoya Lodge	119
Uno Più	294
Vaucluse	134
Villa, The	211
Villa Collini	136
Villa du Fresne	55
Villa Karaka Bay	277
Villa Polenza Boutique Lodge	365
Villa South Pacific	456, 457
Villa Toscana	124
Villa Vittorio	274
Villa-Maria Petit Boutique Hotel	30, 31
Vintner's Haven, The (*Warkworth*)	77
Vintners Retreat (*Blenheim*)	302
Vue Pointe	285
Waiheke Sands Apartment	101
Waimakariri Lodge	387
Waipoua Lodge	62
Wairepo House	346
Waiteti Lakeside Lodge	148
Waiwurrie	25
Wanaka Homestead	458
Wanaka Springs Boutique Lodge	452
Wanaka Stonehouse Boutique	459
Wapiti Park Homestead	366
Warwick House	319
Waterfront Hotel, The (*New Plymouth*)	222
Waterfront Penthouse (*Nelson*)	328
Weldon Boutique B&B	210
West Fitzroy Apartments	403
West Wellow Lodge	177
Westhaven Retreat	355
Weston House, The	400
Westwood Country House (*Wairarapa*)	254
Westwood Lodge (*Franz Josef*)	368
Whare Kea Lodge (*Wanaka*)	460
Whare Ora Lodge (*Ohakune*)	228
Wharekauhau Country Estate	251
Wharewaka Lodge	191
Wheelhouse Inn, The	330
White Shadows Country Inn	472, 473
Wilderness House	412
Wilderness Lodge Arthur's Pass	371, 372
Wilderness Lodge Lake Moeraki	370, 371
Willowridge House	455
Windsor Farm Homestead	362
Woodhaven	264
Woodland Grange (*Kimbolton*)	234
Woodland Park Lodge (*Waihi*)	129
Worcester of Christchurch, The	402

FRIARS' GUIDE TO NEW ZEALAND ACCOMMODATION FOR THE DISCERNING TRAVELLER

Hosts Index

Surname	Page
Adams, Penny	325
Adams, Peter	351
Adams, Ron	14
Akers, Gary & Shirley	178
Allan, Jane	406
Allemano, Giorgio & Margherita	124
Allen, Jan & John	65
Allen, Nick & Ju	250
Allsopp, Jenny & Gerald	342
Amsler, Inge & Edi	41
Anderson, Berta	226
Anderson, Dennis & Sue	78
Anderson, Heather	405
Andrew, Lisa & Philip	266
Andrews, Grace	175
Annesley-Smith, Geoff	115
Arnesen, Helen & Ray	38, 39
Arrowsmith, Martha & Mark	469
Ashman, Graham & Helen	24
Ashton, Rosa & John	128
Ashworth, Colin	378
Axten, Lynne & Graeme	224
Bailey, William	472, 473
Baines, Maureen & Terry	76, 77
Baird, Jenny & John	19
Baker, Cliff & Biba	419
Baker, Fiona & Neville	214
Ball, Denise	368
Ballantyne, Val & Wayne	317
Barbalich, Elizabeth & Zoran	273
Bardebes, Lisa	282
Barltrop, Sue	456, 457
Barnes, Delia	185
Barons, Christopher & Angela	207
Barron, Carrie & Richard	26
Barrow, Nettie & Bill	299
Bateman, Maralyn & Ian	81
Bayley, Tim	312
Beattie, Helen & John	381
Beck, Alex	11
Benseman, Bob	64
Bertogg, Teresa & Guido	292
Biddulph, Noeline	357
Bilbie, Susan & family	275
Binnie, Jan & Murray	391
Birt, Dave	345
Bishop, Mark	112
Bishop, Noeline & Brent	227
Biskind, Sandie & Daniel	52, 53

Surname	Page
Blakemore, Ian	426
Blattner, Bascha & Beat	382, 383
Blaxall, Doug	63
Blewett, Brian & Val	148
Blume, Joan & Larry	206
Boddy, John & Ruth	184
Bohm, Anne & Alan	239
Booker, Carolyn & Ron	118
Boulter, John & Anna	54
Bowley, Cathie & Bob	323
Boyack, Dianne & Paul	262
Bradford, Alan & Laurice	414
Bradley, Jacqui & Clinton	49
Brady, Lindsey & Matthew	461
Brandl, Daniel	11
Bremer, Inge	34
Brennan, Janet	18
Brice, Megan	79
Brinsley, Claire & Andrew	487
Brito, Nalayini	100
Brodie, James & Ann	249
Brough, Steve & Jeanette	485
Brown, Christine & Rod	29
Brown, Nigel & Bridget	488
Brown, Rosemary & Grant	427
Browning, Marg	42
Bulman, Margaret & Derek	479
Burridge, Rosie & Blair	453
Bussell, Susanne & Bruce	459
Butcher, Graham & Lindsay	149
Butler, Natasha	70
Butler, Tom	373
Cairns, Pam, Bernice & Roger	22
Calway, Joy	117
Cameron, Shirley & John	243
Campbell, Jan & Paul	134
Cardie, Patricia & Murray	256z
Carwardine family, The	443
Cheal, Jacqui	38, 39
Christie, Murray	462
Clark, Michael	486
Clark, Yvonne	58
Clarke, Noeleen & Michael	395
Clements, Robin & Sue	390
Clenott, Daniel	237
Clinton, Nicola	327
Cobb, Randall	237
Cockburn, Joan & Ross	492
Colbourne, Christine & Sean	463
Colllini, Margrit	136

Surname	Page
Conder, Anne & James	264
Connochie, Ross	290
Connolly, Phillipa	434
Cook, Barbara	160, 161
Cooper, Margaret & Robert	35
Corbin, Vickie & Rodger	25
Corry, Cliff	413
Costley, Helen & Judith	375
Coubrough, Jim & Liz	412
Cowan, Elisabeth & Evan	169
Cowley, David	165
Crawford, Pauline	183
Creak, Shirley & Michael	133
Creighton, Rosie	435
Curry, Juanita & Scott	234
Dailey, Raewyn & Peter	205
Dalby, Susan & Tony	191
Dale, Rosie	384, 385
Davies, Gareth	100
Davis, Shirley & Alan	265
Daw, Glenys & Brian	254
Day, Donna-Marie	497
Day, Marian & Mike	343
Day, Sue & Tom	229
de Carteret-Bisson, Clare	351
de Gruchy, Deborah & Graham	219
de Jongh, Robbert	307
Deane, Maria & Eric	298
Deavoll, Dennis	476
Delahunt, Kelly	460
Delugar, Anthea & John	114
Desbecker, Robina & Jef	464
Devane, Judy & Peter	268
Dickey, Jenny & Graeme	88
Dickson, Karen	359
Dickson-Hunt, Mary	27
Diedrichs, Russell & Trina	365
Dillon, Mary & Brian	496
Dolan, Angela & Bill	475
Donahoe, Nicole & Chris	62
Donald, Michaela	408
Drought, Sue & Neil	222
Dunning, Chris & Heidi	263
Dykes, Libby	74
Eady, Olaf	10
Earl, Maree & Len	380
Easton, Joyanne & Richard	346
Edwards, Julie	489
Edwards, Malcolm	370, 371
Eggeling, Gloria	340

Friars' Guide to New Zealand Accommodation for the Discerning Traveller

Hosts Index

Surname	Page
Eglinton, Liz	99
Ekdahl, Paul & Pat	225
Emslie, Sheila & Lex	465
Engels, Co	171
Epp, Patti	422
Espie, Dr Peter & Di	441
Evans, Alison	280
Evans, Janice & Ray	309
Fairhall, Kerrie	358
Fairhall, Margaret & Tim	269
Farrin, Neil	446
Farry, Sue & Patrick	490
Fasnacht, Martha & Roland	17
Fawcett, Imogen & Richard	284
Fekkes, Wendy & Marcel	367
Ferrier, Jenny & Nick	319
Ferris, Lyn & Lloyd	145
Findley, Christine	64
Finn, Lyn & Murray	452
Fischer, Robin & Louise	70
Fitzwater, John	318
Fleming, Kathryne	293
Flores, Victor	307
Floyd, Jo & Calvin	396
Fomin, Oksana & Vladimir	431
Foote, Roger & Irene	190
Footner, Halina & Pryme	163
Forde, Jeannette	67
Forgie, Wendy & Robert	152
Fowell, Lorraine	52, 53
Fowler, Judy & Paul	116
Fox, Sue & Stuart	389
Francken, Irina & Nico	438
Franklin, Geraldine & Roy	49
Fraser, Jill & Roger	247
Fraser, Margaret & Bruce	336, 337
Fraser-Wilson, Philippa	504
Freeman, Anthony & Sue	204
Frew, Lynn & John	498
Gambitsis, Decima & John	257
Garewal, Robyn & Manav	198
Garner, Craig	253
Garrett, Bruce	251
Gatenby, John & Carol	347
Gawn, Janet & Bill	368
Geen, Christopher	313
Gepp, Mike	324
Geraerts, Harrie & Barbara	130
Gibson, Teresa	69
Giesen, Liz & Tony	186
Gilfoyle, Vivienne & Brian	85
Gilroy, Maureen & Colin	125
Goord, Richard	384, 385
Gore, Wayne & Suzanne	468
Gow, Jo & John	102, 103
Gower, Jack	180
Grace, Susanna & Christopher	233
Gravatt, Karen	140
Gray, Lyn & Mike	432
Green, Carole & Derek	196
Gresson, Rose & Jeremy	213
Grigg, Christine & Dave	286
Grigg, Deborah	333
Hadwen, Margaret	182
Hamilton, Annabelle & David	220
Hancock, Jeanette & Peter	314, 315
Handcock, Lesley	162
Hannell, Ian	332
Harding, Barbara & Trevor	47
Harding, Carole & Alan	15
Hardy, Denis & Margie	216, 217
Hardy, Shirley & Brent	150, 151
Harris, Michael	472, 473
Harvey, Anthea & Brian	350
Harvey, Noreen & Norm	71
Hay, Pracilla	210
Hayton, Melinda	470, 471
Heffernan, Janice	86, 87
Henderson, Jane & Tony	379
Henderson, Peter & Susan	221
Henderson, Wendy & David	352
Henley, Anne	483
Hetzel, Ralph & Sally	330
Hewetson, Richard	329
Hickin, Caroline & Philip	467
Higgins, Angela	313
Hill, Gerry	107
Hindmarsh, William & Suzanne	90, 172
Hobson, Louisa	413
Hockey, Isabella	407
Hogg, Barbara & Ken	129
Holden, Philip	386
Holland, Kim	197
Holt, Jan & Stan	308
Holtrop, Mieke & Wilfried	288, 289
Hooper, Michael	46
Hopper, Gary & Janice	361
Howard, Linda & Van	218
Howard, Nery	486
Hoyle, Donna	171
Hughes, Jean	192
Hughes, Michael	456, 457
Humphrey, Deborah & Gavin	448, 449
Hunt, Greg	27
Hurst, Claire & Bill	57
Innes, Marian & Greg	61
Isherwood, Sara	334
Jackson, Jane & Martin	123
James, Sally	107
Jarvis, Bridget & Chris	212
Jefferson, Judy & Peter	230
Jenkins, Bev & Robin	425
Jensen, Mark	282
Johnson, Graham	435
Johnson, Heather & Mike	147
Johnston, Margaret & Robbie	320
Johnston, Olivia & Alan	437
Jones, Clare & Peter	335
Jones, Marie & Barry	122
Joslin, Jennifer & John	301
Kavanagh, Juliearna & Killian	424
Kemp, Jill	245
Kennedy, Amanda	23
Kennedy, Liz	244
Kennedy, Tim	106
Keppler, Eckhard	418
Kernohan, Christine	242
Kiely, Louise	482
King, Chris	143
Kirkland, Liz & Andrew	258
Knausenberger, Eva	92, 93
Kopecky, Pam	120
Lapsley, John	470, 471
Lawrence, Dave	497
Leask, Annabel	272
Lee, Ronnie & Andy	84
Lee, Tracie & Kevin	75
Lefferts, Marshall	69
Leniston, Julie & Greg	408
Leung, Mandy	279
Levarre, Venessa & Matt	154, 155
Libline, Jo	302
Lieber, Christine & Franz	344
Lilleby, Tony	12
Lincoln, Warren & Lyn	95
Lindlbauer, Moira & Siegfried	394

Friars' Guide to New Zealand Accommodation for the Discerning Traveller

Hosts Index

Surname	Page
Lindsay, Steve	484
Lineham, Erica & Geoff	255
Loibl, June & George	231
Los, Vikki & David	311
Loten, Drs Jane & David	433
Love, Sharon	153
Lovering, Stella & Colin	276, 277
Lübcke, Hildegard & Ralf	440
Luxton, Rosemary & Peter	135
Lynch, Kerry	181
Lyne, Bronnie & Craig	267
McAuley, Shannon	112
McCallum, Mary & Bruce	263
McConachy, Gael	66
McCormick, Paul	484
McCracken, Sue & Ian	353
McDonald, Maureen & Gavin	174
Macdonald, Heather	194
Macdonald, Neil	215
McDougall, Anne & Fraser	259
McDougall, Stu	404
McEwen, Becky & Rob	176
McGarry, Jackie & Trevor	300
McIndoe, Ian & Frances	104
McKain, Barbara	110, 111
McKeown, Daniel	270
McKirdy, Joan & Greg	109
McLagan, Julie & Rob	261
McLaren, Wayne	406
McLean, Erina & Terry	474
McLelland, Gabrielle & Bruce	98
McLeod, Jay & Bruce	173
McNae, Helen & Kerry	89
McSweeney, Dr Gerry	371, 372
Malcolm, Jan	60
Manson, Christine	165
Marchbanks, Jenny & John	341
Margrain, Daryl & Graham	246
Marks, Alison	10
Marshall, Rebekah	336, 337
Martel, Malcolm	105
Martin, Brian	287
Martin, Kim & Andrew	144
Mason, James	58
Mason, Jenny	480
Mathew, Jill	115
May, Stephanie & Len	400
Mehrtens, Colleen & Roger	420
Meier, Peter & Glennis	43
Milestone, Ian	66
Miller, Teresa & Greg	417
Mills, Carolyn	51
Mills, Glen	197
Milne, Stewart	302
Milner, Valda & John	195
Mitchell, Kay & Trevor	131
Moers, Kari & Bill	478
Moir, Anne & Bob	73
Montagu, Trixie & Murray	363
Montgomery, Matthew & Rose	281
Moore, Sharon & Ian	387
Moran, Matthew	106
Morris, Margy & Dai	415
Morrison, Margaret	20
Morriss, Gloria & Clyde	164
Mouat, Neil	359
Mueller-Glodde, Rolf	34
Muir, Bev & Grant	366
Murphy, Debbie & Justin	356
Murphy, Sandra & Bob	32
Murrell, Jack & Klaske	495
Natusch, Raewyn & Graeme	142
Newbegin, Oliver & Vicki	373
Newman, Beryl & Richard	189
Nicholas, Judith	316
Nichols, Joanna	416
Nickel, Petra & Reinhard	126, 127
Nicklin, Allan & Marilyn	48
Nimmo, Joy	316
Norman, Anette & Anthony	21
North, Shonagh & Roger	458
O'Carroll-McKellar, Joanne	439
O'Keefe, Joanne	137
O'Neill, Gene	99
O'Sullivan, Leon & Rosemary	428
Oltersdorf, Gabi & Sven	68
Orme, Chris & William	208
Owen, Penny & Ashton	401
Oxley, Andy & Graeme	454
Oxnam, Penny	137
Page, George	339
Parker, Bob	416
Parker, Jeanette & Steve	296, 297
Pawson, John	444
Peacock, Robynne & Ron	494
Pearson, Andrew	101
Peat, Sandra	451
Perry, Dave	143
Perry, Sue & Mark	170
Phillips, Alison	310, 321, 328
Pierce, Susie & David	188
Pierce, Ineke & Ashley	423
Pike, Alison & Graeme	157
Piper, Dorothy	370, 371
Piper, Liz & Ray	238
Plüss, Heidi & Werner	291
Potac, Connie	14
Poupard-Walbridge, Gloria	113
Pugh, Janet & Jim	36
Purkis, Diane	287
Quilliam, Carol & Steven	108
Radford, Stacy	344
Radunez, Laura & Roger	16
Rebbeck, Merrilies & Peter	409
Redwood, Maureen & Ron	55
Richards, Andrea	398
Richards, Jeanne	209
Riesterer, Clive	179
Ritchie, Maree	402, 403
Roach, Lewis	223
Robert, Pam	345
Roberts, Elaine & John	285
Robins, Joyce & John	499
Rocco, Gino & Heather	294, 295
Rogge, Sabine	399
Rosieur, Peter	175
Rough, Malcolm & June	200
Rowburrey, John	325
Rowling, Alison & Tom	349
Rozecki-Pollard, Ewa & Keith	436
Ruawai, Polly & Trevor	376
Rumble, Liane & Richard	374
Russell, Annette & Logan	274
Russell-White, Leon	386
Ryan, Colleen	477
Ryan, Val & Kevin	59
Rye, Chris	378
Sanders, Guy	369
Saunders, Anne	371, 372
Savage, Brian	477
Sax family, The	158
Schischka, Melanie & John	82
Scott, David & Jonathan	97
Scott, Karen & Allan	392, 393
Scott, Linda & Ian	168
Scoular, Christine & Peter	167
Seavill, Margaret & Tony	156
Serge, Robert & Masae	44
Sewell, Sandra & Jeff	303
Shand, Tania & Shorty	306

Friars' Guide to New Zealand Accommodation for the Discerning Traveller

Hosts Index

Surname	Page
Sherlaw, Jo	348
Sheiff, Jenny	194
Shortland, Kay & Colwyn	50
Shrimpton, Louise	83
Siegrist-Huang, Evelyne	121
Simpson, Dain	280
Simpson, Kathryn	302
Simpson, Sue & Kerry	193
Sizer, Anna & Ian	28
Smith, Barbara	388
Smith, Keith	140
Smith, Mary & Ian	177
Smith, Nikki & John	377
Smith, Rosalie & Russell	430
Smith, Terry & Julie	132
Smith, Tim	304, 305
Sommerville, Lynda & Wally	271
Sorell, Jenny & Graham	410
Sotiri, Diana & Tiri	228
Southwick, Janet	312
Sowman, Phil	293
Spellmeyer, Toni & Jeff	141
Steeby, Roger & Sonya	240, 241
Stevenson, Bob & Sue	80
Stewart, Angus	183
Stewart, Jan & Dave	235
Stewart, Rhonda & Geoffrey	362
Stompe, Monika & Bruno	355
Storey, Roselyn	96
Strang, Lisa & Colin	442
Stratford, Judy	339
Stratford, June & Murray	501
Summers, Kate & Roy	447
Sutherland, Val & Ross	72
Swannell, Chris	46
Swayn, Diana	203
Swayn, Gilda	201
Sweet, Sue & David	232
Szymanski, Christoph	279
Tait, Iris & Peter	502
Tate, Gary	450
Taylor, James	329
Taylor, Meg	444
Taylor, Tony	402, 403
Te Rakau, Pauline & Heemi	364
Teitell, Cecilia & Ernie	182
Thacker, Judy & Kerry	411
Thiele, Vesna & Tom	491
Thompson, Campbell	260
Thompson, Carol	223
Thompson, Leslie & Ray	199
Thompson, Sally	211
Thorne, Bob & Judy	139
Thorpe, Lorraine & Wayne	455
Tomaszeski, Angela & Troy	159, 187
Townshend, Carol & Colin	166
Trathen, Jo	318
Trathen, Yvonne	322
Trew, Sue & Del	236
Trustrum, Noel & Helen	256
Tuckett, Lesley	290
Turner, Reg	138
van Beek, Lynda & John	429
van den Berg, Johann	119
van der Maat, Anneke & John	146
Van Dyck, Mieke & Catharina	30, 31
Van Valkenburg, George	18
Vansevenant, Sandrine & Peter	33
Veenvliet, Maggie & Adrian	354
Vize, Susan & Des	248
Walewski, Amy & Cornel	202
Walker, Cis & Les	481
Walker, Dawn & George	221
Wall, Dawn & Richard	56
Walsh, Gerard	270
Walter, David	222
Warren, Chris	283
Waterhouse, Marie & Steve	466
Watson, Nicky	332
West, Maureen	179
White, Gail & Tommy	500
White, Robin	310, 321, 328
Wi Neera, Helen & John	252
Williams, Chrystal	324
Williams, Harold	397
Williams, Robyn & Grahame	338
Williamson, Carol & Donald	421
Wilson, Belinda	445
Wilson, Ian	504
Wilson, Jennifer	424
Wilson, Jenny	326
Wilson, Raewyn & Rob	40
Windram, Chris & Mark	91
Wipperfuerth, Ernst	399
Wiseman, Jo	476
Wong, Emily	446
Wood, Terrie & Bill	37
Woodhouse, Margy	180
Worley, Jenny & Bob	331
Wright, Margaret & Doug	503
Wurm, Andy	136
York, Veronica & David	94
Young, Debbie	260
Younger, Wendy	45
Zemla, Elspeth	487
Zissler, Trudy	160, 161
Zwimpfer, Anne	397